亚洲基督教高等教育联合董事会（United Board）与 Henry Luce Foundation 项目
基金及福建华南女子职业学院专项基金资助

春色任天涯

——福建华南女子职业学院外教侧记

International Faculty with Fujian Hwa Nan
Women's College since 1908

主　编：岳　峰　吴瑗瑗

副主编：赖黎群　黄　飞

顾　问：陈钟英　林本椿　苏萌娜

厦门大学出版社
XIAMEN UNIVERSITY PRESS
国家一级出版社
全国百佳图书出版单位

图书在版编目(CIP)数据

春色任天涯:福建华南女子职业学院外教侧记:英汉对照/岳峰等著. —厦门:厦门大学
出版社,2018.10
ISBN 978-7-5615-6869-9

Ⅰ.①春…　Ⅱ.①岳…　Ⅲ.①华南女子职业学院—教师—生平事迹—国外—汉、英
Ⅳ.①K815.46

中国版本图书馆 CIP 数据核字(2018)第 228850 号

出 版 人	郑文礼
责任编辑	王扬帆

出版发行　厦门大学出版社

社　　址	厦门市软件园二期望海路 39 号
邮政编码	361008
总 编 办	0592-2182177　0592-2181406(传真)
营销中心	0592-2184458　0592-2181365
网　　址	http://www.xmupress.com
邮　　箱	xmupress@126.com
印　　刷	厦门集大印刷厂

开本	787 mm×1 092 mm　1/16
印张	38.25
插页	1
字数	860 千字
版次	2018 年 10 月第 1 版
印次	2018 年 10 月第 1 次印刷
定价	198.00 元

本书如有印装质量问题请直接寄承印厂调换

厦门大学出版社
微信二维码

厦门大学出版社
微博二维码

主　编：岳　峰　　吴瑗瑗

副主编：赖黎群　　黄　飞

顾　问：陈钟英　　林本椿　　苏萌娜

编　委：余俊英　　汴　梁　　叶　林　　林　校　　乐荣妹

程铭茜　　林　娇　　林晓鸿　　林丽华　　潘　樱

严　涵　　王　凌　　范圣宇　　董秀苹　　陈　晴

韩艳艳　　余荣敏　　卓小星　　张　琳

Contents

Chapter 1 International Faculty with Fujian Hwa Nan Women's College before 1951

2   I Fujian Hwa Nan Women's College and Her International Faculty (1908—1951)

18   II The First Two Presidents of Hwa Nan College

27   III Summer House: A Token House of Sino-American Joint Education

Chapter 2 International Faculty with Fujian Hwa Nan Women's College after 1984

30   I Here She Came, Owing to Her Love for China—A Story of Mrs. Judith Williamson

36   II California Rose—Dr. Betts Rivét

54   III Let Life Be Beautiful Like Summer Flowers—Recalling Dr. Jeanne Philips

67   IV An Orchid in a Valley—Recalling Dr. Kay Grimmesey

91   V My Reflections: Trimble Boys

160   VI Idealism and Realism of Laihar Wong

第三章　1984 年后的福建华南女子职业学院外教（续）

456　第一节　道德教师
　　　　　　——记格雷戈里·盖尔切教授

463　第二节　普吉特海湾的十三朵金花
　　　　　　——记福建华南女子职业学院与美国普吉湾大学的友谊

479　第三节　玛丽安·戴维斯教授与她的"家政"情结

481　第四节　芬兰黑美丽
　　　　　　——小记福建华南女子职业学院老朋友黑美丽

487　第五节　心中有梦，缘定中国
　　　　　　——记玛莎·苏·托德

497　第六节　唯有爱，永不败
　　　　　　——忆念恩师丽莎

519　第七节　春风化雨，润物无声
　　　　　　——回忆佩罗特博士

525　第八节　记 Sandy

530　第九节　加州阳光
　　　　　　——小记福建华南女子职业学院的老朋友多迪

535　第十节　高雅的郁金香
　　　　　　——记葛·凯伦博士

540　第十一节　一生的坚守：做个有用的人
　　　　　　——记路易斯·罗默博士

第四章　福建华南女子职业学院的外教文化内核

548　第一节　福建华南女子职业学院的外教政策

552　第二节　师者仁心，教无定法
　　　　　　——福建华南女子职业学院外教教学思想探微

561　第三节　福建华南女子职业学院与亚洲基督教高等教育联
　　　　　　合董事会

573　附录　福建华南女子职业学院外教名单

589　参考文献

590　后记

PREFACE 1

A century-old establishment with historical prestige, Fujian Hwa Nan Women's College still stands out with her distinctive features, one of which is her international faculty and their widely acclaimed teaching. But what impresses me most is their dedication to teaching and devotion to the students. In September, 2015, Hwa Nan's Australian teacher Laihar Wong won the 7th Fujian Friendship Award. During the award-granting ceremony some Hwa Nan teachers told me how she had helped students with psychological disorders, paid tuition fee for students with money troubles and done volunteer work for orphanages. I was moved. As our conversation went deeper I realized that Hwa Nan's international teachers were a dedicated faculty. Among all the institutions of higher education in Fujian, Hwa Nan has received the most Friendship Awards from the provincial government and the central government. It is also one of the institutions with the most Friendship Awards in China. This reminds me of Lydia Trimble and her colleagues, who started Hwa Nan from scratch. One good turn deserves another. Although we may not be able to requite their good deeds, I feel obliged to make their contributions known to the world, which are their professional ethics, teaching methodology and friendship with the Chinese people. That is how the idea of writing a book about Hwa Nan's international teachers since 1908 occurred to me. Anyway, academic research is supposed to serve the society.

The Chinese title of the book is a line from a poem dedicated to Matteo Ricci, extolling his service in China, oceans apart from his homeland, Italy. The book is written in both English and Chinese so as to target a wider audience.

This book is a significant contribution to international relations, especially Sino-

Violet Wu, Sa Benmao, Xia Meiqiong , Chen Zhongying and others. Hwa Nan Women's Voc-Tech College, founded in 1984, has inherited this fine tradition. Its international faculty members used to outnumber those in any other university in Fujian Province. Hwa Nan girls got a good exposure to native speakers of English as well as their culture. According to an article in *People's Daily*, Hwa Nan graduates never worry about getting a job, partly because they speak good English. Our international faculty members are not just teachers with state-of-the-art teaching methodology but also role models for our students in their life. They are the dynamo of the college and make the spirit of "sacrifice and service" pass down from generation to generation.

I am sure that this book will help our students better understand the college motto "Having received, I ought to give." and feel proud of Hwa Nan.

Lin Benchun
August 3, 2016

序一
PREFACE

福建华南女子职业学院（以下中文部分简称"华南女院"）是一所百年老校，有相当的历史知名度，至今颇有特色，引人关注。华南特色之一是外教，他们活力四射的教学在社会上广为称道。除了教学，外教还有一个重要的方面需要我们关注：师德与奉献精神。2015年，澳大利亚籍外教Laihar Wong（黄丽霞）获得福建省政府颁发的友谊奖，我有幸听了老师们讲述她如何帮助有心理危机的学生，帮家庭困难的学生交学费，到孤儿院做慈善等事迹，心里一阵感动；再一沟通，意识到华南女院的外教中有相当一批人是来奉献的。在福建省的高校中，华南女院是福建省高校中外教获得中国政府与省政府友谊奖最多的学校，也是全国高校中最多的之一。而1908年美国传教士Lydia Trimble等人筚路蓝缕，以启山林，创建华南，也是感人的故事。中国有句老话，"受人点滴之恩，当以涌泉相报"。我们说不上涌泉相报，但是弘扬师德、关注教育、磨砺教法、见证国际友谊是必需的。于是我萌发了写书做传的念头，记述1908年起在华南女院执教的外教，以学术为社会服务，是为本书的缘起。

明万历进士李日华在《紫桃轩杂缀》中赠利玛窦诗云："浮世常如寄，幽栖即是家，那堪作归梦，春色任天涯。"本书援用其中诗句"春色任天涯"作为书名，以纪念那些不远千里、远涉重洋来异国他乡奉献的外国人。本书以中英双语读本的方式出版，以便扩大阅读面，推进国际化。

本书的编写对国际关系，尤其是中美关系具有重要意义，可以说是中美友谊研究的子课题，从学校的视角纵贯中美人民的百年友谊。中美关系不仅是两国的关系问题，实际涉及全球的安全问题。美国的对华政策是复杂的，中美友谊时时被钓鱼岛、南海等问题蒙上阴影。习近平总书记两次访美，都从民间角度讲述中美友谊，都讲到缘起福州鼓岭的中美友谊，感动千万美国人。宜夏别墅也在鼓岭，主人是华

春色
任天涯
——福建华南女子
职业学院外教侧记
International Faculty with
Fujian Hua Nan Women's
College since 1908

8

南校医、牧师杜医生（Dr. Donly）。他在回国之前将别墅送给了华南女院，使中美人民的友谊借由教育续写；宜夏别墅作为中美合作办学的一个纪念地标留存下来。从1908年起至今，大量的外教来到华南女院，留下了一个又一个感人的故事。外教对华南女院的发展与英语特色起了重要作用，他们的贡献得到政府的充分肯定。他们与华南女院学生及中国教师结下了深厚的友谊，为福建的近代化做出了贡献，使女校至今以自己独特的方式推进福建社会的发展。

本书具有历史学方面的价值。关于华南女院的历史研究，主要有学者朱峰、谢必震教授的论著。华南女院的早期档案由亚洲基督教联合会转交给耶鲁大学神学院。我在耶鲁大学做联合研究员的时候，收集了该部分珍稀档案，本书使用了其中部分资料。本书也具有教学方面的价值。外教的教学生动活泼，颇有实效，总体上得到高度认可；他们当中不乏教学效果出类拔萃的教师，其教学理念与教学方法对于中国教育思想是有益的补充。中美教育理论与教学方法的对比研究可以相得益彰。

本书是集体创作的结晶，课题组是跨学科的队伍，包括英语、历史专业的教师，以满足本书编写不同方面的需要。课题组基于华南女院的早期档案与现在的全面资料及与外教的互动而完成。改革开放后来华的华南女院外教大部分健在，相关传记由他们的学生编写，这些学生现在是华南女院的老师。

本书的撰写得到多人与机构的襄助。感谢亚联董（United Board for Christian Higher Education in Asia）拨款资助该书的出版，感谢袁月兴（Cynthia Yuen）博士对项目申报的协助以及罗安娜（Anna Law）女士的工作。感谢华南女子学院现任院长苏萌娜及其领导班子的支持，使本书的出版得到专项资金的支持。感谢前院长林本椿为本书的编写提供了各类珍贵信息，为发展华南女院的国际化作出的种种努力。感谢理事长陈钟英、许道锋老师在改革开放之际、华南女院重建之时推行外教政策，没有这种高瞻远瞩的视野与锲而不舍的执行，就没有今日华南女院的外教文化。是为序。

岳　峰

2016年4月15日

序二
PREFACE

　　看本书的书稿时，眼前不禁浮现出许多朋友的形象：简·菲利浦、戈登和索尼娅·特林布尔、南希和拉里·摩根、阿曼达·爱基、凯·格里姆斯、贝茨·里韦特、多萝西·麦克迈克尔、葛·凯伦、黑美丽、黄丽霞、多迪·约翰斯顿、邓肯·弗朗斯和特雷莎·泰勒(Teri)、格雷戈里·盖尔切、玛丽安·戴维斯……我1985年开始在华南女院教书，自那以后，便有幸和许多在华南女院教书的外籍老师成为同事，并结交为好朋友。新华南1984年成立，1985年招收第一届学生，阿曼达就是最早来华南女院教书的两个外教之一。我们教同一个班。她每周到我家一次，学习汉语。她是那么和蔼可亲，热情洋溢，学生都非常喜欢她。1987年，我从美国回来，在香港见到她，那时她在《南华早报》当记者。简·菲利浦是美国丹佛大学著名的心理学教授。2012年，她曾邀请我到丹佛她家里住了一个多星期。不料，我回国没多久，就听到她去世的噩耗，令人悲痛欲绝。她在华南女院的朋友们也都非常伤心。她临终还念念不忘我们这些朋友，在遗嘱中交代要用她的钱买山核桃送给华南女院的朋友们，每人一公斤。我至今还记得陪她一起去为学生买VCD机的情景，记得她用自己业余时间为华南女院年轻教师上课，以提高她们的英语水平，还帮助华南女院写了许多基金申请。她不仅是老师还是非常好的朋友；她和蔼可亲，慷慨大方，博学幽默。我当华南女院校长时有幸邀请第一任校长程吕底亚的后人程高登先生来校教书，自那以后他和他的夫人索尼娅每年都来华南女院任教，连他年已鲐背的老父亲鲍勃，也年年来华南，而且年年都捐款给华南女院，直至他2014年期颐之年仙逝。他们真正继承了程氏家族的优良传统，为我们树立了牺牲和奉献的好榜样。南希·摩根是作为富布莱特学者来华南女院任教的，是一位非常优秀的教师。她的先生拉里·摩根本来没有教学经历，在华南女院却成为非常受欢迎的老师，华南女院的经历改变了他的职业生涯。他回国就考了教师资格证，完成了从建筑承包商到教师的转变。学生们非

春色
任天涯
——福建华南女子
职业学院外教侧记
International Faculty with
Fujian Hua Nan Women's
College since 1908

10

常喜欢他们，有的至今还和他们保持密切联系。在我当华南女院校长不久，就有幸接待戴维斯博士，我称她为华南女院的天使，是她帮助华南女院和佛罗里达州立大学建立了合作关系，将十几个年轻教师送到佛罗里达攻读硕士学位。凯伦教授是一位非常严肃的学者。我和她的友谊可以追溯到1986年我在俄勒冈她所在的大学里教书的时候。她的汉语很流利，而且还将几本中文小说翻译成英语。能有这样饱学的教授来授课，学生是很幸运的。盖尔切（Guelcher）教授是我在晨边学院教书时的同事，他被学生认为是最好的老师。华南女院和晨边学院的姐妹关系是第二任校长卢爱德博士在20世纪20年代末建立的。盖尔切教授到华南女院访问和教学，无疑进一步加强了两校的联系。受篇幅限制，在此无法一一讲述我的朋友和他们的每一件事。但我还是不能不讲一下凯和贝茨两位博士。她们在华南女院任教的时间比其他人都长。她们对华南女院的影响是长期和持久的。正如这本书的书名"春色任天涯"说的那样，她们不论到哪里，都能使那个地方美如春色。贝茨和凯还有其他外教无疑使华南女院变得更美丽。我们都可以深深感受到他们的牺牲和对教育的奉献。

我很高兴在岳峰教授指导下编成了这本书，而且还有这么多华南女院年轻教师参加了这项有意义的工作。华南女院有100多年的历史，外籍教师一直是华南女院蜚声中外的一个重要因素。毋庸置疑，1908年由程吕底亚创办的华南女子文理学院有一支很强的外教队伍。没有他们，老华南女院就不可能涌现出那么多杰出的毕业生，如王世静、余宝笙、陈叔圭、许引明、吴芝兰、周贞英、萨本茂、夏美琼、陈钟英等。1984年创办的华南女子职业学院继承了这一优良传统。华南女院的外教曾经比全省任何一所高校都多。华南女院的女生都能接触到原汁原味的英语和英语文化。《人民日报》曾载文，赞扬"华南女儿不愁嫁"，她们一毕业就很容易找到工作，这应该和她们能说流利的英语有关。华南女院的外教不仅有最新的教学方法，她们还是学生人生道路上的好榜样。他们是学校里一股生机勃勃的力量，推动华南女院"牺牲和奉献"的精神代代相传。

我相信这本书将帮助我们的学生更好地理解"受当施"的校训，她们将为华南女院感到骄傲。

林本椿

2016年8月3日

Chapter 1

International Faculty with Fujian Hwa Nan Women's College before 1951

春色
任天涯
——福建华南女子
职业学院外教侧记

春色
任天涯
——福建华南女子
职业学院外教侧记
International Faculty with
Fujian Hua Nan Women's
College since 1908

2

I

Fujian Hwa Nan Women's College and Her International Faculty (1908 — 1951)

Fuzhou, literally "a blessed land" as her name suggests, is a coastal city with a history of thousands of years. She has been actively engaged in international exchanges since the Song Dynasty (960 — 1276) and the Yuan Dynasty (1206 — 1368), and has never severed her ties with the outside world. The Ming Dynasty (1368 — 1644) and the Qing Dynasty (1616 — 1911) saw several mass overseas emigrations. An open, inclusive, innovative and adventurous mentality began to develop.

As one of the five major ports in China that were open for trade in the mid -19th century, Fuzhou became an important gateway for China's exchanges with the west. Missionaries from western countries flocked to Fuzhou, making it an important base for cultural dissemination. Among them were Milton Gardner's parents, who took their son with them to China in 1901. Milton Gardner, who later became a professor of physics in California University, spent his happy childhood in Guling, Fuzhou until the family left in 1911. Milton Gardner had always wanted to revisit his childhood home, but unfortunately was never able to do so due to the circumstances. In the final hours of his life he still murmured the name "Ku Liang, Ku Liang", which is "Guling" in Fuzhou dialect. In 1992, Xi Jinping learned of the story and invited Milton Gardner's widow to visit Guling, a place her husband had developed such an attachment for, and chat with 9 of her husband's childhood playmates, who had all grown into their 90s. This story tells of the strong ties between Fuzhou and the western missionaries.

The missionaries gradually realized that only by changing the traditional thought of the Chinese people could they successfully disseminate Christianity. Griffith John believed that the Chinese people, with their own language, their own sages and philosophers and scholars, were not that ready to worship God unless they were transformed through education.[1] With this in mind missionaries began to set up schools in line with the

---

1 R. W. Thompson & Griffith John. *The story of Fifty Years in China*[M]. London: The Religious Tract Society, 1906:62.

educational systems of their home countries. In 1848, Christian Methodist Episcopal Church established schools for boys and girls respectively. Soon Union Theological School of Foochow, Gezhi Middle School, Ponasang Girls' School, Do-seuk Girls' School and Trinity Middle School were established, paving the way for an institution of higher learning in Fuzhou. The development of women's education was then an urgent demand. The second provost of Hwa Nan College, Ids. B. Lewis (1887—1969) said at an anniversary celebration of Yuk Ying Girls' Middle School, to the effect that missionaries had taken great pains to offer girls an equal access to education in this southeastern city of Fujian and if they had not spent decades on the primary and secondary education of girls, establishing a women's college would not be possible.[2] In the last years of the Qing Dynasty, the Qing government successively promulgated "Regulations for Women's School"and "Regulations for Women's Normal School". Building girls' schools and colleges had become the concern of the government as well.

In the conference of Christian Methodist Episcopal Church in May, 1904, Lydia A. Trimble suggested establishing a women's college in southern China. The conference agreed on the feasibility and necessity of building a women's college in Fuzhou, considering its geographical and cultural conditions.[3] Lydia A. Trimble was made responsible for this cause. She named the college Huan Nang (later changed to Hwa Nan) College, meaning "a college in southern China".

Cangshan district in Fuzhou was an ideal location for the college. Missionaries of Christian Methodist Episcopal Church, Robert Samuel Maclay started a girls' school in Cangshan in 1850.[4] Then Anglo-Chinese College was established here in 1881. The locals generally welcomed girls' schools run by missionaries. In 1908, the prep class for Hwa Nan College began to admit students. Then following the completion of the college's administrative building, Payne Hall (aka Hwa Nan Main Hall), and the student dormitory, Granson Hall, Hwa Nan College was officially established in Fuzhou's Cangshan district. Lydia A. Trimble was made the first provost. The college was committed to training religious leaders from the middle and lower classes, especially women from the rural areas of southern China. However, due to the postponed donation from Anglican Church and American Board of Commissioners for Foreign Missions, the college had been running on meager funds till 1922, and did not offer regular courses until 1917.

Hwa Nan's teachers made great contributions to the college in its early years. The early faculty of Hwa Nan consists of female missionaries, missionaries' female families

2 Xie Bizhen. *A Pictorial of Hwa Nan College* 1908-2008[M]. Fuzhou: Fujian Educational Press, 2008:2. (in Chinese)
3 "Hwa Nan College at a Glance", 1932[A]. Fujian Archives, File Number: 9-1-23. (in Chinese)
4 Wang Yusheng. *The History of Fujian's Education*[M]. Fuzhou: Fujian Educational Press, 2004:296. (in Chinese)

春色
任天涯
——福建华南女子
职业学院外教侧记
International Faculty with
Fujian Hua Nan Women's
College since 1908

4

and some Chinese teachers who had lived overseas. Besides Lydia Trimble, the provost, the international faculty included L. Ethet. Wallace and Katherine Willis. The Chinese faculty included Xie Shaoying, Chen Shugui, Huang Naishan and Wei Jianxiang. Most of them had received higher education, with the foreign faculty mostly graduating from seminaries. However, Hwa Nan's early faculty was rather inadequate. The fact that the major purpose of the college was to disseminate Christianity and many teachers often had to go back to America to deal with church affairs only made the situation worse. Chen Shugui recalled, "Ms. Trimble asked me to teach physics because all the science teachers had left China. I found it absurd. I had never taught physics! But it seemed that I had no other choices."[5] In order to build a strong faculty, Lydia Trimble then began to recruit teachers with various backgrounds, including Wei Jianxiang, once a successful candidate in the imperial examinations at the provincial level, and Wei Naishan, a prominent figure in Fuzhou's modern history, to teach Chinese classics.

Lydia A. Trimble（1863 — 1941）graduated from a teachers' university in the US. She came to China in 1889 and spent 50 years of her life here. She was highly committed to the establishment of Hwa Nan. In 1912, the construction of the main building of Hwa Nan had to stop due to the lack of fund. Lydia Trimble persuaded her brother to sell their home to fund the construction. She busied herself raising funds and facilitating cooperation programs between American universities and Hwa Nan. With limited fund, she managed to hire excellent teachers from America. Indeed, she had personally pulled through Hwa Nan during the most difficult years. She considered Fuzhou a place that she would serve for life. Her student, Hwa Nan's third provost Lucy Wang recalled: "Lydia Trimble was my mentor and my mother. She was the one who had given me a new life. I often forget the fact that she was from America, because she sympathized with Chinese women, saw great capacity in them, and believed that with proper education, they would stand equal and unabashed to any men and women from any countries… She was a woman of far sight. She did not just focus on the improvement of an individual. Instead, she aimed at the general improvement of all Chinese women, one step at a time… Ms. Trimble believed that Chinese women should learn home economics, and picked up some students and sent them to study home economics in America. She also laid the foundation of the music course in Hwa Nan. She made sure that Hwa Nan offered all the courses that were necessary for women, and tried to enhance the subjects that women were generally good at."[6] Another student

---

5 Chen Shugui."Typical Teacher" in Journal of Hwa Nan College—A Memorial of Lydia Trimble[Z]. Nanping: Hwa Nan College, 1941:5. (in Chinese)

6 Lucy Wang. "An Eternal Memory" in *Journal of Hwa Nan College—A Memorial of Lydia Trimble*[Z]. Nanping: Hwa Nan College, 1941:7. (in Chinese)

Lydia Trimble and the third-year graduates of Hwa Nan
Girls' School in 1914

Lydia Trimble in 1941

recalled that Lydia Trimble attached great importance to the practical side of religion.[7] Lydia Trimble embraced the idea that one is supposed to pass on what is given to them. She believed that the purpose of higher education was to serve the people. Hwa Nan was committed to cultivating the students' sense of responsibility over those who had no access to education.[8] In 1922, *Li Xuelou* (aka Trimble Hall),[9] a building named in allusion to her Chinese surname and an episode in Chinese history that tells of reverence for teachers, officially went under construction in commemoration of her contribution to the founding of the college. Lydia Trimble retired in 1925, but did not left China. Her church had arranged for her to go back to America, but Bishop Wilson S. Lewis believed that her best place was China.[10] Lydia Trimble then worked as a consultant to Hwa Nan, supporting the college in various ways. In 1938, when the Japanese navy began to attack *Fuzhou*, the college moved to Nanping (customarily called Yen-ping then), a mountainous city in northern Fujian. Lydia Trimble was seriously ill, but she refused to go Nanping as arranged by the college authority Instead, she stayed in Fuzhou to help with the transferring of school assets. She died in Trimble Hall on August 25, 1941.

---

7 Esther Ling. "A Modern Apostle—A Tribute from the Alumnae"[A]. Yale University Divinity School Library Special Collections. United Board for Christian Higher Education in Asia Archives, Box177, Folder 3217.

8 L Ethel Wallace. *Hwa Nan College:The Women's college of Southern China,* New York: United Board For Christian Colleges in Asia, 1956:33.

9 Now "Peace Hall" or "He Ping Lou" in the administrative quarter of Fujian Normal University.

10 Miss Lydia A. Trimble-Yale University Divinity School Library Special Collections[A]. United Board for Christian Higher Education in Asia Archives, Box176, Folder 3217.

L. Ethel Wallace　　　　　Katherine Willis

L. Ethel Wallace is one of the outstanding teachers in Hwa Nan's history. She was born in the UK. She obtained a BA from Toronto University and an MA from Columbia University. Concerned about China's inadequate higher education, she decided to join Hwa Nan's teaching faculty on the invitation of Lydia Trimble. She successively served as professor of education, dean of teaching affairs and acting provost. She was loved and respected by her students for her amiableness and scrupulousness. They called her Mama Wallace. She spent over 30 years of her life in Hwa Nan, and did not leave the College even after the Sino-Japan war broke out. A grand farewell party was held in her honor when she finally had to go back to the UK due to her illness. She spent the rest of her life writing a memoir of her experience in China—*Hwa Nan College: A Women's College in Southern China*, which was published in New York in 1956. It is a detailed record of her life in Hwa Nan, a valuable document for the study of church colleges for women in China.

Katherine Willis was born into a traditional middle class family. With a wide spectrum of skills and interests, she went to Harvard University to study science of physical culture and sports after she got a BA in Columbia University. Hwa Nan did not have music major or school chorus when she came in 1916. Katherine Willis's athletic and musical talent was given full display in her teaching. The girls made steady progress under the guidance of such a talented teacher. Singing together became a beautiful part of their shared memory. A Hwa Nan alumna recalled that they often went hiking along the Minjiang River, singing "My Boat is Waiting Here" merrily as they enjoyed the beauty of spring. In 1931,on Katherine's invitation, Eugenia Savage, came to Hwa Nan upon her graduation from the University of Southern California. She was an elected member of Mu Phi Epsilon, Pi Kappa Lambda and Phi Kappa Phi. She stayed with Hwa Nan during the war-ridden years and went back to America in 1951.The College then began to offer music programs and spent a small fortune buying phonographs and records. The students were then able to enjoy the world's best music. Katherine Willis taught music and PE and was once in charge of Hwa Nan's student registration affairs. Unfortunately, due to the limited fund, she had to go back to America. She later taught in Syracuse University.

Ella Deyoe was born in Wisconsin. She had received a complete seminary education. In 1921 she came to Hwa Nan to assist Ethel Wallace to teach the course of education, but due to the limited fund she had to go back to America when the College moved inland to Nanping.

Mary Mann was also one of the teachers who worked in Hwa Nan during her early years. Her husband, Horace Mann, used to preach in Massachusetts, but later came to Fuzhou. Mary Mann was responsible for Hwa Nan's religious course. She integrated religious teachings with the students' daily life, which proved an effective pedagogy.

Besides the above mentioned teachers, Hwa Nan's first teachers also include Lula C. Baker, Elsie G. Clark, Roxy Lefforge and some Chinese teachers.

Xie Shaoying was native to Fuzhou. She graduated from Yuk Ying Girls' School in 1893, and went to Morningside College in America for her MA in music. She first taught music in Affiliated School of Hwa Nan College and then in Hwa Nan College. She was the first Chinese teacher in the history of Hwa Nan, spending more than 30 years of her life here. Due to the College's poor conditions, Xie Shaoying had to work on her own in music education over a long period of time, producing a large number of musical students for the College. She was remembered as a loyal and faithful person.

Xie Shaoying

Chen Shugui was also a Fuzhou native. She attended Affiliated School of Hwa Nan College and later obtained her BA in Education in Cornell University and her MA and PHD in education in Columbia University. She came back to teach in Hwa Nan in 1923. She was Chairperson of the College Committee and the dean of the Department of Education. She had practically devoted her whole life to Hwa Nan.

Huang Naishan was born in Minqing, Fuzhou. A legendary figure in China's modern history, he had made great contribution to the liberation of the Chinese nation. In 1991, then Communist Party Secretary of Fuzhou, now China's president Xi Jinping said that he was the pride of all overseas Chinese as well as the pride of the Chinese nation. He appealed to the public to emulate his patriotism, enterprise, and quest for truth and endless pursuit of excellence. Huang Naishan was also an educationalist besides being an overseas Chinese leader and an activist in the Chinese revolution that ended the Qing Dynasty. He was made the provost of Union Theological School of Foochow, Anglo-Chinese College and Peiyuan School concurrently in 1911. In 1919, while he was still busy with his irrigation project, he was invited to teach Chinese classics in Hwa Nan. Then a 71-year-

春色
任天涯
——福建华南女子
职业学院外教侧记
International Faculty with
Fujian Hua Nan Women's
College since 1908

8

old man, his passion for the Chinese classics was not a bit diminished by the fatiguing irrigation project. The students called him "Grandpa Huang".

Wei Jianxiang was native to Ningde, Fujian. A successful candidate in the imperial examinations at the provincial level in 1904, he was well-steeped in Chinese classics and especially versed in writing. Once the magistrate of Gutian, Fujian and a teacher in Anglo-Chinese College, Wei Jianxiang was invited to teach Chinese classics in Hwa Nan in 1924 and was loved by the students for his lively and interesting lessons. Wei Jianxiang retired in 1941 and started a primary school in his hometown. He emigrated to the US in 1949 and died in Cleveland in 1979.

In spite of the adversities, Hwa Nan College grew substantially during the office of Lydia Trimble, from 1908 to 1925. The College offered only one program at first, namely Education, but began to offer Religious Education and Biology in 1924 and Chemistry in 1925, and gradually growing into a comprehensive university with both humanities and science programs. Enrollments grew every year, from 21 in 1920 to 63 in 1923 and 87 in 1925. In 1922, Hwa Nan College obtained a temporary authorization to grant bachelor's degree on behalf of the State University of New York. Hwa Nan gradually developed

International faculty of Hwa Nan College (1913)

A welcoming banquet in honor of Li Houji, the governor of Fujian (1917)

into a women's college comparable with Ginling College. During this period, the College changed her name from "Huan Nang" to "Hwa Nan". Lydia Trimble made a point of building connections with the Chinese government. Li Houji, the first governor of Fujian in the new republican government of China, visited Hwa Nan in 1917 and was warmly welcomed. Then Hwa Nan continued to develop with the support of the government.

Christian Methodist Episcopal Church appointed Ids B. Lewis, a well-known Christian educationalist to be the provost of Hwa Nan College after the retirement of Lydia Trimble.

Ids B. Lewis (1887-1969) once studied in Morningside College and later got her PHD in Education in Columbia University. Tao Xingzhi, a Chinese education guru, acclaimed her as the only one who has insight into women's education in China in those years.[11] Another Chinese educationalist, Yu Qingtang, considered her as a dear friend to China's women's education. Ids B. Lewis embraced liberal theology and believed that the essence of Christian education is the nurturing of fine characters. She believed the only and the fastest way to disseminate Christianity in the East was to train its own Christian leaders.[12]She attached particular importance to women's education and believed that one of the missions of higher education was to groom Christian women for social service.[13] Ids B. Lewis expounded the theory for Christian women's education in China in her monograph *Higher Education of Women in China*. She held that Christian women's education in China served three purposes. The first was to transform the Chinese society with the essence of both Chinese and western culture; the second was to facilitate the self-awakening of China's modern women; the third was to produce religious leaders that are committed to serving the Chinese society.[14] She offered suggestions based on the history and status quo of China's women's education. First, church schools should play a greater role in China's women's education; second, special attention should be

Ids B. Lewis, the second provost of Hwa Nan College (in office during 1925-1927)

---

11 Tao Xingzhi. "15th Anniversary of Women's Education in the Educational System". *The Complete Collection of Tao Xingzhi's Works*, Vol. 1 [M]. Chengdu: Sichuan Educational Press, 1991:467. (in Chinese).

12 "The Foreign Missions Convention of the United States and Canada"[J]. *Woman's Missionary Friend* (May, 1925). Boston: Woman's Foreign Missionary Society of the Methodist Episcopal Church.

13 Ida B. Lewis. "Higher education of Women in China"[J]. *Educational Review* (Oct. 1917). Shanghai: China Christian Educational Association,p.272.

14 Ibid: p. 274.

10

春色
任天涯
——福建华南女子
职业学院外教侧记
International Faculty with
Fujian Hua Nan Women's
College since 1908

given to the education of lower class children; third, women's education should be closely integrated with the social life.[15] These suggestions were highly farsighted and constructive.

Ids Lewis launched a large-scale reform in Hwa Nan College. She developed practical programs in home economics and public health, strengthening the connection between education and real life. She included Chinese teachers in the management of the College and started the practice of governance under Chinese faculty. She promoted Chen Shugui to be an associate professor and appointed her to be the acting principal of Affiliated School of Hwa Nan Collge, considering it the most important event of the year.[16] She lobbied American universities and managed to secure cooperation programs with seven universities, obtaining fund and equipment that Hwa Nan badly needed. Hwa Nan College grew to be a well-known establishment in southern China during her administration.

However, Ids Lewis was confronted with a great challenge shortly after she went into office. A massive campaign aiming at the recovery of the right of education broke out in Fuzhou, demanding to ban all church schools and prohibit their official registration[17]. Hwa Nan College then became the target of criticism and her very existence was crucially threatened. Ids Lewis made a wise decision that sacrificed her own position but saved the College. She resigned as provost and put together a college committee that consisted of five members, all of whom were Chinese. The five committee members were Chen Shugui, the chairperson; Lucy Wang, the dean of teaching affairs; Li Meide, the chief of general affairs; Huang Huizhu, the secretary; Huang Huizhen, who was in charge of the affiliated high school. Lucy Wang later became the provost of Hwa Nan College, which was a new page in Hwa Nan's history.

Hwa Nan College continued to develop under the new leadership. The College was registered as Hwa Nan Women's college of Arts and Science in 1933, with seven departments, which were the Department of Chinese, the Department of English, the Department of Education, the Department of Home Economics, the Department of Mathematics, the Department of Chemistry and the Department of Biology. One year later, Hwa Nan got a permanent degree granting authorization from the State University of New York and continued to grow in prestige in China.

The year after the outbreak of the second Sino-Japan war in 1937, Hwa Nan College was forced to move north to Nanping. However, Nanping was no safe retreat from Japanese bombs. The Japanese air force bombarded the city with growing intensity as the

---

15 Ida Belle Lewis. "The Education of Girls in China"[D]. New York: PhD Thesis, Columbia University, 1919:35-36.

16 "Report of Hwa Nan College"[G]. Foochow Woman's Conference, 1919-1930(1926). Shanghai: Methodist Publishing House, 1931:19.

17 Zhang Zhenqian. "Recollections on the Campaign of Education Right Recovery". *Fujian Cultural and Historical Data*, Vol. 13, P158. (in Chinese).

war went on. Nanping was bombed three times in 1939, which was considered quiet few by Hwa Nan staff members. "We had only 3 bombings last year; one on May 8, another on July 12, the last on September 22. All of them were very close to us and we were very grateful for our dugouts."[18]In 1941, the College was bombed twice in August alone. "We had two bombings in August, one of 3, one of 17 bombs and sirens daily, so that we spent hours at the caves or in them."[19] However, these adversities did not stop Hwa Nan from developing under Ms. Wang's leadership. The following three lists of Hwa Nan's faculty in 1928, 1931 and 1945 showed us the improvement in the teachers' educational background. The number of Chinese teachers was on the rise, until it equaled the number foreign teachers. Lucy Wang recruited both Hwa Nan's excellent graduates and highly competent international teachers. Hwa Nan began to have a very strong faculty.

Table1   Foreign Faculty in 1928[20]

Name	Rank	Educational and Professional Background
Ids B. Lewis	Consultant	BA from Morningside Univsersity, PHD from Columbia University, former educational secretary of American Board of Commissioners for Foreign Missions
Ethel C. Wallace	Consultant, Professor of Education	Master's Degree from Columbia University
Katherine Willis	Professor of PE and Singing, Registrar	BA from Columbia University, studied science of physical culture and sports in Harvard University
Roxy Lefforge	Professor of Religious Studies	Master's Degree from Boston University
Professor Zhang*	Professor of Health Care	DSC from the Johns Hopkins University
Professor Shi*	Professor of History and Mathematics	BA from Cornell University
Elsie G. Clark	Professor of English	MA from Columbia University
Mary Mann	Professor of Religious Studies	BA., studied in Chicago University
Professor Qin*	Professor of Biology	BA and Master's Degree from Syracuse University
Professor Ai*	Professor of English	BA from Northwestern University, studied in Columbia University
Professor Lan*	Professor of Zoology	BA from Syracuse University
Ms. Deng*	Curator of Hwa Nan's library	Grauдated from a teachers' college in the US

---

18 "Excerpts from letters from Hwa Nan Staff Members"(Yen Ping, 1940). Yale University Divinity School Library Special Collections. United Board for Christian Higher Education in Asia Archives, Box177, Folder 3207.
19 Ibid.
20 Zhang Hanshen. "A Survey of Hwa Nan College". *A Selection of Cultural and Historical Data*, Vol. 5. Fu Zhou: Fujian People's Publishing House, 2003:517-519. (in Chinese).

12

春色
任天涯
——福建华南女子
职业学院外教侧记
International Faculty with
Fujian Hua Nan Women's
College since 1908

Name	Rank	Educational and Professional Background
Professor He*	Professor of Botany	Master's Degree from Northwestern University

*Translator's note: Many international teachers assumed Chinese names while they worked in China. However, some of the teachers' English names are no longer available to us. The asterisked names are the transliterations of their Chinese names.

Table2　Foreign Faculty in 1931[21]

Name	Rank	Educational and Professional Background
Ethel C. Wallace	Consultant	Master's Degree from Columbia University
Katherine Willis	Professor of PE and Singing, Registrar	Bachelor's degree from Columbia University, studied science of physical culture and sports in Harvard University, lecturer in Syracuse University
Qin Taoshi*	Professor of Biology	BA and MA from Syracuse University, lecturer in Syracuse University
Zhang Shuqiong*	Professor of English	BA from Morningside University, taught English in Texas and Missouri.
Liu Mali*	Professor of Education	Master's Degree in Columbia University
Deng Huizhen*	Assistant Professor of Music, Curator of the library	Bachelor's Degree from Boston University
Ai Yili*	Professor of English	Bachelor's Degree from Northwestern University, Master's Degree from Wisconsin University, headmaster of a high school in Wisconsin
Ba Meide*	Professor in the Department of Arts	Master's Degree from Columbia University
Elsie G. Clark	Professor of English	Master's Degree from Columbia University, taught English in Massachusetts, New Jersey and Connecticut
Eugenia Savage	Professor in the Department of Music	Bachelor's Degree from South California University

* Transliterations of the foreign teachers' Chinese names.

Table3　Foreign Faculty in1947[22]

Name	Rank	Educational and Professional Background
Albert Faurot	Ass. Professor of Music	MM from Oberlin College
Frances Fulton	Instructor of Music	BA from West Coast State College
Eugene Savage	Assistant Professor of Music	BM from South California University

21 "Table 1 of Hwa Nan College Files"[A]. Fujian Archives, File No. 39-1-5. (in Chinese).
22 List of faculty and administrative staff-A (serving during current semester) & staff-B (On leave)[A]. Yale University Divinity School Library Special Collections. United Board for Christian Higher Education in Asia Archives, Box176, Folder 3196.

Continued

Name	Rank	Educational and Professional Background
Evolyn Troutman	Instructor of Education	BD from Union Thelogical Seminary.
Ethel C. Wallace	Consultant, Full Professor of Education	Master's Degree from Columbia University
Marion Cole	Full Professor of English	MA from Columbia university
Elsie I. Reik	Full Professor of English	MA from University of Wisconsin
Jessie Lacy	Instructor of English	BA from Wesleyan University
Isabelle Lewis	Full Professor of Education	PHD from Columbia University
Elizabeth Mortimer	Instructor of Home Economics	BA from Illinois Wesleyan University

The third provost Lucy C. Wang played the most important role in the development of Hwa Nan during her term of office from 1929 to 1951. Lucy Wang was born into a scholar-gentry family in Fuzhou. Her grandfather was a successful candidate in the highest imperial examinations and was once governor-general of Guangdong and Guangxi provinces. She was brought up well-educated. She entered the prep class of Hwa Nan College in 1913, and later obtained her BA in Education from Morningside University, and her MA and PHD in Education from Michigan State University. Lucy Wang found great truth in Liang Qichao's words: "The long-term weakness of China stems from the absence

Lucy C. Wang，（in office from 1929 to 1951）

of women's education."[23]She followed Ids B. Lewis' educational thoughts and ran the school with the philosophy of "passing on what one has received". She believed the goal of women's higher education in China was to offer Chinese young women education in literature, science, and vocational skills, and to develop in them the willingness to sacrifice for the public good.[24]She added new majors to Hwa Nan, making it a comprehensive university, recruited excellent teacher, and raised funds. In 1937, she traveled to Hong Kong, Guangdong and Southeast Asia to visit Hwa Nan alumni and raise funds. In 1947, the United Board for Christian Higher Education in Asia (here after referred to as "the

23 Liang Qichao. *Collected Works from the Yin-bing Studio*, Book II[M]. Beijing: Zhong Hua Book Company, 1926:14. (in Chinese).
24 "Memorandum of Hwa Nan College" (article 3), 1932[J]. Fujian Archives, File Number: 39-1-6. (in Chinese).

春色
任天涯
——福建华南女子
职业学院外教侧记
International Faculty with
Fujian Hua Nan Women's
College since 1908

14

United Board") held a conference in the US to discuss the revival of education after the war. Lucy Wang gave a report on Hwa Nan's continuous effort in education during the war. After the conference she visited several American universities and delivered speeches on Hwa Nan's educational cause. She was warmly welcomed and Hwa Nan's extraordinary work was highly appreciated. Her effort paid off well, and Hwa Nan was generously funded by American people and Hwa Nan alumni in the US. Lucy Wang continued to devote herself to women's education in Fujian after the founding of People's Republic of China.

Lucy C. Wang in 1937

Leon Roy Peel obtained her bachelor's degree and master's degree in Theology from Boston University. She was assigned to Hwa Nan to teach religious studies by Woman's Foreign Missionary Society. Besides her teaching responsibilities, Leon Peel made great effort to raise funds for Hwa Nan, especially in 1938 when the College had to move to Nanping and was in need of a large fund. She mobilized multiple social sectors to donate for Hwa Nan so that it could tide over the greatest financial crisis since its founding. Her contribution was widely praised.

The first organization she turned to was where she came from—Minneapolis Branch of Woman's Foreign Missionary Society. She received a donation of $2836.68 from the missionary society at the beginning of 1938. She made a detailed report on the three major budgetary expenditures and finally got her missionary society to fund administrative budget and promotional budget.[25]

She also tried to raise funds in Fuzhou. However, she was only able to raise $60 in 1938 in Fuzhou，a city caught up in the turmoil of war.

Leon Peel never stopped her effort to close the $2500 budget gap. In the end she decided to travel to America and asked the United Board for help and she finally got the much needed fund. With the fund Leon Peel had raised, Hwa Nan was then able to move to Nanping, rent a few buildings from the Methodist Church of Yenping and Jianjin High

---

25 B. A. Garside. "Letter to Hwa Nan College" (January 20, 1938)[A]. Yale University Divinity School Library Special Collections. United Board for Christian Higher Education in Asia Archives, Box 177, Folder 3204.

School, converted an old ancestral temple into dormitories, and proceed with teaching during the difficult time.

Miss Grace Davis came to Hwa Nan with Leon Peel and was in charge of the finance and budgetary work. However, she had to go back to America on account of duties at home. Lucy Wang said, "She was a great help to Hwa Nan in delivering our financial statement and budget to the Hwa Nan committee just in time for their meeting, and, especially during this difficult time, her service in America for the College will be greatly needed."[26]

W. P. W. Williams, who had come to Hwa Nan on Lydia Trimble's invitation to help with her missionary work in Fuzhou, was the assistant to Mz. Trimble and stayed in Fuzhou with her when the College moved to Nanping. She looked after Mz. Trimble in her old age and tended the college buildings. Unfortunately, a fire broke out on February 9, 1941 and burned down Payne Hall. Although Ms. Williams had tried to contact the United Board for rebuilding Payne Hall, the reconstruction did not start until 1946 due to the circumstances.

Mrs. Earhart was assigned to Hwa Nan by the Methodist Episcopal Church in 1934 as a professor of music. Due to the financial difficulties after the College moved to Nanping, teachers' salaries were drastically reduced[27] and they sometimes went unpaid for several months, but the Earharts did not give up. After the fire in 1941, Mrs. Earhart returned to America to raise funds for the building's restoration. Mrs. Earhart and her husband finally raised enough fund and asked Ruth Chou to bring it back to Nanping. The teachers and students in Hwa Nan were greatly touched. Lucy Wang wrote to Mr. Earhart: "During these difficult days I often recall Mrs. Earhart's words to me when I was there in 1934 working for the College. She said, 'Hold on, Lucy', and the memory of her encouragement often inspired me still...How splendid it would be if after the war you would help us to re-build Hwa Nan Main Hall or to erect a chapel or a music hall as an Earhart Memorial."[28] Although Mrs. Earhart did not come back to Hwa Nan afterwards, her contributions have been recorded and will always be remembered.

Elsie I. Reik came to Hwa Nan in 1934 and taught in the Department of English, and moved to Nanping during the war. Even during wartime, she managed to make her lessons interesting and make life gratifying. She brought a lot of pictures, poems from Fuzhou, which she used creatively in her classes. When her own supply ran low, she asked

---

26 Hwa Nan News (January, 1939)[A]. Yale University Divinity School Library Special Collections. United Board for Christian Higher Education in Asia Archives, Box177, Folder 3212.
27 ibid
28 Lucy C. Wang. "Letter to Mr. H. Earhart" (February 12, 1943)[A]. Yale University Divinity School Library Special Collections. United Board for Christian Higher Education in Asia Archives, Box177, Folder 3206.

her friend to send pictures from magazines.[29] She asked her friend to send her Christmas presents that she could give to the children and the staff on Christmas.[30]

Miss Margaret Seeck was a professor in child health care, who Hwa Nan's Board of Trustees had recruited from the UK. After she came to Hwa Nan, she launched the Special Child Welfare Project of Hwa Nan's Social Service Program, which was a contribution to the Department of Home Economics during wartime. The teachers and students of Hwa Nan were so reluctant to let her go when she had to return to her country in 1939. Thanks to Margaret Seeck and the social service program, Hwa Nan students became more aware of their social responsibilities.

Miss Marion Cole was a teacher in the Department of English who came to Hwa Nan in 1931. She returned to America because of her illness, but was still concerned about China, a far-away country in the abyss of war. In 1939, she decided to come back to China, but was not able to come back to Hwa Nan because of the Japanese occupation. She taught in the Peiping Language School before she returned to America again in 1951.

Eugenia Savage's friend, Frances Fulton, was a contract teacher for three years in the College Chemistry Department, and she also worked in the Music Department. Her coming in the time of emergency will always be remembered gratefully.[31]

Many Hwa Nan alumni chose to come back to teach in their Alma Mater in spite of the circumstances, helping to maintain Hwa Nan's relatively high quality of education. Among them were Jean Chen, a graduate of Hwa Nan in 1933 and He I-Wu, a graduate of Affiliated School of Hwa Nan College. Jean Chen gave up the opportunity to work in America and came back to Hwa Nan, serving as the dean of the Department of Home Economics after obtaining her Master's degree in Food Economy and Nutriology from the Kansas State College of Agriculture and Applied Science. He I-Wu came back to offer courses in the Physics Department in Hwa Nan after graduating from Morningside University and receiving his M.A. from the University of Chicago. Lucy Wang once said, "we are happy to have in our midst Mr. He I-Wu."[32] Mr. He was important to the Department of Physics during Hwa Nan's most difficult years.

Besides the dedicated wartime faculty, people from other sectors also supported Hwa Nan in various ways. In addition to generous donations, they visited Hwa Nan in person. Many attendees of the Yen-ping Annual Conference in December, 1938, for example,

---

29 Elsie Reik. "Letter to Mrs. Peel" (December, 29, 1938)[A]. Yale University Divinity School Library Special Collections. United Board for Christian Higher Education in Asia Archives, Box177, Folder 3207.
30 Ibid.
31 Hwa Nan News (January, 1939)[A]. Yale University Divinity School Library Special Collections. United Board for Christian Higher Education in Asia Archives, Box177, Folder 3212.
32 Ibid.

Faculty of Hwa Nan College in 1929

Bishop John Cowdy, took the chance to visit Hwa Nan's teachers and students in its temporary site. Colleagues in Fuzhou's educational community, for example, President James L. Ding with Anglo-Chinese College, Mrs. C. J. Lin with Fukien Christian University and Professor Chen with Foochow Trinity College, visited Hwa Nan every year and discussed educational issues with the faculty. Officials in Fujian government also visited Hwa Nan in Nanping, providing strong support for the College.

Hwa Nan moved back to Fuzhou when the anti-Japanese war was over. However, resumption of lessons was unlikely due to the fire that burned down Payne Hall. Fortunately, Hwa Nan received support from both Chinese and American sources. The United Board remitted $50, 000 for the rebuilding, and the Ministry of Education also offered a half-year subsidy. Hwa Nan College was then able to survive and develop in leaps and bounds. The number of students once exceeded 300.

In response to the Three-self (self-governance, self-support , and self-propagation) Patriotic Movement of the Protestant Churches in China, Lucy Wang handed over the seven seals of Hwa Nan College. Hwa Nan's arduous yet glorious 43 years drew to a close.

Faculty of Hwa Nan College in 1950

春色
任天涯
——福建华南女子
职业学院外教侧记
International Faculty with
Fujian Hua Nan Women's
College since 1908

II

The First Two Presidents of Hwa Nan College

Walking into the reception room of the International Faculty House on the campus of Hwa Nan Women's College, I notice the portraits of three women on the wall. They appear so tranquil and dignified. The portraits depict three former presidents of Hwa Nan Women's College. In the middle is the College's first president, Lydia A. Trimble. To her right is second president Ida B. Lewis. Together with the third President, Dr. Lucy Wang, they capably led Hwa Nan through nearly five tumultuous decades.

1. Lydia A. Trimble (1863-1941) — First President of Hwa Nan

Lydia A. Trimble was the first president of Hwa Nan Women's College. Born in Canada near the city of Ottawa, she was the ninth of ten children in her large family. She was a life-long member of the Methodist Church. At age twenty she accompanied her brother, Dr. James B. Trimble, to America and studied in the state of Iowa. Following her graduation from the Iowa State Normal School at Cedar Falls (a teachers' preparatory institution), she decided to become a missionary. Lydia was sent by the Des Moines branch of the WFMS (Women's Foreign Missionary Society) to Foochow [Fuzhou], China in 1889, where she began studying Chinese and training for an evangelistic career that would span over fifty years.

Between 1901 and 1904, Lydia Trimble was on furlough in America, during which time she completed her bachelor's degree at Morningside College in Sioux City, Iowa. In May 1904, while attending the general conference of the Methodist Church in Los Angeles, Lydia presented an appeal to found a college for women in South China. The Women's Foreign Missionary Society Reference Committee

Portraits of the first two presidents of Hwa Nan College

Lydia A.Trimble (1913),
first president (Xie, 2008: 03)

responded with two resolutions, one authorizing the establishment of a women's college in Foochow, and the other constituting a committee consisting of Trimble and two other female missionaries to choose a site, plan the buildings, and decide on a suitable course for study. A board of trustees would oversee their endeavors (Davis, 1991: 22). Thus originated the idea of establishing Hwa Nan Women's College.

In 1908 a preparatory school of Hwa Nan Women's College was established, and Lydia Trimble was appointed president. Two years earlier, in Lungtien[Longtian] [a coastal area in Fukien(Fujian)], she had overseen the building of a girls' boarding school, an experience that helped prepare her for the challenges of building a school in a difficult environment. Wallace (1956: 7-8) recalled that "at the insistence of Bishop Wilson S. Lewis, the resident bishop of Foochow, this small school was called the Foochow College Preparatory of Foochow Women's College. And the name was a constant reminder that the projected college would soon be a reality." Following western practice, a college often developed from a strong preparatory school. However, the actual process of college preparation and construction was slow due to the lack of funds. Nevertheless, donations from churches and friends finally permitted sod to be broken for the campus of Hwa Nan Women's College in the fall of 1911.

An abiding faith that women should have a right to education, and that education could be used to cultivate future Christian leadership, guided Trimble in her efforts to lay the proper foundation for Hwa Nan Women's College and surmount all obstacles and discouragements. In 1914 the college prepared to move from rented quarters and welcome its first class in newly-opened Payne Hall. However, Cranston Hall, the student dormitory, was far from completion and funds were nearly running out. Bishop Lewis

Bishop Bashford laying cornerstone of Payne Hall
(Dec.12, 1911) (Xie, 2008:47)

春色
任天涯
——福建华南女子
职业学院外教侧记
International Faculty with
Fujian Hua Nan Women's
College since 1908

20

Hwa Nan Staff (1913) (Xie, 2008:05)

advised alerting Dr. James B. Trimble of the need for additional funding. Dr. and Mrs. Trimble quietly mortgaged their farm and donated $4000 to Hwa Nan (Wallace, 1956: 15). Thanks to this gift Cranston Hall was successfully completed and opened for occupancy that same year. Both Payne Hall and Cranston Hall quickly gained fame as "architectural gems" for their unique design in Foochow history.

Due to a small faculty and limited teaching materials, the decision was made to restrict the curriculum to the first two years of college work while encouraging third and fourth-year students to study elsewhere until additional staff could be added (Wallace, 1956: 16). In fact, the faculty was so few in number that Miss Trimble was compelled to serve both as president and teacher, holding classes daily from 8:30 to 5:30. After the days' classes she then attended to administrative duties and the translation of textbooks (Campbell, 2005: 335).

In 1916, five students completed their first two years of college studies at the Preparatory School. Four subsequently went on to study in America or Canada, while the other chose to continue her studies at the women's Christian Medical College in Shanghai. Studying abroad was not yet common and the fact that four of five initial graduates were able to matriculate to colleges and universities abroad attested to the school's already high standards of scholarship. It also suggested that the school was ready to complete the transition to offering a four-year course of study leading to a degree. To signify the new mission, the Board changed the name of the school to Hwa Nan Women's College that same year. The following year Hwa Nan began to offer junior and senior-level courses. Hwa Nan

The first college class (1914) (Xie, 2008:9)

could now offer a full four-year course of study, beginning with an education department (Zhou, 2006).

Once again the small number of faculty limited further expansion, and so from 1917 through 1924 the education department was the only department able to offer a complete major. In 1924 two additional majors were added: Religious Education and Biology. By 1925, the curriculum of Hwa Nan's Education Department has consisted of eleven courses: Psychology, Child Psychology, Sexology, School Management, Teaching Principles and Practice in Primary School, Teaching Methodology of Middle School Courses, Present and Modern Educational History of the Primary School, English Teaching Methodology, Music Teaching Methodology, PE Teaching Methodology, and Games Teaching Methods (Zhou, 2006: 2).

Lydia Trimble conferred bachelor's degrees on three graduates at commencement ceremonies in 1921, which indicated that Hwa Nan Women's College had met the proper standards of scholarship in higher education and attained maturity. All three of the 1921 graduates subsequently went on to have noteworthy careers of their own in the field of education.

The college's situation, nevertheless, was still far from satisfaction. Trimble and other administrators worried that Hwa Nan's future prospects would remain constricted unless the school could obtain an official charter from the Chinese government or an American university.Dean of the College Ethel Wallace

Three of the 1921 graduates (Xie,2008:143)

(Lydia Trimble's niece) thus applied for a charter from the State University of New York while on furlough in the United States. Since the Board of Regents of the University was in the practice of granting only one such charter per city in China, and since Fukien Christian University in Foochow had already received its charter, the prospects for Hwa Nan breaking precedent and receiving its own charter seemed slim(Davis, 1991).

When in early 1922 Miss Wallace returned to China, she delegated this arduous task to Miss Katherine H. Willis. Willis, a physical education instructor and chorus director at Hwa Nan, was in New York for further study. Eventually all the paperwork was completed

春色
任天涯
——福建华南女子
职业学院外教侧记
International Faculty with
Fujian Hua Nan Women's
College since 1908

and forwarded on to the Board of Regents of the State University of New York, which granted a provisional charter to Hwa Nan on September 28, 1922. This is an important milestone in Hwa Nan history. The good news and the significant accomplishment it represented greatly heartened the faculty and staff of the college. In a letter of congratulations, SUNY Vice Chancellor Albert Moot offered his praise: "Here, we are glad to find, even in your course of study, that you are broadly far-seeing and progressive. As we read the evidence, you are seeking to make the young women of China think for themselves upon all the great problems that confront progressive leaders among women of China in the future" (Wallace, 1956: 25-26).

Ceremony of Charter Day
(1922) (Xie, 2008:12)

Lydia Trimble tendered her resignation as president of Hwa Nan Women's College in 1925 at the age of 62. During Trimble's seventeen years as president, Hwa Nan had grown from a preparatory school into a college, developing from the stage of offering only first two years of a college curriculum to being able to provide a full four-year course of study, and also secured the all-important provisional charter granted through the State University of New York in the United States. Hwa Nan had progressed slowly but steadily, and thereby laid a solid foundation for its future development. By 1925 the college had also matured physically in that a third building — a residence building — had joined Payne

Hall and Cranston Hall to complete the Hwa Nan campus. Hwa Nan's newest structure was named Lydia Trimble Hall in honor of the president whose great leadership and vision had seen the college so successfully through its formative years.

Payne Hall and Cranston Hall in 1914 (Xie, 2008:51)

Miss Lydia Trimble dedicated herself to Women's education, and to establishing and developing Hwa Nan Women's College. Throughout her life she both advocated and practiced the college motto, "Having received, I ought to give." Although she resigned from her post, her spirit of persistence, unshakable faith, and fearlessness forever left their mark on Hwa Nan Women's College.

2. Dr. Ida Belle Lewis (1887-1969) — Second President of Hwa Nan

Dr. Ida Belle Lewis was born in Blairstown, Iowa in the United States of America. She was the daughter of Bishop Wilson S. Lewis, who served as the second president of Morningside College from 1897 to 1908 before being assigned to residence in Fuzhou from 1908 to 1920. Ida Belle Lewis graduated from Morningside College and received a BA degree in 1909. She then left to become an English teacher at the Sara L. Keen School in Tianjin, China for five years. In 1915 she returned to America and pursued postgraduate studies at Teachers College of Columbia University where she earned her Ph.D. in 1919. She published her book "The Education of Girls in China" that same year. She investigated the situation of women's education in recent China, presented the questions to be solved, and revealed the social reasons causing those problems. She offered specific suggestions, expecting that more efficient educational policies would be made to improve Chinese women's education.

Lewis visited China in 1922 as a representative of the WFMS. Her charge was to survey the educational work of the organization there, with the goal of introducing greater economy and efficiency into its operations (Wallace, 1956: 30). In the course of her survey, Lewis inspected Hwa Nan. She was duly impressed. As she noted in her report to the WFMS: "the dominating factor in the college is its spirit … This spirit is holding through the work of graduates … Efficient, wholly ladylike, they are setting the standards for Christian womanhood from the cities to the far interior out-posts" (Wallace, 1956: 30).

春色
任天涯
——福建华南女子
职业学院外教侧记
International Faculty with
Fujian Hua Nan Women's
College since 1908

24

Given her familiarity with Hwa Nan, it is perhaps not surprising that the Board of Trustees selected Lewis to succeed Lydia Trimble in 1925 as president of the college. However, as Lewis was not scheduled to arrive in China for several months yet, Dean L. Ethel Wallace was asked to serve as interim president.

January 28, 1926 was chosen as the date for Lewis' inaugural ceremony as president, which corresponded with the date of the college's sixth annual commencement. Welcoming the new president, Wallace noted that Lewis was fortunately no stranger to Hwa Nan. In fact, Wallace said, "Dr. Lewis is making her way into the hearts of students and outside people alike. Her deep spiritual

Dr. Lewis and Hwa Nan graduates(1926)
(Xie, 2008:16)

life, her educational knowledge and her ability to speak Mandarin fluently have given her prestige among the Chinese scholars and the love of the students" (Wallace, 1956: 35).

Dr. Lewis proved adept at investigating and studying the educational situation to identify problems and put forward appropriate solutions. In the fall of 1926, in her first annual report as president, Lewis marshalled concrete evidence in summing up the achievements and status of Hwa Nan Women's College. Lewis cited (Campbell, 2005: 340) a total of thirty-eight students having graduated from Hwa Nan. Thirty-four alumnae had worked in Christian schools, where twenty-four continued to serve. Two graduates had

Hwa Nan graduates of 1926 (Xie, 2008:144)

chosen to continue their studies in the U.S., one of whom had expressed interest in eventually returning to her alma mater to teach. Four graduates were studying medicine, three had married, forming Christian families, and another trio remained in mainland China pursuing postgraduate studies. In addition to the Methodist Church, the Baptist, Anglican, Presbyterian, Congregational, and Reformed churches were likewise represented among Hwa Nan graduates. That said, problems remained to be solved. Lewis warned that equipment was lacking in all departments, and she expressed her worries about an overburdened teaching staff; she called for additional faculty to be recruited, especially in the fields of science, music and mathematics.

Clearly being aware of the difficulties facing the college, Dr. Lewis not only strengthened the management inside the college but also took advantage of external resources to promote the college's continued development. Thanks to Dr. Lewis' initiative, Hwa Nan soon established friendly relations and a cooperative relationship with seven "Sister Colleges" within the United States. These seven institutions of higher learning contributed funding, equipment, and/or sent teachers to Hwa Nan. Wallace (1956: 47) later recorded the funds received and the departments at Hwa Nan adopted by each Sister College:

Mt. Union College, Ohio	For Gymnasium	US$2,000
Baldwin-Wallace College, Ohio	For Household Science	1,000
West Virginia Wesleyan College	For Department of Physiology	1,000
Cornell College, Iowa	For Music Department	2,000
Morningside College, Iowa	For Chemistry Department	1,500
Southwestern College, Kansas	For Biology Department	1,500
Missouri Wesleyan College	For Normal Department	300

Dr. Lewis took charge of Hwa Nan during a very turbulent time in modern Chinese history. Nationalist troops entered Foochow early in 1927 as part of their Northern Expedition to reunite the country. A nation-wide movement to protest imperialist aggression in China was also strong at the time, which stirred talk of reclaiming educational sovereignty for China. Hwa Nan's leadership confronted a difficult choice: shut down operations or find a way to accommodate the rising tide of nationalism in China so as to continue Hwa Nan's educational mission. Dr. Lewis clearly recognized that accompanying the larger political revolution brewing in China would come educational and religious revolutions, as well. In consequence, it was only a matter of time before educational administration and finances would need to be turned over to Chinese leadership. Dr. Lewis made the decision to accommodate the changing times, and so, she and Miss Wallace, dean of the college, voluntarily tendered their resignations. The Board of Directors elected Miss Carol Chen, who was serving as principal of the Hwa Nan Middle School, to be the new president; they also tapped Miss Lucy Wang to be the new dean. However, Wallace (1956: 38) recalled, "Miss Chen declined to accept the election and the Board of Directors then appointed a Commission of five to administer the affairs of

春色
任天涯
——福建华南女子
职业学院外教侧记
International Faculty with
Fujian Hua Nan Women's
College since 1908

26

Hwa Nan graduates of 1925 (Xie,2008:144)

the college, with Miss Carol Chen, chairman."

During her year in office Dr. Lewis effected a smooth transition from foreign missionary to Chinese leadership. Prior to resigning, she submitted the annual report to the Board. In it, Dr. Lewis advocated that registration with the government should be carried out as soon as possible to insure the smooth running of the college.

Hwa Nan graduates of 1927 (Xie, 2008:144)

However, from time to time the regulations governing registration were stiffened, and Hwa Nan found itself unable to obtain even a provisional registration until 1933, six years after Dr. Lewis had first raised the matter. Permanent registration would have to wait until the

Hwa Nan commencement in 1927
(Xie, 2008:146)

following year. How it was accomplished will be told in the next chapter on Dr. Lucy Wang's tenure as president.

Although Dr. Lewis stepped down from administrative duties, her heart remained with Hwa Nan. She visited many universities and spoke with many outside groups in America in an effort to raise Hwa Nan's profile and attract support. Xie (2008: 14-15) cites the words of the well-known educator Tao Xingzhi's in paying Dr. Lewis the ultimate compliment: "In recent years, among those who study and know well about Chinese women's education, I've only met one, that is Miss Lewis from America."

III

Summer House: A Token House of Sino-American Joint Education

The Summer House, whose owner was Doctor Rennie with British Embassy in China. The house later belonged to Doctor Donly, pastor with Hwa Nan College, who spent most of his life in Foochow and Nanping, Fujian Province. Before he returned to the U.S., he donated Summer House to Hwa Nan.

Summer House at Guling of Fuzhou (Xie, 2008:144)

Chapter 2

International Faculty with Fujian Hwa Nan Women's College after 1984

春色
任天涯
——福建华南女子
职业学院外教侧记

30
春色
任天涯
——福建华南女子
职业学院外教侧记
International Faculty with
Fujian Hua Nan Women's
College since 1908

I
Here She Came, Owing to Her Love for China
——A Story of Mrs. Judith Williamson

Spring is a season when everything comes back to life, which is reviving my distant memories. My mind has been brought back to the autumn of 1989, when I graduated from the English Department, Hwa Nan Women's College and was recruited by Hwa Nan to work in the Foreign Affairs Office (FAO).

School begins in autumn when new students register and new teachers register report for duty. In the autumn of 1989, I was assigned my first task that I, along with Xu Daofeng, Dean of the English Department and Vice Director of FAO, should go to Yixu Airport to receive Mrs. Judith Williamson and her husband Mr. Andrew Jackson Williamson, both of whom were selected by the United Board for Christian Higher Education in Asia and sent by the Amity Foundation based in Nanjing.

As it was the first time I had dealt with an airport pickup issue, there was no doubt that I was quite nervous, worrying about my oral English and therefore, I hid myself behind Ms. Xu. Beyond my imagination, having claimed their luggage and crossed the security check area, they, wearing a smile, walked directly towards us and spoke to me in standard Chinese "你好！我是朱迪·威廉逊。可以叫我朱迪。" It was not until then that my misgivings were dispelled. Meanwhile, I was given a touch of joy.

The Williamsons

Afterwards when I handled employment visa application for them, I gradually got to know that Judith was born in the city of Aledo, Illinois in the middle north region of the US on November 19, 1932. In 1958, with a major of English she graduated from Cornell College in Mt. Veron, Iowa and received her Bachelor Degree. Between 1962 and 1968, she extended her education by majoring in linguistics in American University of Washington DC and eventually achieved her Master Degree. Also, she studied Chinese in the School of Chinese, the Chinese University of Hong Kong.

Prior to her arrival in Hwa Nan, she had been engaged in teaching for over 25 years. From 1958 to 1964, she taught English in Hong Kong as a missionary from the Methodist Episcopal Church and was also involved in social affairs. Later, during the period between 1964 and 1987, she served as an English teacher in Malaysia and Singapore. Generally, before working for Hwa Nan, she had been committed to sermon translation and other translation activities as a justice and peace maker.

Gentle, learned and refined, Mr. Andrew Jackson Williamson, her husband, was expert in Chinese culture. He was good at Chinese and Chinese calligraphy. He got a Chinese name — Wei Liansheng. We all called him Mr. Jack. He always spoke mildly with a smile on his face. Mr. and Mrs. Williamson seemed devoted to each other. They were so affectionate to each other that they often walked hand in hand, which set a beautiful example for the young.

I delighted in Hwa Nan's employing such highly qualified foreign teachers. Attaching great importance to cultivating teaching assistants, Hwa Nan provided all new teachers with opportunities to further their study and I chose to visit Judith's classes, which lasted three years.

As soon as school began in the fall semester of 1989, Judith started guiding the 54 students from Classes 1987, the English Department to prepare for thesis writing ranging from topic selection, information search, writing to thesis reporting. It took her over four months to complete the job. Despite lots of hard work due to free topic selection such as the Chinese education, national culture, the hundred schools of thought and various sectors and industries, Judith buckled down to guiding each single student

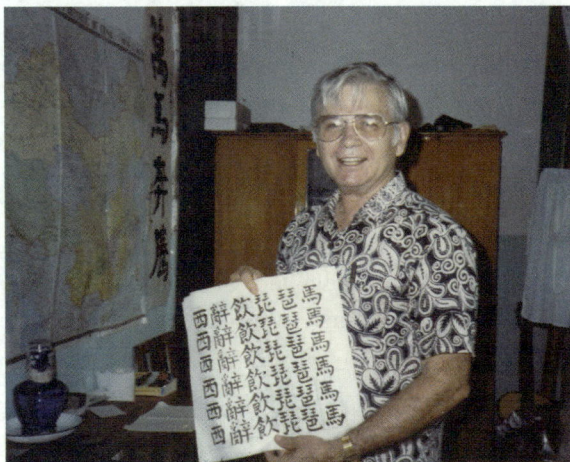

Mr. Jack Williamson and his Chinese calligraphy

春色
任天涯
——福建华南女子
职业学院外教侧记
International Faculty with
Fujian Hua Nan Women's
College since 1908

patiently, even revising punctuations. At the time of the thesis presentation, all the students were amazed at their great progress in historical and cultural knowledge, English writing skills and presentation skills. The 156 graduates in the next two years received her patient guidance alike and her students held her in high regard.

Mrs. Judith Williamsons is delivering a lecture

In terms of teaching content, she took notice of educating students ideologically by means of combining present Chinese situations and current affairs. In early September, 1990 when China, as a whole, was occupied with preparing for the Asian Games our nation had won the bid for, a new semester got started and her first listening and speaking class of that semester revolved around that topic. At the end of the class, as she

The Williamsons are performing a traditional Chinese wedding ceremony

was walking excitedly forward and backward on the platform, she, waving her hands, said to her students "China's winning bid suggests that China is becoming increasingly strong, through which, I can foresee a bright future for China. It is you, young females, who will ensure an even more promising China." Largely encouraged, the students decorated their classroom with some small flags printed with the symbols of the Asian Games and the mascots the next morning.

Judith was a foreign teacher equipped with good teachers' qualities. Strict in working, she took teaching extremely seriously. Meanwhile, she was learned and very experienced in teaching and had standard pronunciation. Moreover, her varieties of flexible teaching methods and great concern for her students also contributed to her success in teaching. No wonder she ranked 1st in the teaching assessment directed at the then foreign teachers in Hwa Nan.

Since the autumn of 1990, she had served as the deputy dean of the English Department. Her conscientiousness was fully manifested. For instance, she often visited many teachers' classes and combined efforts to work on teaching problems with the then foreign teachers who taught the freshmen and the sophomores. In order to ensure better transition of all the listening and speaking courses as well as all the reading and writing courses for 3 years of students and guarantee smooth takeover from teacher to teacher, she felt a strong desire to compile a set of course outlines specially targeted at female students in Hwa Nan, which were successfully completed in her charge. It laid a solid foundation for the Course of English Listening and Speaking to be selected as an excellent course for higher vocational education in Fujian in 1995 and the Department of Applied English to be rated as a high-quality department in higher vocational education of Fujian Province in 2010 (The English Department was later changed into the Department of Applied English).

At the beginning of the 1990s, the top priority for Hwa Nan was to cultivate its own successors, due to the fact that the alumna, who founded the new Hwa Nan, were all above sixty years old. Immediately after her filling the position of the deputy dean, she set about training the young teaching assistants of the Department of Applied English, to whom she delivered lectures for 3 hours on a weekly basis and whom she instructed about how to help students improve grammar. Furthermore, she also gave free conversation lessons to the teaching assistants from the other departments of Hwa Nan with a view to enhancing their English listening and speaking skills. Dr. Jean S Phillips continued her job of training young teachers when Judith returned to the United States.

Not only was Judith an excellent mentor for the young teachers and the students, but also she was a good friend of the old teachers. Aware of the old teachers' wish to improve oral English, she offered to undertake teaching them. In spite of her full class schedule, she managed to fit oral English classes for the old teachers into the intervals between lunchtime every Tuesday and Thursday and afternoon class time.

In response to the social needs, Hwa Nan offered an English speaking course to the public. In defiance of her far exceeding workload, Judith insisted on giving lessons two nights a week like the other foreign teachers. It was attributed to her love for China that she dedicated herself to fostering English language talents for us tirelessly and was always overloaded with work.

She knew about China, liked Chinese and understood our feelings

The Williamsons are participating in a school activity

春色
任天涯
——福建华南女子
职业学院外教侧记
International Faculty with
Fujian Hua Nan Women's
College since 1908

34

pretty well. When told by the American Consulate in Guangzhou over the phone that the Persian Gulf War had broken out, she said to us: "I will go nowhere. It's the safest to stay in China right now. "

Whenever she was invited to attend a banquet or a gala evening held for foreign experts of Fuzhou City by the Department of Foreign Affairs, Fuzhou, she would not like to go, in view of busy work and advanced age. Whereas, she would finally accept the invitations, saying that "It's bad manners to refuse the invitations from the Chinese government". It was a great honor for Hwa Nan to boast such a foreign teacher as Judith who understood China, loved China and took work extremely seriously with high teaching quality.

In 1992, Judith was titled "An Excellent Foreign Expert of Fujian Province", which she deserved.

At 10:05 on Friday morning, June 26, 1992, the Williamsons took Flight 5005 to the US via Hong Kong after 3 years of teaching in Hwa Nan. Going to the airport to see the couple off were Chen Zhongying, Vice School President, Ma Xiufa, Director of Teaching Affairs, Zhen Yuanxu, Office Director, Su Songzhen, Director of Foreign Affairs, Xu Daofeng, Dean of the English Department, He Xiaozhi, a teacher from the English Department, Hou Ruoying, a teacher from the Department of Child Education, Liu Yangzhang, a teacher from the Foreign Affairs Office, and I.

The Williamsons were awarded a silk banner by Hwa Nan Women's College

Twenty four years has passed, but to my surprise, the memory about the Williamsons is still fresh with me. She loved China and everything in Hwa Nan. I sincerely hope everything goes well with her.

（Here I acknowledge the support from the Administration Office, the Foreign Affairs Office and the Department of Applied English of Hwa Nan Women's College.）

Note: At the age of 76, Mr. Andrew Jackson Williamson passed away in the US on October 3, 2005.

The Williamsons are performing a
traditional Chinese wedding ceremony

The Williamsons are interacting with
some students in a field trip

Mrs. Judith Williamson is delivering a lecture

Mr. Jack Williamson is interacting
with the students

36

春色
任天涯
——福建华南女子
职业学院外教侧记
International Faculty with
Fujian Hua Nan Women's
College since 1908

II

California Rose—Dr. Betts Rivét

"Dinglingling" when the school bell rang, there was a vigorous foreign lady with grey hair and a smile showed up at my English Speaking and Listening class."Is this our foreign tea cher?" "Does she give class to us?" "Hi everyone. My name is Betts. I am your teacher!" As we whispered to one another We heard a strong and clear voice as well as careful pronunciation, talking slowly to make sure we could understand her words.The ways she smiled and talked to us nicely and immediately shorten the distance between us. That was my first time meeting with Dr. Marion Betts Rivét.

Personal Honors

Over time we learned a lot about this invigorating elder who was teaching us. She had a doctorate degree of psychology and we were also impressed to learn that Betts had been President of an association of educational psychologists and President of Delta Kappa Gamma (an honor society for women educators). Can you imagine that she also won Most Outstanding School Psychologist (California) and won a Delta Kappa Gamma Scholarship? Betts told us about several convention presentations she had made over the years and they all had to do with self-concept and what effect it had on learning. No wonder her teaching method made us feel good about ourselves and we actually learned more.

When Betts was young she learned how to fly an airplane and has a private pilot's license. She has flown all over the United States and into Mexico. Talking about her hobbies, she has a lot of extensive interests, such as tennis, swimming, camping, stamp collecting, traveling and reading. She has traveled to forty-five different countries. After we heard those things about her, we admired and were attracted to her, not

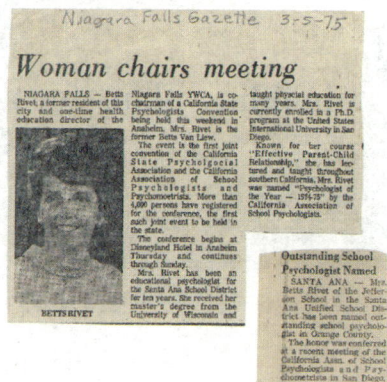

Local newspaper article writing about Betts

only because of her colorful and
joyful experiences, but also the view
how great a life women can have,
which translated into a small hopeful
dream in our hearts.

From 1992 to 2011 Betts taught
over a thousand students at Hwa
Nan. Because of her outstanding
contributions, she received the Fujian
Provincial Friendship Award, the

Betts has flown all over the United States and Mexico

gold medal of the City of Fuzhou Friendship Award as well as the key to the city and in
2006 she was honored to receive National Friendship Award along with forty-six other
foreign experts from eighteen different countries. This is the highest award the Chinese
government set up for encouraging foreign experts. Betts was the only foreign expert from
Fuzhou that year. She was also given the "Honorary Citizen of Fujian Province" in 2009.

Former Prime Minister Wen Jiabao met with the National Friendship Award receivers
in Beijing 2006.

Betts received the National Friendship
Award in Beijing on September 30th,
2006.

Betts at the National Friendship Award celebration in
Beijing on September 30th, 2006.

春色
任天涯
——福建华南女子
职业学院外教侧记
International Faculty with
Fujian Hua Nan Women's
College since 1908

38

Betts received the Honorary Citizen
Award from Fuzhou Municipal
Government on February 10th, 2006.

温家宝总理会见2006年度"友谊奖"获奖外国专家合影

2006年9月30日于人民大会堂

After receiving the Provincial and Municipal Friendship Awards and also the Honorary Citizen Award from Fuzhou, Dr. Betts Rivèt was honored on September 30, 2006 in Beijing when she received the National Friendship Award. Dr. Rivèt was one of 46 foreigners who were given this award and the only person from Fuzhou. Every year foreigners working in China are acknowledged for their outstanding accomplishments on behalf of the Chinese people. At the time of the award, Dr. Rivèt had been a teacher at Hwa Nan Women's College for 14 years.

Betts posing with her awards

Teaching Methods on Pronunciation

On Betts' classes: there was no need to stand up to greet the teacher as we did all the time in primary school and middle school. She always greeted us with a smile on her face. Her class was always flexible and lively. Sometimes she would sit on the table and continued teaching us. We never felt restrained or bored when she was teaching. Perhaps we would get a shock from her suddenly because of her special teaching method to make a point.

Betts sat on the table teaching us

She always planned a variety of different experiences to keep our interest. However, sometimes we would get a "serious warning" because we were not working hard enough on learning. Many memories of her teaching still come to mind, still so lively and interesting.

In the Applied English Department, Betts taught English Listening & Speaking, English Reading & Writing and Free Conversation. Someone heard about her good pronunciation, which led to her being asked to put her voice on a CD describing Fuzhou and surrounding area that would be given to English speaking tourists. And because of her clear pronunciation, patience and skillful teaching, the Applied English Department always arranged her to teach freshmen in English Listening and Speaking. Even though it was many years ago, students still remember how Betts always paid attention to practicing pronunciation and correcting every student's pronunciation. If some students had difficulty pronouncing R or L, she would teach them mouth and tongue exercises and they would try to copy Betts. After that, every time similar pronunciations came up in her classes, she would prod those students to think of what they learned and try again. Another particular pronunciation detail is the difference between N and M at the end of a word. For example, when we pronounced sun or son, usually it sounded like sum. It was the difference between opening or closing mouths for the ending letter, but thanks to Betts' acute listening and sensitive identification of the pronunciation problems during our learning process. She helped us to have a good foundation on clear speech when we were freshmen. The interesting part is that we tried hard to please her.

Teaching Methods on Listening Training

The most common way that Betts used in her classes to teach listening was by giving dictation. Not only did we need to understand what we heard, but we needed to write it down correctly including spelling. Betts usually chose a short interesting paragraph, and she would read it slowly the first time while we looked at it. After collecting the dictation papers, Betts would then expect us to write what she slowly dictated. To be honest, we used to have listening training in high school but only chose an answer according to how much we understood. But her dictations required us to write down every word we heard so some students were afraid of it. Dictation not only tested listening comprehension but also spelling. If students had difficulty, they always had a second chance the next day to improve after studying their mistakes from the first try. A small paragraph in her hands was also used to teach about the subject matter of the paragraph which might be about silk making, about animals, or even about different countries. From my standpoint in Betts' class, if you work diligently you never had any doubt of the outcome. No wonder, she

40

春色
任天涯
——福建华南女子
职业学院外教侧记
International Faculty with
Fujian Hua Nan Women's
College since 1908

often received good evaluations from students year after year with comments such as "strict yet fair and the students learned a lot from the class". She always conducted activities to make her students think and learn something new.

Teaching Methods on Oral English Teaching

Betts particularly paid attention to speaking up which was difficult for us because we were afraid of making a mistake. She would try her best to encourage her students to open their mouths to express. "No answer will be wrong and don't worry about the right words. I will help you." It was the most common encouragement from her. I can remember desks being pushed aside and students forming two circles each student facing a partner. A topic was put on the board and for two to three minutes we talked about that subject with our partner. Then the inner circle walked to their left until told to stop. We had a new partner and continued the subject. She also had students form small groups talking together in class. Betts walked around between us, listening carefully to our conversations, correcting grammar or pronunciation or simply asking a question. She would also write one philosophical statement on the board each week. Betts asked us to express in English what we thought the statement meant to us. Little by little more students felt comfortable to have an open discussion. Two examples of statements are: "One thing you can't recycle is wasted time.""Of all the things I wear, my expression is the most important." Many students who graduated and returned to visit her would recall those moments and could even remember some of the philosophical statements.

Betts' Oral English class

When we talk about oral English, we have to mention one of the specialty courses in Applied English Department at Hwa Nan - Free Conversation. We met in rooms that are inside the International Faculty House where the foreign teachers live and those rooms only had rattan chairs arranged in a semi-circle in order to have a warm and free conversation environment. Betts strongly recommended that there should only be about ten students in a group to attend free conversation at one time. This way it would give each student more time to speak in English. It was a time when Betts wanted every girl to feel uninhibited, not to worry about making mistakes, just speak English, unrestricted stress free.

For myself, actually the most unanticipated experience was the oral English exam. Betts had two students come to the room at an appointed time. At random we would choose a card from many displayed on the table. When we turned the card over, a topic was revealed. Each pair of students was given a minute to quietly think about how they would carry on a five minute conversation about the topic chosen. The focus was on using good grammar, adequate vocabulary, flowing sentences and minimum silence. There was no opportunity to memorize mechanically. We followed much the same routine that we did in class when paired for topic discussion. Even at that time, we had very limited vocabulary, but we learned how to keep a conversation going with our partner by asking questions and talking freely.

Teaching Methods on Speech Contest

Betts always paid great attention on the annual English Speaking Contest. At the very beginning, she would start to organize us to brain storm different topics that could be made into an interesting speech. From the list students chose a topic they wanted to talk about. Then she gave us directions in writing our speech. After we finished writing, she correct them carefully, looking at grammar and content. Betts took each speech and recorded it on tape using her voice. Then she returned the corrected speech to each student along with their speech on tape. We listened to the tape and practiced voice inflection and pronunciation. She always made us feel free to reach her for help when needed. When the time was getting close to the formal first year speech contest, Betts would arrange a preliminary contest in our class. The top three from each class would attend the final contest. In order to make the judging of the preliminary contest fair, Betts would invite other foreign teachers to be the judges. But two weeks before the preliminary contest, Betts did some spot checking to see how well the students were preparing. Unfortunately, in my class many students had not prepared at all. Suddenly she got very upset and disappointed, no more amiableness, instead, serious criticism strongly descended upon

春色
任天涯
——福建华南女子
职业学院外教侧记
International Faculty with
Fujian Hua Nan Women's
College since 1908

42

the class for being lazy. That was the first time and only time I experienced her anger. Thanks for her criticism, we could not be lazy any more and started to work hard. Our hard work paid off. Three students who competed in the formal school contest from my class were the top three winners. When we took the pictures with Betts happily

The top three student winners of a formal school contest from my class

after we had gotten the top scores, we appreciated what she has done for us and learned a lot about what hard work can produce.

Betts also paid attention to a few students who did not work hard or have abnormal behaviors in class. She would talk to them after class and encourage or help them to find out how to solve their problems. After that, if nothing changed, she would use the Chinese way and call the parents. With the help of the Chairman of the Applied English Department an appointment with their parents was made. The description of the problem was interpreted for the parents. The student always attended the meeting. Sometimes you would see the students and parents cry over the situation when they were consulted. The parents appreciated this foreign teacher for talking to them because they could easily see that she was very concerned about their kids. At the same time those students would get touched because of her consulting and change their minds to start learning. On another occasion, Betts found that one of her students was having difficulty in dictation, listening comprehension and spelling. Her many years of teaching experience told her that student had a hearing problem and suggested that her parents to have her hearing checked. The next day the girl came to class wearing a hearing-aid. From that time she improved considerably and successfully completed all classroom activities. The question still remains; why didn't anyone ever find out she had a hearing problem? What Betts has done is more like an extension of education, which is further than what she teaches at class, all because of her love and care about her students.

Teaching Methods on Reading and Writing

Part of Betts' responsibility at Hwa Nan is to teach reading comprehension and writing. She used to divide the ninety minute class into two parts. She spent 1/2 the class reading and the other half writing. The reading half might be short stories or an ongoing book which, when called upon, the student would read a paragraph or two. Often there would be a comprehension test. She also would hand out a story with many blanks and the students were required to fill in the best words. Writing took longer but Betts made it easier by giving them a picture to write about using their imagination to make a story. She also gave them an incomplete first sentence which they would finish and then write about it. Her students definitely had to know what the figures of speech are and how to use them (noun, verb, adjective, adverb, etc.) by recognizing them in sentences.They were also asked to correct sentences. This is not easy for Chinese students because the Chinese grammar is so different but little by little we learned that English grammar and writing became easier and easier.

There was one time, when Betts was explaining a short paragraph using the word "scream". No one knew what that word meant. She decided to show them what a scream was so she opened the window and screamed outside very loudly. After that we saw her smile and she simply said, "Now you know what a scream is." Sometime later, when I got to know a little about educational psychology, I found that Betts' way of helping us remember the word 'scream' is called the Emotional Memory Method.

Experiential Learning

Because Betts has a doctorate in Psychology, she knows how to use Psychology in her teaching. She doesn't use only the Affective but also the Kinesthetic teaching styles to personalized students' learning experiences. For instance, each year from 1993 to 1997, Betts took her students to visit the School for the Blind. She also showed the film that describes the life of Helen Keller, in order to let her students see different ways of learning a language. Starting in 1999, Betts realized that around 90% of her students had never been to the Fujian Provincial Museum, so she began to rent a bus to take each class to the museum at her own expense. She also arranged a guide to explain the information about museum artifacts. She did this continuously until 2003. Later she changed her direction, taking her students to Five Star hotels instead. From 2004 to 2007, she has taken her students to Hot Springs Hotel, West Lake Hotel, etc., in order to observe the interior decoration of the guest rooms, ballrooms, restaurants and the welcoming desk. After the visit the students would write a report on what they had seen and heard and felt. This kind of written work gave the students much appreciation for her. Some students were greatly influenced by this experience so upon graduating from college, they chose to work in the hotels. Obviously this out-of-the-classroom teaching style gave the students fresh insights into life around them.

44

春色
任天涯
——福建华南女子
职业学院外教侧记
International Faculty with
Fujian Hua Nan Women's
College since 1908

Destiny with Hwa Nan Started from 1992

The above teaching methods I have chosen to write about were from my memories when I was a student at Hwa Nan. Others were from my experiences after I worked in the Foreign Affairs Office at Hwa Nan and things Betts told me. I believe everyone who is familiar with Betts will have the same impressions about her as I have. Her distinct character, active attitudes and behaviors as well as her vigorous energy will leave very deep impressions on anyone who comes in contact with her. When people meet her at the first moment and see a lady has grey-hair and a little humpback and they usually would like to ask "How old is she?", "Where is she from?" What is the reason a retired lady came all the way from the United States to Hwa Nan paying her own airfare and getting no salary for teaching? In 1990s the environment at Hwa Nan was very simple and the facility was deficient. What kind of feeling inside her made her to teach at Hwa Nan for nineteen years? She has given so much of herself to Hwa Nan and at the same time has witnessed Fuzhou city's development, traveled extensively throughout China, has received three prestigious Foreign Expert awards and has made many friends. Her life has, indeed, been made richer by her choice to come to China.

Coming to Hwa Nan Women's College all began with a phone call in 1991. The call was from her friend telling her about a college in China that needed foreign teachers. Betts was already 63 years old and was going to retire from education the next year. Betts said, "No, I would never want to teach in China, thank you!" After several more phone calls from her friend, Betts finally wrote to the college for names and phone numbers of other foreign teachers. When calling them, their assessment of the college would influence her final decision. They all had wonderful things to say about Hwa Nan so she decided to take a chance. Her friend go "cold feet" at the last minute and did not come with her. Betts came alone to China to teach English at Hwa Nan. But who knew that because of this first trip to Hwa Nan she would work here so long and hard with her wisdom, passion and professional inexhaustibility and without complaint or regret. She has helped a lot of people and helped the college in impressive ways. Everyone who has met her would be affected by her personality charm. Nineteen years of experience at Hwa Nan also made her retirement life more colorful and joyful.

In 1992, when Betts arrived in China for the first time and walked out the Fuzhou airport, she saw five smiling Chinese women holding a sign that read, "Welcome to Hwa Nan, Betts." They all spoke good English. Maybe teaching at Hwa Nan was not going to be so hard after all, she thought. The first thing happened to her was that she was given a bicycle and she rode everywhere learning about Fuzhou and amazed to see taxis and buses but almost no private cars. Another interesting thing to Betts was that the local people stared at foreigners so she learned the Chinese word "Nihao". From then on, anytime Chinese people stared at her, she would smile and say "Nihao". Their eyes and heads averted immediately.

For the first five years, Betts taught free at Hwa Nan and also paid her own airfare. In 1992, Hwa Nan only has 600 students. Because her psychology background Hwa Nan wanted her to teach in the Pre-school Education Department. She not only taught oral English but also childhood psychology lessons. I remember Betts saying how much she appreciated Ren Jianhong who expertly and untiringly translated her words year after year in psychology class. Betts said, "Teaching psychology was a pleasure; Jianhong made it a thousand times easier."

Retire? Or Coming Back?

It was at the end of the 1996 school year that Betts decided to retire. She was grateful for the things she had learned and had acquired a deep appreciation of China and its people. Even so, it was the time to become reacquainted with her family in USA. She had three married daughters and eleven grandchildren. When she taught at Hwa Nan, the summer time/vocation was the only time to see her family. After Betts actually retired, she was asked to speak at group meetings about China and her teaching experiences. After completed her speeches the most frequently question was asked was "Do you ever think you will go back to China?", "No, I have not thought about it." But always telling people about China made her begin to think about the passion she had for teaching at Hwa Nan, the sense of accomplishment of helping her students and the deep friendships she had made. When those memories came out, unquestionably, she wanted to go back to Fuzhou to teach. So she called the Foreign Affairs Office at Hwa Nan. Xu Daofeng was the director who answered the phone. "I would like to come back to teach, I am not ready to retire yet. Is this ok?" Betts heard a scream from Xu Daofeng who could not contain herself because she was so excited that Betts would return to teach in August 1997.

International Cooperation on Students' Studying Abroad (3+1 Program)

Even though Betts continually taught classes of ever growing numbers of students and correcting homework, she also spent her spare time voluntarily organizing Hwa Nan students to study abroad. As early as 2000, Betts started to organize and launch this program because Centenary College in New Jersey signed a cooperative agreement with Hwa Nan whereby after successfully finishing three years at Hwa Nan a student could earn a bachelor's degree at Centenary College in one year. We called it the 3+1 Program. Betts became the International Liaison officer for Hwa Nan. After that she needed to know

春色
任天涯
——福建华南女子
职业学院外教侧记
International Faculty with
Fujian Hua Nan Women's
College since 1908

46

what they needed to know in order to interview at the American Embassy. So she went to Guang Zhou to talk with officers as well as the Consulate General. Betts met many times with interested students giving all necessary information (cost of tuition/ board and room, IELTS scores required, visa information, table and cultural etiquette) as

Betts with Hwa Nan graduates who studied abroad
in the United States

well as practicing over and over again for the visa interview in Guang Zhou. Without Betts' help, those students could not complete all applications alone for which they would have had to pay high consulting fees to agencies. Betts did this for eleven years helping upwards to 75 students get a BA Degree at Centenary and later at Morningside College (Iowa) and Emporia State University (Kansas). In fact, one student went on to get a Master's Degree and then a Ph.D. To be an elder to work so hard and never expect anything in return is an attribute so admired.

Scholarship Grants that Came Out of Love

Betts not only cared for the learning situation but also the financial conditions of the students. When she was still teaching, she often inquired from the class advisor about the family's financial condition of her students. Anyone who had financial difficulty, but was trying her best to improve, Betts would take the initiative to use her money, and even wrote to her American friends and church friends, so that together they could help solve the financial problem of the family. This would liberate the student and allow her to focus more on her studies. From 2008, Betts has begun using her own living expenses, to help and support needy students who had encountered financial difficulties but had good scores. She did this continuously until she retired in 2011. But her retirement did not stop her financial help. When she retired, she started a foundation in her own name, called the Betts Scholarship. Not only did she put into the foundation the money that she earned from correcting dissertations for students of Tsinghua University, she also added the financial support that her American and Chinese friends gave her. It is an ongoing scholarship so she is still giving her scholarship grants to help the needy. To Betts, starting a foundation does not only mean money, she took the time to understand the students' actual situation, in order to discern more accurately how much scholarship money to be given to each particular student. The process starts with consulting with the Financial Department to find out students who have not paid their tuition fees. Next she asks all Department Heads to recommend and submit transcripts. The qualified students selected are asked to write a brief report

Betts helped students by giving them scholarships in 2009

about their family and about themselves. After that she would ask 3 people to interview the students with her to decide the amount of money to be given to each student (which is paid directly toward their tuition). Presently I am working in the Foreign Affairs Office and have participated in some of the translation of the needed material. Even after retiring, Betts has returned two times to give her scholarship to needy students. I have seen this grey-haired aged lady to be very committed and fair in looking after the smallest details of each procedure. Likewise I have often seen those students who received the scholarship tearfully express their gratitude to Betts. Although Betts has already retired she has not forgotten to give these students her most sincere blessings and encouragement through her scholarship.

Setting up an Agreement with Emporia State University

Joyce Zhou, a former student of Betts, was the first Hwa Nan student to receive an MBA and a Ph.D. She also was one of first students who went to Centenary College to get a BA Degree. Upon graduation after receiving her doctorate, she became Assistant Professor at Emporia State University. Dr. Zhou gave Betts a tour of the university campus during her visit there. Betts and Joyce met with the president who thought a cooperative agreement

Joyce Zhou and Hwa Nan graduates at Emporia State University

春色
任天涯
——福建华南女子
职业学院外教侧记
International Faculty with
Fujian Hua Nan Women's
College since 1908

with Hwa Nan Women's College would be appropriate and to help students from Hwa Nan, they could pay the lower in-state tuition but would necessarily have stay more than one year to earn a BA Degree. Cooperative documents were signed and the following year six Hwa Nan students began their study at Emporia State University. Attending a "university"appealed to the Hwa Nan students and thanks to Dr. Zhou, our students have someone to go to when needed and who watches over them. Many Hvvwa Nan students have stayed to get their Master's Degree at Emporia State University.

Caring for the Expansion of the Campus

Betts not only cared for the students of Hwa Nan, doing her best to teach them well, but also devoted much energy to establish the school's reputation. She often gave suggestions for improvement, and often contributed her own resources to achieve those ideals. In the past, the cook's kitchen in the Foreign Teacher's dormitory at the Yan Tai Shan campus was dark, dingy, with no refrigerator, and coal was used for cooking. Betts created a plan for a new kitchen and with Xu Dao Feng's help, Betts hired a man to build a modern kitchen adding cabinets, gas burners to cook over, a refrigerator to keep left over food, florescent lights and tile counters. Current and past foreign teachers financed the whole project.

There was one land line telephone for three floors at the foreign teacher's house on Yantai-shan Hill. It was inconvenient to expect someone to run to that one phone when it rang. Betts thought that each foreign teacher should have their own phone so after getting cost figures from the Telecommunications Company, the school's governing council spent the money to make it happen. Each teacher paid their own phone bill but the convenience was worth it.

In 2005 the former school president, Professor Lin Benchun initiated plans to build a new Hwa Nan on land in University City. As for the future Foreign Experts' Dormitory, Betts was the one who exerted the most effort to oversee construction details with Lin Benchun. She also helped to organize the detailed arrangements for moving the foreign teachers into their new abode. The school budget was slim, so money for closets, showers and furniture for 20 apartments had to come from other sources. Betts financed a fund raising campaign and over a period of six months, $50,000 US dollars was collected from Hwa Nan supporters in China, USA, England and Canada. When the Grand Opening of the new campus in 2008 took place, all apartments were completely furnished. Betts also took a special interest in making sure that both the foreign teachers' and the cooks' kitchens were completely outfitted with cabinets, water heaters, and all the utensils needed. Later she and Dr. Kay Grimmesey together bought television sets for the foreign teachers' private use. For birthdays and special celebrations, or when academic guests from the United States came, Betts would unreservedly provide all the help she could by decorating the surroundings and by making cakes and pies. She was always joyful as she busily prepared for all these things.

While teaching in Hwa Nan, Betts realized that our school lacked up-to-date English teaching materials. She then bought many books and teaching materials from the United States at her own expense. By doing this she has widened the horizon for our teachers and students, as well as making our English teaching materials much more comprehensive.

Likewise she knew that our school needed many foreign teachers, thus she put an advertisement in an American magazine to inform them of the need for teachers at Hwa Nan. Simultaneously she also created an English website in the United Sates with her own money to promote Hwa Nan. Betts always thought about what was needed to help Hwa Nan. The website existed for ten years and because of that Hwa Nan has welcomed many distinguished foreign teachers to become part of our faculty.

Social Welfare Outside of the School

Other than her great contribution to Hwa Nan, Betts also cared for other people. In 2000 she learned from her colleague, Sue Todd, that there were many poor students in the school for the blind. When Sue retired, Betts went to the Blind School to learn more about their condition. Hence she was able to help solve the financial problems of three siblings. When the weather became cold, Betts took warm clothes to the children. During Children's Day, on June 1, Betts gave them gifts. She also mobilized her Hwa Nan students to volunteer to teach English at the Blind School on weekends. Many of the foreign teachers in Hwa Nan were touched by her love so they, too, began to join her in this ministry of love, giving gifts, clothes and money. Year after year many of these students have graduated to become massage masters, yet Betts did not stop extending her loving support to the newcomers. She said, "I'm just doing what I enjoy doing. Today or the day after I will

Betts visited the Blind School with two other foreign teachers

50

春色
任天涯
——福建华南女子
职业学院外教侧记
International Faculty with
Fujian Hua Nan Women's
College since 1908

continually do it…"

Around the 1990's, the accumulation of garbage outside the campus of Yan Tai Shan had become ugly scenery pilled up on the road, plus, it smelled and rats were daily visitors. Many times Betts tried to talk to sub-district officers through the school's workers in order to solve the problem. Because of her persistence, the Mayor finally took notice of this problem. Although it took a long time, in the end they arranged for someone to come and solve this problem. Not long after that, they changed the public garbage container, bringing much more convenient to the local residents and Hwa Nan teachers and students. It also improved the quality of the air and got rid of the rats.

Besides, Betts was also zealously concerned about the welfare of the city she lived in. She often wrote letters in order to give the city officials feedback on several problems. One letter told of the difficulty for people to see the bus numbers when many buses stopped at the bus station all together. She suggested that numbers be written in bigger print and placed in the lower right hand corner of the front window. The receipt of her letter was acknowledged and the officials replied that they would improve and oversee the problem at the bus stations. Later when Powerlong was built, she saw that pedestrians were in danger as they tried to cross that busy street, which was very dangerous. Therefore she wrote another letter that suggested building a foot bridge that would protect the pedestrians from getting hit by motorists. That letter was also acknowledged with enthusiasm for the suggestion. After a year or so a foot bridge was under construction and when it opened some of us called it the Betts Bridge.

An orthopedic doctor from Number Two Hospital wished to go to the United States to further his medical studies. He was accepted for his residency program at the Medical School of Louisiana State University. Because of his limitation in the English language, Betts recorded audibly several medical books, page by page. By listening to them he learned all that was necessary to pass the three national exams. After 12 years he graduated as a medical doctor in the United States. He is now a famous combined Chinese and Western Medicine specialist in New Orleans in America where he lives with his family. This paragraph is based on the memories of Hwa Nan Excellent Graduate Mrs. Li Xiaowu and her husband.

Retired Octogenarian, Coming Back Visiting Twice

It's worth mentioning that Betts also writes, edits, and publishes her personal annual newsletters. She distributes it to her family and friends, hoping that they may know what she has done during the recent year. In 2011, Betts decided to finally retire from Hwa Nan. One of the main reasons was that she wanted to spend more time writing her autobiography. So in 2013, when Betts was eighty five years old, she completed her autobiography entitled "Bits by Betts: Shadows of My Footsteps.'" In her book there are many chapters telling about experiences of growing up, going to college, marriage, teaching but also things about all she had experienced in China, her teaching experience in Hwa Nan, and her deep love for and remembrance of China.

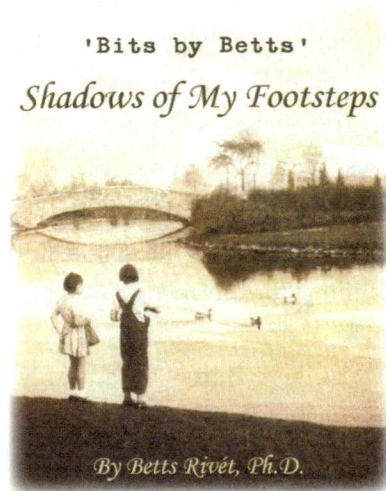

'Bits by Betts'
Shadows of My Footsteps

By Betts Rivét, Ph.D.

Betts' autobiography

When we knew of her leaving, a well prepared farewell party was planned. The Alumna Association started to contact alumna through Applied English Department and Pre-school Education Department. On June 12th, 2011, over 100 former students came to the farewell party. Our former president Professor Lin Benchun made a speech recalling experiences he had working with Betts and thanked her for being a willing and hardworking consultant for Hwa Nan. He expressed, on behalf of everyone, the deep appreciation for all she has done for Hwa Nan and blessed her with joy in her retirement years. Then when Betts gave her farewell speech, she announced that she was starting a scholarship for Hwa Nan students. A journalist from Fuzhou Evening News came in person and wrote a report called "An American Teacher's Fuzhou Love."

Former President Lin Benchun with Betts at her farewell party

Betts giving a speech at her farewell party

Betts came back with Dr. Kay to visit Hwa Nan in October, 2013 when Hwa Nan celebrated its 105 years birthday. Then when Betts was 87 years old, she came back alone in June, 2015, just wanting to see how Hwa Nan was getting along. During these two visitings, she was very willing to join in any class teaching with other Chinese teachers, to

春色
任天涯
——福建华南女子
职业学院外教侧记
International Faculty with
Fujian Hua Nan Women's
College since 1908

52

make some speeches to encourage students to study harder. At the same time, she continued to work on giving her scholarship by assessing and selecting deserving but needy students. Getting closer to 90 years old, she is still planning to return for a visit in 2017.

Betts and Kay returned to Fujian Hwa Nan Women's College on the 105th anniversary in 2013

This is Betts, an amiable and honorable American teacher. She is so many people's scholarly mentor and beneficial friend. She is always full of energy. Her positive and optimistic attitude to life is like a fresh rose that was planted within our hearts. For 19 years, Betts had devoted all her heart and soul to promote women's education in Fujian Province. Because of her desire to build a better education and career for the Chinese women, she did all she could. She never looked

Betts in her apartment when she came back to visit Fujian Hwa Nan Women's College in June 2015

for personal gain. She was selfless in offering herself for the benefit of others (students, the blind school, local residence, and for foreign and Chinese teachers). We have all witnessed this American friend who has highly treasured friendship with the Chinese people. She has always expressed great hope for the higher education of Chinese women, and displayed in her own life an excellent character. From the awards and recognitions she received in China, we can see how diligently she strived in her duties as an educator. She treated people with honesty and integrity. She helped people selflessly. She has shown us that women can both be strong and independent, and if women think, plan, work to overcome obstacles, and be determined to improve, they can have a bright successful future.

Words from Lin Feng

"The first time I met Betts was more than 20 years ago. In 1991, I graduated from a

USA university and came back to teach at Hwa Nan. I started to teach in the same grade and the same course as Betts (freshmen, English Listening and Speaking). So I had more chances to get to know her when we sat together and discussed teaching methods. Even though we lived in different places, leading our own respective lives, we still kept in touch during these 20 years. Every year when we received Betts' newsletter at Christmas time, I was encouraged by her words. Last year we received Betts' phone call telling us that she would visit Vancouver, Canada. She stayed with us for three days, our whole family was very excited. Actually Betts stayed at our house four days and three nights, which gave us a lot of time to talk about our days at Hwa Nan and our decision to move to Canada. Please imagine an elderly lady at the age of 86 who had mastectomy 4 years ago because of mammary cancer and also had two hips been replaced by surgeries. When Betts was 55 she fell down from a horse and fractured her back, leaving her with a very crooked back. But she still carries her own suitcase and travels all over the world. If I did not see her in person, I would guess because of surgeries and a back problem that she would be already a very elderly lady required to stay in bed all the time. However, she is totally different from what I thought. When she visited us, she got up at 7:30 in the morning and kept talking with me and my husband about her experiences in the last 20 years. We showed her the tourist sights and had dinner with friends. We, the younger ones just took our turns to accompany her while some would sneak away to take a short nap. So compared to her, our young people are less energetic. Until now, Betts still goes to the gym three or four times a week as well as going swimming. She also drives her granddaughter to school everyday, joined a book club, plays bridge and has a Sister Reunion (4 sisters in total) often to talk about their lives and how they plan to help people in need. After staying with her for 3 days, I got tips from her about how to keep healthy, live a long life and be happy. Betts' philosophy is to be active, optimistic and dedicated all the time. From Li Xiaowu, Hwa Nan graduate and now works as a Canadian civil servant.

"A person's spirit: Before I saw Betts last year, I imagined that she would look like an elderly person bend over and hunched up. But when she appeared, I just realized she looked almost the same as 20 years ago. She is still vigorous and energetic as well as sharp in remembering things. At the age of 86, she has been to more than 50 countries. During the 19 years she taught in Fuzhou, she received Friendship Awards from Fuzhou, Fujian and the National government. We spent four days and three nights with her and heard many of her stories which benefited us a lot. The most impressive thing about her is the attitude she has for life and for people. Here are two small stories about her. An orthopedic doctor from Number Two Hospital in Fuzhou wished to go to the United States to further his medical studies. He was accepted for his residency program at the Medical School

春色
任天涯
——福建华南女子
职业学院外教侧记
International Faculty with
Fujian Hua Nan Women's
College since 1908

54

of Louisiana State University. Because of his limitation in the English language, Betts recorded audibly several medical books, page by page. By listening to them he learned all that was necessary to pass the three national exams. He graduated as a medical doctor in the United States and is now a famous combined Chinese and Western Medicine specialist in New Orleans in America where he lives with his family. The other story is about her surgery. Three or four years ago, because of mammary cancer Betts had a mastectomy. She had her surgery in the morning and she went out in a wheelchair in the afternoon to visit other patients in the next rooms. She also said actually she could have gone back home that afternoon but there was no one home because her daughter and family had a long-time planned event they had to attend. When she talked about it, there was no complaining about her daughter. She just accepted it as it was. For me, I would never have done it that way. I have learned a good lesson from her about how to treat people sincerely, respectfully and with consideration."（Tr. By Chen Qian）

III
Let Life Be Beautiful Like Summer Flowers
—Recalling Dr. Jeanne Phillips

Jeanne Philips, the seemingly ordinary senior lady, made remarkable achievements to Fujian education. Lots of people were moved by her actions, intelligence, and love. Jeanne was an outstanding and popular foreign teacher. She had taught in Fujian Hwa Nan Women's College for many years with the characteristics of being modest, humorous, and optimistic. Therefore, all the people here loved her very much.

Jeanne Philips was born in Georgia, USA in August, 1929. She got her Ph.D. at

Jeanne with her Friendship Award medal

Washington University. After graduation, Jeanne taught Medical Psychology and Psychiatry in Oregon Medical School. After several years she was promoted to associate professor from instructor. In 1968 Jeanne went to the University of Massachusetts as a professor of psychology and the director of clinical training. She studied in behavior psychology and published a book called

Jeanne and the representative from the University of Puget Sound

Learning Foundations of Behavior Therapy. Since 1971 Jeanne had been a professor of psychology, the instructor of Ph.D. students and also the director of clinical training, until she retired in 1985. Meanwhile, she worked on the editorial board of the *Annual Review of Psychology* as well. She was a member of various committees and committee chairs for the American Psychological Association and published many research theses in psychological journals.

The Indissoluble Bond between Jeanne and Hwa Nan

In 1985, Jeanne had her first teaching experience at Hwa Nan. The accommodation condition was very tough at that time. Since the new Hwa Nan was just founded, there was no special dorm building for the foreign experts. Jeanne's dorm was very simple in a closed-in area in the back of her classroom. It was extremely cold in Fuzhou's winter and there was no heat here at that time. She used to sleep in four layers of clothes, with a woolen hat and two pairs of socks. There was also no water-heater in the bathroom. Jeanne had to go downstairs to get hot water in pails. Jeanne had to exercise to get warm and pluck up courage before taking a bath because it was so cold. Nevertheless, Jeanne never complained about the rough living condition. She was such a considerate person that she really understood the difficulties Hwa Nan had in the first year that it opened its door to students. Jeanne had a firm belief that Hwa Nan would do better and better. She was moved by hospitable people here and forged an indissoluble bond with Hwa Nan.

In 1987, Jeanne came back to teach in Hwa Nan, but this time there had been a dorm building especially arranged for foreign teachers diagonally opposite to the campus. It is a three-floor building with a basement and a yard. Foreign teachers moved in and their living conditions were greatly improved. You would never get to know that Jeanne was a tenured professor in one of America's top-class universities. She simply adjusted to the tough condition silently. You may ask how did Jeanne come to Hwa Nan? Here I'd

春色
任天涯
——福建华南女子
职业学院外教侧记
International Faculty with
Fujian Hua Nan Women's
College since 1908

56

The ground breaking ceremony of the liberal arts building（Jeanne was in a plaid shirt）

Jeanne in the famous English-Chinese writer Elizabeth Comber's lecture

like to mention a famous alumna, the honorary president of Hwa Nan, Dr. Liu Yonghe. Liu was Jeanne's student when she was pursuing her doctor's degree. By Dr. Liu's recommendation, Jeanne came to teach at Hwa Nan as a volunteer. In 1987, Jeanne formally came to teach under the invitation of Hwa Nan. To become a volunteer teacher in Fuzhou, she flew over the ocean ten times. She loved the college and the students by dedicating herself without consideration of pay. She dedicated herself to Hwa Nan and was highly appreciated by the teachers and students. In 1992, Dr. Jeanne Philips was honored by being asked to be an educational consultant for Fujian Hwa Nan Women's College.

Rigorous in Teaching and Caring for Students

Jeanne taught psychology in the Pre-school Education Department at first and then taught Foreign Culture and Listening & Speaking in the Applied English Department. She worked hard and endeavored to do better. She had accumulated abundant experience in training students' listening and speaking skills. She was disciplined, ambitious and devoted to her students. She was fair to every student no matter what level were they at and paid attention to everyone's ability. Let's take Class B, Grade 2000 as an example. The students of this class didn't have good English foundation, which Jeanne eagerly help them overcome. It was hard for them to communicate with a foreigner entering Hwa Nan as a freshmen. As a psychology professor, Jeanne knew what they thought, and understood their shyness and nervousness. She was good at arousing students' enthusiasm for study and always talked with students with a smile, which made her friendliness easily felt. With Jeanne's inspiration and encouragement, the students who dared not speak became more confident to express themselves. By Jeanne's efforts and guidance, the students of Class B, Grade 2000 improved their English. They became eager to speak by raising their hands in the class.

Group picture of foreign teachers with the director Xu Daofeng (Jeanne in the middle of the top row)

In the aspect of teaching, carefulness is the most prominent feature of Jeanne. In addition to the textbook and the teaching plan, she also prepared supplementary materials for the class, which were designed according to the students' actual English level. Starting with the basic phonetics, she helped improve the students' pronunciation. By patiently listening to them, she corrected their pronouncing mistakes. The students tried to intimate Jeanne's pronunciation, attentively practicing and gradually making progress in their oral English. In Jeanne's class, the atmosphere was active, even boring grammar could be easily understood in her relaxing teaching style. The teaching concept upheld by Jeanne was to let her students learn in a relaxing and joyful atmosphere. Therefore, her class was very active and interesting. One of her students recalled that when Jeanne taught the word "giggle", she made the sound of giggle and the whole class giggled. And when Jeanne explained the word "tiptoe", she gently moved forward on her tiptoes. Through Jeanne's vivid teaching, her students memorized these words.They even remember her laughing and humorous behaviors. In order to let students know about the American culture, when western festivals came, Jeanne would introduce the customs of the festival comprehensively. For example, if she met her class on or close to Halloween, Jeanne would bring markers, card board, scissors, and nylon wires and taught the students to make Halloween masks. She told the students to line up and ask for candies from her as they shouted "trick or treat". The classroom was filled with laughter and fun.

Jeanne was full of love and patience for the students. She encouraged the girls all the way. She wrote inspiring words when correcting papers, such as, "You've done a good job", "Well done, keep going", or "You will do better." These words flowed into the girls' hearts like a warm current. Whenever they were a little bit discouraged, thinking of Jeanne's words, they had confidence and morale again. Jeanne paid attention to protecting

春色
任天涯
——福建华南女子
职业学院外教侧记
International Faculty with
Fujian Hua Nan Women's
College since 1908

58

the students' privacy. No matter handing out papers, quizzes or corrected homework, she never asked students to help. She folded the papers and gave them personally to every one without leaking out their scores. In this way, those who didn't get satisfactory scores didn't feel humiliated but even studied harder. In the meantime, the students learned how to respect others and protect other's privacy. The teacher, Dong Xiuping, from the Applied English Department, one of the most popular teacher now, was Jeanne's student. Xiuping said that she learned a lot from Jeanne. Having been a teacher for about twenty years, Xiuping would hand out the paper or quiz in person and told the students not to open others' papers and not to snoop at others' scores. Jeanne was not only teaching conscientiously, but also careful to record the students' growth. At the end of each semester, Jeanne would provide the advisor with a note listing everyone's characteristics, which indicated who improved, who did well and who needed help, etc.

Jeanne's free conversation class was varied in style. Her idea of "learning while playing" was novel

Jeanne made a Halloween party fun(1999)

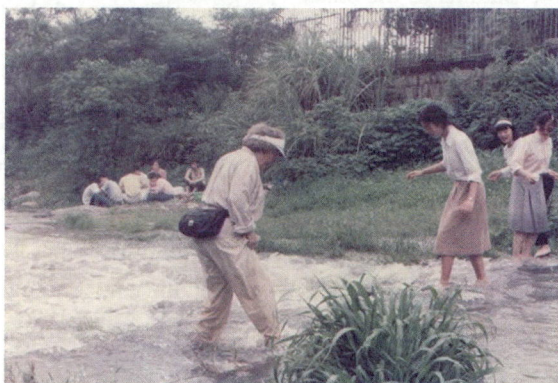

Jeanne and her student, Dong Xiuping

Jeanne and her students in class

in China at that time. In her opinion, young college ladies should be vigorous and enjoy happiness. Sometimes she took the students to the park to get close to nature, carrying on the free conversation in a casual manner. Sometimes she taught the girls how to swim at the swimming pool next to the college. Sometimes she taught the girls how to bake in the foreign teachers' kitchen. And sometimes she even invited them to have meal in the restaurant. Compared with teaching with pictures in the classroom, such immersive teaching allowed students to learn even more. Jeanne never sermonized in front of the students. Instead she set a good example to her students. She was always punctual. She believed that it was more important for college students to learn how to behave themselves than expand their knowledge. Her idea of education and the way of doing things had positive and far-reaching influence on her students. When they became mothers, they kept Jeanne's ideas in mind in educating their children, and let the kids grow up in happiness while obeying the rules.

Besides teaching, Jeanne was considerate and kind to her students in terms of life. It's worth mentioning that Jeanne could remember every student's birthday. Each time when celebrating the students' birthday, she would send nice small gifts to them. Jeanne visited the students' dorms with snacks. She communicated with the students, made friends with them and was concerned about their life. At that time there was a typing course in the Applied English Department. To be skillful, the students were required to practice more with typewriter after class. But the number of typewriters and the open-up practicing time

Foreign teachers and Chinese teachers from Applied English Dept.

was not enough. When Jeanne knew about that, she donated her own typewriter and sorted out a room in foreign teachers' dorm as the typing practicing room for the students. Jeanne regarded the students' matters as her own. Being a teacher is mone meaningful in behavior than teaching. If the teacher affected students with positive behavior throughout their life, he/she would be considered as a significant mentor. When thinking of teachers, many students might not remember what the teachers exactly taught but remember their kindness.

As far as Jeanne was concerned, the freshmen needed an orientation event in order to know more about the college and to make them feel more at ease in a new enviroment. After Jeanne's suggestion, one-week orientation was arranged for the freshmen at Hwa Nan. Jeanne took the first-year students to the Roundabout Park under the Sanxianzhou Bridge and played games. She brought lots of snacks filled in sacks of red, white and

春色
任天涯
——福建华南女子
职业学院外教侧记
International Faculty with
Fujian Hua Nan Women's
College since 1908

60

blue. Young ladies played while eating. Homesickness was replaced with joy. Those who came from the countryside far from Fuzhou were rather homesick at first. But having such a friendly foreign teacher and eating snacks and candies that they had never eaten, they felt better and later built up friendships. Jeanne often took a camera with her because she wanted to take photos for her students at anytime. She recorded the wonderful moments for the girls and then posted the pictures on the wall of the classroom, which made the students feel special. To the students' surprise, Jeanne sent the best photo for each one as a gift before their graduation, and she wrote about the advantages for every person on the back side of the photo. Jeanne thanked everyone who helped her, even if the favor was little. Looking at the pictures, the young ladies felt thankful and reluctant to leave Hwa Nan.

Jeanne's love was broad not only for the students but also for the young teachers in Hwa Nan. She initiated the Spoken English Class for the young faculty. She divided 37 young teachers into 5 small groups and taught them according to their schedules. Because it was hard to have common free time, Jeanne sacrificed her noon time and taught oral English for young teachers. She made coffee and cakes to serve the young colleagues. Young learners studied while they enjoyed delicious cakes in harmonious atmosphere. Each Wednesday noon the young teachers came to Jeanne's room like flying happy birds. They made food and chatted with each offer. Sometimes Jeanne taught them to make sandwiches. Butter on two slices of bread, and then put tuna and lettuce with salad dressing between the slices. And she also taught to make cookies with tuna sauce. Sometimes she made "stuffed eggs". Cut the boiled egg into two halves and remove the egg yolk. Then stir the yolk with salad dressing and put it back into the open part of the half egg. All the western food made the young ladies drool. During the course of making snacks, humorous and amusing Jeanne made everybody burst into laughter. The topic Jeanne used to teach was fresh such as insurance, credit cards and tourism, which the young Chinese teachers had never heard of before although these words are popular now. Tutored by Jeanne, the ladies improved their oral English, becoming more authentic and fluent. Many teachers from Hwa Nan asked,

Jeanne and Dodie with young teachers from the Applied English Dept.

"Have you been abroad?" Actually these young ladies just graduated from Hwa Nan and then worked here. They hadn't been abroad but how could they speak such good English? Answer: in Jeanne's easy and immersive English learning environment.

Jeanne was respected and loved by everyone here. President Chen Zhongying and Xu Daofeng, the director of Foreign Affairs Office cared about Jeanne's living. Every time Jeanne came to Hwa Nan, Xu would go to the airport to pick up Jeanne in person. President Chen took Jeanne to go sightseeing several places such as Fuzhou Forest Park and Xiapu County in Ningde City on weekends. She also taught Jeanne to play Chinese Mahjong, in which Jeanne took great interest. Jeanne asked a Chinese teacher where to buy a bamboo bookshelf. The teacher searched for the bamboo bookshelf by bicycle on weekends and finally found and bought one for Jeanne. At another time, Ms Zhou Ling, who is a good tailor, made two silk blouses for Jeanne. They fit perfectly, Jeanne liked them very much, and she wore them for formal occasions. The parents of students also showed their warm friendship. Mothers brought home-made traditional food at festival times, while fathers took Jeanne to visit places of interest by car. Everything and everyone related to Hwa Nan touched Jeanne. She felt family-like warmth from the teachers, students and their parents. By now you realize that Jeanne's personality, love of people and desire to help others

Jeanne had dinner at the home of President Chen's friend

made it quite easy for her to adjust to and feel at home at Hwa Nan.

Concerned about the Family, Hwa Nan

People here were sincere to Jeanne and she was earnest to Hwa Nan as well. She regarded herself as a member of this big family. On the Double Ninth Festival of 1997, she knew that it was a traditional festival for the elderly, so Jeanne bought kites for the senior teachers and wished them to have a romantic day. She treated them as her sisters. Jeanne often bought things for her "Hwa Nan family." She found it was necessary to buy a video recorder to play English movies, so she went to buy one with Professor Lin Benchun and ask her American friends to send video tapes to Hwa Nan. Thanks to Jeanne, the students could watch original English movies at school. They had improved not only in English listening but also in speaking by imitating the American accent.

春色
任天涯
——福建华南女子
职业学院外教侧记
International Faculty with
Fujian Hua Nan Women's
College since 1908

62

Jeanne in the Christmas party in FAO in 1999

Jeanne with Heimeili and teacher Hou Ruoying

Being dedicated and helpful, Jeanne was concerned about Hwa Nan's comprehensive work and tried her best to support the college. Knowing that Hwa Nan was short of foreign teachers, she wrote to her American friends and introduced Hwa Nan to them. She helped the college recruit foreign teachers and made great contributions in enlarging the team of foreigners. In order to apply for funds from the United Board for Christian Higher Education in Asia, Jeanne drafted the application proposal even though she was quite busy. Later she also found time to teach Wang Ling, who was in charge of foreign affairs, to write proposals for Hwa Nan and made sure that grammar and spelling were correct. According to teacher Wang Ling's memory, Jeanne was an intelligent person with good writing skills and strict logical thinking. Being effective and thoughtful, as she had a great understanding of higher education and pointed out the correct direction for the development of the school. Jeanne was generous and humble. She treated the faculty with a polite and considerate attitude. When others helped her, she would appreciate them. When others needed help, she was sure to help them without asking for anything in return. Hearing that a teaching assistant would further study abroad but lacked grant-in-aid, Jeanne immediately helped her write to an American women organization for the grant. Jeanne paid attention to the impoverished students, for whom she often paid outstanding tuition, or living expense. Those students were always grateful for Jeanne's grant, some of whom went on to be successful in their careers and they repaid society as well. They kept in mind the spirit of giving and receiving, which they had learned from Jeanne.

Help a Teenager Fulfill Her Dream

Jeanne got to know Professor Wang Jing from Foreign Language School of Fujian Normal University because of a working relationship. Professor Wang's daughter, Huang Silu (Lulu) was an excellent student. Lulu was awarded as "Fujian Top Ten Teenager" and "National Top Ten Teenager" in 1995. She also obtained the "Soong Ching Ling Scholarship" and "Huaxing Teenager Scholarship" in 1996. Knowing that Lulu was good at playing the piano, Jeanne suggested that Professor Wang send her daughter to further her piano study in the summer holidays at the Aspen Music School, the cradle of the American Musicians. The best music teachers in the world go there to teach. Enthusiastic Jeanne started to help Lulu with enquiring about the application procedures, materials needed and how to apply for the scholarship. By Jeanne's assistance, Huang Silu flew to the U.S.A and began her study tour of piano in Aspen on June 10, 1999 with full scholarship.

Jeanne treated Lulu with great hospitality in Denver. Then she took Lulu to Aspen three days before enrollment in order to let her become familiar with the environment. They lived in a motel, which Jeanne booked several months ahead because summer Aspen would attract many tourists. As a Chinese saying goes, help people to the end. Jeanne felt responsible for Lulu so she accompanied Lulu to enroll at Aspen Music School with her friend. During the time Lulu was studying in Aspen, Jeanne often called Lulu, asking about her living and study. In order to make Lulu have enough opportunities to play the piano, Jeanne even rented a practice room for Lulu in the campus, which was available for Lulu for three hours per day. Jeanne sent a package to Lulu with a notebook, a pencil and a handmade weekly calendar. She asked Lulu to note down the affairs every day on the weekly calendar and go everywhere with it. Jeanne often drove to Aspen to see Lulu with gifts made in China, and she also bought a clock for Lulu, which could wake her up in time for her lesson. She gave pocket money to Lulu, took Lulu to eat western food, taught Lulu how to use a coin laundry, and she even made a Dollar unit conversion table for Lulu. All of these things never left Lulu's mind. She would forever know Jeanne as a considerate and generous person. Jeanne did everything carefully and she also pointed out the way for Lulu's future study.

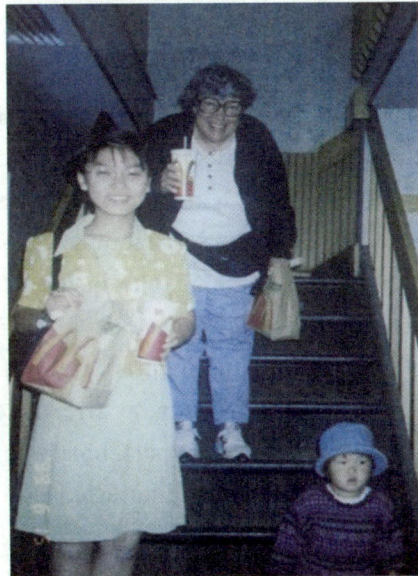

Jeanne with her friend's child and Lulu

Jeanne's Chinese Affection

Jeanne was interested in the long history of China and keen on Chinese culture and art. She invited an art teacher from Fujian Normal College to teach Hwa Nan's foreign

春色
任天涯
——福建华南女子
职业学院外教侧记
International Faculty with
Fujian Hua Nan Women's
College since 1908

64

Jeanne at home in Denvor, U.S.A.

teachers Chinese painting. She also invited a teacher from Foreign Language School of Fujian Normal University to be the interpreter for the art teacher. Jeanne often went to see operas. She was interested in Peking Opera and acrobatics, which made her laugh. She traveled around China on holidays and took part in cultural activities such as Anxi Tea Culture Festival, and Yongding Earth Building Culture Festival. Ancient buildings and special residence could always catch Jeanne's eye. She wandered about the streets and found various arts and crafts, which she was fond of and regarded as a treasure. Jeanne decorated her dorm in Hwa Nan in Chinese style. On the shelf, there were sculptures of her icons, Chairman Mao and Deng Xiaoping, the China's greatest people. On the little table there was mahogany statue of Yue Fei, the Chinese national hero. On the wall there were many things, such as a picture poster celebrating the 50 year anniversary of the founding of the People's Republic of China, a Chinese map, a Fuzhou map, kites made by traditional crafts, a satchel with minority characteristics, congratulation cards from friends, and a bamboo plaque. All the Chinese things she owned were filled with her pride and joy. She described the bamboo plaque as handsome and the kite as pretty. Satisfaction was shown by her words. Jeanne's home in the U.S.A. was also decorated in Chinese style with Chinese paintings, porcelains, arts and crafts. Some were sent by friends, while others were collected by herself. What Chinese enjoyment!

Jeanne was also interested in traditional customs in China. She went to watch the weddings and funerals in Lequn Building, the residence next to Hwa Nan. At that time the foreigners were rare in China, so people curiously surrounded her and looked her up and down. Jeanne didn't feel uncomfortable. Quite the opposite, she was easygoing and friendly. Chinese friends found that Jeanne

Jeanne in Chinese traditional clothes

was attracted to Chinese customs, so if they attended the ceremonies, they would invite Jeanne along. Some weddings took place in the countryside. Cooks steamed rice, washed vegetables and cooked for the whole village. The traditional wedding ceremony was held in the hall. The master of ceremony was congratulating loudly in front of the relatives, and the groom and the bride were serving tea for the elders. Jeanne was inquisitive about all of these. She knew that red stood for celebration in China. In 1993, Year of Rooster, Jeanne took photos in traditional Chinese clothes and sent them to friends wishing them a Happy New Year. Jeanne was like an angel bringing happiness to people, and she always brougt surprises and joy to friends.

Jeanne loved Chinese food very much, such as noodles, dumplings, fried buns and small steamed buns. Snacks in the alleys impressed her and she also enjoyed the pineapple from the fruit stand. Jeanne praised the cooking skill of the foreign teachers' cook. And she often invited her students to have a meal in the local restaurant at the bottom of Yantai Hill. Back in the U.S.A., when Jeanne recalled Chinese flavor, she would go to the Chinese restaurant.

Jeanne with foreign teachers in their dining room

Persisting in Teaching, Reluctant to Part

In 1993 Jeanne was sent to hospital because of asthma and she was diagnosed with high blood pressure. Several girls was chosen from the Applied English Department to take care of Jeanne in turn and acted as interpreters as well. Two weeks later, Jeanne was able to leave the hospital. In return, Jeanne invited the girls who looked after her in the hospital to have western dinner at the Lakeside Hotel. It was their first time to have western food, so the girls didn't know how to order the dishes. They ordered two main courses: steak, and Italian noodles, as well as vegetable salad

Jeanne and her students in Lakeside Hotel

66

春色
任天涯
——福建华南女子
职业学院外教侧记
International Faculty with
Fujian Hua Nan Women's
College since 1908

and soup of mushroom with chicken. Finally, they found the food was too much to eat. At that time, having a meal in a five-star hotel was rare and honorable. Jeanne fully showed her gratitude to the girls.

Leaving the hospital, Jeanne went back and nursed her health for some time in the U.S.A., but she still thought of Hwa Nan. Before long she came back to Hwa Nan after dreaming about

Jeanne and foreign teachers visit Fuzhou Museum

it so much. Yes, she loved this family deeply and was reluctant to leave here. From 1994, Jeanne came to teach successively but her health was getting worse. In 1997, Jeanne was having a rest at home but when she heard that Hwa Nan needed more foreign teachers, she flew to China immediately. Until 2001, Jeanne was hospitalized again and the doctor found something wrong with her heart. This time she had to say goodbye to the class, to her beloved students and Hwa Nan. She went back to the U.S.A. in January 2002. The doctor said she should carry the oxygen bottle from then on. As a result, she couldn't come to China by air. It was a pity that she couldn't come to her second homeland any more.

As an experienced psychologist, combined with her professional knowledge and ability, Jeanne devoted herself to teaching in the alien land, Fuzhou. In the early ten years after Hwa Nan's establishment, she work conscientiously, cultivated a lot of celebrities in society, and made great contributions to Fujian's modernization. In September, 2003 Dr. Jeanne Philips honorably obtained "The Friendship Award" presented by Fujian Provincial Government. This laurel is for those foreign experts who had an outstanding performance in Fujian.

THE FRIENDSHIP AWARD

PRESENTED BY THE PEOPLE'S GOVERNMENT OF FUJIAN PROVINCE, P. R. C.

TO: Ms. Jeanne S. Phillips

The Friendship Award is honorably presented to the above-stated recipient in recognition of her prominent contribution to the modernization drive in Fujian Province.

The People's Government of Fujian Province
The People's Republic of China
September 2003

Jeanne received "The Friendship Award" in 2003

Farewell to Second Homeland, Back to the U.S.A.

After farewell to the second homeland and being back to the U.S.A., Jeanne was not idle and led an optimistic life. She traveled around to visit friends, read books and wrote reviews, or wrote to friends in Hwa Nan expressing her concern about the development of the college. When Jeanne was seriously ill in bed, she kept missing her friends in China. When she saw the mountain walnuts (which originate in Hangzhou, China) given to her by a friend, she thought since people could buy the mountain walnuts in the U.S.A., they could buy such walnuts in Fujian as well for sure. Then she decided to send money to Professor Lin Benchun, the mutual friend between her and Hwa Nan, and asked Benchun to buy boxes of mountain walnuts for her senior friends, including President Chen Zhongying, Ma Xiufa, Director of Dean's Office, and Xu Daofeng, Director of Foreign Affairs Office. They were moved to tears when talking about this.

February 4th, 2014 was a day of great sorrow for Jeanne's friends, because on the day Jeanne departed forever at the age of 84. She was never married, but she devoted herself to the educational career. She loved this career and she greatly contributed to teaching and her students. Being optimistic, humorous and generous, Jeanne was a mentor to everyone who knew her. People were impressed by her spirit of diligence and pursuit of improvement. People were moved by her noble sentiments of selfless dedication and her lofty spirit of willingness to give love to Chinese education.Everybody here respected her, loved her and will remember her forever. Hwa Nan is proud and honored for having had such an outstanding foreign teacher. Dr. Jeanne Philips set a model for the other foreign teachers. It can be said that Fujian Hwa Nan Women's College, her students, colleagues, and friends are far better off having known Dr. Jeanne Philips.

IV
An Orchid in a Valley
——Recalling Dr. Kay Grimmesey

Visiting Kay in Los Angeles

After three years, my son and I crossed half of the United States and met Dr. Kay Grimmesey again on the morning of August 21, 2015 in Los Angeles.

It was the same Kay, elegant in every move and act. I felt again the long-lost warmth and affection when she hugged me with a smile just like before. This may be one of the important reasons that I pay great respect to her. She is very sincere, and you feel totally at ease before her. Without pressure, you will find language no more an obstacle but an easy

68

春色
任天涯
——福建华南女子
职业学院外教侧记
International Faculty with
Fujian Hua Nan Women's
College since 1908

means with which you talk at ease, and she will always understand you. In fact, Kay, gentle and considerate, seems to be able to tell the problems you are facing and the help you would like to get. Her smile seems to tell you, "Don't be afraid. Whatever the difficulty, I am on your side."

During my stay in the U. S. as a visiting scholar, I could better understand what challenges the foreigners from developed countries like Americans would face while living in China since they have been accustomed to an easy life in their countries. What does it take for them to stay and teach at Fujian Hwa Nan Women's College for such a long time when facing the harsh living and working conditions? It is perseverance. The rarest quality in kay is her tolerance. She never complained about the living and working conditions, nor did she impose her standards on others. For 11 years, she had quietly sent forth wafts of delicate fragrance like an orchid in a valley, cleansing and nourishing my soul, teaching me to be grateful, to be helpful whenever necessary, to be tolerant and to be indifferent to fame and fortune.

Kay, 82 years old, picked up my son and me from Four Points by Sheraton, Los Angeles International Airport Hotel to Mount San Antonio Gardens where she lives after driving about one and a half hour. The Gardens cover 30 acres with rows of single-storey apartments. Surrounded by ponds, weeping willows, live oak, bamboo grove, rose garden, the tranquil and beautiful Gardens are fully equipped with Dining Room, Library, Exhibition Hall, Conference Room, Art Center, Health Center, Fitness center, Swimming Pools, Golf Putting Green, Horseshoe... Also, the Gardens offer comprehensive and considerate services with 250 full-time and part-time employees. Just like Kay, the place is telling her story elegantly and free from any disturbance from anyone. Kay lives in a house on her own, in front of which is a little garden full of roses; a little further is a cutting garden where you can take away some flowers as you wish.

Kay's home in Mount San Antonio Gardens

Kay and Huang Fei (English name: Fay) in Mount San Antonio Gardens

A pond

A row of single-storey apartments

The library

The dining room

A golf putting green

Kay does not spend much, nor does she have much savings. She is given to charity and devoted to the teaching in <u>Myanmar</u> for three years and Hwa Nan for 11 years. In 2011, she sold her own house and moved to a retirement home — Mt. San Antonio Gardens. The look of satisfaction on Kay's face made me feel happy from the bottom of my heart.

Blessed is he whose fame does not outshine his truth.

The Old Good Days at Hwa Nan

If you are from Hwa Nan, you definitely will not miss the traces that Kay has left, which is a unique landscape.

Dr. Kay Grimmesey, born in October 1932, worked at Hwa Nan from August 1998

春色
任天涯
——福建华南女子
职业学院外教侧记
International Faculty with
Fujian Hua Nan Women's
College since 1908

70

to March 2011. From 1998 to 2000 and from 2001 to 2002, Kay was sent to teach at Hwa Nan by the Amity Foundation; from 2003 on, Kay continued working at Hwa Nan as a volunteer. As a professional teacher with a doctorate in Education, she had mastered the theories and was quite experienced in teaching English as a foreign language. She taught English Listening and Speaking, English Reading and Writing, Free Conversation in the Applied English Department, and organized extracurricular activities for the students from the whole campus — English corner and English movies. Later, as one of the Department consultants, she devoted herself to the development of the Department. Kay's great effort and persistence contributed greatly to the honors that the Department has gained — the Excellent Department at Fujian Provincial Level in 2010 and the Department with Special Features among private colleges. In October 2008, the English library in Foreign Faculty's House was named after Kay Grimmesey in memory of her prominent devotion to the college. In view of her great contribution to the women's higher education in Fujian Province, Fujian People's Government awarded her the fourth "Fujian Friendship Award" in 2005, and Fuzhou Municipal Government granted her "Fuzhou Friendship Award" in 2006.

In the foreign teachers' photo, three of us were Amity English teachers assigned for two years (1998-2000) to Hwa Nan, part of the Amity Foundation's Teacher Program: Sandy Cullers, Mirzah Rodriguez, and myself. We were there for two straight years without going home during that time. The Amity Foundation is a Chinese non-governmental organization (NGO) based in Nanjing. They were recruiting English teachers from abroad.I met Sandy in New York where we had our first training in the United states as Amity teachers.Sandy and I had never heard of Hwa Nan until we were assigned to Hwa Nan.Then we went to Nantong for the summer (where we met Mirzah) to receive training from the Amity Foundation officials and long-time foreign teachers. All Amity teachers in China joined us at a conference at the end of our summer training. Xu Daofeng met us after we left Nantong, and that is a start of a wonderful relationship.

—Dr. Kay Grimmesey

In 1998, I met Dr. Kay Grimmesey — a plump, soft-spoken middle-aged woman with ear-length curly hair and a slightly-hunched back. She seemed very amiable. She was one of the few senior foreign teachers who held K-12 (Kindergarten to Grade 12) teachers' certificate of California.

Kay and the former president, Dr. Zhang Xunjie, in the English library donated by Dr. Kay Grimmesey (2008)

Kay was awarded the fourth "Fujian Friendship Award" (2005).

Kay visited Lin Zexu Memorial with Betts, Laihar, Marjie, Lis and some Chinese teachers from Hwa Nan (January 2011)

Foreign teachers and Xu Daofeng (the 2nd in the front, then Director of Foreign Affairs Office) (before the Foreign Faculty House, Yantaishan campus, October 1999)

Besides teaching at Hwa Nan, Kay as well as Jeanne Phillips had served as reviewers quietly for a long time for the English textbooks for the elementary school students in Fuzhou.

Over the next 10 years, she left a deep impression on us with her quietness, hard work, uprightness, and caring, and she became our role model. Every year during National Holidays, she would take new foreign teachers in Hwa Nan to Xiamen to spend their holidays, hoping the soft sea wind would blow away their homesickness and comfort them mentally and

春色
任天涯
——福建华南女子
职业学院外教侧记
International Faculty with
Fujian Hua Nan Women's
College since 1908

physically. She would always donate money to the teachers and students who suffered from natural and man-made disasters and give them her shoulders. She is a highly-respected mentor!

—Dong Xiuping (who worked in Foreign Affairs Office at Hwa Nan for about 20 years)

I am honored to be Kay's friend because knowing her has made my life richer. I taught with Kay at Hwa Nan Women's College for 11 years while she was there. Here are some experiences and memories I have of those years with Kay:

Kay and I chose to live on the 4th floor of the International Faculty House and we chose to have our rooms across the hall from one another. The reason for this was that we were quite compatible and liked to get together each evening during the week to watch our favorite TV programs — the news, Dialogue, and Around China. We often shared teaching ideas and ways to inspire students to think.

Kay always went to bed early (always by 10 pm) and was always an early riser (6 or maybe even 5:30 am) to make her way down the hall to get hot water for her morning coffee. Her apartment was always neat and tidy. I always felt that she was not interested in material things.

Kay always dressed professionally in stockings, a skirt and matching blouse and jacket and sometimes long pants. Actually I never saw her wear tennis shoes or jeans or a sporty outfits. Kay is a soft-spoken woman and I found that she never participated in gossip or complaining about anything.

Kay told me that she had troubles with her feet so she wore special shoes that helped alleviate the problem. She knew she walked slowly, but she never complained about walking to the bus station or the long walk to church with Laihar. She never missed a Sunday going to church even though that walk to the bus was VERY taxing for her.

Kay also has a very giving heart. She was so willing to donate huge sums of money to Hwa Nan over the years she taught there. A large embroidered picture she gave to me is very expensive and why did she give it to me? Because she was with me when I was admiring it. I am not the only person she has given gifts of value.

Kay is probably the kindest person I have ever met and always willing to help when asked or when needed. She taught MANY years in Myanmar and was always concerned about the welfare of her friends. While at Hwa Nan, in every Spring Festival vacation she would go to Myanmar to donate money for her friends/former students. Then came the sad day for her when she could no longer enter that country."

—Dr. Betts Rivet (who worked at Hwa Nan for about 20 years)

Kay is a soft-spoken person. She speaks little, but she is a woman of actions. She sees needs and she is quick to act. Also she is a very generous person. Every time she visited Myanmar, she would bring home some gifts for each foreign teacher from Yunnan as she needed to obtain a visa there before proceeding to Myanmar. She would bring reading materials, medicine and money for her needy friends in Myanmar. For the English corner, she wouldn't let me pay her for the candy canes and beautiful certificates for the English Corner committee members. (Note: Kay bought the candy canes and certificates from the USA each year for the English Corner committee members and send them to Hwa Nan.)It was Kay who invited me to be an adviser for the English Corner. To show my gratitude for her years of kindness to others and friendship, I am delighted to take over it after she retired from teaching at Hwa Nan.

She is a wonderful friend and supporter, always appreciative and giving me words of encouragement, a listening ear and praises which I seldom receive from other foreign teachers. Besides all these, she is a very independent person. This is a great quality which all of us can learn from Kay. That's why she could teach in Myanmar and China for so many years, and traveled alone to Myanmar in her seventies during school winter breaks.

I am so blessed and privileged to have her as a friend and colleague in the past. I am sure all her students love her and treasure her friendship.

—Laihar Wong

The responses are unanimous: Kay Grimmesey is quiet, hard-working, humble, kind, generous and completely sincere in her devotion to teaching, Hwa Nan and her Christian faith. She is the very meaning of Kahil Gibran's words: "Work is love made visible." I have really never met anyone quite as genuinely unselfish and principled as Kay. One year when I was unsure about returning to Hwa Nan (in the early 2000s when our salaries were very low) Kay paid for my round-trip ticket to Fuzhou, an impressive outlay of money. Even as I write this, I know she will be chagrined that I disclosed her generosity to me, for fear someone else will feel offended. And, in spite of all my faults, she still claims me as a friend and faithfully sends me both birthday and Christmas cards every year.

—Dodie (full name: Dorene Dorothy Johnston)

Among Hwa Nan foreign teachers, Kay was the only one who holds a doctorate education degree in English language teaching. She had been teaching for a long time and she had rich English teaching experience. Besides, she is amiable, caring, and patient. She is really an exceptionally good teacher who has set a role model for both the teachers and the students. She has a sedate nature, and silently she did many good deeds for Hwa Nan and the students such as donating much money to construct the college and develop education without asking for anything.

—Lin Benchun (Former President of Hwa Nan Women's College, now College Counselor)

1. As a Teacher — Moistens Everything Silently

What makes a great teacher? To pass down wisdom, impart knowledge, and resolve doubts? The engineer of human soul? The whole society expects much of teachers as you can see from the above expressions. Nowadays, it is said that teachers must play a role of actors and directors, which you can barely find in Kay, but what she did has touched the very bottom of our heart and stimulated us to rethink about what makes a teacher.

Kay loves and cares for her students. She took photos of every student and put them on cards along with information written by each so she would get to know the students better. She still has the cards of every student who was in her classes those eleven years. One piece of information was the birthdays of each student so she could make a birthday card on her computer for their special day, which made the students feel the warmth of the home.

Kay has rigorous attitude toward scholarship and she never stops learning. Although she has over 40 years' teaching experience, she sets high standard for herself. Every year she would at least participate in two conferences exploring the innovative ways of English teaching with the participants and thus improving her teaching.

Kay, at her advanced age, firmly walked on the campus, devoting most of her time to the students. She never complained about qualities of the students she had, although there

Kay in free conversation class

may be variations in the students' qualities. Eleven years like a day, she encouraged her students with her gentleness, consideration and patience; she devoted all her love to every student and moistened everything silently just like spring rain. Kay's excellent teaching ability and extensive love gained the respect and support from Hwa Nan teachers and students.

Chen Lu (English name — Alison), a graduate of 2011 from the Applied English Department, Hwa Nan Women's College, now a student in Emporia State University, USA, pursuing her master's degree, recalled Kay with great gratitude, "Kay is my oral English teacher. It's in her class that I had heard such standard English for the first time. I loved her class immediately. Chinese students are shy to speak out, and Kay always encouraged us to do more practice in speaking. She never minded that we made mistakes in her class. Rather, she was always patient, correcting our pronunciation and grammar and

Chen Lu (a graduate of 2011 from Hwa Nan)

providing feedback in time. For so many years, I still can't forget Kay's encouragement. Probably unconsciously influenced by Kay, I have had courage to communicate with foreigners bravely in the past few years in America."

Wang Xiaoyan (English name — Jenny), a graduate of 2009 from Applied English Department of Hwa Nan and 2010 from Morningside College of the U.S.A., the founder of Xiamen USAMILE Industry Co., Ltd. in April 2014, is now residing in the USA expanding her company's business and developing her team abroad. At the same time, she has been working as a fellow in Asian Center, Harvard University since February, 2016. She described this very special foreign teacher as below:

Wang Xiaoyan, a graduate from Hwa Nan, now a research fellow in Asian Center, Harvard University

Kay always smiles from within, gentle and elegant, which gives you a sense of relaxation and enjoyment in her class. Her elegant dress, words and deeds serve as examples influencing us on shaping our image as a woman. Her caring heart, patience and approachability, which we should learn to develop, is admirable.

Besides guiding Hwa Nan students patiently, Kay is also a growth mentor for many young teachers at Hwa Nan. Lin Lihua (English name June), once a teacher at Hwa Nan, affectionately told a story between her and Kay which is rarely known.

In the autumn of 1999, I got to know Kay when she was teaching English Speaking in the Applied English Department for Class A of 99 and I was the class advisor. From then on, we grew from colleagues to cross-age friends. To be precise, she was my mentor who guided my career and spirit on my way.

At the beginning of 2002, there was an opportunity for me to pursue my master's degree in Assumption University of Thailand. I was quite hesitant because my daughter was less than one and half years old. After

Kay knew my worries, she encouraged me to grasp the opportunity to enhance myself while at the same time making proper arrangement. However, the study pressure and my missing for my daughter made me physically and mentally exhausted. To get rid of my worries, Kay insisted on writing to me every month until I completed my study and came back home.

When I came back to China in 2005, I was chosen to take an important post, Director of Business English Department. Kay tried to help me whenever she could. To help develop the core curriculum in the department, she once asked an anonymous donor to purchase the most updated business English books without my knowledge; she spared no pains to support me to apply for and organize "The 3rd International Creative Writing and Literature Conference in Asian Region".

Kay is peaceful, gentle and cultivated, but once I saw that she lost her temper. When she got to know that a foreign teacher had a problem in getting along with a student in my department, she sacrificed her lunch break and went on a special trip from Yantaishan Campus to Shoushan Campus, organizing a meeting with that foreign teacher and me to learn the whole story. She was very angry when she knew that the foreign teacher had offended the student by rude remarks; she severely criticized the foreign teacher to his face and requested that he apologize to the student in his class. This is the only time that I saw Kay was so angry and dealt with the matter severely.

I interviewed Kay when she returned to Hwa Nan in November 2013. She told me that she had been a teacher for 41 years and she was always proud of choosing to be a teacher, the sacred profession. She emphasized that her greatest happiness was "Once a teacher, always a teacher". My good friend Laihar Wong and I both agreed that Kay is the kindest, most caring, most responsible teacher we have ever met, and she is our lifelong role model.

Kay, Laihar, and Lin Lihua

春色
任天涯
——福建华南女子
职业学院外教侧记
International Faculty with
Fujian Hua Nan Women's
College since 1908

78

Zhong Fulian (English name — Alisa) commented Kay as below:

Kay is a learned and refined, sincere and modest teacher who demonstrates her teaching style of moistening all students silently and softly. In 2002, I was very fortunate to participate in a series of workshops about English language teaching skills that she offered to the staff of the Applied English Department. These workshops served as a good model to me when I just stepped on the teaching career immediately after graduation from Hwa Nan. For example, teachers need to stand when giving lectures so that they can have better interactions with their students; the instructions must be clear and concise for the students to follow; teachers should be good listeners so that they can understand what their students are thinking. Kay is our good mentor and our helpful friend. Those old good days with her are just like yesterday.

On the heels of the wind it (Spring rain) slips secretly into the night, Silent and soft, it moistens everything.

—**translated by Gladys Yang, Xianyi Yang**

2. As a Volunteer — Busy Leading Extracurricular Activities

Kay extended English learning to extracurricular activities by organizing different programs, which provided Hwa Nan students a great chance to practice their English and thus improve their English proficiency.

Kay was in charge of the Noon Movie. She would play an English movie for the students on every Monday and Thursday, which greatly stimulated their enthusiasm in English learning. She also donated many English books including a whole set of *National Geographic* to the English Library of Applied English Department. The Noon Movie and the books brought a lot of fun to the students' life and offered great opportunities for the students to get English input.

Besides, as the initiator of English Corner, Kay recruited Hwa Nan students to help organize it. She had meetings regularly with those English Corner student leaders, encouraging them to promote English Corner on and off campus and discussing assignments of the English Corner for each leader. Through learning by doing, the students not only improved their applied English competency, but also got trained for leadership, practical ability, and team spirit.

You Chaoyun (English name — Susan), once a student leader of the English corner of Hwa Nan, mentioned that special experience quite excitedly, "Kay is advanced in years and her legs were not nimble, but we saw her in the English corner all the time, rain or shine. I remember we celebrated Christmas together on a Friday night when I was a second-year student at Hwa Nan. After the Christmas party at the English corner, Kay asked me whether I liked to be one of the English corner leaders like senior students did, and she would recommend me to Laihar if I did. I thought she was not serious about it, but it turned out that Laihar talked with me after class about it and I was so excited! Kay and Laihar provided me with a stage where I was able to build up my organizational ability and improve my oral English; English corner also brought me back many great memories. I admire them greatly. For what Kay, Betts, Laihar, Gordon and Sonia have done for us, what we could do is show our gratitude, thanking them for sparing no efforts to guide us in China after their retirement from the USA."

Kay genuinely cares about her students' feelings and she always tries her best to take care of the specific needs of organizing a high quality English Corner. Please allow me to mention one incident hereby. When the light for the English Corner was too dim, she immediately contacted the college Business Office staff to come and solve the issue. English Corner was usually held between 6pm and 8pm every Friday at the entrance corridor of our college. However, if there was inclement weather, participants could go inside the Administration Building to continue the conversation. Over the years, English Corner has attracted not only many Hwa Nan college students, but also students beyond the campus, including many elementary and middle school students who came to the English

Kay, Laihar with the caretaker near the old Hwa Nan campus and her granddaughter (Kay and Laihar encouraged the girl to continue coming to the English corner, even after it was moved to the new campus.)

Kay, Sandy Cullers, Lin Xiao (English name: Julie) and the students

80

春色
任天涯
——福建华南女子
职业学院外教侧记
International Faculty with
Fujian Hua Nan Women's
College since 1908

Corner because of the excellent reputation. Under the leadership of these dedicated foreign teachers and experts such as Kay, Betts, Gordon & Sonia Trimble, Laihar, graduates from the University of Puget Sound sponsored by the Trimble family Scholarship, Applied English Department have cultivated many excellent graduates. For example: Lin Suhong, a graduate of 2003, is the General Manager of Quanzhou Carle Import & Export Trade Co., Ltd.; Zhang Lin, a graduate of 2008, was selected and offered an internship in Hawaiian Senator Gordon Trimble's Office based on her outstanding spoken English and all-rounded talents. She is now working as an Executive Assistant for the Chief Executive Engineer, GE Aviation (an enterprise ranked on the top Global 30); Wang Xiaoyan, a graduate of 2009, who went to America to further study and then came back to China to establish her own foreign trade company — Xiamen USAMILE Industry Co., Ltd. in 2014. Since February, 2016, she has begun her fellowship position in the Asian Center at Harvard University; Huang Xiaodan, a graduate of 2011, founded Xin Jia Kindergarten in Jin'an District; Zheng Xiaolin, a graduate of 2012, opened her own Quanyou Education Consultation Co., Ltd., in Jin'an District.

I never teach my pupils. I only attempt to provide the conditions in which they can learn.

— Albert Einstein

3. As a Consultant — Forever Support

Kay once said, "I am happy to do whatever is good for Chinese women's education". She has made a significant contribution to the development of the Applied English Department.

Dong Xiuping, a senior teacher and former director of the Applied English Department, recalled that:

Kay bought books from the USA and donated them to the Department with her own pension so that the teachers and the students could read those most updated materials. Kay helped review the English version of the Department Curriculum and different kinds of English documents such as Guidelines for Free Conversation Course, and then she offered constructive advice. She also put emphasis on training young teachers' English teaching skills. She volunteered the workshop about English teaching skills for us. I remember she taught us the theory about multi-intelligence of a learner and the ways to assess the students' learning methods so that we could find

the learning methods suitable for the students This assessing method is still
used by me now.

Kay maintained low profile. She always made silent contribution with
no intention of publicity them. She would not take advantage of her seniority
to throw indiscreet remarks upon others. She was always amiable and soft-
spoken. She always talked to others with appreciation and encouragement.

I have kept in contact with Kay after her "retirement" from Hwa Nan. I will write
to her telling every achievement that the Department and I have made and expressing
my gratitude to her for her constant great support to the Department. In a Language
Department Evaluation hosted by Fujian Provincial Education Department in 2013, the
Applied English and Business English Departments ranked No. 8 among 71 departments
from 35 schools in Fujian Provincial vocational colleges. We were awarded Excellent
Departments with specialty among private colleges and were awarded 100,000 to enhance
our teaching and learning by Fujian Provincial Education Department. I told her about the
good news and said, "We know we would not have had achieved the above without your
great support! Thank you very much for what you have done for us." She replied right
away, "Congratulations! That's exciting news about the awards! That is really fantastic!
You accomplished all that you did all by yourselves! Hwa Nan is so lucky to have you
all. Thank you for thinking that we were in some way a help. I will help in whatever
way I can whenever you ask."

Looking back on the days when I was faced with various pressures and challenges
during these six years, I would think what made me continue to get involved in the
administration and development work of the Department must be teachers like Kay who

Kay and the teachers from the Applied English
Department(Yantaishan Campus, 2002)

Kay and the teachers from the
Applied English Department (Gushan
Mountain, 2003)

春色
任天涯
——福建华南女子
职业学院外教侧记
International Faculty with
Fujian Hua Nan Women's
College since 1908

82

always stand behind me and support me unconditionally and quietly. They seem to tell me, "Don't be afraid. Hold on! I am on your side." How lucky Hwa Nan is! What blessings we are having! How can we give up when we have such a consultant?

"I will help in whatever way I can whenever you ask."—Kay

4. As a Mother —Boundless Love

Kay always provided generous support to the teacher in need. A teacher in the Applied English Department told a touching story between Kay and her:

In 2008, I asked for a three-month leave for family misfortune when our college was undergoing the first-round of Talents Cultivation Level Evaluation. The other teachers in the Department helped me with the tasks I should have done for the Evaluation and other things besides teaching while they were busy dealing with the evaluation affairs. Kay quietly took the English Reading classes for me which totaled ten classes each week. She required that the college should pay me for the classes she taught for me. She carefully graded the students in the class and the final exam, and then calculated every student's score and gave it to me when I returned to work. Kay had 12 classes every week on her own, and she took another 10 classes as a substitute for me, which was toilsome! I always remember it and thanked her from the bottom of my heart. I am very grateful to the people like Kay who selflessly helped me out of difficult situation. I will help those in need like what Kay did for me.

You Chaoyun, a graduate from Hwa Nan, recalled the situation at that time when Kay substituted for other teachers:

Kay substituted in our class once. Her legs were not very nimble, so I wanted to support her with my arms, but she insisted on walking by herself. At that time, I felt so choked up that I was on the point of crying when seeing she stumbled on.

Like a mother, Kay quietly cared for about the ten foreign teachers living in the Foreign Faculty House. She and Betts celebrated a foreign teacher's birthday with a birthday cake and a card signed by her together with other foreign teachers. Every year there would be one or two young teachers leaving their families and friends to come to Hwa Nan, and Kay always gave them special care when they felt homesick; Kay comforted and enlightened them as an experienced Hwa Nan foreign teacher. Marjorie Lodwick, a young teacher at Hwa Nan right after her graduation from the University of Puget Sound, the USA, recalled the stories about Kay:

Kay was a lovely and easy-going person as well as a good friend. I remember how friendly she was and how reassuring kindness she gave to me during my first few days at Hwa Nan. She was soft-spoken, gentle, and went out of her way to make sure that I felt comfortable and welcomed. I remember that her students adored her. She was a great teacher — one that motivated her students with kindness. At English corner planning meetings she never raised her voice, as soon as she started speaking softly, all the students hushed to listen to her. One of my fondest memories of my first semester at Hwa Nan was when Kay, Betts, and Laihar invited me to go with them for a weekend to Gulangyu, Xiamen City. It was so nice to wander around the streets of the island with Kay.

It was more commendable that she also showed her concerns about those female workers who took care of foreign teachers' in their daily life. She would give gifts to them, thanking them for their care for the foreign teachers throughout these years. Kay also cooperated very well with the foreign affairs office; she helped review the English documents and offered many suggestions.

Deliver not your words by number but by weight.

Gleaming Humanity

Kay had been a teacher in the United States since 1955 until her retirement in 1997, except for three years (1958—1961) when she was teaching in Myanmar. She came to Hwa Nan in 1998. You could find the best interpretation of thrifty and generosity in this elder lady: She was thrift and didn't have much savings, but she was always ready to help others — Kay supported several Hwa Nan teachers in pursuing their master's degrees; she donated money to a Hwa Nan student with an incurable disease; every year she bought and sent certificates from the America to Hwa Nan for those student organizers of the English corner; Kay bought a gift for the new-born baby of a teacher in the Department and prepared a card with blessings and signatures of other foreign teachers....

Lin Jiao (English name — Amy), once a teacher in the Applied English Department at

春色
任天涯
——福建华南女子
职业学院外教侧记
International Faculty with
Fujian Hua Nan Women's
College since 1908

Hwa Nan, now a teacher in the USA, recollected the unusual stories between Kay and her with great affection:

I have many sweet memories during my life journey, and I know Kay is definitely one of those who goes beyond thousands of miles to show her unselfish love and concern for an ordinary person like me. Kay is the most gentle and generous woman I have ever seen in my whole life. From the moment I met her at the old Hwa Nan (Yantai Shan) campus till now, it has been more than 17 years. Over these years, she has touched many lives with her tenderness and kindness. She has helped many students and teachers at Hwa Nan not only with her knowledgeable teaching techniques and encouraging guidance, but also with practical and loving deeds.

She has such a caring and thoughtful heart that I would never be able to repay her kindness in all the things she has done for my family, my children and myself. I still remember vividly her handing me that special wedding congratulation card signed by all the international faculty with their best wishes. Besides that, she also highly respected the Chinese traditional custom of giving a red envelope with cash inside. The amount of money she gave took my breath away when I opened it. Five hundred yuan! That's a great amount of money out of her salary.

Another thing that I would never forget happened on the third day after my childbirth, she came to visit us with a beautiful congratulation card. She showed her most sincere care in my newly-born baby-girl and asked whether she could hold my daughter. I was so excited to meet her that I forgot to put a diaper on my baby. It seemed to me that my baby daughter knew instinctively that this visitor is the gentlest woman that she dared to do anything she wanted. Not surprisingly, you already know what happened. My daughter wet Kay's pants within about 5 minutes she's on her laps. And you can also guess what Kay's reaction was, "It doesn't matter. She is so cute."

As time goes on, my family continues to grow and Kay's love for my family and me only grows stronger and more generous. Over the past 17 years, she has never failed once in sending us birthday cards. As I cherished all the cards she sent me, there was one that I hereby would like to elaborate a little more. When I studied the date on the stamp on this special birthday card, it was dated on Oct.5, 2010. How did she know that three years later that Amy (Lin Jiao's English name) would be playing a violin exactly like the one on the birthday card she sent. What a coincidence! No matter she's far away at the other side of Pacific Ocean or on this side, she remembered us in the warmest bottom of her heart. After I finished my Master's Degree, I was offered a new teaching position in another city. When she knew that I needed to rent an apartment to stay during weekdays, she generously donated one thousand dollars to assist me without the intention of letting me know that she did it.

If I could record all the amazing things she did for others, I believe that it would take up all pages of a new book. As for now, that's what I can share. Truly, she is an angel sent to me by the Divine to bless me and to teach me how to be a better person. I know I will never be able to repay what she has done for me. The only thing I can do is to remember her kindness in the songs that I play with my violin. Her life is a living song of quiet spirit and gentle love no matter where she goes and no matter where she is.

Kay generously lent her house to the two college students that she knew for a short time each while they were taking classes nearby when she was teaching at Hwa Nan Women's College. She would go to where she had taught in Myanmar to visit former colleagues and students during winter breaks from Kunming.

She has another good quality — modesty. When you take a look at the English Corner Memo in the Appendix, you would find that she put her signature at the last although she was the English Corners initiator and did the most work. According to incomplete statistics, the funds she used to help students, foreign teachers and facilitate the development of Hwa Nan in recent years totaled RMB 100,000 but she never mentioned it. Had the students, foreign teachers or other young teachers not mentioned about it, we would never know.

The truth, goodness, and beauty of human nature glitter from the inside of quiet Kay. Kay sets the best example to us, which leads us to march forward bravely and firmly. I have been wondering what makes this seemingly weak old lady keep sweet smiles and persist for 11 years at Hwa Nan. This universal love which transcended borders infects me silently, making me feel gratitude for the gift of life and lend helping hands sincerely to those in need.

We have never been lack of love education, but what we need more is the universal love shown by the example of action like her. I want her to know: your angelic smile always stays in my heart, and I believe that it is also branded in the hearts of many people....

春色
任天涯
——福建华南女子
职业学院外教侧记
International Faculty with
Fujian Hua Nan Women's
College since 1908

86

Example isn't another way to teach, it is the only way to teach.

—Albert Einstein

Forever Affection for China

Kay has great affection for China and the Chinese people; she has praised many times the Chinese people's enthusiasm and kindness and the Chinese students' innocence and diligence However, as time went by, Kay had to say goodbye to us in November 2010. I didn't get ready for it, as I always stubbornly believed that she had been connected with the Applied English Department indispensably.

"Retirement" Farewell Party

Dramatically it was me who hosted Kay's farewell party. I was a bit nervous because that was the first time I hosted a party like that, and I also felt honored to do it, for I thought it may be the best gift I could give her. I never regretted hosting the party although I might not make it perfect. The president, the vice president, the senior Hwa Nan teachers, the teachers in the Applied English Department and some of Kay's students came to join the party. Words failed to express our gratitude towards Kay and our reluctance to leave her. Although she is not my teacher in the classroom, I regard her as my best teacher in my life.

Group photo

Former president, Dr. Zhang
Xunjie, presented a gift to Kay

Gordon Trimble, the Honorary Chair, offered remarks

Below are some photos taken on the farewell party.

Very quietly I take my leave
As quietly as I came here;
Gently I flick my sleeves
Not even a wisp of cloud will I bring away.
—by Xu Zhimo

Return to Hwa Nan for the 105th Anniversary

Kay returned to Hwa Nan on September 28, 2013 for the 105th Anniversary ceremony on October 19, 2013 with Betts. She stayed at Hwa Nan for about one month, during which she walked into the classroom of the Applied English Department again to do co-teaching with Chinese teachers as well as joining the English corner on Friday night.

Kay in Huang Fei's class

On October 9, 2013, Kay was invited to the Free Conversation class focusing on the topic "Family" in Class A of 2012, Applied English Department. Kay introduced how American senior citizens led a life after retirement, and then our students also talked about Chinese family's viewpoints on the elderly who spend the rest of their life in nursing homes. They compared the retirement life of the elderly in China with that of in America, through which they had a better understanding of culture and family values of the two countries. On October 23, Kay joined the discussion about the "education" issue with the same students, from which the students gained a deeper understanding of American education. Kay also did co-teaching with Chinese teacher on the topics "how to teach English to young learners by means of stories" and "how to teach writing to young learners". In addition, Kay was invited to the class I was teaching to provide pronunciation guidance and demonstrated choral reading with different activities, which were quite welcomed by the students and were especially effective for the freshmen whose English was poor, because it could help to build their motivation, improve their fluency, and self-confidence. These activities were not complicated and unapproachable at all; they were just like Kay's character — simple but deeply rooted in everyone's mind. Kay's passion for teaching and her wonderful skills are admirable! If only we could go back to the old good

春色
任天涯
——福建华南女子
职业学院外教侧记
International Faculty with
Fujian Hua Nan Women's
College since 1908

88

days enjoying Kay's teaching in her classroom!

Kay had missed her friends in China very much. She was excited to see them again, and she went to Mrs. Xu Daofeng's apartment to visit her and her husband (Xu Daofeng is the founder of the Applied English Department and the former Director of Foreign Affairs Office).

Kay, Betts visited Xu Daofeng and her husband

Yao Yamei (Rose), a graduate of 2002 from Hwa Nan, who had worked in Foreign Affairs Office for many years, has deep affections towards Kay:

> *I was an ordinary third-year student in Kay's class when 911 Attack happened in the USA. I went to talk with her when I saw her stand in the hallway silently. Since then on, I had often talked with her after class because I worried that she might feel lonely, and then we became good friends. I got in more touch with Kay when I worked in Foreign Affairs Office after graduation from Hwa Nan. After she learned that I was hard up for money, Kay encouraged and supported me to pursue my master's degree, which helped broaden my horizons. In my eyes, Kay is a learned, warm, kind wiser with fraternity. Not only did she teach me a lot of knowledge, but also she inspired me with many great ideas. Whenever I think of her, I feel warm. She taught me to be a warm person, warming others as well as myself.*
>
> *Distance makes the hearts grow fonder.*

Great Affection for China

Kay left Hwa Nan for the USA after the school's Anniversary in 2013. Since then, longing has been crossing the Pacific Ocean. Hwa Nan teachers expressed their deep love for Kay in their own ways: While she was studying in America, Xu Ou, the Vice President, went to Los Angeles to visit Betts and they visited Kay together; I went to Los Angeles twice to visit Kay and took her to authentic Chinese food while I was a visiting scholar in America. While Quiet Kay showed her gratitude and excitement implicitly by driving me to her retirement community early in the morning and showed me around her community.

She hides her deep love for China and Hwa Nan in her apartment. You can find many Chinese elements in her room — Chinese landscape painting, Chinese fan, Chinese red and pattern in sofa cushion.... She was thrilled to be invited to have authentic Chinese food. Is it because half of her mind still lingers on in China? When will you come back again? Here at Hwa Nan!

An e-mail from Kay :
From: "Kay Grimmesey"<kgrimmesey@hotmail.com>
Date: 2015/08/22 10:20:02
To: "Fay"<419141732@qq.com>;
Subject: RE: IMG_20150821_115715

Betts, Kay, Huang Fei, and Li Lihua (a graduate of 1997 from Hwa Nan) in Li Lihua's brother-in-law's house, Los Angeles (2016)

The Vice-President, Xu Ou, visited Kay and Betts in Los Angeles (2014)

Fei,
It was wonderful to see you again, and I truly enjoyed meeting your amazing son. Thank you for the photos, for coming to see me, and for the wonderful banquet (it felt like a banquet, not a dinner) you treated me to. I haven't been going to Chinese restaurants here because the food doesn't taste like authentic Chinese food, but the banquet you treated me to was real Chinese food as I remembered it! Thank you for everything!

Love, Kay

Postscript:
Thank Professor Yue Feng for initiating the project Profiles of International Faculty with Hwa Nan Since 1908. I am also indebted to my colleagues and students for their contributions so that I could gather

90

春色
任天涯
——福建华南女子
职业学院外教侧记
International Faculty with
Fujian Hua Nan Women's
College since 1908

many stories happened among Kay and them which are little known by us. I would like to dedicate this article to our dearest Kay in memory of her eleven years' service for Hwa Nan. I believe that I must have missed some very interesting stories about Kay, and I sincerely hope you can write to me about them. I wish I could make up for regret in the second edition of this book.

The Chinese restaurant where Huang Fei treated Kay (2015)

Huang Fei's 2nd visit to Kay and Betts and the restaurant where she treated them, Los Angeles (2016)

Appendix: **Sample of English Corner Memo**

ENGLISH CORNER MEMO OF OCTOBER 19, 2009

TO:Members of the 2008-2009 English Corner Organizing Committee: Amy and Tina from 2007A, Jessie and Nicky from 2007B, Cassie and Sunny from 2007C, Ann and Carrie from 2007D, Wendy and Annie from 2008A, Alice and Tina from 2008B, Christine and Doni from 2008C, and Josephine and Sophie from 2008D.

FROM: Foreign teachers Gina, Laihar and Kay

RE: Meeting set for Wednesday, October 21 at 1 p.m. in the Reception Room of the International Faculty House

Agenda

1. Plan the Halloween English Corner. Sunny and Cassie will be in charge.
2. Feedback on English Corners so far; suggestions for the future
3. Other

Previous decisions on English Corner made 9/18/09

(Present were Tina from Class 2007A, Jessie and Nicky from 2007B, Cassie and Sunny from 2007C, Ann and Carrie from 2007D, Annie from 2008A, Tina from

2008B, Christine and Doni from 2008C, and Josephine and Sophie from 2008D.)

1. There will be two English Corners on the new campus, one on Tuesdays and one on Fridays. We will be responsible for the English Corner on Fridays.

2. It was decided that we would hold English Corner outside the gate near the Administration Building and Bus #89 from 6:00 to 8:00.

3. It was decided to hold two special events: one at Halloween and one at Christmas. Sunny and Cassie will plan the Halloween activities and ask Laihar and Kay for any materials needed (like masks for the organizers) and Annie, Josephine, and Sophie would plan the Christmas activities. There will be a meeting of the organizers before each event to discuss the plans and assign duties.

4. If it is raining at 5:30, English Corner will be canceled.

5. It will be nice to have topics to be discussed in advance each week to help the freshmen. The team members will announce the topic for the following week at the end of English Corner and give them to Laihar or Kay.

Duty Schedule for Organizers

Oct. 23 – Team 3: Cassie and Sunny from 2007C; and Christine and Doni from 2008C

Oct. 30 – Team 4: Ann and Carrie from 2007D; and Josephine and Sophie from 2008D　**(Halloween event)**

Nov. 6 – Team 1: Amy and Tina from 2007A; and Wendy and Annie from 2008A

Nov. 13– Team 2: Jessie and Nicky from 2007B; and Alice and Tina from 2008B

Nov. 20– Team 3: Cassie and Sunny from 2007C; and Christine and Doni from 2008C

Nov. 27 – Team 4: Ann and Carrie from 2007D; and Josephine and Sophie from 2008D

Dec. 4 – Team 1: Amy and Tina from 2007A; and Wendy and Annie from 2008A

Dec. 11– Team 2: Jessie and Nicky from 2007B; and Alice and Tina from 2008B

Dec. 18–Team 3: Cassie and Sunny from 2007C; and Christine and Doni from 2008C

(Christmas event; last English Corner for the first semester)

V

My Reflections: Trimble Boys

Unwrapping the Package

When I pause to recall, invariably my thoughts return to a poem read decades earlier

92
春色
任天涯
——福建华南女子
职业学院外教侧记
International Faculty with
Fujian Hua Nan Women's
College since 1908

at Jiangxi University (renamed Nanchang University since 1993) where I first met foreign teachers. My understanding of Robert Frost's *The Path Not Taken* has evolved with the passage of time and today I can firmly assert that for me the journey is the joy. In 2002 I transferred from Jiangxi Province to Fujian Normal University (FNU), which to me was new place where everything was exciting and inviting. When I rode my bicycle, I frequently passed a college whose name seemed to attract my attention — it was private, non-profit and dedicated to the betterment of women. Later I found a set of three buildings erected in the early portions of the last century that appeared Western in everything but its roof. They bore the names of three Westerners that somehow survived the Cultural Revolution. These buildings also traced their origins to the first women's college in South China — Hwa Nan Women's College (HNC). I was hooked. In 2003 I became one of its part-time English teachers.

China was developing rapidly and Hwa Nan was inescapably caught up with it. The school was expanding enrollment, adding majors and preparing to move to a new campus in University City which is located in Minhou county，15 kilometers from downtown Fuzhou，Fujian，thus, changes came to its reorganization. Half a decade later I became responsible for the Department of Foreign Studies where 10 foreign English teachers were in service. It was rare to have half a dozen foreign experts, let alone one that had received the National Friendship Award, at universities that were 10 times the size of Hwa Nan. Me, a simple country girl getting the opportunity to learn from the very best.

Amazingly three Fujian Friendship recipients were currently on the faculty at Hwa Nan, but I only met two in 2008. They stood in sharp contrast as they could not have been more different. Dr. Kay Grimmesey was soft and gentle. She was a quiet observer who tended to stay behind the scenes until called upon. She led by encouraging others to broaden their thinking. We first met on the street where she told me she had just finished showing her students a free movie and she then invited me to dinner in the Foreign Teachers Compound where I met most of the other foreign experts in an informal setting and had a very enjoyable evening of relaxing conversation.

The second was Dr. Betts Rivet who charged forward with the unwavering determination that somehow seemed to reflect her years' experience as a Physical Education

Kay，Betts & me at Christmas party（2008）

Instructor and later as a Vice-Principal. When a couple of students began to skip her classes, she requested a meeting with their parents and asked me to serve as an interpreter for her. I may have been more nervous than the parents because this was not something we got involved in until something went seriously wrong. But Dr. Rivet was not to be denied. As she would say: "It is better to nip it in the bud. An ounce of prevention is worth a pound of cure." One of the parents, a father who I seemed to recall was a taxi driver, was moved by the depth of Dr. Rivet's concern. The students responded by taking their schoolwork more seriously. And I was truly impressed

Something else happened that Fall, I met Professor Karl Fields. His fluency in speaking Chinese was impressive, but I was in awe that he brought over 20 students from the University of Puget Sound to Hwa Nan to help them experience Chinese culture and have contact with the Chinese people. These students participated in English Corner and interacted freely with our students. I marveled that these were travelers, not tourists, who rode a bus to Gutien where Dr. Fields gave a lecture in the same Hall that Mao spoke before embarking on the Long March. I also learned that financial support from the Trimble Foundation that facilitated this visit. But why Puget Sound and why Fujian Hwa Nan Women's College? Some might find this puzzling. Many have undertaken to compile a narrative. I also have carefully traced the whole sequence of events and decided to give

The Puget Sound & Hwa Nan students getting
to know each other (2008)

President Zhang Xunjie with the Puget
Sound students（2008）

The Puget Sound students（2008）

Betts and Elizabeth Benard from Puget Sound（2008）

an accurate and detailed account so that you may have a complete understanding of what has transpired.

2009 Fall: Three Fish

Everyone has a fish story. I have several because my husband is fond of fishing when he is not teaching science to graduate students. In 2002 when the Fisherman and I walked around FNU we stopped in front of the three Western buildings with the Chinese style roof and stared up at the English names. When we got to Trimble Hall, the Fisherman commented that it was an unusual name, but a name he had met before. After musing for a few minutes, he said that there was a company by that name that had an office in Beijing and sold GPS equipment that you could use even when it was dark and in bad reception. I had no idea what he was talking about until many years later.

The vivid events of 2009 will be forever etched. The tree-lined sketches of our new campus stood in sharp contrast to what greeted us in August. Hot, humid and dusty air; barren earth; and the incessant pounding at a site still under construction grated our senses. We had a new school bus to help Chinese teachers commute from Fuzhou to University City. But it was not so convenient for the Chinese teachers, for it would take them more than one hour to commute by the school bus. We were proud of the International Faculty House in the middle of our campus that overlooks a lake. To our surprise the foreign teachers were not much happier than the Chinese, for in the firs year, the supply of water, electricity and Internet for in first year, Foreign was not stable.

I was sitting in my hot dusty office on the sixth floor hoping for a breeze when a student put a black and white picture of one large and two medium sized fish on my desk. They were obviously dead as they were floating on the lake next to our bridge. I could smell them. It didn't take long to unravel the story that they were dead because of water pollution caused by construction. The teacher — the one with the bright flowers on his shirt — had refused to sign the latest petition of Dr. Rivet. He told her to take a picture and send it. He said: "Nothing would be lost in translation in this way".

Sometimes what you get is not entirely what you expect. This was certainly the case with the Trimbles. Much about them was said; although the majority of which was inferred. I had never met them and I wasn't even sure how to address them. Yes, they came as a pair of unmatched bookends that seem intent to keep an orderly shelf in spite of what might be viewed as a large gulf between them. He had blue eyes and still some hair around the sides that was wavy, light brown. The more he needed a haircut, which was most of the time, the whiter his hair appeared. If he stuck in stubbornness, she embraced it and was continually reminding him of it. He was maybe 1.75 meters tall and while not rotund was at least 90 kilos, while she was lithe and weighed half that. She had a full head of dark brown hair. What should I do to get along with them? He was a state senator from Hawaii. He answered that question for me with his action. He simply stretched out his hand and gripped mine firmly with a smile, and said: "Aloha, I am Gordon and this is my wife Sonia." When he talked, he was usually smiling. As he listened, he would stare at the ceiling. Only the changing expression on his face told me that he was ingesting what I said. When you asked him a question, he would pause, reflect and respond in a deliberate but cheerful manner. But it did not take me long to realize they came as an inseparable set.

When I asked him about his teaching experience, he told me smiling, "English is hard. But I can work at helping students improve their communication skills, and since they will be doing all the work, I am probably more like a coach than a teacher. I know a little about economics and have taught Business Finance and International Trade at the university level. As for business writing — this is something I have been doing for the last few decades. Will you help me gain access to the Computer Lab because everything today is done on a computer?" It was settled — I assigned him to teach 3rd year Applied English students Business Writing, Reading in International Business and Free Conversation. I noted that he referred to *Free Conversation* as *Impromptu Speaking* as it was a skill that could be taught. And with the picture of the fish, he demonstrated that he was more interested in communication than in proving how well he wielded words to express himself in formal English.

Periodically he would stop by the 6th floor to interact with our Chinese English teachers and Vivi, the Department Secretary. He would pop his head in the door and cheerfully say: "Aloha." I found this style intriguing. Usually when someone came unannounced to the sixth floor, they weren't interested in niceties but rather venting or at least unburdening their soul. After a while I got used to his cheery "Aloha" and would ask him if he had a moment. It was during these moments I got to understand them better.

One afternoon Gordon asked for my advice: "Our student Lisa always comes to class on time, sits in the front row, and is dressed as if she were going out to a party after class. But she can't see the board without her glasses even though she sits in the front row. So I have her go to the board to read. She is not rebellious; but she is not there. I checked with another foreign teacher, Laihar who mentioned that Lisa talked about going to school in America next year after she graduates. But she does not study hard and therefore will not pass her courses." Remembering the successful meeting where I served as a translator for Betts, I scheduled a meeting with Lisa the following day. We told Lisa that she was not going to graduate if she did not start wearing her glasses to class and trying really hard. We told her that we were calling her parents to set up a meeting. Lisa said her father was never at home and her mother did not speak Mandarin. My secretary Vivi said: "I speak Fuzhou dialect." When Lisa saw Vivi was serious, she begged Vivi not to call her parents. We said, "Show us." It was like a miracle. She studied, and she asked Sonia and Gordon for extra help. With the help of the two, she turned failure into a C+. But she did not do as well as in one of her Chinese courses. When she heard that Gordon and Sonia were coming back to teach an experimental course in the Spring, she asked permission to be in his class. I refused, so she went and got permission from the Academic Vice-President. Wearing her glasses she again sat in the front row and got the highest grade in the class. Last year I heard that Lisa had received her MA from Centenary College in the United States.

When I invited Gordon to address my class he said something like: "My name is Gordon and my father was born in 1915. Looking at his wife he said: Her name is Sonia and her father was born in 1915. My father was born in Fujian, China. Her father was born in Fujian, China. My last name is Trimble. Her last name is Trimble. She is my sister, right?" (In China the wife maintains her own name but the children take the surname of the father.) And with a straight face he would pause for the reaction. This was Gordon. He was both engaged and engaging.

Gordon and Sonia became a familiar sight in the Applied English Office. A few weeks later Gordon mentioned casually that Bob was coming to Fuzhou and asked if it would be alright if Bob helped him teach. Puzzled as I was, I worked hard at being tactful. How old is Bob (there are many Bobs and I didn't want to assume which Bob, Gordon was talking about.) How was he getting to China? Who was he traveling with? What was he going to teach? He answered: "I wasn't quite prepared for what happened next. My students are preparing for his visit. They need to write five questions to ask him while he is here. Then they have to write what they learned. To prepare I have given the class a copy of this." As he handed me *The Trimble Boys* he said: "This is Dr. Charles Garnet Trimble. This is his son Bob. Bob has two sons. The good son is Charles. And this is the black sheep." As he saw my expression turn he added: "No I did not say Prodigal Son. I said black sheep. They are not the same."

Having read *The Trimble Boys* did not adequately prepare me for what happened next. The writing style was terse and emotionless. It gave me dates and places of an incredible journey. He referred to people; he did not describe them. These were stick figures that needed the body language and expressions that come with words. Gordon and Sonia were in the book. But face-to-face they were so much more alive and exciting. Their enjoyment of life, of people and of the moment stet infectious.

The book did not prepare me for Bob either. Let me recall our first meeting. His walk was unbalanced. He had a walking stick that he carried more as an appendage than something he was actually going to use. His one leg was shorter than the other. Thus as he came toward you his right foot swung out to the side in a giant arc and landed immediately in front or a little to the left of another foot. It was all altogether unbalanced and left some concern as to the actual direction he intended to go. But his pace was hurried and purposeful. Bob had this gaping, toothy grin and he gripped your hand like a steel vise. His face was so weathered by the years that it defied age rather than define it.

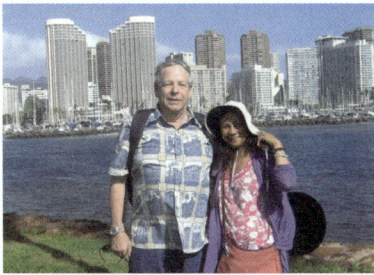

The Trimbles (2013)   Gordon & Sonia Trimble (2013)   Gordon, "the black sheep"
(2016)

The Trimbles and the lady with craftsmanship skill of   Trip to visit Root Carving
cork pictures art in Fuzhou (2013)   Exhibition (2013)

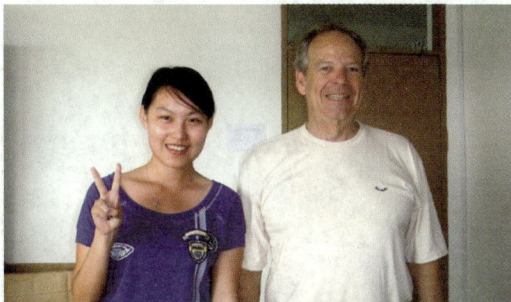

Gordon, the tutor and Vivy, the winner of Hwa Nan   Candidate of Hwa Nan 2009 CCTV Cup Speech
2009 CCTV Cup Speech Contest(2009)   Contest (2009)

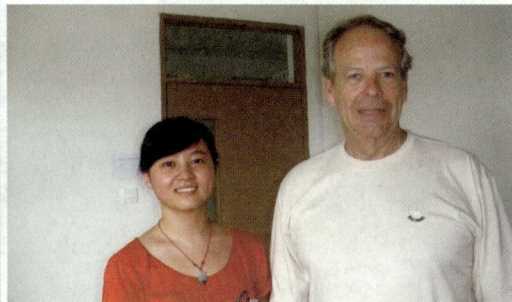

春色
任天涯
——福建华南女子
职业学院外教侧记
International Faculty with
Fujian Hua Nan Women's
College since 1908

98

But his eyes still sparkled and there was excitement in his voice as he spoke which stood in sharp contrast with the rest of his physical appearance. He did not tell me directly his age. He simply took out his driver's license and handed it to me to read. Date of Birth: 15 November 1915. I looked up in confusion. He smiled and said, "look over here at the expiration date." The expiration date was 2020. By then he would be 105. I was stunned. I could not imagine someone still driving at the age of 105. He grinned broadly and added, "Get used to seeing me, for I will be here for quite a while. And I don't need special attention. At that, Gordon smiled and said, "Not to worry, for the next 12 days you will be the entertainment."

Later someone asked, "How old are you?" His face would turn serious, but his eyes were still twinkling. His reply was simple: "We do not use old. The proper term should be mature and I was born in Gutien, Ningde in 1915. Things were different then. And while this is nice, I miss the old China that so many of you are probably trying to forget."

When I needed a judge for the selection of Hwa Nan's candidates for the provincial CCTV cup speech contest the first name that came to my mind was Gordon. He was an attentive listener and his scoring was in line with my Chinese teachers. After the picture taking, he asked three simple questions not targeting at anyone in particular: "When does CCTV release the topic? When does Hwa Nan inform its students of their competition? If your students were interested, how could we utilize time to help them prepare?" This was his style. He asked questions. I could tell he was committed and I liked his attitude. I asked him to coach Vivy (a business English major student) for the provincial competition. During the next three weeks Vivy underwent a remarkable transformation. She reorganized her thoughts, she rewrote her speech and she grew in poise and confidence. Then I knew Gordon was capable. Sonia and Gordon traveled with us on the bus to Xiamen University's new campus in Zhangzhou. There were eight of us in all including the students from FNU. Gordon took advantage of this opportunity to talk to each of the students. He later told me: "If you want a sense of what China will be like a generation from now, talk to students."

He paused and added: "Americans should spend more time coming to China to talk to students."

Bob and Gordon was an interesting pair. They did not talk much to each other. But Bob might suddenly solemnly say: "Life is complex." Gordon would shake his head and reply to no one in particular in an equally somber tone:

Father and son (October 2013)

"Life is simple; it is people that make life complex."

Bob wanted to return to Nanping to again see where he spent most of his first 12 years. Fortunately I was able to get a seat in the car. I wanted to know Bob better. Gordon asked, I accepted. The destination was the site of the original hospital which Bob's father established. For me it was watching Bob and Gordon the two Trimble Boys interact. From listening to them it was not clear who was father and who was son. They did not behave like any father and son I had met before. Bob continued to stare out the window as well journey up the southern side of the Min River. He would describe how many days it took and where the boat was pulled by hand. As we passed the turnoff for Gutien, he wistfully said, "That was where I was born. I don't remember anything but it would be nice to see what it looks like today." And this dream came true in 2013. He enjoyed the excitement when he stood in front of the hospital and again on the top floor as he gazed out at the Min river. Slowly memories started filtering through the passage of nearly half a century. He would mention how he was taught to hold a Ping-Pong paddle and ask how we hold it today. Out of concern, after lunch I tactfully posed a question whether or not he needed to take a rest. His answer was sharp and to the point. "I don't take naps." This guy had flown by himself to China because he wanted to see for himself how much the China in his memory compared to the China of today. He was used to taking care of himself and was more interested in helping others.

To celebrate National Day and Mid-Autumn Festival when Bob being 94 years mature (2009)

When Bob mentioned his desire to see the original site of Hwa Nan again it was my pleasure to keep him company. The Trimble Boys cared more about people who were down-to-earth. They were happy to visit my class of graduate students in Fujian Normal University (FNU). After class, we walked to the original Trimble Hall, took pictures and Bob again repeated that he didn't need to be entertained. My students were amazed that he was genuinely happy eating a bowl of noodles. They were engaged in lively conversation with Bob.

2010 Spring: A Bible Again Opens at Hwa Nan

Gordon and Sonia often asked questions about how we could made Hwa Nan Women's College a better, more attractive place. They used words like: "Who are our customers? How does Hwa Nan build awareness of her brand?" It was just before they

春色
任天涯
——福建华南女子
职业学院外教侧记
International Faculty with
Fujian Hua Nan Women's
College since 1908

100

Pictures being taken with the 2009
postgraduates after class in FNU (2009)

Answer a FNU student's questions (2009)

On the way to have a
simple noodle lunch in
FNU (2009)

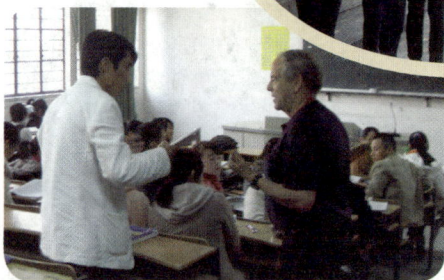

A heated discussion with the
FNU students (2009)

Friendship Award to Gordon Trimble by
Fujian Provincial Government

were preparing to return to Hawaii, I sprung the question: "Would you consider teaching a course entitled *An Introduction to the Bible and Western Culture*?" They were shocked. I went on: "I got the same reaction when I proposed this last year. This is a course that has been taught at FNU. Hwa Nan was started by Methodist. So if any school teaches this course, it should be Hwa Nan and in the beginning who will be better than a Trimble that is directly related to the school's first president?" I showed him the school course catalogue and said, "I would like to first offer it to Applied English and then Business English and finally make it available to every student in the college as an elective course."

There was a long pause. Then he very quietly asked: "When would you like to offer it and for what grade level?" He carefully considered and chose his words slowly and purposefully: "Two conditions: Make sure the Party Secretary knows about this course and when the classes are, and make sure she knows she is welcomed and if she comes I would like her to participate in the discussion." The Trimbles came for five weeks during March and April in 2010. I observed the class on a couple of occasions and at the end of the experiment we decided that it would be better to offer the course to the third year students at the first. And the course continues to be offered and open to both Business English and Applied English as an selective course. It continues to be rated by students as one of their preferred courses. I also told Gordon that words like *apocalyptic* and *charismatic* are probably beyond the students' reach. He replied: "Next time I will be more effective."

When Bob and Gordon walked about the campus during the previous October, something happened. By the time the Trimbles arrived in March there were two new learning areas in the International Faculty House. Gordon said we should drop the term "Faculty" and simple call it the International House where students' learning would be an integral part of this facility. The school adopted his idea. Where bicycles had been previously parked has been developed into a Multimedia Center that the school uses when international groups come to Hwa Nan. Upstairs there is a Writing Lab and two other rooms used for small group discussions. The International House now has the potential to operate during Winter and Summer breaks as a stand-alone facility.

The Trimbles were good at teaching, but for them it was more an hobby than a job. They turned down my request of teaching for the Spring term. They said, "Teaching is very intense. We need time to pause, to reflect, to plan how we can be more effective. We didn't like our teachers in college and we don't want to be like them." I let it go at that.

By summer, some of my Chinese teachers were complaining that how come the

Alumni get-together activity initiated by Gordon (October, 2010)

Trimbles only teach Applied English? Aren't the students of Business English also deserving? I wanted to invite him to teach the second year Business English students. His comment was: "This is stuff I have not done before. I think I can relate more effectively to students with a higher level of English proficiency. Let us make a reassessment at the end of the semester and then talk about how I can be best used for the coming year."

2010 Fall: Evaluation Chart & Lydia Trimble Challenge

We had a new campus whose physical size could meet the Provincial requirement for an institution that had 5000 students. The fact that we had this new campus is a tribute to our former President Benchun LIN. But as one problem goes away others emerge. Students were changing. We were getting fewer students from urban areas and more students from rural areas where the level of primary and middle schools and their learning were not as advanced. Consequently student scores on the Gaokao（Entrance examination to University）were declining. Furthermore student motivation and passion to excel were also waning. This was compounded by the changing nature of those foreigners seeking to teach in China. In the 1990s the people that came to China were motivated by a desire to share and give. By the second decade the pendulum was swinging in the direction of those who came were more concerned with monetary rewards.

This would be the year I got to know the Trimbles much better. I was short of native English speakers and had asked Gordon to teach four different courses to second-year Business English students. I really appreciated that Gordon, with Sonia as his Teaching Assistant, was willing to teach the courses where excellent foreign teachers were desperately needed and wait until the end of the semester to give me feed back as whether it was a good use of his abilities. With four departments to manage, I was constantly hearing concerns from teachers in other departments that they were not getting as many of the best teachers as Applied English. Gordon said, "My objectives remain the same. My students learn business concepts and leadership skills — it doesn't matter what title the course is." Given this attitude, it was not surprising that these students were highly motivated because Gordon and Sonia put forth their best effort.

Not only did the above mentioned heavy teaching tasks Gordon shoulder but there was more to come. To better prepare our students for annual provincial and national English speaking contests, Gordon suggested that we should offer a course named *Presenting in Public*. But how? And when? There was never such a course in our curriculum. Plus in China, public speaking was not being emphasized at all. Yet with his design and help, this course was opened and students from four of our departments were able to have this course. Since the students are from the four different departments, Gordon had to sacrifice his spare time by arranging it every Wednesday evening so that the students could choose it without conflicting with other daytime courses. It is so attractive that two of the English teachers Fay (Head of Applied English department) and Genny went through his course for a whole term without missing one class. the class continues to be offered every year.

As I got to know Sonia and Gordon better, I began to realize that they were both successful at a variety of things before they had decided to dedicate the Fall term to teach at Hwa Nan. Gordon worked as an economist at the Department of Planning and Economic Development and later as a State Senator that represented Waikiki, China Town and Honolulu Harbor. He had devised questionnaires, evaluated the results and used these results to formulate policy. So when we were developing a form to be used by students to evaluate their instructors, I sought his input and incorporated his suggestions in the final form that we still use today (see the following evaluation form). One of his suggestions that I remember was: "Would you recommend this course to one of your classmates?" Unlike many foreign teachers, the Trimbles were fully supportive of student evaluations. Gordon would simply say, "Who is the customer? Yes, grades matter, but most students are able to fairly assess whether their teacher is capable and committed. Most can articulate reasons for why they are unhappy with a particular class." We have been using the questionnaire since then and I still remember the first complaint: "Gordon is in front of us; Sonia is behind us. There is no place for us to hide. We can't even go to sleep or play with our phones The subject is too difficult. There are too many quizzes. Gordon wants us to learn too many words." Even so, it did not matter what course they taught, the students consistently evaluated them among the top three teachers.

Fujian Hwa Nan Women's College

教师教学学生评价表

Teacher Evaluation Form

专业：   班级：

(Department)   (Class)

教师姓名：   课程：   日期：

(Instructor)   (Course)   (Date)

请按以下评估等级如实地对评估项目进行打分:

(Please rate the instructor on these statements according to the following scales)

1、非常不同意 Disagree Strongly	2、不同意 Disagree	3、中立 About Equal Balance Between Agree and Disagree	4、同意 Agree	5、非常同意 Agree Strongly

春色
任天涯
——福建华南女子
职业学院外教侧记
International Faculty with
Fujian Hua Nan Women's
College since 1908

在所选数字栏里打"√"　Tick the number you selected

评估项目 Components	说明 Explanation	非常 不同 意	不 同 意	中 立	同 意	非常 同意
1、组织能力 Organization	教学组织能力强（课堂组织紧凑，连贯，不离题，灵活运用各种教学方法等） The instructor is well organized in his/her teaching. Effective in time management.	1	2	3	4	5
2、知识性 Knowledge	在学科教学中体现了渊博的知识。（知识性强，知识面广，专业基础扎实，介绍本学科新知识，掌握本专业新动态） The instructor appears knowledgeable in teaching his/her subject.	1	2	3	4	5
3、批判性思维或分析思维 Critical/Analytical Thinking	启发学生思维，培养学生批判性思维和分析性思维的能力。 The instructor develops student's thinking and analytical skills.	1	2	3	4	5
4、课堂互动 Instructor-Group Interaction	鼓励课堂讨论和自由提问；营造适宜的课堂气氛。 The instructor encourages class discussion/ participation; Creates an appropriate learning environment.	1	2	3	4	5
5、清晰度 Clarity	用各种方式清楚地传达学科内容。 The instructor communicates the subject matter clearly.	1	2	3	4	5
6、师生联系/关系 Instructor-Individual Student Interaction	建立良好师生关系，关心爱护学生。 The instructor establishes a good rapport with students.	1	2	3	4	5
7、作业 Assignment	作业反映了课程的内容，符合教学目的；作业批判、讲解及时。 The content of assignments reflects the course content and objectives. The assignment is checked and returned on time.	1	2	3	4	5
8、工作态度 Working Attitude	对教学表现出积极的态度。 The instructor shows a positive attitude towards teaching.	1	2	3	4	5
9、责任心 Sense of Responsibility	对学生高标准，严要求。 The instructor is responsible and sets strict demands on students.	1	2	3	4	5

评估项目 Components	说明 Explanation	非常 不同 意	不 同 意	中 立	同 意	非常 同意
10、准时上下课 Punctuality	按时上课，不提前下课。 The instructor is supposed to be punctual to begin and finish each class.	1	2	3	4	5
11、调课频率 Frequency of rescheduling classes	不随意调换课。 The instructor should not reschedule classes frequently.	1	2	3	4	5
12、总体评价 Overall Rating	总体上是一位称职而高效率的教师。 Overall the instructor is effective and competent in his/her teaching.	1	2	3	4	5
	我愿意向其他学生推荐上这位老师开的这门课。 This course taught by this instructor is worth being recommended to students.	1	2	3	4	5
13、总分 Total（65）						

您对该教师改进教学有何建议？

Any suggestions to the instructor for improvement?

感谢您的如实评价！

THANKS FOR YOUR PATICIPATION!

I once asked Gordon what was the most unusual thing he learned as a administrator. He answered without pausing: "Your subordinates feel that they do not need to tell you the truth. Some lie because they do not want to be blamed. Others lie to make fool of someone. But often they simply don't care or think you will never find out what the truth is, so why bother. Others are afraid of you and tell you what you want

Chinese English teachers and international faculty members celebrating Thanksgiving in downtown Fuzhou City (2010)

春色
任天涯
——福建华南女子
职业学院外教侧记
International Faculty with
Fujian Hua Nan Women's
College since 1908

to hear. Still others do not want to do what you expect them to do. That is why I prefer to watch what people do and if I don't have a clue what the answer is I will never ask." I was surprised by his comments. But, after mulling it about for a few weeks, I mentioned to Gordon that one of our teachers had a certificate that indicated he had a PhD from the Grove Academy of New Zealand. The following week Gordon gave me a list of institutions in New Zealand that were authorized to grant PhDs and the Grove Academy was not one of them. Another foreign teacher was asserting that she had a MA from the Grove Academy, but she had never been to New Zealand. Thus we fired three native English speakers and I started to discover that the quality of foreign teachers that come to China was continuously lowered.

Bob at the age of 95 still had a passion for thinking — making small changes to improve Hwa Nan's brand and make the world a better, kinder place. To this end he provided seed money either directly or through the Trimble Foundation that he had established 15 years earlier. Gordon's role was to implement and evaluate and report back to Bob during his annual October visit. This year we began a three-year experiment called the Lydia Trimble Challenge. The purpose was to attract students in Applied and Business English whose English scores were higher in the Gaokao (entrance examination to college, like SAT back in the US) and to take it as an incentive for the rest of the students. The mechanism was to offer five scholarships to the incoming first year students. I was intimately involved in this project and helped to coordinate meetings with the three groups most closely involved — admissions, business and academic departments. We came up with a program that Bob liked and we were convinced that this program would last for three years until the school outsource student recruitment and change her admission policy.

Fall of 2011: Hotline 777 Meets the Trimble Boys

At the beginning of the Fall term, we interviewed and made the final select of the first five Lydia Trimble Challenge recipients. We congratulated them and reviewed their responsibilities to do their best and fulfill Hwa Nan's motto in their outlook and actions— Having Received You Need to Serve Others. These students accepted their responsibilities and worked diligently.

When Bob arrived in October for his 12-day visit, students were eager to show how much they had improved. They exhibited confidence in the style with which they introduced themselves. Again they went into groups of 5 to the Reception Room and interviewed Bob. I enjoyed watching their lively interaction with Bob. Bob also participated in helping our next FLTRP Candidate prepare for the provincial contest. With Bob and Gordon's help, our candidates' confidence and presentation skills grew quickly.

For the candidate this was a transform. Bob would take no credit. He again would remind us that he didn't need to be entertained but came to Hwa Nan to help his younger son.

Sonia & one of the students of the
Applied English Department

The Trimbles with the first five Lydia Trimble
Challenge winners (2011)

The two Trimble Boys were an special couple. One-to-one and in very small groups Bob was an enthusiastic speaker. Facing a large group of people, he would look at his son and say: "Now it is your turn to talk." Bob's love of life was inspiring. What a great role model for people everywhere. An old age does not confine him at home. I wanted other people to hear his story and envision what was possible in life when you are walking around with 95 years' experience. The problem was that Bob was camera-shy. As soon as you put a microphone in his face, he would clam up. He did not think of himself as important. Gordon would say, "Don't worry Bob, this is not about you. This is about experience and helping others to do what they are capable of doing."

Of the people I know in the media, one of my former students was a TV reporter who exuded kindness and concern. I figured if anyone could get Bob to relax and forget the camera it was Lis from the TV news program hotline 777 which had provincial coverage. Lis did what I hoped she would do. And during the interview Bob was impressed with how effectively the cameraman was as an active participant in the process suggesting backgrounds and seeking to have more action. Bob was so taken by Lis and the cameraman that every October he would invite the two to his Birthday Friendship dinner. Over the next four years a total of six different TV news stories by different programs were done on Bob and the Trimble family and it all began with the truly touching story that Lis

春色
任天涯
——福建华南女子
职业学院外教侧记
International Faculty with
Fujian Hua Nan Women's
College since 1908

108

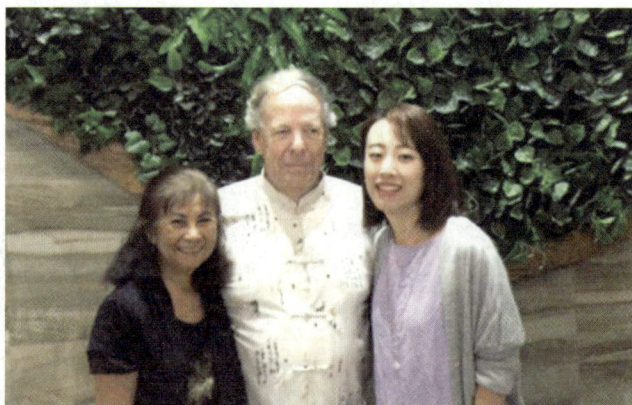

Liz and the journalist from Hotline 777(2015)

put together. I have provided a link to these stories at the end of this chapter. Please refer to the video clip 1. Bob's trip to Hwa Nan.

Hwa Nan- Puget Sound: East Meet West

With the support of the Trimbles and the cooperation of Hwa Nan, 25 students from the University of Puget Sound used our campus for their home base for a month as they studied Chinese history and philosophy. They interacted with our students and learned what Bob would call the real China — not things but people and their history. They participated in English Corner and we held a symposium to highlight differences between the culture of America and that of China.

Gordon declared the beginning of the Forum (2011)

Elizabeth Benard from Puget Sound introduced the Pacific Rim/Asian Study Travel Program (2011)

Sonia& President Zhang issued the Lydia Trimble Challenge Awards to the recipients before the Forum (2011)

Attentive audience at the Forum(2011)

The Trimbles, Elizabeth & President Zhang at Hwa Nan & Puget Sound Forum (2011)

春色
任天涯
——福建华南女子
职业学院外教侧记
International Faculty with
Fujian Hua Nan Women's
College since 1908

Eloquent speaker from Puget Sound at
the Forum(2011)

Excited audience at the Forum break
time (2011)

Eloquent speaker from
Hwa Nan at the Forum(2011)

Interactions between the students from the two
universities (2011)

Puget Sound students with Miss Etiquette from
Hwa Nan (2011)

Puget Sound students joined the graduation
performance of Business English majors (2011)

2012 Fall: A Weight Lifter Comes to Hwa Nan

During the Spring term I got an e-mail from Gordon saying that he had found for us a new native English speaker who had taught English in Germany. He said she was young, energetic and was someone who could inspire our students to think outside the box. He added that she was into sports. I figured that he meant something like golf or tennis. But I found out I was wrong when he forwarded a picture, that Sonia had taken at the Fifteenth State Games in Honolulu. Our students took to Emily so much that she came back to teach a third semester at Hwa Nan.

By the late August, Gordon and Sonia had been in Fuzhou for six years. Having experienced the congestion and smog of Shanghai and Beijing, they preferred Fuzhou because every year it got better and they enjoyed being casual observers of this remarkable transformation. As Gordon would say, "Change is occuring so rapidly that the development in China for one year is worth five or six years elsewhere. If we travel to different places we see they are different but we would not realize the pace of development." Gordon judged this pace by counting the number of cement trucks he saw in every two minutes. Surprisingly he ignored the number of construction cranes. This year he noted: "Most places are wheelchair accessible; five years ago you could not say that. Drivers are getting better, traffic is moving more smoothly and the roads are handling more private cars without appearing more congested. More plants, more hedges and more trees really make Fuzhou a much more attractive place to live in." The same was true for our school campus.

The Trimbles with the students of Pacific Rim/Asia Study Travel Program of Puget Sound celebrating Thanksgiving at Hwa Nan in China (2011)

At the beginning of the Fall semesters when we welcome the freshmen in Business and Applied English Departments, we would introduce our foreign teachers. Gordon always had a well-organized two-three minute presentation. By now I have seen him speak a half dozen time. I remember what he said because while similar they were never the same and for the first few years I got to be the translator because I wanted the students

112

春色
任天涯
——福建华南女子
职业学院外教侧记
International Faculty with
Fujian Hua Nan Women's
College since 1908

to think about what he said. The rooms were large containing over a hundred students. Sometimes he would use a microphone, and he would always stand and speak. The following is a welcome speech given by Gordon for the 2011 year new students.

> *Good afternoon! On behalf of my family, on behalf of all the foreign teachers...Aloha and welcome to Hwa Nan. Your foreign teachers come from many places. They have traveled far in order that you may receive the blessings of a good education. Hwa Nan is special because it is international in origin. It is international in instruction. It is also special because it was designed by women, administered by women to train young ladies that they have a special role to make Fujian, to make China, to make the world a better place.*
>
> *Be proud of your school, be proud of who you are. Work hard, study smart, learn your lessons well in order that our future may be bright. The journey ahead is difficult, but we can realize our dreams if we commit ourselves, remain focused on what is truly important and help each other as we travel into tomorrow. Your foreign teachers are here to help you. But it is up to you to ask. Together we will succeed!*

He seemed never to need to refer to notes or a written speech. When I asked him about this, he laughed and said Sonia would tell him; "Make it short, if you can't remember it, neither will your students." He is more like Winston Churchill who wrote his speeches out and then memorized them. Gordon tries to do the same with his courses.

Weight lifter Emily Brockelman taught 3 semesters in Hwa Nan (2012-2013 school year)

Emily & Fay, head of the Applied English Department (2012)

Several times I had asked him to teach both terms. He would tell me that he need time off to review what had worked and what had not and think of different examples and exercises that would improve students' English. He told me more than once: "As teachers, we know what we say, but we do not know what students have known. I am not here to please students. I want my students to remember even 30 years later that they tried hard and were able to master things that they did not realize they were capable of doing. If I get some bad reviews, that is to be expected. Some students learn no matter what the teacher is like. I would like to keep those from getting bored. But the ones I am really interested in are the ones in the middle. These are the ones that need to be inspired." It did not seem to matter which section I gave Gordon and Sonia to manage, by the end of the semester some foreign teachers would ask me why I always assigned the best students to the Trimbles.

One of our Business English students had Gordon as her teacher during her second year. As a third year student, she was coached by Bob and Gordon for the provincial speech contest. This is what Barbara (Jiapeng HUANG) , who has just finished her master degree in Emporia State University, had to say: "Gordon really has a very good vision for us for our college education. What he taught us then seemed simple, yet it is now a great help for me to study, basic yet meaningful and helpful, like lots of class activities he designed which helped me be more prepared for merging into American university study ."

Barbara finished her Bachelor Degree (study) and began Master in the US

The Trimbles sought to get their students out of the classroom. With more and more students coming from outside Fuzhou city they found that few had been to our provincial museum. So this became a regular activity followed by a picnic lunch with ham and cheese sandwiches in the park that the student made before they departed on the school bus.

Students visited Fujian Provincial Museum with the help of Gordon & Sonia (2012)

The Trimbles lived by Hwa Nan's motto. For them it was: Having received it is now our turn to serve. They viewed giving as enlarging life. And in the spirit of "giving when received", I needed to do more paperwork than my colleagues who were envious of me because they never had a chance to write a letter like this. The following are the e-mails between us.

Thank you for your support

18:14 December 10, 2012 Monday

Dear Sonia and Gordon,

Genny has told me about the 840 Yuan you and Laihar have left with us for the next year's English speaking contest fund. I really appreciate it. Please let Laihar know my heartfelt gratitude for her since she has no e-mail. I will inform all the heads of the departments and the teachers concerned.

I will come to Hwa Nan to have a meeting at 8:50. I am wondering whether you are free late tomorrow morning. I might drop by and say hello to you?

Aloha Alice

Sonia and Gordon never kept the money that the college provided them for tutoring the students to participate in the provincial contests. The money that should go to them was always donated back to the departments for students' extra - curricular activities. Gordon would say, "Do not bring me laud. Actions are what people remember." If it were beneficial to the students and the school, he would try his best to be there. I should add that he stroved to make his classes as vivid as the Hawaiin shirts he wore. You would have no problem spotting him at our

Doc. and Vice President Su Mengna & Gordon at the job fair (2012)

student Job Fair.

The Trimbles are always interested in making connections with others. They want their students to know that English is for living, not just something that rattles around in their head. When the Trimbles are not at Hwa Nan in the Spring semesters, they are looking for ways to connect Hwa Nan to Hawaii or the University of Puget Sound. I didn't know what Bob might have had in mind when Gordon suggested that we see if our Hwa Nan students would be interested in talking face-to-face with students in Hawaii through skype. We used the computer in the writing lab to contact with a middle school in Honolulu (Sacred Hearts Academy.) Both schools were private, for girls only and were approximately the same age and had been established by missionaries. This is how I established a relationship with its Headmistress Betty White. Below is a listing of the original pairs that we connected. These were girls in Hawaii and in Fuzhou that had received scholarships from the Trimbles.

The following are the name list
1 Chris Asano   aasang12@student.sacredhearts.org   shadowflare93
   Rachel Zou   qwreq42@qq.com   rainbowaqq
2 Sierra Fallau   sfallau12@student.sacredhearts.org
   Ellen Zhang   1277803796@qq.com   E187501
3 Nadia Busekrus   nbusekrus@student.sacredhearts.org   nadia.busekrus
   Zoe Xu   328104851@qq.com   babyzoe21
4 Keala Stibbard   kstibbard@student.sacredhearts.org   kealaaumoe1
   Alice Guo   379140914@qq.com   alices1015
5 Lizette Sagun   lsagun@student.sacredhearts.org
   Joy xiao   963251268@qq.com

Below is one of my e-mails with Betty White.
Aloha Alice:
You are a bit ahead of us, but we will catch up quickly.
Let's try for Wednesday, March 21. My understanding is that we will skype at 2 pm Honolulu time, which will be 8 am China time.
Definitely, the girls can skype on their own.
What kind of equipment or set up do you have? Are you projecting the skype onto a big screen or just using the computer screen?
I will not have specific names until Monday morning. My thinking right now is to have 5 girls involved—at least 1 Trimble Scholar. I am thinking of having some of the girls

from our Chinese class involved. What do you think? I will also invite our Chinese teacher to be present.

Let me know what you think.

Aloha,
Betty White
Head of School
Sacred Hearts Academy
3253 Waialae Avenue
Honolulu, Hawaii 96816
808.734.5058, ext 226; cell 808.383-9870

In China we have Chinglish. In Hawaii, its residents are fond of using Hawaiian words when appropriate. If you look at the letter again you will notice that it begins and ends with the word "Aloha". It is a word Gordon throws out when he walks around the campus. If a student answers: "Aloha", then Gordon knows it is one of his current or former students. It is used both orally and in formal writing. It is to express care and concern for the person to whom you are addressing. It can mean: "Hello" or "Good-bye", and Sonia will add that it also means "I love you". Alice is my English name that was given to me by my first native English teacher probably because in her class I was always happy and living in my own little wonderland.

Gordon especially liked the national "CCTV Cup" later being known as "FLTRP Cup" English speaking contest because it had three components—a three-minute prepared speech, a two-minute impromptu speech and a one-minute Q&A. He put it this way: "It would not be too bad if you could do each of these separately but to have to do them all under adverse circumstance really stretches the envelope." He required all of his students to write in good English the CCTV Cup Topic during National Holidays. He used the Impromptu Speaking classes to let each student present one or two speeches each week. As students progressed he would start asking each student questions about what she had just presented. He wanted to know the topic so he could work on topics for both his Public Speaking and Impromptu Speaking classes. So I paid much attention to this and the minute the topic was publicized I would e-mail them to him. In 2012, the topic was "What We Cannot Afford to Lose", I would like to quote the letters between us.

At 2012-05-08 05:22:14

Dear Alice,

Thank you for your e-mail. Thank you again for all your hard work.

We are now checking into the best way to get to Fuzhou.   The price of oil and airfare continues to rise but that is a sign the economies of China and India are continuing to grow so we are happy. We should arrive on or before September 2nd and return on December 16th. Actual flight dates may vary depending upon price and airline connections.   Any thoughts on how difficult it is to fly to Shanghai and take the train to Fuzhou?

Soon you will have the topic for this year's CCTV speech contest.   We are now working on the course outline for Presenting in Public and hope to e-mail this to you so that the potential students can understand what is expected of them.   If they are not willing to put in the time and make a serious effort then the opportunity should be given to those students that are.   The challenge will be in the Impromptu speaking.

Hopefully we can have a teacher's meeting and tour of campus before classes begin. Waiting to schedule this until after the last foreign teacher has arrived is great for the last person but is too late for those that come early and have organized their activities before the classes begin.

We will be showing several movies at night that students in our Bible and Western Culture are expected to attend and write a summary. Thus they will get a few more than the required 34 hours. For the Business Writing class since I only have 24 students I will be meeting with each student individually every other week to go over their writing.

Tomorrow Gordon will be flying to Seattle to spend a week with Bob
With warmest aloha,

Gordon & Sonia

Dear Gordon & Sonia,
Firstly, I would like to check the time you arrive and depart. Where will you arrive on 2nd, September, Fuzhou or Shanghai? And will you return to the US on December 16th? I am thinking if you arrive first to Shanghai, I might find some of my friends or relatives to meet you in Shanghai and stay there overnight, and then take train from Shanghai to Fuzhou, which costs six and half to seven hours day time at the cost of 264 yuan(second class, hard seat) or 316 yuan(first class), please let me know your decision soon.

Secondly I got the CCTV topic for this year which is What We Cannot Afford to Lose, I think we should let the public speaking students know the topic and hopefully do some homework before class.

春色
任天涯
——福建华南女子
职业学院外教偶记
International Faculty with
Fujian Hua Nan Women's
College since 1908

118

I hope too that teacher's meeting and tour of campus will be presented before classes begin. But as far as I know, we have only five foreign teachers next term, including you and Liz from Puget Sound. The rest are Laihar, and the Willie couple , I think.

"Bible and Western Culture" is supposed to be elective/selective course for third year students of Applied English and Business English, yet almost all of the third year students have got full credits for elective/ selective courses. We are now organizing this course in a lecture form in small class. We understand if it were in the first year, many students would select it but their English is poor; this time we changed it to third year, then the students have finished the credits. We (Fay and I) are thinking we might change it to second year students of Business and Applied English Department or keep it a lecture way to have more voluntary students to come. Is it alright?

Lastly, Fay and Genny would like to continue to participate some of your classes like what they did in your public speaking class. Would you give them this chance? I assume they benefit a lot from your class and would like to draw more from your classroom teaching.

with warmest Aloha
Alice

I can still remember parts of the speech that Christine gave because it told me that Gordon wanted his students to achieve whatever goals they set for themselves. Most students from other universities thought they could not live without family, or love or honor, but not Christine. She said something like: "What I can not afford to lose is a simple little word with three 'S', one T, one R and one E. That's right. I cannot afford to lose stress." She talked about learning how to manage stress and in the middle of her speech she alluded to the various rhythms in life when she said with a straight face: "If your mother didn't feel stress, you would not have popped out. If you didn't feel stress you would never go poo. And if I didn't seek stress I would not be here on this stage speaking to you." The judges this year were a group of elder men. They had no idea what Christine was talking about. But I got it and learned that Gordon frequently began his classes by comparing the energy in stress to that in a wild pony. If the students learn how to tame that pony then that energy would propel them faster and further than they could do without it. The students that took this challenge to heart and became successful made me feel proud that I was at the school where Gordon taught about life—knowledge that came not from a book but from experience.

Bob had celebrated his 97th birthday. He had helped develop a writing lab and a multimedia meeting room. Both were equipped with air conditioners to enhance the learning environment. He had helped sponsor a scholarship program to encourage enrollment of students with higher English achievements. But what were Bob and Gordon talking about on their daily walks around the campus? I would learn this soon when we had our meeting to discuss about the annal provincial speech contest. What I liked about the Trimbles is that when they made suggestions for the path forward they were willing to accept the lion's share of what is needed to be done. As the meeting was coming to a close, Gordon asked: "How can we create an environment where students are competing with each other to improve their public speaking skills? The school representative usually comes from Applied English and sometimes comes from Business English. But I am sure that there are students in other departments that would want to and could compete successfully if we provided the right environment.   What if we had an honors class with the most committed students from the school of Foreign Language and Trade? We could call the class *Presenting in Public: Leadership Series* because with the passage of time we might want to integrate other special classes into the *Leadership Series*." He paused, as we reflected on who would be assigned this important task, before he added: 'If you like, I would be willing to teach it for the first five years as we strive to develop a vehicle that would enhance our school's reputation for proficiency in English communication. Unfortunately it was difficult to persuade the administration. ' " As one administrator said: "Why are you going to do all this work? Just pick one student and train her." But with the

Friends joined Bob's 97th birthday
banquet (2012)

The father & the son visited Fuzhou
scenic place (2012)

support of the Chinese teachers, the new course was born. By the end of the school year my Chinese teachers with the input of the foreign teachers had selected 18 students for next year's course.

There was another Trimble tradition that I need to relate. I am not sure when it started but I probably became aware of it in 2009. While Bob was happy with good conversation and a simple bowl of noodles, he came to China to celebrate his birthday. It was his way of giving thanks for everything China had done to shape him as a person and his outlook toward life. I am not sure where he got these ideas but I was always happy to agree with him that it must have been China. The Trimble family began to host their own special banquet in the end of October or early November and the guests including people Bob had met in Fuzhou. There were the Founders of new Hwa Nan that he had first met in 1989. There were government officials, a media journalist and cameraman, a few teachers of Hwa Nan and FNU and some of their current and graduated students. I usually sat with Sonia who helped organize the event to insure that every person felt welcomed in her extended family. There were no speeches, just a simple gathering of those whom Bob had met and not surprisingly no one seemed to be in a hurry to leave. This banquet custom continues to this day. The following is an invitation I received of this year's dinner.

At 2012-10-18 20:15:00

Alice,

Thank you for your e-mail, I just saw your message on my cell phone. I will inform Gordon and Bob. The time for the dinner on the 26 October is 6:00PM. Here is the name of the restaurant.

Kangte Restaurant. In Chinese is 康特大酒店. The address is number 336, Xier Huan Road, Fuzhou. In Chinese is 西二环路336号. The room reservation is vip room 6. In Chinese is 贵六包厢.

Right now I am a little confused. I thought that I told you about the dinner because you were the first person on my list to be invited and because I wanted you to invite Liz and the camera man to the dinner also. There will also hopefully be the five people from the City of Fuzhou I fed in Honolulu two days before we left for China.

Not sure what else I am missing, but the dinner will be a little like what we did last year with some of our students singing at the end of the dinner. No gifts allowed, just great company.

Thanks again for all your help.

Sonia

Touched by the extraordinary contributions that foreign teachers has made for Hwa Nan, Dr. YUE Feng, Dean of the School of the Foreign Languages and International Trade of Hwa Nan as well as Professor of English in Fujian Normal University initiated the project of writing this book. We were stunned to learn that eight foreign English teachers at Hwa Nan have won the Fujian Provincial "Friendship" Awards! And this was more than unusual for only one university in Fujian had more awarded foreign teachers than Hwa Nan. I had come to appreciate that the Trimble family was a gift—an unexpected blessing of the God, which had presented itself. A gift of five generations that began with a very persistent and unconventional woman. I reflected several decades ago that: "An ordinary man accepts the world as it is. Any progress is therefore dependent upon the unconventional ones." Others could have written nice platitudes but I had a responsibility because I had seen them through the hearts of their students, the words of our Chinese teachers and the eyes of their supervisors. They are really people who relished the challenge, who would use at least whatever tools at their disposal to craft a better world, to change one person at a time. To this imperfect world, Bob would proclaim: " Life is wonderful." He paused and then optimistically continued: " I wouldn't want it any other way." If Gordon were in earshot I would hear him add as an aside:"That is good to consider the alternatives." Thus, I began my challenge when I bowed to the responsibility of presenting a complete and frank portrayal of the Trimbles.

Professor Yue reminded me of the several generations of involvement in education that began when Lydia Trimble first landed in China in 1889. What my boss was really telling me is to be sure to give a sense of history when describe the Trimbles because educational cause seems to be something in their DNA. Bob had four generations of admirers of whom I count myself lucky to be one. Bob was born in 1915 in Gutian, Fukien. This was because his father Dr. Charles Garnet Trimble was a physician sent by the Methodist Hospital Board to operate the 80-bed facility in Nanping — the Alden Speare Memorial Hospital.

Dr. Trimble's Aunt Lydia established her first girls' school in Longtien, Fuqing, Fujian in 1890 and she started and became the principal of a second girl's school on Pingtan Island. Later Lydia Trimble decided to establish a women's college. This became the oldest women's college in South China and was called Hwa Nan Women's College, which was located in Nantai Island in Cangshan district of Fuzhou. You can still visit the buildings with its unusual Western and Chinese architecture style in the old campus of Fujian Normal University. These were the original buildings of our school and you can still read the letters "Trimble Hall" that have withstood the tumultuous history of the past century. We cannot help but be touched by this deep and long lasting relationship between the Trimble family and Fujian province. This includes Lydia's niece Ethel

春色
任天涯
——福建华南女子
职业学院外教侧记
International Faculty with
Fujian Hua Nan Women's
College since 1908

122

Wallace who taught and later served as Headmistress of the preparatory school and J. B. Trimble, Bob's Uncle, who served as the engineer who oversaw the construction of this new campus. Robert Trimble was born on 15 November 1915. He grew up in Nanping and Fuzhou until he was 12. Since he spent most of his free time playing with Chinese children, his Fukienese was better than his Mandarin. I found fascinating details of his life in his autobiography entitled simply *The Trimble Boys*. Here he recalls his earliest memory of Guling, Fuzhou, on Page 18.

During the second term we spent our summers in Guling in the mountains near Fuzhou, where many foreign families from that area went to escape the tropical heat. It was about a six-to-eight-hour walk from the city. My mother was carried on a sedan chair with two long bamboo poles lifted with two men in the back and one in the front. This was pretty common practice among wealthy Chinese and foreigners who were not able to, or did not care to walk long distances…Gulling was a wonderful experience for us boys. We were able to interact with other children of foreign business people, as well as from other missionaries of different faiths. I learned how to play tennis while there and how to swim. By this time I had become quite fluent in the Fuzhou dialect and somewhat fluent in Mandarin. Many years later, when I had forgotten most of the Chinese I knew, I was told that some of the words I still remembered were word that I should not have learned and particularly should not have remembered

That's why you could watch that 97 year old Bob visited Guling of Fuzhou this year, and find pretty interesting habits that Bob possessed since his childhood in Fujian.

On page 78, he recalls memories that are more than eight decades old :

While in Fuzhou we visited an old monastery I remembered near our summer mountain retreat at Kuliang.

At the beginning of the last century, many foreigners lived in Guling. Some of them maintained summer cottages where they could escape the heat of Fuzhou. There were swimming pools maintained and even tennis courts. Back then, before the advent of air-conditioning, people escaped the heat by going up into the mountains and leaving the valleys far below. The widely circulated story of an American family named Gardner and President Xi put Guling on the global stage. A less condensed version of this story would include Lydia Trimble, Hwa Nan staff, Dr. Charles Garnet Trimble and many, many more. The Fujian Media group hotline 777 Program gave a special report on Bob's trip back to Guling after an absence of almost ninety years. This report thus kept alive for future generations the voice and tale of this most remarkable person.

Speaking of this living legend Bob, I was shocked to read of his painful adjustment to life in America when he was 12 and the discrimination he encountered at the hands of other teenagers. This may explain Gordon's comment that his mom talk about China but his father never did. That is why he enjoyed being with Bob in Fuzhou because he was hearing stories for the first time. We could read his autobiography page in 21.

It was in Farmington（Illinois）that I was first teased because of my China background. I remember being called "Chink" by the local boys. I knew nothing about baseball, movie stars or cars. I was determined to become an American as quickly as possible. I tried to forget everything about China including the language.

In 1927 Bob and his parents settled in Tacoma, a port city in the State of Washington where he earned money by picking berries and chopping wood during the summer and delivering newspapers the rest of time. He finished middle school at Lincoln High School. (This was the same school President XI visited in 2015.) In 1933, during the great depression, money was scarce so he entered a small local college where he studied chemistry in order to split the cost of the text books with his high school friend. Today, this school is the University of Puget Sound and now I know the origin of connection between Hwa Nan this school. The story gets even better. In the early 1990s, a history professor from Puget Sound that had written a research paper about Hwa Nan accidentally walk into the wrong meeting. The group was debating which Chinese Port City should become their sister city. She was drawn into the discussion and asked to state her preference. She said that the choice was clear cut: "If it were up to me, I would choose Fuzhou." She does not know what happened after she left the room and takes no credit for the

the TRIMBLE *family*

HAPPY NEW YEAR

We are grateful that this time of year carries with it an obligation to remember all that happened for in doing so we get to relive the memories as we finally are pressured to refile them in more coherent digital format.

Here is a picture -- yes we are in China and that is us. It is a custom in Fuzhou that as you acquire wisdom you have a family picture for posterity to remember. And thus this is ours. He didn't smile. He claims that it is not dignified to smile. She thinks that he is being a bit too traditional. You are the judge.

The year began in fulfilling a life long dream. At last we journeyed from the Atlantic to the Pacific by winding up further east than where we started. We travelled through the Panama Canal and imagined how much longer it took ships a hundred and fifty years ago to get all that tea to England by rounding the Horn. We sipped coffee as we pondered.

In February we met up with the same Puget Sound PACRIM students in India that stayed with us at Hwa Nan in December 2011. We traveled with them as they visited the Pink City of Jaipur, and Taj and its baby sister in Agra . What wonderful memories of a world we are very happy to say that we never lived in. Then in March we spent a few days at the University of Puget Sound to review the progress their Asian Studies program has made in the last 20 years.

Christmas Newsletter of the Trimble family in 2012

春色
任天涯
——福建华南女子
职业学院外教侧记
International Faculty with
Fujian Hua Nan Women's
College since 1908

124

eventual decision that Tacoma become sister city of Fuzhou, but she related the story to Bob and he told me. Today along the Tacoma waterfront you can visit Reconciliation Park and Fuzhou Ting. I would like to end this year's main report by something that Sonia sent me as part of their family Christmas newsletter.

2013 Spring September: A Trip to the Well

Now as I look back at 2013, it is slowly emerging as one of my most fulfilling years. But while it was going on there was too much adjusting from moment to moment to allow me to fully appreciate all that was being accomplished. For only my second time have Sonia and Gordon come to Hwa Nan during Spring semester. Bob must have chattered to Gordon during his previous stay so that Gordon made this Journey. It doesn't sound like much — simply planning, taking a trip to the well and giving his June commencement speech. The process started simply enough with e-mails. A few of which I need to share with you. A generation ago Westerners would complain that nothing could be done in China during the 10 days around Chinese New Years. But now we are globalized and firmly in a digital world so the Trimbles use the Internet to anticipate and plan ahead. I was happy to get their New Year's greeting. They mentioned "too many rainbows". In Hawaii, there are lots of rainbows. Sports teams in The University of Hawaii are called the Rainbows. But you don't have rainbows without rain, so what they were actually saying was that it rained too heavily.

At 04:37:56, 2013-02-11 "Gordon Trimble" wrote:

Dear Alice,

In L. Ethel Wallace's book she mentions that Aunt Lydia established a girl's boarding school in Lungtien in 1890. Where is Lungtien? A couple pages later there is also mention that Aunt Lydia in 1905-6 established a girl's boarding school on Bing Tang. Where is Bing Tang?

Happy New Year! We are not late-in Hawaii we are 16 hours behind China or you are 16 hours ahead of Hawaii. We were going to walk to the beach but there are too many rainbows so we will probably wait until afternoon.

Jean is busily engaged in thoughtfully examining many new things but at the same time she is gaining a new appreciation of what she already is and has. She is happy and inquisitive and reflective.

Our very best to the fisherman and both of your families,

With warmest aloha,

Gordon & Sonia

My answer

Wade-Giles romanization system

At 09:43 Feb 16(Saturday), 2013/At 09:43,2013-02-16(Saturday)

Dear Sonia & Gordon,

I am back in Fuzhou so that I could e-mail you at my convenience. Happy Chinese New Year to you since before the lantern festival (Feb 24th) we are still in the Spring Festival holidays.

…

I did some research and found out that we should do some more research on Chinese spelling system before1949 (Mao's regime), that is Wade-Giles romanization spelling system. Because in Wade-Giles romanization, Beijing is Peking, Xiamen is Amoy, Fuzhou is Foochow. I noticed that Bob pronounced in this way in hotline 777 TV shooting. So I am thinking if we could find a dictionary of Wade-Giles romanization system produced before 1949 or a map of Fukien(which is Fujian now) before 1949, that might be a great help for us to know more about LungTien(LongTian???) or BingTang???

By the way the weather here in Fuzhou is much warmer than my hometown Jiangxi which is terribly cold. I love it here !

Aloha

Alice

After nonstop research it came together in May. It was quite accidental. At the same time Gordon and Sonia were also helping to build a bridge between Bob's high school and an Affiliated high school of Fuzhou Education institute to finalize an exchange program. I was happy to serve as a kind of interpreter and liaison.

Re:Re: reply from Principal Cheng Gang and Su Yun and other …

At 11:08 May19(Sunday) ,2013/At 11:08, 2013-05-19(Sunday)

Hi, Sonia and Gordon, when I Baidu (a search engine similar to Google) the relationship of Lydia Trimble and Pingtan No 1 middle school in Chinese, I got a piece of very exciting news that Lydia Trimble was the first principal of Pingtan No1 Exprimental Primary School and this event is listed on the big events of Pingtan History. The primary school was originally named Yu Shu Girl's School and was donated by Methodist

春色
任天涯
——福建华南女子
职业学院外教侧记
International Faculty with
Fujian Hua Nan Women's
College since 1908

126

Episcopal church. I traced Lydia Trimble's work and found out that she was really a great woman who set up Yu Shu Girl's School in 1906(now No1 Experimental Primary School and its another part was developed into No 1 Middle School 6 years later) and in 1908 she became the first president of Hwa Nan Women's College! We should visit these two schools!

...

I am looking forward to seeing you!

Alice

When the Trimbles arrived in June, we went to Pingtan Island. Over a dozen teachers and several school officials came to greet us. The original buildings had long disappeared. In fact, the only thing that remained was the original well that Aunt Lydia had commissioned. After about 15 minutes, Gordon turned to me and said this was perfect. I looked at Gordon and wanted to say: "I found the school. You have seen the original well. What else do you expect." When we were later having lunch with some of the English teachers and school officials, Gordon was asked what prompted this visit. Gordon replied: "This trip will make my father a very happy man. He has been wondering about Lydia's first school from the time we first came to China in 1989. When I confirm to him that it exists and that the original well has been preserved, he will want to come and visit the school. Is it possible that we could come again in late October? " The principal gave Gordon a hard look that turned into a puzzled expression. I understood and said something in Chinese to the effect that Lydia's nephew will come to China every October and travel alone by himself. The principal smiled broadly and said that Lydia's kin were always welcomed. Gordon added: " There may also be some middle school students from Hawaii. " Their English teachers suddenly became excited. One turned to Sonia and said, "Please do come. This will be a motive for my students. It will give them a reason to study English." And suddenly I think I had a better understanding of why Gordon started the dialog between Hwa Nan and Sacred Hearts in 2012.

Then they began a nonstop dialog of what we could do during a ten-day visit. We involved the Alumni Office, the Foreign Affairs Office and of course my staff. We also met with various administrative officials. Gordon

The century old well commissioned by Lydia Trimble (2013)

wanted the students from Hawaii to really get to know their Chinese counterparts so we created the terms of Big Sisters and Little Sisters. The English of Big Sisters quickly improved because they had a compelling reason to speak English. The little sisters from Hawaii would sometimes become big sisters when they were reading children's books to the children of our Alumnae and in the classrooms in Pingtan Island. By the time the Trimbles left, nothing was certain, but at least we had a plan and something to think about over the following four months.

But the highlight of the Spring visit for most students was that in June Gordon delivered our commencement address. It was the shortest speech of the day and as he started to give his speech, in front of the students without notes, the room became very quiet. The Chair of the School Council Chen was siting in the front row and began taking notes. I had suggested that our provincial speech candidate Christine serve as translator. The material of the address was not new to her and she could translate using the skills she had mastered over the two years that she had been a student in Gordon and Sonia's classes.

> *Friends, Fellow Guests, Gracious Hosts*
>
> *It is wonderful to be back in Fuzhou. In 1989, 100 years after Lydia Trimble arrived, I visited old Hwa Nan and stood in awe of what inner strength she had when she resolved to start a women's college. The school motto — Receive to Serve — was and is a challenge to you — its students to remember your responsibility to serve by helping others improve the quality of life for the people of Fujian. The more I thought of what Aunt Lydia was about, the more I came to admire her perseverance. Except for the time spent raising money and promoting Hwa Nan in America, her adult life was spent teaching young Chinese women that the best way to serve was to lead. I have come to appreciate what she instinctively knew: Leadership is an acquired skill. You possess those qualities that enable you to guide others for their benefit and that of society.*
>
> *Life is full of wonderful, unexpected surprises just waiting for you to come along. We are not here to lecture but to share with you, our 10 secrets to happiness and success. Your final exam begins with the conclusion of this ceremony so take out your pen and notebook so that your journey will be met with equal success because you carefully followed these 10 simple steps:*
>
> *1st — Be in control: Control your emotions; don't let them control you. This begins by not retaliating. Getting even with others is a distraction that simply keeps you from doing what is really important. So be in control*

春色
任天涯
——福建华南女子
职业学院外教侧记
International Faculty with
Fujian Hua Nan Women's
College since 1908

128

by forgiving and forgetting the pettiness of others.

2nd — Be happy: Beautiful people have more energy because they smile. Smiling is contagious and life is fascinating because the unexpected is always happening to challenge and test your character.

3rd — Be thankful: Practice being thankful everyday. Little things happen that make you smile. Say 'thank you', if only to yourself. Soon you will find yourself smiling more, being much happier because good things happen when least expected.

4th — Help yourself by helping others: Life was not intended to be easy, but we can make it easier when we work together. It is not "me versus you", but "you and I working together". Reach out to touch someone with your smile or by listening to their outpouring of sadness or grief.

5th — Accept responsibility: Failure is simply not getting it right this time. Be thankful that you have another chance to do better. Only you can tell yourself that you can't. Don't be the one trying to block your own progress! You were given by your creator certain talents. Develop these talents for your benefit and that of society.

6th — Take pride in all you do: There is no job too small or so unimportant that does not merit you full and careful attention. And when you do it, do it with the pride of an artisan. And no matter how well you did it today, when tomorrow comes around, remember you can do it even better.

7th — Believe in yourself: Only when you believe in yourself can others believe in you. Find a quiet time and place where you can pause to reflect. Think about where you are going. Make a list of what you want to do and be prepared to discuss it. Everyone who has succeeded has had a plan that she shared with others. Don't be afraid. No one will laugh at you if you dream and have a plan of which way to go.

8th — Do not worry. Plan, take responsibility, take pride in all you do and then do not worry. Failure is not an end, but a sign post pointing the way to succeed. Worry is a wasted emotion; it accomplishes nothing. It is the noise: ignore it! When you have done your best, relax in the satisfaction that soon you will know what more needs to be done to accomplish your goal.

9th — Stress is your friend: Control stress before it controls you. You control pressure, not by fighting it but by managing it. Do not ignore it, welcome stress into your life with a cheery smile and happy heart. Let it help you be more successful.

10th — Continue learning: You can read, you can write, you can reason; you have the tools for acquiring knowledge. As my father said when I graduated: "Gordon, if you stop learning, some morning you will wake up to discover that the knowledge you have to succeed in a world no longer exits. So continue to learn so that you can communicate with your children and your children's children."

There you have it: 10 easy steps helping you focus on the music and ignore the noise. Life is an incredible journey punctuated by dates. Remember 19 June 2013 as the day you resolved to follow these simple steps into a successful future. Sonia and I congratulate you!

One of Gordon's students, Kay, decided she wanted to write her thesis about the Foreign teachers and how they influenced her. Below is a portion of what she wrote.

FUJIAN HWA NAN WOMEN'S COLLEGE
THE APPLIED ENGLISH DEPARTMENT
ACADEMIC YEAR 2012-2013

The Influence of the Foreign Teachers on Me
艾凤敏 (Kay)
Class: 2010 Class C
Student No.: 201001105
The Applied English Department
Advisor: 赖黎群
I. Introduction
II. The Contribution of Foreign Teachers

1. The Contribution of the Trimbles
Ms Lydia Trimble, the first president of Hwa Nan College put forward the idea to set up a women's college in the south of China to the Methodist Episcopal Church in Los Angeles of the United States in May, 1904. The board of directors of Hwa Nan College of Letters and Sciences was established in early 1908 after a series of consultations and hard work. All students, teachers and Ms Lydia Trimble had made concerted efforts to run the school and yielded achievements which won the high praise in society and education field at home and abroad in this period. The second generation of the Trimbles, Ms Ethel Wallace became a dean of Hwa Nan College of Letters and Sciences in 1914, and her cousin, Fred

春色
任天涯
——福建华南女子
职业学院外教侧记
International Faculty with
Fujian Hua Nan Women's
College since 1908

130

Trimble took charge of constructing magnificent school buildings which made a significant contribution for the early Hwa Nan. In 1989, the third generation of the Trimbles, Mr. Robert Trimble disregarded of friends' discouragements and came to Hwa Nan in the period of turmoil. Why did this American who was quite successful in his many careers come to Hwa Nan? Why was he so attached to Fujian? It is because his father, Dr. Charles Garner Trimble had come to China as a doctor. Mr. Robert Trimble was born in Nanping Fujian and left China when he was 11 years old. He loves the land of his birth, the Chinese children he grew up with and Hwa Nan which was founded by his grandaunt Ms Lydia Trimble. Hwa Nan was re-established in 1985. In order to provide opportunities that Hwa Nan can make academic exchanges with her Western counterpart, Robert Trimble suggested that University of Puget Sound send representatives to sign an agreement with the college. The University of Puget Sound has been sending a teacher every year to assist our college since 1996. Periodically，Mr. Robert Trimble has donated money to our college to buy learning facilities for students and provided help to the economically disadvantaged students. To further commemorate the first president Lydia Trimble of the private Hwa Nan College, Gordon Trimble became honorary Chairman of our college, and the Trimble family set up the Lydia Trimble Scholarship that was designed to encourage students who achieve good college entrance examination scores and got good grades in English to sign up for our college. The scholarship started from 2011, all awarded students who are freshmen and major in Applied English and Business English can get 5000 Yuan individually to pay tuition fees. The scholarship would be available for application for the next three years. At the same time, in order to encourage the students' enthusiasm to learn English, Lydia Trimble Challenge also added a special encouragement to award the 3rd year students who passed CET-6 from the Applied English and Business English Departments with 800 Yuan.

III. The Characteristics of Foreign Teachers
The Trimbles

Mr. Gordon Trimble and his wife, Mrs. Sonia Trimble take good care of their students as they are grandparenting them in Hwa Nan. They always try to refuse some entertainments politely. Instead, they are willing to help students to improve their oral English and writing English, and try their best to improve students' learning and living environment; they always have the best interests of their students at heart. What's more, he taught students, "When you are old, you should give help and concern to young people, not for popularity but help them make the world a better place." He did all this and won the respect from others.

As Ms Lydia Trimble's offsprings, they were inspired by her career of enhancing Chinese women's education, and her love of Hwa Nan. We cannot see an American leader's majesty from Gordon, there is only the child and innocent smile. When a student asked Gordon why came to Hwa Nan? Gordon told the student, "In order to let the people of the world to see the other side of the American — not everyone in the United States is militant as depicted on TV or in movies. He can go all over the world with a peace messenger's identity. I came to China as Hawaii senator, and he represents the friendship between the Chinese and American people." He received the sixth Fujian Province Friendship Award in the late 2009.

2013 Fall: Bob's Best Visit

As time went by, Gordon and Sonia scheduled their departure from Hawaii to Fuzhou earlier and earlier. This year they arrived at the end of the third week in August. They said it was to get used to the weather in Fuzhou. But I thought it had more to do with revising their lesson plans. In any event, it gave us more time to chat. They again asked Vivi to assign them more than the normal weekly load as required. They said that things always came up forcing them to travel unexpectedly and they didn't want to have to make up classes at the end of the semester. When I met Gordon and Sonia, I asked them to push his students a little bit harder because they were lacking motivation. He grinned and replied, "Yes, madam. This year they will get more experience in learning how to manage stress."

We met several times to review his non-standard courses. Gordon announced that he had a serious complaint. I knew what was coming. Someone in administration has decided that writing and reading courses could have 40-50% more students than "Free Conversation". This resulted in three sections of both reading and writing but four sections of "Free Conversation". But I was wrong. Instead of telling me that he had too many students he asked for the rest of his students. He explained: "Every student speaks in every class. They also write in every class. I begin my remedial class in the second week of school. The people who are in this class are the ones that were in the bottom 40% of the quiz last week . And I use the extra class for these students." He got his wish.

I told Gordon that we would be unable to offer "The Bible and Western Culture" because we didn't have enough students. He knew how much effort and time I had spent in obtaining approval to offer this course. He simply said, "Alice, the course is still in the process of development, I need the practice of trying different things before we will

春色
任天涯
——福建华南女子
职业学院外教侧记
International Faculty with
Fujian Hua Nan Women's
College since 1908

132

Sacred Hearts girls trip to Fuzhou Panda
Zoo with the Trmbles & Hwa Nan pair
sisters

Sacred Hearts teachers and students
from Hawaii visited Wuyi Mountain
（Toni，Nicole，Lilly，Angela from
left to right, 2013)

High school students from Hawaii
& the writer experienced the beauty
of WuYi Mountain (Oct., 2013)

know what works best. Besides, I am a volunteer so it really doesn't cost the school much to offer this course." I was very pleased that Gordon's opinion prevailed. Several years earlier Gordon had explained to me that the best followers were also good leaders. He may have been talking about Bob, but Gordon could not have had a better teacher.

We met again to review the proposed trip by Hawaii middle school students from Sacred Hearts Academy. The arrival date was confirmed. With the input of our Chinese teachers we drew up a list of 30 elder sisters from Hwa Nan. Rooms in the Foreign Faculty House were cleaned and assigned. Wi-Fi with passcodes were installed throughout the first floor. We now knew the class schedule for each student and pairing of big and little sisters began so that no student would be absent from the class. Hwa Nan students would accompany Sacred Hearts students and participate in all activities. In addition, the middle school students from Hawaii would read children's stories at a special alumnae event at Hwa Nan as they did during their visit to Pingtan Island. Gordon's class got to take their little sisters to Panda World and the Provincial Museum. This was followed by a picnic lunch the students prepared before boarding the bus. Gordon was surprised to learn on the bus that none of his students had ever seen a panda close up, face-to-face. And I found that at the last moment the group needed an adult to accompany them to WuYi Mountain.

I made a few last minute adjustments to my schedule and got a deeper understanding of major differences between Chinese teenage girls and those from Hawaii.

Being a parent of a teenage girl I once asked Bob about his two boys. He turned really serious: "Of the two, Charlie was really easy. Gordon on the contrary was a problem." He then looked down at his watch and added. We don't have time for me to relate the details. That would take several weeks. But lately I'm very pleased that he has shown some potential. I asked Bob that question at least three times, but every time I got the same answer. What was Bob really saying? Was he trying to tell me to stop worrying about my daughter because in the end she would turn out to be just fine, too?

......

The Alumni Office invited teachers and alumnae with young children to a special event in the Foreign Faculty House where only English was spoken. There were games, the reading of picture books and refreshments. The event was so successful that the school will seek to hold a similar event during the next visit of students from the University of Puget Sound on their Pac-Rim journey of discovery 2017.

Isabel Yeoh & Aimee Park from Hawaii had bamboo rafting on the Nine-Bend Stream of Wuyishan (2013)

While at Hwa Nan, the Sacred Hearts students went to various classes in my four departments. They answered questions about life in Hawaii. We also had designed a cultural exchange to be held in our small auditorium where students told of the history of their woman's school. This was followed by student speeches and then a few cultural dances and songs. The Hawaii girls were truly impressed by how seriously our girls prepared for their performance. There was even a "fashion show". Gordon explained to the girls that this was the first and only chance that these Hwa Nan students

Paper-cutting skill learning with the help of Hwa Nan teacher Zhuoyan (2013)

Hwa Nan/SHA—The East met the West (2013)

春色
任天涯
——福建华南女子
职业学院外教侧记
International Faculty with
Fujian Hua Nan Women's
College since 1908

134

Sacred Hearts girls performanced
at Pingtan (2013)

Chinese children singing & calligraphy
performing (2013)

Sonia in the Sea of Happy Primary Students at
Pingtan Island (2013)

would be able to perform for Bob and they want to make the best impression they can. The performance was covered by our local media. When Gordon was asked to comment on the performances of the students from the two schools, he replied that he considered it more of a cultural exchange that all could appreciate than a competition.

When we went to visit the Pingtan No. 1 Experimental School in June, Gordon and Sonia asked if both groups could sing a song. English teachers in the school liked this idea and so after some discussion the Trimbles proposed that a song by the Carpenters called "On Top of the World" could be done jointly. When the bus reached the No 1 Experimental School we were engulfed in a sea of smiling children. Sonia was literally swept away.

While the adults met to exchange formal greetings, the girls from Sacred Hearts went to classrooms to read picture books that they had brought with them. At the end of the story, they presented the teachers with the books they had brought and then returned to the meeting room for an exchange of songs and dances. The climax of the event came when both groups gathered on stage to sing "On Top of the World".

Sacred Heart had a blog in which the students filed daily reports of all their activities. Thus the classmates, friends and parents could feel the impact of this journey of discovery in the posted pictures that were punctuated with words. Having returned home, they made presentations before adult audiences including Rotary International. I have enclosed a report about this trip that Sacred Hearts Academy published in their school's electronic

The spirit of Lydia Trimble re-united Yuxian, Hwa Nan and Sacred Hearts (2013)

Bob and one of his fans — Me, smiling broadly (2013)

magazine. Note the reference to the financial aids from the Trimbles. Now I know that their support for women's education is more than simply paying homage to the founder of our school. Women's schools are something they believe in. This newsletter described their trip as a life-changing event for the students. And I hope that this means that in the next 10 years they will consider returning to China to teach at Hwa Nan. The Trimbles have a very far-reaching insight into peace and an understanding of people from different cultures. Once they mentioned that they would like to offer an opportunity for the young people in the United States to have direct and cognitive understanding of China from earlier age. Hopefully they would like to teach in Fujian, in China when the young become adults. What an exiting and promising vision. I am always touched by their kindness and greatness.

Sacred Hearts Academy e-parent line

春色
任天涯
——福建华南女子
职业学院外教侧记
International Faculty with
Fujian Hua Nan Women's
College since 1908

136

Across the river from Hwa Nan is Fujian Normal University,the
Trimbles walked there and fished occasionally(2013)

On 1 November we again came together as an extended family to celebrate what we simply called "The 98th". No speeches, but we did watch the young ladies from Sacred Hearts do the Hula and sing "On Top of the World".

The day after Bob's 98th, the Sacred Hearts girls traveled to Quanzhou, an ancient port city with some of Hwa Nan's teachers and their children. The students marveled

Bob at the head table ready for
the 98th celebration to begin (2013)

The Trimble boys at
98th celebration (2013)

Ms Hao and her colleague from municipal
government presented at Bob's 98th
celebration (2013)

Bob's friends from Hwa Nan at his 98th birthday
celebration (2013)

Hwa Nan driver Lin Ping
with Bob (2013)

Toni from Sacred Hearts with
the Trimble boys (2013)

Bob & students from Hwa Nan
(2013)

Milia Libby from Sacred Hearts,
Bob & Zheng Xue from Hwa Nan(2013)

The last picture I took with
Bob (2013)

春色
任天涯
——福建华南女子
职业学院外教侧记
International Faculty with
Fujian Hua Nan Women's
College since 1908

138

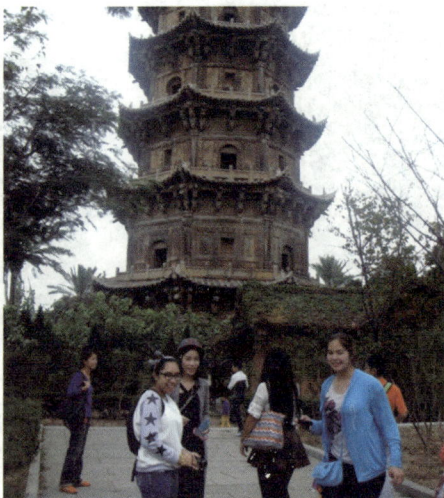

SH & HN trip to Quanzhou (2013)

that a bridge could be made entirely of granite. They visited temples and museums and gained an appreciation for the idea that a nation could be defined not by lines on a map but feelings in peoples' hearts.

School officials from Lungtien heard about Bob's quest to visit each school that had been founded by his grandaunt. Quite unexpectedly, the head of the school, Principal Zhou came to Hwa Nan on 28 November. Hwa Nan administrators took them out for lunch to celebrate the occasion. Then the Trimbles went to Lungtien, Fujian on 6 December to visit the original site of the school which was located next to a church. The school at one time was something that brought the members of the community together, and now it continues to function as a kindergarten. Then we visited the brand new school that was just being completed.

2014 Fall: The Torch Is Passed

During Bob's 98th Celebration, I posed a simple question: "What would you ask for if President Xi suddenly appeared and was willing to grant you one wish?" Without a moment of hesitation, Bob replied: "I would inquire if it were possible to grant a lifetime VISA to anyone over the age of 95 who was born in China and wanted to visit every year the country of his birth." This did not seem unreasonable. I began to think if I can't do that, what else might I be able to do? So I hit upon the idea of making Bob an Honorary Citizen of Fuzhou. At least when he arrived, I could talk about this when he asked me to articulate the vision of Hwa Nan 5 years hence.

So I began to learn something about the procedure. I obtained an application form from the Foreign and Overseas Chinese Affairs Office of Fuzhou Municipal Government. People at Hwa Nan agreed that this was certainly appropriate considering his keen interest in Fuzhou, and his close connection with Lincoln High School and the University of Puget Sound, both of which is situated in Tacoma, the sister city of Fuzhou. But as fate would have it, I was too late. Bob passed away on 28th June, 2014.

The news made everyone silent and sad. Tears fell. Bob, and the two weeks in October that he spent at Hwa Nan had become part of the school culture — it was as old as our relocation to University City. A tradition was born, and it is not defined by time, and even irregardless of the passage of time. Traditions are not to be brought to a sudden termination. Each of us reflects on what Bob had meant to us. I don't know whether think I have mentioned that our office is on the 6th floor with a commanding view of the campus. And once or twice a day Bob would go out and take a walk around the lake so he was easy to notice. Word spread and we would gather at a window to watch his progress and each of us was happy inside that Lydia's nephew still remembered her and what she represented after so many years.

Gordon and Sonia arrived at the end of the third week in August. They were happy to see we had just completed our new sports field. There were some hand rings in the back on which they could swing. I was happy that life would get back to the track. Gordon made sure that his previous students as well as all his current students had known the current FLTRP Speech topic. He commented that those who were the best at the end of the first semester of their second year were not usually the best six months later. How do we work to keep them continuously motivated? As a teacher, I wanted to know the answer as well. was interested in do learning this answer.

Gordon mentioned that Robert would be coming to celebrate Bob's Birthday this year. I liked this idea because meeting Robert would greatly contribute to my understanding of the family and their shared values. I wanted to know what I could do to help. I was told that he was not coming to be entertained. His grandfather had been performing several important functions and it was time for Robert to experience what it was like for his grandfather.

I asked if Robert would like to see the original Trimble Hall. Gordon suggested I invite them to go to my class, and that we should bring Isabella, Hwa Nan's FLTRP speaking contest candidate. Gordon and Robert could each say a few words and Isabella could give her 3-minute speech and answer questions from my students about her speech. Then we could went to a canteen in FNU's old campus. (Loosely translated we could sit about the table and enjoy a bowl of noodles in the tradition of the Grandfather.).

We got a surprising visit from Professor Karl Fields who came to Fuzhou to explore

春色
任天涯
——福建华南女子
职业学院外教侧记
International Faculty with
Fujian Hua Nan Women's
College since 1908

140

the idea of a faculty exchange between the University of Puget Sound and Fujian Normal University. He stopped by Hwa Nan to visit his old acquaintances, the Trimbles. According to their custom, a visit meant walking into the classroom unannounced beforehand and engaging with the students. He later commented how impressed he was that Gordon already knew every student's name, how much poise his students exhibited and their ability to share their opinions confidently in front of the classroom so that everyone in the class could hear. Comments like these made me proud of being at Hwa Nan. And now I was beginning to understand what Bob and Gordon had talked about last October as they walked around campus. In truth Bob was still with us and his spirit was still being felt.

Dean Wang, Professor Karl Fields and Gordon (Oct., 2014)

Bob had envisioned that the faculty exchanges between Puget Sound and Fujian Normal University would also enhance its existing relationships with Hwa Nan. The Foreign Faculty House could serve both to accommodate foreign visitors and host meetings. Relationships are based on people. As Bob put it: "We need to continually reach out to let new teachers become aware of all Fujian has to offer. If we do not, then new faculty will merely focus on what they know and have previously seen—Beijing and Shanghai, which to me is not the real China people should get to know."

Behind the soccer field with its oval track stood a stadium. This three-story concrete structure contained a badminton court, a dancing room, a basketball court and two rooms on the third floor. Several years ago, when Bob saw how isolated the new campus was in University City, he saw to it that the school put up Ping-Pong tables. Hwa Nan took one of the large rooms on the third floor as a Ping-Pong room in honor of Bob. The school put a college that told in pictures and words glimpses of Bob's life in Nan Ping and Fuzhou. Gordon offered brief remarks on behalf of the family at the dedication. Two of these collages were made. The first was put on the third floor of the stadium and the second was mounted on the wall of the multimedia room in the Foreign Faculty House.

Gordon, Robert and Isabella came to the old campus of Fujian Normal University. My class was impressed by Isabella's speech for she performed quite well. Both Robert and Gordon talked about the elements of a good speech and both of them emphasized that it had to be short enough for the audience to remember what you said. I was again realized that Gordon did not just come here and talk; he made adequate preparations instead. He wrote down what he wanted to say and then he practiced it until it sounded like he was talking to you instead of robotically delivering a speech. This added a degree of formality and was more interesting to the students as it seemed like an invitation for them to join the dialogue by asking questions. My students were fascinated by this approach.

Unveiling ceremony for Bob Trimble
Ping-Pong Room（2014）

Dedication of Bob's Ping-Pong Room with Collage
of Nanping and Fuzhou

A college: Glimpses of Bob—
displayed in Bob's Ping-Pong Room
and FAO multimedia room

春色
任天涯
——福建华南女子
职业学院外教侧记
International Faculty with
Fujian Hua Nan Women's
College since 1908

142

We managed to take Robert to Pingtan Island to the newly completed campus of the school that his grandfather and Sacred Hearts students had visited the previous year. And he, too, was warmly welcomed by its teachers, successfully passing the torch to the next generation.

When I was able to talk privately with Robert, the conversation with him was very telling. I didn't anticipate his words so I reprinted them for you to see…

"Robert, did your Dad and Mom force you to come to visit China?" I asked.

"No, they did not force me at all. What they said to me was that teaching in Fujian was what your grandpa was truly dedicated to. Do you have any interest in knowing why?" He answered with a broad smile.

Picture taken in front of the old building of Hwa Nan with Robert & Gordon Trimble（2014）

Robert, Sonia greeted by three Pingtan Teachers (2014)

"Then how about coming to teach in Hwa Nan when you feel like?" I asked.

"I think I will, but I need to wait till my retirement I suppose." He replied.

And finally there was the birthday. This would have been Bob's 99th birthday. When it was time for Gordon to give remarks, I was surprised to see Robert stand up. Then I remembered that Bob had always had Gordon speak for the family at gatherings. So this also was part of their family tradition, just like Lydia Trimble was happy to teach and work with the third Hwa Nan President Lucy Wang. Gordon expressed it this way: "Good leaders make the best followers." They know what it takes and they know how to help before they are asked. Good leadership is about achieving positive results, not about who is in the spotlight. I was very impressed by Robert's speech and that is why I asked for a copy to reprint here:

Let me start by saying I am honored to be here as a guest in Fuzhou, as well as a guest of Hwa Nan Women's college. I am humble to be a part of the legacy my Great, Great Auntie Lydia Trimble envisioned over 100 years ago; as well as being part of my grandfather's legacy. I am here to ensure that legacy of my ancestors continues. As the 5th generation of Trimbles to travel to Fuzhou I reflect on my journey here from Montana, and to put it into perspective of how technology has changed over this past century.

My journey started by boarding a plane in Montana last Sunday morning and arriving in Fuzhou the following Monday night with only 27 hours of travel time. But to think maybe the journey my dear great Auntie Lydia and my Grandfather took from the USA to Fuzhou possibly endured 27 days of travel time to my mere hours. In the mean time during my traveling to Fuzhou, I was in constant communication with mother via e-mail. For every layover, a short message was sent, to ensure her on the progress of my journey. Where as, if Auntie Lydia or my Grandfathers' Family were to communicate of their journey to family members back in the States. their form of communication would take weeks, or even months.

Robert and Council Chair Chen Zhongying (2014)

English club outing in the Fujian Normal University's new campus (2014)

Hwa Nan teachers & the Trimble family at Bob's 99 birthday party dinner(2014)

While here at Hwa Nan, I have observed the enthusiasm of students who were engaged, literally engaged in the act of WANTING to learn; not just learning like a robot because they've been programmed to; but they were active in the learning and teaching process. This gives me great joy to see Lydia Trimble's vision alive and well after a century. My presence here today proves it. Being the 5th generation of Trimbles here in Fuzhou, it is my hope to continue this legacy for many more generations to come.

I should add that one of the funnest things that our students remembered about their time with the Trimbles was the Networking Session. Gordon would give his last lecture—advice for students on how they could lead happier, more successful lives and then for the next two hours, the students were in charge. The only requirement was that they need to speak English in these two hours. And when someone would ask to see something different, I would recommend that they take in the Networking Session in the Foreign Faculty House.

View of Honolulu Harbor with its daily dose of Rainbows (2014)

It was December and the Trimbles had their bags packed and were looking forward to some warmer weather in Hawaii. When they stopped by office, Gordon was grinning broadly. He announced: 'It is settled. My second year students did a terrible job in giving a Power Point presentation and in pretending to be a Wall Street stock analyst. So I gave them a choice. I told them I can give them a grade now or they can choose to do their Last Speech the day before school starts next September. One student wanted her grade now and the rest of them wanted to do the FLTRP topic as their Last Speech next September. In this way they have three months to prepare. I told them that they could send me drafts and I would help them correct the drafts. By the time they arrive on campus they will be ready for the first part of the contest and then we have two months to work on impromptu speeches and extemporaneous Q&A. So this is how he succeeded in getting his students to maintain and improve their English. They wanted to do a good job in the Last Speech. Gordon and Sonia had also been participating in our English Club. This was the creation of one of our Chinese teachers who wanted to give motivated students another opportunity to practice using English in an informal setting. One of my English teachers, Genny, started an English Club open to students who had been enrolled in the School of Foreign Language and Trade. This would supplement our English Corner program to enhance students' impromptu and extemporaneous speaking skills.

15 Fall: Actions Are Turned into Words

Students who opted for their Last Speech would be prepared for the next year's FLTRP topic speaking contest(2014)

The next topic for FLTRP came out in May. It challenged student's ability to relate a dialogue that Chuang Tsu ZI and Hui ZI had 2,500 years ago to their view of the world today. I should not have been more surprised when Gordon confided to me that he had read a similar passage when he was in high school, and the guy he remembered was Chuang Tsu. He said he had no formal instruction on the proper way of interpreting Chuang Tsu's theories, but he was drawn to this philosopher because intuition or a gentle, relaxed perception may contribute more to understanding than a facility to bantering about words. "Sometimes we get so caught up in using vocabulary, proper use of words, and reasoning to arrange language. We forget that when the focus lies in words, understanding is frequently impeded." I am glad he was happy but my angst related to the upcoming evaluation of our school.

In Fujian, schools are subject to a comprehensive review every 6 years. I wanted the Trimbles to present during this evaluation. I had no particular reason. It is just that things seemed to go more smoothly when they were around. I asked Sonia and Gordon to stay on campus until the end of the provincial evaluation. "And when is that going to be?" Gordon asked. "Well, sometime before 31 December" was the best answer I could give at that time. They booked their return flight to Honolulu on the last day of the year. Their explanation was that they would be crossing the International Date Line so that they could celebrate New Year's Eve twice, which was something they had never done before.

I had unexpectedly benefited as a result of the previous evaluation. During the following seven years, our school had been successfully transferred to a much better and larger campus in University City. I welcomed the provincial assessment as an opportunity to find out best way to develope our college in the rapidly evolving arena of college education.

The Trimbles arrived in Fuzhou about two weeks before classes were scheduled to begin. Gordon asked about the Provincial Evaluation. He was very interested in gaining an appreciation for the evolutionary process. He said, "I don't know about China but in Hawaii evaluations are done to justify reorganizations and, sometimes, radical changes in directions. At the colleges and universities I am familiar with, the teachers are the soul of the school and they play an important role in how quickly and in what direction a school will change. The people who get promoted in an organization are the ones who are able to offer cheerier assessments. I had lived through several reorganizations and, personally, my commitment has always been the same. My job is to make my boss look good. I do this by giving her the best possible information I can get and by making sure I try my best each and every time.

The semester began with his previous students giving their "last speech". We had four judges and Gordon was the Question Master. We invited the current speech class

Last speech mock competition (2015)

and anyone who might be interested in competing during the school regular competition normally held in mid-October to observe. During this event, we had a mock simulation of two of the three parts of the actual contest and we were able to train a new set of student helpers. These contestants and Gordon's crop of new students would again be invited to observe the competition at Fujian Normal University, so they could measure the progress they have made during the past 12 months and judge how much more they had to do to be competitive.

Gordon reminded me of Professor Karl Field's visit to Fuzhou. He added: "Bob would be pleased that the faculty exchange has already begun to bear fruit. But in this case the fruit are grapes. Dr. Pierre Ly, an Economics Professor from the University of Puget Sound and his wife Dr. Cynthia Howson are writing a book about the rapidly expanding wine industry in China. Would anyone at Hwa Nan be interested in listening to their presentation?" I talked to teachers in my four departments plus Tourism. Pierre and Cynthia gave a great PowerPoint presentation to a standing room, audience in the Multimedia Room at the Foreign Faculty House only. Gordon commented that their use of a translator improved the communication process because it slowed everything down giving people the chance to reflect before going on to the next thought.

Dr. Pierre Ly from Puget Sound & Dr. Cynthia Howson from Univiersity of Washington Tacoma (2015)

Dr. Howson & Dr. Ly gave a lecture on grape wine research in China at Hwa Nan (2015)

The Trimble family has been devoting themselves to the communication between Chinese and Americans. A lot of detailed work has been done due to the fact that Fuzhou of Fujian Province and Tacoma of Washington state has set up sister city relationship. Last year, that Tacoma City Mayor's visit to Fuzhou recorded by the Hotline 777 was a good case in point.

The Trimbles, with their keen observations, came to Fuzhou to form their friendship with the students of Hwa Nan. Gordon put it this way, "If we put students first, then we need to be willing to help them when they decide they would like to learn. Good students program themselves to learn during assigned class periods but what about the others? Some students are in college simply because their parents want them to be in school. How do we get them excited about learning? You told me a couple years ago I needed to push them a bit little harder to enhance

David Morse, Susan Westberg, & Gordon in front of the original Trimble Hall (2015)

motivation but it may not work well now. So the Trimbles used the National Holidays to work with students that remained at school. They also gave their students homework that needed to be completed before they returned to school. And when the course was supposed to be finished, there were still a couple of students that had given up who needed to be encouraged to get everything finished.

Ling Wang, Susan Westberg, Gordon, David Morse, Alice, Nell before the Hwa Nan Mural (2015)

David Morse & Susan Westberg at Trbimble Hall of Fujian Hwa Nan Women's college(2015)

Gordon regarded Public Speaking as a team sport. He encouraged his students to pick a classmate, someone that was at the same level and then practice with each other: "One of you should be a judge. You know what you can understand and what you cannot. If

English Corner with the Trimbles
during the National Holidays (2015)

Sonia helped students when they had
decided they were ready to learn (2015)

you don't understand, then tell your teammate to explain it differently. Interrupt her in the middle of her speech, tell her to stop and explain. Tell her to talk to you like a friend, not like you are a tree. This way you are competing but you are also growing better together. And whoever does better on the day of the competition will know that she won because her teammates helped her grow faster." The Trimbles took their class to FNU to observe and find out what was possible if only they worked a little harder. His students watched the FLTRP competition. What was of particular interest to them was how the impromptu and extemporaneous parts were performed.

Fujian Normal FLTRP Speech Contest with Hwa Nan
teachers and students (2015)

Perhaps because of Bob's interest in FNU, teachers and students there were interested in the Trimbles as well. This year a group of graduate students who major in history video taped Gordon talking about his, great, great Aunt Lydia. He told them that she was a product of her times. Education for girls had started in the United States a generation before her. The heroines of her day were people like Sojourner Truth and Susan B.

春色
任天涯
——福建华南女子
职业学院外教侧记
International Faculty with
Fujian Hua Nan Women's
College since 1908

150

Anthony. She came from a family of farmers and farmers tended to be more religious than others because they lived at the mercy of the weather—rain and temperature determined what might be produced and determined how much of the potential the family actually harvested. they could get a harvest. There are two parables in particular that could explain her actions. The first—The Parable of the Talents—said she had a responsibility to use her God-given abilities to benefit the society by leaving it with more than when she was born. The second—The Parable of the Sheep and the Goats—led her to select one of only three places in the world where the life expectancy of women was shorter than that of men. Her choice was simple. She chose the biggest country with the largest population of women—China. "I think I can relate to some degree to how she felt. When I was at the same age as her, I joined the Peace Corps because I thought there were better ways to improve the world than sending American troops to fight in Vietnam. The Methodist church helped her get to China while I was helped by the Peace Corps, which took me to Philippines. Different vehicles, similar motivation."

Gordon discussed the motivation of Lydia Trimble of putting
Chinese women first (2015)

This was an important year, for it was time to celebrate Bob's 100th. It was held on the actual date—15 November. Friends that Bob had made during his visits to Fuzhou gathered to reminisce about the old times—the sights, sounds and smells of China a hundred years earlier. Gordon talked with the Principals from Lungtien and Pingtan about another dream. Instead of sending children abroad when they reached middle school, what if there was a better way: a way where the child could become a global citizen while maintaining her Chinese identity and a way that the shock of total emersion in a foreign culture could be alleviated. What he was interested in doing was an experiment with an English teacher from Pingtan or Lungtien who had a daughter in Grade 3 in primary school that was fluent in English. During the Winter Break, there was a five-week period. The teacher and her daughter could stay with the Trimbles. The daughter could be a visitor and placed in the appropriate grade level at Sacred Hearts Academy. The mother could help out in a variety of ways and gain an appreciation of education in a private school in America. Her daughter would gain an understanding of America while being able to see her mother and converse with her mother in Chinese about the activities of the day. If the experience proved positive, the process could be repeated in the following year. And the girl would rejoin the same class with the same students she had met during the previous year. The daughter would be motivated to improve her English when she was in China. In this way, mother and her daughter would gain international understanding as they built foreign friendships. By the time the daughter becomes a high school student she would know the skills she would have to get to be successful in college wherever she decided to go. Gordon said he was looking for some way to test it out. Once the Chinese English teacher had gained experience, she could see if it made sense for six-graders from Sacred Hearts Academy to visit their elementary school and stay with the families of her co-teachers for a cultural exchange. Several found this to be a most intriguing idea. At the head table were the old ladies and the current administrators of Hwa Nan. We also had a table for our friends from Fujian Normal University and another table for former and current students. Many of the celebrants were the same as

Bob's friendship dinner — friends from Pingtan ,
Lungtien & Hotline 777 (2015)

the previous year. It was held on Sunday and people came because they wanted to, not because it was a "work related" function.

The principal of the Lungtien Primary School was so moved by the touching story of Lydia Trimble who ran the Lungtien Primary School and the Trimble family's commitment to teaching in Fujian Province that he wrote a banner and a pair of couplets that he presented to the Trimbles in 2013. He then wrote a poem, which was translated by Ling Wang, the secretary of the College Board and the director of Foreign Affair Office as well as the director of the Personnel Department of our college for the Trimbles. David Morse and Susan Westberg, teachers at Lincoln High School, carried the banner and couplets to the University of Puget Sound of which he is an alumni so that it could be put on display for their Chinese New Year's festivities. Principal Zhou's poem was also displayed with appropriate translations. Below is Gordon standing before the banner and couplets.

Chasing the Dream
By Weirong ZHOU
Principal, Fuqing Lungtien Primary School

There appeared indistinctly a small boat on the blue sea,
From which came an angel on to the desolated beach.
She looked around, for scenery or for friends?
Neither, she was drafting a blueprint for future generations!
Her dream started from here,
From a primitive fishing village enlightened by the flame of wisdom,
More than 100 years have elapsed,
Her successors still carry her torch in a quest,
For treasure or for secrets?
Neither, for writing a new chapter of education!
Dream continues here,
A century old school has students everywhere.
In school, students are growing up happily.
They are playing! They are singing!
They are swimming in the sea of knowledge!
Dreams fly from here.
Thousands of talents will shoulder the responsibilities of society.

Principal Zhou's banner and couplets at Puget Sound
during the Chinese New Years (2016)

As the semester progressed, the details of the Provincial Evaluation started to unfold. I didn't have to explain to the Trimbles that the future of Hwa Nan might well depend on how well our school was received and I wanted to put our best foot forward. There would be about 18 experts from all over China chosen by the Fujian Provincial Education Department who would come to our school to check teaching files, audit classes; interview students and teachers; hold symposia for teachers and observe classroom instructions. Four schools would be evaluated in December and Hwa Nan would be the last one.

At the beginning of December, the schedule was finally set. On Wednesday, 16 December, these experts would arrive on campus. On Thursday and Friday morning they would observe instruction and conduct interviews. Friday afternoon, 18 December, they would have a school-wide meeting in which they would present their preliminary findings. It was dramatic because the people to be interviewed and the classes to be observed would be chosen at the last moment. During the week of the evaluation administrators started getting a bit nervous so we e-mailed our teachers asking them to remain on campus and to start their classes at 8:00 am if possible. We also asked the students to come to class before 8:00 am in case an evaluator came in advance.

Gordon focused on reading and building vocabulary at the beginning of the semester and editing their writing at the end of the semester. He would tell them that the best way to improve was to write at least 125 words everyday. Every student was required to have a new vocabulary notebook and to write down her journal everyday. By the beginning of December, students were reading their drafts out loud individually to Gordon who would ask them questions about the files he had edited. Some students would take six minutes and other students would take 20. Each student wound up getting at least two hours of personalized instruction. Gordon's tutoring began at 7:45 each morning.

When Gordon noticed that the classroom was almost full before 8:00am, he stood up and said: "If you have eaten breakfast, raise your right hand. (One girl raised her hand.) Okay if you have not eaten breakfast, stand up! Now you have 12 minutes to go to the canteen, get something to eat and return to class. I want you to be alert and happy. You have been preparing for the Provincial Evaluation all semester and you are ready. Do not worry. If you are relaxed and happy you will do just fine." The students could see that Gordon was not worried and they were very happy to go to the canteen. The following morning, a student who was waiting to have her essay edited stopped students at the door and only admitted those that had had breakfast. She remembered Gordon telling students: "Stop thinking of yourself as students. Start thinking of yourself as a teacher. Start taking control of you life." She did this quietly and without being told. By Wednesday everyone had eaten breakfast before they came to Gordon's class.

春色
任天涯
——福建华南女子
职业学院外教侧记
International Faculty with
Fujian Hua Nan Women's
College since 1908

Wednesday night I called Gordon to tell him that his writing class had been selected for observation. Gordon said: "Excellent. You are most welcomed. But the moment you enter my classroom you become a participant—a player." People do not remain observers for long when they came to Gordon's class. I remembered what happened to Professor Fields when he came to observe Gordon's teaching: Gordon added this is perfect. Tomorrow is our annual networking session. Every student has prepared a two-three minute presentation on "Three things I have learned during the past 12 months that I can use for the rest of my life".

We entered the classroom a little earlier than 8:30. There were five of us—one provincial expert, Professor HE and four Hwa Nan teachers including one who was going to video tape the course so I could have a record of what happened for future review. Good or bad, I wanted a record, so we could do better next time. After we introduced ourselves to Gordon, we took our seats at the rear of the classroom. As Gordon started walking to the front he noticed something he didn't like. He frowned and I could hear him make a deep sigh. He walked back to Dr. HE and they talked very quietly for a few moments. The eyes of the students and my teachers remained fixed on them, anxious to find out what was happening, because this was certainly not in the script. Dr. HE rose, smiled and said, "How about we have a picture together with a few of your students." They talked in robust, cheery voices so everyone could hear. Dr. HE could tell from the laughter that the students' level of English comprehension was good. By looking at the picture below, you can see that the atmosphere of the class had changed from anxiousness to happy anticipation. Everything went smoothly. Gordon was in control and he chose to influence the ambiance without explaining to his students.

The emcees spoke in clear, cheery voices without reading a script. We were impressed by how relaxed and poised the emcees were. They were much better in their delivery

Getting the class in the right
mood for the Networking
Session (2015)

than the students who functioned as emcees in the big auditorium. The teachers noticed the difference and were delighted. Gordon gave his Last Lecture and then the student presentations began. Dr. HE got to select the first speaker, I the second and one of my Chinese teachers the third. The students spoke, not as robots, but like they were talking to a friend about important things that were happening in their life. Then Gordon would ask them questions and they would answer quickly and smoothly. My Chinese teachers were proud of the stature, good grammar and fluency exhibited by Gordon's students. Then there was a class picture with my Chinese teachers and Gordon's class before Dr. HE had to leave.

Dr. HE was also invited to return for lunch to participate in the ending part of the Networking Session. After we left, the class continued with the program. Half an hour later, Nell WU came up to Gordon and told him that someone in the school administration had' asked him to participate in a group discussion that was going on with a panel of education experts. The class continued and Gordon left with Nell for the administration building.

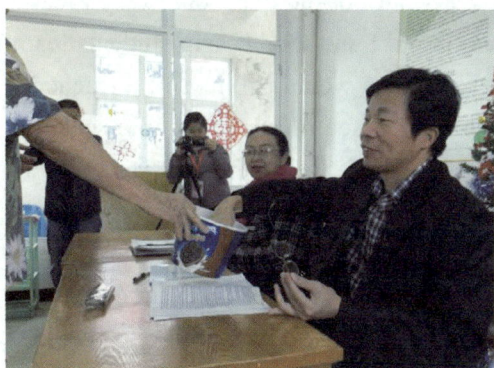

Dr. He of the provincial experts selected the first speaker during the Networking Session (2015)

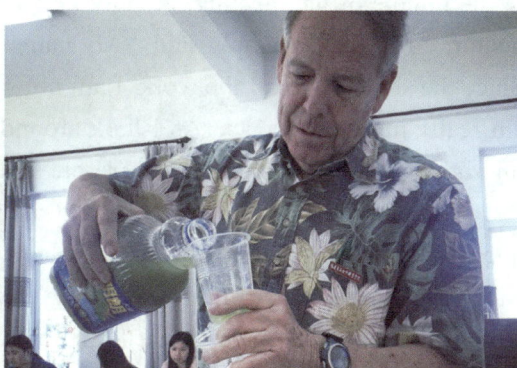

Gordon served the students at the Business Networking class (2015)

Business Networking—observed by the experts from the Fujian Evaluation Team (2015)

春色
任天涯
——福建华南女子
职业学院外教侧记
International Faculty with
Fujian Hua Nan Women's
College since 1908

156

APE Networking Session activity in readings in Int'l Business (2015)

A chair was pulled up to the end of the table where Gordon was about to sit on. Nell sat a little to the left and behind Gordon to translate. Since Gordon had entered the room in the middle of the meeting, he only heard answers but not the questions. When it was his turn to speak, he simply said, "My name is Gordon. I am here to help students learn. Since the students do all the work, I am not sure whether I would call myself a teacher. I am really more of a coach. As I look around the table, I see important people seated to my right and even more important people seated to my left. Seeing the importance of the rest people in the room, it is not clear to me why I am here. Let me answer your second question first. What impresses me most about Hwa Nan is that my students are always eager to learn, so I am proud of having these students. To answer your first question, what I find most satisfying is that I am able to envision what China is going to be like a generation from now through the minds and hearts of my students. I could add that I like what I see. To answer your third question as to what I would most like to see in the future is that more Americans gain a clear realization of what is a real China and that is only possible if they come to China to get to know individuals and get a sense of their collective history. The Great Wall and the Grand Canal are monumental—they make great pictures to show people back home, but these do not begin to tell the story any more than you can understand America by looking at the Washington Monument."

When asked what he thought of male students at Hwa Nan Women's College, he replied: "I come to China to help students. I am a guest in your country and I did not come here to make policy. My job is simple. I take whatever students I am given and try to help them realize that they are capable of doing things that they were unaware of before. I do not have enough experience to give you a fair appraisal."

During the Preliminary Assessment, the educational experts concluded that Hwa

Nan needed to have better students, not more students and they could be more successful by sticking to their brand. They added that Hwa Nan had a wonderful resource in their foreign teachers but they should use this resource more broadly. My teachers were happy that Gordon's class was chosen and that he had also been asked to take part in the panel discussion. I remember what Gordon said, "My job is to make my boss look good and I do that by giving her the best information I can get and I'm doing my best each and every time." I felt relieved that I had successfully put "my best foot forward", because the Trimbles were present during the Provincial Evaluation.

Christmas is celebrated every year at the Foreign Faculty House. Since the Trimbles were here, they volunteered to serve as the official greeters. Christmas dinner is enjoyed every year to embrace our humble origins and remember the important contributions that our foreign teachers have made to our school.

Former President Lin Benchun & Alice being welcomed
to FAO Christmas Dinner (2015)

To me, the Trimbles were a fabulous present — not something that you put on the shelf after you take it out of the box, but companions who could share, listen to and sympathize with as they walked with you on your journey. They were quite different from other foreigners I have known. They were quick to listen and slow to judge. They would tell their students, "Don't give me words; show us through your actions." And our students saw their actions and respected them. They where happy to learn from their students, just as their students were eager to learn from them. Maybe Gordon had learned a lot from Zhuang Zi because he told me one time in a perplexed state: "If you don't understand what people are doing, it does not mean they are irrational. It only means you do not yet understand." The Trimbles have given me encouragement and they have

春色
任天涯
——福建华南女子
职业学院外教侧记
International Faculty with
Fujian Hua Nan Women's
College since 1908

158

helped me view the world trough kinder eyes. To the extent, I have recorded our journey as accurately as possible so that you too might envision what you might have felt if you had journeyed with us. But putting their actions into words is an impossible task. Their deeds are more than words. They have a spirit that uplifts you. I have recorded what they have done and what they have said so that you too can consider how their lives and emotions would also have influenced you. I would shoulder full responsibility for all mistakes including errors of omission. Reminiscing with the Trimbles during the latter part of the semester in order to prepare for publishing this book was a great source of pleasure as we relived the memorable and sometimes more challenging moments. When this record is published, the history will be understood generation after generation. As I reflected I could still see Bob, and know that his presence was reminding us: "Life is wonderful!"

Gorden Trimble in the Eyes of a Student

Interviewing Sonia & Gordon for the book

We addressed Gordon Trimble as "Senator Trimble" at first, but I didn't really get the meaning of "Senator", which may mean "senior" in my understanding. He was my teacher for Business English course and my coach for "CCTV Cup" English Speaking Contest when I was a senior student at Fujian Hwa Nan Women's College. When I knew him, I didn't know those experiences will be magical treasures in my life.

I learned a lot from him, at both professional and personal level, which always influence and benefit my career and make me Execute Assistant in a World TOP 30 Company. I've obtained the concept of women leadership from Senator Trimble by business study and professional presentations. However, I didn't understand why he made every effort to correct minor imperfections; for example, he spent a lot of time in class teaching us how to make handshakes regarding posture, power and eye contact. We practiced again and again to show the professional way as a working woman. I didn't know the effect and meaning until I got the first full-time job. After I got the offer from Siemens, the interviewer mentioned that I impressed him the most among candidates because I delivered my confidence, fortitude and integrity with a proper handshake.

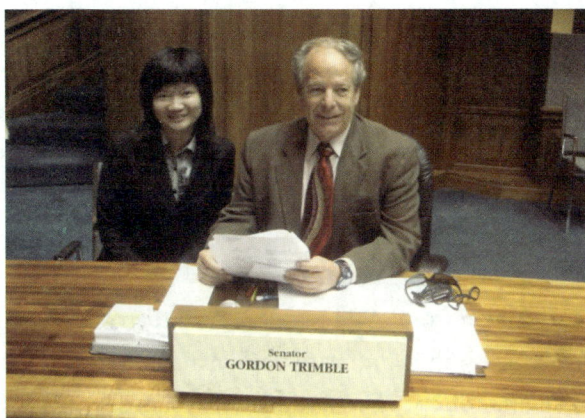

Gordon Trimble and I

Senator Trimble had to go back to Hawaii occasionally for business stuff when he was our teacher. And we thought that we would have less homework. However, Senator Trimble encouraged us to finish double homework during his absence and related examination will be scheduled after he came back to Fuzhou. It was an interesting experience and our English reading and writing skill increased quickly with his help.

During my preparation for 2007 "CCTV Cup"English Speaking Contest when I was a senior student at Hwa Nan, The Trimbles and I got the chance to know each other better. After the contest, I chose to stay in the meeting room and observe each participant's performance instead of hanging out for sightseeing because it was a valuable experience for me. After five years, Senator Trimble told me that he thought "this girl really can go" at the moment, and he would like to offer me an opportunity to learn more, if possible. So, I went to Hawaii, got to know the exact women leadership, and worked with ladies who were smart, independent and charming. The internship has influenced me until today.

Senator Trimble gave us a graduation gift — an article about 7 rules in life. It was intelligence and experience that he wanted to share with us. I was so proud to have such a wonderful coach in my life.

春色
任天涯
——福建华南女子
职业学院外教侧记
International Faculty with
Fujian Hua Nan Women's
College since 1908

160

VI
Idealism and Realism of Laihar Wong

The Australian teacher, Laihar Wong, whose Chinese name is Huang Lixia, was born on September 12th ,1949. It is a great honor that she was awarded the "Friendship Award"of Fujian Province on September 22nd, 2015. Why is she so charming? Let's find it out.

An Educator Who Works Conscientiously

Laihar taught in Hwa Nan from 1993 to 2003. And then she voluntarily went to teach in Guizhou Minzu University in a minority region in 2003. Since 2006, she has been teaching in Hwa Nan again. Totally, she has spent 19 years serving Hwa Nan. She mainly teaches English Reading and Writing, Oral English and English Free Conversation for the Applied English Department. In addition, she has voluntarily organized English Corner activities for years and guided students to participate in English skit contests, English Speech Contests, English Singing Competitions and English Teaching Skills Contests for the School of Foreign Languages and Trade.

When teaching, Laihar always writes down key teaching points on the blackboard even if the chalk dust affects her health and will probably lead to the deterioration of her chronic thyroid problem; therefore, she attaches great importance to keeping her classroom clean. Students are required to clean everything in the classroom with a piece of clean cloth. Her classroom is much cleaner than any other classroom in Hwa Nan. Laihar devotes herself to teaching and corrects students' work carefully. Moreover, she has never given any student up, especially the slow ones in academic learning. For example, she patiently corrected students' pronunciation and promises to make up for the students who asked for a leave from her class. To our appreciation, she has even visited weak students' dormitories. She always encourages students to speak and persuades them not to be afraid of

Laihar was honored with the "Friendship Award" of Fujian Province, 2015

making mistakes. Students have fun attending her class and learning a lot in the meantime. We admire her love, patience and affinity, which are worth learning.

A Granny with a Caring Heart

Laihar is not only a dedicated teacher, but also an elder caring for students. She is amiable and considerate. She is simple but great. She writes down every student's birthday and on each one's birthday, she sends her a gift and blessing and leads the other students to sing *Happy Birthday to You*. Even if some students' birthdays are on holiday, they can still receive gifts from Laihar. She even makes a phone call to students who have dropped out

Laihar served as a judge in the 8th English Singing Competition

The foreign teachers are Laihar, Kennedy, Betts, Bob, Gina and Donald (from the left to the right)

A photo of the First Teaching Skills Competition in 2015

Some foreign teachers and some Chinese teachers were spending a Christmas together. Laihar is the first one on the right

Laihar was teaching in class

春色
任天涯
——福建华南女子
职业学院外教侧记
International Faculty with
Fujian Hua Nan Women's
College since 1908

162

of school because of poverty or other reasons, organizing the whole class to sing *Happy Birthday to You* on their birthdays to wish them a happy birthday. Furthermore, she reasonably comforts poor students in emotional instability and helps them pay off the tuition fee. To our surprise, she remembers every student's name. She often spends a lot of time guiding students to rehearse English dramas and asks excellent students to give a hand to weak students.

Have you ever encountered a foreign teacher who has brought students outside to relax and prepared snacks so as to provide an opportunity for Chinese and foreign students to communicate with each other? The foreign

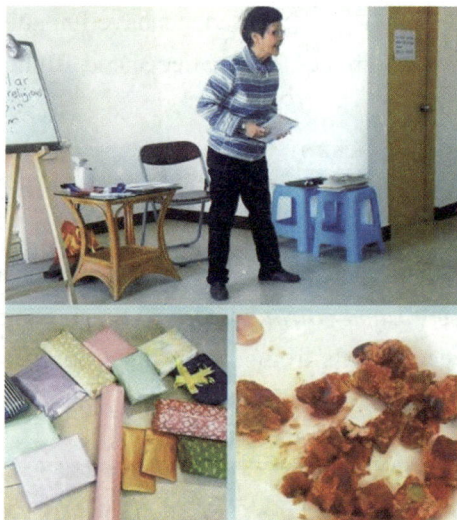

Laihar personally wrapped a Christmas gift for each student

teacher, Laihar, has done all the above for us. She does so many things for us, not because she is rich, but because she regards her students as her kids and she really wants to try her best to help us. From picture 10 to picture 20, you can see the things her students have made and letters they have written to her to show their appreciation to her. I feel so lucky to meet her in Hwa Nan. It is a great honor for Hwa Nan and me to meet her.

English Corner Activities

Since 2010, when Kay, a foreign teacher, retired from Hwa Nan and returned to the US because of advanced age, Laihar has been in charge of all English Corner activities. Every week, she has topics catering to students' needs. With her organization, these activities go with a swing. In order to inspire students to attend the English Corner activities, Laihar holds a party at the end of every semester. For every party, she personally prepares small gifts and snacks. She also asks her friend from the USA to mail some award certificates for the students

Laihar and some students at the English Corner outside the school gate

who help to organize the activities during the semester. If you want to learn English, you can always find Laihar at the English Corner. In spite of all kinds of weather, she is there, waiting for you.

A Deliverer of Love

Laihar is a low-profile, diligent and upright foreign teacher full of love, which impresses us deeply. She is our role model. Every year when the winter vacation ends, she visits the orphanage of Fuzhou, bringing the orphans there some life necessities, ranging from books to snacks. For us, it not only means that we should give a hand to people in need, but also means love can be passed to others.

Laihar wrapped a variety of snacks as gifts for students on the Christmas Day

A student sent a bouquet of handmade flowers to Laihar

A student sent some small handmade Christmas cards to Laihar

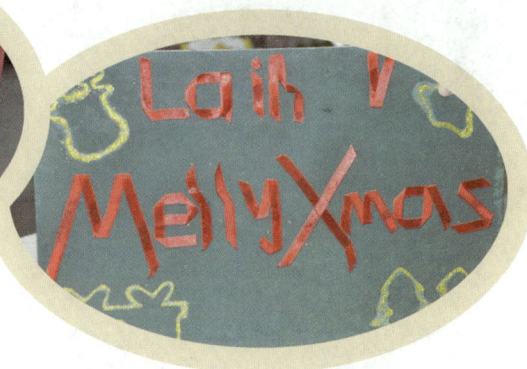

A graduate sent a handmade Christmas card to Laihar

春色
任天涯
——福建华南女子
职业学院外教侧记
International Faculty with
Fujian Hua Nan Women's
College since 1908

164

In view of Wong Laihar's outstanding contribution to women's higher education in Fujian Province, the Fujian provincial government granted Wong Laihar our province's highest honor, the "Friendship Award" in recognition of her brilliant contribution to the economic and social development of Fujian Province.

A student sent a bunch of handmade roses to Laihar

A student knitted a scarf for Laihar

A student made a cross-stitch for Laihar

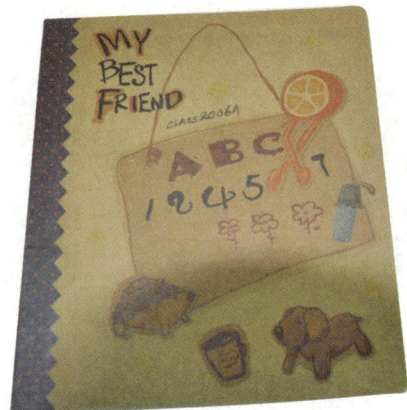

Some students personally prepared a commemorative book full of handwritten blessings for Laihar (from class 2006A)

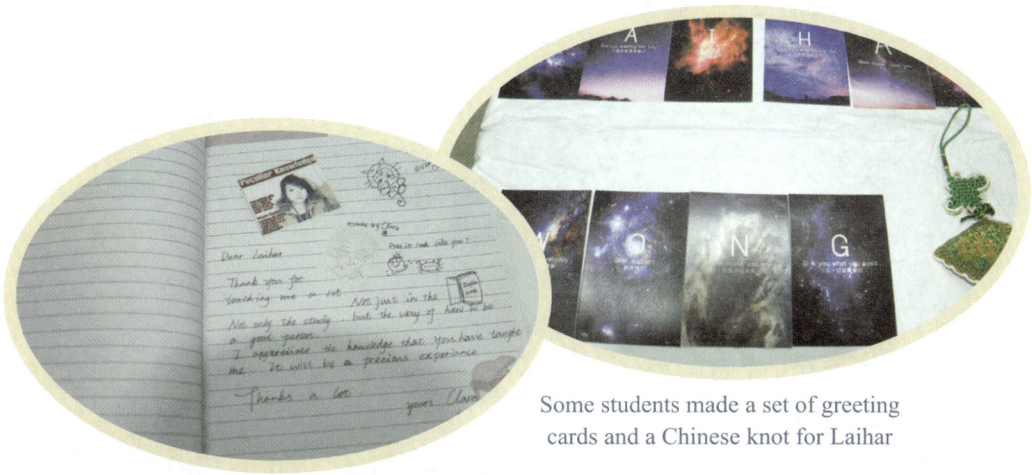

Some students made a set of greeting
cards and a Chinese knot for Laihar

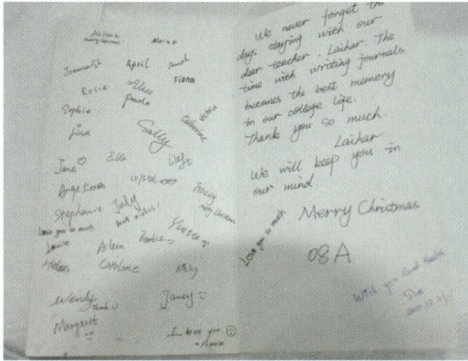

The blessings for Laihar from Class 2008 A,
the Applied English Department

A photo taken with Laihar when
having a free conversation class

A graduate took her kid to visit Hwa Nan new campus and Laihar

Chapter 3

International Faculty with Fujian Hwa Nan Women's College after 1984(Cont)

春色
任天涯
——福建华南女子
职业学院外教侧记

春色
任天涯
——福建华南女子
职业学院外教侧记
International Faculty with
Fujian Hua Nan Women's
College since 1908

168

I

Moral Teacher— Prof. Gregory Guelcher

The first time I saw Professor Greg Guelcher was just after the start of the spring term in 2013, when I was preparing my lessons in the office of the Applied English Department (AED). A tall foreigner with glasses walked into the office with a canvas messenger bag slung over his shoulder in a traditional style popular in the 1970s and 1980s. Vice Dean Lai Liqun (English name, Alice) and Chair of the AED Huang Fei (English name, Fay) received him. Huang Fei introduced him to me and asked me about the course on ICC (Intercultural Communication) that he was to teach, a course I had taught previously. Professor Guelcher struck me as patient, polite, and cooperative.

Prof. Guelcher carried a canvas bag (2013)

I got to know Professor Guelcher better over the course of the next several months. He was born a U.S citizen in Turkey in 1963, where his father was stationed as an Air Force physician. He came to us from Morningside College, one of Hwa Nan's traditional "Sister Colleges". He is a professor of history, and is also very involved in his community as a social activist.

Professor Guelcher taught English and American Culture at Hwa Nan as a Visiting Professor in July 2009, July 2010, and again in spring semester 2013. During his visits, he always brought students from Morningside University with him. In July 2009 he brought his Japanese wife, Yumiko, who taught an Introductory Japanese language class with his daughter, Alyssa. Three Morningside College students he brought — Jordan Aggen, Greg Anderson and Adam Gonshorowski — taught Public Speaking and American Culture courses with some assistance from Alex Guelcher, Greg's son. Morningside students Drake Johnson (2010) and Todd Carnes (2013) accompanied Professor Guelcher during the later visits.

Prof. Guelcher and his family (2009)

Professor Guelcher's students could earn academic credit for fulfilling certain requirements based on their experiences of studying abroad. For example, Drake and Todd completed pre-departure essays about what they anticipated experiencing on their first visit to China and Hwa Nan, and finished a post-trip reflective paper assessing their overall cultural experience. While at Hwa Nan, they both taught classes and assisted several

Prof. Guelcher and Morningside College students (2009)

春色
任天涯
——福建华南女子
职业学院外教侧记
International Faculty with
Fujian Hua Nan Women's
College since 1908

Chinese teachers. By doing so, they earned May Term credit. Alyssa, on the other hand, researched about women in contemporary China. She taped in-depth interviews in English with about a dozen Hwa Nan students. She asked them about the changing roles of women in China today, with a particular emphasis on traditional expectations for women versus what the students themselves hoped to become in the future. Adam worked on a film documentary about Hwa Nan Women's College, which helped him gain acceptance into a prestigious program in film studies in California. Greg Anderson fulfilled his May Term requirement at Hwa Nan, and used what he learned to land an overseas teaching job after graduation. Jordan drew inspiration from teaching at Hwa Nan and later pursued graduate studies.

Hwa Nan changed the lives of these Morningside College students. "In all cases," Professor Guelcher stated, "the students who visited Hwa Nan were expected to immerse themselves in the local culture, and write reflective essays after their return home. These students were greatly affected by their experiences, and consciously used their Hwa Nan experiences to further their educational or career goals. All expressed the wish they could return someday" (Interview with Greg Guelcher, 2016).

Prof. Guelcher presented a lecture to Hwa Nan teachers

Prof. Guelcher, Drake and Hwa Nan students (2010)

The presence of Professor Guelcher, his family, and his students, in return, brought novel experiences to everyone at Hwa Nan. For example, in July 2009, Professor Guelcher came with his family and three students; they lived near the old campus, taught for one month and spent their time outside class touring Fuzhou with their Chinese students as guides. I have excerpted below some stories and photos about their visits from a special feature that appeared in the Fall/Winter 2009 "Morningsider", Morningside College's alumni magazine.

Adam taught the girls poker, while Jordan and Greg combined their classes to teach football and Red Rover. Jordan instructed in football, and it was a real hoot! Jordan used a basketball in lieu of a football. Unfortunately, he hasn't yet learned that when teaching non-native speakers, one must be very precise with one's instructions! Jordan designated a girl as center, and explained how one hikes the ball between one's legs, except for the fact that the center should wait for a signal from the quarterback before hiking the ball. Jordan handed his center the ball, and before he could crouch down in position, she threw the ball between her legs and caught him right where it counts. Jordan doubled over in pain, while the girls doubled over with laughter. At least it broke the ice a bit. Shortly after, while trying to demonstrate a passing route, Jordan got beaned in the head by his over-excited quarterback. Can't fault the guy for trying!

Day Five:
These students are probably the most polite students I have ever met. Though it is only the second day of class, I am so impressed with the effort and ability they put forth in their work. The students were asked to present a symbolism speech using an object that they treasure most. Overall, the students did an amazing job, with most of them having their speeches memorized. Though there were a few mistakes and signs of nervousness, the speeches the students presented were a wonderful beginning to the class.
Jordan Aggen

Day Nine:
I am genuinely impressed with the 31 students in my Japanese class. It is a two-week-long, Monday–Friday, 8:30–11:30 a.m., intensive Japanese language class in 90- to 100-degree temperatures with 60-95 percent humidity on the third floor. We have a few fans on the ceiling. When I go to my classroom around 8:20, almost everyone is already seated and many are studying. I take two 10-minute breaks every day. When I say, "O.K., let's take a break," no one gets up. They just keep reviewing what I have taught that day. I've also tried to dismiss my class a little bit early, but no one leaves until 11:30 anyway. They just keep studying. During the break, students would bring a notebook full of questions. It reminded me of my high school in Japan, but our classes were 50 minutes, not 180. Somehow they can stay focused for three hours in that heat and humidity. What would happen in the U.S. in the same situation?
Yumiko Guelcher 2008

Jordan tought Hwa Nan girls American football (2009)

Prof. Guelcher's Wife, Yumiko and their
daughter at class (2009)

Prof. Guelcher and Hwa Nan students
(2009)

In July 2010, Professor Guelcher brought along student Drake Johnson. Both taught classes in Public Speaking Skills. Drake especially enjoyed clothes shopping in Fuzhou, learning to play badminton, and playing pick-up basketball games with students from Hwa Nan and nearby campuses.

Prof. Guelcher, Drake and Hwa Nan students in summer camp (2010)

Prof. Guelcher and Hwa Nan students played gossip game in the summer camp (2010)

Another pleasant experience in 2013 was co-teaching with Professor Guelcher's student, Todd Carnes. Todd arrived in Hwa Nan in May and stayed about one month. During his visit, Huang Fei and I invited him to join our teaching. The co-teaching model between Chinese and foreign teachers at Hwa Nan had been developed by Huang Fei when Dr. Andrew Pflipsen accompanied two students from Morningside in 2011. Todd taught Comprehensive English with Huang Fei and me. We began by discussing the teaching syllabus and its content, designing activities, and deciding teaching methods. As Todd's supervisor, Professor Guelcher joined in our meetings. But most of the time Professor Guelcher just listened and encouraged Todd to generate his own ideas. Finally, we decided that Todd would be responsible for teaching the cultures of different countries concerning tourism, some part of the reading, and the students' project work. Todd made interesting and attractive Power Point slide shows to motivate students, and provided good advice on project-based English teaching, especially regarding how to improve the evaluation of student projects. Todd also occasionally assisted Professor Guelcher, who recorded the following amusing anecdote in his diary on May 22: "Todd helped me in the afternoon with ELOR (English Listening and Oral Reading) classes. What was funny was that the students in the first class had to remind Todd what my rules for speaking in class were: 'Speak slowly, speak clearly, and speak loudly!' Fortunately, Todd quickly got the hang of it." Todd learned something, too. In May 2016, Todd e-mailed to Prof. Guelcher, he commented: "Funny story, I am now tutoring students in software development. I think this is partly a result of my experience in China."

It was very nice working with Professor Guelcher. When the spring term of 2013 came to an end, he sent me a gift by e-mail: his teaching plan and notes for the ICC course. He hoped they might prove helpful in developing the course in the future. From his gift I learned that Professor Guelcher was good at using discussion questions to get students to really think about what they had read in their textbooks, and apply the lessons led to

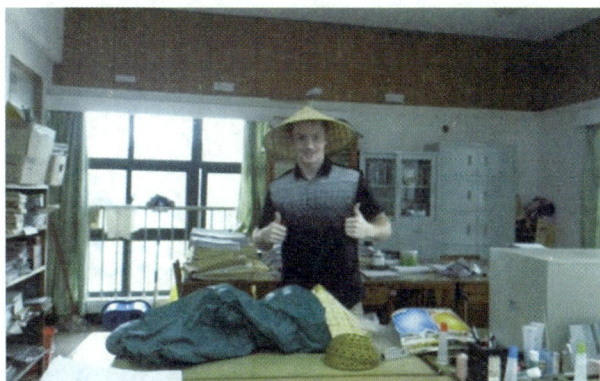

Todd Carnes is keen on Chinese Martial Art (in AED Office in 2013)

Huang Fei and Todd co-teaching (2013)

real life situations. Some students even kept their graded assignments for future reference. In addition, student evaluations at mid-term featured many positive comments about Professor Guelcher and his classes. Students described him as patient, careful, responsible, interesting and humorous, gentle, active, considerate, good tempered, and handsome. Regarding his classes, students especially appreciated that Professor Guelcher emphasized proper pronunciation and tried to help them improve their oral English, and that he always prepared good lessons with rich teaching contents, and that he paid close attention to the interaction between teacher and students. As one of their final tasks, students were asked to recreate a textbook lesson involving a toast speech at a farewell dinner. One group of students composed and presented the following toast in honor of Professor Guelcher:

"Classmates, we are very happy to have Greg with us tonight. For the past three months, he has taught us English. He is a friendly and patient

春色
任天涯
——福建华南女子
职业学院外教侧记
International Faculty with
Fujian Hua Nan Women's
College since 1908

174

teacher. He always planned fun activities and told funny stories. Without Greg's help, we can't get second place in the English skit contest. He was like a father. Without Greg we can't enjoy studying English. Here's to Greg – Cheers!"

Prof. Guelcher commented on the English Play Contest (2013)

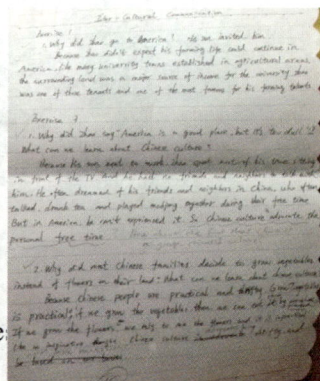

One student's assignment with Prof. Guelcher's comments(2013)

appearance but also in daily deeds and actions, which were often subtle. One day, for example, I met him on my way to the International Faculty House. As we were walking along, we approached a trash can. Professor Guelcher bent down to pick up some litter near the trash can and casually tossed it in. His behavior seemed so natural and his actions so fluid, and it was all over in a second. Nobody else noticed, not even some students passing by. Weeks later, however, when I mentioned Professor Guelcher's trash-picking deed to one of my classes, the students weren't surprised. They told me they often saw him with a big plastic bag picking up trash on the weekends, especially around the big pond in the center of campus. One student even took a photo of Professor Guelcher picking up garbage and uploaded it to her Wechat website, which inspired much animated discussion among the students and taught them a valuable lesson. Students began calling him "Moral Teacher".

Prof. Guelcher picked up garbage along the lake of Hwa Nan (2013)

One Hwa Nan student, when participating in a provincial speech contest in December 2013, included the Moral Teacher as an example to support her argument that Confucius always highly praised moral actions motivated by a sincere moral sentiment. The question master of the contest asked her an impromptu question based on this example in order to lead the audience to a fuller understanding of morality. Later, when I mentioned to my students that I was writing some stories about Professor Guelcher, they began sending me a lot of their own messages and pictures of him via QQ. A number of students mentioned they had kept their assignments with Professor Guelcher's comments written on them. A sampling of student remembrances appears as below:

"For every class meeting he sat outside the door of the classroom waiting for students, and greeted us as we entered."

"He did a good job teaching us. He was a careful and strict teacher, but the test was fair and not too difficult."

"He assigned us group work in class, helping to cultivate our team-work spirit."

"He sometimes played basketball or badminton on the playground and often joined in our activities, such as Girls Day on March 7th or English Corner."

"He would share with us stories of campus life at Morningside College."

"He cared about the environment, and didn't just talk about it. We often saw him carrying a plastic bag and picking up garbage around the pond."

"He liked to study Chinese history, particularly the People's Liberation Army."

"He liked drinking Longjing green tea."

"He liked to take pictures everywhere with his camera. He called himself a 'photo guy.'"

Aside from the three teaching visits, Professor Guelcher also came to Hwa Nan on two earlier occasions for non-teaching duties: in May 2008 with the first delegation from Morningside College, which presented the gift of two "friendship" trees to the college, and

Prof Guelcher showed photos to students(2013)

春色
任天涯
——福建华南女子
职业学院外教侧记
International Faculty with
Fujian Hua Nan Women's
College since 1908

176

again in October 2008 for the Centennial Anniversary Celebration of Hwa Nan Women's College, during which time both colleges signed an official exchange agreement. One of the friendship trees was planted in front of the Practical Training Building on Hwa Nan's new campus. It has since grown strong, like the relationship between Hwa Nan Women's College and Morningside College.

Both colleges signed the Exchange Agreement (2008)

Morningside College delegation and Hwa Nan staff (2008)

Former President Zhan Xunjie of Hwa Nan and Provost William Deeds of Morningside College (2008)

Planting "FriendshipTree" (2008)

The "Friendship" Tree at Hwa Nan campus from Morningside College (2016)

Professor Guelcher has developed a special appreciation for Hwa Nan and its staff and students.He wrote: "Hwa Nan Women's College has become like a second home to me,and the staff a second family! The FAOs, Nell and Jessica, are the very best and take such good care of the foreign teachers! To take but one example: while at Hwa Nan in spring 2013, I turned fifty years old. That is a major milestone in one's life, and normally in the U.S. we have a big celebration with family and close friends. But obviously that wasn't going to happen with me being so far away in China! When the FAOs and teachers at Hwa Nan found out, however, they quietly arranged a birthday party for me, an evening of delicious Chinese food, wonderful companionship, and even a surprise birthday cake. So rather than being a sad day, it was one of my most memorable birthdays ever! Whenever possible, I talk about the history of Hwa Nan and share photos and stories with my Morningside students. I look forward to returning and seeing all my Hwa Nan friends again."

Celebrating Prof. Guelcher's fiftieth birthday at Hwa Nan (2013)

II

Thirteen Golden Flowers from the University of Puget Sound —The Friendship between Fujian Hwa Nan Women's College and the University of Puget Sound

In September 2015, President Xi Jinping paid his first visit to the United States, which was his first state visit to the USA since he had become China's president; therefore the whole schedule attracted everyone's attention. One stop on his visit was to Tacoma,

春色
任天涯
——福建华南女子
职业学院外教侧记
International Faculty with
Fujian Hua Nan Women's
College since 1908

178

Washington. Tacoma, a port city in the south of Puget Sound, is located between Seattle and Olympia, the state capital. In 1994, Tacoma and Fuzhou City became sister cities, which was promoted by the then Fuzhou municipal Party committee secretary Xi Jinping. There is an unexpected story with regard to the establishment of friendly relations between Tacoma and Fuzhou. A former history professor at the University of Puget Sound, Suzanne Barnett, accidentally went to the wrong room when looking for her meeting, and overheard Tacoma municipal officials discussing which city was to be established as a city to have friendly relations with Tacoma. The teacher took it upon herself, as if it were up to her, to say the city must be Fuzhou. Unexpectedly, the teacher's unintentional words became reality.

Fuzhou and Tacoma became sister cities on November 16, 1994. The two cities have been carrying out various exchanges in the fields of economy, education, sports, trainees, etc. over many years.In the years of 1996 and 1997, the two cities exchanged officials. Two parties repeatedly visited each other and conducted several discussions on the issues of trade and investment, cultural exchanges and other fields. In

Trimble Family with President Susan Pierce (third on the right) and Professor Suzanne Barnett (second on the right)

1998 a photo exhibition called "Tacoma: Past and Present" was held in Fuzhou. In 2000, a delegation of 48 people from Tacoma participated in the Cross-Straits Fair for Economy and Trade as well as international dragon boat races. In 2001, a delegation from Fuzhou joined in the Mohair Festival and the dragon boat race hosted by Tacoma. In 2006, the Fuzhou municipal cultural delegation went to Tacoma to participate in international music festivals and other activities. In 2011, Fuzhou Pavilion, which is located in Tacoma China Union Park was-donated and constructed by Fuzhou, won the United States International Sister Cities Association Art and Culture Innovation Award for that year. The calligraphy of the sign on the Fuzhou Pavilion was designed by Mr. Chen, Fenwu, a famous calligrapher from Fuzhou.

While the two cities have been booming with exchanges and interactions, the University of Puget Sound in Tacoma and Fujian Hwa Nan Women's College in Fuzhou also have established relations. These two schools are tied together by the vigorous efforts of the Trimble family. Four generations of the Trimble family have had a relationship or connection with Fujian in one way or another for over 100 years. Lydia Trimble, first generation of Trimble family, was the first foreign president of Hwa Nan Women's College. Bob, a representative from the third generation of the family was born in Gutian, Ningde of Fujian.His father returned to the United States in 1927 and served as a doctor at the University of Puget Sound. Bob graduated from the University of Puget Sound; therefore he also has a deep connection with the University of Puget Sound. This background allowed the Trimble family to actively promote the exchanges and cooperation between the two institutions. The University of Puget Sound is a private university, which focuses on students' ability to think both critically and creatively. Fujian Hwa Nan Women's College, founded in 1985, is a three year vocational college aiming to cultivate students with high-quality skills and talents. The two educational institutions are academically different, so one may think, "How can the two of them start a type of exchange program?" The answer is found within Fujian Hwa Nan Women's College's long term and renowned international background. Many foreign teachers come to teach at Hwa Nan every year since the founding of the college. It was then decided that the University of Puget Sound would start sending selected young female graduates to Hwa Nan to be part of the growing relations.

In November 1996, Fujian Hwa Nan Women's College officially signed the memorandum with the University of Puget Sound. Puget Sound English instructor at Hwa Nan indicated the intention to provide a woman graduate to teach English on a reasonable basis of occurrence, currently every other year (but possibly every year at some time in the future). The relationship between the University and the College acknowledges historical resonance between the two institutions, fits the College's educational goals, and extends the University's undergraduate program in Chinese studies. Selection of the Puget Sound English Instructor will be examined by a competitive application process at the University and approval by officials of the College and appropriate government authorities. The teaching program will be determined by officials of the College. The University will be responsible for arranging the Instructor's travel to and from Fuzhou and assuring major health insurance during the time of appointment. The college will provide the Instructor with room, board, laundry service, routine medical attention, assistance in securing entry into China, and assistance in initial arrival at (as well as final departure from) the College. This memorandum of understanding will be in effect for an indefinite period unless cancelled by an appropriate official of either the College or the University and may be modified at any time with the mutual consent from both parties.

春色
任天涯
——福建华南女子
职业学院外教侧记
International Faculty with
Fujian Hua Nan Women's
College since 1908

180

Puget Sound English Instructorship at Hwa Nan

MEMORANDUM OF UNDERSTANDING

Hwa Nan Women's College
(Fuzhou, Fujian, China)
and

The University of Puget Sound
(Tacoma, Washington, USA)

By this memorandum the University of Puget Sound formally establishes the intention to provide a woman graduate to teach English at Hwa Nan Women's College for a ten-month appointment on a reasonable basis of occurrence, currently every other year (but possibly every year at some time in the future). The relationship between the University and the College acknowledges historical resonance between the two institutions, serves the College's educational goals, and extends the University's undergraduate program in Chinese studies.

1. Selection of the Puget Sound English Instructor will be by a competitive application process at the University and approval by officials of the College and appropriate government authorities.

2. The teaching program will be as determined by officials of the College.

3. The University will be responsible for arranging the Instructor's travel to and from Fuzhou and assuring major health insurance during the time of appointment.

4. The College will provide for the Instructor room, board, laundry service, routine medical attention, assistance in securing entry into China, and assistance in initial arrival at (as well as final departure from) the College.

The memorandum between the two schools

The University of Puget Sound is very strict and cautious in selecting appropriate English instructors. Since Hwa Nan is a women's college, only female graduates are accepted. The candidates need to provide transcripts to the University of Puget Sound as well as two letters of recommendation. In addition, a personal statement is a must. Within a 500-600 word statement, the applicant must indicate their interest in the teaching position at Hwa Nan and why they qualify for the position. The applicant also needs to mention her academic ability and personal preparedness relating to any Chinese culture, language, and current affairs courses taken at Puget Sound. After submitting the application, an interview will be conducted by the committee. Once completed, the committee will select a final candidate for the position. The selection process is usually finished in the spring of the year, ard then the teacher will perform the instructorship. The staff from both schools will work together to prepare necessary paperwork for the work visa for the teacher to work in China.

An important requirement for the applicant is having the interest and basic background in Chinese culture, therefore, all the teachers that have been sent to Hwa Nan have already had different levels of Chinese language before they come. Most of them may have even had a short-term study experience in China. After selecting the teacher, a TEFL training course will be arranged for the teacher before she arrives in Fuzhou. TEFL refers to teaching English as a foreign language, which is a certificate qualifying the teacher to teach students whose native language is not English in non-English speaking countries. The China State Bureau of Foreign Experts conducts the current TEFL certificate training course that is attended by the most recent Puget Sound teachers. A TEFL or TESOL certificate is a requisite for a foreigner to teach in China if they have less than two years teaching experience. It is not very difficult to get a TEFL certificate, for one can either complete the course online or in a more traditional classroom setting. We know the University of Puget Sound values this program since they are willing to provide the teachers an opportunity to travel all the way to Beijing for training.Training in Beijing gives the instructor an idea what kind of Chinese students she is going to meet as well as providing many details about living and working in China, which undoubtedly offers a great help for those who are far from home so that they can adjust themselves as soon as possible. With the rapid development of China economy and its opening up policy, China attracts more and more foreigners to work here. Therefore, the requirements for foreign teachers set by China State Bureau of Foreign Experts have become even stricter. In addition to a TEFL certificate, two years of teaching-related experience has become one of the requirements. The University of Puget Sound communicates regularly with Hwa Nan, so these qualifications are known while applying for the instructorship.

When the two schools signed the memorandum, a concern regarding sending a young female teacher every year was brought to their attention. The program is fully granted by the Trimble Foundation. With the continuous effort by Bob and his son Gordon Trimble, everything has been going very smoothly.The University of Puget Sound informs the instructor that she can extend her contract if she wants, and she can still gain the support from the Trimbles. In addition, Gordon mentioned many times to Puget Sound, if there is more than one suitable candidate, do not hesitate to send more than one! Because of the generous support of the Trimble family, teachers have been able to continuously come to Hwa Nan to teach every year since 2010.

In the early years, most foreign teachers came to teach at Hwa Nan as volunteers; therefore, they are much older than students. The English instructors sent by Puget Sound are women who just graduated. All of them are only 22 or 23 years old when they come to Hwa Nan. They are young, beautiful, kind, and generous with good education and good manners. They have no trouble making friends with their students.Their appearances always impress the students on the campus. The University of Puget Sound has sent a total of 13 young female teachers so far. Let us call them the thirteen golden Puget Sound flowers!

Early before the signing of the formal memorandum, Puget Sound piloted the first female teacher, Catherine Lee Showalter. Her term was from August 1994 to August 1995. She is tall, but is always seen in pictures bending down attentively listening to the students, this idea gave a different impression to students who just were not used to foreign teachers. She has curly hair and is very enthusiastic with the students, but a little bit shy. Students understanding of the cultural differences between China and America started from the English reading and writing course. She printed out the scripts of the Joy Luck Club to students and showed the movie. The students had a more intuitive understanding

182

春色
任天涯
——福建华南女子
职业学院外教侧记
International Faculty with
Fujian Hua Nan Women's
College since 1908

of the differences between Chinese and American culture through the film. She also guided the students to read the story of Robin Hood and watch movies. During the spare time, she encouraged students to do creative writing and helped them edit the campus magazine *Sunshine Girl*. Gradually, students' talents in English writing was encouraged.

Trimble family with Catherine at Hwa Nan

Trimble family visited Catherine at Hwa Nan

During the year of 1996 when the two schools signed the memorandum, Puget Sound sent the second teacher, Jennifer Patterson, to Hwa Nan. She worked from August 1996 to June 1997. In 1998, Morley Megan became the first teacher to continue the second year teaching after the one-year agreement was extended. In August 2000, she transferred to another college to continue teaching in China. The following two teachers were Carrie Ann Richardson and Tyler Alison Bruno. Both of them stayed for a year.

Jennifer Patterson

Megan Morley

Carrie Richardson

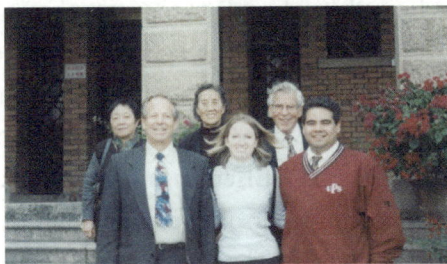

Trimble family with
Tyler Bruno

In 2004, the sixth teacher was McLeod Marian, who stayed at Hwa Nan for two years. Then in 2005, the University of Puget Sound sent Lisa Long to teach for a year. It was the first time and the only time Hwa Nan had two Puget Sound graduates teaching at the same time. From 2004 to 2006, there were quite a few young female teachers in Hwa Nan. In addition to Lisa and Marian, Lisa's sister Mikiko Long, Shannon Rise sent by Jian Hua Foundation, and several young Japanese teachers came to Hwa Nan, forming a big family.

The following experience is shared by Marian, which was published in the spring 2005 Asian Studies Expands from the University of Puget Sound.

When I visited America during my winter break the question I was repeatedly asked was, "How's China?" I appreciated and understood everyone's interest, China is a strange and curious place to most people, but of the hundreds of answers that ran through my head I usually went with the simplest, and "It's good." And China is good. It's great, especially for foreigners, who are treated like celebrities. A surprising number of Chinese in Fuzhou have never seen a non-Chinese face, so encountering a foreigner on the street is an event for them. Constant staring and whispers of "laowai" (foreigner) have become part of the background of my life here, although there are moments when I would give anything to just blend in. Our strange faces, and the light eyes and hair of some of my friends and coworkers, have opened a number of doors, sometimes literally, in the city. When we wander down the small alleys in the older sections of Cangshan, our district, and peer into the entryways and courtyards, the women sweeping the steps or washing the dishes will eye us up and down

Marian、Lisa Long、Mikiko Long、Jessica、Sachika、Moyoko

Gordon and Sonia Trimble with Lisa and Marian

春色
任天涯
——福建华南女子
职业学院外教侧记
International Faculty with
Fujian Hua Nan Women's
College since 1908

184

then ask if we would like to come inside and look around. The openness of the people here and little incidents like this keep me from being overwhelmed by the challenges of living in China. I live in a big house with most of the foreign teachers from Hwa Nan, so it's like living in a tiny UN or a mini-America. I revel in the familiarity of the language and behavior, particularly on Thanksgiving and Christmas, but I regret the insularity of our little "nation." I feel quite sure that my Chinese would be much better right now if I was not living with a dozen English-speakers, although my Japanese has improved a lot (thanks to the two Japanese teachers who live in the house). Luckily, Fuzhou is easy to travel around, particularly by bus, which at one yuan (1 dollar=8 yuan) provides many opportunities to explore the city. I feel comfortable in Fuzhou, know my way around well enough to give directions to other people and have even been mistaken for a resident of Fuzhou a few times. I'm looking forward to the rest of the spring term and starting my second year at Hwa Nan next September. Hopefully by then I'll have come up with a better answer than "It's good."

Lisa Long, the seventh English instructor, has a very close relationship with Hwa Nan. In 2008 and 2011, she came to visit Hwa Nan with two groups of students from the University of Puget Sound. At Puget Sound, Lisa became familiar with the Hwa Nan Instructor's position sponsored by the Trimble family and she always thought that she would apply for the program upon graduating from university. As an Asian Studies major, she studied Chinese during her undergraduate studies and had studied in China before. Unfortunately, the timing of the program through Puget Sound did not align with her timing after she completed her Masters in Teaching, so she decided to apply independently. Once she learned that it was possible to apply independently, she encouraged her newly graduated sister to also apply to become an English Instructor at Hwa Nan Women's College. The fellow teaching at Hwa Nan at that time, Marian McLeod, was Lisa's good friend and when she told

Gordon Trimble and Lisa Long

Lisa that she would extend her fellowship for another year Lisa became even more excited about moving to Fuzhou. Lisa was also very keen on working at Hwa Nan a instead of at other institutions in China, because as a student at Puget Sound, she received scholarships from the Trimble family many times. Knowing that she would never be able to repay the family for their generosity, which was so crucial to her education, she felt that providing service to an institution that is so strongly supported by the family could be an action that could accurately convey her gratitude.

Mikiko Long is Lisa's older sister. Lisa convinced her to apply and teach at Hwa Nan because they always undertook adventures together since they were young. It seemed appropriate that they would also embark on the chance to move and teach in China together. Mikiko did not attend the University of Puget Sound. She is a graduate of Colorado State University and has always been interested in languages and cultures. Although she studied Spanish and studied in Central America, she was very excited about moving move to China and living in Fuzhou for a year.

When Lisa arrived at Hwa Nan, she had just completed her Masters in Teaching, so she felt very prepared to teach the students at Hwa Nan. She thought that this was how all the overconfident young teachers would feel. But Lisa quickly realized that while her training and education was a huge asset, nothing prepares one for teaching other than as teaching itself. Her students were all very excited and eager to learn English, but most of them were also very shy. Her biggest challenge was finding ways to encourage them to speak out louder than a whisper. She tried to incorporate fun activities, interesting topics, and opportunities to share personal experiences within her lessons to encourage more to speak. Although not directly related to speaking and listening (which were Lisa's subjects),

Lisa and Mikiko Long with Gordon Trimble

春色
任天涯
——福建华南女子
职业学院外教侧记
International Faculty with
Fujian Hua Nan Women's
College since 1908

186

she also tried to encourage her students to analyze and think critically. So while it means more work for herself, she was continually altering the content of her lessons to push students to think deeper and broader about life and their place in it.

In 2006 and 2008, Puget Sound sent their eighth and ninth teachers, Eva Tam and Lan Nguyen respectively. Lan Nguyen is a Vietnamese American, who was also the last teacher Hwa Nan received at the old Yan Tai Shan campus.

Lan gave the speech

Eva Tam visited the West Lake Park with
other foreign teachers

The tenth instructor, Marjorie Katherine Lodwick, was the first Puget Sound teacher to move to the new Hwa Nan compus located in University Town.She prefers to be called Marjie. Marjie is a goldilocks full of energy, she is also friendly, industrious, and hard working. We found many of her characters more like a Chinese girl than a typical American girl. Marjie's passions are well presented in the class. When students didn't understand her, she would use a lot of hand gestures and body languages to help describe what she talked about. In order to let the students experience Western festivals, she asked her parents in the United States to send dyes used to color Easter eggs. When the students finished coloring the eggs, Marjie hid eggs in the lawn in the front of the international faculty building. Students very much enjoyed the egg hunting activity. What moved her students most was that Marjie cut off her hair to help children in need of hair in the United States. During her teaching at Hwa Nan, she volunteered to lead an English club to help students practice oral English after-school or during the weekends. She also accompanied another foreign teacher, Laihar, to English Corner every Friday night. Marjie majored in biology, so she is very good at recognizing animals and plants in the natural world. Thanks to her friendly and cheerful personality, she always got along well with other Chinese colleagues. It is no wonder why Marjie stayed at Hwa Nan for a second year to teach, for she truly found a home here. In August 2012, she finished her teaching at Hwa Nan and then was placed in Indonesia as a Peace Corps volunteer. Peace Corps is a large US government program that has been sending volunteers to more than 140 countries (today there are 63 countries with active programs) for over 50 years. Gordon Trimble was also a Peace Corps volunteer in the Philippines, where he met Sonia. Marjie's assignment was teaching English in a small rural high school and training local English teachers in East Java, Indonesia. She served until the summer of 2015. In July 2015, she was able to visit China again, and it was absolutely wonderful for her to reunite with her students who had become women, to see where their dreams had led them to and to reminisce about old school days.Currently, Marjie is working with the National Park Service in the US. It is a government organization that oversees all of the National Parks and monuments in the US (including places like Yellowstone, the Grand Canyon, and The White House). She is an interpretive ranger at the Chesapeake and Ohio Canal National Historical Park about 15 miles outside of Washington D.C.. She spends her days educating and informing visitors of the parks' unique history and natural setting both at the visitor center and out on trails.

Marjie cut her hair

Marjie with her students

Elizabeth Whitaker is also a blonde. She is tall with a very cute smile.She was shy, but was never afraid to ask Chinese colleagues for any suggestion. She actively participated in students' activities as well as assisted Laihar with English corner every Friday night. Liz comes from Oregon and majored in Economy and Chinese in Puget Sound. Her interest

春色
任天涯
——福建华南女子
职业学院外教侧记
International Faculty with
Fujian Hua Nan Women's
College since 1908

188

Liz was handing out candies

Quincy with former President Lin Benchun

in Chinese started from overseas exchange programs in the Rotary International Young People in high school. Like Marjie, Liz continued to teach at Hwa Nan for a second year. The twelfth teacher, Kennedy Holt, came to Hwa Nan for only a year and returned back to the states for graduate study in July 2015. Currently, Quincy Livingston, the thirteenth instructor, is teaching at Hwa Nan. Quincy majored in Chinese Language and Culture with a minor in biology at Puget Sound. She continues to represent the Puget Sound blonde girls. Her grandfather was born in Fuzhou and grew up there until ten years old before returning to the United States. Quincy has been attracted by the Chinese artwork collected by her grandfather since she was young. The special family connection fueled Quincy's interest to teach in Fuzhou. Quincy is very considerate. She is currently enjoying the teaching and the life in Fuzhou.

Can you imagine these girls in their early twenties leaving their family and motherland, and traveling all the way to a completely new and strange environment for a year or perhaps two years?How much passion they must have for the amazing oriental cultures that China possesses? How much courage, confidence and responsibility they must have to stand in front of thirty students or more?Therefore, we can understand those girls who can't wait to return home after a year's teaching. At the same time, we are very grateful for those young instructors who are willing to stay for another year. The whole Hwa Nan community, from school administrators to students always try to give the Puget Sound teachers more care and attention. Once a vice president saw a Puget Sound teacher ordering noodles at a food stalls at the Student street, she kindly reminded the teacher of the food hygiene. Teachers from English departments always communicate with teachers from Puget Sound, accompanying them on a campus tour as well as informing them what kind of students they are going to meet. Other experienced foreign teachers always provide advice and suggestions to help the young girls adapt to cultural differences. Young staff from the Foreign Affairs Office also goes out for a walk or talk with these young girls. Students are always warmly inviting teachers to visit their hometowns and sharing local specialties with those teachers.Even our cook gives special consideration to the Puget Sound girls.For example, one teacher liked to eat eggplant, so our cook prepared the braised eggplant when she had meals in the dining room. Another example was that another teacher was afraid of bones and didn't eat drumsticks, the cook took careful note of this. The Foreign Affairs Office deliberately leaves the best room in the international faculty house for the Puget Sound girls to try to help them adapt to their new life. Since the Puget Sound teachers share the same room year after year, the new teacher can feel the warmth from the previous teacher.

The friendship between the University of Puget Sound and Hwa Nan has been strong for more than 20 years thanks to the generosity of the Trimble family. Although most of the students they have taught are all over the world, the teacher-student bond will have a definite impact and influence on their lives in the future. As the memorandum said, once it is signed, there shall be no specific end date, meaning the friendship will continue to grow.

The cooperation between Puget Sound and Hwa Nan is far more than sending female instructors. In 2008 and 2011 Hwa Nan hosted two groups of nearly 30 Puget Sound students as part of their Asian study program. The Asian study program is called the Pacific Rim/Asia Study-Travel Program, which is abbreviated as the PAC RIM program. Every three years, a group of students from the University of Puget Sound ventures out into the world for nine months of rigorous academic and personal inquiry. Visiting eight Asian nations, the group engages in a vast multicultural experience that forces them to confront novel systems of culture, economics, politics, religion, and philosophy. Asian classrooms and hands-on education extend the limits of the regular curriculum taking place on campus in the U.S.. Prior to start of the program, students must complete courses related to Asian studies. Throughout their year in Asia, the students have first-hand exposure to numerous cultures, including the Republic of Korea, Nepal, Vietnam, Japan, India, the People's Republic of China, and other sites chosen in conjunction with the expertise of the Director. The PAC RIM Program students usually achieve a more nuanced understanding of Asian cultures than other students in the university. Moreover, the careful meshing of itinerary and course work fulfills overall academic objectives of the University, and the challenges of the moveable classroom and changing faculty within a general context of novelty

春色
任天涯
——福建华南女子
职业学院外教侧记
International Faculty with
Fujian Hua Nan Women's
College since 1908

190

meet co-curricular objectives. While they were visiting China, they made the longest stop in Fuzhou rather than in metropolitan cities like Beijing or Shanghai. On the Eve of Thanksgiving in 2008, more than 20 students travelled all the way from Mongolia to Fuzhou and celebrated Thanksgiving Dinner with the Hwa Nan community. Since it was the first time to entertain so many guests, the Foreign Affairs Office teachers and foreign teachers prepared beforehand to make arrangements for accommodation, even picking the proper beddings and mattress fit for American people. Since we were celebrating Thanksgiving, one of the most important holidays, the Hwa Nan teachers began to roast turkeys under Betts' guidance one month before their arrival. One month before Thanksgiving, the seasonings and gravy were delivered to Hwa Nan, and all the turkeys were purchased from Metro in Fuzhou and even Xiamen. The ovens in the Foreign Affairs Office were not enough, so a bigger oven was borrowed from the Food and Nutrition Department. In addition to turkey, pumpkin pie is a must for a delicious Thanksgiving dinner. Betts and another teacher from the Foreign Affairs Office went to the five-star Shangri-La Hotel to order some pumpkin pies. Everything was ready. Everybody was anticipating the arrival of the group. At the Thanksgiving dinner, Chinese and international friends gathered together at the Lucy Hall in the old campus to celebrate the festive season. During the feast of the authentic American Thanksgiving dinner, Puget Sound students began to share their gratitude. A student was thankful for those students who traveled with her and helped her all the way long; someone thanked Obama for being the president; some thanked the University of Puget Sound for providing them with the opportunity to study abroad; some people were thankful for Hwa Nan for making them feel at home. And someone thanked the turkey and the pumpkin pie, which they had never tasted before. It turned out that the pumpkin pie served in Shangri-La and American pumpkin pies were completely different!

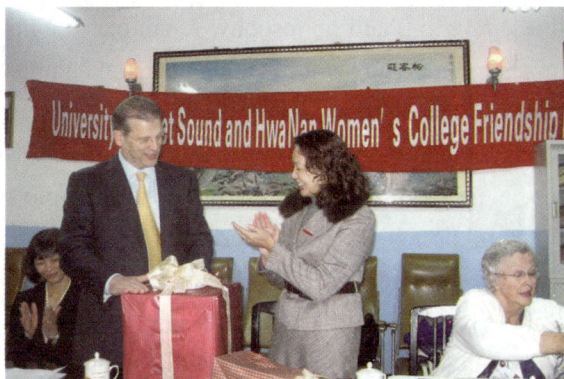

Two schools celebrated the friendship in 2008

The PAC RIM program was led by several teachers including the program director, Elisabeth Benard, an accompanying doctor, and the project liaison, who is also our old friend, Lisa Long, the seventh Puget Sound teacher. They spent almost three weeks at Hwa Nan. They visited the local famous scenic spots like Gushan. Professor Lin Benchun and foreign teacher Dodie were invited

University of Puget Sound and Hwa Nan Friendship Day

as guest speakers to introduce to them (Chinese history and culture). More importantly, the students were able to complete a course in Fuzhou, for Hwa Nan arranged a classroom for them. The teacher who taught this course was Professor Karl Fields, who was also the director of Asia Studies at Puget Sound. The course he taught covered the topic of Asian politics. During this course, the students visited the famous Gutian Conference site, which is a milestone for the Chinese Red Army. Professor Karl Fields lectured a vivid lesson at the site. After the tour in Gutian, the group took the opportunity to visit Yongding and the earth tower of Hakka. All the students were amazed by the ancient Chinese construction technology.

Hwa Nan was afraid that these young students would have trouble in a completely strange country, so excellent students were chosen from Applied English Department to help them. The students took them to the school cafeteria and showed them local delicacies.They took them on the bus, which only cost one yuan to search for the local life. Some hospitable students even invited their partners to their home. Ron Thomas, the president of the University of Puget Sound, came from the United States to meet his students in Fuzhou. If you were lucky, you would have seen them either on the old campus, student street, or by those old buildings in Cangshan from late November to mid December 2008.

Three years later in 2011, another group of Puget Sound students travelled from Vietnam to Fuzhou at the same time right before Thanksgiving. This year students arrived two days before Thanksgiving. They worked together to a make big Thanksgiving feast. Some students went shopping, some students made pumpkin pies, some students decorated

192

春色
任天涯
——福建华南女子
职业学院外教侧记
International Faculty with
Fujian Hua Nan Women's
College since 1908

the dining room while others were roasting turkey or made other food. The night before Thanksgiving, the kitchen in the International Faculty House was busy all night. Students wrote down their words of thanks on thank you cards. This year we were glad to welcome back our old friends,Professor Elisabeth Benard and Lisa Long. In addition, Professor Benard' husband, Nima, paid his first visit to Fuzhou. This year, their course study in Fuzhou was concerning Asian religions. Professor Deborah took her students to visit Wufu Town, a small town in Wu Yishan, where Zhu Xi, a master of Neo-confucianism, had lived for more than 40 years. The students visited Zhu Xi Alley, and Ziyang Tower. Some students also went to see the impressive Dahongpao. Some students commented that this was the best show they have ever seen in their lives. This year, Hwa Nan also arranged for every Puget Sound student to have a Hwa Nan partner to help her adapt to local life. A gala was also organized by Hwa Nan students to celebrate the Sino-American friendship. With the help of the Trimble family, students from the two schools jointly organized the forum, "West meets East "with the theme of changing the world. At the forum, students from China and the United States exchanged ideas reflecting the friendship between the two peoples. After they left Fuzhou, the students went to Hong Kong and they had a short break there.Some students returned to the United States and met their family, some students stayed in Hong Kong, some students traveled to other Asian countries such as Cambodia and explored the mysterious oriental culture. Before their departure, students enjoyed the hospitality of Fuzhou people. The Puget Sound teachers told the Foreign Affairs Office that Fuzhou was the only stop that brought home-like warmth to their students. Unfortunately, after 2011, the University of Puget Sound temporarily cancelled the trip to Fujian for the PAC RIM program due to the project curriculum adjustment. However, since the Trimble family is still communicating with them, we believe that, perhaps in the near future, we will have a number of Puget Sound students on the campus again.

With the casual words of Professor Barnett, Fuzhou and Tacoma formed a strong everlasting friendship. The Trimble family is responsible for closely connecting Hwa Nan Women's College and the University of Puget Sound together. In the past twenty years, which is just a drop in the bucket in human history, we have seen the rise of a better relationship between China and the United States. In the early 1990s, Fuzhou people watched foreigners just like watching pandas. Twenty years later, the prosperity of foreign exchange makes the streets full of blonde hair and blue eyes. We watch our students with pride and we are deeply thankful for those who make efforts to promote this strong friendship, for those who help keep the mutual understanding between the two schools, and for those who work together to make PAC RIM program successful in Fuzhou.And of course, please never forget, the thirteen golden flowers, who came from the other side of the world to spend many unforgettable and irreplaceable moments with our students.

When the author was completing this chapter, the University of Puget Sound shared the exciting news that Amy Bodner has been selected as the fourteenth English instructor. She will be joining us in September 2016.

Students visited the Xiamei Village
located in Wuyishan City

Students prepared for the
Thanksgiving dinner

Students visited Wuyishan Mountain

春色
任天涯
——福建华南女子
职业学院外教侧记
International Faculty with
Fujian Hua Nan Women's
College since 1908

194

Students from both schools
had a celebration

Students had a tour in Xiamen

The group pictures taken in front of the administration
building of Hwa Nan

III

Professor Marian Davis and Her Affection for Home Economics

Professor Marian Davis, a master of Clothing Design from California University, the U. S. A., a PhD of Home Economics from Ohio State University, Professor of the School of Science in Clothing, Textiles and Consumers, College of Human Sciences, Florida State University (FSU),Coordinator of International Home Economics. At the beginning of the rejuvenation of the new private Hwa Nan Women's College, Professor Davis came to Hwa Nan to conduct a research. She showed great concern about the departments regarding home economics such as Nutrition and Food Science, Childhood Education and Clothing Design. Since 1987, she had visited Hwa Nan Women's College once a year for several years, holding academic workshops for the students of Clothing Design Department, conducting questionnaire for home economics research, consulting the materials about the history of Hwa Nan, and interviewing Hwa Nan teachers and students. In 1991, Professor Davis published her first research paper about Hwa Nan Women's College named "Home Economics Heritage and Promise in China: A College Reborn" in the periodical of Home Economics. She explored the history of Hwa Nan Women's College in depth from the perspective of the development of home economics. She started with the great concern about the education of home economics by the early administrators of Hwa Nan Women's College and thus they invited the U. S. home economics teachers to set up home economics course; she then described the facts that young teachers were sent to Canada and the U. S. for Master's Degree in home economics in 1916 and 1929; she also included the formal establishment of the Home Economics Department in 1932, and the cancellation of the program after the adjustment of Chinese colleges in 1951. Based on these facts, she analyzed the practical significance of the existence of home economics and the conflict between "American style" and "Aristocratic" home economics and the demand of working people in New China, and she argued that the reason of the cancellation of the home economics program was that the then Chinese government did not are have all rounded awareness of the basic functions of the home economics in enhancing people's life and welfare. Home economics is closely related to everybody's life. The great impact

春色
任天涯
——福建华南女子
职业学院外教侧记
International Faculty with
Fujian Hua Nan Women's
College since 1908

196

of China, a leading power with one fifth of the world population, is international.

The rejuvenated private Hwa Nan Women's College developed three independent departments, namely Nutrition and Food Science, Childhood Education and Consultation, Clothing Design, based on the home economics department from the original Hwa Nan College of Letters and Sciences. Professor Marian Davis conducted detailed surveys regarding the enrollment, curriculum design, teaching methods and graduate employment direction of the three departments while she was at Hwa Nan. Above all, she thought that the setting up of these courses indicated the hope of rejuvenating home economics, but she also felt that generally these "newborn" departments were not highly connected, lacking recognition of home economics, the professional focus was on the application of manufacturing, commercial and economic areas rather than the application of family life with people as the center. She emphasized again and again the necessity of the existence of an integrated home economics focusing on enhancing people's life quality. Her suggestions of establishing a well-established home economics department was approved by Hwa Nan leaders.

Professor Davis considered it vital to solve the problem of lack of teachers in a private women's college that first ran home economics program when she saw many part-time teachers at Hwa Nan, so she actively boosted cooperation between Hwa Nan Women's College and College of Human Sciences (formerly as Home Economics College), FSU, the USA. She accompanied President Yu Baosheng to examine FSU, the U. S. A. in 1987. With Professor Davis's help, Hwa Nan Women's College was admitted to the International Union of Home Economics. Hwa Nan was the first college in China that had joined the world home economics organization, through which Hwa Nan teachers got a better understanding of the world by attending international exchange activities.

Hwa Nan and FSU, the U. S. A., signed the first memorandum of cooperation in 1990, which provided a chance for Hwa Nan to assign the initial three young teaching assistants who taught at Hwa Nan after graduation there to pursue a master's degree and a visiting scholar to conduct academic exchange.

In September 1995, Dr. Davis came to Hwa Nan again to carry out her research work and she conducted three workshops about clothing design. In July 1996, Dr. Rolston, President of College of Human Sciences, FSU, and Dr. Davis visited Hwa Nan. Both sides made an initial agreement to continue accepting five young teachers to study in FSU and to cooperatively found modern home economics department.

Hwa Nan Women's College had already sent 8 young teaching assistants to do further study in the U. S. A. and these teachers obtained their master's degree in Nutrition and Food Science, Childhood Education, and Clothing and Textiles. Most of these teachers took

Professor Davis's course, International Home Economics, as an elective course while they were studying there, which enhanced their awareness of the relationship between their major areas and home economics and thus laid a foundation for their future teaching and research in China.

FSU offered great assistance to Hwa Nan Women's College during the cooperation periods. College of Human Sciences, FSU, donated hundreds of professional books to Hwa Nan Women's College. Professor Davis called upon the professors from different departments in her college to found a mentor team to provide guidance for the relevant departments and train young teachers at Hwa Nan. As a professor of Textile and Clothing Department, Professor Davis donated the clothing design wallcharts made by her students and the teaching aids and slides made by herself to Hwa Nan Clothing Design Department for teaching purpose. Hwa Nan's visiting scholars and teaching assistants studying in FSU received Professor Davis's enthusiastic and selfless help in study and life while studying in the U. S. A. Every year she applied funds from different Foundations for the young Hwa Nan teachers so that they could get the opportunities to participate in academic activities regarding home economics held by American Home Economics Association.

After more than 10 years' attempt, Hwa Nan was finally approved to found Home Economics Department in 2002. Professor Davis was overjoyed with the news and she actively helped the Home Economics Department with the curriculum development despite her ill health after the surgery; she collected a large volume of curriculum materials by all means as the references of the curriculum design for Home Economics Department, guided the teachers of Home Economics at Hwa Nan to localize the curriculum to adapt to Chinese situation; and assisted the construction of the laboratories for Home Economics with her own money.

Professor Davis made great contributions to the development of home economics in China and her dedication to Home Economics greatly impressed Hwa Nan educators,young and old. Although home economics is still in its primary stage, an increasing number of scholars have joined its research team. The veil of home economics is lifted gradually and it has gradually showed its charm. We believe the prospect for home economics is promising.

春色
任天涯
——福建华南女子
职业学院外教侧记
International Faculty with
Fujian Hua Nan Women's
College since 1908

198

IV
Black Beauty from Finland
——A Profile of Elisabet

Black Beauty is not really black, but very beautiful. Black is translated from her family name "Köhler", which means the man who holds the coal. Beauty comes from her first name "Elisabet", which combines "beauty" or "Mei", a very common character for Chinese female names. Black Beauty, or Heimeili, comes from Finland. Her full name is Elisabet Rantschukoff. On December 8th, 1988, at the invitation of the United Nations Development Program, Heimeili came to teach at Hwa Nan as a volunteer. She went back to Finland on June 7, 1989 after finishing the spring semester. After a summer break, she came back to Hwa Nan on August 27, 1989. After one year's teaching, she finished her teaching assignments and went back to Finland on June 27, 1990. Her students' first impression on her was that she loved all Chinese elements, especially traditional style clothes Qipao. Her students recalled that before their graduation they were asked to take group pictures in the Yantaishan Park, which is next to Hwa Nan campus. Heimeili mentioned that she would give them a surprise. On that picture day, she showed up wearing an elegant Chinese Qipao, which impressed all students. They thought it fitted her well and was a really beautiful scene when a young foreign beauty wore it. Heimeili even said that she would love to take Qipao back home as a souvenir. Many years after she came

Students and Heimeili in Qipao

back to Hwa Nan, Hwa Nan faculty still can feel her love for Qipao, for on every formal and important occasion, she would dress in Qipao.

Before Heimeili came to Hwa Nan, she had worked in Sweden at Ericsson Company (a multinational telephone company) for seven years as a training consultant, responsible for the company's secretarial training programs. She felt that she wanted to do something else and thought she would move back to Finland, however, at the same time she had been interested in China for many years and felt that she wanted to go there someday but she did not know how. Anyway, she moved back to Finland in September 1987 and started working at the Swedish People's Party of Finland. During the summer 1988, there was an ad in the biggest newspaper in Finland that UN was looking for a Secretarial Skills Instructor who could work at Hwa Nan, Fuzhou. It felt like her destiny, so she applied to become Finland's candidate for the UNDP (United Nations Development Program) project in China. UNDP was looking for one to be in Beijing and one in Fuzhou. As China has just started to open to the outside world, there was a huge need of training for people who would work in joint-ventures especially in offices of shoe factories. Heimeili went through a long and detailed admittance process including submitting written application, taking personal tests during a whole day. This was all done through the Finnish Foreign Ministry and then she was elected to be Finland's candidate for the position. Though she doesn't hold a MBA, nor is she a native speaker of English, the Chinese education commission chose her! Heimeili was the first (and the only) United Nations Volunteer from Finland who went to China. There came other projects in other countries after this UNDP-project.After being selected, Heimeili went through a two weeks preparatory course in Finland at the Ministry. By the end of November 1988, she was sent to UN's headquarters in Geneva for a few days to meet some officials to discuss the coming project and get more information about how UNDP worked in China. She came to Beijing in December 1988. In Beijing she stayed for one week. After that, she came to Hwa Nan.

In the early 1990s, Heimeili was at her thirties when she came to teach at Hwa Nan, just a little bit older than her students. She tried to get closer to her students, thus she always came to students' cafeteria to have lunch with them, which unconsciously improved students' oral English. Although her native language is Swedish, Heimeili practiced with her students in English a lot. She took them to walk around the West Lake Park or had meals at the famous Shanghai Western Style Restaurant at that time. Students took these opportunities to practice their language skills with dictionaries. Heimeili's academic background focused on foreign-oriented secretary, therefore, the courses she taught in Hwa Nan were more concerned with secretary combined with English language. In the early 1990s, foreign secretary was quite new to China, which had just opened the door to the world. Students were trained not only in foreign language but also in office automation system. Back at that time, there were no computers yet. Students learned to type through typewriters and to master the theory and practice of being a qualified secretary. It was the first time for students to be exposed to new ideas and knowledge, students felt it a valuable

春色
任天涯
——福建华南女子
职业学院外教侧记
International Faculty with
Fujian Hua Nan Women's
College since 1908

200

chance and kept memorizing the course they took and the teacher who taught them after they enter into career. Heimeili was also very proud of her students. She mentioned that the most remarkable experience was that when she sent all the third year students to practical training. They all used their contacts to find a work place for a month and she prepared them with questions before they went. During that month, she visited everyone of them. She went by bike all over Fuzhou to meet and interview them and see if they needed any help. It was the most memorable and wonderful thing she did together with her students. Owing to her academic background and professional trainings, Heimeili always gave students suggestions regarding to their behaviors, and taught her students what was respect. Chinese students like to peek the roster which teachers put in the platform. They were caught once by Heimeili, which made her very angry. After flying to a rage, she told students that these were private and should be respected by others. Students were scared by her anger, but they also learned what respect is.

After leaving China for many years, Heimeili started her career and got married like Chinese women. Taking care of her family and working hard kept her from returning to China. In 1996, she changed her job and started to work as International Coordinator at Swedish Polytechnic, Finland (since 2006 Novia University of Applied Science).During this period, she developed international contacts in Europe and Asia, therefore, she thought she should use her old contacts in Fuzhou to explore cooperation possibilities. She contacted her old friend Shi Yin at the Fujian Provincial Department of Education to see if both sides could find some common ground. She actually visited Hwa Nan in 1997 and discussed a possible cooperation contract. After that, she came to Fuzhou (and every time visited Hwa Nan) for six times, including 2006 when she came with the president of the University to attend Fujian Normal University's centennial anniversary. They did

Heimeili practiced shaking
hands with students

Student Chen Qian
and Chen Lulu

Heimeili was listening to a student's speech

sign a cooperation contract with Hwa Nan but unfortunately it did not result in any student or teacher exchange activities. However, Novia has had cooperation with Fujian Normal University, Fuzhou University, College of Traditional Chinese Medicine and Fujian Medical University. Every time she came, she would always visit Xu Daofeng and some of her other old friends like Shi Yin, Chen Chunsu and some of her old students who have become her really good friends.

Shirley, SHI Yin, who has been working for the International Cooperation Office of Fujian Provincial Department of Education, shared her memories with us:

I met Heimeili in the summer of 1989, when the Fujian Foreign Affairs Office organized the first Longyan Pickup Festival for foreigners who were teaching in Fuzhou. Since then, we have been keeping in touch from 1997 to 2005, Heimeili served as the director of the international department and information department in Swedish Polytechnic, Finland (now renamed " Novia University "). Thanks to her continuous efforts, Fuzhou University, Fujian Normal University, Fujian Medical University, Fujian College of traditional Chinese medicine and Fujian Hwa Nan Women's College set up various exchanges and cooperation with Swedish Polytechnic, Finland, University of Vaxjo, Sweden (now renamed " Linnaean Oslo University "). In the May of 1998, Mr. Chen Kongde, the Deputy Director of the Provincial Education Commission, led a delegation to Finland, Swede, and Denmark. The delegation included Mr. Zeng Minyong, the president of Fujian Normal University; Mrs. Ye Huiling, Vice Party Secretary of Fuzhou University; Mrs. Chen Liying, the president of Fujian Medical University, Mr. Du Jiam, the president of Fujian College of Traditional Chinese Medicine; Mr. Li Candong, the director of International Cooperation Office of the College of traditional Chinese Medicine., Shi Ying, the staff of the Foreign Affairs Office of Fujian Provincial Education Commission. The delegation visited several universities and conducted discussions concerning faculty and students exchanges.

In the October of 1998, the president of Swedish Polytechnic, Finland paid a visit back to several universities in Fuzhou with the exchange agreements signed. Since 1998, the delegation of Fujian Provincial Education Department piloted the visit to Nordic countries, programs related to faculty and students' exchanges have been going smoothly.

In 2013, Heimeili wrote to her student,

Delegation visit to Finland

202

春色
任天涯
——福建华南女子
职业学院外教侧记
International Faculty with
Fujian Hua Nan Women's
College since 1908

former Hwa Nan president Dr. Zhang Xunjie, expressing her desire to return to Hwa Nan to teach for a semester. She had a very tight work schedule in Finland, therefore, she had been preparing for coming back to teach for almost a year! Heimeili worked for Nils Torvalds, member of Parliament at European Parliament, an active Communist and radio reporter who was elected as the member of the Central Committee of the Communist Party of Finland. The Torvalds family belongs to ethnic minorities in Finland, which account for 6% of the Finland people in Sweden. Actually, Nils Torvalds's son earned much fame than his father. His son is named Linus Torvalds, who is the inventor of Linux, one of the world's most popular computer operating systems, and the cofounder of this scheme.

August 27, 2014, Heimeili came back to the campus after 20 plus years. She planned to teach for a semester. Owing to her working experience and background in foreign-oriented secretary, she was arranged by the School of Foreign language and International Trade to teach in the Applied English Department. Heimeili enjoyed returning back to the campus, and sharing her learning experience with students. In addition, this return gave her more opportunities to meet with her former students and old friends. What a pleasure for her and the people who have known her! Heimeili shared with us the differences between her teaching experience in 1988 and 2014. In 1988 they had typewriters with ribbons that the students used. There were no books about Office Administration in English or Chinese. She had to prepare all the teaching material herself. She typed all texts, exercises and exams and then used a blueprint-machine to get them copied to her students. There was no copying machine, DVD, computers, etc. At that time, when she asked her 213 students how many of them had been to an office, less than 10 answered yes. Some of them answered that they had been to a post office. Many of the students had not had any foreign teacher teaching them, so it took some time until they got used to the teacher. They had

Heimeili with former President,
Dr. Zhang Xunjie

Heimeili with former President Chen
Zhongying

Heimeii visited the old FAO building in 2014

Heimeili visited the room she used to
stay in the old FAO building

blackboards and chalk. In May and June when it was very hot and humid, the chalk almost melted in her hand when she tried to write something. In 2014 the teaching facilities were all upgraded. It was all computers and I-pads as well as very good and contemporary books were provided. The books contained all exercises, texts and tests needed. Everyone is used to foreigners and foreign teachers. Still some of the students were very shy to speak, but more open to suggestions to work in groups and do presentations. What's more, there were whiteboards which made it much easier, except when you used a permanent filt-pen.

However, something happened out of everyone's expectation. During the National holiday, Heimeili felt uncomfortable at one midnight.She was sent to the provincial people's Hospital, and then transferred to the provincial hospital. During her stay at hospital, teachers from the Foreign Affairs Office and the Applied English Department took turns to look after her. Her good friends, Shi Yin, from the Provincial Education Department and Chen Chunsu, from Fujian Medical University,visited her almost every day. Former president, Zhang Xunjie also visited her many times. It was very regrettable that her asthma led to pneumonia. After talking to her family, her doctors, and her boss, she made a hard decision to leave China. Heimeili didn't want to give her Chinese friends too much trouble, so, she left Fuzhou once again in October 27, 2014 with great regret. We don't know when to see her again after this leave.

Heimeili had a rest after going back to Finland. During this time, she always thought of those colleagues who helped her when she was ill. At the end of 2014, she wrote a letter to Hwa Nan, which indicated that she made a donation of 5,000 yuan to reward teachers from the Applied English Department for the five consecutive years since 2015.

春色
任天涯
——福建华南女子
职业学院外教侧记
International Faculty with
Fujian Hua Nan Women's
College since 1908

204

V
Dream of China
——Ms. Martha Sue Todd

Martha Sue Todd in China

1988.8—1992.7	Teaching in South East University
1992.8—1995.6	Teaching in Fujian Hwa Nan Women's College
1994.9	Won the prize of "Fujian Provincial Excellent Foreign Expert"
1995.8—1997.8	Teaching in Fujian Medical University
1997.8—2000.7	Teaching in Min Jiang University
2000.8—2001.6	Teaching in Fujian Hwa Nan Women's College
2004.6.13—7.2	Visiting Fujian Hwa Nan Women's College

Martha Sue Todd, born in 1920, was a Christian who is notably devout. She had a belief that "God had a place for me to serve in China". She dreamed of serving in China for many times when she was young. However, her dream did not come true, for World War II interrupted her plans to come to China.

Sue and her husband

Sue got acquaintance with her Mr. Right, Carl Glenn Todd during the following years. They got married and enjoyed forty-one years together before Carl passed away in 1985. After getting married, Sue became a mother with one son, later a grandmother with two grandchildren.

Three weeks after her husband's funeral, Sue learned that her son's mother-in-law was diagnosed with inoperable cancer. In order to free her daughter-in-law to take care of her dying mother, Sue took the responsibility of looking after her grandchildren. Fourteen months later, her daughter-in-law came back to assume full duties of her home and children. Sue started to look for other ways to make herself useful.

At that time, Sue's dream to go to China came back again. In her mind, she thought coming to China was her destiny. All she had done in her life were considered as preparing for her plan to come to China. When Sue learned from the Baptist Foreign Mission Board that teachers could come to China to teach English, she was so excited, happy and enthusiastic. She submitted her application without any hesitation and been approved for being qualified. Her dream of coming to China has finally got realized when she was getting close to 70.

Farewell to the United State, Sue, at the age of 68, took on the plane headed for China in August, 1988.

Coming to China, Serving in Hwa Nan

Amity Foundation, based in Nanjing, created in 1985, on the initiative of Chinese Christians headed by Bishop K. H. Ting, is made up of people from all walks of society, aiming at improving Chinese social public good such as education, social welfare, medical health, community development and environmental protection and disaster management.

The founding of Amity was such a joyous news for the newly founded Hwa Nan. Amity has been an angel for Hwa Nan ever since then. They sent Native English teachers, from one to three at a time almost every year, to voluntarily teach at Hwa Nan.

Amity makes Christian involvement and participation in meeting the social needs and is devoted to China's social development, social service and openness to the outside world.

As a connected Chinese organization of the Baptist Foreign Mission Board, Amity sent Sue to teach at the Southeast University in Nanjing at the beginning. In 1993, Sue was assigned to Fujian and started her serendipity with Fujian Hwa Nan Women's College.

It was the sixth year since Sue had been in China when she came into my college life. She was 73. Though she had passed her seventy, she didn't look like an old lady. Our impression on her in class was always energetic, gentle and mild. Out of the class, she seemed like our grandma, always concerning with our life, our study and our vexation.

Unforgettable Love

Sue is a teacher full of love. She cared about every one of her students. On her first class of each semester, she always took photos for each student, and marked the names, numbers, birthdays of the students beside their pictures developed and posted in a notebook.

春色
任天涯
——福建华南女子
职业学院外教侧记
International Faculty with
Fujian Hua Nan Women's
College since 1908

206

Went picnic with students

When there was a student's birthday, Sue always asked all the students to sing "Happy Birthday" to her in class. She always prepared birthday card for the student. Every time when Sue came back from home visiting in America during the holiday, she brought a lot of small presents to distribute to students at the beginning of the semester. In her spare time, Sue often purchased many cooking materials and took students to their kitchen to teach them how to make western food like cookies and cakes, and she often took students to Chinese restaurants and western fast food restaurants like McDonald and KFC. She always paid for the students.

Sue was really concerned with students and thought a lot of them. When any of them fell into trouble or was absent from classes, she would ask the others to write to encourage her and con-sole her. When someone got sick, she would have a warm greeting for her when she came back to school.（*Lin Lihua*，*1995*）

Creative Teaching

Sue's class was always easy and relaxed. One could hardly feel dull in her class. Sometimes Sue got students to do exercises. Sometimes she taught students a song and sang together with them. Sometimes she made students play little games. One special class deeply impressed many of my classmates, we could still remember even until now. In the middle of the class, Sue suddenly announced that we would leave the classroom for about half an hour. The requirement from her was obeyed quietly. Then she carried a tape recorder, pressed the "record" button, walked out of the classroom in the front. We all followed her, went out of the school, down the hill of Yantai Shan, passed by the Liberty bridge, walked along Guanhai Road and Meiwu Road, reached Chanshan Cinema, went through Yantai Shan Park, came into school and finally got back to the classroom. After we sat down in our seats, Sue started to play the recorder. We were required to listen, recall and write down what we have heard, what we could imagine, what we thought and how we felt. When we finished writing, we were then asked to share and communicate orally with each other. Sue's teaching perfectly integrated into the real life, which made all of the students learn a lot with great interest.

Sue's free conversation classes were always flexible and closely related to students' real life. In order to create a good language environment, to make students practice using English in life experience, Sue put her class everywhere, sometimes in the kitchen of Foreign Affairs Office, in her living room or in the video room; sometimes in the market or in the park; sometimes in the church or in MacDonald. In her class, students often acquired English and used English unconsciously. With Sue's influence, speaking English became such a natural thing for her students. Speaking English out loud was no longer a problem for even the shyest students after so many life practice. Out of question, Sue's language training was proved to be very successful.

Free conversation

In teaching writing, Sue focused on teaching creative writing. Usually she would give students a topic, inspire them, and elicit their ideas by using the method of brain storming. Students would then be required to discuss and share ideas. Normally Sue would stop the discussion when it became lively. She would then ask students to calm down to think and start writing. By using this method, Sue not only stimulated students' fervor of thinking and discussing, but also encouraged students to learn from each other, and to make progress together. In her writing class, we were assigned to write poems, songs, stories and dreams. Owing to Sue's patient instruction and advising, my first English auto biography, which recorded my life before I was 23, finished successfully in her class.

One good example for song revising is the Christmas song "Twelve Days of

208

春色
任天涯
——福建华南女子
职业学院外教侧记
International Faculty with
Fujian Hua Nan Women's
College since 1908

Christmas". Sue asked students to revise it according to Chinese traditions and characteristics. Here shows the different versions:

1. A partridge in a pear tree ------------------------ long life noodles
2. Two turtle doves ------------------------------------ chopsticks
3. Three French hens ---------------------------------- red banners
4. Four calling (colly or collie) birds ---------------- dragon boat
5. Five golden rings ----------------------------------- bicycles
6. Six geese a'laying ---------------------------------- fluttering kites
7. Seven swans a'swimming ------------------------- beautiful Chinese jackets
8. Eight maids a'milking ----------------------------- silk scarves
9. Nine ladies dancing -------------------------------- babies laughing
10. Ten lords a'leaping -------------------------------- juicy jiaozi
11. Eleven pipers piping ------------------------------ smooth pearls
12. Twelve drummers drumming -------------------- -bowls of rice

Letter writing is another teaching tip that Sue used a lot. She found every reason for students to write a letter. For Christmas, writing to Santa Clause; for beginning of semester, writing to the freshmen; for New Year, writing to their parents or friends. Sue asked all her family members to be the pen pals of her students. The letters posted in her biography includes those written to her son, her daughter-in-law and her grandchildren.

"In our International Business English class, we were asked to design different packages for different kinds of products or draw a logo for our future company. She also asked us to make advertisements, and draw posters for our sales promotions. Then she would give a special exhibition in our classroom. We really learned much from her classes and improved our practical skills. "（Lin Lihua，1995）

In Sue's opinion, practice listening to English with different accents is especially important for learning good English. Therefore, Sue always tried her best to create opportunities for the students good to listen to and speak with foreign people coming from different places. She often invited her foreign colleagues, foreign friends she got to know in Fuzhou and those who came to Fuzhou and visited her to walk into the classroom and share all kinds of information with her students. When her grandson and his friend came to visit her in 2001, she asked them to speak to students in English classes about the life of young people in the USA.

Loves for All

Sue is so affable and kind that she saw everyone as her family member. Whenever there is a need, she would try her best to provide selfless help. Those who have received her generous help and assistance are countless. She visited students in the School for the blind and paid full tuition of 4500 RMB for three children almost every year when she was in Fuzhou. She went to see the orphans in the neighborhood and brought gifts and happiness to those children. In order to support people, Sue used up her stipend almost every month so that she had to withdraw money from her previous savings for living.

Many students who had graduated invited Sue to attend their weddings, which Sue never refused. Besides, she even helped students by acting as the priest to host western style weddings for them.

Attending wedding in 1999

Plenty of former students kept in touch with Sue. Many of them became Sue's forever friends. May is one perfect example. She even flied to America to visit Sue in recent years. Hereby I attached her article written for Sue:

Martha Sue Todd—Who taught me more than English

Martha Sue Todd——a name I will never forget. She was my teacher of third year when I studied in Fujian Hwa Nan Women's college. But in my heart she is more than a teacher. After graduation, we still kept in touch until now. In other words, we have had more than 20 years' friendship.

Until now I can still recall her classes which are distingushed from others'. Apart from normal class teaching, sometimes she taught us in the park; at McDonald's(She paid for every one of us); at the teacher's kitchen (cooking class)etc. I always felt that her classes were very interesting and (her tone and her pronunciation) were easy for us to grasp daily English. I remember once I went to her apartment in Teacher's Education College, there I met another teacher from the USA, she asked me why I had American Southern accent. She answered for me, " Because her English teacher is from Southern USA." Later, she told me she was so proud of me.

After my graduation, though she was transferred to other college, we still met once a week. We talked a lot, listened to each other.

She often came to my home to visit my family and had dinner with us. She had good relationship with my family.

春色
任天涯
——福建华南女子
职业学院外教侧记
International Faculty with
Fujian Hua Nan Women's
College since 1908

210

After she went back to USA, she had visited China once again in 2004. She told me she was old and wanted me to visit her when possible. So I went to see her in Feb 2009. We had good time.

I have a daughter, her name is Esther. Sue named her Esther after her grandma's name. She told me it means the shinning star. As a mother, I always wonder how to teach my daughter well, so we talked about this problem over e-mails. Sue gave me some advice. Here is one of her e-mails:

Sue & May

Taken on June 2, 2001 (several days) before she left China. My grandparents, my parents , my sister, my bother-in-law, my niece, Sue，Matthew (Sue's grandson), Mary(Matthew's classmate) and me.

Dear May,

The way to help Esther is to act the way you want her to behave. Small children learn poor ways to act from adults. You speak softly to her and she will do the same. I am sure you do that already. Use good manners and she will do like she sees her Mom and Dad doing.Her poor habits could be coming from being in the day care with other children who act in an unacceptable way. You set the example you want her to follow and she will develop good manners.

Teach her when you say "No" that you mean NO. Small children always have to learn what is acceptable and what is not. They have not lived long enough to know so the adults have to teach them by living the way parents approve.

I know you love her as does your Mom but the two of you can help her and I feel you will. Be firm and kind. You can do that.

I hope these suggestions will help you to be in control.

Love to you and all your family,

Grandma Sue

May and Sue in a restaurant . May and other friends in Sue's home in Creek, North Carolina in 2009

This year she will have her 96th birthday. I wish her have more and I am arranging my trip to visit her again.

I only have one sentence to describe her, that is: She taught me more than English.

—by May, Zheng Meifang in Fuzhou

Teaching & Inspiring

Just as Zheng Meifang said above, Sue is not just a patient English teacher. She is more like a life mentor guiding directions for the students. She not only taught students English, but also inspired them to study, live and work positively and healthily with her behaviors and words. Many words she mentioned are so instructive that they are influencing people even until now.

Whenever Sue met someone who was quitting because of difficulties, she always said, "There is no 'impossible' for everything, only if you are not willing to try."

Mr. Zheng, who got to know Sue on a bus when offering his seat to her, was invited by Sue to share Chinese immigrants' working experience in New York with her students in the class. His life changed after knowing Sue and one of her excellent students, who is now his three cute boys' dear mother. Mr. Zheng recalled, "Sue made me feel, or I should say she made me learn the importance of family, the contribution to the society and know that learning is for living better, etc. I did learn a lot from her. I might do the same as her. When I retire in the future, I would also teach."

春色
任天涯
——福建华南女子
职业学院外教侧记
International Faculty with
Fujian Hua Nan Women's
College since 1908

212

"I appreciate what she said about being happy by making someone else happy." A line quoted from June's article in 21st century in 1995. Sue often helped other people. But she did not do it only by herself. She would take students with her and let them experience the joy of helping people. For example, she encouraged students to donate to Hope Project; she recommended students to voluntarily teach English in nearby primary school where there is no English teacher; she took students to see orphans together. When she found her students start helping people themselves, she always felt so happy and proud.

Trip with students

"Though one may be old in years, one should keep young inside all the time". Sue showed us with her actual deeds that being old shall not be the reason for the cease of fighting and pursuing for one's dreams. Only when one always keeps young in mind and keeps working till the end of our lives, can our life value be extended endlessly.

Sue has once been interviewed by Lin Haichun, on the topic of "By the Age of Thirty", her speech were enlightening:

By the Age of Thirty

By the age of thirty, most of people have completed their education. They are ready to begin their life work. They have set goals for themselves. Those goals could change as years come and go, and they are pretty well established in their jobs.

By the age of thirty, most people have developed independence from their parents, and are pretty much self-supporting, operating by themselves, achieving the personal goals they have set for themselves and pursing their chosen work.

So, by the age of thirty, I believe most people begin to realize their responsibility more and begin to serve in organizations and also can serve into his country. Some of them in leadership position, in government by this time on local level, state level, whatever.

Also, by the age of thirty, many people have the responsibility to take

care of their parents, because they have become older, and unable to take
care of themselves physically, emotionally or maybe financially.

By the age of thirty, I believe many people begin to think of their
future more by setting aside some of their earnings for future goals and
future needs. People have established their own families by the age of
thirty, but not everybody. They begin to think of educating their child or
their children as the case may be.

I think the age of thirty is the wonderful milestone in a person's life,
because you have completed much by that time, and you have many years
ahead of you to serve and achieve your goals.

So, if you can't be twenty-nine and can't be thirty -one, then, the age
of thirty is the best age to be!

—From Lin Haichun,Accompany with Microphone

Closing

After 13 years' service in China teaching English in universities and colleges, Sue was then in her eighties and was no longer allowed to continue working. She had no choice but to say goodbye to her so-called "second home country" in June 2001. After that she managed to come back once to visit Hwa Nan in 2004, enjoying so much in meeting her loved friends and students. After that, Sue went back to America and has been staying with her family since then.

Here quotes Sue's words from the epilogue of her biography "Never Too Old To Climb Walls", which published in 2007:

Visiting Hwa Nan again in 2004, Sue and Shirley

春色
任天涯
——福建华南女子
职业学院外教侧记
International Faculty with
Fujian Hua Nan Women's
College since 1908

214

My childhood dream of serving God in China had finally become a completed reality. One regret—it was not longer.I still miss the bicycle bells, loud voices on the streets, vigorous singing in the churches, noisy children during break time at schools, horns blowing as buses roared through crowded streets dodging pedestrians and cyclists, and early morning loud and mournful music when a Buddhist neighbor had passed away. Most of all, I miss the visits of inquiring students…

Sue wanted to stay longer and contribute more to China. She missed China a lot.

As an ending, I would like to share with you one word that Sue emphasized to us in the class. "A woman's life is not considered as complete until she experiences marriage, giving birth and growing children." As I see it, Sue has a complete life not just because she had married, had a good career and a warm perfect family, what is more important, that she managed to pursue and realize her childhood dream at the age of 68, after she had presumed her family responsibilities well enough. Therefore, I would love to comment that Sue's life is not only complete but also wonderful and brilliant. As an optimistic, positive, kind, considerate, modest woman with strong will, Sue is a good model for all women. Martha Sue Todd, the more I dig into her stories, the more I admire her. May God bless her and wish her safe & sound in her first homeland America.

VI
Only Love Will Never Fail
—Memories of Mentor with Mixed Feelings

Impression on Lisa: A teacher with students all over the world

Lisa is an American who grew up in New Zealand. She is the eldest sister of a family with three daughters. From September 1994 to June 1995, she taught three English courses to the students majoring in the Applied English of Class A, Grade 1994，Fujian Hwa Nan Women's the College. Now, all the 28 students of the Class A recall Lisa with all sorts of feelings.

Lisa Ravenhill, the third one from the right in the front row, with Class A, Grade 1994

Huang Sheng, who works at the Taikoo (Xiamen) Aircraft Engineering Company Limited passionately pours out how she misses Lisa:

The year 2015 has passed and I miss Lisa more than ever before. Last year, jumpsuits were quite popular of China and the first jumpsuit-wearer I encountered was Lisa, my fair foreign teacher of Fujian Hwa Nan Women's College. I believe that Lisa's figure would also cross the mind of my classmates whenever they see jumpsuits.

As I said, Lisa was my first foreign teacher in Fujian Hwa Nan Women's College and her impact on me is undoubtedly the greatest.

At the first sight, I was amazed at her youth, blonde hair and blue eyes, and I wondered why such a pretty young lady was willing to spend her best years in China. She amazed me time after time over the next days. Then my amazement transformed into admiration, for I saw her wisdom, her gentleness...She never shouted at us or pounded the desk with outrage, but she was the strictest teacher I ever met in my life. In the first lesson, she spoke to us frankly that she didn't want to see Chinese-English dictionaries in her class. If she saw us look words up in dictionary in her class, she would throw it out of the window. Then, gingerly, I started a journey of learning with the most earnest attitude in my life in Fujian Hwa Nan Women's College...It was the most fruitful journey of learning.

Lisa's courses only lasted for a year, but during our three-year study in the College she cared about us all the time and her door was always open to us. Until now, though time and space separate us, I believe she

春色
任天涯
——福建华南女子
职业学院外教侧记
International Faculty with
Fujian Hua Nan Women's
College since 1908

still cares for us just as she did in the past. And Lisa has always been our prettiest teacher, friend and sister!

Shen Chaochen，who has already got two children, gives her own descriptions of Lisa:

Lisa Ravenhill, who was my first foreign teacher, had left me a very deep impression. She was so elegant with long blonde hair and blue eyes, just like a character of Hollywood movie. Unlike the other Americans I saw, she was completely a lady. You would never see her be mad or laugh out loud. She not only taught us knowledge but also cared about students.

I can still remember that I felt sick once and I couldn't concentrate on study. Lisa asked me carefully about it and gave me suggestions. I was really grateful about that. Her classes were attractive, especially free conversations. She taught us how to make cookies and asked us to share with each other. We also made Easter eggs and gave blessings to our roommates. We had so much fun during her classes. Those beautiful memories were really treasures of my life!

Cheng Xiaoxia, the principal of Fuzhou New Step English Training School and manager of Fuzhou Orlando Trading Co., Ltd., recalls:

Talking about Lisa, I cannot help thinking of words like beautiful, dedicated, professional, considerate...

I put beautiful in the first place, because it is my first impression on her. It was a sunny day, a fair-skinned lady in a blue-green dress wearing a pair of white casual flat shoes, with her blond hair left loose, walked into the classroom gracefully with light steps. And her blue eyes seemed to be clearer. She looked so different from Chinese teachers! All my senses were engaged immediately — that there should be such a beautiful foreign woman teacher in the world! Needless to say, I was all ears in her class.

Lisa not only looked nice, but delivered excellent lessons. Attending her class was a unique enjoyment. With her fair-sounding voice, our minds would stroll in the ocean of English, having a taste of exotic customs. She used to encourage us that where there is a will, there is a way. "As long as you work hard, you will be able to get good grades!" Moreover, she often reminded us of self-discipline. On her classes, what she taught us was not only English communication skills, but also all sorts of basic etiquette, such as meeting and greeting, table manners, conversation niceties and business etiquette. Her vivid words would enlighten me all of a sudden. I have benefited a lot from the basic common sense which has helped me to communicate freely with foreigners throughout my future work and life.

Wang Xiaoyan, an English teacher in Fuzhou Gezhi Middle School, shares her feeling:

> *Ms. Lisa Ravenhill was the first foreign teacher in my life who taught me listening and speaking; reading and writing in Grade One, and she was also one of the most important foreign teachers who opened the door of a new world for me. In my mind, she is a very responsible and kind teacher whose lectures were very colorful and interesting. Although I have graduated for more than 20 years, I can still remember many of them; still remember the happiness she brought to me. It is really a good memory.*
>
> *Here my heartfelt gratitude goes to Ms. Lisa Ravenhill who is just like my respected supervisor and elder sister keeping on encouraging me and guiding me. I will love her and remember her forever.*

Lin Jiao who married an American says that:

> *Of all the college teachers I have, Lisa is definitely my favorite. Of all the blessings I have been receiving, Lisa's blessing has been the most meaningful one in my life. She is the most influential teacher I have ever had. She is a teacher who not only passes knowledge to her students with her best teaching expertise, but also inspires her students to think deeper about life and to search zealously for truth. She models what she teaches and she plants the seed of pursuing a holy and purposeful life in my heart. I believe I am who I am today largely because of what I have learned from her.*
>
> *Above all, she is a teacher who has transformed my mind and led me into a life direction that I would have never known. Her love for teaching and her guidance to me and other classmates has impacted us in a way she could never imagine. My deepest gratitude goes to this remarkable lady— Lisa Ravenhill. Every time, I think of her, one of my favorite English songs that Lisa introduced to us, The Rose, appears in my mind. She is indeed a beautiful rose in my heart.*

春色
任天涯
——福建华南女子
职业学院外教侧记
International Faculty with
Fujian Hua Nan Women's
College since 1908

Zheng Yan, who once worked for Nestle (China), Import Group (formerly Xiamen International Airport Group Company), has traveled to Southeast Asia in recent years, committing herself to the cross-border cooperation of independent travel routes to Cambodia, Taiwan, etc. She tells the secret she has hidden for over 20 years:

I remember that in the first year of college, I was a playful girl and often absent from class. Lisa was very unhappy. She came to talk with me very seriously. At the beginning, I turned a deaf ear to her words, but gradually I listened to her. Strangely, at that time, I trusted her and confided all my past experience to her. She understood, but eventually gave me a criticism with some advice on life. She said, 'we cannot change our personality, but we can change the way of doing things.' Her golden words have exerted a lasting impact on me.

I still remember one Christmas; we pasted the words "Merry Christmas" vertically on the door of the classroom. Lisa came and for a while she couldn't understand what it meant. Until then, I did not know that the English alphabet couldn't be written vertically.

Honestly, I really miss her. Once, I saw a lady who looked like Lisa at the Bangkok Airport, and nearly rushed over to her. However, after a closer look, I found it was not her after all.

Time flies, and the memories are still vivid in her mind. Ji Yumei, Sales Manager of Xiamen Winfree Import & Export Trading Co., Ltd.，who has been successful in her career, expresses her gratitude to Lisa:

Lisa Ravenhill was the first foreign teacher in my life, a beautiful young woman coming from the other side of the ocean. She came to us with the love of God, asking for no rewards and fearing no hardships.

I do not know whether we were the first or second class she taught, but she was one of the teachers that I won't forget all my life. I have graduated from college for almost 20 years and been engaged in my romance, my marriage, my baby and my career in recent years. However, when recalling my three years in Fujian Hwa Nan Women's College at my leisure, the figure of Lisa always comes readily into my mind. She taught us Listening, Speaking, Reading and Writing and gave us many lessons every week. In my reminiscence, she was always smiling and most often more of a sister than a teacher to us.

As a country girl, I used to speak a Southern Fujian dialect before I went to Fuzhou for college. My Mandarin pronunciation was not standard at all, let alone the English I learned from secondary school. I could read and write, but I seldom opened my mouth to speak a sentence in English. It should be no wonder that my English pronunciation was also quite poor. I remember that Lisa used to correct my pronunciation over and over again with great patience in class. She would not walk away to the next student with smiles until she heard the right pronunciation. It was because of her encouragement and influence that I dared to speak English and got interested in it. Since my graduation, I have been engaged in foreign trade which often involves communications with foreigners. I know my English still has a Southern Fujian accent, but despite that, I can rely on it to get a very good job. After years of hard work, I have my own career and have achieved the so-called financial freedom in good time. Therefore, I feel grateful to her forever.

In the blink of an eye, eight years have passed since I last met Lisa at the anniversary celebration of my college. Nonetheless, I know she is still teaching in Kunming, China, keeping on sowing the seed of love. I cannot help cheering up every time I think that more Chinese students will experience her great love. I believe that Lisa is simply an angel that God sent to the earth to spread love, the great love in her heart that she is always willing to give. Many of the things she taught us was knowledge that can't be obtained from books. It was really lucky for me to have such a foreign teacher.

I haven't done any writing for nearly two decades. But now I have this opportunity to express how I feel about Lisa. Unfortunately, I am not a good writer with fancy words to express my true feelings in my mind. To put it in a nutshell, I am grateful to her all my life!

Lin Ying, the then class branch secretary of the League, has this picture present before her:

Time is a huge tree growing with winding and twisting branches, while life is the bird flying in and out. On an ordinary Saturday I went, as I usually did, to the studio at the foot of Yantai Hill to pick up my daughter who was there learning the art of painting. When my car passed the gate of the College standing tall on the hilltop, I tirelessly pointed it out to her, and talked endlessly about my college years. The person I talked the most about was my dearest Lisa. My first memory was answering a question in

春色
任天涯
——福建华南女子
职业学院外教侧记
International Faculty with
Fujian Hua Nan Women's
College since 1908

220

one of her classes. She wanted to see if we had remembered her full name. I blurted it out and got praises from her. I had never had this experience in my prestigious middle school where the students were all excellent. Now I found that I could gain such recognition from teachers. My first handwork was in a free conversation class in which Lisa taught us how to make animal-shaped cookies step by step. It made me feel that language learning was not about memorizing words or grammar, but building a bridge of communication between people. As for my first participation in the English speech contest, she revised my draft again and again and gave me a lot of encouragement. She believed that to appeal to the audience, speeches should be delivered sincerely with the simplest and most natural feelings rather than exaggerated tones and facial expressions. On my first visit to her warm and perfumed room, she wanted me to see her as a good friend (now it is called bosom girlfriend) instead of a teacher. We sat down and talked about the boy next door that I had adored for a long time. I haven't confided this secret to anyone before, not even my parents and sisters. She encouraged me to pursue my own dreams, even if the success could not be guaranteed. After failing the college entrance examination, I got lost on the path of life. But finally, a light broke in upon me and I opened my heart to let her in. It was her love that lighted up my way forward and made my steps assertive. I talked about these bygones with my daughter who regarded them as stories. She asked me curiously, "Is Lisa pretty?" And I said, "Sure. She is the most beautiful woman I have ever met in the world. Despite the vicissitudes of time, she will always live in my heart.

Dear Madam, I want to proudly tell you that I have never forgotten your lesson of love after my graduation. I work hard and I'm good. God bless you! Though far apart, we will meet again someday..."

★Konstantin Ushinsky, the father of Russian pedagogy once said: "The power of character is an irreplaceable wealth. The impact of a teacher's character on his/her students is an educational power that cannot be replaced by any textbooks, moral maxims or punishment and reward systems."

Devote Herself without Asking Anything in Return

Approach Lisa: Time wrinkles her skin as she dedicates herself to the course of education

At that time, Ms. Yang Fang who taught College English, was our head teacher. She

Yang Fang (a TCSL teacher in China Lingua School of Singapore)

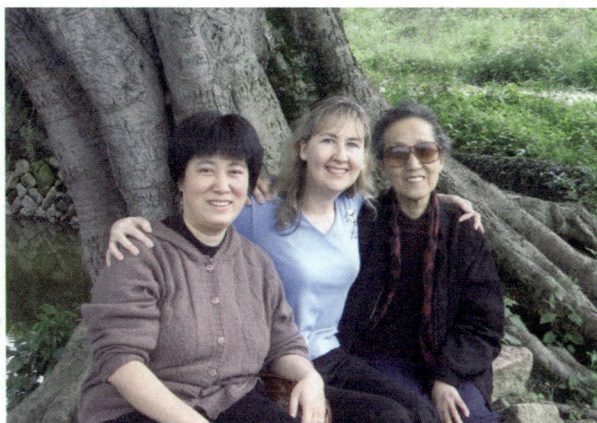

From left to right: Dong Xiuping (a teacher who worked for the Foreign Affairs Office of Hwa Nan for nearly two decades), Lisa Ravenhill, and Xu Daofeng (the former director of the FAO)

has been working in Singapore since 1998. This is her description of Lisa.

"I remember Lisa, the very elegant lady with a fair-sounding voice. She was always smiling and very patient with her students when they needed her explanations."

Dong Xiuping, who has worked at the Foreign Affairs Office for over 20 years, shares her memories with us:

> *When it comes to Lisa, we will think of her elegance, her serious teaching attitude, her concern about students, and the harmonious relation between her and her students. Before she decided to work in Fujian Hwa Nan Women's College, she went to Taiwan to learn Chinese for a year at her own expense in order to better understand her students and communicate with them later.*

He Xiaozhi, the former director of the Applied English Department, speaks highly of Lisa:

> *In my impression, Lisa had a clear plan for the teaching contents. Take the English Free Conversation as an example. She would begin with a simple start, such as an introduction to your family, introduction to your friend, introduction to your teacher, then gradually add something more complicated. She followed the simple-to-complex model in arranging her teaching content into a plan.*

In addition, she adopted a student-centered pedagogy, making use of the cooperation-

春色
任天涯
——福建华南女子
职业学院外教侧记
International Faculty with
Fujian Hua Nan Women's
College since 1908

mode teaching. One kind of cooperation is between the teacher and students. Although it is based on students, the teacher plays a significant role. Another kind of cooperation is between students. In a student-to-student cooperation, the one who has learned faster and better will help the other one so they can encourage and inspire each other. This went well, especially in the beginning. For those freshmen who had not got accustomed to college life, the methods she used were very good for motivating the students instead of terrifying them.

For teaching practices, Lisa always focused on motivating students as a teacher. This doesn't mean she motivated herself and talked a lot, but found ways to motivate students to learn as a teacher. This was a very good way for the students to be generally active in class and feel happy in learning. Sometimes, if the student couldn't answer the question, Lisa would not hold on to the question but turn to something else. This is the part that teachers should play. When the teacher's focus is shifted to something else, the terrified and nervous student is able to calm himself/herself down.

Lisa was very strict with her students. She would give her students the topic to discuss in advance and ask them to prepare, like searching for information and reading relevant books. She would require them to think independently and make their own preparation for the topic. In this way, the students could be prepared in advance and be active in class, leaving people a deep impression. Moreover, Lisa was good at creating a relaxed class atmosphere, which helped her students overcome their nervousness. When the students were stuck in speaking, she would gradually intervene, as if she knew what they really wanted to talk about. Then, she would continue the topic and guide the students to think. Thanks to her patient guidance, the students were happy to talk and laugh in her class. Lisa's classes were also full of encouraging sentences and various activities. Take the free conversation course for example, Lisa would sometimes take the students to the river park, sitting there and talking naturally about whatever they saw in the park. After a semester, the students who attended her classes would really improve their English, and after graduation, three years later they could speak English fluently.

Dr. Betts Rivet, who has worked with Lisa for several years, recalls:

I have known Lisa Ravenhill since 1992 when she became a foreign teacher with me. There were 14 foreign teachers at that time. We were completely volunteers and that continued for 4 years. We never received any pay from the college and we paid our own travel expenses. Lisa is definitely a people person. She was instrumental in planning events for the foreign teachers such as birthdays, Christmas, Valentines Day and Easter parties. Leadership skills were a natural part of her everyday life. Her positive demeanor, her articulate speech, the kind, caring expression in her face attracted people to her.

I am not familiar with "inside the classroom Lisa". However, at that time the foreign teachers only had typewriters to use to prepare lessons, exams, and handouts for our students. So we all had to share time on the two typewriters that were available. Our teacher's library was the source of much of the material that we used in the classroom. Lisa was very diligent in her preparation for her classes. It was not easy in those days because it was completely up to the foreign teachers to decide what to use for teaching. In her case English as a Second Language. Since there was no specific guidance, I remember her sharing some of her lesson plans and organizing the material she used for her next year classes. In 1992 there were only about 650 students enrolled in Hwa Nan so our classes were small.

Perhaps by contacting students who had her as a teacher, you would find out her manner of teaching, how she organized the classroom, her student/teacher relationship. Was she innovative, check out her evaluation, go into the archives and look at her grade books, but the best would be student comments. I know it was long ago but I still keep in touch with some of my students who graduated in 1994 and 5. I can take a guess and say that Lisa was an excellent teacher…a model teacher…a teacher that created a positive learning environment in the classroom…who was always well prepared… and showed her love of teaching.

Come to think of it, I remember Lisa did some things with her

From the left to the right: Lisa Ravenhill, Betts Rivet, Michelle Long and Mary Logsdon

春色
任天涯
——福建华南女子
职业学院外教侧记
International Faculty with
Fujian Hua Nan Women's
College since 1908

224

students. I am remembering she would go shopping with them, maybe went to parks to fly kites, watch the Dragon Boats, etc. Well, if you talk to her students you will find out.

Mentor and Friend, as Good as Wine

The freshman days with Lisa were full of easiness, joy, and fun...

In addition to class time, Lisa allowed us to come to her any time after class. So, we would dine together, play together and share with each other...

As an outgoing person, Ji Yumei depicts her memories of Lisa first:

Sometimes, Lisa would play a trick. On April Fool's Day of my freshman year, she suddenly visited our dormitory along with several foreign teachers. They brought a lot of toilet paper and hung the paper all over the place. It wasn't until then that I knew foreigners were allowed to be mischievous on this day! She was a big sister who would play with her students. I remember the day that we invited her and the other teachers to go to the river park with us, and the precious photo we took together. She was also with us when the whole class went to Eighteen Streams Scenic Resort, and to McDonald's... Today, these photographs are all my precious memories.

On Lisa's birthday, the whole class went to the McDonald's in Taijiang District for a celebration.

Lisa at the Eighteen Streams Scenic Resort

At the River Park

Lisa with her students at the McDonald's

Celebrating Lisa's birthday at the McDonald's

Celebrating Lisa's birthday at
the McDonald's

Lisa (left) and Michelle (right)

Lisa with Lin Xiao

This is our beloved Lisa. She sows the seeds of spring, dreams and strengthens with the noblest emotion of human-love. She is like a gardener who sows with languages, plows with crayons, waters with sweat and takes care of her students with heart and soul!

Next, let's go to Lisa's class to enjoy the wonderful course, appreciate her art of teaching and experience her personal charisma!

★Georg Wilhelm Friedrich Hegel, the famous philosopher once said, "In the eyes of students, their teacher is the best idol". Teachers are the moral example admired and mimicked by students. Knowledgeable people become teachers while integrity makes them examples.

Teaching with Soul, Getting Better and Better

More about Lisa: Fallen flowers that decay but nurture the new buds are not heartless at all

In September 1994, as a freshman, we were delighted to have foreign teachers. At that time, Lisa taught us three courses, namely, English Listening and Speaking, English Reading and Writing, and English Free Conversation. Each course had its own characteristics. Thus, we were very fond of her class. Let's take English Reading and Writing and English Free Conversation for example.

English Reading and Writing: Feeling the pulse of life and setting sail to the future

In my impression, the College English class at that time was focused on reading like this: Teacher introducing relevant cultural background → Students' answering the set questions after a timed reading → Teachers' explanation on difficult points; while the writing mode goes as follows: Explanation of writing requirements → Introduction to writing skills → Time for students' writing → Presentation of composition→ Teacher's comments.

Lisa's reading and writing classes, however, were different from the traditional teaching mode. She emphasized a teaching method focusing on students' own interpretation of the written materials. She believed this approach was conducive to improving the students' English competence, so that the students no longer needed to worry about an absolute or singular way to comprehend the written material, which helped to arouse their interest in reading and writing in English, as well as cultivate their ability to appreciate English articles and to write in English.

Lisa adopted flexible teaching methods in her English reading class. She suggested following several principles in the reading process:

(1) Read fully

When teaching reading, Lisa suggested that we should enter into the article itself, indulging ourselves in the author's language to experience the beauty of the article itself.

(2) Read the content rather than the language

It is important to learn the usage of language during reading, but the ultimate goal of reading is to grasp the meaning and significance of the article. If you read an article but cannot grasp its meaning, it is useless no matter how much reading you have done. At the time, Lisa encouraged us to re-read an article so as to grasp its meaning.

(3) Guess and Prediction

Lisa used to say that in reading, the meaning of a word is determined by its context. Paying attention to the context is a very good reading strategy which will help us to make reasonable guesses that are both grammatically correct and meaningful with our language sense.

In addition to the above suggestions, Lisa would look for some topics related to the selected articles for the reading task, and raise various questions for us to answer. Those imaginative and challenging tasks would make us excited and the whole class full of heated discussions.

Her pedagogy was not only flexible, but kept up with the times. She adopted the latest teaching methods of the time suitable for students at a certain level—fluency being first. This approach focuses on the fluency in reading, writing and speaking, putting fluency in reading first in teaching and emphasizing fluency more than accuracy in speaking and writing training. The theoretical basis is as follows:

The input hypothesis developed by Stephen Krashen stresses the importance and significance of language input as well as the intrinsic link between language input and language learning from the perspective of language acquisition. He believes that the language input is a necessary prerequisite for language acquisition. The input is of primary importance. Understanding a large amount of comprehensive input is seen as the only mechanism that results in language acquisition. Krashen also summarizes the requirements for optimal input:

(1) Comprehensibility

To comprehend the input of language materials is a requirement for language acquisition. "Comprehensibility" refers to the understanding of meaning rather than the understanding of form. The language input should be slightly more advanced than the current level of the learner.

(2) Interesting and relevant

Meaning must be processed to make the language input more conducive to language acquisition. The more interesting and more relevant the language materials are, the easier it is for the learner to acquire a language unconsciously.

(3) Not grammatically sequenced

Krashen believes that it is important to have enough comprehensible input regarding language acquisition. Learners do not need to acquire a language in strict accordance with grammatical sequence, because language acquisition is a natural process in a natural environment where learners are exposed to a lot of comprehensible input.

春色
任天涯
——福建华南女子
职业学院外教侧记
International Faculty with
Fujian Hua Nan Women's
College since 1908

228

(4) Enough input

The quantity of language input is the material premise and basis of language acquisition. There is no language acquisition without a lot of language input. In this process, learners will naturally absorb a lot of useful language materials and linguistic knowledge.

This idea was fully embodied in Lisa's reading and writing classes:

(A) Selecting the most appropriate reading materials according to the level and interest of junior college students

According to the views of Krashen's Input Hypothesis, Lisa took the requirements for optimal language input into consideration when selecting language materials. In order to make the language input more interesting, she first selected a large number of classic novels and some popular books as learning materials instead of textbooks that focused on language knowledge. The novels carefully selected by Lisa were all first-class works such as *Anne of Green Gables, Dead Poets Society, Ben Hur,* and *Back to the Future.*

(B) Attaching equal importance to reading and writing in coursework

Every day we had to finish Lisa's reading assignment independently, and do oral and written exercises on our own. In addition to the reading tasks, Lisa also asked us to do the corresponding writing exercises. One was called the Reading Log which meant to summarize the main events or plots of the segments we read in two to three sentences. Another was to write Double-entry Journals, in which the left entry was for the sentences that we felt interesting, important or incomprehensible in the reading material, while the right entry was for our views and opinions about the excerpted sentences. The right entry usually included the following content: (1) Your own feelings and thoughts; (2) To associate the event in the text with your own life experience; (3) To express your views on the part you have doubts; (4) To give your comments on the features of the characters. As a student, I felt this kind of coursework aroused our interest in reading, built our confidence in expressing our thoughts, and improved our writing skills.

(C) Various classroom activities

Lisa would check the students' reading through a variety of listening and speaking competency-based classroom activities encompassing the reading materials. The main kinds of activities were: (1) Group activities. Students would have group discussions about the key and difficult points of the reading materials to improve their speaking and listening. (2) Dialogue with partner. Two students would play the two roles or choose the topics in an article to discuss. (3) Speed Prediction. Students would be put into small groups and the teacher would raise questions about the reading materials. Then the students needed to find the answer as a group and elect a representative to answer the question. Lisa's class put special emphasis on students' participation with students playing leading roles in most of the classroom activities, such as group activities, personal statements, group discussions and role plays that count on the active involvement of students. Lisa's role in the class was only as a guide.

(D) Learning by free writing

Lisa used to ask us to write two journals a week, expressing our thoughts and feelings freely without paying too much attention to the form of the language. Misspellings and grammatical errors were excused. Lisa told us that in the writing process, we should pay more attention to the fluent expression of thoughts rather than grammar. I think Lisa's training is conducive to the cultivation of students' language competence, especially to the improvement of writing skills.

(E) Applying multimedia technology in reading and writing classes

At that time, Lisa played us the videos of *Anne of Green Gables, Dead Poets Society, Ben-Hur* and *Back to the Future*. The sound and videos enriched the reading of black and white novels, making them more vivid and helping us to understand the language of those novels so as to improve our reading speed and quality.

When dealing with our writing assignments, Lisa's didn't cling to the grammatical errors or make correction, but responded to the content of our writing. She always made informative comments on our weekly journals, having heart to heart exchanges and communications with us. We could write anything we wanted in our journals, and she would communicate with us in a timely manner.

Next, let's appreciate two representative masterpieces selected by Lisa.

The First Selection: *Anne of Green Gables*—Healthy Personality

Lisa selected *Anne of Green Gables*, a 1908 novel by the Canadian woman writer Lucy Maud Montgomery. The story takes place in Avonlea—a fictional community in Canada. In the orphanage of Nova Scotia, there is a girl called Anne Shirley who lost her parents soon after she was born and spent her childhood in strangers' homes and orphanages. At the age of 11, she was mistakenly sent to Matthew and Marilla Cuthbert, a brother and sister who had intended to adopt a boy to help Matthew run their farm named Green Gables. Through a misunderstanding, the orphanage sent Anne Shirley. This little girl was not the favorite type of Marilla. Full of the yearnings for new life, Anne quickly fell in love with Green Gables and its surroundings, but at first, Marilla said the girl must return to the orphanage. This drags Anne from the heaven of joy into the depths of despair. Nevertheless, Anne doesn't lose hope for life. Instead, Anne is happier than ordinary people and she is innocent, passionate with all sorts of wonderful fantasies. As an

春色
任天涯
——福建华南女子
职业学院外教侧记
International Faculty with
Fujian Hua Nan Women's
College since 1908

230

imaginative child, Anne sees the brook, roses, even trees as beautiful lives and regards her shadow and echo as close friends communicating with her in her world. Her imagination is also full of romantic color, for the cherry-tree is her "Snow Queen"; the apple is her "red sweeting"; the avenue is the "White Way of Delight"; "the cheerful brook" laughs under the ice; her reflection in the mirror is a girl who has been enchanted; the echo from the valley is her close friend called Violetta who likes to repeat her words...! What a sweet and innocent child of imagination!

Anne loves fantasy and she is also an optimistic and positive girl. Facing miserable life and experiences, she doesn't grumble at all, always smiling at everything. Marilla once asked Anne: "You have so many miserable experiences, how can you take so much joy in life? " Annie replied seriously: "Life is very much like a mirror: if you smile upon it, it smiles back upon you; but if you frown and look doubtful on it, you will get a similar look in return. Why not live each day happily? It can also make parents feel at ease in heaven."

Anne is characterized by a trait that few people have — gratitude. In order to repay Marilla and Matthew, she sets a lofty goal: to be admitted to Queen's Academy and win the Avery Scholarship. To this end, she studies hard. Her hard work pays off finally. With dreams coming true, Anne has become the pride of Marilla and Matthew. However, Matthew dies after learning shock news and Marilla is filled with sorrow by his death. After graduating from Queen's Academy, Anne gives up her dream of college and teaches at the Avonlea School to take care of Marilla. Just as Anne said: "There was always the bend in the road! 'God's in his heaven, all's right with the world.'"

When talking about Lisa's reading and writing lessons and the novel "*Anne of Green Gables*", the students of Class A, Grade 1994 had various views. Chen Hong, HR and Finance Supervisor, Xiamen Office of Hong Kong Rhodes Architectural Stone Co., Ltd. recalled, "In Lisa's reading class, I really liked the protagonist of the novel, Anne. Her story told me something that we didn't have, which is to keep graceful and smiling at all times."

Zheng Yan said, "After reading this novel, my English vocabulary and reading quality greatly improved. Anne's story touched me a lot and I learned that we should be kind to others, so they will treat us in the same way."

"The novel had a great impact on me. Like Anne, the protagonist of the novel, I am not a good-looking girl but I have an unyielding spirit. I am as active and energetic as a boy. Anne doesn't grow up with a good background, but she is strong-minded and always smiling and working hard and strong. I decided to try my best to overcome my weakness in writing, challenging myself in English writing. When I was writing an English book review, I felt words naturally appearing in my brain and I could write them out without hesitation." Huang Sheng added, "Anne has a strong yearning for knowledge and learning and I have been moved by her positive, enterprising spirit. She sets an example for me."

Anne of Green Gables is really a classic novel moving tens of thousands of kind-hearted souls. Anne has strength and courage, kindness and frankness, optimism and persistence, diligence and efforts. All of these are good qualities. We should learn from her perseverance, innocence, and virtuous soul. Many thanks to Lisa for selecting such a masterpiece which helped us to complete a tremendous amount of reading and writing tasks with joy and ease. What should be appreciated is that Lisa led us to a sea of English in which we could constantly absorb the nutrition of the English language like a sponge, enriching our minds and souls, cultivating our tastes, and improving our personalities.

The Second Selection: Dead Poets Society —Beacon of Life

This was the second masterpiece recommended by Lisa. After watching the video and reading the script, we were overwhelmed by irrepressible excitement. This film exerted an endless impact on the depths of our hearts. We had never met such a special fictional teacher as Mr. Keating.

The setting, Welton Academy, is a traditional school with plenty of elite graduates. For over a hundred years, the school had adhered to four tenets, namely, tradition, honor, discipline and excellence. The arrival of a new teacher changes everything. And it is this new comer that brings novel ideas as refreshing as a spring shower to the students. John Keating, a alumnus of Welton (Hell-ton), who is fond of poetry calls himself captain. Without the traditional rigidity that kills humanity, he discards traditional teaching methods and gives every lesson with humor and boldness which allows his students to have deeper understandings about life and themselves. He encourages his students to think independently, and free from the shackles of tradition. In the first lesson, Keating asked the students to come out of the classroom and listen to the voices of their predecessors in the hallway. He tells them to rip out their poetry books which are full of dead theories. He takes the students outdoors to experience the real "conformity". He asked everyone to stand on their desks and look at life in a different way. Mr. Keating is soon accepted by every student. They like having a teacher who is so different.

Upon learning that Keating was a member of the unsanctioned Dead Poets Society while he was at Welton, the boys restart the club which becomes their spiritual sanctuary. Henry David Thoreau once said, "The Dead Poets was dedicated to sucking the marrow out of life". Poetry, beauty, romance and love are the meaning of our life. The members of the society read poetry and verse in turn, singing and laughing cheerfully, and living their lives on their own terms.

春色
任天涯
——福建华南女子
职业学院外教侧记
International Faculty with
Fujian Hua Nan Women's
College since 1908

232

I went to the woods
because I wanted to live deliberately,
I wanted to live deep
and suck out all the marrow of life,
and put to rout all that was not life,
and not when I had come to die,
discover that I had not lived.

A student called Neil writes this poem on the title page of his poetry collection and he learns to recite it. How happy a man will be to know what he wants to do at a young age. Tears well up in Mr. Keating's eyes as he reads the poem after Neil's suicide. Neil loves acting and tries to break free from his father's control to participate in the play. However, his wonderful performance does not change his father's mind. Knowing that he will be transferring to a military school and has to give up acting, Neil commits suicide. Murmuring "I was good. I was really good," Neil dies at a cold blizzard's night.

We thought that Neil's death might have changed something, but it didn't. Welton adheres to its four tenets as usual. Cameron, a member of Dead Poets Society, gives his friends away. They blame Neil's death on Mr. Keating which results in Keating's dismissal and the disbandment of Dead Poets Society. In the final climax, Mr. Nolan takes over teaching the class and Mr. Keating interrupts the class to collect personal articles. Before he leaves, a timid student Todd, stands on his desk and salutes Keating with the words "O Captain! My Captain!". Over half the rest of the class does the same. Keating thanks the boys and departs with smiles.

This concludes the film. The sound of Scottish bagpipes and drums is so exciting. It would be a great tragedy if the boys failed to stand on the desks. Their gesture touches Keating deeply and moves everyone. We marvelled at the boys' courage. Mr. Keating wins the day. The final standing up is an outbreak of emotion, demonstrating a fearless rebellious spirit.

In an era of constraints, Mr. Keating is a proper weirdo and rebel in most people's eyes. However, in the eyes of his students, he opens a window for them and gives them a different perspective for life. His unique way of teaching allows his students to savor the beauty of literature. This is a teacher who overturns the traditional concept of education and frees his students from the cage of spoon-feeding education. Amidst the gaze of amazed students, he keeps talking about how to live deliberately.

Just like Mr. Keating in the film, Lisa was also a captain guiding the young students with her teaching. She adopted lots of teaching methods that allowed her students to learn a lot, not only to get knowledge, but also pleasure. Teaching and learning is a process of communication. When the process becomes interesting, the result will be quite different. Lisa paid much attention to the development of our personalities, protecting us from outdated teaching theories that undermined our natures. The purpose of education is to help every knowledge-thirsty person to find his/her own value and live a better life. This is the teaching philosophy that Lisa advocated. She lived up to this philosophy in her teaching practice. She influenced us with her charisma, constantly encouraged us to think independently and to look at things in a different way, helped shape us to be better individuals, told us how to make decisions for our life and to "look before you leap", as well as to shoulder responsibilities.

"Two roads diverged in a wood / and I took the one less traveled by / And that has made all the difference." Lisa's teaching was just like a spring shower, quietly exerting a lasting impact on each of her students.

English Free Conversation: Love and Care

English Free Conversation was a course unique to us at that time. The class was divided into four groups with seven students in a group. Each group took a 45-minute lesson in which the students played the leading roles, enjoying full freedom to talk about the topics Lisa gave us. In Lisa's conversation class, there were various wonderful activities which were just her style. She would take us to the McDonald's (just opened in 1994) located on the other side of Jiefang Bridge in Taijiang District of Fuzhou, and we would eat and chat about anything we liked. She would also take us to the kitchen in the Foreign Faculty House and make a variety of pastries there. In one special class, she had us to play the card game of UNO. This was completely new to us. Lisa explained the rules for the game, and told us that all communication had to be done in English.

Lisa told us, UNO is a popular card game originating from Europe and favored by young people all over the world. It is a game that tests the players' concentration and reaction, as well as logical thinking. Then she told us the rules of the game. To begin with, each person draws a card and the one with the largest card value becomes

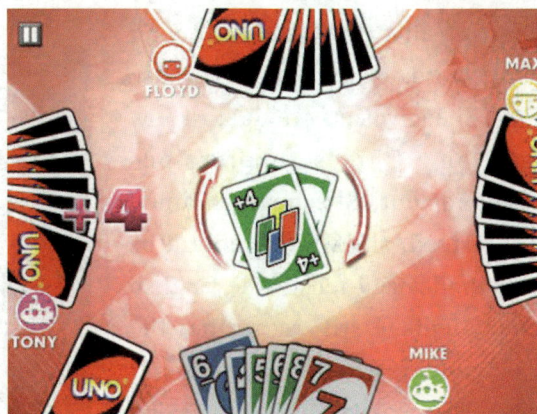

UNO Card

春色
任天涯
——福建华南女子
职业学院外教侧记
International Faculty with
Fujian Hua Nan Women's
College since 1908

the dealer. The dealer deals each player seven cards and places the remaining cards face down in the center of the playing area as the "draw stack", then the top card (it must be a card with number; if not, keep flipping) of the deck is flipped over and set aside to begin the discard pile. The player to the dealer's left plays first, and play proceeds clockwise around the table. On a player's turn, he/she must play a card matching the discard in color, number or symbol or play an Action/Wild card. For instance, if the first player plays a card numbered 3 in red, the next player must do one of the following: (1) play a card numbered 3; (2) play a card in red; (3) play a Skip/Reverse/Draw Two card in red; (4) play a Wild/Wild Draw Four card. If the player doesn't have any card mentioned above, he/she must draw the top card of the deck. Then it is the next player's turn to play card. A player who plays his/her next-to-last card must call "UNO" as a warning to the others. If the player forgets to call "UNO", he/she must draw two cards. The first player to discard all of his/her cards is the winner of the hand. We listened carefully to Lisa as she patiently explained the rules. It really surprised us that we were able to understand Lisa's explanation about the rules of the game effortlessly.

Recalling this, Huang Sheng said: "UNO is an interesting game. I have been playing it with kids until now. I get cheerful and confident as I play UNO for it is the only card game that I can play. When playing UNO in the conversation class, I could relax and reduce my that nervousness. As the game became fiercer, you just couldn't help but open your mouth and speak. In retrospect, this was really a good way of teaching which integrated learning with playing. We gradually overcame our fear and shyness and spoke out in English as much as possible. Step by step, our oral English improved unconsciously. So did our confidence in speaking English."

"Lisa's conversation classes were very interesting. She encouraged us to open our mouth and speak and offered different topics each time for us to talk about freely. Occasionally, we would encounter some words or expressions whose English equivalents we didn't know and some Chinese expressions 'slipped' out. She never blamed us. Instead, she would remind us with smiles and tell us the English equivalents. I still remember the free conversation class at Easter when she cooked a lot of eggs and asked us to draw patterns on them.

Drawing patterns on eggs at Easter

When the drawings were done, we took photos. Every time I see this photo, I feel as if it happened yesterday," Ji Yumei recalls.

When it comes to Lisa's free conversation class, Cheng Xiaoxia has something to say. "Lisa's free conversation class was very appealing to me. Students in the class were divided into groups and went to the kitchen in the Foreign Faculty House. We would make tempting desserts like cakes and biscuits while doing English conversations — this is something I had never experienced before. Haha, the delicious biscuits were my favorite! We would decorate eggs on Easter and make lovely pumpkin pies on Thanksgiving...

However, once in a free conversation class, I was called out alone by Lisa whose blue glowing eyes seemed to be darker in the sunshine. She talked with me very seriously, Xiaoxia, you are a cadre of the student union, the role model for others. Other students will pay attention to your speeches and behaviors. Do you feel it appropriate to communicate with your classmates in Chinese in my class? I don't think so, for other students may follow suit.' With my face suddenly flushing with shame, I apologized to her again and again. Then, a smile of delight immediately came into Lisa's charming eyes. I was very grateful to her for not embarrassing me by criticizing me in front of my classmates. This talk left a deep impression on me and always reminds me that teachers should give consideration to the self-esteem of students and pay attention to their tone."

There is an old Chinese sayings that goes, "He who is true to himself is sincere in his deeds" and "wisdom demonstrates itself by speech". Sukhomlynsky once said, "The school learning is not about putting knowledge from one mind into the other mechanically, but about the ongoing soul communication between teachers and students." Lisa's free conversation class was not only about the exchanges of knowledge between teachers and students, but also the emotional exchanges of the two sides. Lisa treated us with love and care. Everything she did was out of her love for us. In order to achieve a good learning effect, Lisa would give us an encouraging look and smile and have frank talks with us again and again, comforting and warming our hearts. In her class, I always felt it was her cordial and amiable smile that shortened the distance between us. Her vitality, emotion, and passion all affected us a lot. As a result, we could

春色
任天涯
——福建华南女子
职业学院外教侧记
International Faculty with
Fujian Hua Nan Women's
College since 1908

236

enjoy learning English with ease and delight in an atmosphere featured by harmony, warmth, amity, joy, coziness and affection.

Lisa, you are the bridge that connects separate mountains, leading us to the peaks of achievement; you are the ivy, tough and slender, directing us the way to the cliff top where precious herbs grow. Here is a Chinese poem dedicated to you, which goes, "No matter how much toil it may need, it is worthwhile seeing the trees bear fruits. It is easier to grow flowers than to cultivate talents. Without the silent dedication, there is no bloom of art and knowledge in the world. There's nothing in life that makes a talented person happier than having a mentor."

★Confucius once said, "Living with a good company is like entering a room of scented orchids whose fragrance is unrecognizable as time passes for one has become part of it."

Back to the College for the Anniversary Celebration

Lisa came back to Hwa Nan for the 100th anniversary celebration held in 2008.

From left to right: Lisa Ravenhill, Huang Sheng, Ji Yumei, MichelleLong, Xiao Chune

Lisa Ravenhill (the first from the right)

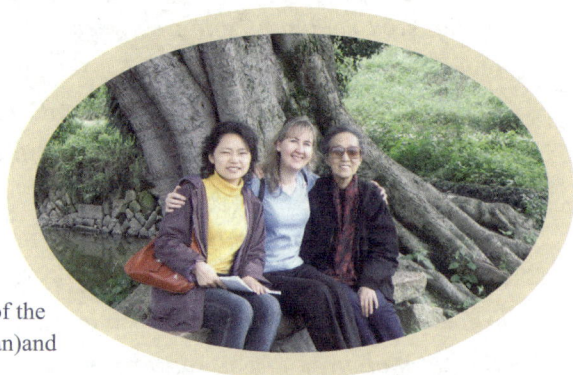

Lisa with Wang Ling (Director of the Personnel Department of Hwa Nan)and Xu Daofeng

Lisa Ravenhill (the fourth from the left of the back row)

Lisa with Zhang Xunjie (the former president in Hwa Nan)

Listen to Mentor's Best Teaching

Dialogue with Lisa: After endless mountains and rivers that leave doubt whether there is a path out, suddenly one encounters the shade of a willow, bright flowers and a lovely village.

Linxiao: Dear Lisa, could you please tell us your own education background and your family?

Lisa: With an English father and an American mother, I have the advantage of knowing both British and American English. My family traveled quite a lot growing up so I got to experience a lot of different cultures and also see that English was truly an international language. I studied Home Science at Otago University in New Zealand, Vocational Home Economics at Texas Woman's University in the United States, and got a Teaching English as a Second Language qualification through the University of the Holy Land, Israel.

Linxiao: How did you know Hwa Nan and why did you come here to teach without any pay? Lisa: I read about Hwa Nan in a professional science journal and realized that my educational background fit in with Hwa Nan's home-economics based program. Since I had already planned on coming to teach in China and was interested in education for women, this college seemed an obvious choice. What I gained in experience, knowledge of a new place and culture, and the chance to befriend Chinese people was far more valuable to me than any amount of money. I believe we are all blessed to be a blessing to others, so I could heartily concur with the original motto of Hwa Nan: "Having received, I ought to give."

Linxiao: Before you came to Hwa Nan for teaching, I found that you went to Taiwan to learn Mandarin for one year. What is your philosophy by doing so?

春色
任天涯
——福建华南女子
职业学院外教侧记
International Faculty with
Fujian Hua Nan Women's
College since 1908

238

Lisa: A friend advised me to take "stepping stones" towards my goal of living in China, and studying Mandarin Chinese in Taiwan for a year was one of those stepping stones. I believe that studying Mandarin gave me a lot more empathy towards language learners in general, as well as giving me some insight into Chinese culture.

Linxiao: From Dr. Betts Rivet, I came to realize that when you taught Hwa Nan students between 1992 and 1996, you were actually a teacher as well as a curriculum planner. You were involved in content selection, methodology, materials selection and adaptation and assessment. You developed a learner-centred curriculum, which is a collaborative effort between you and students, since they were closely involved in the decision-making process regarding the content of the curriculum and how it was taught. Such a curriculum will contain the following elements, namely, planning (including needs analysis, goal and objective setting, learner grouping), implementation (including content selection and gradation, methodology and materials development) and evaluation.

In the three courses you taught us in 1994 and 1995, *Reading and Writing, Listening and Speaking,* and *Free Conversation*, how did you handle these elements? Could you please share some idea with us?

Lisa: Having taught Hwa Nan students since 1992, two years previous to Class A 1994-1995, I felt fairly certain that I understood the English level of the average first year student and what they needed to focus on in order to improve their English. My goal was simply to get the student *to believe that they could learn English* and grow in that confidence. To that end, I used whatever materials I found personally interesting and actually wanted to teach (because no student is going to pay much attention to a boring lesson taught by a bored teacher), and I hoped that my students would find the lesson equally interesting and my enthusiasm for the English language infectious!

Linxiao: Methodology, which includes learning activities and materials, is generally the area where there is the greatest potential for conflict between teachers and learners. In a learner-centered curriculum, it is crucial that any conflict be resolved. Evidence from recent studies documenting widespread mismatches between teacher and learner expectations is examined. Since, as we have noted, a good many of learners are likely to have fixed ideas about course content, learning activities, teaching methods and so forth, it seems that teachers will continually have to face the problems of deciding to what extent to make compromises. However, if programs are to be learner-centered, then learners wishes should be canvassed and took into account, even if they conflict with the wishes of the teacher. When you taught us, did you have met some conflicts with us? If so, how did you solve these conflicts?

Lisa: I'm glad to say, "No, I did not have any conflicts with my students over the methodology, activities or materials I taught." This is not to say that I made all the best choices but that I was teaching (first year) college entrants who had few if any fixed ideas or expectations regarding their English courses. I had the advantage of being the first foreign English teacher these students had ever had so everything I did seemed new and exciting!

Linxiao:As we all know, given the constraints that exist in most learning contexts, it is impossible for teachers to teach learners everything they need to know in class. With so little class time, teachers must use it as effectively as possible to teach learners those aspects of the language which the learners themselves deem to be most urgently required, thus increasing surrender value and consequent student motivation. Take the course *Reading and Writing* as an example, when this kind of thing occurred in your class, what measures did you take to solve this problem?

Lisa: It wasn't a matter of solving the problem, but of prioritizing the basics and giving the students a good foundation that other English teachers in the 2nd and 3rd years could build upon. To that end I focused on the enjoyment one gains from reading, and the ability to look for clues and key ideas in the reading material, i.e. the opening paragraph, headings, bold type, italics, use of graphs, pictures and questions, as well as the context of new worlds.

Linxiao: In education, the teacher as *professeur* has come under some suspicion as a possible agent of authority which seeks to maintain the power of privilege, schooling pupils into obedient compliance. We know that the exercise of authority in interaction is different from the exercise of authority in transaction. In interaction, the teacher—as *professeur*—claims a superior and dominant position by virtue of a role which has been socially ascribed to him or her: "I am your teacher. By the authority vested in me I have the right to ask you to behave in a certain way, whether you like it or not. And you, in your role, have the obligation to obey." So the exercise of authority in interaction is more or less authoritarian. But the teacher as *enseignant* exercises authority in transaction by virtue of the achieved role of expert. His or her authority is based on professional qualification. Dominance derives from the claim to be able to teach, to make the transaction successful in respect of its specified objectives. In this case there is no assertion of right but a claim to knowledge : not "Do this because I tell you and I am the teacher and I know what's best for you". Transactional exercise of authority, therefore, is more or less authoritative. Meanwhile, the increase in learner-centred activity and collaborative work in the classroom does not mean that the teacher becomes less authoritative. He or she still has to contrive the required enabling conditions for learning, still has to monitor and guide progress. In the process of teaching in Hwa Nan, what is your attitude to the roles of teachers and learners?

240

春色
任天涯
——福建华南女子
职业学院外教侧记
International Faculty with
Fujian Hua Nan Women's
College since 1908

Lisa with the students crossing a stream hand in hand

Lisa: I understand the role of teacher as both an authority in interaction and transaction, but I tried to come across more as a guide or mentor in the lives of my students. This was not hard for I was also a young teacher and therefore still learning how to teach! Not only that but I was learning how to teach *Chinese students*, which meant I was learning about their culture, background and worldview. That's a humbling position to be in and counteracts the notion that I as a teacher always know what's best!

Linxiao: We know that evaluation is the final component in the curriculum model, and evaluation is a wider term, entailing assessment, but including other processes as well. These additional processes are designed to assist us in interpreting and acting on the results of our assessment. The data gathered from evaluation assist us in deciding whether a course needs to be modified or altered in any way so that objectives may be achieved more effectively. If certain learners are not achieving the goals and objectives set for a course, it is necessary to figure out why. We would also wish, as a result of evaluating a course, to have some idea about what measures might be taken to remedy any shortcomings. Evaluation, then, is not simply a process of obtaining information; it is also a decision-making process. In the courses you have ever taught, what are your actual practices for that?

Lisa: In addition to quizzes, tests and exam scores which gave some data for evaluating a course, I would conduct personal interviews or "chats" with each student to try and ascertain why they were not achieving the desired goal or objective of confidently listening, speaking, reading and writing in English. As a result it was usually obvious what I as a teacher needed to do to help that student improve, and more often than not the difficulty faced by one student was indicative of problems that all the students were struggling with. At that stage I might review a lesson, or re-teach a lesson in an entirely different way, coupled with a great deal of encouragement for the students!

Linxiao: In the course *English Reading and Writing*, you selected four videos for us to watch, which were *Anne of Green Gables, Dead Poets Society, Back to the Future, and Ben Hur*. In the meantime, you printed out all the original materials for our reading tasks and then we did the hot and deep discussion in the class. After that, I remembered that you produced the assessment paper for us so that it would help us better understand the videos and the novels. I wondered why you made the selections of the four. What exact expectations did you have ever had by doing so?

Lisa: There was nothing too academic about these movie selections because at that time in China there were not a lot of video choices! (It is not like today where there is unlimited access to DVDs and movies on the internet.) I simply liked these movies myself because they were character driven, had a good message and came from a variety of genres. I expected my students to learn something from each movie that would positively influence their future lives.

"Tomorrow is always fresh with no mistakes in it."

Linxiao: Through the courses you taught, I found that you actually had incorporated the target culture into your teaching unconsciously. On Christmas Day, you let us know why westerners celebrate this festival and who Santa Claus is. You gave each of us Christmas cards and Christmas presents, and we had Christmas dinner and sang Christmas carols together. Throughout the whole academic year, you introduced us to all the western festivals and spent them with us so we could also experience, Valentine's Day, St. Patrick's Day, Easter, April Fool's Day, and Thanksgiving etc. It is undeniable that culture and language are inextricably intertwined. This point is strongly supported by Kramsch (1996) as he stated unequivocally "language and culture are from the start inseparably connected".

242

春色
任天涯
——福建华南女子
职业学院外教侧记
International Faculty with
Fujian Hua Nan Women's
College since 1908

Similarly, Sapir (1970:207) says "language does not exist apart from culture, that is, from the socially inherited assemblage of practices and beliefs that determines the texture of our lives". One of the major ways which intangible culture is mediated, interpreted and recorded is through language. Interestingly, language appears to be the most representative element in cultures.

By the same token, culture is the indispensable context for language use. Without cultural contents, foreign language instructions are "as dry as a bone". For foreign language students, language study seems meaningless if they know nothing about the people who speak it or the country in which it is spoken. As culture is an integral part of language and in return language is also an integral part of culture, it is virtually impossible to separate culture from language. To put it frankly, teaching a foreign language cannot be without introducing the target culture.

Secondly, we are absolutely convinced that culture constitutes a firm foundation of successful communication. As a matter of fact, culture not only dictates who talk to whom about what and how communication proceeds, but also helps interlocutors encode messages and understand conditions and circumstances, understand which various messages may or may not be sent, noticed or interpreted. Put simply, linguistics alone is not enough for learners of the target language to be competent in that language (Kraner, 1999). Language learners need to be aware, for example, of the culturally appropriate ways to address people, express gratitude, make requests, and agree or disagree with someone in different contexts. They should know that behavior and intonation patterns that are appropriate in their own speech community may be perceived differently by members of the target-language-speaking community. Therefore, it is the teachers' responsibility to help learners understand socially appropriate communication. In your teaching, you have done so perfectly. Could you please provide your own philosophy on this so that all of us could hear your own voice here?

Lisa: Actually, I consciously incorporated some aspects of both western and international culture into my teaching because I wanted my students to get to know me and understand what I thought were important stories, attitudes and beliefs from my background. In turn, it may have enabled them to see their own culture differently or even in a better light.

As already stated, language and culture are deeply rooted, and one cannot be separated from the other. I had, therefore, to teach my students more than just English words, sentences and phrases. I had to teach them the *culturally appropriate and natural usage* of those words, sentences and phrases. Not only would this help them to communicate effectively with me and other English speakers in the future, but it would make sure they did not say or do something inappropriate and embarrass themselves—a very important issue for a "face-saving culture" like China.

Finally, I wanted my students to find the English language enjoyable, so I used aspects of western and international culture to make my lessons fun and stimulating.

LinXiao:From 1992 to 1996, you taught here in Hwa Nan. At that time, the teaching and living conditions were actually very poor. What was your own feeling towards that and how did you overcome them then? Except teaching, what else did you do in your spare time?

Lisa: I felt it was a privilege to be in China and the staff of the Hwa Nan Foreign Affairs Office were so welcoming, kind and helpful that I was barely aware of the poor living conditions. Again, my life was so rich in experiences and friendships that I did not need to focus on what I didn't have! There was the occasional rat, bouts with food-poisoning, no-water Mondays, no international phone line (and definitely no internet in those days), but these type of "hardships" just made for great China stories!

Most of us also know that poverty has very little to do with poor living conditions. Real poverty comes from a lack of meaning or purpose in life. Teaching at Hwa Nan gave me plenty of both purpose and meaning!

Foreign teachers in Mawei, Fujian. Lisa on the left of the back row

In my spare time I got to know Chinese people (most of whom I am still friends with till today!), explore the city of Fuzhou and take trips to other famous places in Fujian Province, try all the local foods, socialize with other foreign teachers, read, cook, take photos and do cross-stitch. I also got to be an actress in three Chinese movies!

Linxiao: Since 1996, you have taught students at different ages and English levels in Kunming. Could you please share some of your teaching experience there?

Lisa : I came to Kunming to set up and run a full-immersion English language campsite where all the activities were taught and conducted in English. This was a great

244

春色
任天涯
——福建华南女子
职业学院外教侧记
International Faculty with
Fujian Hua Nan Women's
College since 1908

opportunity, not only for the students to experience a total English language environment but for me to learn a lot of new organizational skills. I also worked for many years in an English language night-school where professionals could study after work.This job included preparing students for the IELTS (International English Language Testing Systems) test. Lately I have been teaching English to private students, most of whom have moved overseas to live and work.

Linxiao: I was wondering why you continued the career as a teacher in Kunming for more than 20 years and why you chose China instead of the other countries as your working place.

Lisa：I don't know if I chose to teach in China or if it was chosen for me, but I love living in China. Rather than develop my *career*, I chose to make a *life* here—which I believe is a lot more important. It is an abundant life because I get to do what I love and I love what I do! After all, and I hope my former students will all remember this, it doesn't matter what language we speak, if we do not have love we are only resounding gongs and clanging cymbals. Only love will never fail.

Ai Wo in Fuzhou

Appendix 1 : *Oh Captain! My Captain!*, Walt Whitman, From Dead Poets Society

> *O Captain! my Captain! our fearful trip is done,*
> *The ship has weather'd every rack, the prize we sought is won,*
> *The port is near, the bells I hear, the people all exulting,*
> *While follow eyes the steady keel, the vessel grim and daring;*
> *But O heart! heart! heart!*
> *O the bleeding drops of red,*
> *Where on the deck my Captain lies,*
> *Fallen cold and dead.*
> *O Captain! my Captain! rise up and hear the bells;*

Rise up--for you the flag is flung--for you the bugle trills,

For you bouquets and ribbond wreaths--for you the shores
a-crowding,

For you they call, the swaying mass, their eager faces turning;

Here Captain! dear father!

This arm beneath your head!

It is some dream that on the deck,

Youve fallen cold and dead.

My Captain does not answer, his lips are pale and still,

My father does not feel my arm, he has no pulse nor will,

The ship is anchord safe and sound, its voyage closed and done,

From fearful trip the victor ship comes in with object won;

Exult O shores, and ring O bells!

But I with mournful tread,

Walk the deck my Captain lies,

Fallen cold and dead.

VII

Spring Rain Nourishes Gently, So Does Her Love for Fujian Hwa Nan Women's College
—In Honor of Dr. Mary Carol Perrott

Distance cannot separate the persons who are destined to meet even when they are thousands of miles apart

With the mission from Amity, Dr. Mary Carol Perrott (Dr. Perrott) came all the way to China from America in 1996 and began her two-year teaching at Hwa Nan, which started her friendship with Hwa Nan that has lasted two decades.

First meeting with Dr. Perrott

In early 1990, English speaking was one of the great barriers to many Chinese in their

春色
任天涯
——福建华南女子
职业学院外教侧记
International Faculty with
Fujian Hua Nan Women's
College since 1908

246

English learning. It was lucky for us to learn English at Hwa Nan, with many opportunities to get in touch with foreign teachers, typically native English speakers, which provided the chance for us to overcome the difficulties listening to English and improve our spoken English as well. In our memory, we were nervous before the foreign teachers' classes and would ask ourselves "Can we make it?" in the first semester at Hwa Nan. Hearing the news that Dr. Perrott would teach us, we were excited on one hand, for it would/provide a chance for us to communicate in English in a real context. On the other hand, we felt nervous and many of us were afraid of poor communication, typically those who did not come from the downtown cities but the remote villages, which offered a poor circumstance for English learning. Their poor pronunciation was one of the key factors that made them nervous. Their teachers seldom spoke English in class, or they would speak English with strong dialect or incorrect pronunciation, and the result was that many of their students spoke English poorly.

With complex feelings, we were looking forward to the meeting with Dr. Perrott. Our memory of the first meeting with her is still fresh. That day, we came to the classroom earlier than usual, and we were surprised to find that Dr. Perrott was already there. She was around 50 and was of medium height in a pear-shaped figure. She had a fair complexion with a short brown hair around her ears, and on her prominent nose stood a pair of black round glasses, behind which was a pair of big brown eyes, understandable and amiable. She had rosy lips and pretty white teeth, with a big smile on her round pink face. She was as lovely as a doll. Her endearing sense of graciousness and warmth drove away our nervousness and worries in few seconds. "Good morning, ladies. My name is Mary Carol Perrott. You may call me Dr. Perrott. Well, do you know of a bird called parrot? Yes, that is a similar pronunciation.It is easier for you to remember my name if you connect my name with it. That is me, Dr. Perrott." Her humorous opening self-introduction made us relaxed, and it lightened the classroom atmosphere.

Then it began a rush of self-introductions in class. We felt relaxed and interested in her first class. From then on, with the encouragement from Dr. Perrott, we overcame our timidness, and began to love English and the courses taught by Dr. Perrott, typically the course of English speaking and listening. Thanks to her encouragement, we built up our confidence. Thanks to her support, we were motivated to learn further in English. Thanks to her guidance, we had a clearer target in our English learning. Thanks to her help and efforts, we conquered the difficulties in English pronunciation one by one, and practiced our English speaking and listening in a persistent way. After the short first term, we achieved big progress in English speaking and listening.

Taken at the Amity training in Hefei, Anhui before coming to Hwa Nan

The Seasons Staying with Dr. Perrott

Dr. Perrott began the tour of teaching us with the song "Little Teapot" in September. "Im a little tea pot, short and stout. Here's my handle, here is my spout." She had a unique teaching method, which was warmly welcomed by students. She made the performance while she was singing, with her right hand on her waist and left hand making the shape of the teapot. Her performance created a humorous air in class, which made us joyful and relaxed.

In winter, sometimes we could have oral English classes at the faculty house, Dr. Perrott would turn on the heat, and offer us hot cocoa on the chilly days. We would feel warm both inside and outside our bodies after having the hot drink. It was one of the most beautiful scenes in winter in our deep memory, staying with Dr. Perrott, considerate and enthusiastic, in a room full of the cocoa aromas. It was our great yearning to have oral English class with Dr. Perrott in winter.

Many Chinese found it difficult to pronounce /θ/ and /ð/, so did Hwa Nan ladies. Dr. Perrott created a way to tell them apart. She lighted a candle, and demonstrated the pronunciation of the words in pair with /θ/ and /ð/ ,and invited us to find what would happened on the candle. Before she read the words, she closed the curtain and turned off the light, making the room dark. After that, she pulled the candle near to her mouth, with its flame in parallel line.Then she demonstrated the pronunciation. The flame danced and became weak by the air coming out when she pronounced /θ/ ; while the flame stood motionlessly when she read /ð/, with a movement in the throat and no air out of her mouth. Finishing the demonstration, she invited students to practice and find the right way to pronounce /θ/ and /ð/. With the candle in a dark room, we found its flame dance now and then when we did the pronunciation practice in that class. The creative and interesting teaching method made Hwa Nan young ladies remember deeply the pronunciation of /θ/

春色
任天涯
——福建华南女子
职业学院外教侧记
International Faculty with
Fujian Hua Nan Women's
College since 1908

and /ð/, which is most challenging for oriental English learners.

Once the winter vacation was ended, we looked forward to take Dr. Perrott's class in February, just like the grass waiting for the sunshine when the spring approaches. We would feel excited when we heard her footsteps on the way to the class as usual. That was the first class after the vacation, we were eager to see her, for she would

Dr. Perrott sat on her bed made up with sheets and blankets brought from USA

share her stories, her life in her holidays, her trips, and her gain and reflection etc. It was enjoyable to listen to her stories. She also told frankly about her life experience, including her marriage. Because of love, she married to a man named Larry who was much older than her. Sadly, less than 5 years later, he left the world early, leaving her alone. However, she was not lonely because she considered her niece and the students as her children, and she led a full life. Her knowledge, love and dedication made her life wonderful and rich. We could figure out her independence and strong will from her experience. Apart from the stories she shared, she would give us some guidance, such as not falling in love with a married man, which had high possibility of ending with tragedy, for it was quite easy for this kind of man to cheat a lady with little social experience.

The May in Fuzhou is hot and stuffy, but we could sense the coolness in that season when staying with Dr. Perrott. She would arrange for her students to go outside the classroom during the weekends or the time after the final exams, and she would treat us at McDonald's, which offered western food . She would push us to practice oral English in ordering and speaking about the food in the real context there.

How the wonderful time flew! Here came a farewell time in hot June when cicadas sang. At the faculty house, Dr. Perrott prepared a warm farewell party for us. When it was time to say goodbye, she gave a big and warm hug to each of us, with tears in her eyes. Before our leaving, she reminded us, who would graduate soon from the college and enter the society, of the responsibilities as an adult, and of the duties on our behaviors, and of the best performance showing at work as Hwa Nan ladies.

The Impression of Dr. Perrott

Dr. Perrott was our favorite teacher. Her classes were alive and full of fun, with a variety of teaching methods. It was enjoyable and enlightening at her classes, which were always full of laughter. She would forgive our minor mistakes in English learning. She loved us in a special way and pushed us to learn further, and we did improve our English speaking and listening in the enjoyable and relaxing learning context.

As a teacher from Amity, Dr. Perrott has a great dedicated spirit which was owned by few people. It was the spirit that supported her and pushed her to do her teaching well. In her teaching career, she showed her responsibilities, her love, and her dedication, which brought good fortune to Hwa Nan ladies. For those who were weak in English, she would help them whenever she could. Also she would donate her salary to help those who were poor. Meanwhile she focused on collecting English material, and would buy the useful learning resources at her own budget, and then provided them for the class before donating to the school. We were lucky to be her students. And we would get small gifts from her now and then, either in the teaching performance or outdoor activities, which was envied by students from other class. Thanks to her, we overcame the fear in English speaking and listening. Thanks to her, the road of our English learning was full of fun. Thanks to her, we were able to use the authentic English material to learn English in a more effective way. Thanks to her, we improved ourselves. We learned not only the English knowledge, but also the positive attitude toward life.

> *She was a teacher who touched us and she treated her students in a fair way. She never judged her students from their appearance. She also was not partial to any of her good students, and did not ignore the poor and weak students. (Pengken, her student)*
>
> *She is a good educator. She has always been a very dedicated, organized, and creative teacher, and she arranges her life in a good organization. (Amy, Lin Jiao, her student and colleague as well)*
>
> *Dr. Perrott is a good teacher, who would always be kept in my heart. Her independent, strong will, affection towards life and career, and dedication encouraged us greatly and pushed us to move forward in our lives. Many teachers at Hwa Nan, Chinese or foreigners, including Dr. Perrott, set up the shining models and provided me different spiritual nutrition which helped me grow up in a strong way, and finally made me become an independent, strong-willed and professional woman in modern society. (Celina, Zhuo Xiaoxing, her student)*

In short, she is a dedicated teacher. She cared about the growth of her Hwa Nan ladies and loved her students, and supported Hwa Nan education in many detailed ways. She

春色
任天涯
——福建华南女子
职业学院外教侧记
International Faculty with
Fujian Hua Nan Women's
College since 1908

made us realize what the responsibilities were and what love was. Her joining as a teacher and educator was a blessing for Hwa Nan. She was enthusiastic and optimistic. Though she earned a Doctorate in Psychology (Ph. D.), she kept on learning other courses and earned two professional Masters degrees (M.B.A. and M.Div.) , which were interesting and useful for her future. Her constant self-improvement made us first get in touch with the concept of continuing education throughout one's whole life.

Showing Her Love and Support to Hwa Nan Like Spring Rain Nourishing Gently

Since the first year of teaching, Dr. Perrott had been making genuine efforts to support English education at Hwa Nan and the ladies there.

1. Enriching English teaching and learning by showing original English Movies at noon time

With the benefit of her extensive background, Dr. Perrott made efforts to help numbers of Hwa Nan students in various ways. One of these was using media to show the original English movies without Chinese subtitles to improve students' spoken English and to enrich students' understanding of English and American cultures. At that time, the original English videos were very expensive, Dr. Perrott bought them at her own expense and showed them to the students before donating them to Hwa Nan. "As her student, I was very thankful for her. She was my senior year reading and writing teacher who in particular organized the Noon Movie event in the language lab. I remembered I would grab my lunch from the cafeteria as quickly as possible and rushed to watch the movie while eating my lunch." (Amy, Lin Jiao)

The Noon Movie program attracted more and more Hwa Nan ladies, including those Non-English majors. "After my graduation, I became a teaching assistant in the English Department and in 1998 I continued to run the Noon Movie program. Many students from the English Department would agree that they benefitted a great deal from watching the original English movies. I can honestly say that my spoken English improved a lot because this unique offer. She used her own money to purchase those movies and donated them to the college."(Amy,Lin Jiao)

2. Purchasing more than one hundred Longman English Dictionaries for students

After teaching at Hwa Nan for a year, Dr. Perrott realized that it was very important for each of her students to have a English-English dictionary whether in the classroom or after school as a homework reference. "After some extensive research, she ordered more than one hundred Longman English-English dictionaries from Hong Kong using her own money for all of her students. The total cost of those dictionaries exceeded more than a thousand dollars."(Amy, Lin Jiao)

3. Encouraging and supporting her students to take English exams and get certificates

When teaching at Hwa Nan, Dr. Perrott cared greatly about the students' learning progress. She used to encouraged her students to learn and improve English from various aspects. With rich experience, she had sharp views and foresight. Apart from developing fluent oral English, she proposed that Hwa Nan ladies should take part in exams to get the certificate in English. To make us more competitive in future talent market, she again gave the financial aid to support us to take part in WSK, a national English test, and she felt proud of us when we made outstanding achievements.

The Friendship as Teacher and Students

When Dr. Perrott left Hwa Nan, we tried to remember our respectful teacher in different ways as her students.

> *For many years, I have kept my English name Celina Zhuo on my business card, which was given to me by Dr. Perrott. I keep my connection with her in this way, in order to remember the special nourishment she gave me.*

In contemporary society, it is popular to use cameras and mobile phones, yet seldom were they used in middle 1990s. However, Dr. Perrott took many pictures together with the wonderful ladies at Hwa Nan. We remembered her in our own ways, and we kept in touch with her by writing letters in a traditional way before she left for Japan, and after that the school address was one of the key ways for us to keep contact. It was thoughtful that she would visit us when she returned to visit Fuzhou. It was warm to find out she would order some dishes that were our favorites when we gathered together. It was moving that she had been caring about her students' growth and development. It was joyful that she would give us some surprise.

> *I was specially pleased that she gave me a big surprise in 2005 when I studied abroad for a Master's Degree in Bangkok, Thailand. That was a biggest pleasant surprise to me! Dr. Perrott and her new husband, Mr. Clifford Bell came there for their honeymoon. They called me and came to my school to visit me. How considerate of her to visit her student studying abroad! That touched me greatly, for few teachers had ever given me such a surprise and showed such care about my growth. Words could not express my gratitude to her. That unforgettable event would exist in my deep memory. (Ann, Yan Han, her student)*

春色
任天涯
——福建华南女子
职业学院外教侧记
International Faculty with
Fujian Hua Nan Women's
College since 1908

252

Every time we caught her lovely smile, we found small gap between our ages. We would enjoy listening to her stories of traveling around the world and her rich experience, which broadened our views on the world. The longer we kept the relationship as teacher and students , the further we realized that her devotion to her students put across the spirit of Hwa Nan: "Having received, you must give ".

We have been separated from each other for more than 10 years, but Dr. Perrott's voice and smiling image are as fresh and alive as ever. Her constructive guidance still rings in our ears. We are encouraged by her independence, affection towards life and work, and her dedication, which guide us to develop ourselves and go further on our lives. She has carried on the spirit of Hwa Nan and implemented it with many positive deeds in details, nourishing the earth of Hwa Nan, and guiding Hwa Nan young ladies as we walked out of confusion and entered a new world of self-respect, self-esteem and self-reliance for modern women.

2016 will witness 20 anniversary of our meeting with Dr.Perrott. We write this article expressing our respect and longing to our dear teacher. We hope the writing find her live a happy, peaceful,and healthy life in America.

Dr. Perrott and her husband Clifford Bell in 2014 with their Chinese-American god-children with their grandmother and Maltese/Shih Tzu dog, Sadie Bell

VIII
Thinking of Sandy

I don't know Sandy's Chinese name and I think she probably doesn't have one. In fact, she wasn't officially my teacher and I have never sat in her classes. It seems not very appropriate for me to say that she's a foreign teacher. Anyway, she was the first foreign teacher who had come to my class without any notice in advance, and I was very surprised her visit. It was then that we first met. In a blink of an eye, that took place about twenty years ago. What happened that day still vividly remains in my memory and we are still friends after so many years. I believe that we will be friends forever. It was my fortune and honor to have met Sandy, because not every foreign teacher left good

Sandy and Kay

impressions on us. What's more, we don't become friends with foreign teachers easily. After I came to Australia, I myself become a foreign teacher to the Aussie students. I have met all kinds of students and I do not become friends with all of them. That's why I feel that I am the lucky one.

While I was a graduate student in Fujian Normal University, my professor recommended me to teach a course called "Selective Reading in English and American Literature" to self-taught students. I was extremely nervous at that time and I used to sweat easily under stressful situation. Although I maintained my excellent GPA, I didn't really have much classroom teaching experience. This course was one of the most difficult courses among all the examination subjects. Usually there were about one hundred students who registered and came to listen to this course. Honestly speaking, I was not very sure about myself during the first class that I found my shirt saturated by my own perspiration

春色
任天涯
——福建华南女子
职业学院外教侧记
International Faculty with
Fujian Hua Nan Women's
College since 1908

254

right after I finished the class. Fortunately, I learned to overcome the nervousness after a couple more classes and I was able to relax and to teach with ease and confidence. Another thing is that I think I am pretty conscientious about what I was doing. As soon as I agreed to teach the course, I had started my instructional planning not only during the weekdays, but also in the weekends. I took full use of my weekends during the semester to prepare for this course and I wrote down the comprehensive lesson plans beforehand. Due to no access to the Internet in those days, I remembered that I would go to the university library and resources center in our department every day to use the encyclopedia or other kinds of resources to help with lesson planning. The staff in the resources center commented that a hard working teacher like me surely conducted outstanding classroom instruction and teaching. Maybe it was my enthusiasm and zeal that I successfully fulfilled my teaching obligation. Otherwise, I myself would not give a very high score for my own course. When I reflected on those teaching days, I believe that now I have a much deeper and better understanding of those works of literature due to more than two decades of living and teaching experience in both China and Australia. In this journey, I have not only become experienced but also felt the richness of societal warmness and in some cases the indifference among human beings. As the saying goes, art is life and life is art. My understanding about life and literature has both changed drastically compared with what I had twenty years ago.

I forgot which lesson we were on that night and I didn't notice any differences at the beginning of the class. Since the auditorium was so large that when I was standing behind the podium the students looked like a dark cloud in front of me. Those self-taught students were so internally motivated that they always paid great attention to teachers and it was rare to find any student being disruptive or absent-minded. In the middle of the class, I realized that it seemed that there was a foreign teacher sitting in the last row. I was quite puzzled since I didn't know who the person was and why she was there. But I continued to carry out my class until the intermission point. During the interval recess, I walked to her and politely asked who she was and how come she decided to come to my class. Sandy's original plan was not to disturb my class and she probably had hoped that she would not be noticed by me, and that's why she chose to sit in the last row, but she was eventually spotted by me. (Good eyesight, haha! I still don't wear glasses after so many years.) With her gentle and sweet smile, she told me that she was a foreign teacher from Fujian Hwa Nan Women's College. One of her teaching assignments was to teach the course called "Reading and Writing". A good number of her students had taken the self-taught exam and one of the courses they had been working on was my "Selective Reading in English and American Literature". While Sandy was checking her student's journal writing, she discovered that those students thought highly of the teacher who was teaching the course, which arose Sandy's curiosity and interest in finding out what kind of teacher the students were describing and what he was teaching as well. Therefore, she followed Amy, who was a teaching assistant at Hwa Nan and was taking the course at that time, to this class. (Oh, no wonder!) We only talked briefly and then I went back to the podium to complete that night's second period of class. Once the class was dismissed, students quickly left for their own homes or dormitories. I again walked to the last row of the big auditorium and told Sandy that I was very pleased to meet her. I asked whether I could walk with them and Sandy gladly accepted it. Three of us, Sandy, Amy and I left the classroom and we talked all the way until we came to the gate of Fujian Normal University. There I said goodbye to them. It was around 9pm in the night. From the classroom to the gate, the boulevard was decorated with all kinds of trees, such as camphor, mango, yulan magnolia, or other unnamable ones. The evening breeze brought the wonderful fragrance from those trees. Even after I have been away from Fuzhou for so many years, wherever I reminisced about Fujian Normal University, the fragrance from those trees was always in my mind. It seems that only in the night time that we could smell the dainty fragrance.

I have forgotten what we had talked about that night. I do remember that I received a letter from Sandy in a couple days. In the letter she expressed her appreciation of my allowing her to be in my class that night. (Frankly, do you think that I would ask her to leave under the circumstance? Someone takes time to come and sit in my class is indeed a compliment for me.) She invited me to visit Hwa Nan Women's College and her telephone number was provided at the end of the letter. (There was no phone in my dormitory and cellphone was a rare thing in those days. There was only one phone in the building keeper's office in the whole building. While we were self-studying at night, we would often hear the loud voice calling someone who had phone call from outside.) I immediately went to a public phone booth to give Sandy a call, telling her that I was very happy to receive her letter and I was planning to visit her for sure. Honestly speaking, I didn't know where Hwa Nan was even though that I had been in Fujian Normal University for about five or six years. I thought this would be an excellent opportunity for me to know more about the College. Later when came to Australia, I read a book called *Hwa Nan College: The Women's college of South China* by L. Ethel Wallace. To my surprise, I discovered that Hwa Nan Women's College was an outstanding university. When I turned to the pages with building pictures, I found that they were the most familiar buildings that I saw so many times when I was a student in Fujian Normal University. Those buildings originally belonged to Hwa Nan Women's College. Each building had its own name: Cranston Hall, Payne Hall, Trimble Hall, etc. The Trimble Hall has two Chinese names (程氏楼，立雪

春色
任天涯
——福建华南女子
职业学院外教侧记
International Faculty with
Fujian Hua Nan Women's
College since 1908

楼) indicating two connotations: one was in memory of the founding president of Hwa Nan College, Miss Lydia Trimble (程 氏); the other one (立 雪) was to echo a famous story: "*Cheng* (Cheng Yi) *Men* (door) *Li* (standing) *Xue* (in snow)" (程门立雪) in Chinese history. The story is from *History of Song – Biography of Yang Shi*, "Yang Shi and You Zuo went to see Cheng Yi, a famous Confucian scholar at that time. Cheng was having an afternoon nap when Yang Shi and You Zuo respectfully stood outside the door in the severe snowy weather. When Cheng woke up, the snow was already one foot deep." This idiom is later used to describe Chinese students' respect for their teachers as well as their determination to pursue their studies. It is indeed a very appropriate name for a building in university. These buildings were named after the donators or the founders. After 1949, those buildings were renamed as "Democracy Building", "Peace Building", "Victory Building" etc. Do they really mean anything? The new names look more like empty political slogans. But that is not the worst case, for our dormitory building at that time did not even have a name-it was called "No. 19". The Music Department building of Fujian Normal University was also the old building of a Christian school called Do-seuk Girls' School (陶淑女中), founded by the English Anglican Church in 1890. The whole campus of Fujian Normal University was built on the bases of these Church schools or universities.

The original name of Hwa Nan Women's College was Hwa Nan Women's Letters and Sciences College. It was founded by the Woman's Foreign Missionary Society of the Methodist Episcopal Church in 1908. It was one of the 13 Christian universities in the Republic of China era. The campus of Hwa Nan Women's College was located exquisitely on the top of Yantai Mountain. It was named Women's College because all the students were female. Sandy showed me around the campus and then invited me to the top floor of the teaching building. I had thought that she would intend to show me her classroom. However, as soon as I finished climbing the stairs of steps, I realized why she wanted me to be up there. In front of me was the Min River flowing peacefully, the white clouds in the blue sky gently floating, cargo ships and cruise ships sailing calmly on the water, with a couple of birds flying freely in the sky. Once in a while, you could hear the birds chirping and singing on the birches of trees nearby. What a splendid scene! What a contrast between the small campus and the panoramic view of the city! I said to Sandy that compared to Fujian Normal University, Hwa Nan was much more beautiful. Sandy responded with smiles and she said that's why I would like you to be up here and see it with your own eyes.

Since then on, we became good friends. The relationships among human beings are miraculous sometimes. My English proficiency was average at that stage (maybe not much better even now) and Sandy didn't know any Chinese except Hello and Thank You, but we were talking like old friends. We both felt super comfortable with each other and we didn't feel we had to be someone else. Sandy knew that I had always been eating in the school cafeteria and I wanted to improve the quality of my meals. Therefore, she particularly invited me over to the International Faculty House to dine with her. What's so special about this meal was that she herself cooked a western style one. To me, that was my first time to eat western meal and I was curious about everything that she did. I have forgotten most of the dishes she prepared, but one thing that I would never forget was the way she cut the vegetables, especially the cucumber. For most of Chinese people, we lay the cucumber on the cutting-board and slice them. However, Sandy did it very differently. She held both the cucumber and the knife in her left hand, and pushed the cucumber towards the knife. The same way she dealt with the eggplant. I asked her why she was not afraid of cutting her own finger and she replied that she had got used to this way of cutting since it was a habit that she had developed since her childhood. I studied for a while and really wanted to try her method, but I didn't dare. Many years later when I was in Professor John Minford's kitchen watching him slicing the potato, I found that his way of cutting was also very different from that of many Chinese. He told me that one of the standards for British people to judge whether the chef's skills were good or not is by the peeling of potatoes. Although from the perspectives of cultural differences, these aspects are minor ones, they are indeed very interesting.

At one time I was invited by Sandy to have a meal with her at the Hwa Nan International Faculty House's Dining Hall, which was specifically arranged for foreign faculty. I eat with all foreign teachers together. The dishes were prepared by the chef. For me, this was another good opportunity to get to talk to Sandy and other foreign teachers in English. I remembered that there were very few foreign teachers in Fujian Normal University. During my four years of undergraduate study, I only had two foreign teachers, and one of them apparently did not know what he was teaching. I simply didn't know why he was there. The number of foreign teachers was much smaller than that of Hwa Nan. One of the most important elements to learn a foreign language well was to have opportunities to communicate with native speakers. Since universities or colleges have decided to have English majors, one of the reasonable expectations from students would be to have native speakers as their English teachers. However, it also depends on the quality of the foreign teachers' professional background and commitment to teaching. There were all kinds of international faculty. Not every foreign teacher was excellent. I learned that night that there were foreign teachers from America, Malaysia, Singapore and the Philippines. They were all very friendly. Although compared to Sandy, I found they were not as amiable. Maybe it was because I was more familiar with Sandy then.

春色
任天涯
——福建华南女子
职业学院外教侧记
International Faculty with
Fujian Hua Nan Women's
College since 1908

258

Another time Sandy formally invited me to dine with her in a restaurant situated on the top the Yan Tai Mountain. I recalled that when I was about to finish eating everything on my plate, Sandy said: "You are a good boy, you are cleaning your plate." I smiled and thought to myself: "Is cleaning my plate worthy of her praise?" It was such a natural thing for me to clean up my plate and I had never wasted food unless that I was severely sick and I was not able to hold any food down. Otherwise, I would never throw food away. I once joked that if all the students at Fujian Normal University ate like me, there was no need to hire someone to do cleaning in the dining hall. Every time when I saw the sink filled with leftover waste, I felt upset. One of the poems recited by every elementary school student was "Who knows the food on our plates? Every grain comes from farmers' hard work." For God's sake, there were so many people in the world still in need of food and they were in huger.

While I was a graduate student, I often had tonsillitis for unknown reasons or maybe it was caused by too much fatigue. One time I was having a fever so I rested on the bed in the dormitory. Suddenly Amy brought me a bag full of things. It was Sandy who asked her to bring me food. In the bag, there were mashed potatoes and jello. Sandy wanted me to know that these were foods that I could eat even I had a sore throat. Although I didn't really have a good appetite under the circumstance, I did eat them all. I remembered that it tasted very well because there was butter in the mashed potatoes. The jello was slightly pink and not very sweet. It was frozen in the refrigerator and it tasted cool. Now I've lived in Australia for five or six years, every time when I make mashed potatoes, I always like to add butter. I believe it was the good impression I had from Sandy's mashed potatoes dish. She actually didn't need to cook those special dishes for me, but she did it anyway. Her actions of caring and concerns for a sick person like me made me feel the days of being sick were no big deal. I don't know whether she cared about her students and colleagues the same way, but for me, I could feel the long-waited family warmth from her, a foreign teacher. Therefore, it became one of the unforgettable memories.

My thesis for Master Degree was the Comparison between *A Dream of Red Mansions* and Henry Fielding's *Tom Jones*. My understanding of comparative literature was quite shallow then. It was hard to come up with high quality level of thesis when you were still a young postgraduate student. Even later when I completed my Doctorate dissertation, it was merely an academic training experience. I remembered that it was the second year of my graduate program, I went to Beijing and Shanghai for research materials (some of my classmates went to Guangzhou) once I chose my topic. I went to Beijing Library, Peking University Library, and Beijing Normal University Library where later I frequently visited when I was studying for my Doctorate degree in Beijing. I gathered as much materials as

I could for my thesis but I still lacked several important books. Upon hearing my troubled situation, Sandy volunteered to help me do research. I gave her a list of books needed. Sandy sent the list to her daughter who was in America. In a very short time, I received all the books on the list. I asked Sandy how much I owed her. She said that they were gifts for me. She wouldn't accept money from me. We, as graduate students, were by no means in good financial situation at that time. When I was in Beijing doing research, I stayed in the cheapest motel, the basement inn, or stayed at the dormitories of those universities with former classmates' permission. In whatever way we could save penny, we would try our best to do so. Beijing Library charged two dimes or two quarters for one page and I thought that was very expensive. Receiving this bag of precious books, I really didn't know how to thank Sandy for her kindness and help. Since I had all the needed materials and references, I completed my thesis in a couple months. Usually the thesis was required to be submitted by March or April of the year you are supposed to graduate. I finalized my thesis in November in previous year instead. (Another incentive for me to have my thesis completed was to be able to focus on the preparation for the admission examination for my doctorate study.) Amy helped me type the manuscript (I was still writing with my pen and paper then. Only after I arrived in Beijing, I began to use computer.) Sandy helped me with proofreading and corrected many errors. I mentioned Sandy in my thesis acknowledgement particularly. Without her great support, I would not have been able to finish my thesis so efficiently. Later I went to visit Sandy in her apartment at the International Faculty House, she allowed me to read one of her daughter's e-mails. It turns out that her daughter bought all the books on the list except one due the expensive cost of the book. One particular statement from her daughter's e-mail was "Or if you like him that much, you can buy it for him." The expensive book titled *Rereading the Stone* by Anthony Yu was also highly recommended by Professor John Minford many years later. It probably cost 30 to 40 US dollars and for me that was a huge amount of money if you know that our monthly stipend as a graduate student then was about 400 RMB. The emphasis here was not on the amount of money, but it reflected how much Sandy liked me and her personality of willing to help others in need with all the efforts she could.

In 2000, I graduate from my Master's Degree program and in the same year I was admitted to the doctorate program at Beijing Normal University. Sandy was very happy for me to have the opportunity to further study in Beijing. At the same time, she told me that she would need to leave for home soon because she needed to go to California to take care of her younger brother who was very ill. I had always thought that Sandy would stay in Fuzhou for a couple of more years. Upon hearing this unexpected news, I was sad. However, I knew that I myself would be leaving for Beijing in the near future, I thought

春色
任天涯
——福建华南女子
职业学院外教侧记
International Faculty with
Fujian Hua Nan Women's
College since 1908

260

it would be hard to see her again. Before our departure, Sandy gave me a gift, a simple display on the desk. She told me that it was a hand-made craft by her friend. On the top of the gift was a star with the caption "Believe in yourself" three words on the display. Even now I am still not very confident in myself so I should say that this gift from her was the perfect one for me. It has been 15 years since I received this special gift from Sandy and it has always been with me. This gift traveled with me from Fuzhou to Beijing, and then from Beijing back to Fuzhou, and finally came to Australia with me and it is still on my study desk here in Canberra.

When I was studying in Beijing in 2001, I received a special Christmas present. Inside the card of "For You, Son" was Sandy's own handwriting: "Dear Son Shengyu, Hope you have a Happy New Year and a wonderful Lunar New Year. Enclosed is a little something to help you celebrate. Love from Mom Sandy." Enclosed was a twenty US dollar bill! It was the first time that I had ever received a gift like that and I cherished so much that I saved it for a long time. During my doctorate study years in Beijing, she sent me a Christmas card every year. I occasionally sent some Fujian tea to her while she was still in California taking care of her brother. Later she moved back to her home in Missouri. I began to use the computer after I arrived in Beijing and gradually I started using e-mail. Sandy rarely sent e-mail to me although I received many of her handwriting letters. I think she understood the restrain of internet access then that she would send me some interesting articles, such as Gao Xinjian's Nobel speech, Ha Jin's book prize reports, etc. She highly recommended me a website called South China Morning Post, saying that was a very good channel for her to understand what was going on in China.

In 2005 I was very lucky to get Houghton Library of Harvard University's Visiting Scholarship and I stayed there for a month. During my stay there, I really wanted to visit Sandy. Sandy was very excited when I called her and she was also very happy for me that I was at Harvard. She told me that she would help me find economical airplane tickets and checked when would be convenient for me to come to see her. Later she suggested that since I only had one month, I had better stay in Harvard and nearby. It would take at least a week for the trip to Missouri and back to Boston if I want to spend a few days with her. I did take her advice and only went to New York to visit Rutgers University where I stayed at Professor Barbara's home for two days. Professor Barbara took me to tour the New York city for a whole day. The rest of that month I stayed at Harvard and nearby area. I was in America and I didn't get to see her in person, every time when I think of that decision, I would always think that I should make a different one.

All the cards that Sandy sent to me over the years are being kept on my bookshelf. On one of them is the following sentence: "Your efforts will always reward you, maybe in unexpected ways." A life without setbacks is impossible. Life is usually filled with ups and downs. Whenever encountered with challenges, it is better to take them as temporary storms. They will always pass. "Without a storm, how can a beautiful rainbow be seen?" It seems to me that Sandy was a single mother but I have never heard her complain about anyone. In order to take care of her younger brother who was ill she sacrificed her own career. She invited her granddaughter to come and stay with her during her high school years in order to provide a better living condition for her. Every time when I think of her warm smiles and her generosity for others, I sense her amity and warm-heartedness. I bought an Australian made wool scarf and sent it to her on her seventies birthday. She called me and thanked me for the special gift and specifically commented on the nice bright red color which matches many of her clothing. Upon hearing that she liked my present, I was super happy.

Sandy had her own house in Cassville, Missouri. She invited me to visit her many times. However, I never realized my trip to the house and visit her in person. When I was planning to visit her in my sabbatical year, Sandy told me that she had sold her house and needed to more to an apartment in the city of Springfield. Not being able to see her own house in Cassville was a pity, but when I come to think of Sandy's age, I realized that it was more convenient and more realistic for her situation because having a house means lots of responsibilities not only in time, but also in energy and cost: such as mowing the lawn, tending the fences, pruning the bushes, and taking care of the landscape and gardening. Sandy had planned to visit me in Australia, but it had not come true yet. It seems that friends are more often far away from each other than being together, not even mentioning that we are separated by the big continent and ocean. Even with the most convenient airline services, it would take at least three to five transfers in flight for us to see each other. Although we are thousand miles away, we still keep in touch with each other. We call each other sometimes and it is so good to hear her familiar voice while thinking of her gentle smiles. I indeed miss her after we said goodbye to one another in Fuzhou, China fifteen years ago. I genuinely wish her good health and long life. I sincerely hope that I will meet her in person in the near future.

春色
任天涯
——福建华南女子
职业学院外教侧记
International Faculty with
Fujian Hua Nan Women's
College since 1908

IX
California Sunshine
—Hwa Nan's Old Friend Dodie

Dodie's full name is Dorene Dorothy Johnston, however she loves to be called Dodie. She comes from sunny California. Her cheerful personality and understanding heart always brought us the warmth of the sunshine from California. For the most part of her career, Dodie was involved intensively in providing various social services in the United States, including serving as a consultant or counselor in the special education schools. Dodie started her teaching career at Hwa Nan in 2000. In the following ten years, she continued to come back 7 times in 2002, 2003, 2004, 2005, 2008, and 2011. Undoubtedly, she is respected as Hwa Nan's old friend. Dodie's interest in teaching at Hwa Nan started in the 1990s. At that time, Dodie read an article in a professional journal published for school psychologists. The article was written by Betts, who used to teach at Hwa Nan for many years and was urging school psychologists who were interested in China to come to Hwa Nan and teach. Dodie wrote to Betts that she was interested but not retired yet, and would keep it in mind. A few years later, Betts and Dodie finally met at an International School Psychologists Conference in Australia. Betts continued to encourage her to come to Hwa Nan and teach. In 2000, Dodie finally decided to do so. Since that year Betts had stayed in the states for a semester,Dodie was afraid that she would be all alone without one person she knew. But then she met Sue Todd and Jeanne Phillips and Sandy (who later had to go home to take care of her brother) and Carrie and all the lovely and kind Chinese teachers and Xu Dao Feng and Amy. Dodie knew that she would never be lonely at Hwa Nan at all!

Dodie had almost no teaching experience before she came to Hwa Nan, but everyone was so helpful. The first year girls she was teaching were very enthusiastic and motivated so. Dodie quickly learned how to keep their attention. But she had to spend every night planning what to do the next day, Because she wasn't experienced and confident, she was always one step ahead of her class. In Dodie's opinion, The students in 2000 were so sweet and innocent. She'd never met young adults like them! They were eager to learn, respectful of age and of teachers and of foreigners. They were so unsophisticated that they could have a lot of fun learning to speak English because they were willing to play.

She didn't mean they were silly, just unsophisticated in a charming way and open to new experiences and ways of thinking. They colored Easter eggs and baked Chocolate chip cookies and had sincere discussions during Free Conversations.

Because of the international culture created by Hwa Nan for many years, the college became a meeting venue for faculty from different places to travel thousands of miles just to meet a bosom friend. Dodie met Jeanne Phillips when she taught at Hwa Nan in the year of 2000. Sometimes you just know when you meet someone, from the way they use words or their sense of humor, that you're going to be great friends. Jeanne and Dodie liked each other right from the first

Dodie with her favorite daffodil in class

time they met and built a very special friendship. When Jeanne was unable to return to China, Dodie visited her in Colorado. Dodie admired her intelligence, her optimism in the face of her disability and her deep love for China. When Jeanne Phillips passed away in 2013, Dodie was the first one to convey this message to Hwa Nan community.

In 2002, the second time Dodie returned to China, Jeanne and she decided to try something new. They both thought it would be better for the students group together in them in classes according to their levels. Jeanne and Dodie gave every incoming first year girl a quick test to assess their level of English and divided them into 4 groups: one advanced English learners, one slow English learners and two averages. Dodie took the advanced kids and an average class, Jeanne took an average class and the slower learners. Well, both of them forgot the fact that all the contests and competitions were done together as a class (instead as individuals like in America). The kids in Dodie's advanced class won all the contests and competitions because they were bright, hard-working students. It suddenly began to look like a very bad idea to have all these high achievers in one class, because they overpowered all the other classes. It should not have been done in this way, Jeanne and Dodie were very embarrassed and sorry for their decision.

As for this teaching trial, the advisor from one of the average classes commented that this trial was good for teachers to manage the class and conduct the teaching schedule. However it created pressure for students. Meanwhile, it doesn't have any advantages

春色
任天涯
——福建华南女子
职业学院外教侧记
International Faculty with
Fujian Hua Nan Women's
College since 1908

Dodie with her students

for the slow class to participate in English contests when competing against higher level classes. Although teachers tried very hard to avoid the truth, students were sensitive. Unless these two classes were taught by different teachers, students will not be treated as differently. For classes with classmates at almost same study level, communication is easy and progress steady. However, for the mixed classes, good students can also motivate the slow students. The experience shared by the advisor from the slow class indicated that it was good for teachers to schedule the teaching plan. this arrangement did have drawbacks for students. When students found out that they were labeled as slow students, the whole class felt depressed and avoided communications with other classes. Most students were at the same level in terms of academic performance. It was hard to find a role model or a leader. Fortunately, foreign teachers at that time were very devoted and responsible. After adjusting to new expectations, students can keep on the track. Besides, students at that time were very diligent and hard working. They were brave in the face of challenges and never gave up. Gradually, the whole class made impressive academic outcome. It is hard to judge whether it is good or not for group teaching. Teachers or students hold their different views. After the trial in 2000, there was no group anymore. Despite its merit or drawbacks, we could feel deeply

Dodie with former President Zhang Xunjie at the welcome dinner

how much efforts Jeanne and Dodie had put on their students. It is no wonder they still think of this trial and feel very sorry after many years.

Well, let's just forget the embarrassment. Dodie kept wondering what on earth kept her coming back and forth to teach at Hwa Nan for seven times? In her younger days her life had been intense. She had married, had children, divorced, returned to university to get her Master's Degree, moved to the mountains, married again, got her first job as a School Psychologist, became very involved in her community (sang in the Music in the Mountains chorale, was on the board of two environment protection organizations, as well as a literary organization, and the local ski club), became a whitewater river guide and a mosaic glass artist...She was riding the tide of Women's Liberation! But then her kids grew up and went off to college and got jobs, she got too old to do wild rivers. She also retired from her job in the public schools and then she was tired of trying to save rivers and keep her county rural, and life became too insipid and a little boring. She wanted new challenges and a new passion.

Coming to China gave Dodie that challenge she needed and Hwa Nan College gave her even more: a strong sense of participating in a long history stretching from Lydia Trimble to the young faculty and the students. Teaching was a challenge for her because she had never done it before and she was thankful for the support from seasoned teachers like Sue Todd, Jeanne Phillips and Betts Rivet. She loved the feeling of living in a dorm with people of all ages. Hwa Nan attracted so many interesting and lively people to teach and visit there! Here in America her friends were all about the same age, with the same political beliefs and values and interests. At Hwa Nan, she met such a wide spectrum of ages and personalities!

And how friendly were the staff at Hwa Nan! Hwa Nan staff were all so accommodating, willing to be friends with foreign teachers, even though Hwa Nan staff had to do all the talking in English. The cultural differences were huge and she is quite sure there were many times our Chinese colleagues felt impatient with the foreign teachers, but they rarely showed it. Dodie has so many good memories of outings with the young teachers, of cooperation from everyone, of Xiu Ping and Rose and Xu Dao Feng in the old Foreign Affairs Office helping foreign teachers with travel arrangements, of the dear cook preparing yummy meals. Even though the setting changed completely at the University Town, Nell and Jessica and the new cook brought that tradition of care and help to the new campus. Dodie's friends who taught at different campuses were all jealous of how friendly and supportive Hwa Nan was to its foreign teachers.

Dodie changed, as time passes. As she became a better teacher, she set higher standards for herself and her students and that made her work harder. The students

春色
任天涯
——福建华南女子
职业学院外教侧记
International Faculty with
Fujian Hua Nan Women's
College since 1908

266

became sophisticated and worldly and care about make-up and clothes and "image"...more like Western teenagers, more interested in their cell phones than the lessons. By 2008 Fuzhou was more like a big American urban center, shopping malls were everywhere, the old neighborhood was torn down and Hwa Nan moved to the University town. The college got bigger, more formally managed

Dodie with her Hwa Nan colleagues

(which was good and necessary), the young faculty took on more responsibility and were busier...little time for friendly get-togethers. Dodie felt glad the college was so successful and thriving, but it had changed too much for her to teach.

Dodie with the students from Hwa Nan and the
University of Puget Sound

Dodie had a one day tour in Yongtai,
Fujian with other foreign teachers

Dodie is currently staying in the States. She wrote a book about how was China. This is the little introduction she gives when someone asks about her book: "My book is called How Was China? part of it is memoir, another is part short story, and another part is travelogue. There are lively chapters of history, too, because the century-old college where I taught off and on for 10 years provides the time frame for me to understanding China's sharp rise to power and affluence. Stories from the everyday lives of my students and colleagues are full of humor, depth and resilience. Lacing it all together is a vivid narrative of my adventures, from the classroom to the neighborhood, to provincial villages. After reading this book, you'll never look at China the same way again!" With the approval of Dodie, several paragraphs from the cover summary of this book are provided for reading, below.

What happens when a handful of elderly Chinese matriarchs resurrect their beloved college from educational ashes of the Cultural Revolution? Who are the optimistic young adults who attend the new Hwa Nan College for Women? And how does a retired psychologist with no ESL training muddle through a decade of teaching them English, only to discover that she, herself, has been the student?

How Was China? answers those questions with humor, honesty and intelligence. Part memoir, part history, part vignette, this book puts a human face on a China you've never seen before. You will wander the neighborhoods of old Fuzhou, delighting in the street life, sample the wares of the markets and watch while students turn into workers, then wives and mothers. A short but lively history of the college itself illuminates events that led to the triumph of the Communist Party and China's rise to power and affluence.

How Was China? Paints an intimate portrait of two different generations of women. You read their stories, visit their villages and even glimpse their futures as the author returns again and again from 2000 to 2011 to observe and comment on the changes in the neighborhood, the culture and her pupils.

X
Elegant Tulip—Dr. Karen Gernant

The tulip symbolizes elegance, fraternity, intelligence and capability, therefore, comparing Dr. Karen Gernant to the tulip is appropriate. Karen Gernant was born in May, 1938 in Michigan, USA. In 1959 Karen got her bachelor's degree in English and History. After graduation, she planned to put what she had learned into practice, so she started to

春色
任天涯
——福建华南女子
职业学院外教侧记
International Faculty with
Fujian Hua Nan Women's
College since 1908

268

teach. With great interest of learning, she continued studying while working and earned two master's degrees, one from Michigan State University in Political Science in 1963, and another from University of Oregon in 1970 in Asian Studies. At that time Karen thought she hadn't learned as much as she wanted, so she decided to pursue the doctoral degree. Where there is a will, there is a way. In 1980, Karen got her Ph.D in history with the major field of Asian history, especially modern Chinese history. Her dissertation was on *The Long March*. I think you might be shocked at Karen's education experience and say, "Wow!".

Before coming to China, Karen was a professor teaching history in Southern Oregon University (SOU). She had taught Chinese history for nearly 20 years since 1982. From then on she became inextricably connected with China and deserved to be called a "China expert". In her teaching career, she introduced China as one of the four great ancient civilizations to her students, and introduced the five thousand years of Chinese history as well. In order to help more American people get to know China, Karen did research on Chinese women, gave lectures about China, and did her best to build bridges between Chinese and western culture. In addition, she presented papers at international academic conferences, such as papers on the Long March at conferences in Manila and Singapore, a paper on Chinese folklore at a conference in Bangkok, a paper on the life of women on Meizhou Island at a conference in Hong Kong, and a paper on the goddess Mazu at a conference in Putian. All of these showed that Dr. Gernant had made a deep research on Chinese history, even on Fujian folk custom. If we compare Karen's study on Chinese history in her doctoral period to the seeds planted in her heart for her dream to come to China some day, her teaching, the lectures and the papers were the rooting and sprouting of the seeds.

After many years of research on China, Karen's dream came true in September, 1979. At that time the reform and opening up policy was just implemented in China, and Karen got a chance to introduce Chinese history and culture to the foreign tourists on a cruise ship, which docked in Shanghai and in a northern port serving Tianjin and Beijing. Karen gave the tourists some ideas of China's extensive and profound culture, as well as its centuries-old history. They were happy to learn about the culture that they were seeing first-hand. Karen

Karen in Oregon

felt lucky that she could make her dream come true and put the knowledge into practice. Karen said she loved China and still does. Recalling her impression and feelings about China at that time, she said, Chinese people were very curious about foreigners. Once she stopped for a moment to change the film in her camera, dozens of people formed a circle around her looking her up and down and asking many, many questions. This occurred even in Shanghai, which at that time was nothing like the metropolis it is today. There was only one multi-story hotel in the city, maybe 15-18 stories, and this was considered amazing at that time. There wasn't much traffic, so she could easily walk around in both Shanghai and Beijing. The cruise trip left her a good memory. Three months later, Karen left China reluctantly with a little sadness because she had no idea when she would be able to return to this beloved country again.

From January to June, 1987, Karen served as resident-director of the Oregon State System of Higher Education study program at Fujian Normal University (FNU). This was an exchange program that allowed several scholars from Fujian to pursue advanced degrees at Oregon universities, while undergraduates from Oregon universities could study Chinese language at FNU. As the resident-director for the Oregon students, Karen came to China with the students. She tried to help the students adjust to living in Fuzhou. She not only took care of the students, but also helped Chinese teachers plan various field trips to Xiamen, Quanzhou and Wuyi Mountain. Being the liaison, Karen got to know some teachers at FNU and made good friends with them. Karen was moved by Chinese friends'

warm hospitality, so she applied to be the resident-director in the program again in the following year. By writing recommendations, Karen helped one teacher from FNU go to the U.S. to study in 1988 for his Ph.D., at the University of Michigan. Later the same year, Karen also arranged for another teacher from FNU to teach Chinese at SOU. Thanks to Karen's great efforts, the exchange program went smoothly.

In the early 1990s, Karen was instrumental in bringing about a faculty exchange program between SOU and FNU, which allowed 12 faculty and administrative staff from FNU to teach or

Chinese craft given by Karen's friend

visit SOU for periods of one to nine months. Similarly, it allowed 12 faculty members from SOU to come to FNU for periods usually of about three months' duration. In order to push forward the faculty exchange program between Fujian and Oregon, Karen shuttled

春色
任天涯
——福建华南女子
职业学院外教侧记
International Faculty with
Fujian Hua Nan Women's
College since 1908

270

back and forth between the places. She enhanced the academic exchanges between the two countries, helping more FNU teachers to further study in Oregon. Due to her significant contributions to Fujian's education, Dr. Gernant was honored with the "Fujian Provincial Government's Friendship Award" on September 29, 1999. It is especially worth mentioning that this was the first time the award was granted in Fujian.

Karen received "Fujian Provincial Government Friendship Award" in 1999

Karen retired from SOU in 2000. After her retirement, she came to teach in her second hometown — Fuzhou. She taught in Fuzhou for half a year and went back to the U.S. for another half year. She was a visiting professor at FNU teaching a writing course for graduate students from 2001 to 2003, and she taught spoken English to English majors in Concord University College of FNU from 2004 to 2006. As Karen's good friend, Kay Grimmesey, a foreign teacher in Hwa Nan Women's College, often invited her to have lunch together at the foreign teachers'

Karen at Qing Yuan Mountain, Quanzhou in 1983

dining room of Hwa Nan, she got to know some other foreign teachers and faculty. On Kay's recommendation, Karen came to Hwa Nan to teach free conversation in February, 2008. With the careful and rigorous attitude, Karen chose some suitable topics for students to discuss and tried to create a relaxed and happy atmosphere. Her free conversation was not only abundant in content but also varied in style. Sometimes she asked her students to answer questions printed on the cards. She threw a little ball and asked those who caught the ball to answer questions. Or she listed the vocabulary on the blackboard and asked the students to make sentences. In addition, she gave an opening of story, for example, "Two girls were walking on Student Street yesterday…", then the students would continue the story by their creativity. Sometimes on a sunny day, Karen would take the students to have the free conversation at the Yan Tai Hill, which is next to the college. After Hwa Nan's moving to the university town, Karen came again to teach free conversation to two classes in Fe March, 2010. Many girls were too shy to open their mouths because they were afraid of making mistakes. In Karen's opinion, the teachers need to encourage the students, cultivate the students' confidence, and never correct their mistakes.

When talking about Hwa Nan, Karen said, twenty years ago, she was told by her friend, Jeanne Philips that Hwa Nan graduates were highly sought after for jobs requiring English skills. It was widely believed that Hwa Nan students had the best English skills that could be found in this province. They were highly motivated and hard-working. Therefore, Hwa Nan students were able to get very good jobs after graduation. However, during the years, when Karen taught in Hwa Nan, she found some students were not studying hard enough and this disappointed Karen. Karen thought the girls were all sweet and good kids. She thought that the women who founded Hwa Nan are admirable. They provided a good place where young women could be educated. During the late 1980s and early 1990s, foreign teachers received no salary from Hwa Nan and they had a real sense of contribution. And the so-called "old ladies" were the same. They didn't have salaries, either. They devoted their time and energy because they believed in Hwa Nan. In addition, Karen believes that most of the faculty now are also very much dedicated to the school and the students.

As we know Karen is knowledgeable about China, what's more, she is good at Chinese language. She started learning Chinese as a graduate student at the University of Oregon in 1968. She studied Chinese in an intensive program in Taiwan in the 1970-1971 academic year. Of course she learned complex characters there. In addition, Karen relied almost exclusively on Chinese language sources for her Ph.D. dissertation on the Long March, which helped her with reading skills and learning simplified characters. As for speaking, it's really been her time in Fuzhou that has helped her with speaking. In the late 1980s, not many people here spoke English. Karen had to speak Chinese as much as possible if she wanted to get along without a translator.

Karen translated folk tales and published them in 1995 with New York Interlink Press under the title "Imagining Women: Fujian Folk Tales". Later Karen and Chen Zeping, professor of Chinese linguistics at FNU, have collaborated on translating several books of contemporary Chinese fiction for U.S. publishers such as Chinese writer Can Xue's books, *Blue Light in the Sky* and *Five Spice Street.* The two translations were respectively published by New Directions Publishing Corporation and Yale University Press. Professor Chen and Karen have also translated more than 40 contemporary Chinese short stories, mostly for U.S. literary magazines. Because Karen is good at both Chinese and English, she was invited to be the English language consultant for *A Handbook of Translations of Fujian- Related Terms and Expressions,* which was chiefly edited by Chen Xiaowei,

春色
任天涯
——福建华南女子
职业学院外教侧记
International Faculty with
Fujian Hua Nan Women's
College since 1908

272

Karen and the Chinese writer, Can Xue

a professor of Fuzhou University. Karen offered some corrections for the book, which became the teaching reference for the interpreting course of English majors. Besides, much earlier, Karen served as an English-language consultant for Fujian TV. In 2014, she also assisted the Fujian Foreign Affairs Office with translations, particularly translations related to travel and tourism.

As a teacher, Karen offered a helpful hand to Chinese students. Many students got her help these years. She wrote strong recommendations and provided some financial support for a student at FNU to go to SOU to complete her bachelor's degree. She also provided housing for her during part of the time she was there. Karen and her friend Louis Roemer provided school tuition for a middle school student in Fuzhou for about three years, and then helped with her college tuition for three years. When warm-hearted Karen heard of

Karen and the students in Tantou, Fu'an

Karen's Chinese home, which
she bought in 2000

an organization named "Fujian Kids", which especially helped kids from impoverished families. she contacted the organization immediately and expressed her willingness to help. Since 2006, Karen provided financial support for six children in Fu'an Jinzhuotou Primary School until they graduated. Some of them continued to get Karen's support in middle school. Karen also encouraged one student to attend Hwa Nan after she finished high school and supported her in her first year at Hwa Nan. At that time to visit students in Jinzhuotou, Karen had to go to Fu'an by train first and took another 1.5 hours by car to Jinzhuotou. Fatigued by a long journey, Karen still felt happy because she could give a hand to others. Teacher Karen's love offered much energy to the kids in their studying and alleviated their families' burden. In addition, Karen made contributions toward: a heart surgery fund for orphans; improvements in classrooms for the disabled; and new clothing for the school children. She dedicated herself selflessly and silently, and has found her life here immensely rewarding.

Karen is enthusiastic, sincere and easygoing. She has lots of Chinese friends. Recently she opened her WeChat, by which she often communicates with friends. Karen's emotion toward China is like a trickle and will last long. She settled down and bought her own house in China. Her Chinese home is decorated in Chinese style. I talked with Karen and occasionally had some tea, which made me feel comfortable. I didn't feel the culture but felt like chatting with an experienced senior friend. We are lucky and proud to have such a mentor. Karen's story is like a precious and intriguing book. Louis Roemer, Karen's good friend, said, "Karen is a kind, wise and energetic person". Indeed, Karen is like a gorgeous and noble tulip. Her wisdom made her know China well, her fraternity let her help a great number of people, her fragrance is scattered all over Fujian and her talent has promoted the development of Fujian's education.

XI
Being a Useful Person—Dr. Louis Roemer

Getting to Know Dr. Louis Roemer

In the summer of 2006, the Foreign Affairs Office (FAO) recommended to me a new American teacher with a thick folder, in which was his eight-page resume. He

春色
任天涯
——福建华南女子
职业学院外教侧记
International Faculty with
Fujian Hua Nan Women's
College since 1908

274

was introduced as Louis Roemer, professor, Doctor of Applied Science (Electronic Engineering), engineer, expert in radar and communications with 35 years of teaching in American universities. Amazingly, he's got nearly 100 achievements including research papers, published books and patents. Would such a big shot like to come to teach in such a small college? I questioned, but the staff of FAO said yes, definitely. Then I contacted him by e-mail to invite him to teach English Thesis Writing. He was delighted to accept and told me he would arrive in Fuzhou on August 24. Ignoring the jet lag, he wanted to make an appointment with me on the afternoon of August 26 to talk about the new semester.

I went to meet him in the living room of FAO. He looked like Santa Claus, tall, joyous and kind with white beard. He was very energetic and witty though in his seventies.

Louis was raised as an army brat, as his father was an army officer. He spent his childhood in the Panama Canal Zone and in the State of Maryland. In World War II, his father was in the Philippines, and he lived in California. Later, he moved to Delaware to attend the University of Delaware, majoring in physics. Then after 3 years of military service as a US Marine, he went back to the Universty of Pelanare and earned a master's degree and a doctorate in applied physics and electrical engineering. After graduation, he taught at the University of Akron (in Ohio) for 21 years, and in 1989, he was recruited by Louisiana Tech University (in Louisiana) as director of the Electrical Engineering Department in addition to teaching and research. He also took part in some projects in the National Aeronautics and Space Administration (NASA) and the American Society of Engineering Education (ASEE). Industrial experience in radar and communications helped him gain practical experience.

When he retired from Louisiana Tech University, he wanted to continue being useful. He considered the US Peace Corps, but they processed paperwork too slowly. A friend from China arranged for him to teach at Qingdao University of Science and Technology (QUST) for a year. After returning to the US, he realized that he missed being useful, so he wanted to return to China. While searching for a position, he got a telephone call from Dr. Betts Rivet, then teaching at Hwa Nan, asking whether he'd like to teach English there. He was

Louis's dream-building trip

pleased to accept the invitation. He has made many friends in Fuzhou, and he's been happy contributing here for more than 10 years.

Teaching Students with Love and Strictness

English Thesis Writing was Louis's first course at Hwa Nan. There were eighty students from the Business English Department in the Class of 2004. It was a tough job for him to instruct and correct so much. Furthermore, this was also his first time in Fuzhou, so it was a big challenge for him to stay in such a so-called "hot pot". The weather was so hot that he sweated all over when arriving at the simply-equipped classroom with only one fan in the front. However, he cared about the students so much that he directed the fan towards them. As a result, he got sun-stroke and had a fever. He had to visit doctors here and there, but he never missed a period during his illness. In a word, he put all his heart into the course, helping each student select the thesis title, draft the outline and proposal, and write rules of thesis writing. He also met regularly with each student to make corrections, and very delicately, he sent me an e-mail a week to report on the students' progress.

One day, a staff member from the FAO noticed Louis sitting at the computer and shaking his head with a frown on his face. He was checking the students' research papers, and he found some of them were plagiarized. He felt very disappointed, and said, "I have to report it to the director." He immediately came to me and gave me a computer disk and a notebook. The disk contained samples of thesis papers and citations. On the cover of the notebook, Louis had written, "SUGGESTED BUSINESS THESIS TOPICS 2007.4.14 ROEMER LOUIS (FOR NEXT YEAR)." Opening it, I found that he came up with 20 topics regarding Fuzhou. At the end of the notebook, he left a sincere message like, "I want our students to be good. I want Hwa Nan to have a justly known good reputation, as well as the students".

It was really tough for him to handle this course with the group of students who had low English level and poor writing skill, but Louis was successful. All the students succeeded in the thesis defense. In addition to teaching, he voluntarily helped with all aspects of thesis preparation, such as writing the instructions for thesis defense, and scheduling presentations.

Giving Help with Endless Love

"It's always a pleasure to share with others and help others as much as I can." Louis always said so and did so.

As a former staff of FAO recalled, when Louis first arrived at Hwa Nan Women's College, his daughter who taught Law in Xi'an Jiaotong University sent him home appliances and some bedding. But Louis found that the FAO had made all of these things available to him and other foreign teachers. Therefore, he didn't need the things his daughter had sent, and he gave all the things to members of the support staff at Hwa Nan. Colleagues in FAO advised him to keep some for his convenience, but he said it was more important to give them to those who needed them more as the dining room had appliances for all the teachers' use.

Now, Louis's former neighbor at Hwa Nan still remembers how her daughters pent her first Christmas. During the Christmas season, Christmas stockings could be seen everywhere around the FAO. The little girl felt curious and asked why. Her mother said if she behaved well, Santa Claus would put gifts in the stocking for her. Louis's neighbor just blurted out whatever came into her mind, but on Christmas Day, the child got up early to see whether Santa Claus had put gifts in the stockings on the door. At that moment, her mother was very worried about it as she had not put anything in them, and she was afraid that her daughter would be very disappointed about it. To her surprise, her little girl was very happy to find many gifts inside, such as toys, fruit and chocolates. She thought things ended then, but since the child thought of herself as a good girl, and so Santa Claus should come to visit her every day. Every day she behaved well, greeted everyone, and did what she could do. Louis still took his role as Santa Claus. So the days when he stayed in China were all this little girl's Christmas Day because the socks on the door were always full of presents. Now, she has grown up, she and Louis have become good friends. At this, Louis's neighbor said gratefully that it was not difficult to do the good deed once or twice, but it was quite difficult to do it all his life. This is Louis who was always ready to help others, even children.

Louis's neighbor's niece came too Fuzhou to live with her, in order to receive better education. One day, a thief stole her niece's tuition. Louis and his best friend talked this over and decided to pay the youngster's tuition. So they supported her from seventh grade to her graduation from nursing school. Actually, the neighbor declined several times, but they always insisted and said they were doing just a small thing. The youngster has now grown up and is a nurse in a local hospital. She considers Louis her grandfather and goes to see him when time permits.

Dr. Karen Gernant, whom Louis met after he came to Fuzhou, is his best friend. They have the same hobbies, and similar values, and they both like China very much. They have common interests such as reading, listening to music, going to operas, plays and movies, attending art exhibits; traveling; walking; and cooking or baking. Speaking of Louis,what made him full of praise is that he is kind, considerate, thoughtful, articulate, and witty.One of the things that impressed her most about him when they first met was his telling her that he learned Braille in order to help a blind classmate with his homework. What's more, learning Chinese at any age is a little daunting. But Louis has surprised her and others by learning to communicate in Chinese and memorizing many Chinese characters. Furthermore, he has a knack of getting along with kids, which may be rather rare in elderly American men. She likes watching him interact with children — with his grandchildren or students who all adore him.

Louis's neighbor's niece came to Fuzhou to live with her in order to receive better education

In 2010, Hwa Nan moved to the new campus in the university town, and the transportation was not convenient. Then Louis had to quit his teaching job on campus. However, to be useful was still his pursuit. He volunteered to help some kids of Hwa Nan faculty with English every weekend in the old FAO, until the FAO apartment was sold in 2013. A teacher of the Applied English Department said with appreciation, "Louis is very kind and modest, and never struggles for fame and money. What impressed me most was his patience with the kids. He would use very vivid and interesting body language to help the kids enjoy learning English. His smile was always as kind as Santa Claus, which made the kids feel close, and they all called him 'Grandpa' courteously. English became interesting to the kids because of his efforts. I respect him for his generous love for the Chinese kids."

In early 2011, I got a warm call from the former FAO staff, asking me whether my daughter needed a foreign teacher's help with English. She told me that Louis would like to help those who needed it and I was very delighted. I e-mailed him and recommended some other faculty's kids to join his class. He was very happy to accept it and said he would like to give his tutoring as a gift for the kids for a very simple reason that he has got a lot of help from Chinese

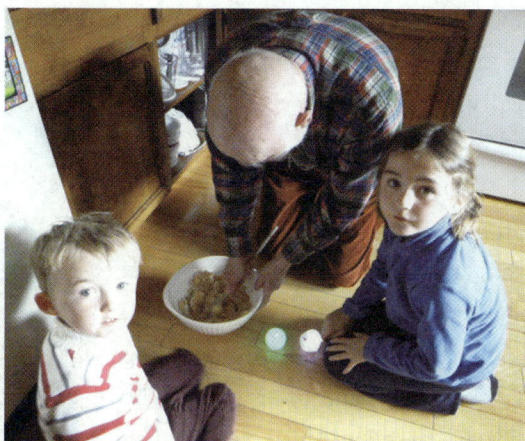

Staying happy with a childlike heart

春色
任天涯
——福建华南女子
职业学院外教侧记
International Faculty with
Fujian Hua Nan Women's
College since 1908

278

friends and it was time to give something in return. But what I could not imagine is that he should stay with these kids every Saturday from then on without any pay. He teaches them the functional skills of English and widens their reading gradually. He plays games and drama, goes shopping and visits the art centre with them. In addition, he teaches them how to learn English while having fun cooking and baking. In order to expand the kids' reading, he creates stories for the kids to activate their interest and guide them to be good. He puts every kid into his stories and teaches them to appreciate China's culture and contributions to scientific development. By now he has composed nearly 80 stories, which have been published locally in two books as gifts to his friends, his students and students at Hwa Nan, hoping they can benefit from these stories.

"Five years ago, I learned from a good friend that one of her American friends was a volunteer teaching an Oral English course for the kids. To be honest, I felt very excited and took my daughter to join this special class. Over there, I got to know this kind and respectable old man—Louis Roemer. In the past five years, this tall and vigorous gentleman would always show up on time and stay happily with the kids in the Saturday afternoon class. He teaches the kids not only the English words and expressions, but also how to dye cloth. In his spare time, he takes them to his apartment to cook western food or to METRO to figure out the weight and prices of the products, showing the children how to be wise in shopping and home finance management. In his class, children have learned things that they cannot acquire from Chinese class. The kids are always looking forward to his joyful class on the weekend. Though I am not a Christian, I have to say, 'Thank God for sending us such a kind and warm-hearted foreign friend!' His concern and help are a big part of my life, encouraging us to get along with people in kind and friendly ways. His spirit of universal love has nothing to do with religion or nationality. I'd like to express our sincere gratitude to Louis on behalf of the kids and their parents, 'It's really nice to know you!'" A kid's mom said.

The kids always call him Grandpa Louis affectionately after class, and give him their best regards and appreciation at every festival. Looking at their gradual growth, he is very happy, and often says, "The kids are excellent, and their English is far better than American kids."

Staying with Chinese kids

"Grandpa" and kids

He is advanced in age, and we don't want him to get tired, but he always says, "Though I am old, I am very delighted that I am still useful for the kids. Growing up together with them, I never feel I'm getting old."

Walking around Fuzhou with Pleasure

Somebody says, "Loving a city is because there is someone he loves in it." However, Louis says, "Every year I come back to Fuzhou because I love all here." He likes the vigor of Fuzhou and loves this flourishing city. He says what he likes most is to wander in the streets and alleys to feel the deep and long history, witnessing the changes and treasuring the warmth and friendship of Fuzhou.

The two theatres sitting side by side in the neighborhood are the places that he usually visited to watch performances, which is believed to be a window to learning Fuzhou's traditional culture. In the morning market of Student Street, he enjoys walking through the crowds to buy fresh fruit and vegetables. He also enjoys going to the Art District behind the Shida campus. He always loves to stop and talk with the workers whom he meets in the factory. Sometimes, walking from Minjiang Park to the Flower Park, he enjoys the beautiful scenery and the joy of seeing children and their parents and grandparents. While wandering around, he would occasionally step into a temple for its quietness or a taste of the delicious vegetarian food. walking through mud and old roads, he delights in how the people adjust to the new roads and buildings.

Seeing the rapid changes every day makes him as excited as the residents in the city, and he often records the moment at every corner with his camera. When anyone needs help along the street, he always provides help promptly. All these are the reasons he enjoys walking around Fuzhou.

Why does Louis still like to stay in China to search for and pursue his dream

春色
任天涯
——福建华南女子
职业学院外教侧记
International Faculty with
Fujian Hua Nan Women's
College since 1908

280

at such an age? He explains, "Life is like a journey, and to be useful is a need of all people. I regard it like planting trees. We all enjoy the shade of trees that planted by our predecessors. As we get older, we must plant trees for people that we will not know. Hopefully, the world will be better for the efforts we put out. We cannot control the lives of others, but we can hold doors open, show a better way, and help others achieve their goals. I view it as a responsibility, but it is more of a pleasure. An old quotation goes, 'Education is a fire to be kindled, not a pot to be filled'. If students want to learn, we should help them. If the students are not motivated, the most that we can do is wish them well in their journey. Sooner or later, one learns life's lessons."

Chapter 4

Heritage Culture of International Faculty with Fujian Hwa Nan Women's College

春色
任天涯
——福建华南女子
职业学院外教侧记

春色
任天涯
——福建华南女子
职业学院外教侧记
International Faculty with
Fujian Hua Nan Women's
College since 1908

282

I
Fujian Hwa Nan Women's College Policies Related with International Faculty

In Oct. 1984, the existing Fujian Hwa Nan Women's College (Hwa Nan) was founded by the alumna of Hwa Nan Women's College of Letters and Science and its Affiliated High School under the leadership of Dr. Yu Baosheng. Hwa Nan carries on the fine tradition of international exchange and cooperation. Since its establishment, the college has received strong support from international organizations such as the United Board for Christian Higher Education in Asia (UBCHEA) and Women's Division (now United Methodist Women) of General Board of Global Ministries (GBGM) of the United Methodist Church, as well as the provincial and municipal governments,the Amity Foundation and its Board of Trustees in Hong Kong. Since 1985, Hwa Nan has recruited more than 80 foreign teachers from countries such as the U.S., U.K. and Australia with the help of UBCHEA and the Amity Foundation.

To get a better understanding of the policies and management for the foreign teachers, we interviewed the following people: Professor Chen Zhongying, President of the College Council, Professor Lin Benchun, Adviser of College Administrative, Xu Daofeng, former Director of Foreign Affairs Office (FAO), He Xiaozhi, former Director of the Applied English Department, Ma Xiufa, former Director of Teaching and Academic Affairs Office.

Since its reestablishment, Hwa Nan has highly valued the recruitment of foreign teachers. Hwa Nan leaders were fully aware of foreign teachers' indispensable role in HNWCLSAHS, and alumnae of HNWCLSAHS, such as Dr. Yu Baosheng, called on the heritage and esteem of the tradition of incorporating foreign teachers into the faculty. Memory fragments of those bygone days came back to Professor Chen Zhongying, President of the College Council when she was interviewed. She said, "President Yu placed a high value on the involvement with foreign teachers. She located her office in Foreign Faculty Building for convenient communication with foreign teachers. After meetings with us, President Yu would go to Foreign Faculty Building to talk with foreign teachers with a cup of tea in hand. In that way, she would get foreign teachers' immediate feedback or suggestions." Deeply influenced by President Yu, President Chen Zhongying also put emphasis on the establishment of a team of foreign teachers.

Xu Daofeng remarked during the interview, "Foreign faculty is a unique feature of HNWCLSAHS. They guarantee consistent teaching activities and teaching quality, especially for the English Department." Therefore, at the beginning of the reestablishment of Hwa Nan, President Yu Baosheng and Professor Chen Zhongying, as well as other alumnae of HNWCLSAHS, recruited foreign teachers to work at Hwa Nan through a variety of ways.

In the initial phase, UBCHEA gave much help to the new college by assigning several foreign teachers to teach there. Some had even taught at the Hwa Nan Women's College of Letters and Science (HNWCLS); other candidates were recommended by UBCHEA or the foresaid foreign teachers. These foreign teachers brought vigor and vitality into Hwa Nan.

Xu Daofeng (2012)

Ma Xiufa (the 1st, the 1st row), Chen Zhongying (the 2nd, the 1st row), He Xiaozhi (the 1st, the 2nd row) , Zheng Yuanxuan (the 4th, the 2nd row) and three teachers from the Applied English Department

春色
任天涯
——福建华南女子
职业学院外教侧记
International Faculty with
Fujian Hua Nan Women's
College since 1908

284

Chen Zhongying, President of the College Council

Serving as President of Hwa Nan, Professor Lin Benchun continued the tradition of attracting foreign teachers. He improved the communication with UBCHEA, asking them for help in sending more excellent foreign teachers to work at Hwa Nan for the benefits of the students. He also e-mailed and sincerely invited Gordon Trimble, the descendant of Lydia Trimble, the first President of HNWCLS, to come and visit Hwa Nan. The Trimble family has developed a hundred years' friendship with Hwa Nan. In fact, Gordon Trimble and his father had already been to China several times to trace their roots before President Lin Benchun contacted them. Gordon, then a U. S Senator from the State of Hawaii, accepted the invitation with delight! During a legislative recess, he came to teach at Hwa Nan with his wife, Sonia, following his ancestors' footsteps. While serving as a senator

for the State of Hawaii, Gordon took an active part in promoting the cooperation between Hwa Nan and the University of Puget Sound in Tacoma, Washington, which is the sister city of Fuzhou. Since 1994, the Trimble Foundation, with Gordon Trimble as President, has sponsored one graduate from the University of Puget Sound to teach at Hwa Nan every two years, and has sent 25 students to Hwa Nan for academic and cultural exchanges.

President Lin Benchun was awarded an honorary doctorate by Morningside College.

Foreign teachers are treasures of Hwa Nan. Hwa Nan has made every

Dr. Yu Baosheng (L2), Xu Daofeng
(L4) and the foreign teachers

Dr. Yu Baosheng and Jean Phillipse (L1)
celebrated Christmas with foreign teachers

Xu Daofeng and Su Songzhen entertained
Judy Marton (1998).

Xu Daofeng picked up Jeanne Farrer (L3)
at the airport (2000).

Xu Daofeng with a foreign teacher's
family: Leslie Hill (mother), Jessica Hill
(daughter) and James Kirby (father)

Xu Daofeng, FAO teachers and the
foreign teachers

春色
任天涯
——福建华南女子
职业学院外教侧记
International Faculty with
Fujian Hua Nan Women's
College since 1908

286

effort to provide a comfortable environment for them, thoughtfully caring for them both in the classroom setting and in life. As Director of FAO, Xu Daofeng had taken care of foreign teachers for many years when Professor Lin Benchun was President of Hwa Nan.

According to He Xiaozhi, former Director of the Applied English Department, every foreign teacher earnestly wrote syllabus, lesson plans and teaching reflections, among which there were many creative ideas. He Xiaozhi collected foreign teachers' teaching materials and filed them so that the young Chinese teachers could learn from the materials, as well as exchange and discuss ideas with the foreign teachers to improve their teaching methods. Xu Daofeng actively encouraged foreign teachers to take a lead in organizing extracurricular activities such as English Corner, English Speech Contest, and English Play Contest. She also encouraged foreign teachers to be involved in students' study and life.

All foreign teachers live in the Foreign Faculty Building, and they are like a big family. Cooks are hired to prepare nutrition-balanced meals for the foreign teachers; there is also a kitchen for them if they would like to cook for themselves. Daily laundry service is also provided. This tradition originated from the old HNWCLS. The tradition was maintained even when HNWCLS campus was moved to Nan Ping during the period of the War of Resistance Against Japan. If a foreign teacher was sick, other teachers in FAO would go to the hospital to take care of him or her. FAO would communicate with every foreign teacher and then schedule a trip during holiday according to his or her interest. The foreign teachers have been to the places inside Fujian Province such as Gushan Mountain, Kwu Ling, West Lake and Xiamen. The FAO staff developed an excellent relationship with foreign teachers.

While Xu Daofeng acted as Director of FAO, she used to organize welcome party or farewell party for the foreign teachers. Xu Daofeng would modestly ask the foreign teachers who were going to leave for suggestions as to how FAO could do better to serve the coming foreign teachers. She eloquently expressed her sincere hope for their future return to teach again at Hwa Nan. At all times Xu Daofeng did her best to meet foreign teachers' needs in teaching and in life. She said, "Managing, caring and serving foreign teachers is my duty and my pleasure."

President Lin Benchun (2004-2007)

Since the establishment of Hwa Nan, a strong sense of belonging has developed among the foreign teachers because Hwa Nan has done its best to satisfy

Former President Lin Benchun and Gordon
Trimble

President Lin Benchun, Gordon
Trimble and Sonia Trimble

Robert Trimble (L4 of the 1st row),
Gordon Trimble (L3 of the 1st row),
Sonia Trimble (L2 of the 1st row)
and other foreign teachers

their needs while they work in the college. They feel well understood and respected by FAO staff; therefore, they dedicate themselves to Hwa Nan selflessly. They teach students according to their aptitude; not only enhancing their overall qualities, but also teaching them the proper ways to behave in society. They have forged profound and enduring friendship with Chinese teachers at Hwa Nan. Dr. Kay Grimmesey occasionally sent Sudoku or Circle-A-Word Collection to Xu Daofeng. She hoped the books would enrich Xu Daofeng's life. This also shows Xu Daofeng's excellent work for foreign teachers from another perspective. In 2003, Xu Daofeng was awarded "National Excellent Individual in Employing Foreign Teachers" by the State Administration of Foreign Experts Affairs.

Adhering to the spirit of "Having received, I ought to give", Hwa Nan has cultivated a batch of excellent female college students with rich foreign teachers' resources and strong

春色
任天涯
——福建华南女子
职业学院外教侧记
International Faculty with
Fujian Hua Nan Women's
College since 1908

288

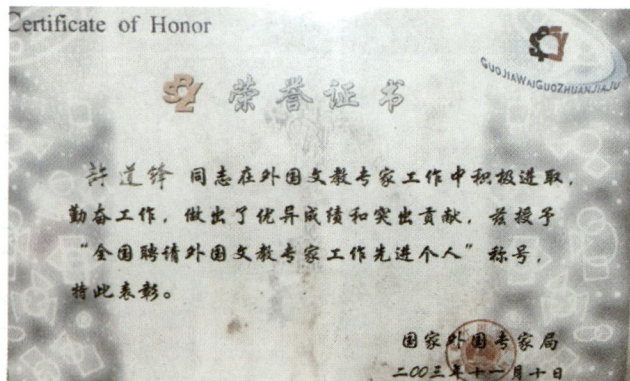

荣誉证书

许道锋 同志在外国文教专家工作中积极进取，勤奋工作，做出了优异成绩和突出贡献，获授予"全国聘请外国文教专家工作先进个人"称号，特此表彰。

国家外国专家局
二〇〇三年十一月十日

State Administration of Foreign Experts Affairs Awarded the Certificate of "National Excellent Individual in Employing Foreign Teachers"to Xu Daofeng.

support from all sectors of the society. The teaching quality as well as Hwa Nan graduates' capabilities have been widely recognized by the society. Consequently, Hwa Nan has gained increasingly positive attention over the years. On Sept. 27, 1990, a nine-people delegation led by Xi Jinping, Secretary of the Fuzhou Municipal Party Committee (now CPC General Secretary), inspected Hwa Nan. Xi said to President Yu Baosheng, "Thank you for cultivating so many talents for Fuzhou. We will continue to support Hwa Nan. I hope that you will reflect on and summarize the experience of running a college by social forces. Write to me if you ever meet any difficulties, and I will bring together the relevant personnel to solve your problems." In 1992, Hwa Nan was invited to attend a conference on private education held by the Ministry of Education. President Yu made a speech on "emancipating the mind and exploring bravely — Hwa Nan has found a way to run a private college" at the meeting, putting forward the important role of the foreign teachers.

On Sept. 27, 1990, Xi Jinping, Party Secretary, CPC Fuzhou Municipal Committee (now General Secretary of CPC Central Committee) inspected Hwa Nan, and was accompanied by Dr. Yu Baosheng and Professor Chen Zhongying.

The influence of Hwa Nan lies not only in its characteristics as a women's college but also in its overall comprehensive strength. The impact of the foreign teachers on this strength is profound. Below are the foreign teachers who were awarded the National and Fujian Provincial Awards.

Award	Name	Gender	Nationality	Year
National Friendship Award	Betts Rivet	Female	American	2006
Fujian Friendship Award	Betts Rivet	Female	American	2001
Fujian Friendship Award	Jeanne S. Phillips	Female	American	2003
Fujian Friendship Award	Kay Grimmesey	Female	American	2005
Fujian Friendship Award	Gordon Trimble	Male	American	2010
Fujian Friendship Award	Laihar Wong	Female	Australian	2015
Foreign Expert Award	Judith H. William	Female	American	1992
Foreign Expert Award	Martha Sue Todd	Female	American	1994
Fujian Honorary Citizen	Betts Rivet	Female	American	2010

II

Dedication, Variation and Appreciation —A Probe into the Educational Thought of the International Faculty in Fujian Hwa Nan Women's College

The classes given by the international faculty with Hwa Nan are characterized by vitality and engagement. Hwa Nan's graduates always have cherished deep feelings for their Alma Mater and have had fond memories of their time with the foreign teachers. Curious about the international had teachers' way of teaching, I conducted an e-mail interview with them on the following questions.

春色
任天涯
——福建华南女子
职业学院外教侧记
International Faculty with
Fujian Hua Nan Women's
College since 1908

290

1. What is your philosophy of teaching?

Ms. Elisabet Kohler came up with four A's:

Attendance = always attending the classes

Activity = as active as possible because this is the only way to learn

Appreciation = it is not enough to learn, appreciation require insight both in mind and heart

Awareness = the knowledge acquired should be put in practice and shared to others.

Dr. Louis Roemer proposed a formula:

(a) figure out what the student needs.

(b) determine what resources are available for the task.

(c) prepare materials to meet this need.

(d) determine whether the message got through to the student.

(e) go back to step a.

Laihar Wong : My philosophy of teaching is to impart useful and practical knowledge to students and to influence students to change for the better by examples so they make a significant contribution to society.

Senator Gordon Trimble:I have never given that much thought to philosophy. Students started coming to me when I was 12 or 13 and started asking me to explain what the teacher said. I grew up helping people learn. I do not look at it from the perspective of me talking but getting them to explain to me what something means until they are able to explain it comfortably in their own words. This does not make me a teacher because the person learning is doing all the work. I think of myself as more of a cheerleader or a coach. Perhaps kids started coming to me because I didn't take notes in class, squinted at them intently and listened carefully before talking. They assumed these were the characteristics of an intelligent person. I didn't see the need to explain to them that what I did had little to do with intelligence. I believe that anyone who seeks to improve is important. They have ideas and feelings—and will grow faster when they sense that they as a person are respected.

Dr. Betts Rivét: If a person wants to be a teacher, there are certain personal qualities that are essential and are also the essence of my philosophy of teaching.

They are: a desire to show a <u>sincere interest in each and every student</u>(academic improvement, getting to know something about them, willingness to help when needed), never criticize a student = instead, find something to praise them about, have positive energy in the classroom (in other words, don't just sit and teach — walk around, be near students AND come into the classroom with a happy, smiling hello), make the class interesting but at the same time challenging for the students (be creative to get them to "think"— not boring), be strict but fair, to find ways to motivate the students through field trips (I took my classes to tour museums and 5 star hotels) and games plus unusual activities and competition, and to encourage and make each class group seem special. You can't accomplish any of these if a teacher does not think positively, have a sincere love for all students and prepare well for each class.

Ms. Dodie Johnston: I believe students learn best when they trust their teachers and when they are not afraid to take chances. Creating a bond between teacher and student allows the information to flow freely between the two without anxiety. I was assigned to teach spoken English but also tried to teach the students to have confidence, to believe in their abilities and to think more broadly in ways that would benefit themselves and society.

It was important to make the content of each class meaningful to the students and to seek ways to personalize teaching materials. Kids learn best when they are really interested in the content of each class. Motivating students with personal stories, non-threatening competitions, and positive feedback was part of the challenge. *What* I taught was dictated by the curriculum, but I could choose *how* I taught the material. I tried to make my classes student-centered.

Second language learners make progress through a combination of basic drills on language fundamentals, the introduction of new vocabulary and grammar, *as well as* participatory activities that require the use of new material being presented. I tried to include a daily opportunity for personal expression for every student in my classes…lots of discussion, argument and presentations.

Each student comes into the classroom with different abilities, family background and school experience. I tried to recognize those factors when new material was being presented and to make sure that no one felt ashamed of their performance if they were making an effort to participate. I used frequent quizzes to check student progress and give students the chance to strengthen weaknesses. I tried to convince them that tests helped me gauge the speed of instruction and to see who needs extra help.

Dr. Karen Germant: When I taught history at Southern Oregon University, I thought that when students are actively engaged in the learning process, they retain the subject matter better. Therefore, my teaching evolved to a point where I assigned a great deal of

春色
任天涯
——福建华南女子
职业学院外教侧记
International Faculty with
Fujian Hua Nan Women's
College since 1908

292

reading and then used class time for focused discussions of the readings. The students had to be prepared because their participation in discussions counted toward their grades in the class. I dispensed with formal examinations. Instead, I asked the students to write essays on their choice of one of two or three questions. Often, the questions asked them to take stands on an aspect of the history. Which side they took was much less important than how they supported the position they took — how they used the evidence.

Language classes probably do not lend themselves as well to this teaching method or philosophy, because one is teaching skills more than content. Still, it's essential that students learning a language participate in class (maybe especially important in oral English and free conversation classes). In these classes at Hwa Nan and, earlier at Xiehe, I asked each student to participate in each class session. I understand that some students are shy (I was, too, when I was young), so I tried to create a nurturing, encouraging environment. I asked students not to criticize one another, or laugh at each other, and I generally didn't criticize or correct students in class, either. I also told the students that listening well was part of conversing, and I wouldn't let them whisper to one another while someone else was talking. (Sometimes, to check their listening, I would ask them what someone else had just said.) My goal in free conversation classes was for the students to become comfortable in speaking English and for them to communicate. Communicating doesn't have to mean speaking perfectly. If I could understand what a student was saying, that was good enough. If some students asked to be corrected, I did so. Though pronunciation drills aren't very interesting, students in free conversation classes felt the need for them. I began each session with these drills — and in those drills, I did correct the students. Or I asked them to correct each other. I also generally drilled them on one sentence pattern each class period, to try to instill correct grammar without making a point of correcting the students.

At Hwa Nan and Xiehe, I tried to make the classes fun. When the students could find humor in what they were saying and when they were laughing, they seemed to relax and learn more readily. When laughter rang in the room, I felt that the students were learning, because I think it shows progress if one can play with words or be humorous in a foreign language.

I also did my best to speak as little as possible, so that the students could use the class time to speak English. Sometimes, to make sure each student had more time to talk, I divided them into small groups.

I saw myself as not only a teacher, but perhaps more important (not sure about this), a cheerleader. I felt it was my job to increase their confidence, and so I tried to give them positive feedback about their use of English. If I didn't forget, I almost always ended each class session with a general statement about how well they were doing or how much progress they were making (even if it wasn't always true). I could see that this pleased them. (I'm not sure, however, that it spurred them on to do better.)

Their answers boil down into the following points. First, teaching is a matter of attitude, a devoted attitude. Second, teaching is a matter of involvement. Third, to promote student involvement, teachers have to prepare activities that motivate students.Fourth, to ensure sustainable learning, teachers are supposed to offer sincere academic and spiritual support. I would strongly advise Chinese English teachers not to make the class a place of competition, where strong competitors win while those who need help become losers. In the long run, the confidence that teachers help nurture in students could be more important than knowledge or skills.

2. How Do You Make Your Class Interesting?

Elisabeth Kohler：Well-prepared classes with plans on both WHAT and HOW: I thought of the topic to be conveyed but also on which didactical method would be the best for that actual topic. I think an ideal lesson is when there are the following ingredients:

（a）I explain what we are going to cover during the class.

（b）We go through words, idioms and conceptions to see if everyone has understood what it is all about.

（c）Comments or questions are dealt with.

（d）Discussions in small groups/larger groups about the topic.

（e）Individual exercises or small group exercises which can be written or practiced orally.

（f）Presentations within the small group or for the whole class.

（g）Feedback from me and peer classmates how the presentation went (pronunciation, voice, body-language, logic of the topic presented)

I emphasize very much on activity both in small groups and big groups but there should also be time for individual reflection. The reflection helps the students to understand the topic and let it "sink in".

Louis Roemer: I look for materials that interest me. The materials should be accessible to the student, within the student's ability to understand. Trying to estimate the student's interest is the difficult part of that.

春色
任天涯
——福建华南女子
职业学院外教侧记
International Faculty with
Fujian Hua Nan Women's
College since 1908

294

LaiHar Wong：

Here are a few things I would do:

（a）Teach from what students know to what they don't know.

（b）Select topics that are relevant, interesting and thought-provoking .

（c）Avoid topics that are mundane and unmanageable for students.

（d）Add humor in your teaching – explain words, give an illustration, tell stories, joke with students.

（e）Try to involve students to participate in your teaching so the TTT (teaching-talking- time) is not high.

（f）Be enthusiastic and well- prepared all the time.

Gordon Trimble: Learning is difficult. I focus more of the learning process than trying to think of what things students might consider interesting. Quite frankly it is the students that make a class interesting and set the tone and the bar. Students have an attention span of perhaps seven minutes. Occasionally they need to stand up and stretch to clear their head and get oxygen to their brain. And they need to be engaged by reading, writing and speaking. It is difficult but when they see they are improving they are more willing to work a little more. I take time to explain why knowing this or being able to do that will make them a happier, more successful person. I try to relate learning to what life is like after college. Students seem to be engaged in learning when the class seems to unfold in a spontaneous manner, the direction of which they seem to have an influence. The more they write every day the better their writing becomes. The more they speak every day the better this communication skill becomes. We do not think of ourselves as models to be replicated. There needs to be a large degree of spontaneity and excitement and this is only possible when teachers develop their own style.

Betts Rivét: I **changed activities** several times during the hour and a half class period. I taught Reading/Writing and Speaking/Listening and often did small group activities (4 students in a group) and I always **walked around** to listen, help, suggest, question. I used pictures to **incite thinking** of stories/conversation and even used an opening sentence to have students finish the story. **Each week** I always started with a **philosophical sentence** I put on the board asking <u>what it meant to them</u> = interaction between teacher and students grew phenomenally as the semester progressed (Example: 'Life is too short to wake up with regrets.') Also I got permission to take my class(es) on **field trips** (I paid for the bus) and the students learned =museum tours, 5 start hotel tours. Then they wrote about the trip and shared their views with another student. Another activity was (in pairs) each had a copy of the <u>same picture that was different</u> in some way and they had to **question** each other to find the 8 or 10 differences. Another thing I remember is **telling personal stories** and living experiences related to the topic or reading for the day. This helped students see what they were studying had relevance to their own lives.

Sometimes the class had to be just **speeches** or a **vocabulary** test or just **writing** a story from a picture I gave them. I brought MANY reading books from USA so my reading classes read stories and wrote a short outline (which they had to learn to do) and gave their opinions. Whatever I did with my students, they were **kept busy**. IF I had 5 minutes at the end of a class, I would always do a hangman word game using the blackboard or white board… each student giving a letter until someone guessed the word.

I wanted to be **fair to all students** no matter their skill level. Everyone had a chance to be better than they were even if I had to work with them individually. I wanted them **to be the best they could be** and I told them that. "I will not allow you to fail." Some didn't know what their "best" could be so I set out to prove it to the ones who needed more attention. It paid off more often than I can count.

Dodie Johnston: Since the idea in oral English classes is to get students talking, I would try to build my lessons in vocabulary and grammar around subject matter that would interest young women of their backgrounds. Starting with things we knew best, like our families, our hometowns, our food preferences, etc. and then branching out into broader subject made working with the basics of spoken English lively and fun.

Each morning one student presented an idiom or phrasal verb to the class. We sang traditional rounds and Beatles songs. I brought in architectural drawings, asked them to design their dream house and tell us about it. We described the ideal vacation to each other. I had them tell me Chinese folktales. In small groups we discussed issues brought up in the lesson.

They made up endings for stories I told using colorful descriptive adjectives. They designed new products or services and tried to sell them to the class. I brought the China Daily into class, had each of them select a story that interested them and then summarize for the class and speculate on its implications. I brought in National Geographic magazines and had them pick a country that interested them and convince the rest of us we should go there, too. Each small group had a rotating facilitator (who made sure everyone got a chance to talk) and a reporter (who shared the information back to the class).

I never sat down. While presenting new material I was often at the black board, but most often I was roaming up and down the aisles or dropping in and out of the groups with

春色
任天涯
——福建华南女子
职业学院外教侧记
International Faculty with
Fujian Hua Nan Women's
College since 1908

296

questions and suggestions. This kept the class dynamic and everybody participating and speaking English.

Karen Germant: I tried to use different methods, some of which I note in #1 above.

The interview on the second question can be summarized with two words: variety and personalization. If the teacher is not by nature humorous, how can he or she teach in an interesting and engaging way? Well-trained teachers know that variety is the golden remedy. Variety means planning a number of different types of activities and where possible, introducing students to a wide selection of materials so that learning is always interesting, motivating and never monotonous for the students.

In foreign language teaching, textbook materials are customarily stories of others, with whom students may not easily identify. However, personalization is one very effective way of enhancing motivation. By this, we mean making language learning content personally meaningful. If personal experiences, feelings, values and opinions of individual learners are integrated into the teaching content, they will be fully engaged in the tasks and more likely to be motivated to learn the target language.

3. How Do You Deal with Cultural Differences While Teaching in China?

Elisabeth Kohler : I have always tried to be open-minded, curious and sensitive about other culture's way of thinking, behavior and expressions. As I am trained in body language it is easy for me to pick up on non-verbal expressions though I do not always understand what is said (in Chinese). If something remains unclear the best thing is to ask and say: "My dear, I now get an impression that you are confused/angry/happy/sad. Is this a right interpretation?" And if you have not perceived the person's state of mind right, it is better to clear it up by asking so you can go forward in harmony.

Every culture has its own specific facial and bodily gestures which you simply have to learn. But that is the intriguing part of meeting people from other cultures!

If you are curious and eager to learn another person's way of thinking, the easier you get along with everyone.

And you should always respect other people and their culture. Never put yourself on high horses and think that your culture is the only good one. There are good things and bad things in every culture. That is probably what makes us all human!

Louis Roemer: I try to keep the materials relevant to the students' interests and their ability to comprehend. When the differences appear to be a problem, I try to address why they have a problem.

Laihar Wong : When I encounter cultural difference, first of all, I figure out what is right or wrong, If the culture of another country does not affect my faith or conscience, I try to respect, understand and uphold the country's culture. Sometimes I find it hard to keep silent and tolerate like most Chinese in China when something is not right because of my personality and upbringing. I tend to speak my mind at times. Nevertheless, I try to be like the Chinese in the presence of authoritative figures.

Betts Rivét: Forty-five years ago I became a charter member of the International School Psychology Association. We had a conference in a different country every summer. To date I have traveled in 48 different countries. To tell you the truth, I never felt uncomfortable in any country. Yes, even China. I adjust very easily. The word **adjust is the key.** I didn't feel I had to SOLVE any cultural differences. I simply ADJUSTED to where I happen to be. I lived in Puerto Rico for 14 years which is Spanish. I piloted my own plane into Mexico with doctors and dentists to medically minister in small villages. I even learned to bargain in China by myself. Another word I had better add to getting along in foreign lands and that is **LEARN their ways** and join them. "Do in Rome as the Romans do" as the saying goes. It's easy!!!!!! ☺

Gordon Trimble: On the first day of class I want my students to recognize three things. First, life is difficult. Second they need to use the energy in stress to give them the power to succeed. And, they should think of themselves as a movie starlet and I am the director for the next 4 ½ months. They are going to have many different parts to play. 'Get out of your comfort zone and try new things. See what fits best for the new you. By the end of the semester you will be able to adjust your actions so there is a better fit with the real you.' We are separated by gender and at least a couple generations. I do not think, nor do I look at my students through cultural glasses. I am interested in them growing into something that will work successfully for them in whatever culture they chose to work and live. Diversity for us is the preferred alternative. When I meet you I notice that you have two eyes, a nose with four fingers and a thumb on each hand. I assume that you are at least as good as me and I will strive to work hard enough so that you will not presume me to be inferior. I use my eyes to get around without bumping into things; I use my brain to envision. I think of people as individuals and I want to understand what they think and feel. This is a much slower process than simply labeling people by some arbitrary cultural tag. So we come to China to learn from our students and to share our experiences with them. It is up to them to see what is useful to them and free to ignore the rest. We are not interested in changing China. We do seek to build a platform from which to make connections, to

春色
任天涯
——福建华南女子
职业学院外教侧记
International Faculty with
Fujian Hua Nan Women's
College since 1908

build bridges by which we can better understand and communicate with one another.

Dodie Johnston: I don't see cultural differences so much a problem to be solved, but more as social conventions to be considered and understood in a larger context. At first I was amazed and a little shocked at some things Chinese people did casually: throat-clearing and spitting in public, pushing and shoving while waiting for service or admission, cheating on homework or exams, laughing at accidents or conflicts. But as I began to know people as individuals and friends I understood they were kind, polite, hospitable people who were just following traditional ways of behavior left over from a much more difficult time. Life had been very hard for ordinary Chinese people for centuries and some of the things I saw as rude or pushy had been necessary for their survival.

For instance, foreigners often had to depend on our Chinese friends or colleagues to "run interference" for us (for instance, in a bargaining situation) because we weren't tough enough. I cringed when I saw a parent making his Down Syndrome child beg in a train station or shopkeepers sweeping their commercial garbage into the street and I constantly made a big fuss about not cheating in my class. But what do I know about the conditions that drive people to this behavior? The complexity of Chinese society can sometimes be overwhelming and de-humanizing, at least to an outsider who doesn't understand it. What I *do* understand is the disregard for rules when so many rules are enforced arbitrarily or not at all.

The more I returned to China, the more I tried to become flexible in my judgments and to accept that, while I was in their country, I needed to accept how things were done and try to understand why, rather than feeling frustrated or angry. I'm sure this is often true for Chinese people getting used to American ways when in the U.S.

Karen Germant: I tried to empathize and understand from the point of view of the students here. But sometimes, I felt obligated to challenge their assumptions of what was acceptable. When I taught graduate students written English at Shida, I encountered a fair amount of plagiarism. As I recall, I failed them on those papers and told them that they risked failing the class if they plagiarized. I explained that if they were in the west, they could even be expelled from the college for plagiarism. I'm not sure that they believed me, and some continued to plagiarize, but I felt I had to make these points.

At Hwa Nan, one cultural difference had to do with regulations set by the department (or the college itself?). If a student received a failing grade, the instructor had to continue giving the student exams until the student finally passed. I believe that most of us (maybe all of us) teaching at Hwa Nan saw this as punishment for the teacher. Ultimately, most of us weren't willing to coddle the students to this extent. So if a student should have failed, we instead assigned the lowest passing grade (60) to that student.

Another cultural difference has to do with guanxi. Some students didn't care if they learned anything or not, because they had guanxi and were sure they would get jobs regardless of their grades at Hwa Nan. I don't think there's much that can be done about that.

I was disappointed and discouraged when students clearly weren't putting much time and effort into studying. And they cheerfully acknowledged this. "What do you do with your time?" I asked. "Listen to music, go shopping, sleep, go online, play games," and so forth. When I mentioned that in the U.S., we expect students to study two hours outside class for every hour in class, they were incredulous. (Of course, students here are also in class many more hours than students in the U.S. When the students told me how many hours of classes they had, I was less upset about the minimal studying. Or at least I understood it better.)

More than twenty years ago, I was obliged to compile a textbook of English for vocational schools in Fujian Province. Quite a few lessons in the textbook dealt with cultural differences, an unfamiliar concept to many people of that time, when international exchanges were not as intensive or extensive as today. In a seminar on my textbook, I was asked to justify my suggestion of adapting ourselves to western culture. Some people thought it showed a lack of cultural confidence. So much has changed in the twenty odd years. Intercultural communication has now become a must in English teaching. While Chinese people are seeking to approach western products or service through domestication, westerners also try to adapt their products or services through what is now called localization. The website of Nokia, for instance, features different styles for different cultures, with a blue background for European countries and a red one for China. The East and the West are beginning to adopt a positive attitude towards cultural differences on the basis of mutual understanding for mutual benefit. Everything, good or bad, happens for a reason. This is the basis of understanding.

Cultural differences are less of an issue in a university setting when compared with other sectors, particularly in Hwa Nan, where the international faculty is full of love, empathy and tolerance for students. As the writing of the book is coming to the end, some authors are talking about their feelings for Hwa Nan's international teachers, their love, respect and gratitude for them. These feelings transcend cultural differences.

300

春色
任天涯
——福建华南女子
职业学院外教侧记
International Faculty with
Fujian Hua Nan Women's
College since 1908

III
Fujian Hwa Nan Women's College and the United Board for Christian Higher Education in Asia

Before 1949, Christian missionaries established 13 Christian colleges and universities in China. They are Yenching University, Shantung Christian University (cheeloo),Soochow University, St. John's University, Hangchou Christian College, West China Union University, Huachung University, University of Nanking, Fukien Christian University, Hwa Nan College, Ginling College, Shanghai University, and Lingnan University. Although small in number, these colleges and universities had very high starting points and a level close to contemporary general universities in Europe and the USA, playing an exemplary role in guiding China's educational modernization. Hwa Nan Women's University was founded in 1908 by the Methodist Episcopal Church (known as the United Methodist Church after 1939) as Hwa Ying Women's School and was renamed Hwa Nan Women's University (HNWU in short) in 1916. In 1912, funded by the American Christian Women's Evangelistic Association, the university was built at No. 8, Shangsan Road, Cangshan District, which is now the Cangshan campus of Fujian Normal University. When registering with the Ministry of Education of the Republic of China in 1928, HNWU was renamed Hwa Nan College (HNC in short) because it did not meet the requirements of at least three schools of a general university. In 1951, the college merged with Fukien Christian University to found a new Fuzhou University and renamed Fujian Normal College in 1953 and Fujian Normal University in 1972. In 1984, the alumna of the original Hwa Nan College and the Attached Middle School reestablished the college and founded the private Fujian Hwa Nan Women's College, located at No. 6, Lequn Road, Cangshan District, Fuzhou.

The United Board for Christian Higher Education in Asia (UBCHEA) is a non-profit NGO headquartered in New York, USA. Founded in 1922, it was a joint office in New York, USA set up by three Christian colleges and universities in China in the beginning, and it gradually developed into the United Board for Christian Colleges in China. It raised funds and developed overall development planning and policies of higher education in

North America for the 13 Christian colleges and universities in China. The efforts of the United Board won the approval from the Chinese government. It worked on a number of Christian higher education projects in cooperation with the government and also attracted cooperation and assistance from many American colleges and universities. The United Board made its contribution to the modernization and internationalization of China's higher education and the exchange of Chinese and Western cultures. Unable to continue its work in China after 1951, the United Board shifted its efforts to other Asian courtiers and regions outside China's mainland, and renamed the United Board for Christian Higher Education in Asia. Today, the United Board works in partnership with over 80 institutions of higher education across 14 countries and regions in Asia.

In her book *Hwa Nan College*, Ethel Wallace gave a description of the support of the United Board to Hwa Nan College: "After the end of the Japanese invasion to China, Dr. William P. Penn, the Field Representative of the United Board and Dr. Robert J. McMullen, Secretary of the United Board paid a visit to Hwa Nan in the spring and summer of 1946 respectively. In 1947, the Hwa Nan Committee of the United Board allocated $50,000 for the rehabilitation of the burned Payne Hall. In the same year, Hwa Nan obtained the equipment for a science laboratory with the help of the United Board. In short, after the end of the Anti-Japanese War, the United Board gave us significant support to resume education in Fuzhou."

The United Board was formally invited to return to China in 1980. Our China Program continues to be the largest part of the United Board work, with the most partner institutions, grants, and sponsored projects. The reestablished Hwa Nan renewed its relationship with the United Board in 1984 and opened a new chapter of the cooperation between Hwa Nan and the United Board. For three decades, the United Board has always given Hwa Nan consistent companionship, silent concern and great support, making outstanding contributions to its construction and development. The close, family-like cooperation between Hwa Nan and the United Board has three major reasons. First, the timing matches. The United Board was formally invited to return to China in 1980, while Hwa Nan was reopened in 1984. Second, the identity fits. Of all the 13 Christian colleges and universities in China, Hwa Nan is the only independent private college reopened, and is a product of China's reform and opening up, full of vigor and vitality. Its independent and private identity is identical with that of Hwa Nan, which soon gained approval and special attention from the United Board. Third, the goals coincide. After resuming its work in China, the United Board focused its efforts on training teachers, which coincided perfectly with the urgent need of the new Hwa Nan. Reestablished by the alumna of Hwa Nan and the Attached Middle School, the college had difficulty in attracting young teachers

春色
任天涯
——福建华南女子
职业学院外教侧记
International Faculty with
Fujian Hua Nan Women's
College since 1908

due to the stiff personnel assignment policy of China at that time. The only way out was to invite a number of outstanding graduates of Hwa Nan to stay in the college, continue their studies and training, and obtain higher degrees until they became qualified as a teacher in universities and colleges. Led by Ms. Yu Baosheng, Dean of the College, the alumna of Hwa Nan spared no effort to seek ways of further study for young people, and cultivate fresh blood and successors for Hwa Nan. Given the circumstances of higher education in China at the time, it was impossible for young teachers to get a higher degree in China. Sending outstanding teachers to study abroad and get a higher degree within the shortest possible time with the financial support of the United Board was not only the tradition for cultivating the college's successors, but also a very sensible choice at that time, which received a positive response from the United Board.

For three decades after its reestablishment, Hwa Nan has kept frequent contacts with the United Board. The college had a visit from both the President and Vice President of the United Board as well as regular ones from the China Program Director of the United Board. During the visits, they communicated with the school leaders, young teachers, and students to learn the development and needs of the college. On the other hand, the college leaders also paid a visit to the United Board's headquarters in New York and its office in Hong Kong, and had a talk with officials of the United Board in the interval of international conferences organized by the United Board. It is worth mentioning that Dr. Light, the President of the United Board, together with 8 members of the Board of Trustees, paid the college a visit and inspection from November 14th to 15th, 2002. Xu Ou, the young assistant to the Dean, made an introduction of the old and new Hwa Nan and Wang Ling, another Assistant to the Dean, made a report on Hwa Nan, the higher education as well as the women's education in China. All the Board of Trustees was very impressed by the visit. In her letter of thanks, Anne Ofstedal, the China Program Director, said that at the board meeting held after the visit, the board members were full of praise for Hwa Nan's development and its efforts to train young teachers.

List of Contacts between Hwa Nan & the United Board

1986	Dr. Lauby, President of the United Board, paid the college a visit and gave students a lecture. Mr. Lin Benchun accompanied to be a translator.
21/1-30/1/1987	The College was invited as the sole representative of China to participate in the Seminar of Women's Higher Education in Asia held in Paya University, Chiang Mai, Thailand and presided over by the United Board.
7/4/1993	Roger Johnom, President of China Committee and professor of Wellesley College, USA, paid us a visit and discussed issues concerning the plan for arranging teaching practice in the College for university graduates who were going to proceed to get a Master's degree.
18/5/1993	Mr. Wen Dehui, President of the United Board paid us a visit, went to the hospital to visit Dean Yu Baosheng, and discussed the arrangements of supporting young teaching assistants to study in the USA and sending foreign teachers to the College with the College's leaders, staff of the Foreign Affairs Office and the director of the Applied English Department.
7/5/1994	Anne Ofstedal, the China Program Director, visited our college.
19/1/1995	Professor Kate Parry, from the United Board's teachers training course in Nanjing University, shared with our teaching assistants for English majors her teaching experience in the USA and China, and answered their questions on "how to organize listening & speaking and reading & writing courses".
12/2/1995	Chen Qionglin, Deputy Dean of the College, was invited to be a visiting scholar for six months at Florida State University, USA.
20/7/1995	Dr.David Viednetr, Wen Dehui, President of the United Board and Professor Ding Yanren from the Education Division at Amity Foundation paid us a visit and discussed the funding for the College.
9/1997	The United Board provided a special scholarship of U.S $5000 (equivalent to 40,000 Yuan) for poor students (101 students in total) enrolled in 1997 through the Amity Foundation.
24/7-26/7/1999	China Program Director of the United Board, Ms.Anne Ofstedal, paid the College a visit.
21/3-22/3/2001	China Program Director, Ms.Anne Ofstedal, paid the College a visit and inspection.
8/3/2002	The Vice President of the United Board, Dr. Rita Pullium, accompanied by its China Program Director, Ms.Anne Ofstedal, paid the College a visit and inspection.
14/11-15/11/2002	Dr. Light, President of the United Board, together with 8 members of the Board of Trustees, paid the college a visit and inspection.
5/2003	Wang Ling, the assistant to the Dean, paid a visit to the headquarters of the United Board.
20/3-3/4/2005	When attending the 2005 board meeting in Hong Kong, Chen Zhongying, the College President, Lin Benchun, Dean of the College,Wang Wei, Secretary, Xu Daofeng, Director of the Foreign Affairs Office, and Wang Ling, the assistant to the Dean, were invited to visit the Hong Kong Office of the United Board.

春色
任天涯
——福建华南女子
职业学院外教侧记
International Faculty with
Fujian Hua Nan Women's
College since 1908

304

24/9-29/9/2005	The Third International Conference and TESL（Teaching English as A Second Language）Workshop themed as "Creative Writing and Literature in English Teaching" sponsored by the United Board and organized by the College were held in Fuzhou City, Fujian Province.
8/3-10/3/2006	Dr. Birgit Linder, China Program Director, visited the College.
17/8/2006	The College had a visit from Vice Consul Mr. Daniel Cletus Gaush, Economic and Political Department of the Consulate General of US in Guangzhou, entrusted by ASHA Foundation, USA.
22/9/2006	The College had a visit from the US Consul General in Guangzhou, Robert Goldberg, the Political & Economic Consul and the Press & Culture Consul, accompanied by officials from the provincial Foreign Affairs Office.
10/2008	Avron Boretz and Birgit from the United Board, came to Hwa Nan for the 100th anniversary celebration.
1/2009	Jonathan Wolff, the Donation Manager of the United Board, paid a visit to the College and discussed ASHA project.
1/2/2010	The College had a visit from Patricia Stranahan, President of the United Board, and Jonathan Wolff, the Donation Manager of the United Board.
12/6-16/7/2011	A young teacher, Wu Yuanyuan of Hwa Nan, participated in the Institute for Advanced Study in Asian Cultures and Theologies (IASACT) held in Hong Kong and sponsored by the United Board.
11/3-13/3/2012	Dr. Nancy Chapman, the President of the United Board, and Ricky Cheng, the Vice President of the United Board came to visit Hwa Nan. Ricky Cheng had a face-to-face exchange and sharing themed "Concepts, Principles, Strategies and Methods of Raising Funds for Universities" with the College's leaders, middle-level administrators and staff from the Development Office and the Alumni Office.
1/11-2/11/2012	The College's library got the acceptance and review of the ASHA plan by the officials from the American Development Plan Department. The results of the plan were well recognized by the officials from the funder.
19/8/2012	Ms. Xiong Zhou, China Program Director, came to visit Hwa Nan. Zhang XunJie, Dean of the College, Xu Ou, Deputy Dean of the College, Wang Ling, Secretary-General of the Council, Zheng Huiling, the Chief Librarian, and Wu Yuan Yuan, Deputy Director of the Foreign Affairs Office, participated in the discussion.
8/2014	Vivica, Asia Program Director，visited Hwa Nan and discussed faculty programs.
8/2015	Cynthia, Asian Program Director, paid a visit to Hwa Nan and made a discussion on UB Programs.

The United Board has spared no effort in supporting Hwa Nan in training young teachers, and has developed many leaders, middle-level administrators, academic leaders and core teachers for Hwa Nan. Besides providing funds for training, the United Board also shows concern for the teachers' development and work in Hwa Nan. Now Hwa Nan could independently survive with its young and middle-aged core teachers. Hwa Nan had strong team of teachers, who helped make the transition from the old Hwa Nan to a new

Dr. Lauby paid a visit to Hwa Nan in the spring of 1986.

Mr. Joseph Sprunger, China Program Director, came to visit Hwa Nan.

Dr. Birgit Linder, China Program Director, visited Hwa Nan in 2006.

Dr. Nancy Chapman and Ms. Ricky Cheng had a visit in Hwa Nan in 2012.

Hwa Nan, and embarked on a new chapter. The United Board support mainly came in the form of project funding. Hwa Nan would apply for projects with the United Board, and make a report on the development of the College, the implementation of the projects and the use of funds to the United Board each year. Its good implementation of the projects, and frequent and effective communication with the United Board gained the appreciation and trust of the United Board. Basically, all of its projects, which mainly focused on the teachers training at home and abroad, as well as traning administrators, would get the United Board's support. In the beginning, for overseas studies, teachers were sent to get a higher degree in Florida State University, USA; and at home, 3-4 young teaching assistants were sent to study in higher colleges and universities each year. Later, overseas studies mainly took place in relevant colleges and universities in Thailand and the Philippines liaised by the United Board. Still later, as the United Board shifted its efforts of teacher training to colleges and universities in the less developed central and western regions, and as the young teachers of Hwa Nan got a higher degree group by group, Hwa Nan shifted

春色
任天涯
——福建华南女子
职业学院外教侧记
International Faculty with
Fujian Hua Nan Women's
College since 1908

306

its focus of projects to community service, scientific research and leadership training. Two deans and two vice deans of the College were sent in succession to attend the UB Fellow project held by the United Board. They went to the colleges and universities in the USA and Asia respectively for visits and studies for a semester, and participated in a week-long summary exchange organized by the United Board, thus improving their management and college running capacities.

Talking of the United Board's support to Hwa Nan in the young teacher training, a figure must be mentioned, Ms. Anne Ofstedal, the long-time China Program Director at the United Board. When in office, Ms. Anne Ofstedal played a significant role in the United Board's support to Hwa Nan in the young teacher training. Low-key, soft and firm, Ms. Anne Ofstedal always bore the interest of the College in mind, offered timely help, and gave the College firm, sustained and suitable support. The following is a list of overseas studies funded by the United Board.

List of Fujian Hwa Nan Women's College Overseas Studies Funded by the United Board

	Departments	Names	Projects	Colleges and Universities	Majors	Duration	Commencement Date & Ending Date
1	The Applied English Department	Li Xiaowu	Bachelor's Degree Study	Virginia University of Lynchburg, USA	Business Administration	1year	8/1989-5/1991
2		Zhang Hua	Master Degree Study	Florida State University, USA	Multilingual and Multicultural Education	2 years	8/1991-12/1993
3		Lin Han	Master Degree Study	Florida State University, USA	Child Development	2 years	8/1992-12/1994
4		Wang Ling	Master Degree Study	Florida State University, USA	Library and Information Science	2 years	9/1995-12/1997
5		Dong Xiuping	Master Degree Study	Florida State University, USA	Multilingual and Multicultural Education	2 years	1/2002-12/2003
6		Huang Fei	Master Degree Study	Assumption University,　Thailand	English Language Teaching	2 years	9/2003-1/2005
7		Zhao Hui	Master Degree Study	Hiroshima Jogakuin University, Japan	English Language and Literature	2 years	4/2002-4/2004
8		Yan Han	Master Degree Study	Assumption University,　Thailand	English Language Teaching	2 years	9/2004-1/2007
9		Pan Ying	Master Degree Study	Assumption University,　Thailand	Business Administration	2 years	12/2006-12/2008

308

春色
任天涯
——福建华南女子
职业学院外教侧记
International Faculty with
Fujian Hua Nan Women's
College since 1908

	Departments	Names	Projects	Colleges and Universities	Majors	Duration	Commencement Date & Ending Date
10	Fashion Design Department, Shoes and Hats Department	Xu Ou	Master Degree Study	Florida State University, USA	Apparel Merchandising	2 years	9/1999-12/2001
11		Zhou Ling	Master Degree Study	Hiroshima Jogakuin University, Japan	Clothing Life	2 years	4/2004-3/2006
12		Yu Rongming	Master Degree Study	Florida State University, USA	Fashion Design	2 years	11/1998-11/2000
13		Lin Lihua	Master Degree Study	Assumption University, Thailand	English Language Teaching	2 years	9/2003-1/2005
14	Business English Department	Lin Xiao	Master Degree Study	Assumption University, Thailand	English Language Teaching	2 years	9/2004-1/2007
15		Zhu Qing	Master Degree Study	Ateneo De Manila University	English Language and Literature Teaching	2 years	6/2006-8/2008
16		Yang Shuqing	Master Degree Study	De La Salle University, Philippines	Educational Leadership and Management	2 years	9/2006-10/2008
17	International Economics and Trade Department	Lin Xiaohong	Master Degree Study	Centenary College, USA	Business Administration	2 years	9/2004-9/2006
			Academic Exchange	New York, USA	Women's Higher Education Seminar		5/2008
18	Tourism Department	Chen Weiwei	Master Degree Study	Assumption University, Thailand	Tourism Management	2 years	12/2006-12/2008

	Departments	Names	Projects	Colleges and Universities	Majors	Duration	Commencement Date & Ending Date
19	Food and Nutrition Department	Zhang Xunjie	Master Degree Study	Florida State University, USA	Food Nutrition and Exercise Science	2 years	12/1993-12/1995
20		Su Mengna	Master Degree Study	Florida State University, USA	Food and Nutrition	2 years	8/2000-12/2002
21	Preschool Education Department	Cai Qiaoying	Master Degree Study	Florida State University, USA	Child Development	2 years	1995-1997
22		Ren Jianhong	Master Degree Study	Florida State University, USA	Family and Child Science	2 years	6/2004-8/2006
23	Preschool Education Department	Ren Jianhong	Visiting Scholar	Hong Kong Baptist University		Half year	9/1999-5/2000
24	College's Leaders	Wang Ling	Visiting Scholar	Randolph-Racon college, USA	Leadership Training	1 semester	2/2003-5/2003
			Visiting Scholar	Ewha Womans University	Leadership Training	1 semester	4/2004-6/2004

310

春色
任天涯
——福建华南女子
职业学院外教侧记
International Faculty with
Fujian Hua Nan Women's
College since 1908

	Departments	Names	Projects	Colleges and Universities	Majors	Duration	Commencement Date & Ending Date
25	Business English Department	Lin Xiao	Academic Exchange	Bangkok, Thailand	The 25th International Thailand TESOL		20/1/2005 -22/1/2005
			Academic Exchange	Manila, the Philippines	Higher Education International Symposium on Women's Leadership in Asia		3/12/2007-8/12/2007
26		Zhong Fulian	Academic Exchange	Manila, the Philippines	Women's Education and Gender Equality		12/5/2008-26/5/2008
27		Yang Wenyan	Further Education	University of Manila, Philippines	English Language		9/2007-11/2007
28	Fashion Design Department, Shoes and Hats Department	Yu Rongming	Academic Exchange	Sain Scholastica College, the Philippines	Gender Equality Education		6/2006-11/2006
			Academic Exchange	Luzern, Switzerland	The 21st International Annual Conference and the 100th Anniversary of the International Federation for Home Economics (IFHE)		26/72008-7/30/2008
29	Food and Nutrition Department	Su Mengna	Visiting Scholar	Maryknoll Women's College of Manila, the Philippines	Leadership Training	1semester	1/2007-5/2007

	Departments	Names	Projects	Colleges and Universities	Majors	Duration	Commencement Date & Ending Date
30	Department of Basic Courses	Yao Guangping	Academic Exchange	Manila, the Philippines	Women's Education and Gender Equality		12/5/2008-26/5/2008
			Visiting Scholar	Fu Jen Catholic University	Leadership Training	1semester	2009
				Lingnan University	Leadership Training	1semester	2010
31	College's Leaders	Zhang Xunjie		Hong Kong	Asian University Leaders Program (AULP) of UB		6/2/2009-11/2/2009
				Indonesia	Leadership Forum		26/7/2010-1/8/2010
			Academic Exchange	Hong Kong	Asian University Leaders Program (AULP) of UB		24/1/2011-28/1/2011
				Hong Kong	Asian University Leaders Program (AULP) of UB		2/2/2012-6/2/2012
32	College's Leaders	Xu Ou	Visiting Scholar	Faiefield University, USA	Leadership Training	1semester	9/2014-1/2015
			Visiting Scholar	Seoul Women's University, South Korea	Leadership Training	1semester	3/2016-6/2016

List of Projects Funded by the United Board (1997-2017)

	Teacher Training Abroad	Staff Welfare	Teacher Training in China	Scientific & Teaching Research, Publications	Scholarships	Leadership Training	Library Automation	Visiting Professors	UB fellowships	Conferences	Total
1997-1998	26,000	19,590		2,000	5,000						52,590
1998-1999	34,000	21,000	10,000	5,000							70,000
1999-2000		15,000	6,000	3,670							24,670
2001-2002	42,217		4,813			6,600	7,118	8,700	15,000		84,448
2002-2003	82,950		5,788			6,270					95,008
2003-2004	33,762		15,000	8,487				1,100	13,500		71,849
2004-2005	10,070		8,000								18,070
2005-2006	31,300									18,000	49,300
2006-2007			13,750					6,000	12,500		32,250
2007-2008	29,457.14		5,438						12,600		47,495.14
2008-2009	2,300		7,114						12,700		22,114
2010-2011				1,100							1,100
2012-2013				3,000							3,000
2014-2015									15,000		15,000
2015-2016				5,000					15,000		20,000
2016-2017				26, 400							26, 400
											633, 294.14

In 2007, out of great trust, the United Board proposed and supported the College in hosting an international conference in the old Shoushan campus, which was the only international conference held by us after our reestablishment and was a milestone in the history of our foreign and academic exchanges. On December 17th and 18th, 2007, the "Asian Women and Social Work" International Conference hosted by the United Board, organized by Hwa Nan, and co-organized by the College of Society and History, Fujian Normal University and Social Work Research Center of Yunnan University, was held in Hwa Nan. Both Professor Lin Benchun, College Dean and Dr. Linder, China Program Director at the United Board, delivered speeches of welcome at the opening ceremony. Mr. Xiang Rong, Director of Social Work Research Center of Yunnan University gave the keynote speech on research of Chinese Feminist Social Work Education. During the seminar, nearly 30 experts and scholars engaged in social work education from 9 countries and regions exchanged ideas on theories and practice of social work education. The "Women and Social Work in Asia" course outline was formulated, and a mechanism for cooperation and exchanges in research of social work education and student service learning were also established in the seminar. The international seminars promoted Hwa Nan College's communication and exchanges on social work for women with domestic and foreign scholars, and helped to integrate social work education for women into the College's curriculum.

Another significant contribution the United Board made to the College was its critical role in building the library. As early as 2001-2002, the United Board allocated $7118 for library automation. With the money, the library purchased computers and ILLAS system, initiated the setup of machine-readable books data base and realized automated

International Conference: "Women and Social Work in Asia" organized by Hwa Nan

春色
任天涯
——福建华南女子
职业学院外教侧记
International Faculty with
Fujian Hua Nan Women's
College since 1908

borrowing. In 2007 and 2008, the United Board and the College worked hand in hand to apply for ASHA plan — the library internet-based learning plan with United States Agency for International Development. ASHA i.e. American School and Hospital Abroad, a plan under USAID, provides assistance to schools, libraries, and medical centers outside the United States. ASHA receives applications once a year, which must be submitted together by a United States organization and a foreign one. In 2008, ASHA accepted the College's application and provided us with a fund of US $400000. During 2009-2012, the construction of the library under the plan was conducted in two stages. From September 2009 to June 2011, equipment and software such as the reception desk, access control systems, servers, storage devices, book shelves, tables and chairs, self-service print, copy and scan systems and equipment, e-reading room devices and management software, anti-virus software, e-books, VOD-demand systems and resources were purchased and installed. From October 2011 to June 2012, a remote access management system, three-seat steel chairs, air conditioning, books monitors, books, and a security monitoring system were purchased and installed. By the end of October 2012, all equipment, software and books purchased under the ASHA plan have all been put into use, and benefited all students and faculty. The results of the plan passed ASHA's inspection.

All faculty of Hwa Nan is deeply touched by the contribution the United Board has made. The staff sent to study abroad had great gratitude towards the United Board and deep love for the College. Most of them returned to the College on schedule, stuck to their positions, and became the backbone of the College. We'd like to dedicate this article to the United Board on behalf of all the staff who got assistance from the organization for its sustained and selfless help and support, and great efforts in training young teachers for the College. As the construction of the new campus came to an end in recent years, our financial pressures have been released to some extent. The College decided to donate a small capital to the United Board annually since 2014, to express our gratitude towards it. What's more, it shows our preservation of the school motto of "Having received, I ought to give", whose essence lies in selflessness, dedication, and giving instead of taking.

第一章

1951年前的福建华南女子职业学院外教

春色
任天涯
——福建华南女子
职业学院外教侧记
International Faculty with
Fujian Hua Nan Women's
College since 1908

316

第一节　华南女子文理学院（1908−1951）与外教

古语曰："闽在海中，闽中山在海中。"福州是有着千年历史文化积淀的"有福之州"。早在宋元时期便积极开展形式多样的对外交流活动，且从未间断；明清以降更是产生了数次海外移民潮，使得福州形成了开放包容、开拓创新的优良传统。

五口通商后，福州成为中西交流的重要前沿，西方传教士纷至沓来，将福州作为文化传播的重要传播据点。如已故美国加州大学物理学教授弥尔顿•加德纳1901年随父母来到中国，在福州的鼓岭度过了快乐的童年时光。1911年回到美国后，他立誓要再回到孩童时的故园去看看，临终前也不断念叨着"Kuliang, Kuliang"。1992年，在时任福州市委书记习近平的安排下，加德纳夫人终于如愿前往丈夫在世时心心念念的鼓岭，并且与九位年届九十的加德纳先生儿时的玩伴们围坐在一起畅谈往事。这个故事反映出近代福州对西人，尤其是对传教士群体的巨大吸引力。

西方传教士们在漫长的传教过程中，逐渐意识到只有改变中国人原本的传统思想才能取得更好的传教效果。杨格非认为，中国人有自己的语言，有自己的圣人、哲人、学者，唯有教育才能改变他们，让他们信奉上帝。[1]正因西人对在华教育活动的重视，来闽西方传教士纷纷根据本国教育制度开设各类学校，早在1848年，美以美会便在福州开设了男塾、女塾，而后福州保灵福音院、福音精舍、格致中学、文山女中、陶淑女中、三一中学等先后建立，这使得在福州建立高等院校成为可能。同时，发展女子教育事业因其必要性、迫切性成为当时福建社会的必然选择。正如华南女院第二任校长华惠德（Ids. B. Lewis, 1887—1969）在参加福州毓英女中的校庆时所说，传教士们已经在福州做了很多努力，使得女子也能享有平等的受教育的权利，如果没有教会女子初等、中等办学方面几十年的辛勤耕耘，也不可能创办教会女大学。[2]清末新政时期，清廷接连颁布《女子学堂章程》和《女子师范学堂章程》，女校建设得到了官方的重视。

1904年5月，在美国洛杉矶举行的美以美会总议会会议上，程吕底亚女士提出了在中国华南地区建立女子大学的设想，会议做出了"从福州地理与文化上之观察，均

1　R. W. Thompson & Griffith John: The Story of Fifty Years in China, London: The Religious Tract Society, 1906: 62.

2　谢必震.图说华南女子学院1908~2008[M]，福州：福建教育出版社，2008: 2.

认为有设立高级女校以提高女子教育之必要"[3]的决定，由程吕底亚女士负责大学的相关筹备工作。而后她将即将组建的女校命名为"华南女子学院"。

　　福州仓山地区的女学开设较早，1850 年美以美会传教士麦利和罗伯特·塞缪尔·麦克莱（Robert Samuel Maclay）的夫人便在仓山开办女塾[4]，1881 年著名的鹤龄英华书院亦在仓山建立。当地人对于女子教会学校的接受程度较高，成为女子大学理想的所在地。1908 年华南女院预科班开学，1914 年坐落于福州仓前山岭后路的华南女院行政楼彭氏楼及学生宿舍楼谷莲楼相继建成，华南女子文理学院最终落成，程吕底亚女士被任命为第一任校长。学校的主要目的旨在培养中下层女子宗教领袖，尤其是华南地区农村妇女。然而事与愿违，原本答应提供经济援助的美部会及圣公会却一再延误捐赠款项的发放，导致华南女院的资金供给十分紧张，直到 1917 年才开设正规的大学课程，1922 年后学校的经济情况才有所好转。

　　在华南女院的初创阶段，许多优秀的教师为其发展做出了巨大的贡献。这一时期的华南女院教师组成成分十分复杂，大多为外国女传教士或外国传教士眷属，也有少数归国华人，外籍教师除院长程吕底亚女士外，还有如华惠德、和爱德等，中国本土教师有谢绍英、陈叔圭、黄乃裳、魏建祥等。她们大多有过一些高等教育（外籍教师以神学院为主）经历，但华南女院成立初期的师资力量处于较为薄弱的水平。同时，建立初期的华南女院依旧将传教布道作为自身的第一目标，许多教师常需回国处理教会相关事物，使得学校教师更为紧缺，据陈叔圭后来回忆，有一次，程吕底亚"来告诉我学校所有的理科教师都走了，物理学没有人担任，她叫我来代替，我听了很莫名其妙，因为我从来没教过物理学……最后我只好答应了"[5]，程院长逐渐意识到了这个问题的严重性，采取"不拘一格降人才"的策略，大胆聘用了前清举人魏建祥负责国学专业的教学工作，而后又聘请了近代福州名人黄乃裳讲授国学，取得了良好的效果。

　　程吕底亚（1863—1941）毕业于美国西福特尔师范大学，1889 年来到福建进行传教工作，一待便是 50 年。她积极推动华南女院的创办，1912 年华南女院主楼因工程款告罄而被迫停工，程吕底亚万分着急，最后动员自己的哥哥将程氏祖居变卖，并无偿将钱款捐助给华南女院进行校舍的建设；她奔走各地为学校进行各类筹款活动，积极联系美国高校开展合作教学，在资金极为有限的条件下聘请优秀教师赴学

3　私立华南女子文理学院一览.福建省档案馆，1932 年，档案号39-1-23.
4　王豫生.福建教育史[M].福州：福建教育出版社，2004：296.
5　陈叔圭.典型的教师[M].华南学院校刊——程前校长纪念专号.南平：华南女子文理学院，1941：5.

春色
任天涯
——福建华南女子
职业学院外教侧记
International Faculty with
Fujian Hua Nan Women's
College since 1908

318

校教学，和华南女院一起经历了创建初期那段最艰辛的岁月。她一直将福州作为自己终生服务的地方。她的学生，华南女校第三任校长王世静深情回忆道："程前校长是我的恩师，我的慈母，也可以说是引我到新生之路上的唯一领导者。我忘记她是美国的女子，因为最同情于我国女子，首先发现我国女子有绝大的能力，如果施以教育，不让于任何男子，更比任何女子没有愧色的，就是她！……程校长有着先知先觉的眼光……她培植中国女子，不仅谋其自身改善，而且在由小及大、由近及远，谋普遍之改善……程前校长当日，早已见到中国女子，应该学习家政，并在历届学生中选派留美专攻家政，音乐一门也是她奠定基础。程前校长苦心焦思，凡是女子应有的学科，绝对不使缺乏，女子特长的学科，更设法谋其增加。"[6]另一位学生则记得程校长十分强调宗教的实践部分。[7]程吕底亚很赞同"受当施"的理念，认为高等教育的宗旨是为人服务，华南女院致力于培养对于未受教育同胞的责任感[8]。1922年纪念其建校功绩的"立雪楼"[9]正式破土兴建，取"程门立雪"一词以示纪念。1925年，已过花甲之年的程校长光荣引退，然而她并未因此离开中国，当时美以美会曾安排她回国的，但会督卢思义却认为她应该留在中国。[10]程吕底亚后来一直担任华

首任校长程吕底亚（1908—1925年在任）

6 王世静.永远刻在我的脑海中[M].华南学院校刊——程前校长纪念专号.南平：华南女子文理学院，1941:7-8.
7 Esther Ling. A Modern Apostle— A Tribute from the Alumnae. Yale University Divinity School Library Special Collections.United Board for Christian Higher Education in Asia Archives, Box177, Folder 3217.
8 L Ethel Wallace, Hwa Nan College: The Women's college of South China. New York: United Board For Christian Colleges in Asia, 1956:33.
9 "立雪楼"即今日福建师范大学校部"和平楼"。
10 Miss Lydia A. Trimble, Yale University Divinity School Library Special Collections. United Board for Christian Higher Education in Asia Archives, Box176, Folder 3217.

南女校顾问，以各种方式支持学校发展。1938年，已患重病的程吕底亚拒绝了学校提出的让其一同北迁南平的方案，决定留在福州协助学校进行教学物质的转移工作，1941年8月25日病逝于华南女院立雪楼。

华惠德是华南女院历史上杰出的教师之一，她生于英国，先后获得加拿大多伦多大学文学学士学位及美国哥伦比亚大学硕士学位，毕业后深感中国女子高等教育的羸弱，受程吕底亚校长的邀请毅然来到华南女院教书，历任华南女院教育学教授、教务主任、代理校长等职位。她教学严谨、待人和蔼，深受学生的爱戴，被学生们亲切地称为"华妈妈"。她在华南女院从教超过30年，在战争中也从未离弃这所学校，1941年因病回国，全校师生为她举行了盛大的送别仪式。华惠德也依依不舍，回到英国后，她用余生将其在中国的经历写成回忆录《华南女校：一所中国南方的女子大学》并出版（纽约，1956），在其中她详细记述了她与中国华南女院的情缘，为中国女子教会大学研究工作提供了非常宝贵的资料。

和爱德出生于美国一个传统的中产阶级家庭，从小兴趣广泛、涉猎颇多。她毕业于美国哥伦比亚大学理学专业，后又赴哈佛大学进修体育学，于1916年来到华南女院授课。在她赴校之前，华南女院并没有音乐专业，也没有校办的合唱团，和爱德在教学中充分发挥她的专业特长，将体育与音乐相结合。学生们在这位充满音乐天赋的老师的指挥下演唱功底日益精进。同时，音乐极大地丰富了女生们的课余生活，一起歌唱成为每个华南女院学生难以忘怀的美好记忆。据校友回忆，女学生们常结伴到闽江畔踏春，她们边感受春的气息，边放声欢唱"我的船儿在这里等着"。在和爱德的邀请下，1931年美国南加利福尼亚大学音乐学院毕业的施曼姿老师来校任教，她音乐造诣很深，是国际音乐家联谊会组织、全美高校音乐荣誉社团、全美学术荣誉社团成员，在战火纷飞的岁月里她一直留守学校，直到1951年回国。后来学校开设公共音乐专业，花重金购买了留声机及唱片等，让女学生们在课堂上感受到了来自当时世界前沿的音乐风尚。和爱德先后教授音乐及体育课程，曾任华南女院注册部主任，后由于经费问题无奈回国，在美国雪城大学担任讲师。

李戴耶出生于美国威斯康星州，在美国接受了完整的神学教育，于1921年到华南女院协助华惠德女士进行教育学课程的教学。然而，1937年后由于华南女院内迁南平，经费紧张，李戴耶不得不返回美国。

明茂丽也是华南女院早期教师之一，她的丈夫明霍利曾长期在马萨诸塞州传教，而后来到福州。明茂丽负责华南女院的宗教学课程，她力求将宗教教义与学生的日常生活相结合，在教学中取得了良好的效果。

春色
任天涯
——福建华南女子
职业学院外教侧记
International Faculty with
Fujian Hua Nan Women's
College since 1908

320

卢师姑（Lula C. Baker）　　　　　　　黄乃裳

其他教员还有卢师姑、康师姑、罗黎唏等。此外，教员中还有不少中国人。

谢绍英是闽县（今福州市区）人，1893年毕业于毓英女学，1896年赴美国晨边学院学习，获得音乐硕士学位。回国后她先在华南女院附中教授音乐课程，而后成为华南女院的音乐教师，她是学校历史上第一位本土教师，由于初建的华南女院办学条件较差，谢老师不得不长期独担重任，为学校培养了大批的音乐人才。她为华南女院工作30余年，学生们称她为谢师姑，人们赞许她忠信可嘉。

陈叔圭亦是闽县人，曾在华南女院附中就读，先后获得康奈尔大学教育学学士学位，哥伦比亚大学教育硕士、博士学位，1923年回华南女院任教，先后任院务委员会主席、教育系主任。她将一生都奉献给了华南女校。

黄乃裳出生于福州市闽清县，是一位富有传奇色彩的中国近代人物，为中华民族的解放做出了杰出的贡献。1991年，时任福州市委书记的习近平同志曾对他高度评价："黄乃裳先生是全体华侨的骄傲，也是中华民族的骄傲。"并号召大家进一步学习和发扬黄乃裳的三种精神，即"爱国主义精神""艰苦创业精神""不懈探索、追求进步精神"。事实上，黄乃裳也是一位教育家，1911年他被推举为福州福音、英华、培元三书院的教务长，后于1919年受聘为华南女院教师，当时他正带领福州人民建设"福斗圳"，但劳累丝毫没有影响71岁的他对于国学的热爱，被女学生们亲切地称为"黄爷爷"。

魏建祥是松吉乡罗峰村人，光绪二十九年（1903）举人，先后担任古田县知事、英华中学教师，1924年受邀前往华南女院教授国学，他国学基础深厚，文笔尤佳，堪称"意精词湛，锋发韵流"，上课生动有趣，深受学生们的喜爱。1941年魏建祥光荣退休，回家乡兴办罗峰小学，1974年病逝于克里夫兰。

在程校长领导期间（1908—1925），华南女院师生克服了种种不利因素，使学校取得了长足的发展。在学校成立初期，只有一个专业，即教育主修专业。随着学校的发展，1924年成立了宗教教育学和生物学专业，1925年更增添了化学系，学校逐渐成为兼有文理学科的综合性大学，入学人数逐年增多，从1920年的21人增添至1923年的63人。到程院长退休时已有87人进入华南女院学习。此外，华南女院还将校名由"Huan Nang"改为"Hwa Nan"，并且取得了美国纽约州立大学理事部的临时特许证，学校规模进一步扩大，成为与金陵女子大学齐名的女子高等学府。同时，程校长注重加强与中国政府的联系。1917年，在程校长的邀请下，民国第一任闽督李厚基前往华南女院探望学生，受到了热情的欢迎，学校也在民国政府的支持下不断发展。

华南女院早期外籍教师合影（1913）

程吕底亚退休后，美以美会指派著名基督教教育家卢爱德女士出任校长。

卢爱德（1887—1969）曾就读于美国晨边学院，后获得哥伦比亚大学教育学博士学位。陶行知称她为"近几年唯一在中国女子教育上有研究的人"[11]，俞庆棠也将其称为中国女子教育史上的"良友"。卢爱德信奉自由派神学，坚持基督教教育便是人格培养的教育。她认为基督教团体在东方实现基督教化的过程中，为他们培养自己的基督教领袖是最快且唯一的途径[12]，她对女子教育极为重视，强调培训积极服

11 陶行知.女子教育在学制上占领地位之十五周年纪念.陶行知全集（卷一）.成都：四川教育出版社，1991:467.
12 "The Foreign Missions Convention of the United States and Canada", Woman's Missionary Friend (May, 1925), Boston: Woman's Foreign Missionary Society of the Methodist Episcopal Church.

春色
任天涯
——福建华南女子
职业学院外教侧记
International Faculty with
Fujian Hua Nan Women's
College since 1908

322

务的基督妇女应该是大学的使命[13]。在她的著作《中国女子高等教育》一书中，卢爱德系统阐述了基督教女子高等教育在中国发展的理论，首先是进行基督教女子高等教育的三个目的：（1）使用中西文化之精华改造中国社会；（2）促进中国新女性的自我觉醒；（3）培养乐于为中国社会服务的宗教领袖[14]。而后她根据中国女子教育的历史和现状，提出了在中国发展基督教女子教育的一些建议，包括：（1）提高教会学校在中国女子教育系统中的地位；（2）不应忽视中国贫下阶层子女的教育问题；（3）中国女子教育不应与社会生活脱离[15]。这些建议具有高度的建设性与前瞻性。

　　因此她在华南女院进行了大范围的改革。首先是调整院系，她积极发展公共卫生系、家政系等实用型专业，力求做到教学与生活相结合。其次她启用本土教师参与学校管理层的建设，开创了华南女院"华人治校"的优良传统。如卢校长对青年教师陈叔圭极为关爱，不仅将其提拔为副教授，还任命她为华南女院附中代理校长，并称"这项任命是本年度我校发展的最重要进展"[16]。此外，卢校长积极游走于美国大学，为华南女院争取经费，在她的努力下有7所美国大学与华南女院建立了合作关系，为学校带来了办校急需的设备和经费。在她的带领下华南女院不断发展，在华南地区有着很高的知名度。

第二任校长卢爱德（1925—1927年在任）

13　Ida B. Lewis. "Higher Education of Women in China", *Educational Review*. Shanghai: China　Christian Educational Association,1917(10):272.

14　Ibid: p. 274.

15　Ida Belle Lewis. *The Education of Girls in China*. New York: PhD Thesis, Columbia University, 1919:35-36.

16　"Report of Hwa Nan College", Foochow Woman's Conference, 1919~1930(1926). Shanghai: Methodist Publishing House, 1931:19.

然而，卢爱德上任不久便遇到了重大的挑战。1927年福州爆发了声势浩大的收回教育权运动，要求"严格取缔教会学校并禁止其注册立案"[17]，华南女院成为众矢之的，面临着停课解散的命运。关键时刻，卢爱德做出了一个"舍小家护大家"的决定，她主动辞去校长职位，在校内成立"五人校务委员会"，成员均为中国人，其中陈叔圭为主席，王世静以委员身份兼任教务长，李美德以委员身份兼任庶务长，黄惠珍以委员身份兼任中学主任，黄惠珠以委员身份兼任秘书。最终，王世静成为华南女院的新掌舵人，学校也开启了崭新的篇章。

新的华南女校并未停止前进的步伐。1933年华南女子学院改名为"私立华南女子文理学院"，设中文、外语、教育、家政、数理、化学、生物7个系。一年后，纽约州立大学授予华南女院永久特许状，再一次扩大了华南女院在中国的影响力。

1937年日寇全面侵华，次年华南女院被迫北迁延平（即南平市延平区），并且不断遭遇日军机的狂轰滥炸。随着抗战的持续，日寇的轰炸频率越来越高。1939年南平遭遇三次轰炸，这在华南女院教职工看来算是比较平静的了："一次在五月八日，一次在七月十二日，一次在九月二十二日，三次轰炸都离我们非常近，幸亏我们都躲在防空洞里。"[18]而到了1941年，仅八月份学校便被轰炸两次，"八月份我们受到了两轮轰炸，一轮三枚炸弹，另一轮则多达十七枚，每天都拉响防空警报。我们只好连续几个小时待在洞旁，或直接躲进洞内"。[19]在这样艰苦的情况下，华南女院在王校长的带领下并未退缩，反而在困境中不断发展，从1928年、1931年、1947年三张教职工列表（分别见表一、表二、表三）中我们可以发现教师学历越来越高，中外教师的比例由最初的外教占优变为中外平衡，这反映出王世静校长不仅积极引进优秀的华南女院毕业生，同时积极招揽外国高水平人员参与学校建设，形成了人才荟萃的局面。

17　章振乾.收回教育权运动的回忆、福建文史资料（第13辑）.福州：福建人民出版社，1986:158.
18　"Excerpts from letters from Hwa Nan Staff Members"（Yen Ping, 1940）, Yale University Divinity School Library Special Collections. United Board for Christian Higher Education in Asia Archives, Box177, Folder 3207.
19　Ibid.

春色
任天涯
——福建华南女子
职业学院外教侧记
International Faculty with
Fujian Hua Nan Women's
College since 1908

表一　1928年华南女院外国教员履历表[20]

姓名	职务	资历
卢爱德	顾问	美国晨边大学文学学士、哥伦比亚大学博士、前美部会教育部干事
华教授	顾问、教育学教授	美国叨伦大学文学学士、美国哥伦比亚大学硕士
和教授	体育唱歌教授兼册记	美国哥伦比亚大学文学学士、美国哈佛大学体育科毕业
罗教授	宗教教授	美国波士顿大学硕士
张教授	卫生教授	美国约翰·霍普金斯大学理科博士
施教授	历史、数学教授	美国康奈尔大学文学学士
康教授	英文教授	美国白提斯大学文学学士、哥伦比亚大学硕士
明教授	宗教教授	美国德包大学文学学士、芝加哥大学肄业
琴教授	生物教授	美国塞列克士大学文学学士、硕士
爱教授	英文教授	美国西北大学文学学士、哥伦比亚大学肄业
蓝教授	动物学教授	美国塞列克士大学文学学士
邓女士	图书馆主任	美国师范学院毕业
河教授	植物学教授	美国莺蒙大学文学学士、西北大学硕士

表二　1931年华南女院外国教员履历表[21]

姓名	职务	资历
华惠德	顾问	加拿大多伦多大学文学学士、美国哥伦比亚大学硕士，历任华南女院教务主任及代理院长
和爱德	体育唱歌教授兼册记	美国哥伦比亚大学学士，哈佛大学体育科毕业，美国塞列克士大学讲师
琴陶世	生物教授	美国塞列克士大学文学学士、硕士，曾任美国塞列克士大学讲师
张淑琼	英文教授	美国晨边大学文学学士，曾任美国得克萨斯州学校和密苏里学校英文教员
刘玛利	教育学教授	哥伦比亚大学硕士
邓惠贞	音乐系助教，兼任图书馆主任	美国波士顿大学学士
爱以利	英文教授	美国西北大学学士、威斯康辛大学硕士，曾任美国威斯康辛州一所中学的校长
巴美德	艺术系教授	美国波芒拿大学文学学士、哥伦比亚大学硕士

20 张涵深.私立华南女子文理学院概况.文史资料选编（第五卷）.福州：福建人民出版社，2003:517—519.
21 私立华南女子文理学院呈请立案用表之（一）.福建省档案馆，档案号39-1-5.

姓名	职务	资历
康慎德	英文教授	美国白提斯大学文学学士、哥伦比亚大学硕士，曾在美国马萨诸塞州遮而寺学校、坎诺提克省桥波学校和新泽西州东阿莲学校当英文教员
施曼姿	音乐系教授	美国威廉参大学学士，曾任美国南加利福尼亚大学音乐教师

表三　1947年华南女院外国教员履历表[22]

姓名	职务	资历
Albert Faurot	音乐系副教授	美国欧柏林大学音乐学硕士
Frances Fulton	音乐系讲师	美国西海岸州立大学音乐学学士
施曼姿	音乐系副教授	美国南加利福尼亚大学音乐学学士
Evolyn Troutman	教育系教授	美国纽约协和神学院学士
华惠德	顾问、教育学教授	美国叨伦大学文学学士、美国哥伦比亚大学硕士
Marion Cole	英语系教授	美国哥伦比亚大学文学学士
Elsie I. Reik	英语系教授	美国威斯康辛大学文学硕士
Jessie Lacy	英语系讲师	美国卫斯理大学文学学士
Isabelle Lewis	教育系教授	美国哥伦比亚大学博士
Elizabeth Mortimer	家政系讲师	美国伊利诺伊州卫斯理大学文学学士

　　在这一时期对华南女院的发展产生最重大影响的，毫无疑问是在职25年的第三任校长王世静女士（1927—1951在任）。王世静（1897—1983）出生于福州一个望族家庭，她的祖父是清道光年间（1821—1850）进士，官至两广总督，在这样的书香家庭中，王世静从小便受到良好的教育。1913年入华南女院预科就读，先后获得晨边大学教育学学士、密歇根州立大学教育学硕士及博士。王世静极为赞同梁启超"吾推及天下之积弱之本，则必自妇人不学始"[23]的观点，积极实践卢爱德女士的教育思想，提出"受当施"的办学理念，强调"本中华民国教育宗旨以栽培中国女青年得受文学、科学上、职业上之高等教育并养成牺牲服务之高尚人格"。[24]她不仅关心学校师生发展，不断健全学科门类，引入高素质教师提高教学质量，同时东奔西走为学校募捐，如1937年她前往香港、广东、东南亚等地探访华南女院校友，为华南女

---

22 List of faculty and administrative staff-A (serving during current semester) & staff-B (on leave), Yale University Divinity School Library Special Collections. United Board for Christian Higher Education in Asia Archives, Box176, Folder 3196.
23 梁启超.饮冰室文集.中华民国十五年九月中华书局铅印本，第二册，第14页.
24 私立华南女子学院组织大纲（第三条），福建省档案馆，1932年，档案号39-1-6.

春色
任天涯
——福建华南女子
职业学院外教侧记
International Faculty with
Fujian Hua Nan Women's
College since 1908

326

院的发展募款；1947年，亚洲基督教高等教育联合董事会在美国召开战后复兴会议，王世静在会上报告了华南女院在抗战期间坚持办学的情况，会后还到各大学演讲，备受欢迎和赞赏，许多美国人士和华南女院在美校友纷纷解囊相助。中华人民共和国成立后，王校长一直关心福建女子教育发展，把一生都奉献给了福建的教育事业。

王世静（1927—1951在任[25]）

Leon Roy Peel毕业于美国波士顿大学，先后获得神学学士、神学硕士学位，1927年她被女子海外传教会派往华南女院担任宗教学教授。在校期间，她在出色完成教学任务的同时，积极为学校募捐筹款。尤其是1938年学校被迫迁往南平，需要大量经费支持，Leon Peel动用了各种社会力量为学校捐款，让学校度过了建校以来最大的财政危机，一时传为华南女院之佳话。

她的第一个求助对象便是自己的母会——女子海外传教会明尼波利斯分会。1938年初，她顺利收到差会捐助的2836.68美金款项。而后，她向差会详细列举了学校三类主要预算的使用情况，在和差会协商后，最终差会同意进一步对华南女院行政预算、建设预算两方面进行经费资助[26]。

同时，她还在福州当地积极开展募捐活动。然而此时的福州一片兵荒马乱，1938年华南女院竟然仅募得60美元。Leon Peel老师一直为了学院剩余的2500美金预

25　其中王世静于1927~1929年在美进修，由陈淑圭代理校长一职。

26　B. A. Garside. "Letter to Hwa Nan College" (January20, 1938). Yale University Divinity School Library Special Collections. United Board for Christian Higher Education in Asia Archives, Box177, Folder 3204.

算缺口不断努力。最终她决定只身前往美国寻求亚联董的帮助，最终如愿以偿。正是因为Leon Peel的巨大努力，华南女院能够顺利迁往南平，出资借用南平卫理公会几所房子及私立剑津中学的校舍，同时将一个旧祠堂改造为宿舍，继续进行教学活动。

　　Grace Davis和Leon Peel一起来到华南女院负责财务及预算工作，1939年9月因为需回国处理一些事务离开华南女院，王校长说："她做了很多工作，使得财政和预算报告得以及时提交给校委员会会议讨论。尤其是在这样艰难的时候，我们特别需要她在美国为华南女院工作。"[27]

　　W. P. W. Williams是第一任校长程吕底亚的助手，1928年在程吕底亚的邀请下来到福州协助其开展传教工作，并在1938年追随程前校长留守福州华南女院，她不仅照顾年老体弱的程前校长，而且承担起了打扫校园的工作。1941年2月9日，一场大火烧毁了彭氏楼。之后吕威廉积极联系亚联董试图对校舍进行修缮，遗憾的是受限于当时的情况，这项工作直到1946年后才着手进行。

　　Mrs. Earhart是美以美会派往华南女院的教师，1934年她前往华南女院，担任音乐系教授。而后虽然学校因战事北迁，教师待遇极差[28]，甚至有时会数月拿不到工资，但哈特夫妇并未放弃。1941年彭氏楼被烧毁后，哈特返回美国为学校募捐经费进行大楼的重建工作。最终她和丈夫哈特先生成功募集到资金，并委托Ruth Chou将善款带回南平。这让全体华南女院师生极为感动。在给哈特丈夫的信中，王校长写道："在那艰难的日子里我常常回忆起1934年她与我在华南女院共事时对我说的话：'Lucy，要挺住。'她的鼓励至今给我极大的鼓舞……要是战后你能帮我们重建彭氏楼，或者建一座教堂或音乐厅来纪念哈特，那该多好。"[29]可惜的是，哈特女士再也没有机会重返华南女院任教，但她对学校发展做出的贡献却被记录了下来。

　　Elsie I. Reik于1934年来到华南女院任教，负责英语系的教学工作，1938年随学校迁往南平。在战火纷飞的年代，她还费心把课上得生动有趣，让生活充满喜悦。她从福州带去大量照片、诗歌，创造性地在英语课堂上使用。自己带的图片不够用时，她让朋友给她寄各种杂志图片供教学之用[30]。她还让朋友给她寄圣诞节礼物，以

27　Hwa Nan News (January, 1939)，Yale University Divinity School Library Special Collections. United Board for Christian Higher Education in Asia Archives, Box177, Folder 3212.

28　根据《私立华南女子文理学院呈请立案用表之（一）》（现藏福建省档案馆，档案号39-1-5），战前外籍教师月收入333元，而战后随着海外教会与学校的交流阻绝，外籍教师的月收入下调至100元。

29　Lucy C. Wang. "Letter to Mr. H. Earhart" (February 12, 1943),Yale University Divinity School Library Special Collections. United Board for Christian Higher Education in Asia Archives, Box177, Folder 3206.

30　Elsie Reik. "Letter to Mrs. Peel" (December, 29, 1938), Yale University Divinity School Library Special Collections. United Board for Christian Higher Education in Asia Archives, Box177, Folder 3207.

春色
任天涯
——福建华南女子
职业学院外教侧记
International Faculty with
Fujian Hua Nan Women's
College since 1908

328

便送给当地的孩子和员工[31]。

Margaret Seeck是华南女院董事会从英国引进的儿童护理学的教授，她到校之后，很快便着手开展华南女院特殊儿童社会服务培训项目，推动了特殊时期华南女校家政系的发展。1939年，玛格丽特女士因事回国，华南女院的师生们都极为不舍。社会服务培训课程的开设使得华南女院的学生更具有社会责任感，在这一方面完全应感谢玛格丽特。

Marion Cole是华南女院英语系教师，1931年来校任教，1938年因病返回美国治疗，然而她依旧深爱着大洋彼岸那个饱受战火摧残的国度。1939年她返回中国，但是由于日军的阻挠，她没能再次回到华南女院，只能前往北平语言学校执教，1951年再次回国。

施曼姿的好友Frances Fulton也在华南女院任职，从1936年起在化学系任教三年，同时还常常兼音乐系的工作，她在华南女院最艰难的时候给予女校的支持永远值得感恩[32]。

另外，还有许多华南女院的毕业生毅然选择回到母校任职，使得华南女院的教育一直处于较高水平。如华南女院1933届毕业生Jean Chen，毕业后赴美国堪萨斯州立大学农业与应用科学研究所深造，获得食品经济及营养学硕士学位，之后她放弃了留在美国的机会，回到母校任教，担任家政系主任；He I-Wu毕业于华南女院附中，先后获得晨边大学物理学学士学位、芝加哥大学物理学硕士学位，后和Jean Chen一样回华南女院任教，王校长曾深情地讲："我们很庆幸何先生在我校任教。"[33]这从侧面反映了何老师对于困境中的华南女院物理系的重要性。

除了这些在战时女子高等教育第一线辛勤工作的教师们，很多社会人士也用实际行动支援华南女院的建设。他们不仅在经费上尽可能地提供支持，而且还对学校进行实地探访。许多宗教人士，如Cowdy主教在出席1938年12月的南平传教年度会议后前往华南女院临时所在地和师生们亲切交流；很多福州教育届的同行，如英华书院的James L. Ding、福建协和大学的Mrs. C. J. Lin、福建三一学院的陈教授等，每年都会去学校交流学习。此外，当时的福建省官员也经常会前往南平探视学校，给予巨大的支持。

---

31 Elsie Reik. "Letter to Mrs. Peel" (December, 29, 1938), Yale University Divinity School Library Special Collections. United Board for Christian Higher Education in Asia Archives, Box177, Folder 3207.

32 Hwa Nan News (January, 1939) , Yale University Divinity School Library Special Collections. United Board for Christian Higher Education in Asia Archives, Box177, Folder 3212.

33 Ibid.

　　抗战胜利后，华南女院从南平迁回福州。然而学校主楼彭氏楼的烧毁给学校的复课带来了极大的困难，可喜的是华南女院的复校工作得到了中外多方的支持，美国联合董事会汇款5万美元作为彭氏楼的重建经费，教育部也给予学校半年的办学补助款。这使华南女院得以继续招生办学，学校迎来了又一次腾飞，学生人数一度突破300人。

　　1949年新中国成立，学校积极响应"三自爱国运动"，1951年王校长代表学校交出7枚校印，华南女院结束了她艰难而又辉煌的43年。

1950年华南女院教职工合影

第二节　春风化雨总关情
——记福建华南女子职业学院前两任院长

　　走进华南女院校园专家楼的会客厅，赫然入眼的是墙上三幅女子的画像。她们显得宁静而尊贵。画像上画着的是华南女院前三任院长。首任院长程吕底亚位于中间，她的右边是第二任院长卢爱德。这两位女院长连同第三任院长王世静引导华南女院走过了时局动荡、风雨飘摇的近半个世纪。

春色
任天涯
——福建华南女子
职业学院外教侧记
International Faculty with
Fujian Hua Nan Women's
College since 1908

330

程吕底亚（1863—1941）——华南女院首任院长

程吕底亚是华南女院首任院长。她出生于加拿大渥太华附近，家有兄弟姐妹十人，程吕底亚排行第九。她是美国美以美基督教会成员，二十岁时跟随其兄长 Dr. James B.Trimble 游学于美国艾奥瓦州。从美国西弗特而师范学校（师范学院的预科学校）毕业后，她决心成为一名传教士。1889年，受美国美以美会海外女布道会得梅因支会派遣来到中国福建，开始了她在华50余年的传教办学生涯。

1901年至1904年间，程吕底亚回美国休养，同时在美国爱艾奥瓦州苏市的晨边大学攻读学士学位。1904年5月，她参加了在洛杉矶举行的美以美会总会议。在会议上，她申请在中国南方建立一所女子大学。美以美会海外女布道会委员会同意了她这一请求并做出以下决定：其一授权在福州建立一所女子大学，其二由程吕底亚和另外两位女传教士三人组成一个委员会，负责选定大学的地

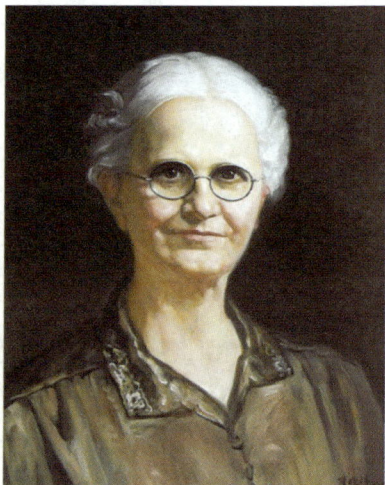

程吕底亚，华南女院首任院长

址、规划校园建筑并决定适宜的课程等事宜，由托事会督导她们的工作（Davis, 1991: 22）。这便是建立华南女院的最初来由。

1908年，华南女院的预科学校成立，程吕底亚被任命为校长。任预科学校校长前两年，她在福建沿海地区龙田建立了一所女子寄宿学校，积累了在艰苦环境中办学、创业的经验。据华惠德（1956: 7- 8；2005：8）回忆，当年"在福州美以美会会督卢思义的坚持下，这个小小的学校被称为福州女子大学预科。这个名字经常提醒大家那计划中的大学将很快地变成

1912年兴建中的华南女院彭氏楼
（谢必震，2008：48）

1912年建设中的彭氏楼
（谢必震，2008：49）

1912年兴建中的彭氏楼和谷莲楼（左边）（谢必震，2008：49）

现实"。按照西方惯例，大学往往都是由预科发展而成。因缺乏资金，大学的筹备和建设进展缓慢。然而，在教会、各方朋友的捐助下，华南女院于1911年秋开始破土动工。

程吕底亚治校期间，抱着女子应该享有受教育的权利，并培养基督教会女性领导人才的执着信念，克服万难，为华南女院的良好发展打下了坚实的基础。1914年，大学结束了在条件简陋的租赁屋子办学的日子，即将搬进新落成的彭氏楼，准备开始招收大学一年级新生。然而，宿舍楼谷莲楼因资金告罄远未完工。卢思义会督建议将学校的资金需求告知程吕底亚兄长James B. Trimble 博士。程氏夫妇悄悄地抵押了他们的农场，将4,000美元的款项捐给华南女院，使得谷莲楼得以在当年建成使用（华惠德，1956: 15）。不久彭氏楼和谷莲楼被称为"建筑瑰宝"，两座建筑的独特设计是福州历史上前所未有的。

因师资、教学设施等条件制约，当时大学决定只招收一二年级两班学生。学生读完这两年课程后，学校鼓励她们到其他地方完成三四年级课程（华惠德，1956:16；2005）。事实上，当时师资严重不足，程女士既当校长，又兼授课老师。她从早上8：30至下午5：30给学生授课，下课后她还要处理行政工作并翻译一些教材。（Campbell, 2005: 335）

春色
任天涯
——福建华南女子
职业学院外教侧记
International Faculty with
Fujian Hua Nan Women's
College since 1908

程校长和第三届高中毕业班（1914）（谢必震，2008：9）

　　1916年共有五名学生完成了大学一二年级课程，随后有4名学生到美国和加拿大留学，另外一名进入上海基督教医科大学继续深造。那时出国留学是稀罕事，而华南女子大学首批毕业的五位学生中有4位得以被海外的大学录取，这证明学校培养的学生知识基础扎实，已具备开办完整的四年大学课程的条件。为体现这一提升，董事会将校名改为华南女院。次年，华南开设了大学三四年级课程。至此，华南女院开设了四年制本科的全部课程，首先开办教育系。（周艺芳，2006）

　　囿于师资力量的不足，教育系自1917年开设以后的六年间是学校唯一的学系，直至1924年，学校新增了两个专业：宗教教育专业和生物专业。1925年教育系开设的课程共11门，包括心理学原理、儿童心理学、性学、学校管理法、小学教授原则及练习、中学课程教授法、近代小学教育史、英文教授法、音乐教授法、学校体操教授法、游戏术。（周艺芳，2006：29）

大学毕业班（1916）（谢必震，2008：10）

程校长与附中毕业生（1924）（谢必震，2008：13）

　　1921年的毕业典礼上，程吕底亚授予三位首届毕业生大学文凭。这标志着华南女院已经成熟，完全具备实施高等教育的条件。日后这三名毕业生均从事教育工作，成绩骄人。

　　首届大学毕业典礼之后，大学的情形并不十分乐观。华南女院并未获得中国国家教育部或美国大学的注册承认，程吕底亚及学校其他管理者意识到这一局限必将影响华南女院日后的发展。鉴于此，教务长华惠德女士（程吕底亚外甥女）趁当年回美休假之机，着手向纽约州立大学评议会申请注册许可证事宜。申请工作并非一帆风顺，甚至机会渺茫，因为华惠德女士得知纽约州立大学评议会只向一座城市发放一个许可证，而该大学已经向福州的福建协和大学发放了许可证。（Davis，1991）

教务长华惠德（谢必震，2008：5）

　　1922年初，华惠德休假期满回到华南女院，她将这项艰巨的任务转交给和爱德负责。和爱德在华南女院担任大学物理教学和合唱团的工作，当时她正在纽约进修。经过艰难的申请准备工作，申请文件最终上呈到纽约州立大学评议会。评议会在1922年9月28日同意给予华南女院临时许可证。这是华南女院办学史上的一个重要里程碑，这一成就鼓舞了华南女院的师生，大家信心倍增。纽约州立大学副校长穆峙先生在其祝贺信中赞道："……根据女士（华惠德女士）所条陈的意见，和该校所设立的学科，足见主持该校教育的人，实属眼光长远，思想前进，其所栽培之中国女子将来必能应付一切问题与责任，不失为妇女领袖的地位。"（华惠德，1956：25-26；2005：25）

春色
任天涯
——福建华南女子
职业学院外教侧记
International Faculty with
Fujian Hua Nan Women's
College since 1908

获纽约州立大学特许证后留念（1922）
（谢必震，2008：12）

程校长和毕业生留影（1924）（谢必震，2008：15）

　　1925年，年逾花甲的程吕底亚从华南女院校长任上引退。在她担任校长的17年间，华南女院从预科学校发展成为本科制大学，从设立大学一、二年级课程开始，到设立完整的大学四年课程，再到最终获得美国纽约州立大学特别许可证书，步步维艰，但步步扎实，为日后华南女院的发展打下了坚实的基础。至1925年，校园第三座楼——宿舍楼完工，与彭氏楼和谷莲楼连为一体，校园主体建筑建设竣工了。程吕底亚卓越的领导才能和眼光使大学在初创时期获得巨大的成功。为了纪念她为华南女院做出的杰出贡献，1925年完

纪念程吕底亚老校长来华50周年（1939）（谢必震，2008：34）

工的新宿舍楼被命名为"程吕底亚楼"，后来又称立雪楼。

程吕底亚女士毕生致力于女子教育事业，致力于建设与发展华南女院。她倡导并实践了校训"受当施"。她虽然辞去了校长职务，但是她坚持不懈、坚韧不拔、不畏困难的精神和品质永远留给了华南女院。

卢爱德（1887 — 1969）——华南女院第二任院长

卢爱德出生于美国爱荷华州布莱尔斯敦市，美国晨边大学校长、福州美以美会会督卢思义之女。1909年她毕业于美国晨边大学并获文学学士学位。毕业后来华任教，在天津Sara L. Keen 纪念中学教学五年。1915年回美国入哥伦比亚大学师范学院读研究生课程，于1919年获得教育学博士学位。同年，她出版了论著《中国女子教育》。通过调查研究，她在书中详细阐述了中国近代女子教育的状况及面临的种种问题，揭示了产生诸多问题的社会根源，并提出具体建议，希望教育界和当局能实行更有效的教育政策以发展中国女子教育。

卢爱德博士，华南女院第二任院长

1922年她以美以美会女外洋布道会代表的身份来华考察该教会在中国开展教育工作的情况，希望实现更经济、更有效率的重组。（华惠德，1956：30）于是她访问并考察了华南女院。因此在接任华南女院校长之前，她对该校已有相当了解，从她对华南女院的报告中可见："华南女子大学的特质在于她的精神。……华南精神体现在毕业生的工作中。……她们办事有效率，有淑女风范，从城市到边远地区，她们确立了基督教女性的标准（华惠德，1956：30）。"

卢爱德了解华南女院，1925年，美国托事部顺理成章地选派她担任华南女院第二任校长。因有其他事宜未了，她未能立马上任，董事会决定在此几个月期间由教务长华惠德代理校长一职。

1926年1月28日卢爱德到任，学校为她举办了就职典礼，这一天还举办了第六届毕业典礼。在欢迎致辞上，华惠德表示卢爱德不是外人，相反地，她说："卢博士深得人心。她虔敬的精神、教育学知识和一口流利的汉语使她获得中国学者的尊敬和学生的喜爱（华惠德，1956：35）。"

卢爱德善于对教育状况进行调查与研究，并从中发现问题，从而提出解决问题

春色
任天涯
——福建华南女子
职业学院外教侧记
International Faculty with
Fujian Hua Nan Women's
College since 1908

336

毕业留影（1925）（谢必震，2008：16）

的方案。1926年秋，在第一份校长年度报告中，她用具体数据总结了华南女院自办学以来所取得的成就和办学状况（Campbell，2005：340）：共有38位学生从华南女院毕业，其中有34名校友曾在基督教会学校工作过；现有24名校友在基督教会学校继续服务；两名校友在美国进修，其中一名将于1927年回到母校工作；四名校友在学医；三名校友已结婚，组建了基督教家庭；另三名在中国内地攻读研究生课程。学院的学生除美以美会外，还有浸信会、安利间会、长老会、公理会等其他改革宗的学生。分析了学校办学条件后，卢爱德明确提出学院亟待解决的问题：所有的系都要增添设备，所有的教职员工已经是超负荷工作，必须增聘教师，尤其是科学、音乐和数学教师。

对于学院面临的困难，卢爱德不仅从加强学校管理工作着手解决，她还将眼光投向外部的办学条件，积极寻求外界教育资源以促进学院的发展。在她的努力下，最终促成了华南女院与美国7所姊妹大学建立友好合作关系。这7所大学为华南女院

毕业班的女生（谢必震，2008：17）

提供经费、设备，或为各系派遣教师。华惠德（1956：55；2008：43）详细记录了这7所姊妹大学和华南女院相对应的系和专业及资助经费：

俄亥俄州联合大学负责运动馆　　　　　　　2000美元

俄亥俄州保灵华莱士大学负责家政系　　　　1000美元

西弗吉尼亚卫斯理大学负责物理系　　　　　1000美元

艾奥瓦州康奈尔大学负责音乐系　　　　　　2000美元

艾奥瓦州晨边大学负责化学系　　　　　　　1500美元

堪萨斯州西南大学负责生物系　　　　　　　1500美元

密苏里州卫斯理大学负责师范　　　　　　　 300美元

卢爱德担任华南女院校长期间，正值国内局势动荡时期。1927年初，国民革命军入闽，福州各界掀起了反文化侵略、收回教育权的运动。华南女院面临着艰难的抉择：停办或是顺应形势交出教育权使华南女院继续开办。卢爱德意识到，伴随着中国政治革命，教育和宗教改革势在必行，教育的管理权和财政权都应该移交给中国人负责。最后，卢爱德做出了顺应形势的决定。她和华惠德教务长自愿辞去行政职务。校董会任命华南女院附属中学校长陈叔圭为大学校长，王世静为教务长。然而，华惠德（1956：38）回忆说："陈女士不愿意接受校长一职，校董会遂决定任命以陈叔圭为主席的'五人校务委员会'统筹处理全校事物。"

卢爱德任内完成了学校领导权由外国传教士向华人顺利移交的转变过程。离职前，她向校董会提交了年度报告。在报告中，她强调学校必须尽快完成向政府登记注册的工作，以保证学校能够顺利地继续办学。然而，注册工作未能顺利进行，政府的注册要求不断提高，直至6年后的1933年，学校才成功地得到政府的临时注册，并于1934年获得正式立案，这其中的艰辛曲折将在王世静任院长章节中叙述。

离职后，卢爱德仍心系华南女院，在美国各高校和社会团体中四处奔走、演讲，力求扩大华南女院的知名度，吸引人们的关注和办学支持。谢必震（2008：14—15）引用著名教育家陶行知先生对卢爱德的高度评价："'这几年来，在中国女子教育上有研究的人，我只遇到一位，这一位就是美国露懿士（卢爱德）女士。'（《女子教育在学制上占领地位之十五周年纪念》，《陶行知全集》卷一）"

春色
任天涯
——福建华南女子
职业学院外教侧记
International Faculty with
Fujian Hua Nan Women's
College since 1908

338

第三节　宜夏别墅：中美合作办学的纪念性地标

在福州鼓岭可以看到宜夏别墅，英文名是Summer House。这房子的主人、建造者是英国领事馆的任尼医生（Doctor Rennie），后归属在福州和南平度过了大半生的杜医生（Doctor Donly），他是华南女院的校医、牧师。回国时，他将别墅赠予华南女院；但由于种种原因，房产证一直没办好，2005年福州市政府将此地划归华南女院，见下图：

如今的宜夏别墅作为中美合作办学的一个纪念性地标被留存下来，见证外教对华南女院的贡献与当代华南女院的发展延续。

华南女院前院长林本椿教授带华南外教在宜夏别墅参观

华南女院中国老师带家属在宜夏别墅举行活动

第二章
1984年后的福建华南女子职业学院外教

春色
任天涯
——福建华南女子
职业学院外教侧记

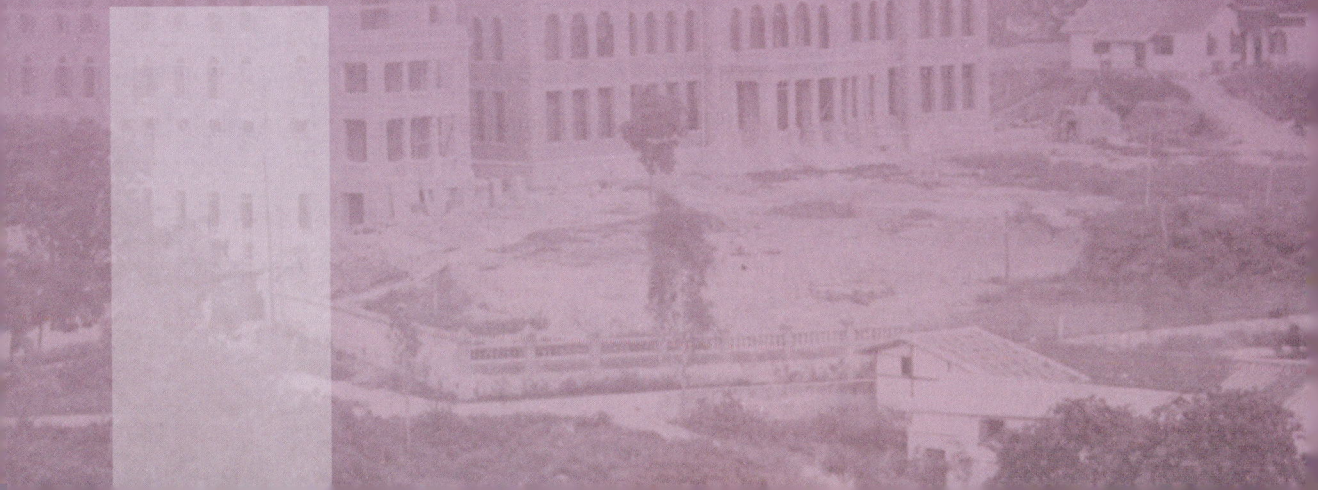

春色
任天涯
——福建华南女子
职业学院外教侧记
International Faculty with
Fujian Hua Nan Women's
College since 1908

340

第一节　因为爱中国，她来了

——记朱迪丝·威廉逊

　　春天是万物复苏、生机勃勃的时节，久远的记忆也被唤醒，思绪带我回到了1989年秋天。那年我刚从福建华南女子职业学院的实用英语专业毕业，并留校，是外事处一名年轻的工作人员。

　　秋季是新学年的开始，是新生、新教师报到的时刻，所以我上班接到的第一项任务就是和实用英语专业主任兼外事处副主任许道锋老师一起到义序机场迎接由亚洲基督教高等教育联合董事会（The United Board for Christian Higher Education in Asia）选派，通过南京爱德基金会（The Amity Foundation）派来的朱迪丝·威廉逊（Mrs. Judith Williamson）和她的丈夫安德鲁·J.威廉逊（Mr. Andrew Jackson Williamson）。

　　因是第一次接机，心里难免忐忑，很担心自己的英语无法应对，所以就躲在许

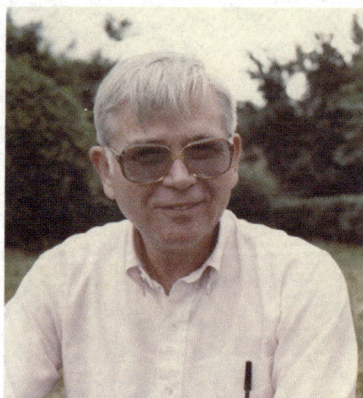

威廉逊夫妇

主任身后。可是没想到，威廉逊夫妇取完行李，步出安检线，笑容满面，直朝着我举的接机牌走来，"你好！我是朱迪丝·威廉逊，可以叫我朱迪"，一口标准的汉语，完全打消了我的担忧，多了分欣喜。

　　随后在给他们办理工作签证的事宜中，我逐渐知道了朱迪是1932年11月19日出生于美国中北部的伊利诺伊州阿莱多（Aledo）市。1958年毕业于艾奥瓦州的康奈尔

学院（Cornell College），主修英语，获学士学位。1962年至1968年在华盛顿特区的美利坚大学（American University）选修语言学，并获硕士学位。1964年在香港大学中文学院进修中文。

　　来华南女院之前，她有超过25年的教学经验。1958年至1964年间，作为美国卫理公会的宣教士，在香港教授英语，并从事社会事工。1964年至1987年间，在马来西亚和新加坡担任英语教师。1987年到来华南女院之前，她一直做布道和公义和平使者翻译工作。所以不足为奇，她的英语、广东话和普通话都那么棒！

　　她的丈夫安德鲁·J.威廉逊先生是一位性格温驯、十分儒雅的中国通，中文功底很深，能写一手好毛笔字。他有个中文名——卫连胜。大家都叫他Jack老师。他总是面带微笑，说话轻声细语。他们夫妇十分恩爱，常常携手而行，给年轻人留下很美的榜样。

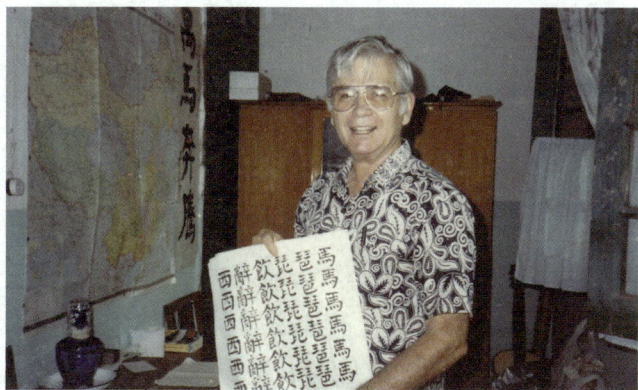

Jack老师和他的毛笔字

　　我为我们能聘请到如此高资质的外教而高兴。注重培养助教的华南女院，给我们新留校的老师继续充电的机会，我自然选择了听朱迪老师的英语课，这一听就是三年的时光。

　　1989年秋季一开学，朱迪老师就对54位87级实用英语专业的学生进行撰写毕业论文的指导，从确定选题、查资料，到写作、论文汇报，整整花了4个多月的时间。由于论文是自由选题，涉及面很广——中国教育、民族文化、诸子百家，各行各业，包罗万象，朱迪对每篇论文的形成都加以悉心指导，从字句到标点符号都一一做了修改。学生在班上一一做论文讲演时，都惊讶地发现自己在历史文化知识、英语的写作与讲演方面有了长足进步。接下来的两届156位毕业生同样受到朱迪老师的悉心指导，学生十分敬佩她。

春色
任天涯
——福建华南女子
职业学院外教侧记
International Faculty with
Fujian Hua Nan Women's
College since 1908

342

朱迪老师在授课

在教学内容方面，她最能注意到结合中国的实际对学生进行思想教育。记得1990年9月初，我们举国上下正为第一次申办成功的世界瞩目的亚运会做准备时，新的学期开始了。朱迪老师开学第一个星期的英语听说课的教学材料便是围绕北京亚运会的内容而设计的。在这个单元即将结束的时候，她登上讲台，一边激动地走来走去，一边挥动着手臂对同学们说："中国有能力举办亚运会，说明中国的强大，这使我看到中国的希望和未来，而你们这些年轻的女同学们，会使中国的未来更充满希望。"学生们深受教育和鼓舞，第二天上课时，教室里已挂上印有亚运会标志和吉祥物的小旗子了。

朱迪老师是一位具备良好教师素质的外籍教师。她工作作风严谨，教学极度认真负责，教学能力很强。她知识面广，语音极为标准，教学经验丰富，教学方法灵活多样，而且非常关心爱护学生。这些因素使她的课堂教学十分成功。学校进行教学评估时，她名列外教的榜首。

威廉逊夫妇表演中式婚礼

1990年秋季开始，朱迪老师担任了实用英语专业的副主任工作，她那认真负责、严谨的工作作风更加充分地表现出来了。她经常下班听课，和担任一、二年级的外教共同研究教学问题。她感到为了使三个年级段的英语听说和英语读写课衔接得更好，为了使新旧教师更替时能衔接得更顺，必须编写出一套具有华南女院特色的教学大纲，这项工作在她的主持下完成了，为1995年英语专业的"英语听力与口语"课程获福建省高校优秀课程，2010年应用英语专业（实用英语专业后改为应用英语专业）被评为福建省高职精品专业打下了坚实基础。

20世纪90年代初，华南女院最迫切需要解决的是培养接班人的问题，因为创办新华南女院的老校友都已年过花甲。朱迪担任副主任后，立即着手抓实用英语专业助教的进修培训工作。她每周为年轻助教开班上课3小时，并指导她们如何做好辅导学生学习英语语法的工作。对于其他专业的助教，也开展每周一节的英语口语自由谈话课，提高助教们的英语听力和口语会话能力。这工作在她回国后，其他外教像简·菲利普博士都做了很棒的传承。

朱迪老师不仅是年轻老师和学生的良师，也是老教师们的益友。当她知道老教师也想提高英语口语能力时，主动提出愿意承担老教师班的教学工作。因为她的课程表已经排满了，老教师口语班的上课时间只能化整为零，安排在每周二、四午餐后至下午上课前的休息时间。

当时学校应社会的需要，开办业余英语口语培训班，她的工作量已经大大超过了，但是，她还要求与其他外教一样承担每周两个晚上的教学任务。因着对中国的爱，她不知疲倦，超负荷地为我们培养外语人才。

威廉逊夫妇参加学校活动

**春色
任天涯**
——福建华南女子
职业学院外教侧记
International Faculty with
Fujian Hua Nan Women's
College since 1908

344

她了解中国，喜欢中国人，在感情上与我们相通。当海湾战争爆发，广州美国领事馆打电话通知她这个消息时，她对我们说："我哪儿也不去，现在在中国最安全。"

每逢大节日，外事部门邀请本市外籍专家参加宴会或晚会时，她因年纪大、工作忙不想去，但最终还是应邀出席了，她说："这是中国政府的邀请，不去没有礼貌。"像朱迪老师这样理解中国，热爱中国，教学水平高，工作极度认真负责的外籍教师实在是难得，是华南女院的荣幸。

华南女院授予威廉逊夫妇锦旗

1992年，朱迪老师荣获福建省优秀外国专家称号，她是当之无愧的。

1992年6月26日星期五上午十点零五分，威廉逊夫妇结束三年在华南女院的教学，搭乘FL5005航班经香港回国，当时到机场送行的有陈钟英副院长、马秀发教务长、办公室郑元珣主任、外事处苏松珍主任、实用英语专业许道锋主任、英语专业何孝智老师、儿教专业候若英老师、外事处刘杨璋老师和我。

24年过去了，我惊讶记忆怎么这么清晰，只因为她爱中国，爱华南女院的一切。希望她一切安好！

（本篇文章资料的取得得到华南女院院办，院外事处及应用英语专业的支持，特此鸣谢！）

注：2005年10月3日安德鲁·J.威廉逊在美离世，享年76岁。

第二节　加州玫瑰
——记贝茨·里韦特博士

　　"丁零零"，一阵清脆的上课铃声响起，只见一个头发花白、精神矍铄的外国老人面带微笑地出现在教室里。"这是我们的外教吗？""是她给我们上课吗？"同学们交头接耳，小声地询问着。"Hi everyone. My name is Betts. I am your teacher!"（大家好，我叫贝茨。我是你们的老师。）洪亮的嗓音，中气十足的发音，为了照顾我们的听力能力而有意放慢的语速，还有她那笑容可掬的样子，一下子拉近了我们之间的距离。这便是我初识贝茨·里韦特博士（Dr. Marion Betts Rivét）的场景。

个人荣誉

　　眼前这位神采奕奕的老人，不仅获得过心理学的博士学位，还曾任加利福尼亚州心理学协会主席，Detta Kappa Gamma国际妇女教育组织主席。你能想象她还曾在加州获最杰出教育心理学家奖，国际Detta Kappa Gamma（DKG）奖学金吗？发表过《语言交流对儿童自尊的影响》《关于学习上自我理想的影响的研究发现》《建立于父母子女关系中的自我理想》《自我理想和智力，它们的关系及对学习的影响》等会议论文。在年轻的时候还有私人驾驶飞机执照。说到爱好就更广泛了，网球、游泳、野营、集邮、阅读都是她的兴趣所在。而且她还去过45个国家呢。当我们听到这些信息的时候，都对她充满了无限的敬佩之情，原来女性也可以有这么丰富多彩的人生经历，同时也在我们的心里种下小小的希望种子。

　　从1992年开始在华南女院教书至2012年退休，因为她卓越的贡献，先后获得第二届福建省友谊奖，福州市友谊奖及福州市

贝茨和她所驾驶的私人飞机

春色
任天涯
——福建华南女子
职业学院外教侧记
International Faculty with
Fujian Hua Nan Women's
College since 1908

346

"荣誉市民"称号。2006年她又荣获国家外国专家局授予的国家友谊奖。这是中国政府授予在华工作的外籍专家的最高荣誉。当年共有46名专家获奖，贝茨是唯一一位来自福州的外国专家。2009年又再次获得福建省"荣誉市民"的称号。

教学方法之语音练习

在贝茨的课堂上，没有"报告，请进"，也不需要起立问好。有的只是轻松活

2006年9月30日贝茨在
北京荣获国家友谊奖

贝茨获得的部分荣誉

2006年10月1日贝茨参加福建省国庆招待会

泼的课堂气氛，时不时，她还会习惯性地坐在桌子上，以一副优哉游哉的姿态继续她的讲课内容。在她上课的时候，你不会觉得拘束，也永远不会觉得无聊，反而会被她出人意料的教学方法惊得不知所措，或是被她那丰富多彩的人生阅历所折服，当然也有可能经历因为不认真学习而被"狠狠教训"的下场。许多不同的回忆，此刻都渐渐地浮现在眼前，还是那样生动有趣。

在应用英语专业，贝茨主要教授英语听说、读写、自由谈话等课程的教学内容。早在20世纪90年代，就有单位请她录制音频作为介绍福州和周边地区的英文材料，供来访的外籍游客使用。也正是因为她语音非常清晰，在教学上既有耐心又有方法，所以应用英语专业通常都安排她负责大一新生的英语听说课程，主要包括语音训练、听力训练、口语能力培养等。说起语音训练，虽然时隔多年，但至今回忆起来还是印象深刻。每次课上，贝茨都非常注重语音练习，耐心地纠正每个同学的语音。如果有同学在发R和L音上有困难，贝茨就会让她们做口舌操，或者模仿她的发音进行练习。有时还会用上她的休息时间，为这些同学做个别辅导，仔细地告诉她们发音要领，不厌其烦地纠正，直至她们能正确发音为止。在日后的课堂上，每逢遇到类似的语音，贝茨还会特别留意提醒，看她们是否真正掌握了。贝茨对于每个细节都不轻易放过。同学们很容易混淆M和N的发音。比如在读sun或者son的时候，常常读成sum，看似好像只是一个尾音开口和闭口的区别，但是如果仔细听辨，的确能发现其中的不一样。也正是因为贝茨有如此敏锐的听力能力和对口型的辨识度，一次次纠正同学们不够规范的读音，才帮助大家从大一就打下了清晰准确地发音的基础。

教学方法之听力训练

关于听力方面的练习，贝茨最经常使用的教学方法是听写。不仅要求大家听懂，更要大家能准确地写出来，包括单词的正确拼写。贝茨通常会选择一段有意思的小短文，先将文章读一遍给大家听，以便留下一个整体的印象，然后开始进入听写的环节。说实话，在高中阶段，我们接受的听力练习大多都是听懂原文，能作出正确选择就可以了。而现在的听写，则要求将听到的短文一字不差地写下来，不少同学心里直发怵。这既考查对原文的理解，又考查单词的拼写能力，以及对同音异义词的辨识度。当然这样的教学目的不是难倒学生，而是通过这样的方式促进单词的识记和拼写能力，提高听力理解能力。因此在听写过程中，她会重复朗读，在大家熟悉原文的情况下，她还会时不时地"偷梁换柱"，悄悄地改变原文的单词，测试大家是否真正地掌握。针对不同学习程度的学生，她总是很好地兼顾，通过之前的学习，

春色
任天涯
——福建华南女子
职业学院外教侧记
International Faculty with
Fujian Hua Nan Women's
College since 1908

348

隔天再给学习进度慢的学生一次测试的机会。小小的一篇短文在她的手上，通过不同的教学方法，居然演变出不一样的效果，真是用心啊。这也难怪在每年的评教当中，她常获得"严格但又不失公平，也让学生收获多多"的好评。她总是运用课堂活动帮助学生思考，不仅在听力、口语教学中，在阅读和写作上也是如此。

教学之口语教学

在口语课上，贝茨特别重视大家开口说英文。她会尽一切可能鼓励学生开口表达。"No answer will be wrong."（没有什么回答会是错的。）是她常挂在嘴边的鼓励。组织开放性的话题，让班级中的学生分组或两两对话，在规定的时间内交换谈话对象，继续原来的话题和不同的同学交谈。而她自己则在我们中间走动，仔细认真听我们的对话内容，便于及时纠正。每周她都会写一则富有哲理的语句在黑板上，然后请我们用英文解释对这句话的理解或现场讨论。例如：One thing you can't recycle is wasted time（不能被重复使用的东西就是被浪费的时间。），Of all the things I wear, my expression is the most important（对于所有我能随身携带的东西，表情是最重要的。）。很多学生在毕业之后，返校看望贝茨的时候，都经常和她一起回忆那段边讨论，边用英文思维思考的时光。

说到口语课，不得不提的就是华南女院应用英语专业的特色课程——自由谈话课（free conversation）。就连教室都搬到外教们生活的专家楼了，教室里没有课桌，只有一排藤椅呈半圆形环绕着——为了创造一个更加温馨自由的谈话氛围。自从贝茨开始承担这门课程以后，她向学校强烈建议，将已经是小班教学的自由谈话课班级再次进行分组，以达到每组大约10人的规模。这样就能更好地为学生提供比较充足的时间阐述自己的观点，也能更快速地发现学生的问题，提供及时的帮助。

就我个人而言，我最期待的就是口语考试了，因为贝茨的口语考试考查的是口语表达能力，不需要任何死记硬背。我们按顺序，依次进入谈话室，贝茨还会事先准备一张小方桌，在桌上摆一小摆件，为小小的谈话室增添了温暖的气氛。然后从桌子上抽出一张话题卡，一同参加考试的两位同学有1分钟的时间准备，然后开始围绕之前抽到的话题进行5分钟的两两对话。考查的内容包括语法是否准确、词汇量的大小、句子流畅度和停顿次数的多少。在平时的口语课上我们也是按同样的标准来训练的。尽管当时单词量有限，但不影响我们自由地表达想法。

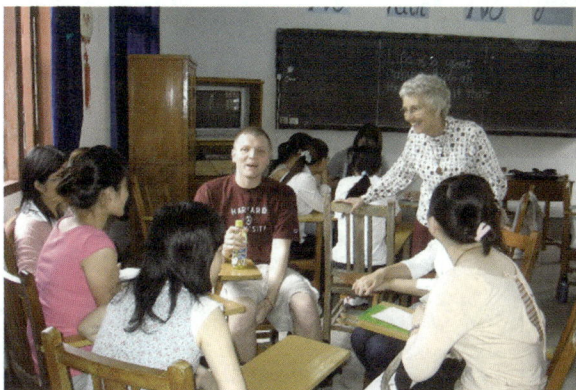

贝茨请来访的美国学生参与她的口语课堂

教学之演讲比赛

对于每年一次的英语演讲比赛，贝茨格外重视。一进入准备阶段，她就开始组织我们思考比赛的主题，在班级内进行讨论，帮助我们寻找写作的方向。在我们完成写作后，贝茨开始仔细批改，校正语法问题。开始练习的时候，贝茨事先将每个人的演讲稿分别录制在不同的磁带里，让我们带回去，以便课后对照她的朗诵来练习。如果在发音方面遇到任何问题，都可以随时请她指导。临近比赛，她还会先组织一次预赛，优胜者才能参加专业内的决赛。为了保证预赛结果公平公正，贝茨又特意从其他班级"借来"外教作为我们的评委。就在距离预赛开始不足两周的时候，贝茨抽查部分同学的准备情况，却意外地发现大部分同学都没有准备好，甚至还有人还没开始准备。此时的贝茨一改平时和蔼可亲的样子，十分严厉地把我们教训了一顿，批评大家的不努力。这是她第一次对我们生气，也是唯一的一次。因为这次的"敲打"，同学们再也不敢偷懒了，纷纷投入紧张的准备中。"功夫不负有心人"，我们班的同学在决赛中分别取得前三名的好成绩。当贝茨开心地看着我们获得的成绩，和我们拍照的时候，我们也由衷地感谢她的辛苦付出和良苦用心。

对于不太用功的学生或者在课堂上表现不正常的学生，贝茨也会留意她们，课后找时间和她们约谈，鼓励她们或是帮助她们解决学习中的问题。如果还没有收到理想的效果，贝茨就会采取中国化的行动——请家长。通过应用英语专业主任约见学生和她的家长，请人帮忙现场翻译，有时候会出现学生和家长一起泪洒现场的场面。家长们很喜欢这个这么关心自己孩子的外国老师，学生也被贝茨的这种良苦用心所感动，从此开始认真学习。还有一次，贝茨在上课的时候屡次发现一个学生反应不太正常，通过询问本人，甚至和家长沟通也没有什么明显进展。但是凭着多年

春色
任天涯
——福建华南女子
职业学院外教侧记
International Faculty with
Fujian Hua Nan Women's
College since 1908

350

的教学经验，她推断这位同学的听力可能有问题，建议家长带她去做个检查。第二天上课的时候，这位同学戴着助听器来上课，参与度明显提高不少，原来她们之前一直都没发现她的听力有问题。其实她所做的这些都是延伸教育，远超过在课堂上所传授的知识，而且是发自内心地关心学生。

教学之阅读写作

贝茨除了负责上英语听力和口语课程，还经常承接英语阅读和写作课程。她通常将90分钟的课堂时间一分为二。在英语阅读部分，贝茨会准备一些小短文，或是励志的书，将学生每4个分成一组或者就直接两两分组，完成阅读后进行讨论，检查学生们是否理解阅读的内容，有时还会出题测试——完形填空或是选词填空。在写作课上，贝茨通常会要求学生在课堂规定时间内完成一则短文的书写。或提供一张照片，让学生通过想象来完成写作；或是一个半命题作文。不仅如此，在课堂上贝茨也注重单词的识记、拼写，以及在句子中如何正确地使用单词。中文和英文的主要区别有很多，其中之一就是英文讲究不同词性的使用，而中文却不明显。所以贝茨注意在造句上强调英文的词性，有时候通过句子改错的方式加以训练。虽然改错对中国学生来说是很困难的，但通过一点一点的语法学习和写作练习，学生们逐渐上手了。

记得有一次，贝茨在讲解一篇小短文的时候，提到单词scream。班级里的同学大都面面相觑，一时不知何意。贝茨看出大家的问题了，于是悄无声息走到窗边，趁大家还埋头冥思苦想的时候，冲着窗外大喊一声，所有人都被吓了一跳。当我们反应过来的时候，发现她正冲我们笑呢。原来如此！从那以后我深深地记住了这个"特别的"单词。只是日后才知道她是运用情绪记忆法帮助我们识记这个单词，而这种方法源自教育心理学。

体验式教学

由于贝茨是心理学的博士，所以更加懂得如何自如地运用这些方法，不仅是运用情绪记忆法，她更经常运用动作记忆法，让学生们在户外，在不同场所去学习和体验不一样的知识和信息。比如：从1993年起至1997年，贝茨开始带学生们去盲校参观，还放映描述海伦·凯勒生平故事的电影，让她们了解不同的学习语言的方法。从1999年起，贝茨发现大约90%的学生都没去过福建省博物馆，于是开始自掏腰包付车费，带着她的学生们去参观，并联系讲解员为她们讲解。这一做法一直持续到2003年。后来她调整方向，带她们去参观五星级酒店。这次的转变，同样源于贝茨发现她的学生们几乎没有去过五星级酒店。从2004年起到2007年，她带着学生们去过温泉大饭店、西湖大酒店，参观那里的室内布局、大厅设置等。她事先将班级内的学生按小组分好，然后再按小组分批前往。参观回来的我们是要写观后感的，将我们的所见所闻和体验都写下来，这样的写作训练引来不少同学的好评。更意想不到的是，有些同学正是因为在学生时代对酒店管理留下良好印象，在大学毕业之后选择在大酒店就业。可想而知，这样的教学和体验带给学生时代的我们多少新鲜感。

缘起1992年

以上提到的林林总总的教学方法，有些来自我在学生时代的回忆，有些是我在华南女院外事处工作中亲眼所见，还有些是贝茨告诉我的。我相信每个熟悉贝茨的人，对她的印象都会如我一样深刻。因为她鲜明的个性、积极努力的态度和作风、旺盛的精力都很容易给我们留下深刻的印象。大家一见到满头白发、略微驼背的她，总喜欢问"她几岁了呀？来自哪个国家啊？什么时候来福州的？来福州多久了？为什么来福州呢？"。是啊，是什么让一位已经过了退休年龄的老人，不远万里从美国来到福州，甚至在初期是自愿自费在华南女院教书。初期的环境是那般简陋，设施是那般缺乏，是什么样的情谊让这位老人一待就是19年，为华南女院做出那么多

丰富的课外生活之一：
2006年贝茨和其他外教
一起学剪纸

丰富的课外生活之二：
2006年贝茨和其他外教参观茶厂

丰富的课外生活之三：
2006年贝茨和外教们游厦门之
人力三轮车体验

春色
任天涯
——福建华南女子
职业学院外教侧记
International Faculty with
Fujian Hua Nan Women's
College since 1908

352

的贡献，成为福州发展的见证人，更被国家外国专家局授予国家友谊奖。这一切使她晚年的生活更加丰富多彩！

这就要从1991年的一个电话说起了。有一天，即将退休的贝茨接到她的朋友埃莉诺·柯丽芬（Elinor Kniffin）的电话。柯丽芬说她在阅读一篇文章的时候，看到一则消息，说是中国有一所大学需要外籍教师，地址在一个叫作福州的城市，学校是华南女院。她希望贝茨陪她一同前往教书。当时的贝茨对此完全没有兴趣，于是很直接地回绝了她的邀请。但是埃莉诺再三劝说，于是贝茨只好提出和在华南任教的外教们联系，以便找到下一个拒绝的理由。一个月之后，贝茨收到5位外教的信息，她一一给她们打去电话。令人惊讶的是，没有一个人对华南女院做出负面评价。此时的贝茨有些动摇了——或许值得去华南女院看一看。于是她给埃莉诺打电话，表示愿意和她一同前往，但是只待1年。当华南女院接受了她们的简历，一切都准备妥当的时候，埃莉诺却无法与贝茨同行，贝茨只能只身前往。

当1992年贝茨终于踏上福州这片土地的时候，一出机场，就看见5个中国老师微笑着举着一面横幅，上面写着"Welcome to Hwa Nan, Betts"（贝茨，欢迎来华南女院）再加上她们流利的英文，贝茨在心中暗想或许在华南女院教书并不是太难吧。当时的福州是什么样的社会状况呢？据贝茨回忆说，举个最简单的例子，那时的福州只有两座跨江大桥。一座是解放大桥，另一座就是闽江大桥了。满大街看到的都是自行车，鲜少看见私家车的身影。不久，贝茨也学会骑着自行车在福州的街道里穿梭。在20世纪90年代，外国人在福州并不常见，每当贝茨走在马路上，总有许多人盯着她看。有一次，两个十几岁的男孩一边走一边回头看贝茨，只顾着回头看她，一不小心就撞上了停在路边的卖香蕉的板车上，打烂了好些香蕉，气得摊主直跳脚。出于礼貌，贝茨还从摊主那里买了点香蕉以示补偿。还有一次，一个骑自行车的中年男子一边骑车一边不停地回头看贝茨，结果骑上了马路牙子，一头栽进了灌木丛，也令贝茨觉得尴尬。渐渐地，贝茨学会了一个技巧，每当有人侧目的时候，她就对他们微笑着说"你好"。这下大家便会迅速地避开目光了。

最初来华南女院的5年时间里，贝茨不仅无偿教书，而且还自己承担往返机票的费用。1992年的华南女院只有600名学生。由于贝茨是心理学博士，又长期从事心理学的研究和教育工作，所以一开始华南女院安排贝茨在学前英语专业上课，不仅上英语口语课，后期也逐渐开始上儿童教育心理学的课程，直到她从华南女院退休为止。她特别感激任建红老师年复一年地为她的儿童心理学课程做翻译。贝茨说："教授儿童心理学是一种乐趣，建红将这门课翻译得简单易懂。"

退休？还是重回？

完成了1996学年的教学任务后，贝茨有了想要从华南女院退休的想法。她很感恩在华南女院所学到的一切，以及在中国的所见所闻和所遇到的人。但是她还是想多花一些时间陪伴在美国的家人。毕竟她有3个已经成家的女儿和11个外孙、外孙女。在华南女院教书的这些年，她只能在假期回国探亲。虽然有许多的不舍，但她还是艰难地做了这个决定——回国。当她回美国，享受和家人、友人相聚的时光时，大家最感兴趣的就是她在中国的经历。最经常被问到的问题就是："你还打算回去吗？""不打算了。"贝茨坦然地回答。可是当这个问题一次次地被问到，尤其是一次在教会的分享中被问及，她的脑海里闪过许多在华南女院的画面。在华南女院教书时的激情、帮助学生时的成就感，以及与她们建立的深厚友谊，还有那些热情善良的中国人、纯真好学的学生们。这一幕幕在眼前浮现时，她才知道短短几年的时间，已经让她对这个学校、那里的师生产生了割舍不下的感情。毫无疑问，贝茨决定要重回华南女院教书。

国际合作之"3+1项目"

除了在课堂上孜孜不倦地教学，在课后认真备课批改作业，贝茨还利用课余时间义务承担起华南毕业生赴美留学的事情。早在2000年，贝茨就率先开始组织和开展这项工作了。可能在当时的社会，这也算是先例了吧。1999年我院与美国森坦纳瑞大学（Centenary College）签订了校际间的合作项目（简称"3+1项目"）之后，贝茨就开始主动承担了这个项目的跟进工作。所谓"3+1项目"就是森坦纳瑞大学和我院签订协议，内容包括在华南女院学满3年并获得毕业证书的学生，在取得相应的雅思成绩后，森坦纳瑞大学承认申请学生在我院学习的部分学分并同意转学分，如果选择森坦纳瑞大学的个人学习专业（Individual Study），毕业生只需在美学习一年时间，成绩合格即可获得森坦纳瑞大学学士学位，大大缩短了学习时间，也节省了许多费用。在两校间的协议下，我院2000届毕业生首次开始尝试赴美留学。在此之前，贝茨已经认识来华南女院访问的罗伯特·弗瑞尔（Robert Frail）（原美国森坦纳瑞大学国际部主任，文学教授），通过他获得了许多赴美学生需要了解的信息和材料，包括学费、生活费、未来的专业学科课程、如何才能在一年内拿到学士学位等。贝茨还自费前往美国驻中国的广州领事馆，约见了广州领事馆的工作人员和总领事，了解相关的情况和信息。（值得一提的是这位美国驻中国广州领事馆的总领事在次年来访华南女院，参观了正在建设中的华南女院新校区，也会见了贝茨和第二批有

春色
任天涯
——福建华南女子
职业学院外教侧记
International Faculty with
Fujian Hua Nan Women's
College since 1908

354

贝茨和时任院长以及美国森坦纳瑞大学的老师们一同
会见2006届申请留学的学生

意向赴美学习的学生。）贝茨就是这样一点一点地收集信息，帮助学生们准备出国前的资料，她还和学生们准备应对面试有可能出现的问题。从一开始向学生宣传学校的优惠政策，收集有意向参加出国留学"3+1项目"的学生名单和学习情况，向学生介绍美国姐妹校的情况，指导学生如何填写申请材料并邮寄，到后来森坦纳瑞大学审核通过学生的申请材料后，又开始积极指导学生进行签证面试的实战演练。虽然签证官通常只会问三到四个问题，但是贝茨却准备了整整40道的问题让学生去反复练习。这其中的每个环节她都参与和协助，甚至小到网上转账这样的小细节，她都一一帮助。可以说如果没有她的帮助，学生们是很难独立完成这些申请工作的，或许要支付大笔的咨询费和中介费。可是贝茨分文不取，而且坚持了整整11年，一直到她2011年从华南女院退休为止才将出国留学的事情移交。她先后帮助了75位华南女院毕业生赴美留学，分别在美国森坦纳瑞大学、美国晨边学院和美国恩波利亚大学获得学士学位。每次看到学生们顺利通过签证，赴美学习，她比谁都高兴。一个古稀之年的老人，如此地用心付出不求回报，真是让人敬佩。

爱心资助之奖学金

贝茨不仅关心学生的学习状况，也关心她们的生活。她在教学期间，长年不定期地主动了解班级里学生的家庭经济状况。遇到有经济困难，又努力上进的学生，贝茨会主动自掏腰包，还会写信给远在美国的朋友或者是美国教会中的朋友，一同帮助学生缓解家庭经济压力，好让她们可以更专心地学习。从2008年起，贝茨开始用自己的生活费，奖励并资助那些品学兼优但又遭遇经济困难的学生，一直坚持到2011年她从华南女院退休为止。退休并不意味着结束，从2011年开始贝茨以自己的名义设立贝茨奖学金（Betts Scholarship），不仅将她平时帮助修改清华学生论文赚取的稿费全部用在奖学金上，还从热心教育事业的中美友人那里得到资助，进一步增加奖学金的金额和帮助对象的数量。设立奖学金，对于贝茨而言，不仅投入资金，还要亲力亲为地去了解学生的实际情况，准确地甄别衡量每个学生将获得的奖学金金额。这其实是一项巨大的工程：先是从学院的财务部门找出欠费的学生，将这些学生的信息上报给对应的专业，请专业主任提供该学生的学习情况，并邀请专业主任出具书面文件介绍学生平时的生活状况和学习情况。对于被筛选出来的学生，要求他们用书面方式简要地介绍下自己的家庭情况，尤其是经济状况。最后邀请外教和资助者参与面试，最终确定给学生最适合他们的奖学金。现在身为外事处工作人员的我，也曾参与部分材料的翻译工作，又一次看到满头白发的老人依然富有干劲、认真地对待每个细小的环节，也常常看到最后手拿奖学金的学生们是怎样含着眼泪向贝茨表达感激之情的。虽然已经退休的她不知道什么时候还会重返华南女院，但她总是不忘为这些学生送上最真诚的祝福和鼓励。

牵线恩波利亚大学

即使如此忙碌，贝茨也没有停下她为华南做贡献的脚步。在华南女院陆续和美国森坦纳瑞大学、美国晨边学院签订校际合作协议之后，贝茨的另一举动无疑又为华南毕业生打开了一扇门。这份协议最终得以签订，最初源自华南女院优秀毕业生周鑫，她是华南女院首批赴美国森坦纳瑞大学留学的学生，后来在美国查普曼大学攻读硕士学位，在获得博士学位后，以副教授的身份进入美国恩波利亚大学工作。周鑫带贝茨在恩波利亚大学参观，拜访了有意促进两校校际合作的校长，在贝茨的大力推动下，两校达成了校际合作协议。协议中有一项条款，规定华南女院的毕业生在恩波利亚大学学习期间按州内标准，而非留学生标准支付学费，这大大节省了华南女院毕业生在美求学的费用。在协议签订之时，已有6名华南女院毕业生申请赴恩波利亚大学求学，有不少学生在学成之后，留下来继续攻读硕士学位。

关注学院发展

贝茨不仅关心华南女院的学生，致力于教学事业，还对学院的建设倾注了大量的心血，经常向学院提出建设性的意见，也常常自己出资完善设施。位于烟台山校区的专家楼，尤其是厨房设备比较简陋，1995年贝茨为了改善外籍教师的生活环境，利用回美休假之便购买了许多厨具供我院外教使用，而后又自行设计并请人装修了专家楼的大小厨房。还找人一起去了电信公司，让每个外教房间有电话可以独立使用，大大地方便了外教的生活。（她时刻关注着学院的发展，为华南女院的发展建言献策。）2005年，时任院长林本椿教授特别聘请她为我院的顾问。她对新校区的建设很关心，刚做完髋骨置换手术后就拄着拐杖出现在新校区的工地上。对外教们

**春色
任天涯**
——福建华南女子
职业学院外教侧记
International Faculty with
Fujian Hua Nan Women's
College since 1908

356

将来的新居——专家楼，她更是最出力的一个，参与了每个装修设计的细节，协调专家楼的搬迁工作、入住后的整理完善工作，并捐赠了舒适现代化的厨具。由于学校经费有限，她又四处筹款，在短短六个月时间里，筹集到5万美金捐款。在2008年新校区正式投入使用时，专家楼内的20套公寓在贝茨的大力帮助下，完成了最后的装修布置工作。她亲自监督橱柜、热水器等的安装，后来她又和外教凯·格里姆斯（Dr. Kay Grimmesey）一同出资购买了8台电视供外教使用。每年的圣诞节，或是遇到美国友好院校的师生来访，贝茨都是不遗余力地帮忙，无论是布置环境还是亲自下厨烹饪，贝茨总是满心欢喜地准备着、忙碌着。

贝茨整理的专家楼图书馆一角

贝茨出资捐赠的外教厨房

任教期间，贝茨发现我院缺乏原版英文教材，就自费从美国邮购了大量教材，并利用回美探亲的机会搜集有关教材带回华南女院赠给相关专业的师生，开拓了他们的视野，充实了学院的外语教学教材。她还了解到我院需要大量外籍教师，就在美国报刊上刊登招聘广告，同时自费出资建立华南女院海外英文网页以宣传华南女院。在她连续付费10年期间，这个海外的英文网站已吸引多名外教慕名前来任教，为华南女院外教队伍的扩大做出了重要的贡献。

2008年5月8日《福州晚报》报道贝茨的事迹

心系校外

除在华南女院的巨大贡献外，贝茨还关心身边的人和事。2000年，从同事苏·托德（Sue Todd）那里得知市盲校有许多贫困学生后，热爱慈善事业的她来到盲校了解情况，当即帮助三兄妹解决了学杂费、生活费等问题。从那以后，贝茨便成了盲校的常客。天气转冷，贝茨就给孩子们送来

贝茨带着华南女院的2名外教为市盲校的孩子们
送来了崭新的冬衣

衣服；"六一"儿童节，贝茨给孩子们送来礼物；盲学生们有困难，她就解囊相助；她还动员她在华南女院的学生利用周末到盲校义务教英语。华南女院的不少外籍老师被贝茨感动了，纷纷加入了爱心行动，送衣送物，出资帮助特困生完成学业。7年来，贝茨和她的盲学生们结下了深厚的情谊。贝茨帮助过的盲学生毕业了一届又一届，她仍坚持着帮助盲童的爱心之旅。"我只是做了自己想做的事，今后我还会继续下去……"贝茨说。

20世纪90年代，烟台山校区外的公共垃圾场呈现"脏、乱、差"的现象。她通过学院的工作人员向街道管理部门一次次地反映问题，请求解决。正是因为她的坚持，当时的市长都关注到了这一问题，出面协调，虽然前后花费了不少时间，但最终街道管理部门专门安排人员上门勘察，不久就开工扩建，将原来敞开式的绿皮箱，改建成了一个封闭式公共垃圾场，方便了当地的群众和华南女院师生，也改善了那里的空气质量。

贝茨和年轻外教在校园开展义卖活动，筹集资金用于
捐赠贫困学生和市盲校学生

春色
任天涯
——福建华南女子
职业学院外教侧记
International Faculty with
Fujian Hua Nan Women's
College since 1908

358

不仅如此，她对于自己生活的这个城市也充满了热爱，希望她小小的建议能改善城市建设的问题。她是这么想的，也是这么做的。她时常写信反映问题，比如公交车在进站的时候，乘客难以看到叠加的车号，她建议是否可以增大车号并将车号放置在前挡风玻璃的右下角。她的信件不仅被收到了，相关部门还认真地给她回信，感谢她的关心和支持，表示会加强公交车二次进站的监督管理工作。她看见刚建成的宝龙城市广场人车混行，危险系数很大，又写信建议增设人行天桥，后来我们欣喜地看见宝龙的人行天桥矗立在那里。

再次退休，两次返校

值得一提的是，贝茨每年还自己编辑、排版、印刷她私人的Newsletter（年报），寄给她的家人和朋友，希望他们借此机会可以了解她在过去一年中的经历。到了2011年，贝茨最终决定要从华南女院退休，其中一个主要原因就是她想用晚年时间完成她的自传。因为在华南女院太过于忙碌，她担心无法专心写作或拖延了成书的时间。虽然有太多的不舍，但是她深知人生有时候需要做出取舍。2013年，时年85岁高龄的她完成并自费出版了自传 *"Bits by Betts" Shadows of My Footsteps*（《贝茨的点滴生活——记我的足迹》）。她在自传中提到了很多在中国的见闻体验、在华南的教学经历和她对这片土地深沉的爱和思念。

欢送会后的师生校友合影

贝茨将剪好的剪纸穿在身上

来参加贝茨欢送会的校友和在校师生坐满了会场

当我们得知贝茨即将离开，一场为她精心准备的欢送会悄然开始预备。学院校友办通过应用英语专业和学前教育专业开启联系校友的工作。确定时间、布置场地、联络校友的准备工作在有条不紊地进行。6月12日，大家怀着不舍和感恩之情前来参加欢送会，我院的前任院长林本椿教授在会上深情地回顾了他和贝茨共事的经历，也表达对这位老教师的感激和祝福。《福州晚报》的记者亲赴现场采访，发表了一篇题为《一位美籍教师的福州情缘》的文章。

《福州晚报》2011年6月28日题为《一位美籍教师的福州情缘》的报道

春色
任天涯
——福建华南女子
职业学院外教侧记
International Faculty with
Fujian Hua Nan Women's
College since 1908

360

2015年贝茨返校时受邀担任应用英语专业首届教学技能大赛评委

此后，贝茨依然心系华南女院的建设和发展，2013年10月，正值我院105周年校庆之际，她和前外教凯相约再次返校参加校庆活动。2015年6月，已经87岁高龄的她依然只身返回华南女院，想要来看看现在的华南女院又有哪些喜人的变化。两次返校，她都积极参与专业的教学活动，开设讲座，鼓励学生继续努力学习，也继续开展她的奖学金的筛选和评定工作。

这就是永远充满激情和活力的贝茨，一位可亲可敬的美国外教，许多人的良师益友。她和她积极乐观的人生态度，犹如一株玫瑰鲜艳地绽放在我们的心头。19年来，贝茨为华南女院的发展付出了许多心血，她所做的努力全是出于她对中国女子教育事业的热爱。她不计个人报酬和个人得失，无私地奉献着自己。我们也见证着这位美国友人对中国人民的崇高友谊、对中国女子高等教育的美好愿望，以及她个人的高尚人格。从她在中国获得的这么多荣誉，不难看出她是如何努力地教书育人，真诚待人，无私助人。她热爱运动，爱好广泛，她让我们看到女子也当自强自立，也当勤奋拼搏，一样能够迎来美好的未来。

2015年6月贝茨再次返校

优秀校友、贝茨好友林峰回忆

最早认识贝茨应该是二十几年以前的事了。1991年那年，我从美国留学学成归国返母校教书，刚好与贝茨一同教英语专业一年级新生的英语听力与口语课程，所以有机会在探讨数学的过程中慢慢地认识和了解她。在这二十几年里，虽然我们生活在不同的地方，各自有着不同的生活轨迹，但我与贝茨一直保持着联系。每年读贝茨寄来的圣诞书信更是让我深受鼓舞。去年的这个时候，收到贝茨要来温哥华的电话，我们全家3口都非常开心。贝茨在我们家呆了三晚四天，整个过程让我们得到了很多的激励。各位想象一下：一位86岁的老者，三四年以前因乳腺癌动了手术把整个乳房切除，两个大胯骨全部换过，年轻时骑马摔下来落个至今走路驼着背的后遗症……你说这样的人有可能还一个人拎着行李东飞西走吗？如果我没有亲眼见过，我一定会以为这个人现在十有八九是卧床不起了。但是，情况恰恰相反。贝茨在我们家三天，每天早上都是7：30起床。之后，她就没有歇过，一直不停地说话，给我和先生讲她这十几年经历的人与事。搞得我和先生两个"年轻人"一个陪谈，一个溜到二楼卧室悄悄地小睡一会儿。和她相比，我和先生的精力明显被比了下去。贝茨现在每个星期仍然坚持去健身房3到4次，使用不同器械锻炼，外加游泳。此外还每天早晚接送外甥女，参加读书俱乐部，同时还和姐妹们举行每周一次的午餐聚会，聊聊各自的生活，讨论如何帮助有需要的周边朋友。经过三天和贝茨一起生活，通过观察，我得到了她健康、长寿和开心的秘诀：开朗，积极，乐观向上并且乐于奉献。（李小武／文）

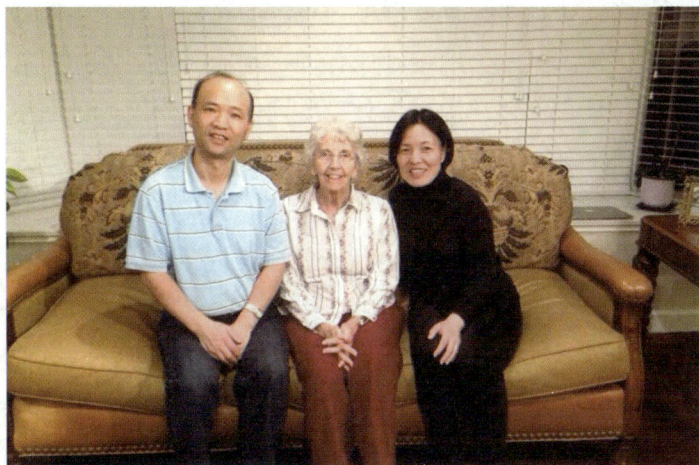

优秀校友李小武和她的先生林峰与贝茨在加拿大家中的合影

春色
任天涯
——福建华南女子
职业学院外教侧记
International Faculty with
Fujian Hua Nan Women's
College since 1908

362

去年在见到贝茨之前，我想象她一定是弯着腰，弓着背，一副老态的样子。没想到出现在我面前的她却和20年前的模样差不多，仍然是精神抖擞，说话敏捷。86岁高龄的她，走遍了世界上50多个国家。在福州教书育人的19年里，多次被授予省、市和国家级友谊奖。和她朝夕相处了3晚4天，听她讲了很多人生的故事，受益匪浅。感触最深的是她对人生的态度。在这里分享她的两个小故事。她曾经资助一个从福州市第二医院来美求学的骨科医生。由于语言问题，在这个医生几乎放弃学业的时候，贝茨给了她一个"实在"的帮助。她将整本医学课本一页一页地录在磁带里，让这个学生带回家慢慢地听，慢慢地去琢磨。十几年过去了，这位福州医生现已成为美国当地小有名气的中西医结合的医生。贝茨三四年前得了乳腺癌并做了整个乳房切除手术。上午进手术室，下午就坐着轮椅去隔壁房间探望其他病人。她还说本来当天下午就回家的。没有回家的原因是因为家里没人，女儿一家刚好那天外出旅游。她谈话的样子一点也没有责怪女儿的意思。要我一定做不到！我从她身上学到了真诚待人、体谅别人的功课！

第三节　生如夏花之璀璨
——记简·菲利浦博士

简·菲利浦，这位来自美国看似再平凡不过的老人，却在她的后半生为福建的教育事业做出了不平凡的贡献，她用她的行动、她的智慧、她的爱心打动着许许多多的人。简在华南时是一位非常优秀并且受欢迎的外教，因为她在华南女院教书很多年，为人谦和、风趣幽默、乐观豁达，大家都很喜欢她。

简·菲利浦于1929年8月生于美国佐治亚州，1957年于美国华盛顿大学取得博士学位。博士毕业后在俄勒冈州医学院教心理医学和精神病学等课程，1968年简到马萨诸塞州立大学担任心理学教授兼任临床训练主任，专门研究行为心理学，还出版了书籍《行为疗法的基础》。1971年起在美国丹佛大学心理学任教授、博士生导师、临床训练主任，直至1985年退休。在此期间兼任美国《心理学报》的主编，在美国心理协会担任各种委员会主席，并多次在心理学期刊发表研究论文。

简和华南女院的外教
们（简在第二排中间）

2001年简在专家楼参加圣诞晚会（第二排左二）

刘永和博士在华南女院给儿教专业的
学生上课（刘博士在美国是简的学生）

简和外教，以及外事处许道锋主任在专家楼前合影

简与华南女院的不解之缘

　　1985年简第一次来到华南女院进行短期访问和教学，当时住宿条件非常艰苦，因为新华南刚创办不久，还没有外籍专家宿舍楼，简的宿舍是很简陋的。福州的冬天非常寒冷，美国的冬天室内有暖气，而这里什么都没有，只有一间空荡荡的宿舍，玻璃窗被风刮得砰砰直响，冷飕飕的，晚上睡觉要穿着4件衣服，戴着帽子，穿两双厚袜子。那时候的洗手间里都还未安装热水器，必须在楼下烧了开水，提到楼上

**春色
任天涯**
——福建华南女子
职业学院外教侧记
International Faculty with
Fujian Hua Nan Women's
College since 1908

364

兑自来水，每次洗澡前都要鼓起好大的勇气，做好热身运动才可以开始。尽管这样，简却从来没有抱怨过如此简陋的住宿环境，因为她深知华南女院办学之初的难处，她就是这么一个善解人意的人。简有一个信念，她相信华南女院会越办越好。热情友好的华南女院人也深深地打动了简，因此简与华南女院结下了不解之缘。

到了1987年，简正式来华南女院任教时，华南女院在学校斜对面专门给外籍专家安排了宿舍楼，那是一个有院子、有地下室的3层公寓楼，外教搬进去后，住宿条件改善了许多。你也许怎么也不会想到，在中国默默适应艰苦环境的简其实是美国一流高等学府的终身教授。也许你会问简怎么会来到华南女院的呢？这里我要提及一位华南女院的著名校友、当时的名誉院长刘永和博士，因为当年简曾是她的博士生导师，所以受刘博士的引荐，简来到了华南女院担任志愿者。从1987年简应华南女院之邀正式前来任教起，她先后10次远渡重洋作为志愿者来福州教书。她热爱华南女院，热爱师生，不计报酬，乐于奉献，为华南女院倾注了她的心血，深受学院师生们的赞扬。1992年，简·菲利浦博士被聘为华南女院教育顾问。

治学严谨 爱护学生

简·菲利浦博士先后在福建华南女子职业学院学前教育专业教授"心理学"和应用英语专业教授"外国文化""听力与口语"课程。她工作踏实勤恳、精益求精，

欢迎著名英籍华裔作家韩素音女士
来举办讲座（简帮学生拍照）

院领导、外教与韩素音女士合影（简在第二排中间）

在训练学生听说技能方面积累了丰富的经验。她严于律己，事业心强，对学生倾注了满腔热忱，无论是优等生还是后进生，她都做到一视同仁，因材施教。例如英语专业2000B班是英语底子比较薄弱的班级，简投入了大量的时间和精力。当时2000B班的同学作为大一新生，但要开口说英语，特别是还要与外籍教师交流，这对于学生们来说真不是件容易的事。作为一名心理学教授，她明白学生的思想，理解学生心里的那丝畏惧，体谅学生的紧张。她特别善于调动学生的积极性，从来都是面带微笑地跟学生交谈，让学生们倍感亲切，在可爱的简的带动和鼓舞下，连那些原来因害怕说错不敢开口讲英语的学生也放下了胆怯，逐渐地树立起自信心，是简让大家开口说英语的。在简的精心辅导和教育下，学生们的英语水平有了明显的提高，能讲出一口标准的英语，甚至有时候在课堂上还会争先恐后地踊跃发言。

在教学方面，细致、认真是简最突出的特点。一堂课上除一本通用的教材以及教案之外，还有她为学生所准备的补充材料，这些材料都是根据学生实际水平而设计的。先从基本的音标入手，从语音方面不断强化教学，耐心倾听学生读英语，并且不厌其烦地纠正学生发音的错误。学生努力模仿简的发音，用心地反复练习，逐渐地在口语方面取得了或多或少的进步。简的课堂气氛十分活跃，枯燥的语法在简的谈笑间变得通俗易懂。简秉持的教学理念是让学生在轻松愉快的氛围中学习，她的课生动有趣，据她的学生回忆，当简教到giggle这个单词时，自己嘴里也发出咯咯的笑声，同学们都忍不住咯咯地笑了起来。当教到另一个词tiptoe的时候，简踮起脚尖，轻轻地往前走，正是她如此形象生动的教学，让学生至今都还记得这些单词，甚至记得她当年的一颦一笑，一举一动。每到西方的节日，为了让学生了解美国文化，简都会仔细地给学生介绍节日的习俗。例如万圣节的时候，简带了马克笔、卡纸、剪刀和尼龙线，让学生画鬼脸、做面具。她让学生们排队找她要糖果，边排队大家边喊："不给糖，就捣蛋。"班级里充满了欢声笑语，其乐无穷。

简对学生富有极大的爱心和耐心。她总是鼓励学生，会在批改试卷时写上一些鼓励的话语，如"你做得很好""不错，继续努力""你一定能再提高"等，这些温暖的话语就像一股暖流从学生的心里流过，每当她们有些气馁的时候，想起简的话，立刻就充满信心和斗志。简还很注意保护学生的隐私，不论发放试卷、小测，还是作业，她从来没有让学生帮忙，而是将试卷对折，亲自一张一张地发给每一位学生，以避免成绩外泄。她这种做法，让考得不理想的学生不但没有因为成绩不如别人而羞愧，反而更加努力学习。同时也教会了学生如何尊重她人，保护她人隐私。华南女院应用英语专业的董秀萍老师，是现在学生们最喜爱的老师之一，当时也是简的

春色
任天涯
——福建华南女子
职业学院外教侧记
International Faculty with
Fujian Hua Nan Women's
College since 1908

366

学生。董老师说，简发放试卷的这种细微行为，让她受益很深，当老师20年来，只要显示成绩的作业或测验，她都会亲自发到每一位学生手中，还特意交代学生们不要私自翻阅他人的东西，也不要偷窥同学的成绩。简不仅教学兢兢业业，还十分用心地了解和记录学生成长的情况。每到学期末，简都会给班主任提供一份清单，上面详细列出每位学生的特点，哪些同学取得了进步，哪些同学成绩较优秀，哪些同学在学习上还需要帮助，等等。

简的自由谈话课形式可谓是丰富多样，她的"玩中学"的教学理念当时在中国是非常新颖的，她认为年轻的女大学生们应该朝气蓬勃，她们这个年龄就应该拥有快乐。有时她会带学生到公园接触大自然，和学生们促膝谈心；有时去学校隔壁的游泳池教女生们游泳；有时是在专家楼的外教餐厅和学生们一起做烘焙，甚至还请学生去餐馆吃饭。如此身临其境的英语教学，比起坐在教室里看图片教学，学生们吸收的效果更加显著。简在学生面前从来不说教，但却以身作则，注重守时，从不迟到。她认为，大学生学知识固然重要，但更重要的是要学会做人。她的教育理念、为人处世方式给她的学生们带来了积极并且深远的影响，以至于她的学生后来为人母时，在教育自己的后代时都牢记着简的理念，让孩子在快乐中成长，但是做人要有规矩。

1993年简和华南女院的余宝笙院长一起为
先进班级颁发奖状

简在上自由谈话课

除教学以外，简在生活方面对学生们细心周到、无微不至。值得一提的是，简记得每位同学的生日，每次给学生过生日，她都会送上精美的小礼物。她还带着零食到宿舍看望学生，与学生谈心、交朋友，询问学生各方面的生活情况。当时实用英语专业有一门"英文打字"课程，需要学生课外用打字机多加练习。但是学校提供的打字机以及打字练习的开放时间不能满足同学们的需求，简了解到这种情况后，就主动贡献出自己的打字机，并在专家楼整理出一个房间，作为学生的打字练习室，让学生们有空就去练习。只要是学生的事，她都当作是自己的事，只要能帮到学生的地方，她都尽量想办法。其实，一个老师只懂得教学，并不算什么，但是如果她能用自己的言行影响学生一辈子，这才是良师益友。很多学生多年后回想起老师，也许不记得当时老师教过她什么，但是一定会记得老师的好。

简认为新生刚进大学，在正式开始学习之前，应该对新生进行教育与指导，帮助她们认识、了解学校，让她们轻松地适应新环境。后来华南女院在每年新生报到后都安排一周时间进行新生教育，这也是源于简的提议。简带着大一的学生到三县洲桥下的环岛公园做游戏，她还为学生们准备了许多吃的，装满了红、白、蓝三麻袋，同学们边吃边做游戏，在欢乐中忘却离家的伤感之情。当时很多同学来自山区，离开家那么远，的确有些想家。可是看到这么热情友好的外教，吃着以前没有吃过的零食和糖果，有的甚至是从遥远的美国带来的，她们心里感到无比甜蜜。简常常随身携带照相机，心思细腻的她善于随时捕捉学生的一举一动，记录下精彩的瞬间，然后把照片贴在班级的墙上，让学生感觉到班集体生活的快乐与温馨。在学生毕业前夕，她送每位学生一张拍得最好的照片并且在后面写上她所看到的这位学生的优点，她感谢每个人曾经对她的帮助，哪怕是一点点微不足道的小事。学生们看着简拍的照片，心中无比感动，甚至有种舍不得离开华南女院的感觉。

简的爱博大宽广，不仅热爱学生，对青年教师也十分关心。她主动举办青年教

简与刚留校在外事处工作的董秀萍老师促膝谈心

简喜欢在假期带学生出去游玩

春色
任天涯
——福建华南女子
职业学院外教侧记
International Faculty with
Fujian Hua Nan Women's
College since 1908

368

职员英语口语培训班，将37位青年教师分成5个小班，根据每个班的不同特点进行教学。因为老师们的时间不好统一，简只好牺牲自己的午休时间，来教年轻老师英语口语。她常常亲自煮咖啡，还准备好自制的糕点热情款待大家，让老师们边享用美味的糕点，边学习英语，课堂气氛十分融洽。老师们一到周三中午，就像快乐的鸟儿一样飞到珍妮的房间，因为大家要一起做好吃的，一边做一边用英语交谈。有时简会教大家做三明治，在两片切片面包上涂抹黄油，中间加金枪鱼和生菜，还有沙拉酱。有时是用饼干，中间夹着吞拿鱼酱。有时是把蒸熟的鸡蛋分成两半，取出中间的蛋黄加上沙拉酱再放回蛋白中。总之，美味的西式点心，让中国年轻老师们垂涎欲滴。制作西点的过程中，风趣幽默的简常常逗得大家哄堂大笑。简当时给助教们上课的话题非常新颖，如保险、信用卡、旅游等，虽然这些词在如今十分普遍，但在当时的中国大家却都还没有接触过。经过简的悉心辅导，青年教师在口语方面得到显著的提高，他们的英语口语变得更加纯正、地道和流利。华南女院的很多英语老师都曾在外面被人称赞过英语口语很好，都曾被询问是否有出过国的经历。其实，当时这些老师刚留校工作，根本没有出国深造过。在简创造的如此轻松，如此原汁原味的语言环境中怎么能不练就一口流利的英语呢？

简在华南女院受到师生们的爱戴，陈钟英院长和外事处许道锋主任对简的生活起居体贴入微。简每次来华南女院，许主任都亲自去机场迎接。陈钟英院长则利用周末带着简去福州森林公园、宁德霞浦等地游玩，还教简打中国麻将，简可感兴趣了。简曾经随口问一位中国老师哪里可以买到竹制的书架，这位老师花了几个周末，骑车找遍榕城才寻觅到这样的书架。服装专业的主任周玲老师手艺娴熟，她为简量身制作了两件丝绸面料的衣服，简穿在身上不仅合身而且感到很舒适。简虽然很喜

1993年简参加华南女院全体教职工的合影（第二排左四）

欢，但只在重要场合才舍得拿出来穿。学生的家长也常常给简带来他们的暖暖情谊。逢年过节，学生的妈妈常给简送来亲手做的中国传统佳肴，而学生的爸爸则利用假期开车带简参观名胜古迹。这些来自华南的点点滴滴都让简感动万分，她从师生们、家长们身上感受到了暖暖的家人般的温馨。

心系华南　视为家园

华南女院人诚心诚意对待简，简对华南女院也是情深义重，把自己视作华南女院这个大家庭的一分子。在1997年的九九重阳节，简听说这一天是中国传统的敬老节，便买了许多风筝送给学院的老教师们，祝大家过个浪漫的老年节。她与华南女院的老教师们情同手足。她也常常自掏腰包，为"家"添置物品，她觉得"家"里应该购买录像机来播放英文原版录像，以便于学生们学习英语，于是自己掏钱在林本椿教授的陪同下去购买录像机，并委托美国的朋友寄来录像带。托简的福，英语专业的学生们在学校里可以看到原汁原味的美国电影，不仅提高了英语听力，而且模仿电影对白的腔调也有助于提高口语水平。

爱岗敬业、乐于助人的简对华南女院各方面的工作都十分关心，并且尽自己所能给予极大的支持。当时学院需要大量的外教，简就到处写信给她的朋友，向她们介绍华南女院，帮助华南女院招聘外教，为华南女院外教队伍的扩大做出了巨大的贡献。为了让华南女院能够向亚联董组织申请资金资助学院的各项开支（如教师培

简与普吉湾的代表以及华南女院的老教师们

简在华南女院与芬兰Swedish Polytechnic职业大学签订交流协议时发言

春色
任天涯
——福建华南女子
职业学院外教侧记
International Faculty with
Fujian Hua Nan Women's
College since 1908

370

养资金），简在繁重的教学任务外，加班加点为我院写申请草案。后来还抽空指点当时负责外事的王凌老师如何为学校写草案，并且帮她修改草案。据王凌老师回忆，简是一个非常有智慧的人，写作功底强，思维缜密。她办事高效，有思想，十分了解高等教育，为我们学校的发展指出了正确的方向。简为人谦和，没有任何架子，常常以礼貌周到的态度对待学校的职员们；每当需要别人帮助时，她都会对帮助她的人表达充分的尊重和谢意。当别人需要帮助时，她总是尽心尽力地给予帮助，不求回报。当得知英语专业的年轻助教到美国世纪大学进修的助学金不够用时，简立即写信给美国妇女组织请求对方给予资助。简非常关心学院的贫困生，经常帮她们缴纳欠交的学费或者给生活费资助她们，这些学生多年以后一直对她心存感激，也以自己的爱心来回报社会，因为她们牢记华南女院"受当施"的精神，并且也从简身上传承了这种精神。

帮助他人放飞梦想

由于工作关系，简认识了福建师范大学外国语学院的王晶教授。王教授的女儿黄思路是个非常优秀的学生，1995年曾被评为福建省"十佳"少年和全国"十佳"少年，1996年获宋庆龄奖学金、华兴青少年奖学金。当简得知路路弹得一首好钢琴，便建议王教授在暑假送女儿去美国音乐家的摇篮——爱斯本音乐学校学习钢琴，她说那里有最好的师资。于是热心的简开始帮路路张罗，打听音乐学校录取程序，需要准备哪些材料以及如何申请奖学金等事宜，在简的倾力帮助下，1999年6月10日，黄思路带着申请到的全额奖学金，张开梦想的翅膀飞到了美国，开启了赴爱斯本的钢琴学习之旅。

简在丹佛的家里热情友好地接待了路路，并在音乐学校报到时间的前三天送路路到爱斯本熟悉环境，让路路住在一家汽车旅馆。由于爱斯本是旅游胜地，细心的简怕夏天的旅游旺季订不到房间，特意提前几个月就订好了旅馆。中国有句俗话说："帮人帮到底。"简就是一个负责到底的人，她和美国的朋友把黄思路送到爱斯本音乐学校报到。路路在爱斯本的学习过程中，

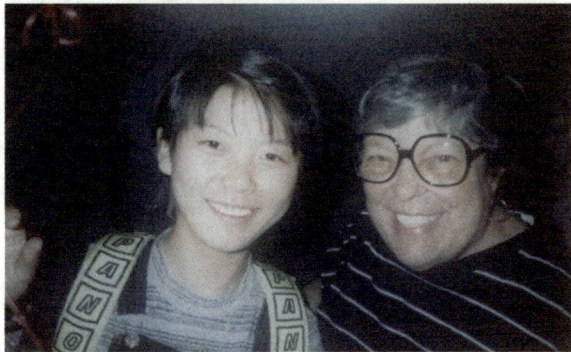

简与黄思路

简经常打电话关心路路，了解路路的生活和学习情况，为了让路路能够有充足的机会练琴，简在校园里帮路路租了一间琴房，每天可供路路使用3个小时。简还寄了一个包裹给路路，里面有一个笔记本、一支铅笔，以及简亲笔制作的每周记事表格。她嘱咐说，一定要把每天的事情记在笔记本上，随身携带，免得误事。简多次亲自前往爱斯本看望路路，为路路买了好多中国货，还买了闹钟以防路路睡过头。她给路路带去了零花钱，带路路去吃西餐，教路路用投币洗衣机洗衣服，甚至写了一张美元单位换算表让路路贴在钱包里。所有这一切让黄思路觉得简真的太好了，不仅对她关怀备至，慷慨解囊，还把每件事情都办得那么认真细致，并且为路路将来的学习指明了方向。

简的中国情结

简对中国悠久的历史充满兴趣，热衷于中国文化和艺术。1990年简从福建师范大学请来一位美术老师到华南女院教外教画中国画，如牡丹，还请了一位师大外语系的教师来当翻译。她常常去看戏剧，对京剧的变脸、杂技非常感兴趣，看得哈哈大笑。简利用假期到中国各地旅游，积极参与文化活动，例如安溪茶文化节、永定土楼文化节等。各地古老的建筑和特色的民居总会锁住简的目光，她走街串巷淘回各种各样的工艺品，爱不释手、视为珍宝。简把在华南女院的宿舍布置得充满浓厚的中华气息。她在厨架上摆着她崇拜的中国伟人毛泽东、邓小平的塑像；小茶几上放着中华民族英雄岳飞的红木雕像；墙上挂着庆祝中华人民共和国成立五十周年的宣传画、中国地图、福州地图，还有中国传统手工艺制作的风筝、具有少数民族特

简在美国丹佛的家中

简十分喜爱中国菜

春色
任天涯
——福建华南女子
职业学院外教侧记
International Faculty with
Fujian Hua Nan Women's
College since 1908

372

色的小挎包，墙上还贴着许多中国朋友寄给她的
贺卡。甚至中国人用来装东西的竹匾也被简用来
当装饰品挂在墙上。这些中国特色的宝贝在简看
来，似乎是有生命的，她用美国人形容男性英俊
的词"handsome"来赞扬她的竹匾，用形容女性
美丽的词"pretty"来夸奖她的风筝，喜爱之情溢
于言表。简在美国的家也同样充满中国风味，摆
挂着许多中国字画、瓷器、工艺品等，其中有很
多是她的中国朋友送的，有的是她自己收藏的。
她真的是一位中国迷啊！

简身穿她喜爱的中国传统服装

简对中国的民俗风情也特别感兴趣，华南女院烟台山校区隔壁的乐群楼里的邻
居家有红白事，她都会去看，了解风俗。当时来中国的外国人非常少，人们看到外
国人感到十分稀奇。所以当简到居民家里参观的时候，人们把她围成里三层外三层，
眼里充满了好奇。可是简却一点儿也不觉得不自在，相反，她非常平易近人、和蔼
可亲，对居民表现得十分友好。中国朋友们看到简对中国的习俗这么感兴趣，如果
参加婚宴都会带简去。有的婚宴是在农村举行的，厨师们在村子里蒸饭、洗菜、烹饪，
新郎新娘在大厅里举行传统的结婚仪式，喜娘在新人的亲朋好友面前大声贺喜，新
人拜见长辈，简对这一切感到好奇。她了解到红色在中国代表喜庆，于是在1993年，
到照相馆穿戴上中国传统服饰凤冠霞帔拍了几张喜气洋洋的照片，并把冲洗出来的
照片送给好朋友，祝福朋友鸡年快乐。简就像送快乐给人间的天使，她总是给朋友
带来惊喜和乐趣。

简对中国的美食情有独钟，面条、饺子、煎包、小笼包这些传统特色小吃总是
百吃不厌。小巷深处的福州风味小吃每每让她回味无穷，就连水果摊上的菠萝她也
吃得津津有味。她总是对专家楼厨师做的饭菜赞不绝口，烟台山脚下的香喷喷饺子
馆是她当时常带学生去的地方。回到美国后，每当简想念中国的美食，她就会去中
国餐馆寻找中国的味道。

多年带病坚持教书　依依不舍离开

1993年简因哮喘发作，被送进医院，医生查出她还患有高血压。学校派英语专
业几个学生轮流去医院照顾她并且为她担任翻译。住院半个月后，简出院了。为了
表示感谢，出院后她特地请这几个到医院照顾她的学生一起去西湖大酒店吃西餐。

简邀请在医院照顾她的学生吃西餐

当时在五星级酒店里吃西餐对于中国人来说是很罕见也是很荣幸的，简充分表示出了对大家的感恩之心。

出院后，简回国调养了一段时间，却一直心系着华南女院，不久又再次来到这个令她魂牵梦萦的地方。是的，她已经深深地爱上了这个大家庭，离不开这里的家人。1994年起，简又陆续来华南教书，但是她的身体每况愈下。1997年，哮喘缠身的简正在美国丹佛的家中休养，当她听说华南女院当时正缺外教，立即拖着病体"飞"到华南。直到2001年，简再次住院，被诊断出心脏也有问题，这才依依不舍地离开讲堂，告别了学生，辞别了华南女院，于2002年1月回到美国，因为医生说她从此必须背着氧气瓶生活，所以她无法再乘坐飞机来中国，这对简来说成了一个遗憾，因为她不能再回到这片她认为是第二故乡的土地。

外事处主任许道锋老师带领外教参观
福州市博物馆

2003年9月简·菲利浦获得福建省"友谊奖"

春色
任天涯
——福建华南女子
职业学院外教侧记
International Faculty with
Fujian Hua Nan Women's
College since 1908

374

作为一名资深的心理学家，简结合自己的专业知识与才能在异国他乡的福州潜心教学、无私奉献。在华南女院创办早期10多年的时间里，兢兢业业，辛勤耕耘，为社会培育出了许许多多人才，在福建现代化建设中做出了卓越的贡献。2003年9月，简·菲利浦博士被福建省人民政府授予福建省"友谊奖"，这是福建省人民政府给予在福建地区有突出表现的外籍专家的一项殊荣。

简的笑容总是灿烂的

辞别第二故乡回美国后的简

辞别第二故乡回国后的简并没有闲下来，依然过着积极乐观的生活。她常常四处旅游看望各地的朋友，有时会在家里看书、写书评，有时会写信给华南女院的老朋友，关心华南女院发展的状况。简在美国病重卧床时，心里还时刻惦记着华南女院的朋友们。一位朋友送给她产自中国杭州的山核桃让她补身体，她心里想在美国都能买到杭州产的山核桃，那福建一定也能买到吧。于是，她特地从美国捎钱给她和华南女院共同的朋友林本椿教授，让他帮忙买几盒山核桃送给华南女院的老朋友，其中包含陈钟英院长、教务处马秀发主任和外事处许道锋主任。回想起这件事，三位老教师都热泪盈眶。

2014年2月4日对于简的朋友们来说，是个悲痛的日子，因为在这一天，简永远地离开了大家，享年84岁。简终身未婚，却将自己的一生奉献给了教育事业。她热爱这份事业，为教育为学生倾其所有。乐观、幽默、豁达的简对于每一个人来说都是一位良师益友，凡是与简接触过的人都会从她身上感受到那种孜孜不倦、不断进取的精神，都会被她无私奉献的高尚情操和愿为中国教育事业献出爱心的崇高精神所打动，都可以看出她拥有一颗金子般的美好的心灵。每个人都尊敬她，喜欢她，并永远记住她。华南女院为曾经拥有如此卓越的外教而感到自豪与荣幸，简·菲利浦博士也为其他外教树立了楷模。可以这么说，华南因有了简·菲利浦博士而蓬荜生辉，简的学生、同事和朋友们因认识了简·菲利浦博士而生活得更加精彩。

第四节　空谷幽兰

——记凯·格里姆斯博士

寻访洛杉矶之家

2015年8月21日，在横穿了大半个美利坚合众国之后，我和儿子在洛杉矶见到了阔别三年之久的外籍教师凯·格里姆斯博士。

凯举手投足间还是那么优雅，如往日一样，她微笑着给了我一个拥抱，让我重新体验到那久违的温柔和慈爱。这也许是我敬爱这位老太太的一个重要原因吧。她十分真诚，你会发现自己在她面前非常放松，没有任何压力。你可以跨越语言的障碍，侃侃而谈，而她总是能够理解你。其实，温柔、善解人意如她，无需你开口，似乎已经明白你面临的困难和需要的帮助。她的微笑好像告诉你："不要怕，有什么困难，我就在你身边。"

在美国访学的日子里，我更加明白了来自发达国家如美国，过惯优裕、舒适生活的外教，在中国会面临着怎样的不适应，在面临发展中国家尤其是私立学校华南女院的艰苦生活和工作条件时，她们要有多大的毅力坚守在华南女院这片土地。更为难得的是，凯从不抱怨学校的生活、工作环境，也不把她的标准强加在别人身上。11年来，她就这样像一株空谷幽兰，默默地发出淡淡的清香，滋润我的心田，荡涤我的心灵，使我学会心存感恩，真诚帮助别人，宽以待人，淡泊名利。

82岁的凯一大早就亲自开车来到洛杉矶国际机场福朋喜来登酒店接我们。大约一个半小时后，我们到了她居住的老年社区——圣安东尼奥花园（Mount San Antonio Gardens）。这个花园占地面积30英亩，多数是一层屋顶的公寓，环境清幽，有鱼池、垂柳、竹林、玫瑰园等；各种设施配套完善，

凯在圣安东尼奥花园的住所

春色
任天涯
——福建华南女子
职业学院外教侧记
International Faculty with
Fujian Hua Nan Women's
College since 1908

376

有餐厅、图书馆、展览厅、会议室、艺术中心、健康中心、室内健身中心、游泳池、小高尔夫球场、掷蹄铁套柱游戏运动场等；专兼职员工共250人，提供的服务周到、全面。就像凯一样，这个宁静的社区优雅地诉说着她的故事，谁也打扰不了她。凯住在一个联排的单人小别墅，门前是一个种满了玫瑰花的小花园，不远处是一个供社区居民随意采摘的花园。

凯积蓄不多，非常节俭，但她不仅乐善好施，还曾在缅甸义务教学3年，在华南女院服务11年。2011年，她卖掉房子，住到圣安东尼奥花园老人社区。看着凯一脸满足的表情，我感到由衷的欣慰。

有福之人，是因为他的真实比他的名誉更耀眼。

忆往昔华南岁月

如果你是华南女院人，你一定不会错过凯在华南女院留下的足迹，不会错过那道独特的风景。

凯·格里姆斯博士，1932年10月出生，自1998年8月至2011年3月在华南女院工作，1998年至2000年以及2001年至2002年由爱德基金会派遣来华南执教，2003年开始以志愿者身份自费在华南女院教书。作为科班出身的教育博士，凯有着丰富的英语作为外语的语言教学理论和实践。她承担应用英语专业中英语听说、英语读写、英语自由谈话等课程教学，为全校的学生开发英语第二课堂活动——英语角和英语电影。之后作为该专业的教育顾问之一，她为专业的发展献计献策。她的努力和坚持赢得了师生的广泛赞誉，也为应用英语专业2010年获得"福建省职业院校精品专业"、2013年荣获"福建省民办高校优势特色专业"等的荣誉称号奠定了坚实的基础。2008年10月，福建华南女子学院以"凯·格里姆斯"命名外教楼里的英文图书馆，以纪念她为我院教育事业做出的突出贡献。鉴于凯·格里姆斯博士多年来对福建省女子高等教育事业做出的特殊贡献，福建省人民政府授予她2005年度第四届福建省"友谊奖"，2006年福州市政府又授予了她福州市"友谊奖"。

在全体外教合影中，其中有三个是爱德基金会教师项目派来（华南女院）任教两年（1998—2000）的：桑迪·卡勒斯（Sandy Cullers），米尔扎·罗德里格斯（Mirzah Rodriguez）和我。我们在华南整整待了两年，中间没有回过家。爱德基金会是总部设在南京的一个中国非政府组织。他们从国外招聘英语老师。我第一次见到桑迪是在纽约，我们在那里接受了作为爱德基金会教师在美国的第一次培训。桑迪和我在分配到华南女院之前，从没听说过华南女院。接着，我们暑期去南通（在那里我们碰到了米尔扎）接受爱德基金会工作人员和资深外教为我们进行的培训。暑期快结束时，爱德基金会在中国的所有其他老师和我们一起参加了一个会议。我们离开南通后，许道锋老师来见我们，从此我们结下了深厚的友情。

——译自凯·格里姆斯博士

1998年我见到了凯·格里姆斯博士——卷发齐耳，背微驼，身材微胖，语气轻柔的中年女老师，她给我很亲切的感觉。她是极少数持有加州K-12年级教师资格证书的资深外教。除了在华南女院任教外，凯还和简·菲利普（Dr. Jeanne Phillips）担任编委，长期默默无闻地为福州小学生英语课本质量把关。

在以后10多年的共事中，她的默默无闻，勤勤恳恳，一身正气，爱心满满，给我们留下了深刻的印象，成为我们学习的榜样。每年国庆黄金周，她都带新到华南女院执教的外教去厦门旅游度假，让柔软的海风吹散乡愁，让身心得到安慰。对遇到天灾人祸的学生和青年教师们，她都会慷慨解囊，并给予心灵的安慰。她是位让人敬佩的师长！

——董秀萍（在华南女院外事办工作近20年的老师）

我很荣幸成为凯的朋友，因为认识她使我的人生更加丰富。我和凯在华南女院共事了11年，以下是我跟凯这些年来的一些经历和零星回忆：

凯和我选择住在外国专家楼的第四层，我们是对门邻居，隔着走廊相望。这么选择是因为我们相处得相当愉快，我们喜欢每天晚上一起收看我们最喜爱的电视节目——新闻、《对话》和《走遍中国》。我们常常在一起分享教学的一些想法，以及激发学生进行思考的办法。

凯总是早睡早起。晚上10点前一定睡觉，早上一般6点，甚至可能更早5：30就起床，穿过走廊，去拿热水泡咖啡喝。她的公寓总是很干净、整洁。我总是感觉她对物质的东西不感兴趣。

凯穿着总是很职业化：长筒袜、短裙、配套的衬衫、夹克，有时着长裤。事实上我从没见她穿过网球鞋或牛仔裤或整套运动装。凯是一个柔声说话的女子，我发现她从不在背后说别人的坏话或是抱怨任何事情。

凯跟我说过她的脚有些问题，所以她穿特别的鞋子来减轻问题。她知道

春色
任天涯
——福建华南女子
职业学院外教侧记
International Faculty with
Fujian Hua Nan Women's
College since 1908

378

自己走得很慢，但从不抱怨到公交车站要步行的一段路程，也不抱怨跟黄丽霞（Laihar Wong）一起要走很长的路才到教堂。虽然走到公交站对她来说很费劲，但是她从来没有错过一次教堂的礼拜。

凯总是有一颗乐于给予的心。在华南女院教学期间，她乐意捐赠大笔的钱给华南女院。她给了我一张很昂贵的巨大的刺绣画。她为什么要给我呢？因为当我陶醉于这幅画之时，她就在我旁边。除我之外，她还赠送贵重的礼物给别人。

凯可能是我见过的最善良的人。当有人请求帮忙或有人需要帮忙时，她总是愿意帮助。她在缅甸从教多年，总是很关心她在那里的朋友过得好不好。在华南女院教学的十几年里，每到寒假她都会带着钱去缅甸给她的朋友和以前的学生。接着，令她很伤心的日子来了——她再也不能进入那个国家。

—— 译自贝茨·里韦特博士（在华南女院服务近20年的外籍教师）

凯是个轻声细语说话的人，她说得很少，但她付诸行动。一旦她看到别人需要帮助，她马上就行动。她也是一个非常慷慨的人。每一次去缅甸之前，她都会到云南取得签证，从那里为每个外籍老师带回一些礼物；她会为缅甸的朋友带一些阅读的材料、药品和钱。英语角委员会成员会得到糖果棒和漂亮的证书，而她不让我为此付钱。（注：凯每年从美国购买糖果棒和漂亮的证书并邮寄到华南女院。）凯邀请我成为英语角的指导老师。自从她从华南退休后，我为了感念她多年来对他人的善意和友谊，很高兴地接管了英语角。

她是一个很棒的朋友和支持者，常怀感恩之心，给我鼓励，善于倾听和赞扬他人，这一点在其他外籍教师身上我未曾多见。此外，她是一个非常独立的人，这是我们都可以从凯身上学习的一个优秀品质。这也就是她能在缅甸和中国从事教学这么多年，70多岁时在寒假期间还能独自去缅甸的原因。

我是如此有福、如此幸运——有她这位朋友和同事一起走过这些年。我相信她所有的学生都敬爱她并且珍惜与她的友谊。

——译自黄丽霞

谈到凯，大家的看法是一致的：她很安静、勤奋、友善、大方，而且她全身心地献身教学、华南女院和她的基督教信仰。她很好地诠释了纪·哈·纪伯伦的话"工作是看得见的爱"。我从来没有遇见过一个像凯一样真正无私和有原则的人。2000年（那时的薪水很低）当我不太确认是否要回华南女院（教学）时，凯为我支付了到福州的往返机票，一笔价格不菲的费用。当我在写这件事时，我知道凯会因为我把她对我的慷慨泄露出去而懊恼，因为她害怕会冒犯别人。而且尽管我犯了世俗的错误，她仍然认我为朋友，每年准时给我寄来生日和圣诞卡片。

——译自多琳·多萝西·约翰斯顿

　　华南女院外教中，凯是唯一有英语语言博士学位的老师，长期从事英语教学，有丰富的英语教学经验，而且她和蔼可亲，充满爱心，诲人不倦，真是一位不可多得的好老师，是学生和同行教师的典范。她处事低调，从不张扬，默默为华南女院和学生们做了很多好事，捐资助学，捐资建校，从不图回报。

——林本椿（曾担任华南女院院长，现任学院顾问）

师者——润物细无声

　　师者何为？传道授业解惑？人类灵魂的工程师？社会对于教师角色的期望之高可见一斑。当今社会有人提出老师必须要像演员和导演，这两个特征在凯身上也许不容易找到，但她的行动却深深地打动了我们，让我们重新思考何以为师。

凯在自由谈话课上（2005年）

　　凯热爱、关心学生。她给每个学生照相，把照片和学生手写的信息贴在卡片上，以便她能更好地了解每个学生。她至今还保留着11年来她教过的每个学生的卡片，卡片上的信息包括每个学生的生日，这样她就可以在那特别的日子用她的电脑为学生制作一张生日贺卡，让身处异乡的学生感受到家一样的温馨。

　　凯治学严谨，从不间断学习。虽然有着40多年的教学经验，但是她对自己的教学水平要求甚高，每年她至少参加两次会议，和与会者探讨英语教学的新思路，孜孜不倦地提高自身的专业素养。

　　年届高龄的凯，每天迈着坚定的步伐在教室与宿舍间来回，她把一天中大部分的时间奉献给了学生。生源素质起起落落，她没有抱怨过，11年如一日，用她的温柔、善解人意、耐心去鼓励学生，一如既往地把爱倾注给每一位学生，正所谓"润物细无声"。凯精湛的教学水平和广博的爱心赢得了我院教师及学生的爱戴和尊敬。

　　现在美国恩波利亚州立大学攻读硕士学位的2011届毕业生陈璐回忆起凯，满是感激：

春色
任天涯
——福建华南女子
职业学院外教侧记
International Faculty with
Fujian Hua Nan Women's
College since 1908

380

凯是我的英语口语老师，在她的课上我第一次听到如此正宗的美国英语，我一下子就喜欢上了她的课。中国学生羞于开口，凯总是鼓励我们多练习。她从不介意我们在她的课堂上犯错误，总是耐心地纠正我们的发音和语法并及时给予反馈。这么多年了，我还忘不了凯对我的鼓励。在美国这么几年，我能勇敢地与外国人交流，或许就是凯的潜移默化给我勇气。

王小燕（英文名字为Jenny），2009年华南女院应用英语专业毕业之后留学美国晨边大学，2014年4月创办厦门中美汇实业有限公司，现在美国拓展公司的海外业务和团队。同时，从2016年2月起，她还是哈佛大学亚洲中心的一位研究员。她这样描述这位很特别的外籍教师：

凯总是带着由内而外的微笑，柔和而优雅，让人感觉坐在她的课堂里是一种放松和享受。她端庄的打扮和优雅的言行举止更是一种言传身教，无形中影响着我们对于女性自我形象的塑造。她的爱心、耐心和亲和力更是让我们钦佩，值得我们学习。

除耐心教导华南女院的学生之外，凯还是华南女院许多年轻教师的成长导师。曾在华南女院任教的林丽华老师深情地讲述了她与凯之间一段鲜为人知的故事：

认识凯是在1999年秋季，她当时担任99级实用英语专业A班的"英语听说"课程，而我是这个班的班主任，从此我们从同事变成了忘年交，确切地说，她是我一路成长的职业导师和心灵导师。

2002年初正好有个机会前往泰国易三仓大学读研，我当时很犹豫，因为我女儿还不满一周半，凯知道后便鼓励并建议我妥当安排，把握机会去提高自己。然而，一出国门，学习压力和思念孩子一度使我身心疲惫，是她坚持每个月给我来信，为我排忧解难，直至学成回国。

2005年初回国，我被委以重任，负责商务英语专业。凯处处为我伸出援手，她曾经默默地在美国找到一个匿名捐赠者，采购最新的商务英语书籍赠送给我专业，帮助核心课程建设；全力以赴地支持我申请并顺利组织"亚洲地区第三届创意写作与文学的国际学术会议"。

凯为人一向平和、温文尔雅，但有一次我见到她生气了。得知我专业的一位外籍教师和学生关系处理不好时，她牺牲了午休时间，专程从烟台山跑到首山校区召集我和那个外教开会，了解事情原委，得知那外籍教师是出言不逊引起学生不满时，她非常生气地当面批评了他，并要求他在班上向学生道歉，这是我唯一一次看到凯如此生气且严肃地处理事情。

2013年11月凯回华南女院，我有机会采访了凯，谈话中，她说到从事教育41年了，她始终很自豪自己选择了老师这个神圣的职业，特别强调"一日为师，终身为师"是她最大的幸福。好友黄丽霞和我一致认为，凯是我们见到的最善良、最有爱心、最尽职的好老师，是我们一生学习的楷模和好榜样！

钟福连老师是这么评价凯的：

凯是一位儒雅、真诚、谦逊的师者，彰显润物细无声的教学风格。2002年，我很幸运地参与了凯在教学之余为我们实用英语专业全体老师开设的英语教学技能系列讲座。这一系列讲座给刚刚留校任教的我起到很好的示范作用，如教师必须站着授课，便于和全班学生互动交流；教学语言必须清晰简练，便于学生模仿跟读；课堂上得善于倾听，便于领悟学生的心理。凯可谓我们的良师益友。共处的记忆，犹如昨天。

随风潜入夜，润物细无声。

志愿者——繁忙的课余

凯还把英语学习延伸到第二课堂，积极组织各种活动，以不同的形式促进学生把英语用到实践中，转化为英语应用能力，为华南女院学生英语水平的提高提供了极好的条件。

她负责午间电影的活动，每周一到周四中午都给学生放映一部原版影片，极大地调动了学生的英语学习热情。她还向应用英语专业的英文图书馆捐赠了很多原版书籍，包括全套的《国家地理》杂志等。午间电影和这些宝贵的图书给学生课外带来了很多的乐趣，为学生的英文输入提供了难得的条件。

凯、外教黄丽霞和学生尤超云

春色
任天涯
——福建华南女子
职业学院外教侧记
International Faculty with
Fujian Hua Nan Women's
College since 1908

382

此外，凯作为英语角的牵头者，她招募华南女院的学生参与英语角的组织工作，定期召集学生召开筹备会议，发动学生做好宣传广告工作和英语角当天的组织工作。在这过程中，通过做中学，学生不仅提高了英语应用能力，领导能力、动手能力和团队合作能力也得到了很好的锻炼。

华南女院英语角曾经的学生组织者之一——尤超云，颇为兴奋地谈起那一段特殊的经历：

凯老师的年岁已高，腿脚也不是很灵便，但每次在我们的英语角仍然都可以看到她那坚守的身影，风雨无阻。记得我刚上大二的一个星期五的晚上，我们在一起过圣诞节。活动结束后，凯老师问我想不想也像学姐一样做个英语角的组织者，她说她可以向丽霞推荐我。本来我以为她只是说说而已，结果第二个星期丽霞老师真的在课下找我说了这件事，当时我非常激动。凯和丽霞老师给了我一个舞台，这个舞台极大地锻炼了我的组织能力和口语表达能力，英语角还带给我许多美好的回忆……高山仰止，景行行止。对于凯、贝茨、丽霞、程戈登夫妇（Gordon Trimble and Sonia Trimble）等老师的无私奉献，我们这些学子唯有感激，感激他们在人生颐养天年之时，来到中国尽心尽力地教导我们。

2001届毕业生周鑫博士，
美国恩波利亚州立大学商
学院副教授

2003届毕业生林素红，
泉州卡尔进出口贸易有限公司
总经理

2009届毕业生王小燕，
哈佛大学亚洲中心研究员

2011届毕业生黄晓丹
创办福州市晋安区新嘉幼儿园

2012届毕业生郑小玲创办福州市
晋安区全优教育咨询有限公司

凯很重视学生的感受，注重做好细节问题以吸引学生参加英语角。比如，英语角的灯光不够亮，她就想办法联系学校总务处及时处理。英语角在每周五晚上6点到8点于校门口进行，逢下雨就移到校内。多年下来，英语角吸引了华南女院的学生，很多外校的学生包括小学和中学生也慕名而来。在凯、贝茨、戈登和索尼娅、丽霞、程式家族派来的外教（美国普吉湾大学毕业生）和其他外教的精心教育和帮助下，专业为社会输送了许多优秀毕业生。比如：2001届毕业生周鑫博士是美国恩波利亚州立大学的副教授；2003届毕业生林素红担任泉州卡尔进出口贸易有限公司的总经理；2008届毕业生张琳因为出色的英语口语和良好的综合素质被选去美国夏威夷州程戈登参议员办公室实习，毕业后在上海工作，现在担任全球30强的通用电气航空集团工程部总经理秘书；2009届毕业生王小燕因流利的口语被选送到美国深造，并于2014年在厦门开办自己的贸易公司——厦门中美汇实业有限公司，同时她从2016年2月份开始还是美国哈佛大学亚洲中心的研究员；2011届毕业生黄晓丹创办福州市晋安区新嘉幼儿园；2012届毕业生郑小玲创办福州市晋安区全优教育咨询有限公司。

> 我从来不教学生。我只是尽力为学生提供他们能够学习的条件。
>
> ——爱因斯坦

顾问——永远的支柱

凯曾经说过："凡是对中国女子教育有益的事，我都乐意做。"她对应用英语专业的发展做出了积极的贡献。

应用英语专业的资深教师、原专业主任董秀萍老师回忆：

为了让老师和学生看到国外最新的英语学习资料，凯用自己的退休金从美国买了书捐赠给专业；凯认真审核专业培养方案的英文版、各种英文材料的翻译稿，积极提出修改意见；她还重视培养青年教师的英语教学能力，为我们开设英语教学技能讲座。记得讲座中她曾经讲到学习者的多元智能理论，教我们为英语学习者进行学习方法的测试，让每个学生找到适合自己的学习方法，这份测试至今我还会用到我学生身上。

她很低调，做事从不张扬，总是默默无闻地付出。她不会仗着自己是老教师就会对他人指手画脚，总是和蔼可亲，低声细语，以欣赏的态度、鼓励的眼神和人交谈。

**春色
任天涯**
——福建华南女子
职业学院外教侧记
International Faculty with
Fujian Hua Nan Women's
College since 1908

384

我始终与从华南女院"退休"的凯保持着书信往来。每当专业建设和我个人取得成就，我就会写信告诉她，并且表达对她一直以来大力支持专业工作的感激。2013年应用英语专业和商务英语专业在全省专业建设评估中位列第八（71个专业参评），被评为优势特色专业，得到省教育厅十万元奖励进行专业建设工作。我写信告诉了她并说："我们知道没有您的鼎力支持，我们不会取得这些成绩。非常感谢您一直以来的帮助。"她马上回复："祝贺你们！得到这些奖励真是令人激动！太好了！这些奖励是你们通过自己的努力取得的！拥有你们真是华南女院的一大幸事。谢谢你认为我们外籍教师在某些方面对你们有所帮助。只要有需要，我会随时以任何形式来帮助你们。"（译自凯的邮件）

回想起来，我觉得自己这六年来能够面对专业建设中出现的种种压力和挑战，坚持下来的源动力，一定就是像凯这样永远站在我背后、无条件、默默支持我的老师吧？她们好像在跟我说："不要怕，坚持住！我就在你身边。"华南女院何其有幸！我们何其有福！有顾问如此，我们怎能轻言放弃？

> 只要有需要，我会随时以任何形式来帮助你们。
>
> ——译自凯

妈妈——无疆的大爱

对于需要帮助的老师，凯总是鼎力相助。应用英语专业一位教师讲述了一段感人的往事：

2008年正值学校接受第一轮人才培养水平评估，我因为家里突然发生变故，请了三个月假。专业里其他中国老师忙于评估事务，她们帮我承担了专业分配的评估任务和一些其他事务，凯则默默地接下了我三个班的"英语阅读"课共计10课时，并且不计酬劳，让学校继续把课酬算给我。期末还认真地计算好了每位学生的成绩，并且认真负责地把学生的平时表现和期末成绩记录了下来，在我回校时交给了我。凯自己一周要上12节课时，还接下了我的10节课，真是太辛苦了！我一直记着这件事，由衷地感激她。正是因为有像凯一样的老师无私地帮助了我，所以我心怀感恩，我也要像她一样用爱心去帮助需要帮助的人。

华南女院毕业生尤超云回忆起凯当时帮忙其他老师代课的情形：

记得有一次，凯来我们班代课，她腿脚不是很灵便，我想过去搀扶她，但她坚持自己走上来。那时，看着她蹒跚的步伐，我鼻子有点泛酸。

在校园湖边的专家楼里，住着大约10位来自世界各地的外籍教师，凯像妈妈一样无声无息地关心着其他老师。她和贝茨出钱买生日蛋糕，并一起附上其他外教的签名。每年总有一两个年轻的外教，远离家人和朋友，万里迢迢来到华南女院教书，难免会想家，凯对他们总是很关心，并以过来人的身份开导他们。玛乔丽·洛德威客，美国普吉湾大学毕业后就来华南女院任教的一位年轻教师，回忆起关于凯的故事：

凯是一个很可爱的人，很容易与她共事，是我的好朋友。我记得在我刚到华南女院的那几天她带给我的友善和安慰。她柔声细语、温文尔雅，轻轻地走路，以确保带给我舒服和受欢迎的感觉。我记得她的学生很喜欢她。她是一个了不起的老师——一个用善良激发学生的老师。在英语角跟学生组织者开会时，她从来不大声说话。她一开始轻声说话，所有的学生就安静下来认真听她说话。我第一学期在华南女院的最温馨的记忆之一是凯、贝茨和丽霞邀请我跟她们周末一起去鼓浪屿的事情。在那个岛上跟凯一起走在街上，感觉多么美好啊！

更为可贵的是，她对照顾外教生活起居的女工友们也很关心，逢年过节，都给她们送上礼物，感谢她们多年来对外教的照顾。对于外事处的工作，凯也是积极配合，提供了很多意见和建议，帮外事处做好各项英文文件的审稿工作。

言不在多，而在有物。

熠熠发光的人性之美

凯自1955年开始在美国从事教师工作直到1997年退休，期间在缅甸教学3年多（1958年至1961年），1998年来到华南女院工作。节俭和大方在这位老太太身上得到了最好的诠释：她生活很勤俭，拥有的积蓄并不多，然而她却乐于资助别人——凯资助多位华南女院老师攻读研究生学位；捐助一位身染绝症的华南女院学生；每年从美国买英文的奖状，寄到华南女院发给帮忙一起组织英语角的学生；凯为专业教师刚出生的孩子买礼物、贺卡，并请其他外教写上祝福语和签名……

曾任教于华南女院应用英语专业，现在美国担任教师的林娇无比深情地回忆起

春色
任天涯
——福建华南女子
职业学院外教侧记
International Faculty with
Fujian Hua Nan Women's
College since 1908

386

了她与凯之间不寻常的故事：

在我生命旅途中有很多温馨的回忆，我知道凯一定是那其中一个，她经过万水千山的跋涉来到我身边，向我展示她对于我这样一个普通的人的无私的爱和关心。凯是我一生中见过的最温柔、最大方的女性。从我第一次在烟台山华南女院校区见到她到现在，已经有17个年头了。这些年来，她用温柔和善良感动了很多人。她不仅教学技能精湛，善于引导学生，而且她还用实际的、充满爱心的行动帮助了许多华南女院的学生和老师。

她有一颗关心别人、善解人意的心，我觉得我永远也无法回报她为我家庭、孩子和我所做的一切。我仍然清晰地记得凯递给我那个特别的结婚祝贺卡片，那卡片上写满了全体外籍教师的最美好的祝愿和签名。她还十分尊重中国给红包的传统，给了我一个红包。打开一看，我惊呆了。500元！当时对于她的工资来说，这是一大笔钱。

还有另外一件事情是我永远也忘不了的。我女儿出生的第三天，凯带着一张漂亮的贺卡来看我。她对刚出生的小女孩显示出极大的兴趣，问我是否可以抱抱我的女儿。看到她，我很激动，忘记给孩子放尿片了。我觉得我的女儿可能本能地知道这位访客是最温柔的女性，她可以"恣意妄为"。接下来发生的事情想必你不难猜到——在凯的膝盖上还未过五分钟，我女儿就把凯的裤子尿湿了！你也可以猜到凯的反应："没关系，她太可爱了！"

随着时间的流逝，我的家庭继续成长着，凯对我的家庭和我的爱越发强烈和大方。在过去的17年来，她没有一次忘记给我们寄生日贺卡。我珍惜她所寄给我的所有贺卡，其中有一张贺卡我想在这里特别说一说。仔细观察这张特别的生日贺卡里邮戳上的日期，我发现是2010年10月5日。她怎么知道三年后艾米（林娇的英文名字）会拉小提琴，那个跟她的生日贺卡上的一模一样的小提琴？真是巧合！不管是在遥远的太平洋彼岸或者同在太平洋的这一侧，她把我们记在心底最温暖的地方。完成硕士学位后，我在另一个城市得到了一个教学的岗位。当她知道我需要租一套公寓，以便周一到周五工作日可以在里面休息时，她慷慨地捐了1000美元帮助我，并且无意让我知道是她捐助的。

如果我要把她为别人所做的好事都记录下来，我相信可以写成一本书。目前，我就分享这些。我知道我永远也无法回报她为我所做的一切。我唯一能为她做的是记住她的善良——在我用小提琴弹奏的乐曲里面。不管身在何处，她的生命都是一首静谧的、灵与温柔的爱之歌。

凯来华南女院教书的时候，她曾把自己在美国的房子无偿提供给她认识的、在那里求学的两个大学生暂时居住。在昆明的寒假期间，她会到缅甸她曾经任教的学校看望以前的同事和学生。

如果你仔细观察附录的"英语角会议备忘录样本"，马上会发现她的另一个闪光点：谦虚。英语角是她组织起来的，她做了最主要的工作，但在署名时她总是把自己放在最后。据不完全统计，她近些年在帮助学生、外教、华南女院发展等各方面提供的资助至少达十万元之多。要不是这些受过她资助的学生、外教和其他青年教师提起，这些事情至今都不为人所知。

在沉静的凯的身上，人性中的真、善、美熠熠发光。凯为华南女院人做了最好的榜样，引领着我们勇敢地、坚定地走下去。我一直在思索：是什么让这位看似柔弱的老太太保持恬静的微笑和十一年的坚守呢？这种超越国界的、普世的大爱，无声地感染着我，使我感恩生活的馈赠，对有困难之人真诚地伸出援手。

我们从来就不乏爱的教育，稀缺的是像她这样用实际行动展现出来的一种普世的大爱。我想让凯知道：您天使般的微笑，永远留在了我的心里，相信也留在了很

凯发表告别演讲

凯、任建红副院长、赖黎群系副主任

凯和徐欧副院长

凯和杨淑琴

凯和黄飞

凯和陈晴

春色
任天涯
——福建华南女子
职业学院外教侧记
International Faculty with
Fujian Hua Nan Women's
College since 1908

388

多人的心里……

树立榜样不是教育的另一种方式；它是教育的唯一途径。

——爱因斯坦

斩不断的中国情思

凯对中国和中国人民有着深厚的感情，她曾多次称赞中国人的热情善良和中国学生的纯真好学。但是，随着岁月的流逝，2010年11月，到了凯不得不跟我们说再见的时候了，我是完全没有心理准备的，因为我总是固执地认为她一直是与应用英语专业连在一块儿的，必不可缺。

"退休"告别晚会

颇具戏剧性的是，那场告别晚会居然是我主持的，这是我人生中第一次组织那样的晚会，心里不免紧张，但同时也觉得很荣幸，我想那可能是我送给她的最好的礼物了，所以尽管晚会主持得不尽完美，但我从来没有后悔。院长、副院长、华南女院老教师、系里的老师和凯的部分学生参加了那场告别晚会。三言两语难以道尽大家对凯的感恩和依依不舍之情。虽然我不是凯真正意义上的课堂上的学生，但是我把她视为我此生最好的老师。

凯、外教黄丽霞和董秀萍一家

凯再次走进应用英语专业的课堂

返校参加校庆

凯和贝茨于2013年9月28日专程从美国回华南女院参加学院2013年10月19日举行的105周年庆典。凯在华南女院逗留了约一个月，她除参加了我们每周五晚上的英语角之外，还应邀再次走进应用英语专业课堂。

2013年10月9日，作为嘉宾的凯被邀请到2012级应用英语专业A班的自由谈话课上，围绕主题"Family"展开讨论。凯向大家介绍了美国老年人退休后的生活，而学生也用英语畅谈了中国家庭对老人到养老院安度晚年的看法。大家对中美老人晚年生活进行比较，从中对双方的文化、家庭观念有了进一步的了解。10月23日凯还参加了该班以"教育"为主题的讨论，让学生对于美国教育有了更深入的了解。凯还以"如何用故事进行少儿英语教学"和"如何进行少儿英语写作教学"为主题与中国老师共同授课。凯还被邀请到我执教的班上对大学一年级学生进行英语发音的指导，通过不同的活动让学生齐声朗诵，受到学生的喜爱。这些活动对英文基础薄弱的一年级学生特别有效，能够提高她们对英文阅读的兴趣、英文阅读的流利度和增强学生说英文的自信心，但这些活动一点也不复杂，不会给人难以企及的感觉；它们就像凯的性格一样——简单朴实却深入人心。凯对教学的热情和精湛的教学技能真是令人敬佩！要是时光能够倒流，我们可以经常坐在凯的教室好好地享受她的课该多好啊！

凯十分想念中国的朋友。再次见到老朋友，她非常激动。她还登门拜访了许道锋老师和她的先生（许道锋是华南女院应用英语专业的创始人，原外事处处长）。

2002届毕业生姚亚美（英文名Rose）在外事处工作多年，对于凯有着深厚的感情：

发生9·11事件那年，我是凯的班上一个普通的大三学生，下课时我看到凯安安静静地站在走廊上，就走过去问候她。因为担心她孤单，之后我就经常下课了找她聊天，我们成了好朋友。留校后，我在外事处工作，跟凯有了更多的接触。得知我想攻读硕士学位但经济上有困难，凯鼓励并赞助我继续深造，让我的视野更加开阔。在我眼里，凯是一位善良、温暖、博爱、博学的智者。她不但教给我很多知识，也让我学到了许多美好的理念。每次想起她，都会让我感到温暖。她让我学会了做一个"暖人"，温暖自己也温暖他人。

距离使两颗心靠得更近。

春色
任天涯
——福建华南女子
职业学院外教侧记
International Faculty with
Fujian Hua Nan Women's
College since 1908

390

难舍中国情缘

老太太于2013年参加校庆之后再度离开华南，回到美国。从此，大洋的两岸添了几多思念。华南女院的年轻老师用自己的方式表达着对凯深沉的爱：2014年在美国学习的徐欧副院长专程到洛杉矶拜访了贝茨，之后贝茨和徐欧副院长一起去看望凯；2015年在美国访学的我两次前往洛杉矶拜访了凯，带她去吃了正宗的中国餐。而沉静的凯含蓄地表达了她的感激和兴奋——一大早开车把我接到她的老年社区并带我参观了整个社区。她把自己对中国、对华南女院的深深的爱藏在了她的公寓里。她的房间里遍布中国元素——中国山水画、中国的扇子、中国的沙发靠垫……她会为了吃一顿正宗的中国菜激动不已。她多半是把一半的心思留在了中国吧？何日君再来？华南女院续情缘！

译自凯的一封来信：

飞，

再次见到你的感觉真是太好了！我也真的很喜欢见到你那令人惊叹的儿子。感谢你发给我的相片，感谢你来看我，感谢你请我吃的美食宴会（我觉得那不是晚餐，是宴会美食）。我很久都没有去中国餐馆了，因为我自己去过的那些中国餐馆吃起来不像真正的中国菜。但是你这次带我去吃的宴会美食是我记忆中的，真正的中国菜的味道。

爱你们的，凯

第五节　印象程氏家族

开启尘封的历史

当我回首往事，不禁想起三十多年前在江西大学（现南昌大学）读书时，首位外教介绍的美国著名诗人罗伯特·弗罗斯特那首名为《未选择的路》的诗歌。随着时间的流逝，我对这首诗有了更深入的理解。现在，我更加坚信，我选择的是快乐之旅。2002年，我从江西省辗转调到福建师范大学，这于我又是一个崭新的地方，充满了刺激和挑战。骑自行车上下班时，我常常路过一所学校，不禁被其中具有西式建筑风格的三座大楼吸引，据说这些经历文革余生的大楼建立于20世纪之初，得名于三位西方人士，属于中国南方第一所女子学院——华南女子学院（HNC）。2003年我成为华南女院的兼职英语教师。

中国处在快速发展的进程中，华南女院当然也不例外。华南女院扩大了招生，增加了新专业，准备搬到位于大学城的新校区。重组随之而来，五年后我接手了十名外教所在的外语外贸系，担任教学和管理工作。即便在规模为华南女院十倍的大学里，多不过6位外教，更别说10位了，而且其中还有一名得过国家"友谊奖"的外教。

目前，还有3名福建省"友谊奖"的获得者在华南女院任教。2008年，我遇见了两名性格迥异的外教，一位是凯·格里姆斯博士（Dr. Kay Grimmesey），她和蔼可亲，温柔敦厚，一向是个安静的观察者，甘居幕后，总是鼓励别人开拓思维。我初遇凯时，她刚刚结束自费教的电影课程，邀请我去外国专家楼的餐厅共进午餐，在那里，我还遇到了其他外教，因为是非正式的场合，我们无拘无束，聊得非常开心。

另一位是贝茨·里韦特博士（Dr. Betts Rivet），她精明强干，曾在美国的学校担任过体育教导员和副校长。一次，当她发现自己教的学生逃课时，立即要求会见学生家长，并让我做翻译。那时我比家长还紧张，因为除非事态严重，我们一般是不会要求家长来校的。但是她说一不二："凡事要早做准备，防止事态恶化。"我记得当时学生的父亲是一位的士司机，深为贝茨的用心所感动。自此，学生认真对待学业。此事令我终生难忘。

与贝茨在圣诞时的合影
（2008年12月）

与凯在圣诞时的合影
（2008年12月）

贝茨和普吉湾大学的伊丽莎白·贝纳德
（2008年11月）

春色
任天涯
——福建华南女子
职业学院外教侧记
International Faculty with
Fujian Hua Nan Women's
College since 1908

392

来自普吉湾大学的学生
（2008年12月）

华南女院学生与普吉湾大学学生联欢
（2008年12月）

那年秋天，还发生了一件事情。我遇到了卡尔·菲尔德教授（Karl Fields）。他一口流利的汉语，令人印象深刻。更令人感动的是，他组织了20多名大学生从美国的普吉湾大学来华南女院体验中国文化和人情。这些学生参加了英语角的活动，和女院学生自由互动。他们是来游学，而不是来旅游的。菲尔德教授带他们坐长途班车去古田，在长征出发前毛泽东发表演讲的地方给他们上课。我了解到是程氏基金促成了这次的行程。但为何是来自美国的普吉湾大学的学生，又为何到华南女院来呢？有些人觉得很奇怪。很多人认为有必要记叙一下。我仔细追踪了事情的来龙去脉，决定提笔书写，以便世人周知。

2009年秋：三条鱼的故事

许多人都有和鱼有关的故事，我也不例外。我先生闲暇时的爱好是钓鱼。早在2002年，我们在师大的校本部楼前散步时，曾注意过大楼外墙上镌刻的字，走到程氏大楼时，先生说这个姓氏非同寻常，他曾经见过。思忖片刻，他说，北京有家公司出售这个名字的GPS设备，即便你在伸手不见五指的黑夜中、在信号不好的地方，也能用该设备。我真不知道他在说什么，直到多年后才对此有所了解。

每当回忆起2009年发生的那一幕，仿佛历历在目。8月的华南女院新校区，绿树成荫，空气潮湿，校区建设并未全部完工，地面杂乱，空气中布满灰尘，工地上不停响着震耳欲聋的敲打声。有校车接送教职工来往于市区和新校区之间，但通勤要花一个多小时，令中方老师上下班非常不方便。同样，遭遇不便的还有外教，他们入住在新区静湖边的外国专家楼，大楼高耸，不过第一年供电和网络都不太稳定。

那时我在6楼落满灰尘的办公室办公，又闷又热，一天有个学生把一张照片放在我的桌面上，照片上是一条大鱼和两条小鱼，翻着白肚，在桥边的湖上漂浮着。我想到，平时路过那里也闻到一股怪味。到底发生了什么呢？由于施工和水质问题，湖中出现了很多死鱼，贝茨博士因此希望发起联名请愿书告知各位校领导，解决这一问题。然而，其中常常穿大花衬衣的那位外教，拒绝在贝茨博士的请愿书上签名。他说应该拍照发给大家，而且说："这样要表达的意思才一目了然。"

有时候你所得并非你所愿。对于程氏夫妇（Mr. & Mrs. Trimble）来说，尤其如此。有关他们的传言甚嚣尘上，不过多半属于臆测。我也并未见过他们。我甚至不确定该如何与他们打交道。他们看上去似乎根本不是来自于同一个星球的人。丈夫程戈登有着蓝色的眼睛，头上长着些波浪般的淡棕色卷发。大多数情况下，当他的头发长得越长，颜色就越淡。当戈登过于固执己见，太太索妮娅就会提醒他。戈登身高约1.75米，保持得好的时候体重大约90公斤。索妮娅则身材纤细，体重不及他的一半，她满头棕褐色头发。我该如何与他们相处呢？

这位来自夏威夷的参议员用行动回答了我的问题。他伸出手，坚定地与我握手，并微笑着说："阿罗哈，我是程戈登（Gordon Trimble），这是我妻子程索妮娅（Sonia

程氏夫妇在华南女子学院第一任校长
程吕底亚画像前合影（2005年）

相亲相爱的程氏夫妇（2011年5月）

程氏夫妇参观福州著名小吃
——同利肉燕在福州西园村的生产车间（2013年12月）

春色
任天涯
——福建华南女子
职业学院外教侧记
International Faculty with
Fujian Hua Nan Women's
College since 1908

394

Trimble）。"他说话的时候通常带着微笑，而当他倾听时，则会盯着天花板看。我只有从他表情的变化判断他对我谈论的是否感兴趣。每次向他提问时，他会停顿一下，思考片刻，然后以最幽默的方式回答。不久我就明白了，原来他们夫妇俩无法离开彼此。

我问他教学经历，他笑着告诉我说："英语真不容易学。但我会帮学生们学习沟通技能，学习是学生的事情，所以我更像个教练。我略懂经济，也教过大学水平的商务、金融和国际贸易。近几十年来，我从事的一直都与商务写作有关。如今，所有事情都得在电脑上完成，你能否帮我找一间计算机房呢？"最终我安排他教应用英语专业大三的"商务英语写作""国际商务阅读""自由交谈"三门课程。我注意到他把"自由交谈"当作即兴演讲课，将之变成一种可以教授的技能。他展示的那张鱼的照片表明，与用正式的英语表达相比，他更注重沟通技巧教学。

他时不时会到6楼办公室来，与中方英语老师和教学秘书陈晴交流。他每次来访，会在门口探出头来，开心地说："阿罗哈！"我觉得这很有趣。通常而言，6楼的不速之客一般对这种礼仪细节不感兴趣，只是希望他们来发发牢骚，放松心情。慢慢地，我习惯了他那声快乐的"阿罗哈"，开始和他一起聊天。在这个过程中，我对他们有了更多的了解。

一天下午，他告诉我："我们班的丽萨上课从不迟到，每次都坐在前排，衣着考究。她近视却不戴眼镜，根本看不到黑板。我让她到讲台上来大声朗读，她也没意见，但总是心不在焉。我和另外一名外教黄丽霞（Laihar Wong）聊了聊，她说丽萨毕业后要去美国留学。但她学习不用功，根本没法通过考试。"我想起了我担当贝茨的翻译和家长的那次成功的交流，就安排第二天见丽萨。我们告诉丽萨如果她不认真学习将无法毕业，我们想见她的家长。丽萨说她父亲很忙，母亲只会说福州话。我的秘书陈晴说："我会说福州话。"当丽萨发现陈晴是认真的，她就恳求陈晴不要联系她父母。我们说："那就看你的表现了。"奇迹很快发生了，她开始努力用功，拜托索妮娅和戈登在课外辅导她。在他们的帮助下，她的英语科目都及格了。但是她有一门中文课程考试还是不尽如人意。当她听说戈登和索妮娅春天会回来开实验课时，丽萨就请求加入这个班。我不同意她的请求，但是她找到副校长，副校长最终答应了她。她戴着眼镜，坐在前排，最后成了第一名。去年我听说丽萨已经从美国世纪大学获得硕士学位。

我觉得程氏夫妇对教学有独到之处，特别是程戈登，他是凭自己的努力竞选成为美国夏威夷州参议员的，我希望他能将自己丰富的人生经验与更多人分享，鼓励更多的年轻人。

我于是邀请他到我在师大任教的班级发表演说，激励学生。

"我叫戈登。我的父亲生于1915年。"他转身望向他妻子，"她叫索妮娅，她的父亲也出生于1915年。我父亲出生在中国福建，她的父亲也出生在中国福建。我姓程，她姓程。那么她就是我的妹妹了，对吧？"（在中国，妻子保留娘家的姓，但儿女跟父亲姓。）说完后他停下来，看着大家吃惊的脸。这就是戈登，他总是乐在其中。

索妮娅和戈登成为应用英语办公室一道亮丽的风景。几周后，戈登随口提到他父亲鲍勃会来中国，能否让他父亲也帮忙上课。我心存疑惑，想问又得把握分寸。鲍勃（又名程闽岱）的年纪到底有多大？（我不太确定系里到底有多少个叫鲍勃的，戈登说的又是哪位鲍勃）他怎么来中国，与谁一起来，他要教什么？戈登说："我也没做特别的准备，只是让我的学生做一些准备。鲍勃来时每个学生要向他问5个问题，随后写下自己的收获。为此我准备了一份资料。"他将《程氏家族》一书交给我，指着照片说："这位是查尔斯·加纳医生，这是他的儿子鲍勃。鲍勃有两个儿子，其中较乖的是查尔斯，另一个儿子则不是省油的灯。"他发现我的表情变了，补充说："他不是个败家子。我说的是不让人省心。这可不一样。"

我仔细阅读了《程氏家族》，但是对接下来发生的事情还是有点始料未及。这本书笔触简洁干脆，主要内容是时间、地点、事件，描绘了一位老先生的一段神奇的历程。书中提到了许多人，但都只做了一些简要介绍，很少细节叙述。书中还提到了索妮娅和戈登。与他们面对面交流时，他们享受生活、热情待人、活在当下的生活态度，非常有感染力。

与鲍勃的会面也让我大吃一惊。第一次见面时，他走路一瘸一拐，手里的拐杖，看起来更像是个装饰品。他的腿脚虽有问题，走路时左右摇晃，但他的步伐急促而果断。他常常露齿而笑，握手时刚劲有力。他的脸虽饱经风霜，却难辨具体年龄。他的双眼熠熠发光，声若洪钟，气质不凡。他并未直接告诉我他的年龄，只是拿出驾照给我看。他出生于1915年11月15日。我迷惑地看着他，他笑了笑，说："看看有效期。"有效期到2020年为止，那时他已105岁。我大吃一

笔者第一次与鲍勃合影，他时年94岁
（2009年10月）

春色
任天涯
——福建华南女子
职业学院外教侧记
International Faculty with
Fujian Hua Nan Women's
College since 1908

396

惊，无法想象105岁的人还在开车。他笑道："你要习惯，我会在这里多待一会儿。我不需要特殊对待。"听到这儿，戈登笑着说："别担心，接下来你会成为开心果。"

后来有人问他"老人家，您高寿？"时，他会变得脸色凝重，不过眼中很快露出诙谐的闪光。他的回答很简单："我们不说'老'，我们说'成熟'。我1915年出生于福建宁德，那时的情形与现在大不一样。现在固然不错，但我更怀念彼时的中国，现在大部分人不像我这样念旧。"

福建省"CCTV杯"（现名外研社杯）英语演讲选拔赛需要评委，我当时想到的第一个人选

程鲍勃（又名程闽岱）与时任校长的
陈钟英教授合影（1998年）

就是戈登。他善于倾听，评分与中国英语老师一致。演讲活动一结束，他就提出了3个问题，不针对任何人：这个比赛的题目什么时候公布？女院什么时候通知学生？若学生有兴趣，我们该如何利用好时间帮助学生？这就是他行事的风格，他喜欢直接提出问题。我看得出来他有想法，也欣赏他的做事态度。我请他辅导入围省赛的一名商英专业的学生——叶柳莺。在接下来的三周里，叶柳莺的英语水平有了很大的提高。她重新组织了思路，重写了演讲稿，她斗志昂扬、信心满满。我现在终于了解戈登的能力了。程氏夫妇和我们一起坐长途班车到厦大新校区——漳州校区参加比赛。加上福建师大的三位选手和指导老师，一行共有8人。戈登借此和每位学生交流沟通。后来他对我说："若想知道下一代的中国发展将会如何，那就和学生谈谈吧！"他停顿了一下，补充道："美国人应该多来中国与学生聊聊。"

程氏一家为华南女院"CCTV"杯英语演讲
选拔赛做裁判（2009年9月）

程氏父子俩很有趣。他们不善言辞。鲍勃也许会突然很严肃地说："生活是纷繁复杂的。"戈登听后会摇头，以同样严肃的语气，说出不针对任何人的话："生活是简单的，复杂的是人。"

南平之行令我印象深刻，不久之后我们还去了师大老校区。鲍

勃故地重游，其中发生的一些事情让我永生难忘。我想更深入地了解鲍勃。戈登拜托我安排同行，我乐意奉陪。我们要去的是（当年鲍勃的父亲开办工作过的）那家医院。对我而言，这是观察程氏父子互动的好机会。光听他俩对话还真难分清谁是父亲，谁是儿子。与我所认识的其他父子的关系相比，他俩是最不一样的一对。

华南女院和福建师大参赛选手以及指导老师在厦门大学嘉庚学院（2009年10月）

我们沿闽江向西而行，鲍勃一路睁大眼睛看窗外的风景，他说从前，乘坐纤夫拉的船，在闽江上要花好多天，才能从南平到福州。当我们经过古田时，他惆怅地说："这是我的出生地，但我什么也不记得，我真希望有一天能去回顾一下。"2013年他实现了这个愿望。当他站在医院的楼顶凝望闽江时，他满心激动，记忆慢慢穿过长达半个世纪的时光。他提起小时候有人教他握乒乓球拍，问这种握法现在是否还有。午饭后我拐弯抹角地问他是否需要休息。鲍勃的回答直截了当："我不用午睡。"这位94岁高龄的长者一个人独自坐飞机来到中国，因为他想亲身体验如今的中国与记忆中相比有何变化。他习惯于独立自主，对帮助别人更是热心。

当鲍勃提起他想再度拜访华南女院校区原址时，我也很高兴能与他同去。程氏父子更关注脚踏实地的人。他们也很高兴能旁听我在福建师大老校区教的课程。课后我们一起去参观程氏大楼原址并拍照留念（也就是我开头提到的那三座大楼之一，是华南女院首任校长——鲍勃姑婆程吕底亚时代建立的），鲍勃再次强调不用给他特

非同寻常的程氏父子（2013年11月）

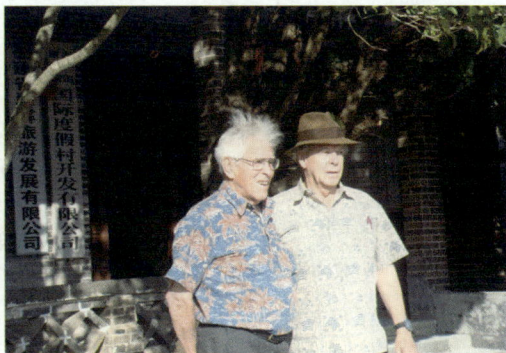

古田寻访出生地之旅（2013年10月）

春色
任天涯
——福建华南女子
职业学院外教侧记
International Faculty with
Fujian Hua Nan Women's
College since 1908

398

殊待遇。当我的学生发现鲍勃只吃一碗面条就很开心时，感到非常诧异，学生们和他聊得很开心。

2010年春季：华南女院再次开设"圣经"课程

戈登和索妮娅常常会和我们一起探讨，应该如何把华南建设得更加美好，更加富有魅力。他们常说：咱们的顾客是谁？华南女院如何打造自己的品牌？在他们打算回夏威夷之前，我问他们："你们愿意教'《圣经》与西方文化'这门课程吗？"他们听了大吃一惊。我继续道："去年我向校领导提出时，得到的反应与你们如出一辙。师大开设过这门课程，而华南女院是百年前卫理公会开办的一所大学，华南女院应是最适合开这门课程的学校。没有谁能比程氏家族的后人更适合上这门课程了，因为第一任校长就是程氏先人程吕底亚。"我把培养方案中的课程介绍给他们看，我想首先在应用英语和商务英语专业中开设这门课程，以后还可以开成全院选修课。

戈登听后愣了许久，然后轻声问："你希望何时开始上课？给几年级学生上课？"

经过仔细思考，戈登很认真地说："我有两个条件：（1）确保学校的党委书记知道有这门课程，也让他或她知道何时上课；（2）我很欢迎党委书记来听课，并参加课堂讨论。"2010年3月到4月期间，程氏夫妇在华南女院待了5周。我去听了几次课，经过尝试，我们决定还是作为选修课，在应用英语和商务英语专业三年级上学期开设这门课程。没想到这门课程大受欢迎。我曾告诉戈登像"启示录的"和"神授的"这类词太虚了。他说："下次我会选择更实际和实用的表达词汇。"

鲍勃和戈登去年10月在校园里散步时发生了一件事情。3月份戈登夫妇来新区时外国专家楼有了两个新的学习中心。戈登说我们应该去掉"专家"这个词，把外国专家楼的名字改成国际学习中心，让这个设施为学生服务。学校接受了他们的意

戈登和鲍勃在师大回答学生提问（2009年10月）

戈登在师大为非英语专业研究生演讲
（2009年9月）

程戈登荣膺福建省政府颁发的
"友谊奖"获奖证书（2009年获评）

与2009级历史专业研究生陈文庆合影
（2009年10月）

程氏父子与我任教班级学生合影
（2009年10月）

与2009级经济学院学生合影
（2009年10月）

见。以前存放自行车的地方被改造为一间多媒体学习中心，供国际友人来华南女院讲学时使用，楼上的写作实验室和另外两间小教室用作小组讨论。国际学习中心现在能作为独立的设施，在寒暑假开班。

程氏夫妇擅长教书育人，对他们而言，这更是爱好而非职业。当我邀请他们来上春季学期的课时，他们拒绝了，理由是："教书是很紧张的。我们需要时间修整、反思，考虑如何提高效率。我们不喜欢从前上大学时教我们的老师，我们不想像他们一样。"我只好作罢。

到了暑假，有些中国老师在抱怨：为什么程氏夫妇只教应用英语专业的学生？难道商务英语学生不够优秀吗？于是我就想让他们教二年级的商务英语专业学生。戈登回答："这是我以前未教过的学生。我想，给英语水平更高的学生上课更有效果。上完一学期后我们再来重新评估，看我明年上什么更好。"

2010年秋季：评估表和程吕底亚奖学金

我们拥有了新的校区，规模符合省级要求，可容纳约5000名学生。这要归功于

春色
任天涯
——福建华南女子
职业学院外教侧记
International Faculty with
Fujian Hua Nan Women's
College since 1908

400

我们的前任校长林本椿教授。但一波未平，一波又起。生源发生了变化，来自城市的孩子越来越少，而来自农村的越来越多，她们的水平不过初中或小学，学习能力不强。所以高考成绩偏低。更糟糕的是，她们的学习动力和学习热情日渐消退。雪上加霜的是，来中国教学的外教也发生了变化。20世纪90年代，来中国的外教大都感召于分享和给予的理念，但现在，看重物质回报的外教越来越多。

2010年我对程氏家族有了更进一步的了解。

我们外教短缺，我请戈登教商务英语大二学生的4门不同课程。我特别感激戈登能解决燃眉之急，并让索妮娅做他的助教，每到期末，还及时向我反馈对他的教学任务分配是否合理。因为有应用英语、商务英语、国际经济与贸易、商务经纪与代理4个专业的外教要安排，常有老师抱怨说除应用英语外，其他几个专业没有安排足够优秀的外教。戈登说："我的教学目标是不变的。我要教学生学习商务概念和领导才能——这与课程的具体名字关系不大。"心怀这样的态度，加上戈登和索妮娅他们一心一意地专注教学，他们所教的学生学习积极性、主动性都很好。

戈登不只是承担了上述繁重的教学活动，还有更多其他的工作需要他完成。为了让学生更好地为全国、全省的大学生英语演讲比赛做准备，戈登建议开设"英语演讲"课。但是怎样开？什么时候开？在我们的教学培养方案中从未有过类似的安排。长久以来，公共演讲课程在中国的大学并不受重视。在戈登的规划和帮助下，学校面向外语外贸系4个专业的学生开设了英语演讲课程。因为学生来自4个不同专业，白天上课会发生冲突，戈登只能牺牲自己的业余休息时间，在每周三晚上课。这门课大获成功，一直延续到现在。应用英语专业主任黄飞和乐荣妹两位老师还全程旁听了一个学期的课，一堂课也没落下。

戈登在校友会聚会活动上做主旨发言
（2010年10月）

随着了解的深入，我发现戈登夫妇来华南女院任教前，在很多方面已有所建树。戈登以经济学家的身份，在美国夏威夷州规划和经济发展部门工作过，后来又当选为美国夏威夷州参议员，代表怀基基区、唐人街和火奴鲁鲁港，设计问卷调查，评估并使用调查结果，制定相关政策。所以当我们要制定一套学生评估教师的评估表格时，我寻求他的帮助，并将他的建议融入评估表中，一直使用到现在。（评估表如下所示）

Fujian Hwa Nan Women's College
教师教学学生评价表
Teacher Evaluation Form

专业：　　　　　　　　　　班级：
（Department）　　　　　　　（Class）
教师姓名：　　　　　　　　　课程：　　　　　　　日期：
（Instructor）　　　　　　　 （Course）　　　　　　（Date）
请按以下评估等级如实地对评估项目进行打分：
（Please rate the instructor on these statements according to the following scales）

1. 非常不同意 Disagree Strongly	2. 不同意 Disagree	3. 中立 About Equal Balance Between Agree and Disagree	4. 同意 Agree	5. 非常同意 Agree Strongly

在所选数字栏里打"√"　Tick the number you selected

评估项目 Components	说明 Explanation	非常不同意	不同意	中立	同意	非常同意
1. 组织能力 Organization	教学组织能力强（课堂组织紧凑，连贯，不离题，灵活运用各种教学方法等）The instructor is well organized in his/her teaching. Effective in time management.	1	2	3	4	5
2. 知识性 Knowledge	在学科教学中体现了渊博的知识（知识性强，知识面广，专业基础扎实，介绍本学科新知识，掌握本专业新动态）The instructor appears knowledgeable in teaching his/her subject.	1	2	3	4	5
3. 批判性思维或分析思维 Critical/Analytical Thinking	启发学生思维，培养学生批判性思维和分析性思维的能力 The instructor develops student's thinking and analytical skills.	1	2	3	4	5
4. 课堂互动 Instructor-Group Interaction	鼓励课堂讨论和自由提问；营造适宜的课堂气氛 The instructor encourages class discussion/participation; Creates an appropriate learning environment.	1	2	3	4	5
5. 清晰度 Clarity	用各种方式清楚地传达学科内容 The instructor communicates the subject matter clearly.	1	2	3	4	5

春色
任天涯
——福建华南女子
职业学院外教侧记
International Faculty with
Fujian Hua Nan Women's
College since 1908

评估项目 Components	说明 Explanation	非常 不同 意	不同 意	中立	同意	非常 同意
6. 师生联系 / 关系 Instructor-Individual Student Interaction	建立良好师生关系，关心爱护学生 The instructor establishes a good rapport with students.	1	2	3	4	5
7. 作业 Assignment	作业反映了课程的内容，符合教学目的；作业批改、讲解及时 The content of assignments reflects the course content and objectives. The assignment is checked and returned on time.	1	2	3	4	5
8. 工作态度 Working Attitude	对教学表现出积极的态度 The instructor shows a positive attitude towards teaching.	1	2	3	4	5
9. 责任心 Sense of Responsibility	对学生高标准，严要求 The instructor is responsible and sets strict demands on students.	1	2	3	4	5
10. 准时上下课 Punctuality	按时上课，不提前下课 The instructor is supposed to be punctual to begin and finish each class.	1	2	3	4	5
11. 调课频率 Frequency of rescheduling classes	不随意调换课 The instructor should not reschedule classes frequently.	1	2	3	4	5
12. 总体评价 Overall Rating	总体上是一位称职而高效率的教师 Overall the instructor is effective and competent in his/her teaching.	1	2	3	4	5
	我愿意向其他学生推荐上这位老师开的这门课 This course taught by this instructor is worth being recommended to students.	1	2	3	4	5
13. 总分 Total（65）						

您对该教师改进教学有何建议？
Any suggestions to the instructor for improvement?

感谢您的如实评价！
THANKS FOR YOUR PATICIPATION!

我记得他有一个建议是：你是否愿意将该门课程推荐给你的同学？程氏夫妇非常支持学生评估教师，而不像其他外教一样会排斥。戈登只问："客户是谁？是的，评分很重要，大部分学生都能对任课老师是否有能力、是否负责做出公正的评价。大多数学生不喜欢某一门课程都会有一定理由。"我们一直在使用这个问卷表。我还记得早期的学生抱怨："戈登上课站在前面，索妮娅在后面，我们无处可藏，没法睡觉，也没法玩手机。这门课程太难。测验太多。还有，上戈登的课，要记的新单词太多了！"即便如此，无论他们教哪门课程，学生对他们的评价一直在所有外教中名列前茅。

我曾问及戈登，作为管理者，最特别的事情是什么。他不假思索道："部属向你隐瞒事实。有些人撒谎是因为害怕被责备，另一些人撒谎是为了让别人出丑。但通常他们只是不在乎或者是认为你永远也不会发现真相，所以撒谎。还有一些人怕你，所以只告诉你你想听的话。最后的一类人是不想做你希望他做的事。这就是为什么只有在我通过观察他人的行为，了解了事情的原委，才会发问。"对于他的这番话，我很是吃惊。经过几周的思考，我提起有个外教拿的是新西兰Grove Academy的博士学位证书。一周后，戈登给了我一份新西兰有授予博士学位资格的大学名单，其中并没有Grove Academy。还有一个外教信誓旦旦地说她有Grove Academy的硕士学位，但她从未去过新西兰。因此我们一口气开除了3名母语为英语的老师，我也是从此才开始感觉到来华的外教素养发生了变化，这种情况一直持续到现在。

95岁的鲍勃还是乐于思索——做些小事来提升华南女院的品牌，让世界变得更加美好。为此，他直接提供启动资金，把他15年前设立的程氏基金作为奖学金。戈登的任务是实施、评估鲍勃的想法，并于每年10月向鲍勃汇报。今年我们启动了为期3年的"程吕底亚挑战"奖学金，目标是吸引高考英语成绩高的应用英语和商务英语专业学生，以此激励班上的其他同学努力学习英语。具体做法是每年给5位符合一定条件的新生提供奖学金。我亲自参与这个项目，与3个紧密相关部门——招生、管理和教学部门的负责人讨论协调事宜。我们提出了一个具体计划，鲍勃和我们都确信可以实施3年，直到学校招生政策改变。

2011年秋：热线777遇见程氏家族

秋季学期一开学我们就面试了入学新生，并挑出5位程吕底亚奖学金获得者。我们恭喜这5位姑娘，嘱咐她们牢记华南校训——受当施。这些学生肩负重任，努力勤奋。

春色
任天涯
——福建华南女子
职业学院外教侧记
International Faculty with
Fujian Hua Nan Women's
College since 1908

404

戈登与2010年参加英语演讲赛的
师大学生合影（2010年10月）

外语外贸系英语老师与鲍勃和其
他外教的合影，鲍勃时年95岁
（2010年10月）

　　鲍勃10月份来到中国，开始了为期两周的福州行。5个获奖的女孩向他展示所获的成绩。她们充满自信地进行自我介绍。她们组成五人小组，到接待室与鲍勃面谈。我非常开心地看着她们和鲍勃互动。鲍勃也兴致勃勃地帮助参加福建省大学生英语演讲大赛的华南女院选手。在鲍勃和戈登的帮助下，入选选手信心大增、进步神速。这对于选手来说是一次绝好的机会。鲍勃从不居功自傲。他又提醒我们千万别热情款待他，他说他是来华南女院帮助戈登的。

　　程氏父子是一对很奇特的父子。一对一谈话或者人少的情况下，鲍勃讲起话来滔滔不绝，但是面对一大群人的时候，鲍勃会看着儿子说："该你说了！"鲍勃对生活的热爱十分鼓舞人心。无论走到哪里，他都受人敬仰。他不会因为年事已高就不出门。我很想让其他人听听他的故事，了解一个饱经世事的人，以及他过去95年的传奇人生。问题在于鲍勃羞于面对拍摄镜头，一看镜头他就会变得语塞。他也并不认为自己很重要。这时戈登就会安慰他说："没事，鲍勃，你不是主角，只是分享经验，让别人了解你而已。"

　　我所认识的媒体人中，有一位

程氏夫妇及张迅捷院长与首批荣获"程吕底亚奖学金"
的5位同学（2010年10月）

鲍勃与我作为班导师的学生们合影，
他时年96岁（2011年10月）

应用英语专业2011级学生周玲和戈登合影
（2011年11月）

我从前教过的学生，她善良而有爱心。我想最适合采访鲍勃的就是这位林黎倩，她在福建电视台经济频道《热线777栏目》工作，这个节目的收视面覆盖全省。林黎倩果然没让我失望。在采访拍摄过程中，摄影师积极参与，为选取最佳的拍摄背景和角度不断变换拍摄角度。鲍勃对她印象也很深刻。鲍勃非常欣赏林黎倩和摄影师的这次报道，此后，在每年10月程氏家族的友谊宴上，都会邀请他们俩。在接下来的4年里，鲍勃和程氏家族共上了6次电视，而这一切都始于林黎倩向大家讲述的动人故事。

华南女院与普吉湾：东西方相遇

在程氏家族的资助下，华南女院迎来了25位来自美国普吉湾大学的学生，他们来华学习中国历史和哲学。他们与华南女院学生互动，了解鲍勃心中真正的中国——不单是表面呈现出来的物质文明，更重要的是内在的精神文明，包括这里的人和历史。普吉湾大学的学生参加华南女院的英语角活动。我们还特地为他们举办了一场大型研讨会，展示中美文化之间的区别。

春色
任天涯
——福建华南女子
职业学院外教侧记
International Faculty with
Fujian Hua Nan Women's
College since 1908

406

林黎倩、戈登和我
（2011 年10月）

戈登宣布华南—普吉湾研讨会开始（2011年12月）

普吉湾大学项目负责人伊丽莎白介绍相关情况
（2011年12月）

普吉湾学生在研讨会上做演讲
（2011年12月）

研讨会上认真听讲并思考的听众
（2011年12月）

华南女院学生在研讨会现场做演讲
（2011年12月）

普吉湾的学生与外语外贸系商英
学生在毕业会演上的互动表演
（2011年12月）

热烈讨论问题的听众（2011年12月）

2012年秋季：举重运动员来到华南女院

在春季学期的时候，戈登发来一封邮件说他帮华南女院找到一位新的英语教师——艾米丽，她在德国教过英语。他说她年轻、活力四射，并且能够激励学生跳出常规思考问题。他补充说她爱好运动。我还以为这位新老师喜欢高尔夫球或网球，但看到他们发来的照片时，我发现我想错了，下面是索妮娅在美国第15届举重运动会上为艾米丽拍的照片。我们的学生非常喜欢艾米丽，她在华南女院教了两年。

到8月底，戈登和索妮娅来榕已经第6个年头了（我是在2009年才与他们有亲密接触，事实上，他们2005年就来过华南女院教书）。他们体验过北京以及上海的雾霾和交通堵塞，所以他们更愿意选择在福州停留，因为这儿一年年变得越来越好，他们更愿意做见证变化的观察者。正如戈登所说："变化太大了，中国一年的发展抵得过其他国家五六年的发展。我们常去不同的地方旅行，也会觉察到变化和发展，但感觉不到具体的发展步调。"戈登以每两分钟内经过的水泥车数目来计算城市发展的步伐。但他不愿计算建筑工地起重机的数目。今年他注意到："大多数地方已有了轮椅通道；5年前很少看到。司机的素质提高了，路况越来越好，私家车的数量在增加，道路不算太拥挤。满目的绿色植物、树丛和大树让福州变成一个更加宜居的城市。"华南女院的新校区也变得越发漂亮。

每年秋季新生入学教育时，我们一起欢迎应用英语和商务英语的一年级新生。

春色
任天涯
——福建华南女子
职业学院外教侧记
International Faculty with
Fujian Hua Nan Women's
College since 1908

408

举重运动员艾米丽·布洛克曼在华南女院任教两年
（2012年、2013年）

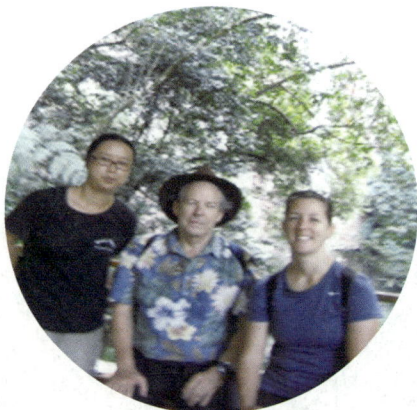

艾米丽永泰赤壁游
（2012年11月）

我们会一一介绍中外教师。戈登每次都会应邀发表精心准备的两分钟的演讲。至今我已经亲自聆听了6次。他的演讲我都记得，因为他每一次的内容并不一样。我一般做即时翻译，因为我想让一年级大学生思考戈登说的话。这个见面会通常有一百多号人。有时候他用麦克风，但是他总是站着演讲。请看戈登在应用英语专业迎接2011级新生会上的发言。

下午好！我代表我的家人和所有的外籍教师向大家问好！你们好，欢迎来到华南女院！我们的外教来自世界不同国家，我们远道而来是为了让你们接受良好的教育。华南女院很特别，因为她实行国际化办学和国际化教学。她的特别还在于她是由女性筹建，由女性管理，办学宗旨在于培养女性人才，为福建、中国和世界的美好明天做出应有的特殊贡献。

为你们的学校感到骄傲吧！为你们自己自豪吧！为了让我们的将来变得更加美好，努力学习、高效学习。前方的道路虽是坎坷的，但只要我们认清真正重要的事情，互相帮助，坚持不懈，就能够实现梦想。作为学校的外籍教师，我们是来这里帮助你们的，但是关键还取决于你们是否愿意主动开口。让我们一起努力，携手走向成功。

他好像从来不用看讲稿或笔记。我问他是怎么做到的，他大笑起来，说是索妮娅跟他说："别说太长了，如果你记不住，听你演讲的学生又怎么能够记得住？"他在这方面很像丘吉尔，先写好稿件，然后背诵下来。戈登备课也是如此。我好几次请他春季学期也来上课。他总是说他需要时间调整准备，思考上过的课程中的教学方法，哪些奏效，哪些失效，再仔细考虑补充更好的范例和练习，来提供给学生学习。他不止一次说："作为老师，我们当然知道自己在讲什么，但我们并不知道学生听懂了什么。我来教书并不想讨好学生。我想让学生30年后还记得他们曾经努力过，能够掌握他们以前认为不能够做到的内容。如果对我的教学评估分数不高，那在意料之中。总会有学生想学习，不论老师怎样。我会尽量不让课堂变得枯燥乏味，但我真正感兴趣的是那些成绩处于中间的同学。他们需要激励。"我分配什么学生给戈登和索妮娅确实很重要，到期末，有些外教会问我，为什么总是把最好的学生分配给戈登。

有个商英专业的学生二年级上过戈登的课，三年级代表华南女院参加全省英语演讲比赛，戈登成为她的指导老师。这位学生叫黄佳芃，她刚在美国恩波利亚大学获得硕士学位。她感慨地说："戈登眼光很远，教的东西当时看来没有什么，等我来了美国之后才发觉原来是很基础的东西，对我适应这里的新环境很有帮助，包括举办的活动，也让我对美国文化有了大概的了解，帮助我更好地融入美国。他们对学生态度好，教我们演讲。还有，他有社会工作经验，他懂商业，所以他教的东西比较实用。他的启发点比较独特，不是照搬书上的理论。"

程氏夫妇尽量带学生走出课堂，参观，实践。许多外地学生从未到过福建省博物馆，所以戈登和索妮娅总是让学生事先和他们一块儿准备好包着火腿和奶酪的三明治作为中餐，大家一块儿坐学校班车参观博物馆，这成为他们带每届学生的固定节目。

程氏夫妇带领他们的学生去参观福建省博物馆
（2012年11月）

商务英语专业2012届毕业生黄佳芃，
2015年获美国恩波利亚大学毕业证

**春色
任天涯**
——福建华南女子
职业学院外教侧记
International Faculty with
Fujian Hua Nan Women's
College since 1908

410

程氏夫妇以华南女院校训要求自己。对于他们来说，得到过，故该给予。他们认为给予可以丰富人生。我每年也因为"受当施"的校训精神，要多做一些文字工作。我周围的同事因此很羡慕，他们从不涉及此类事情。下面是我们的电邮通讯。

主题：感谢您的资助
时间：2012年12月10日，周一

亲爱的索妮娅和戈登，

荣妹已经告诉我，你和黄丽霞为筹备明年英语演讲比赛留下了840元。真是太感谢你们了！因为黄丽霞从不用电子邮件，请代我向她表示感谢。我会把这件事情告诉给所有专业主任和相关老师。

我8：50来华南开会。你们明天上午晚些时候是否有空？我想顺便和你们聊聊。

阿罗哈，爱丽斯

每年，戈登和索妮娅都把他们辅导学生参加全省演讲大赛的课时津贴捐献出来，用于资助系里学生参加课外活动。戈登常常说："最高的赞扬也比不上行动。"只要对学生和学校有利，他都竭尽全力。此外，他不断拓展他的教学内容，如同他那五颜六色的夏威夷花衬衫一样丰富多彩。在学生招聘市场会上，你一眼就能认出戈登。

程氏夫妇总是乐于与人打交道，且做了许多牵线搭桥的工作。他们想让学生明白：英语可用来谋生，而不是闲置在大脑里的东西。程氏夫妇春季学期一般不在华南女院（他们秋季学期来华南女院教书），就在美国努力促成华南女院与夏威夷或

戈登参加学生招聘会（ 2012年11月）

普吉湾大学之间的交流。我不知道当戈登向鲍勃提出建议，让华南女院的女孩和夏威夷的女孩面对面沟通时，鲍勃作何感想。网络视频电话成了她们的沟通工具。我们用写作实验室的电脑跟夏威夷火奴鲁鲁圣心女子高中沟通。这两所私立院校都只招收女生，学生年龄大致相仿，都由传教士所建立。我也与该校的校长保持通信联络。以下是最初两校获程氏奖金的女生两两结对的名单。

下面是具体名单：

（1）克丽丝·阿斯诺与邹丽巧

（2）西拉·法劳与张丽珍

（3）娜蒂亚·巴斯克鲁斯与徐宝琼

（4）凯拉·司迪巴与郭丽英

（5）莉泽特·萨港与肖燕娟

以下是我和圣心女校校长贝缇·怀特的通信：

阿罗哈，爱丽斯，

你们动作比我们快，但我们会迎头赶上。

3月21号（星期三）如何？也就是火奴鲁鲁时间下午2点，中国北京时间上午8点。

孩子们可以自己聊天。

你们用什么设备？用大屏幕投影视频，还是在电脑上视频？

我这边的名单要到星期一才能出来。我目前考虑让5名女生参加会面——其中至少有一位是程氏奖学金获得者。我还想邀请我们的中文老师参加。你意下如何？

请让我知道你们的想法。

阿罗哈，贝缇·怀特

夏威夷圣心学校校长

在中国我们有中式英语。在夏威夷，合适的时候，大家喜欢用夏威夷语。如果你把信的内容读一遍，就会发现信的开头和结尾都用了"阿罗哈"这个夏威夷语中的词。戈登在校园里也常用这个词。如果学生也回以"阿罗哈"，戈登就知道，这一定是他以前教过的学生。这个词在口语中和书面上都可以使用，表达对对方的关心和问候。这个词的意思是"你好"或"再见"。索妮娅会补充说，还有一个意思是"我爱你"。"爱丽斯"是我的英语名字，这是我的第一位外教为我取的，因为我当学生的时候无忧无虑，在自己的奇境世界里漫游。

春色
任天涯
——福建华南女子
职业学院外教侧记
International Faculty with
Fujian Hua Nan Women's
College since 1908

412

戈登特别中意"CCTV杯"全国英语演讲大赛。比赛由三个部分组成：3分钟定题演讲，2分钟即兴演讲和1分钟自由问答。如果可以分别完成，比赛就并不十分困难，但要在紧张的氛围中完成三个环节，压力非常大。他要求所有学生在国庆期间写好比赛题目要求的内容，并安排每位学生每周做一到两次课堂演讲。当学生取得进步后，他会开始提问题。他想把这些题目用在演讲课和自谈课上。所以我每年要认真跟进比赛，题目一公布，就通过电子邮件告知他们。2012年的题目是：我们无法失去的是___。

以下是我们之间的电子邮件。

亲爱的爱丽斯，

感谢来信。再次感谢你的辛勤工作。我们正在为返回福州的最佳路径而做准备。燃油费和机票费用大涨，这表明中国和印度的经济持续上行。我们对此很高兴。我们预定9月2日或之前抵达福州，12月16日返美。实际飞行日期将随着机票价格和航线而变。届时我们想取道上海，坐动车回榕如何？

今年全国英语演讲比赛的题目不久就要公布，我们正在准备英语演讲的课程大纲（我们会把准备好的大纲发给你），希望有潜力的学生能明白我们对他们的期望。如果他们不愿意花时间努力，那机会就应该让给其他更努力的同学。这个演讲比赛最难的部分应该是即兴问答环节。我们希望学校能在开学前召开外教例会，并组织外教环校园游。这可以等最后一个外教到校后，再作安排。这对于这最后一位外教而言是件好事，但对早到并提前备好了活动的老师而言，就显迟了。选"《圣经》和西方文化"课程的学生将观看电影，并撰写影评。这样能收到比安排34学时更大的教学效果。我的商务英语写作班只有24个学生，我每隔一周会单独指导每一位学生，仔细查看她的习作。

明天戈登要飞到西雅图和鲍勃共度一周。

阿罗哈，戈登和索妮娅

我的回信：

亲爱的戈登及索妮娅，

首先，我想确认一下你们抵达福州和离开的时间，抵达日期显示是9月2日星期天，是抵达福州还是上海？是12月16日星期天返回美国？我想，你们若取道上海，我可以找我的亲朋好友在上海接待你们，然后你们坐大约7个小时的动车回到福州，一等座316元，二等座264元。请把你们最后的决定告诉我。

第二，今年演讲题目是"我们无法失去的是___"。我想我们应该让学生知道题目，提前准备。但是据我所知，下学期我们只有5个外教，其中包括你们和普吉湾大学的丽姿。还有黄丽霞、魏莉和马丁。

"《圣经》和西方文化"课程本来开在应用英语和商务英语专业大三上学期，是一门全系公选课，可是几乎所有三年级学生都已经修满了公选学分。我们想以讲座形式开设这门课。我们都知道如果这门课在一年级开设，选修的学生会很多，但大一学生英语水平普遍较差，所以我们改在三年级开设，可是他们课程又修满了。黄飞和我决定把这门课开设在大二下学期，或者开成讲座，让更多想听课的学生来参加，可以吗？

最后，黄飞和乐荣妹从你的课堂以及教学方面获益良多，想象以前听你的"英语演讲"课程那样，继续听你的其他课程。可以吗？

阿罗哈，爱丽斯

我现在还记得林雪的部分演讲内容，因为她的演讲告诉我，戈登想要他的学生们实现自己设定的目标。其他大学的大部分学生都认为离开家庭、爱或是荣誉，自己就无法生存，但林雪不这样认为。她讲的是："我不能失去的东西由三个S，一个T，一个R和一个E组成，没错，我不敢失去的是压力。"她谈了如何学会处理压力，她一脸正经，发言充满了节奏感："如果母亲没有压力，你不可能从母体生出来；如果你没有压力，永远无法排除体内废物。如果我不寻求压力，我就没法像现在这样，站在讲台上面对你们。"那年的评委们年纪比较大，他们没听懂林雪在讲什么。但是我听懂了，我知道戈登常常上课时把压力中的能量比作野马，如果学会驯服它，在压力之下，野马跑得比没压力时更快。能有记住这种挑战、获得成功的学生，让我对学校里有戈登这样的老师感到骄傲，他教授有关人生的事，这是来自实践而非书本中的知识。

鲍勃今年已经过了97岁生日。在他的帮助下，有空调设备的写作实验室和多媒体中心建成了，他资助高考英语成绩好的新生。但是父子俩平日里在校园里散步时都聊些什么？有关这点，之后我们讨论年度全省英语演讲比赛时就会得到答案。我非常欣赏程氏家族的一点是，当他们就前进的方向做出建议时，通常会在将之付诸现实时，做出最大的贡献。开会结束时，戈登问道："我们要怎样才能创造出学生能够互相竞争，提高公共演讲能力的环境？我们学校选出的代表通常是应用英语或者

春色
任天涯
——福建华南女子
职业学院外教侧记
International Faculty with
Fujian Hua Nan Women's
College since 1908

414

商务英语专业的学生。但是我敢保证，如果我们提供正确的环境，其他专业的学生会愿意来，进行有效的竞争。我们在全系选出最愿意努力的优秀学生，开设'英语演讲以及领导艺术系列'课程，怎么样？因为随着时间的推进，我们可以将其他特别课程增加到'领导艺术系列'中去。"我们在考虑能完成这个任务的人选时，他停了停，然后补充道："如果你愿意，我可以先教5年，期间我们要努力开发出用英语交流提升学校名声的方法。"但令人吃惊的是，这个建议很难说服校方高层管理者。因为有个管理者说："你们为什么要做这么多？只要挑选一个学生，专门培训她就好了。"但是在中教的支持下，新的课程还是诞生了。到学年末，中教和外教一起选出18个学生，参加来年的演讲班课程。

程氏家族还有个传统，我想有必要记叙一下。我不确定是从什么时候开始的，但我是2009年开始意识到的。能和大家见面聊天，鲍勃就感觉非常开心，他满足于一碗面条。他来中国庆祝他的生日。这是他用自己的方式，在感谢中国对他和他世界观的塑造。我不确定鲍勃是怎么有那些想法的，但是我同意他的观点，确实是中国成就了他。程氏家族每年在10月底或11月初，以自己特别的方式，宴请大家，客人包括鲍勃在福州认识的所有人：有他于1989年华南女院复办时结识的创始人，有政府官员，有媒体记者和摄影师，有华南和师大的教师，有他们目前在教和已经毕业的学生。通常是三代，或四代同堂。程氏家族的人分坐在不同的饭桌上。我常和索妮娅坐一桌，她负责组织整个活动，确保这个大家庭中的每位来客宾至如归。没有演讲，只是鲍勃认识的人坐在一起聚会聊天，大家也不急着离席。这个聚会的习惯一直延续至今。下面是我2012年收到的邀请函。

艾丽斯，

感谢你的来信。我刚看到你发给我的短信，我会转告戈登和鲍勃。聚会时间是10月26日晚上6点。酒店的名字是康特大酒店，地址是西二环路336号，贵六包厢。

现在我有点糊涂了。我想我已经跟你提了聚会的事情，因为你是我邀请名单中的第一个人，我希望你帮我邀请林黎倩和摄影师。应该还会有五个市政府的客人，我们来中国前两天，在火奴鲁鲁请他们吃过饭。

不知还有没有忘记什么，但是我们的聚会和去年的一样，结束时会有学生表演唱歌。不要带礼物，人来就好。

谢谢你的帮助。

阿罗哈，索妮娅

程氏父子游览福州合影
（2012年10月）

参加鲍勃97岁生日晚宴的戈登、摄影师、电视台制片人
和张琳（曾赴夏威夷参议院实习）（ 2012年10月）

　　外语外贸系系主任（及福建师范大学教授）岳峰博士被外教对华南女院所做出的杰出贡献深深打动，发起了这本书的编写项目。我们非常惊喜地发现，华南女院拥有8位获评省级"友谊奖"的外教！华南女院获奖的外教数量位居全省第二。我逐渐意识到程氏家族弥足珍贵——他们仿佛从天而降。这份五代人传承的宝藏，始于一位坚韧而不认常理的女性。几十年前我思考过："常人只能接受事实。所以任何的进步只能依赖于不认常理的人。"我有一种责任感，因为我通过学生的内心、其他中教以及管理者，看到了程氏家族的用心。他们是喜欢挑战的人，尽其所能，使用一切方式，每天让这个世界变得更加美好，哪怕每次只改变一个人也好。面对这个不完美的世界，鲍勃会说："生活是美好的。"停一会然后乐观地接下去说："好得不能更好了。"如果戈登听到了，他会补充说："思考别的可能性也是不错的。"就这样，我开始承担起完整而真实地展示程氏家族面貌的责任。

　　岳峰教授提醒我，程氏家族自1889年程吕底亚来到中国起，就开始了持续好几代人的教育事业。他真正想告诉我的是，当我描写程氏家族的时候，字里行间要有历史感，因为从事教育已成为他们基因中的一部分。鲍勃的仰慕者年龄范围横跨四代人，我有幸也是其中一个。鲍勃1915年出生于福建古田，因为鲍勃的父亲查尔斯医生是卫理公会派出的医生，他在南平一家有80个床位的医院担任外科医生——口士吡哩医院（曾改称中华基督教南平卫理医院，现南平市第一医院）。

　　查尔斯医生的姑姑程吕底亚1890年在福建福清垄田开办了第一所女子学堂，在

春色
任天涯
——福建华南女子
职业学院外教侧记
International Faculty with
Fujian Hua Nan Women's
College since 1908

416

平潭岛担任了第二所女子学校的校长。接着程吕底亚决定建立一所女子大学。这就是中国南方历史最悠久的女子大学——华南女院，位于福州仓山区的南台岛。你还可以在福建师大老校区看到那几座非同寻常，兼具西式和中式风格的大楼，也就是我在开篇提到的那三座大楼。

这是华南女院原址，现在还可以找到"程氏大厅"的石刻字迹，它经历了百年风雨。我们不禁为程氏家族和福建的深厚渊源深深触动。这其中还包括程吕底亚的侄女伊赛尔·华莱士，她一开始是教员，后来做了预科学校校长；还有程J.B.，程鲍勃的叔叔，就是他担任工程师，建造起这座新校园。程鲍勃出生于1915年11月15日，在南平和福州长大，12岁前他大部分时间都在和福建的孩子自由玩耍，他的福州话比普通话还要流利。我在他的自传《程氏家族》中发现他一生中有很多令人着迷的细节。参见书中第18页中，他对鼓岭最早的回忆：

我们第二学期在福州近郊的鼓岭山上度过酷暑。很多附近的外国家庭都在那儿躲避炎热的夏天。从城里走过去要6到8个小时。我妈妈坐在由木竹做成的躺椅上，由前面一人、后面两人抬着。这在当时对于很多走不动或不想走路的中国或西方富人是很普遍的做法。对于我们男孩子来说，鼓岭是个美妙的地方。我们可以和其他外国孩子玩耍，或者是同有着不同信仰的传教士交流。我在那儿学会了打网球和游泳。那时候我能说非常流利的福州话，以及一些国语。多年后我忘却了大部分的中文，其中我印象最深刻的一些福州话据说是不该学的，更不该记住。

这就是为什么当你看到97岁高龄的鲍勃今年游鼓岭的时候，会有从小在福建养成的习惯。请看后面视频附录3——《鲍勃的鼓岭之行》。

在《程氏家族》一书中（第78页），他回忆了80多年前的经历：

我记得在福州的时候，我们游览过一座历史悠久的寺庙，就在鼓岭避暑地附近。

上世纪初很多外国人在鼓岭住过。还有一些老外建了别墅，躲避福州炎热的夏日。这儿有游泳池和网球场。那时，空调还未发明，人们都到山上来避暑，远离山下谷地。广为流传的习近平主席与名叫加纳德的美国人之间的故事，使鼓岭享誉全球。与鼓岭有关的故事里也有程吕底亚、华南女院员工、查尔斯·加纳·程医生和其他更多人。福建广播集团《热线777》节目做了鲍勃1990年后再度游览鼓岭的专访。这个报道可以让未来的人们视听这位传奇人物的音容笑貌。

说起这位活生生的传奇人物鲍勃，他12岁回到美国时，经历了痛苦的调整期，并且受到其他同龄小朋友的歧视，我读后感到震撼。这解释了为何戈登说他妈妈常常提起中国，而鲍勃却从不曾提起。这也是为什么戈登特别喜欢和父亲在福州度过的时光，因为鲍勃说的很多故事，戈登也是第一次听说，我们来读读他在自传第21页写下的内容。

正是在伊利诺伊州的法明顿，我第一次因为中国背景而受到嘲笑。我记得被当地男孩叫作"中国猪"。我不懂棒球，也不知道电影明星，更不认得名车。我下定决心，要尽快融入美国。我试着忘却中国，以及中文。

1927年鲍勃和他父母在华盛顿州的港口城市塔科马市安顿下来，那时他夏天摘草莓，劈柴挣零花钱，其他时间送报纸。他在林肯高中读完中学。1933年，正逢经济大萧条时期，那时生活拮据，他进入一所当地比较小的大学学习化学，以减少学习费用。这所大学就是如今的普吉湾大学，现在我终于明白了华南女院和这所大学之间的关联。还有更有趣的事呢。早在20世纪90年代，普吉湾大学有一名历史教授写过关于华南的书，她偶然间进错了会议室。会议室中的人正在争论塔科马应该和哪座中国沿海城市缔结为姊妹城市。这位教授被他们的讨论吸引住了，她阐述了自己的想法，她的选择简单明了："我选择福州。"这位普吉湾大学的教授不知道她离开后会议室中发生了什么，对于最后的结果（塔科马和福州结为姊妹城市）她也不觉有自己的贡献。但是她把这件趣事告诉了鲍勃，鲍勃告诉了我。如今，你可以沿着塔科马海滨，参观协和公园和福州亭。我把索妮娅发给我的家庭欢庆圣诞年度汇总罗列在下面，作为这一年报告的结尾。

程氏家族2012年度庆祝圣诞的家庭简报中文如下：

程氏家族，

新年快乐！

这是照片感恩的时刻，我们以电子数据的形式记录下这一年中的一切生动美好的回忆。

这张是我们在中国拍摄的。福州有个习俗，当你收获智慧，就会拍下全家福，

春色
任天涯
——福建华南女子
职业学院外教侧记
International Faculty with
Fujian Hua Nan Women's
College since 1908

418

以便后人铭记。这就是我们的全家福。戈登拒绝露出笑容，他说笑则显得不够体面。索妮娅觉得他太传统，各位看官来评判好了。

这一年始于圆梦。而最终我们从大西洋回到太平洋，来到出发点的东方。我们到巴拿马旅行；想想150年前，绕行好望角，买到中国茶叶要花费多少时间。我们边喝茶边想。

二月份我们在印度和普吉湾大学环太平洋研究项目的学生相聚，2011年时，我们在华南住在一起。我们和他们一起参观了Pink City of Jaipur，戈登四月和五月去看望了鲍勃，六月和鲍勃一起修整他在shaw岛上的房子。

经过两年热烈的讨论，我们终于改造了厨房。以前我们的厨房是个原始山洞，我们拆掉了几堵墙，现在我们洗碗时就能欣赏到火奴鲁鲁国际机场起飞降落的飞机。

8月28日我们出发去华南女院。能看到学生们性情和善、开心快乐、愿意学习，真是觉得很值得。近年来学生学习动力有点不足，但是看上去健康多了。我们的学生很高兴能和鲍勃在华南女院进行两周的互动。鲍勃和中国的新朋老友们庆贺了他97岁的生日。今年12月28日鲍勃会到夏威夷火奴鲁鲁迎接新年。我们的儿子罗伯特还在蒙大拿州的Billings，今年没有会面，明年再去看他。我们祝贺大家圣诞快乐，新年健康。

爱你们的，索妮娅和戈登

the TRIMBLE family

HAPPY NEW YEAR

We are grateful that this time of year carries with it an obligation to remember all that happened for in doing so we get to relive the memories as we finally are pressured to refile them in more coherent digital format.

Here is a picture -- yes we are in China and that is us. It is a custom in Fuzhou that as you acquire wisdom you have a family picture for posterity to remember. And thus this is ours. He didn't smile. He claims that it is not dignified to smile. She thinks that he is being a bit too traditional. You are the judge.

The year began in fulfilling a life long dream. At last we journeyed from the Atlantic to the Pacific by winding up further east than where we started. We travelled through the Panama Canal and imagined how much longer it took ships a hundred and fifty years ago to get all that tea to England by rounding the Horn. We sipped coffee as we pondered.

In February we met up with the same Puget Sound PACRIM students in India that stayed with us at Hwa Nan in December 2011. We traveled with them as they visited the Pink City of Jaipur, and Taj and its baby sister in Agra. What wonderful memories of a world we are very happy to say that we never lived in. Then in March we spent a few days at the University of Puget Sound to review the progress their Asian Studies program has made in the last 20 years.

2013年春季学期：古井探访之旅

当我回顾往昔时，2013年是最富有成就感的一年。时过境迁，当时发生的事情还历历在目，我常常会回想起当时的成就。戈登和索妮娅在春季学期也来到福州，这是我第二次看到他们。鲍勃一定跟戈登唠叨了许久，才让他下定决心春天来。这听起来并没有什么，只是做一个计划，进行一次寻访古井之旅，以及在毕业典礼上听戈登发表演讲。一切都是从电子邮件来往开始的，我将其中几封拿出来与大家分享。二三十年前，春节期间来中国旅游的外国人会抱怨无事可做。现在已经全球化了，我们身处电子时代。程氏家族可以用电子邮件与相关的各方进行商量和规划。我很高兴能收到他们的新年祝贺，邮件中他们还提到"彩虹太多"。在夏威夷彩虹经常出现，夏威夷大学的运动队名字就叫彩虹。没有雨就没有彩虹，他们说彩虹太多，实际意思是雨下得太大了。

亲爱的爱丽斯，

在华莱士的书里，她提过程吕底亚婶婶1890年在Lungtien开办过一所女子寄宿学校。那Lungtien在哪里呢？几页之后，还提到程吕底亚婶婶于1905—1906年间还在BingTang开设过一所女子寄宿学校。BingTang又在哪里呢？

祝你们新年快乐！我们这里时间并不晚——夏威夷时间比中国延后16小时。我们想去散步，但是"彩虹"太多，所以我们下午再去。

……

阿罗哈，戈登、索妮娅

我的回信：

亲爱的索妮娅、戈登，

现在我已回到福州，可以随时给你们回信。祝你们春节愉快，在这里到正月15日前，即2月24日前都属于过年。

……

我做了些功课，发现有必要研究毛泽东时代前——也就是1949年前——的中文拼写体系——威妥玛式拼音法。因为在威氏拼法里，Beijing（北京）是Peking，Xiamen（厦门）是Amoy，Fuzhou（福州）是Foochow，我发现在《热线777》专访鲍勃的节目中，他说福州时发出的是Foochow。所以我想如果我们能找到1949年前的威氏字典，或者是1949年前的福建地图，对弄清楚Lungtien（Longtian）和

春色
任天涯
——福建华南女子
职业学院外教侧记
International Faculty with
Fujian Hua Nan Women's
College since 1908

420

BingTang，会有极大帮助。

阿罗哈，爱丽斯

　　经过不断搜寻，我终于在五月找到了答案！这个发现很偶然。那时程氏夫妇正致力于帮助鲍勃的母校——林肯高中与福州教育学院附属中学牵线搭桥。我有幸帮忙翻译和联络。

　　嗨，索妮娅；嗨，戈登，当我百度程吕底亚和平潭第一中学时，得到一条非常令人兴奋的好消息，那就是程吕底亚是平潭第一实验小学的第一任校长，这件事被列在平潭重大历史事件中。这个小学最早叫毓淑女子学堂，由卫理公会捐资建造。当我追溯程吕底亚的事迹时，发现她是位极其伟大的女性，她1906年建立毓淑女子学堂（即现在的第一实验小学，部分发展为第一中学），两年后她又成为华南女院第一任校长。我们要去参观这些学校！

　　6月的一个周六，我们来到平潭。平潭第一实验小学几位领导及学校的十几位老师迎接了我们。学校原址早就不见了踪影。事实上，唯一留下来的是当时程吕底

百年前程吕底亚带领大家挖的井（2013年10月）

亚带领大家一起挖的水井。15分钟后，戈登对我说："这一切真是太好了。"我看着戈登，很想说："我发现了这个学校。你看到了最早的那口井。还有什么遗憾的呢？"中午和学校的领导，以及英语老师进餐时，大家问戈登，是什么促成他的这次行程。戈登回答："这会让我父亲非常开心。我们1989年第一次来中国时，他就想了解程吕底亚建立的第一所学校。我们晚些时候大约在10月份，再来一次，好不好？"校长疑惑不解地看了戈登一眼。我明白了，就翻译给他听，让校长知道程吕底亚的曾侄子每年10月会来中国，那个季节他大都独自旅行。校长脸上绽开了笑容，说学校非常欢迎程吕底亚的后人。我说可能还会有些夏威夷中学的学生顺便来访。听到这儿，英语老师们很兴奋。其中一位对索妮娅说："请夏威夷的学生们一定要来，这样可以带动我们学生的学习动力，让他们懂得学习英语的重要性。"突然间，我明白了戈登去年发起华南和夏威夷圣心女校学生交流的意义。

程氏夫妇拜访平潭第一实验小学（2013年6月）

他们开始了为期十天、马不停蹄的对话之旅。华南女院的校友会、外事处，以及外语外贸系的许多同事都参与其中。我们也和不同的行政官员打过交道。戈登很想让夏威夷的学生了解同龄中国人，所以说法是"大姐姐和小妹妹的交流"。女院英语专业的大姐姐们英语水平进步神速，因为她们懂得学好英语的重要性。来自夏威夷的小妹妹们给校友的孩子，以及平潭实验小学的孩子朗读和阅读文章时，又成为"大姐姐"。而到程氏夫妇返美时，一切并未确定，但是至少我们做了这样的计划，在接下来的四个月里可以好好谋划。

戈登春天来访，最精彩的时刻是他向2013届毕业生发表毕业致辞。那是当天最

春色
任天涯
——福建华南女子
职业学院外教侧记
International Faculty with
Fujian Hua Nan Women's
College since 1908

422

短的一场演讲，戈登面对学生演讲，没有看笔记，整个会场非常安静。学校理事会会长陈忠英边听边做笔记。我建议参加全省英语演讲大赛的林雪同学担当翻译。她并非第一次读到演讲稿，她运用在索妮娅和戈登课堂上学到的知识，翻译得很不错。以下是演讲内容：

程戈登在2013届学生毕业典礼上的致辞

各位亲爱的朋友，尊敬的来宾，华南女院的领导：

很高兴借此机会又回到福州。1989年，在我的曾姑母程吕底亚来到福建100年后，我第一次参观了华南女院旧校区，我对她当年决心创办女校时的信心和勇气充满了敬畏。学校的校训是"受当施"，无论是在过去还是现在，对于华南女院的学生来说，这都是一个挑战。请记住你们的责任：通过帮助别人提高福建人民的生活质量。我越去思考程吕底亚曾姑母的作为，我就越发地钦佩她的坚持。她不但去美国筹钱创建华南女院，还把她的大半辈子都花在了中国青年女子教育事业上。她告诉我们：最好的服务方式是领导。我慢慢领会了她直觉就知道的事情：领导才能是后天习得的。领导特质可使你为他人和社会谋福利。

人生充满了乐趣，有很多意想不到的惊喜将一路伴随着你。在这里不是说教，而是要与你们一同分享通往幸福和成功的10个秘密。毕业典礼的结束就是你对这些秘诀检验的开始，所以拿起你的笔和本子，记下并谨遵以下10个简单的步骤，你的旅程将会充满收获。

第一，掌控情绪：学会做情绪的主人，而不要被情绪所掌控。掌控情绪始于不报复不记仇。报复和记恨只会分散你的注意力，使你没办法去做一些真正重要的事，所以请原谅并且忘掉别人的小错误，控制自己的情绪。

第二，保持快乐心情：微笑的人更具活力、感染力，生活因挑战而充满了乐趣。

第三，懂得感恩：学着每天感恩。一点小小的事情也可以让你微笑，即便是对你自己都不忘说一句"谢谢"，很快你就会发现你经常笑脸盈盈，越来越快乐，因为好事总是不期而至。

第四，助人亦是助己：生活并不总是事事如意，但相互帮助就可以让事情变得更加简单。不是所谓的"我与你竞赛"，而是"我与你合作"。可以用你的微笑或者用心倾听去抚慰他人。

第五，承担责任：失败只不过是这一次没做好。要为你有另一个机会做得更好而感恩。除非你告诉自己你办不到，否则不要阻止你自己取得进步！造物主给了你一些天分，为了你和社会的利益，请把这些天分发挥出来。

第六，为自己做的每一件事而骄傲：勿因事小而不付出百分百的努力。当你努力的时候，请带着匠人的自豪感去做。无论你今天把工作干得多出色，记住：当明天到来的时候，你还可以把它做得更好。

第七，相信你自己：只有当你相信你自己，别人才会相信你。找一个安静的时间，以及能让你停下来思考的地点。想想你将要去哪，将你想做的事情罗列一个清单，并且做好和别人讨论这个计划的准备。每个成功的人都曾和别人分享过自己做过的一些计划。不要害怕，如果你有梦想并且有个规划，知道往哪走，没有人会取笑你。

第八，不要焦虑：做出计划，承担责任为你所做的事而自豪，不要焦虑。失败并不意味着终结，而是通往成功的路标。焦虑只是无益的情绪，它不会带来任何益处。它是噪声，撇开它吧！当你已经尽了你最大的努力后，满意地放松片刻，很快你就会明白，为了实现自己的目标，你还需要做什么。

第九，压力是朋友：学会控制自己的压力，不能让压力来主宰你。要通过管理压力而不是对抗压力来控制压力。不要忽视压力，用愉快的微笑和快乐的心情欢迎压力来到你的生活中，让它帮助你变得更成功。

第十，不断学习：你可以阅读，也可以写作或是推理，你有获取知识的工具。正如我毕业的时候，我的父亲说过："戈登，如果你停止学习，有一天早上醒来的时候，你会发现，你不再拥有在世界上获得成功的知识。"所以继续学习吧，这样你才有办法与你的儿孙辈交流。

戈登在2013届毕业生典礼上致辞（应英毕业生林雪现场翻译）

春色
任天涯
——福建华南女子
职业学院外教侧记
International Faculty with
Fujian Hua Nan Women's
College since 1908

424

现在你拥有了能帮助你专注于乐音、忽视噪音的10个简单的方法。生命是以日期记录的不可思议的旅程。把6月19日作为你决心遵循这十个简单的步骤迈向成功的第一天，索妮娅和我在此祝贺你们！

戈登教的2013届学生中，有一个叫艾凤敏的学生，因为受到其他外教和戈登的影响，毕业论文以此为主题，以下是其中的部分内容：

福建华南女子职业学院
应用英语专业
2012—2013学年
外籍教师对我的影响

> 艾凤敏（Kay）
> 班级：2010 C 班
> 学号：201001105
> 应用英语专业
> 指导教师：赖黎群

一、介绍
二、外教的贡献
程氏家族的贡献

程吕底亚女士是华南女子学院第一任校长，1904年5月，她向美国洛杉矶的卫理公会提出在中国南方建立一所女子大学。经过一系列协商和准备，华南文理学院校董会于1908年成立。所有的学生、教师，以及程吕底亚一起做了大量的工作，取得了非同寻常的成就，获得同时期国内外教育界和社会各界的好评。第二代程氏家族成员——艾瑟尔·华莱士在1914年担任华南文理学院教务总长，华莱士的堂兄程弗莱德负责建设了学校大楼，为早期女院做出了重大贡献。1989年第三代程吕底亚后人——程罗伯特（即程鲍勃）不顾朋友的劝阻，在1989年造访福建。为什么他如此钟情于福建？这是因为他父亲——查尔斯·加纳·程曾经在福建行医。程罗伯特出生于福建南平，离开中国时11岁。罗伯特热爱他出生的那片故土，以及曾经一起长大玩耍的中国朋友，他也惦记着姑婆程吕底亚建立的华南女子学院。1985年华南复办，为了加强华南与西方在学术上的交流，程鲍勃建议他的母校，美国普吉湾大学与女院签订派出代表的协议。普吉湾大学从1996年开始，每年向我们女院派送一位英语教师。程鲍勃定期捐资资助学院购买教学设备，资助经济上有困难的学生。为了更好地纪念第一任校长程吕底亚，程戈登担任华南女子学院名誉理事长，程氏家族设立程吕底亚奖学金，鼓励高考英语成绩好的学生报考我院。这个奖学金从2011年开始，向来自应用英语和商务英语专业的新生发放，优秀的学生可以获得5000元奖学金。奖学金适用三年。同时，为了鼓励学生学习英语的热情，也增设了程吕底亚特别奖励金，奖励通过六级英语考试的三年级商英和应英专业学生，每人可获800元奖学金。

三、外教的特点

1.程氏夫妇

在华南女院教书时，程戈登先生和他妻子程索妮娅像长辈般照顾学生，他们总是礼貌地回绝娱乐活动，一直致力于提高学生英语口语和写作能力，不遗余力地改善我们学习和生活的环境。他们将学生的利益牢记于心。而且，他们还教导我们："你们以后变老，也要关心和帮助年轻人，不是为了让他们喜欢，而是要帮助他们，让世界变得更加美好。"他们言行一致，受到其他人的尊重。

程吕底亚对中国女性教育事业做出了巨大贡献，作为程吕底亚的后人，程氏夫妇深受激励。当同学问起他们为什么来中国时，戈登说："想让人们看到美国人的另外一面——并非每个美国人都像电视或电影里描绘的那样好战。美国人也可以作为和平使者走遍世界各地，我作为夏威夷参议员来到中国，代表中美两国人民之间的友谊。"2009年底，他获得第六届福建省"友谊奖"。

2013年秋季：鲍勃最好的一次来访

相比以前，戈登和索妮娅来福州越来越早。2013年8月的第三个周末，他们就到了。他们说要习惯福州的气候，但我觉得他们更想为新学期课程做准备。总之，无论如何，我们有更多的时间来交流。像以前的学期一样，他们请求教学秘书陈晴安排比每周额定工作量更满的时间表。因为总有事情需要他们外出，他们不想到期末再来安排补课。看到程氏夫妇后，我请他们要多给学生以压力，敦促学生努力学习。他露齿而笑，说："遵命。今年学生会得到更多的经验，学会处理压力。"

我们碰面好几次，讨论他的非标准化课程。戈登说要投诉，我知道他是什么意思。管理层认为，相比小班教学的"自由交谈"课，大班教学的"写作和阅读"课程可以多让百分之四十到五十的学生上课。这导致阅读和写作分成三个班，而自由

春色
任天涯
——福建华南女子
职业学院外教侧记
International Faculty with
Fujian Hua Nan Women's
College since 1908

426

交谈则分成四个班。但我猜错了，他并未抱怨我给他太多学生，他反而要求教多出来的一个班的学生。他解释说："每个学生上课要练习口语，他们每节课也要写作文。第二周开始，我用业余时间给学生补课，这个班的学生上周小测的成绩居后百分之四十。"我答应了他的要求。

我跟他说，因为学生不够，开不了"《圣经》与西方文化"这门课。他非常清楚这门课程是费了很大功夫和精力才获准开设的。但他只说："爱丽斯，课程还需要完善，在弄清楚到底如何上好之前，我得试试不同的教法。而且，我本身也是志愿者，所以开这门课程，学校也不用额外破费。"我很高兴最后实现了戈登的建议。几年前戈登对我说过，最好的追随者也是最好的领导。戈登也许是在说鲍勃，没有比鲍勃更好的老师了。

我们专门碰头讨论夏威夷圣心女校来访的行程，确认她们到达的时间。和中方老师一道，我们确认了华南女院30位"大姐姐"的名单。外国专家楼打扫得一干二净，一楼安装了Wi-fi，并设有密码。我们了解每个学生的课程表，让大小姐妹在不缺课

笔者与圣心女校师生游览武夷山
（2013年10月）

游览武夷风景的圣心女孩
白依敏、胡玉兰和郑嘉雯
（2013年10月）

圣心的何安琦游览武夷山
（2013年10月）

的情况下结对交流。华南女院学生将陪伴圣心学生参加所有活动。此外，圣心女校的学生还在特别举办的校友会活动上，为孩子们朗读故事。去平潭实验小学的时候，也朗读了英语故事。戈登的班级还带着小妹妹们参观了福州海峡熊猫世界和福建省博物馆。随后，他们一起吃了自备的野炊式午餐。在公车上，戈登才发现学生们之前从没有亲眼见过大熊猫。最后，他们要去武夷山游览，由于赴武夷山的时候需要一位成年人随同，我在最后一刻做了时间上的调整，担当陪同。此行让我对中美女孩之间的区别有了进一步了解。

作为一名少女的妈妈，我忍不住问了鲍勃对两个儿子的评价。他严肃地说："在两个儿子中，查理很乖。戈登则是个问题少年。"他低头看看手表，然后补充道："我没有时间讲述有关戈登的细节，那要花上几天几夜。但是最近他终于展示出了潜力，我非常开心。"这个问题，我问过鲍勃三次，每次得到的答案都一样。鲍勃到底想表达什么呢？他是在告诉我，不要老是担心我自己的女儿，因为最终她一样会长大。

由于忙碌，我错过了宁德古田之旅。在传教士活动编年史中记载着"1895年古田教案"的地址，当时其中一位传教士被困在山崖上，得到非斋教村子村民的救助和保护。程氏一家来到传教士被救的村子，参观旧址，了解当时的事件详情。

1989年鲍勃回到福建，在去南平的路上，中途停在古田吃午饭。他抬起头，看见巨大无比的人工湖，得知在1950年代，整座小镇被水淹没，所以他当年出生的小镇已经迁移。可是今天他才知道其他的事情。以前山顶的建筑现在在湖底。雨季时，这是一座小岛。秋季湖水降低时，人们可以从湖堤穿行而过。因为山顶上的砖瓦房是医院，所以曾经是人们希望的灯塔。1915年11月15日正是在这家医院，鲍勃来到这个世界。对于我而言，遗憾的是没有能够看到鲍勃脸上的表情，分享他的开心。

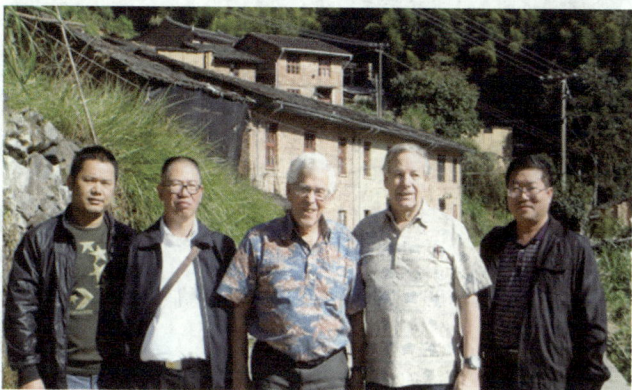

参观古田教案中传教士获救的小山村（2013年10月）

**春色
任天涯**
——福建华南女子
职业学院外教侧记
International Faculty with
Fujian Hua Nan Women's
College since 1908

428

而且，戈登不用补那天的课，因为他已经预先完成教学计划。鲍勃是对的——戈登确实有潜力。

校友办邀请老师们和校友们带着自己的孩子，到华南女院外国专家楼参加英语亲子活动。大家一起阅读绘本，吃点心。这个活动很成功，学校打算在2017年度普及湾大学环太平洋发现之旅的活动中再次举办类似活动。

在华南女院，圣心女校的学生进入外语外贸系四个不同专业班级的学习课堂，与此同时，她们也回答有关夏威夷的问题。我们设计了文化交流活动，活动在小礼堂开展，热闹非凡，华南女院的学生谈论了女院的历史。接下来是学生演讲，最后是文化舞蹈表演以及歌曲演唱。华南女院学生事先进行认真排练，夏威夷女孩对此十分感动。活动还穿插了一场服装表演。戈登对圣心女孩解释说，这是第一次也是唯一一次的机会，华南女院的"大姐姐们"为鲍勃致敬，所以她们全力以赴。当地媒体进行了现场报道。当记者问及如何评价两校之间的表演比赛，戈登说活动的目的是文化交流，而不是比赛竞争。

当我们6月份到平潭第一实验小学参观时，戈登和索妮娅问能否让双方合唱歌曲，他们的英语老师很支持这个提议，经过讨论，程氏夫妇建议让两校学生一起演唱卡朋特兄妹的《世界之巅》。当汽车来到实验小学时，我们进入了一片欢乐的海洋。索妮娅是真的被淹没了。

圣心女校学生参加校友孩子返校
"亲子阅读日"活动

参加"亲子阅读日"活动的孩子黄晨翔
与鲍勃合影留念

华南女院与圣心女校学生表演歌舞（2013年11月）

　　当大人们见面寒暄时，圣心的女孩们进入课堂，给小朋友们朗读她们自己带来的故事。讲完故事，就把书转送给老师，然后来到大礼堂进行歌舞文化交流。当两校的孩子合唱《世界之巅》时，活动达到高潮。

索妮娅沉浸在平潭第一实验小学孩子们
欢迎的海洋中（2013年11月）

中国孩子表演唱歌和书法
（2013年11月）

程吕底亚精神促成华南女院、圣心和毓贤
（平潭第一实验小学前身）三校团聚

程氏父子与平潭第一实验小学领导合影
（2013年10月）

春色
任天涯
——福建华南女子
职业学院外教侧记
International Faculty with
Fujian Hua Nan Women's
College since 1908

430

圣心女校开了一个博客，记录她们每天的活动行程。所以她们的同学、朋友和父母都能从照片，以及标注的描述中，感受到这次发现之旅。回去之后，她们向家人、朋友，以及扶轮社进行了演讲汇报。下面我附上她们学校的电子报对此行的报道。请注意程氏家族进行了资助。现在我才理解程氏家族对女性教育的支持，我们不仅仅是向华南女院的缔造者表示敬意。女子学校是程氏家族的生命的一部分。这条新闻通讯将圣心女校学生们的这次访问称作"改变人生之旅"。我希望在未来十年里，她们会考虑再次来访中国，到华南来教书。程氏家族对于和平和不同文化下的人们的理解有着非常敏锐的洞察力。他们曾经提到，要给美国年轻人提供来访中国的机会，让她们早早地对中国有认知和理解。希望她们未来能回到中国，来福建教书。这是多么令人感动和有前瞻性的愿景！我被他们的善心和伟大深深打动。

圣心女校家长电子读物中文翻译：

学生们分享中国之行的美好回忆

十月份下旬，8位圣心女子高中的学生到中国福建省游学。1月23日，她们在Clarence T.C. Ching做了一场特别的分享演讲报告。

SACRED HEARTS ACADEMY
e-parentline

January 2014 | Vol. XVV, No. 22

Students share memories of time in China

In late October, eight Academy High School students traveled to *Fuzhou Province* in *China*, and on January 23, they shared their experiences, memories and perspectives at a special presentation in The Clarence T.C. Ching Student Center.

At the presentation, the group also expressed their appreciation to the members of the school community who made the trip possible, including teachers and parents. And, at the top of the list was *Robert Trimble*, (from back right) *Sonia Trimble* and *Gordon Trimble* and their namesake *Foundation*, which sponsored the two-week trip in an attempt to foster student exchange programs between China and America.

On this trip, the students were teamed up with "big sisters" from *Hwa Nan Women's College*, where they also stayed.

The students all agree this was definitely a life-changing experience, and they are forever grateful for the unique opportunity to be "fully immersed" in the Chinese culture.

The Trimbles, teacher *Lilly Zhang-Micco* and *Director of Student Activities Toni Normand* coordinated all the details for the trip.

To view more about the students' China experience, go to *http://china102013.blogspot.com.*

ABOVE: Head of School Betty White, Lilly Zhang-Micco, Toni Normand, Gordon Trimble, Sonia Trimble and the students who traveled to China; *LEFT:* During their fall trip, the Academy students participated in a Cultural Exchange Day at Pingtan Experimental Primary School, sharing songs and even a hula with the young Chinese students.

圣心女校家长电子读物

演讲中，她们也表达了对学校、老师和家长促成此行的感谢之情。程罗伯特、程索妮娅、程戈登，以及以他们的姓为名的程氏基金位列感谢名单之首。他们资助了这次"两周之旅"，想以此推进中美交换项目的建设。

旅行中，他们和华南女院的"大姐姐"结对，并在这个大学住宿。

程氏家族、张丽丽老师和学生活动中心的托尼·若尔曼协调了相关细节。欲了解更多详情，请访问网址：http://china102013.blogspot.com.

11月1日，我们参加了鲍勃98岁生日的庆祝会，这个大家庭为他庆祝。活动中没有演讲，我们观看了圣心女校学生表演的呼啦舞蹈，还唱了《世界之巅》。

华南女院前院长、师大英语教授林本椿与
98岁鲍勃合影庆生（2013年11月）

程氏父子和来自福建省政府的朋友
（2013年11月）

夏威夷圣心女校的学生胡玉兰、杜妮可
和我一起与98岁的鲍勃合影留念
（2013年11月）

春色
任天涯
——福建华南女子
职业学院外教侧记
International Faculty with
Fujian Hua Nan Women's
College since 1908

432

程氏一家和他们当时教的学生在聚会上合影
（2013年11月）

商务英语专业学生参加鲍勃的生日晚宴
（2013年11月）

福建省政府"友谊奖"三位获得者贝茨、
凯和黄丽霞参加鲍勃生日晚会
（2013年11月）

外事处铭茜老师与鲍勃合影
（2013年11月）

时任外事处副处长的吴瑗瑗
老师与鲍勃合影
（2013年11月）

原教务处处长马秀发老师与鲍勃
合影（2013年11月）

和圣心女校学生学习使用夏威夷手势语 "small shaka"
（2013年11月）

福建师大教授、阳光学院外语学
院院长杜昌忠老师与鲍勃合影
（2013年11月）

　　鲍勃98岁生日聚会结束后，我们到泉州这个古老的港口城市参观游玩，圣心女校和华南女院的一些老师带着自家的孩子同行。学生们很诧异地发现整座桥都是用花岗岩打造的。大家参观了寺庙和博物馆，深深体会到：一个国家不是以版图来定义，而是以人民内心的感情来定义的。

　　有时候，最好的会留到最后。事情虽并不总是如此，但没有人会不同意，对鲍勃而言，2013年秋季之旅是最重要的。他亲眼见证了夏威夷学生与中国"大姐姐们"的互动，深感教学相长的道理。他惊喜地发现自己1915年11月15日出生的医院还屹立着，他怀抱希望，要在来年到福清龙田去程吕底亚担任首任校长的学校去访古探幽。在他98岁生日时，他不禁感慨：人生真的很美好！

　　龙田小学的领导听说鲍勃希望参观他姑婆建立的学校后，学校的周校长11月28日专程来到华南女院。女院领导带他们一起外出进餐以庆祝。接下来，程氏夫妇于

圣心女校学生与华南女院部分师生共赴泉州之旅（2013年11月）

春色
任天涯
——福建华南女子
职业学院外教侧记
International Faculty with
Fujian Hua Nan Women's
College since 1908

434

华南女院前任校长林本椿教授、龙田小学周校长和戈登的合影（2013年12月）

12月6日访问了福清龙田，早期学校的原址位于教堂附近。这个学校曾经是社区成员的聚集中心，现在是他们社区的幼儿园，仍然能把大家聚集在一起。我们参观了刚落成的新校区。

2014年秋：传递火炬

鲍勃98岁生日时，我曾提出一个简单的问题："如果习主席突然出现在这里，让你许一个愿望，你会许什么愿望呢？"鲍勃毫不迟疑地回答："我会询问他，能否给出生于中国的95岁以上的外国人永久签证，以便老人去参观出生地。"这不无道理。我开始想，如果做不到这点，那我能做些什么呢？我突然想到，可以为鲍勃申请福州荣誉市民。至少当他再来向我问起5年后华南的愿景时，我可以跟他聊聊这个。

所以我开始了解相关程序。华南女院对此也甚表赞同，这个申请是理所当然的。我从福州侨办领取申请表，考虑到他对于福州的兴趣和贡献，他和高中母校林肯中学以及普吉湾大学的关系，这两个学校位于华盛顿州的塔科马市，而塔科马是福州的姊妹城市。然而遗憾的是，这一切太迟了。鲍勃在2014年6月28日就辞世了。

听闻这个消息，大家一片寂静，眼泪止不住地夺眶而出。鲍勃本人和他10月在华南女院逗留两周已经成为华南女院文化历史中的一部分了，这一传统从我们搬入大学城新校区的时候就开始了。新的传统诞生了，传统不受时间的定义限制，传统与时间无关。传统将永远传承下去。我们大家都在回想，鲍勃对于我们到底意味着什么？不知道我提到过没有，我的办公室在行政大楼6楼，在那里可以俯瞰全校校园。鲍勃每天会到湖边散步一两次，很容易看到他。只要他一出现，大家都会来到窗前，看他散步。大家都很高兴，因为时隔多年，程吕底亚的侄子还记得她和她的精神。

戈登和索妮娅今年8月的第三个周末来到福州。他们看到校园新的运动场建成，很高兴，后面还有吊环可以供他们锻炼身体。生活终于恢复了正常。戈登确保他以前以及目前的学生都要知道"外研社杯"演讲比赛的题目。他说，那些二年级上学期末成绩最好的学生，一般6个月后就不是成绩最好的学生了。我们如何让她们保持学习动力不减呢？作为老师，我也很想知道答案。

戈登说，他的儿子罗伯特今年会来庆祝鲍勃的诞辰，我想认识罗伯特，他能帮助我们更好地了解他们的家庭。我问我能帮上什么忙。一问才知道他也不是来享受的。他的爷爷曾发挥过重要作用。是时候让罗伯特来感受他爷爷的人格魅力了。

我问罗伯特是否愿意去参观程氏大楼原址，戈登建议我邀请他来听我的课。我们还应该带上Isabella，她是华南女院"外研社杯"演讲比赛的候选人，戈登和罗伯特会分别在课上讲几句话，给Isabella三分钟时间进行演讲，然后回答我学生提出的问题。最后我们来到师大老校区食堂，吃了鲍勃吃过的大蓝边碗的面条。（简单地说就是我们围坐在桌旁，像爷爷那样吃面。）

普吉湾大学的卡尔·菲尔德来到福州，探索应该如何与福建师大开展教师交流项目的时候，还特地拜访了我们华南女院。他到华南女院来会见了老朋友——程氏夫妇。作为他们的习惯之一，他们会在事先未经告知的情况下走进教室，与学生互动。他后来评论说，他感到十分惊讶，因为戈登竟然记得每位学生的名字，他的学生展示出自信的姿态，以及她们敢于走到教室前面大声发表观点，让班上人人都听得见。这样的评论让我引以为豪。现在我开始明白去年10月鲍勃和戈登在湖边散步时讨论的事情。确实，鲍勃与我们同在，我们可以随时感受到他的精神。

鲍勃预见到普吉湾大学和福建师大之间的教师交流也会加强普吉湾与华南女院既有的良好关系。外国专家楼既可以为外国来访者提供膳食，也可以主办会议。关系是以人为基础的，正如鲍勃所说，我们要继续让新教师意识到福建是大有可为的，而不是让新教师只注意广为人知的地方——北京和上海。

福建师大外事处副处长王绍祥博士、
卡尔·菲尔德教授以及戈登（2014年10月）

**春色
任天涯**
——福建华南女子
职业学院外教侧记
International Faculty with
Fujian Hua Nan Women's
College since 1908

436

华南女院的椭圆形风雨操场后面是径赛馆。这个三层楼的水泥结构包括室内羽毛球场、舞蹈房、篮球场，以及三楼的两个房间。几年前，当鲍勃看到大学城新校区比较偏僻的时候，他建议搭建乒乓球桌。考虑到鲍勃从小打乒乓球，也喜欢乒乓球，华南女院将3楼较大的一个房间，专设为鲍勃乒乓球比赛室。学校特意定制了一块展览板挂在墙上，用图片和文字描述了鲍勃在南平和福州的生活情境。在纪念室落成典礼上，戈登代表家族做了简短讲话。

总共有两块展板，一幅放在风雨操场三楼的鲍勃纪念室，另一幅挂在外国专家楼多媒体教室的墙上。

华南女院程闽岱（鲍勃）乒乓
球室揭牌仪式（2014年10月）

展览墙——挂在风雨操场径赛馆3楼的
鲍勃乒乓球比赛室（2014年10月）

纪念鲍勃的乒乓球室落成
（2014年10月）

戈登、罗伯特和Isabella来到福建师大老校区。我班上的学生对于Isabella的演讲印象深刻，说她讲得很好。罗伯特和戈登都向我的学生们提过做好演讲的要素，他们俩重点强调：要让观众记住演讲内容，就必须缩短演讲时长。我突然意识到，戈登不只是说，他也做了准备。他把想讲的内容先写下来，然后进行反复练习，直到听起来像是在向你演讲。这就增加了一些正式性，学生听起来也感觉更有趣，因为像是邀请大家提出问题加入对话。我的学生被这种方法深深地吸引了。

我们和罗伯特一行来到平潭岛实验小学新近改建的校区，他爷爷程鲍勃和圣心女校的学生去年来参观过这里。罗伯特受到老师们的特别欢迎，我仿佛看见火炬成功地传到了程氏家族的下一代。

我和罗伯特私下的聊天是很有趣的，我没想到他的回答会是这样，所以写出来给你们看看。

"罗伯特，你是否是在爸爸和妈妈的强迫下来中国的？"我问。

"不是的，他们根本没有强迫我。他们只是跟我说，你爷爷一直致力于福建教育，你是否有兴趣了解其中的原因？"他咧嘴大笑。

"那你有空时是否愿意来华南女院教书？"

"我想我愿意，但是可能要等到我退休的时候吧。"他答道。

最后我们举行了生日晚餐聚会。今年鲍勃应该99岁了。当轮到戈登讲话时，我很诧异地看到发言的是罗伯特。我想起了鲍勃，他总是在家庭聚会时让戈登发言。所以这也是传统的一部分，就像当年程吕底亚也将校长的职责传承给华南女院第三任校长王世静一样。戈登用让罗伯特发言的方式表达他对程吕底亚的纪念。好的领导总是会获得追随者，好领导懂得需要付出什么代价，并且在别人提出请求前，就知道要如何帮助别人。好的领导追求达到正面的效果，而不追求成为聚光灯下的焦点。我对罗伯特的发言印象深刻，所以我向他要了讲稿，具体内容如下：

首先，很荣幸成为福州和华南女院的客人。我将诚惶诚恐地继承百年前我的曾曾姑婆程吕底亚展望直至今日的遗志，以及我爷爷的事业。我来此是为了确保我祖先的意志得以传承。作为程氏家族来榕的第五代，我仔细考虑了我从蒙大拿州到这里的旅程，想到在过去一个世纪中，科技进步了很多。

上周天上午，我在蒙大拿登机，开始了福州之行，周一晚上到达福州，一路上只花了27个小时。但是仔细想想，我亲爱的曾曾姑婆和我爷爷从美国到福州可能需要27天。旅行期间，我同时通过电邮和我妈妈保持联系。每次中途短暂停留，我都

春色
任天涯
——福建华南女子
职业学院外教侧记
International Faculty with
Fujian Hua Nan Women's
College since 1908

438

给母亲发送信息，让她了解我的行程。可是在我曾曾姑婆和我爷爷的时代，要和远在美国的家人联络，需要花好几周甚至几个月的时间。

在华南女院，我看到热情的学生忙碌而充实，她们将对学习的憧憬付诸行动。她们并非像机器人那样，被程序控制，机械地进行学习，而是积极参与到学习和教学的过程中。很欣慰，程吕底亚的事业百年后得以延续。我今天能够来到这里，也证明了这点。作为程氏第五代，我希望能在接下来的岁月里续写传奇篇章。

罗伯特和华南女院陈钟英理事长
（2014年11月）

罗伯特和华南女院老师在鲍勃生日晚会上合影
（2014年11月）

福建师大老校区校部参观程氏
大楼之行（2014年10月）

在福建师大新校区举行的户外英语俱乐部活动（2014年11月）

　　我要补充一点，学生能够记住的最有趣的事情之一，是与程氏一家外出参加英语俱乐部活动。戈登先向大家发表演讲——"如何让生活更幸福，更成功"。然后由学生负责安排接下来的活动，唯一要求是这两个小时内只能说英语。如果有人想了解与众不同的教学方法，我会推荐他们去外国专家楼多媒体教室，体验和观察戈登的商务社交部分的教学内容。

戈登的商务写作课的商务社交部分
（2014年11月）

　　戈登每次来办公室，都笑得很开心。他说："一切搞定！我二年级的学生做的PPT和假扮的华尔街的股票分析师都糟糕得很。所以我让她们选择：是选择现在获得一个学分，还是选择来年即明年2015年9月我回来，给她们最后一次演讲机会，之后再给成绩。只有一个学生现在就要成绩。其他人都愿意明年9月再以'外研社杯'演讲题目作为演讲课的最后考核题目。这样她们就有三个月的准备时间。我请她们把演讲稿发给我来帮助她们修改。这样当她们回到学校时，就已准备好演讲的第一部分。我们有两个月时间来为即兴演讲和回答问题做好准备。"这就是戈登成功让学生保持和提高英语水平的秘诀。戈登和索妮娅想做好最后的演讲，让学生们一直参加英语俱乐部活动。英语俱乐部是我们的乐荣妹老师在外语外贸系主持开办的，作为英语角的补充，目的是提升学生即兴演讲和回答问题的技能。

戈登、索妮娅和选择来年参加"外研社杯"题目做最后演讲课考核的学生合影（2014年12月）

春色
任天涯
——福建华南女子
职业学院外教侧记
International Faculty with
Fujian Hua Nan Women's
College since 1908

440

2015年秋：行动转化为语言

5月份，"外研社杯"英语演讲题目颁布了。这次的题目是有关2500年前庄子和惠子看待世界的对话，考查学生们如何看待当今世界。当戈登告诉我他中学时读过类似文章的时候，我感到十分吃惊。他记住的是庄子。他说他在这方面并未受过相关的正式引导，但他被这位思想家吸引，是因为直觉，或者说是一种温和放松的知觉，这更有利于促进理解，而不仅仅是用玩笑戏谑的语言。"有时候我们沉迷于用词汇、恰当的词汇用法，以及理智来安排语言。我们忘了当我们专注于单词时，理解常常会受到限制。"他高兴，我也高兴，但是同时对于即将来临的评估，我又隐隐担心。

在福建省，高校每隔6年左右要迎接专家的综合评估。我希望评估期间程氏夫妇在华南女院。没有特别的理由，只是若他们在，我便心安。我请索妮娅和戈登在华南女院一直留到12月底，等学院评估结束后，再回美国。"评估在什么时候呢？"戈登问。"嗯，应该是12月下旬，月底前。"这是我当时能给出的最接近的时间。他们订了年底最后一天返回夏威夷的机票。他们解释说，这样他们就可以庆祝两次新年了，这对他们来说，还从未经历过。

上一次的评估学校受益匪浅。在接下来的7年里，女子学院在大学城发展得更快更好。我们欢迎省教育厅来评估，并以此找到我们学院适应快速变化的大学教育的最佳方法。

程氏夫妇在新学期开学前两周来到福州。戈登咨询省级评估的具体内容。他很有兴趣了解评估过程。他说："我并不了解中国的情形，但是在夏威夷，评估是为学校重新组织进行解释性阐述，有时候是为了方向性的改变。在我熟知的大学，教师是学校的灵魂，学校往哪个方向发展，发展速度多快，老师在其中起着至关重要的作用。在一个组织中，能够获得提拔的人应该能够提供更鼓舞人心的评估结果。我经历过好几次的重组，我个人的承诺一贯如此，我的工作就是要让上司更加体面，我会给上司最好的信息，并确定每次都尽全力而为。"

这个学期以学生完成上学年留下的"最后一次演讲"为开端，我们请了4位评委，戈登负责提问。我们邀请新的演讲班学生，以及其他任何有兴趣参加10月份中旬学院常规比赛的同学来旁听。在这场模拟比赛中，我们选择了实际比赛中的两个部分，同时训练新同学。这些选手与戈登新近担任班级的学生到时又会受邀到福建师大去参观真正的比赛，这样学生们可以检测自己在过去一年以来进步的程度，判断自己还要付出多大努力，才能更有竞争力。

紧接上学期的模拟英语演讲比赛
（2015年9月）

皮埃尔·李博士以及辛西娅·豪生博士来访
（2015年11月）

戈登提醒我说他父亲鲍勃的母校普吉湾大学的卡尔·菲尔德教授已到访福州，与福建师大探讨两校教师的交流互动。戈登说："鲍勃会很高兴看到教师交流结出果实，不过这次的果实是葡萄。"原来，来自普吉湾大学的经济学教授皮埃尔·李博士，与他的妻子辛西娅·豪生博士正一起编写一本关于中国葡萄酒产业快速发展的书。"他们夫妻俩是这方面的专家，华南女院有人愿意听相关讲座吗？"戈登问我。我同4个专业的教师进行了沟通，加上旅游专业，有5个专业的老师有兴趣。皮埃尔和辛西娅在外国专家楼的多媒体教室进行了PPT演讲报告。戈登建议配备翻译，这更加有利于沟通，因为这样可以放缓节奏，让大家在下个问题前有机会思考。

李博士和豪生博士为华南女院师生阐述他们对中国葡萄酒产区的研究报告（2015年9月）

春色
任天涯
——福建华南女子
职业学院外教侧记
International Faculty with
Fujian Hua Nan Women's
College since 1908

442

程氏家族一直致力于帮助中美两国人民之间的沟通交流，由于福建省福州市与华盛顿州塔科马市是姊妹城市，程氏家族对于两市的交流做了很多具体工作。如塔科马市长到访福州时接受福建电视台《热线777》的采访一事就是他们促成的。

程氏家族带着他们的友谊和关注来到福州，来到女子学院。戈登这样说："如果我们将学生置于首要的位置，那当他们愿意学习的时候，我们要愿意帮助他们。好的学生会自律，能主动完成课堂任务，但是其他的学生怎么办？有些学生上大学是因为他们的父母想要他们去学校。那我们如何使他们对学习感兴趣呢？几年前，你告诉我给他们压力，增强他们学习的动力，但这个办法已经用了这么长时间了。"所以，程氏夫妇决定辅导国庆不回家的学生，也给回家的学生布置了作业。当课程结束时，还需要鼓励几个要放弃学习的学生，激励她们完成学习任务。

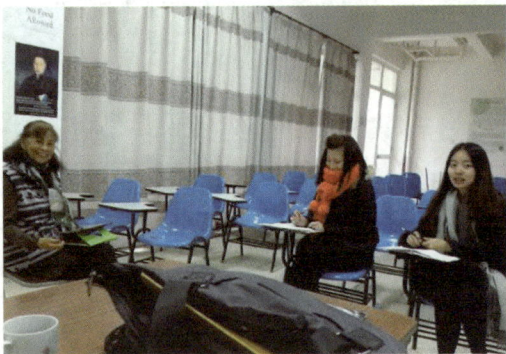

索妮娅辅导落下课程的学生（2015年12月）　　戈登带领女院师生观摩师大英语演讲比赛现场
（2015年10月）

也许因为鲍勃对福建师大感兴趣，所以师大老师和学生对于程氏家族也很感兴趣。今年有几名师大学历史的研究生录制了程戈登谈他的曾姑婆程吕底亚的访谈视频。戈登说程吕底亚是时代产物。美国女性教育从程吕底亚前一代人就开始了。她那个时代的英雄人物是索杰娜·特鲁斯和苏珊·安东尼。程吕底亚来自农村家庭，农民比其他大多数人更有宗教信仰，因为他们看天吃饭——风雨和气温决定了他们能够收获什么，会遇到什么虫害，特别是蝗虫、野鸟带来的灾害以及闪电引起的火灾，这些都有可能影响整个家庭的庄稼收成。有两个寓言尤其能解释她的行动。第一个是按才干接受责任的比喻——说她有责任运用上帝赋予的能力，去做对社会有益的事，使社会比她出生时更加进步；第二个是分羊的比喻——引导她在当时世界上仅有的3个女性寿命低于男性寿命的地区中进行选择。程吕底亚直接选中妇女最多、

国土面积最大的国家——中国。我想从某种程度上我能理解她的感受。我在与她相同的年纪，加入了美国和平护卫队志愿组织。因为这与美国派部队到越南打仗相比，是一种更好的改善世界的方法。卫理公会帮助她来到中国。对我而言，是和平护卫队志愿组织，使我来到菲律宾。我们的途径不同，但目标相同。

今年是很重要的一年，因为要庆祝鲍勃百岁诞辰。在11月15日鲍勃生日那天，我们举行了聚会。鲍勃来福州期间认识的朋友一起回忆了美好时光——100年前中国的风景、声音和味道。戈登向来自龙田和平潭的校长们谈了另一个梦想：不是让孩子们中学时出国，而是考虑更好的方法——一种让孩子成为世界公民，同时又保有中国身份，减缓遭受外国文化冲击的方法。戈登感兴趣的是和平潭或龙田的英语老师一起进行实验，让英语老师带上能说一口流利英语的小学三年级的女儿，寒假到夏威夷住上五周时间。英语老师和她的女儿可以住在程氏夫妇家。女儿可以到圣心女校合适的年级上学。妈妈可以用不同方式帮忙，加深她对美国私立小学的了解。英语老师的女儿可以和妈妈在一起，每天在日常活动中与女儿交流。

晚餐聚会——2015年11月15日纪念
程鲍勃诞辰100周年

戈登与师大研究生探讨程吕底亚将女性教育置于
最重要的位置的意义（2015年12月）

春色
任天涯
——福建华南女子
职业学院外教侧记
International Faculty with
Fujian Hua Nan Women's
College since 1908

444

如果这种方法积极有效，那来年可以再次进行。女孩可以重新加入上一年来时的同一个班级学习。这样女孩回到中国后，也还有兴趣提高英语水平。这对母女在与外国朋友建立友谊的时候，也能获得国际级别的理解力。到女儿上高中的时候，无论她想上哪里的大学，她都知道在大学需要掌握什么样的技能。戈登说他想试试这个办法。一旦中国英语老师获得经验，老师就知道让六年级的圣心女校学生来参观中国小学（食宿由中方合作提供），在教师家做文化交流的做法是否切实可行。饭桌上好几个人都觉得这个主意有吸引力。坐在晚宴主桌的是华南女院早年的毕业生和现任领导。我们这一桌中有4名来自福建师大的老师，还有一桌是程氏夫妇以前和现在教的学生。许多来宾往年也来过。鲍勃生日聚会是在周日举办的，应邀前来的人们都很开心，因为这个聚会与工作无关。

龙田小学校长有感于程吕底亚在龙田建立女子学堂的事迹，以及程氏家族对于福建教育事业做出的贡献，于2013年创作书法对联作品赠送给戈登。他还写了一首诗歌，由时任校理事会秘书王凌老师翻译。大卫·摩西和苏珊·韦斯特贝格都在林肯高中任教，他们帮忙把对联带回普吉湾大学，因为鲍勃是普吉湾校友，这副对联可以在春节展示，以示祝贺。周校长的诗歌已翻译成地道的英语，下面是戈登与字画的合影留念。

追梦

作者：福清市龙田中心小学校长周位荣

蔚蓝大海，一叶扁舟若隐若现。

荒芜沙滩，下凡女神左顾右盼。

是赏景？是访亲？

是描绘千秋伟业蓝图！

梦，从这里开始……

原始渔村，燃起智慧火光。

历史长河，奔腾不息漂过百年。

火炬传人，茫茫人海寻寻觅觅。

为寻宝？为探秘？

为续写树人宏伟篇章。

梦，从这里延续……

春节期间戈登站在周校长送的书墨（赠给普吉湾大学）前留念（2016年2月）

追梦一族，传播人生至上真理。

百年老校，根深叶茂桃李芬芳。

和煦阳光，普照学子快乐成长。

在锻炼！在歌唱！

在畅游知识无边海洋！

梦，从这里放飞……

社会重担，万千栋梁担当！

开学以来，省教育厅的评估工作也慢慢展开。我无须过多地向戈登解释这次评估结果对学校的重要性，我只想做最好的准备。省教育厅邀请了18位来自全国各地的专家进校评估。他们来检查教学档案，旁听老师上课，观察学生学习，与学生面谈，召开教师座谈会，观察课堂指导。有4所大学需要接受评估，华南女院是其中最后接受评估的大学。

12月初，评估具体细节基本敲定。12月16日，星期三，专家们进入华南女院。星期四和星期五上午，专家进入课堂听课，并召开座谈会。星期五下午召开全校会议，反馈初步评估结果。因为在最后一刻才能确定听课的教室和参加座谈会议的人员，所以很有戏剧性。评估的最后一周，学校管理层非常紧张，发出邮件请老师务必待在校园内，有可能的话，最好将早上的课程提前到8点。我们也请学生8点前进入课堂，以防有专家提前来听课。

在学期初，戈登集中于教授学生阅读技巧与增加她们的单词汇量，到期末他则致力于提高学生的写作水平。他告诉学生，提高写作的最好办法是每天写至少125个单词的文章。每个学生按照要求准备了一个单词本，每天写日记。到12月，学生们就可以大声对戈登朗读她们自己的文章，然后由戈登对经过他修改打印出来的讲稿提问。他的辅导从每天早上7点45分开始。对有的学生的回答辅导要花6分钟，对其他的学生则要花20分钟。平均而言，一个学期下来，每个学生接受戈登的辅导时间至少为两个小时。

戈登注意到8点前教室里就坐满了学生，他站起来说："吃过早餐的同学请举右手。"一个女孩举手了。"好，如果没吃早饭，请站起来！你们有12分钟时间去食堂买点吃的再回到班里。我希望大家高兴起来，同时也要小心。这个学期以来你们一直在为省专家评估做准备，你们已经准备好了，不用担心。如果你们放松又开心，就会表现得很好。"学生们发现戈登一点也不严肃，她们很高兴地去了食堂。第二天

春色
任天涯
——福建华南女子
职业学院外教侧记
International Faculty with
Fujian Hua Nan Women's
College since 1908

446

早上，早早来等戈登修改文章的学生在门口把关，只有吃了早餐的同学才可以进教室。她记得戈登曾告诉过大家："不要把自己当成学生。从一开始，就把自己当成老师，开始管理和控制自己的生活。"她悄悄地去做了，而没有人强迫她这么做。到了周三，每个来上戈登课程的同学都吃过早餐。

星期三晚上，我打电话告诉戈登，他的写作课程被专家选中观摩。戈登说："好极了！非常欢迎！但是你一进我课堂就是参与者——表演者。"来旁听戈登课程的人不会旁观太久。"明天是我们年度商业活动社交课程。每个学生上台做2～3分钟的演讲，题目是：过去一年中我学到的三件让我终生受益的事情。"

8点半前，我们进入了教室。共有5个听课的人——一位省级专家，何教授和4个华南女院的老师，其中包括一个进来录视频的，这样以后有记录可以参看——无论好坏，我想要录像，这样下次能做得更好。自我介绍后，我们在教室后面坐下。当戈登走到讲台上时，他发现了自己不喜欢的东西。他皱起眉头，我听到他深深叹了口气。他回到何博士旁，悄悄地说几句。我们的目光都焦急地落在他们身上，想知道到底出什么事了，因为这肯定在计划外。何博士站起来，笑着说："我们来合影怎么样？"他们声音很大，人人都听得见。从学生的笑声中，何博士看得出，学生的英语水平很高。看看下面的照片，你就会发现课堂气氛从紧张严肃变得开心而又充满期待。一切都很顺畅，戈登掌控着局面，他没有跟学生明说，但是却把控着氛围。

为商务写作班"商务礼仪社交"课程营造良好
的课堂氛围（2015年12月）

戈登亲自为参加"商务礼仪社交"
课程的同学服务（2015年12月）

主持人用清晰欢快的声音宣布活动开始，她并未照稿件朗读。我们对主持人的轻松自如印象深刻。她们的主持比在大礼堂做主持的学长表现得更好。老师们注意到这种区别，非常高兴。戈登做了演讲之后，学生们开始发表演讲。何博士选择第一位演讲者，我选择第二位，另外一名老师选出第三位。学生们发表演讲时，不像呆若木鸡的机器人，而仿佛是在对朋友说她们生活中发生的重要事情，然后戈登会问她们问题，学生们则及时而流畅地回答问题。中国老师为戈登的学生演讲的仪态、准确的语法和流利的陈述感到自豪。在何博士离开前，我们和戈登的学生一起合影留念。如下图所示。

中餐后，何博士被邀请回来继续旁听商务社交课程。何博士离开教室后，课程继续。半个小时后，外事处主任吴瑗瑗来找戈登，告诉他学校管理层请他参加由专家举行的座谈会。商务社交课程按计划继续进行，索妮娅留下来上课。戈登和吴瑗瑗一同赶去行政楼。

"商务社交礼仪"课程接受省评估专家观摩（2015年12月）

戈登在会议桌的尽头拉出一张椅子，坐了下来。吴瑗瑗坐在戈登左后方，为他做翻译。因为戈登是在会议中途加入的，轮到他发言时，他简要地说："我叫戈登，到这个学校来帮助学生学习。因为在学习的是学生，我不确定我是否能被称作老师。我应该更像个教练。各位都是重要人物，我不清楚为什么我在这里。我先回答你们的第二个问题。华南女院给我印象最深的是我的学生都很好学。有她们做我的学生，我感到自豪。至于第一个问题，通过我学生的眼睛和思想，我能够预见到，从现在算起，下一代中国将会怎样。我补充一句，我喜欢所见的一切。第三个问题，我最想看到的未来是，我希望有更多美国人对真正的中国有清楚的了解，而这只有当他们亲自来中国，熟识一个个具体的中国人，体验中国的社会文化，方能了解中国。长城和大运河是了不起的，人们游玩后会拍照欣赏，但是这没有什么意义，就像只参观华盛顿纪念碑，也不能了解美国人。"

春色
任天涯
——福建华南女子
职业学院外教侧记
International Faculty with
Fujian Hua Nan Women's
College since 1908

448

商务英语社交礼仪活动进行中（2015年12月）　学生与戈登流利进行商务社交沟通（ 2015年12月）

当问及他如何看待华南女院招收男生这个问题时，他说："我来中国帮助学生学习。在你们国家我是个过客，我不是来制定政策的。我的工作简单明了，有什么学生就给什么学生上课，帮助他们发现到未曾意识到的潜能。对于你提出的具体问题，我没有足够经验来做出合理的解释。"

在第一次评估期间，教育专家提到华南女院需要更好的生源，而不是更多生源。如果华南女院能够坚持自己品牌特色，会更加成功。他们强调说华南女院外教资源丰富，但应该更充分地利用这一资源。我院老师很高兴戈登的课被选中，他也受邀参加座谈会。我记得戈登说："我的工作是让上司体面，我尽可能给出最好的信息，每次我都尽力而为。"由于我成功的前瞻性挽留，省级评估期间，程氏夫妇都在华南女院，因此我如释重负。

每年我们都在外国专家楼庆祝圣诞节。因为戈登今年也留了下来，他们自愿做迎宾员。每年圣诞聚会我们都欢聚一堂，缅怀我们谦逊的先祖，感念外教对于学校做出的贡献。

对我而言，程氏夫妇出现在我生命中，于我是一种幸运——他们不是能从箱子里拿出来炫耀的收藏，而是在前行的旅途中，可以共同分享友谊的伙伴，我们互相倾听，乐意理解。他们有别于我熟识的其他外教。程氏夫妇善于倾听，但不急于下判断。他们会教育学生们说："不用信誓旦旦，行动才是最重要的。"学生们都看得到程氏夫妇的所作所为，而且敬慕他们。程氏夫妇也很开心能从学生身上学到东西，正如学生渴望从他们身上学到东西。也许戈登从庄子那里学到许多，因为他有一次曾困惑地对我说："你不明白人们在做什么，并不表明他们是不理智的。只能说明你还不理解。"程氏家族给我极大鼓励，帮助我以他们善良的眼光看待这个世界。在他们的帮助下，我才能比较全面地记录下我们一路的行程，如果你们与我们一路同

前任校长林本椿教授、我与程氏夫妇欢度圣诞合影
（2015年12月）

行，我一定能想象到你会感受到什么。但是，将他们所做的一切全部付诸语言是不可能完成的任务。

　　他们的善行无法用语言表达，他们拥有鼓励人心向上的精神。我尽力记录下他们的行为和话语，这样你们也可以有所思考，有所获益。如果出现任何错误（包括省略错误），我愿意承担责任。在后半个学期，为编辑出版这本书，我们一起回忆过往难以忘却、充满挑战的时光，真是件开心快乐的事情。这段经历出版后，可以让后人了解这段历史。当我回想时，鲍勃仿佛就在眼前，他与我们同在，并不断提醒我们："生活是如此美好！"

程戈登和我——学生张琳的回忆

　　认识Gordon Trimble（程戈登）的时候大家都叫他"Senator Trimble"，可是我当时并不知道"Senator"的真正意思，以为它就是"Senior"。他是我大三学年商务英语的老师，也是当年我在"CCTV杯"大学生英语演讲比赛时的指导老师。我和他的师生之缘，充满了有趣又奇妙的色彩。

　　大专学历的我，成长到今天，任职于全球30强总监秘书，很大程度上得益于他对我的教导。从课堂上学到的商务知识，专业的语言表达，让我认识到女性也可以有影响力。不到20岁的我对此疑惑，却也认真学习；而今回头看，却是受益匪浅。他曾经花不少时间来教导我们与人握手的礼仪，从伸手的姿势、力道到眼神，一一把关，他想要我们呈现给对方的是，女人可以像男人一样专业，而不仅仅是花瓶。在我进入西门子工作之后有一个有意思的插曲：一位技术专家提及，当时面试时和

春色
任天涯
——福建华南女子
职业学院外教侧记
International Faculty with
Fujian Hua Nan Women's
College since 1908

450

你握手，觉得这个女生很不一样，很坚毅。我在心里笑了，在心里再次感谢您。

大三时他仍然在夏威夷担任州参议员一职，有时需要回美国一段时间处理事务，作为学生，我们还以为他不在的这段时间，我们的课业可以轻松不少。"Too young, too naïve"恰如其分地描述了我们。Gordon留下了他任教时双倍的作业，并叮嘱我们不要偷懒。之后我们再也不敢期待他远行，但是我们当时并不知道，英文阅读和书写能力就在这样高压的环境下迅即提高了。

我的夏威夷实习之行，在5年之后终于得到一个正面的肯定。2007年的"CCTV杯"英语演讲比赛，也是我学生生涯中最后一场专业性比赛，对此我非常珍惜。我婉拒了和他们一起外出的邀约，在自己的演讲结束之后选择继续留下直到整场比赛结束，并记录下了自己的心得。这一切被他看在眼里，觉得应该给我更多一点向外看的机会，就有了之后那玄妙的传奇。在夏威夷短暂的实习时光，我真正接触到了所谓的女性力量，认识并有幸和多位女性共事，欣赏到她们的独立、聪明和个人魅力。这段经历深刻影响着我的职业行为，也因此让我在进入外企之后被多次评价为得体从容。

Gordon在我们毕业的时候写了一篇文章，我相信这是他宝贵人生经历的浓缩，是他愿意给予后辈分享的锦囊。他的理念和观点会一直影响着我的职业生涯和人生。我很骄傲，也非常珍惜有一位这么棒的导师出现在我的生命里。

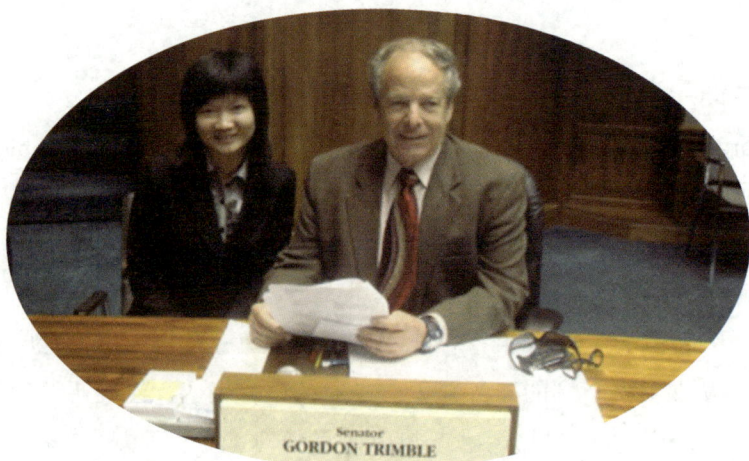

张琳在夏威夷州参议员办公室实习

第六节　丽霞老师的理想与行动

我院澳大利亚籍外教Laihar Wong，中文名黄丽霞，生于1949年9月12日，她于2015年9月22日被授予福建省"友谊奖"荣誉称号。外教Laihar为何有如此大的魅力？让我们去仔细探究一番吧！

兢兢业业的育人者

外教Laihar从1993年至2003年间来我院任教，2003年赴贵州民族学院义务支援少数民族地区的英语教学，并于2006年重返我院教书至今，在我院任教已达19年之久。主要教授应用英语专业"英语阅读与写作""英语口语""英语自由谈话"等课程。此外，她多年以来自愿组织华南女院英语角的活动，指导学生参加外语外贸系英文小品比赛、英文演讲比赛、英文十佳歌手比赛、教学技能大赛等。

Laihar每节课都在黑板上用粉笔仔细地写下教学内容，然而粉笔灰会影响健康，还会导致她犯老毛病而无法正常上课，因此Laihar特别重视教室的卫生，每次课上完都要用干净的布擦洗干净。估计华南女院没有一间教室会比她上课的教室更为干净整洁了。Laihar非常敬业，每次作业都认真批改，从来没有因为任何一个学生基础不好或反应慢而放弃她们。口语课上总是不厌其烦地帮助学生纠正发音，她会因为担心请假同学落下功课而单独为她们补课，也会照顾学习能力较弱的学生，在课后给她们进行辅导，有身体不适而不方便去教室上课的同学，Laihar也会亲自去学生的宿舍给她开小灶。她总是鼓励学生要勇于开口，不要害怕犯错误。她的课堂总是充满趣味，又可以学到很多。她的爱心、耐心和亲和力更是让我们钦佩，值得我们学习。

关怀备至的老奶奶

Laihar不仅是一名敬业的老师，更是一位用心关怀、爱护学生的长辈。她的爱很亲切，却无微不至，她很朴实，却透露着伟大。每一个学生的生日她都会认真记下并且送上礼物与祝福，还会带领班上学生一起唱生日歌，即便学生的生日是在假期，也会补上礼物。有学生因为贫困等原因休学了，她也会打电话祝福她生日快乐，

春色任天涯
——福建华南女子
职业学院外教侧记
International Faculty with
Fujian Hua Nan Women's
College since 1908

452

华南女院外教Laihar荣获2015年度福建省"友谊奖"

让全班同学在电话边齐唱生日快乐歌。她会花时间安抚情绪不稳定的贫困生并帮助其交学费。她能够记住并准确叫出每一个学生的名字，包括已经毕业了的学生。她关心生病请假的学生并询问她们的康复状况。她花费大量私人时间指导学生排练英语话剧，并校正她们的发音，再三嘱咐同宿舍口语或英语能力较高的学生要帮助基础薄弱的学生。

试问有哪一个外教会带上他所教的学生一起出去游玩并细心地为我们准备自制三明治，就是为了创造学生与外国交换生之间的交流以提高我们口语呢？而这所有的一切，我们的外教 Laihar 都为我们做过。她做这些事情不是因为她足够富有，而是因为她不只把我们单纯地当作学生，更是将我们当作她的孩子，她付出她的家来关怀每一个学生，尽她的一切能力帮助我们。很庆幸可以遇见她，遇到她是我们的荣幸，也是华南女院之幸也！

风雨无阻的组织者

自从2010年起，外教Kay因为年事已高，退休回美国后，Laihar就一直义务担负着组织英语角的工作。她每周都会精心制定英语角的试题，考量难度是否与学生的能力相符。在她的带领下，每周的英语角活动都开展得有声有色。为了激励学生积极参与英语角的活动，英语角每学期的最后一期都是Party活动，Laihar亲自准备糖果等小礼物，她还设计许多活动及奖励的环节。她每年都会请美国的朋友从美国邮寄奖状，颁发给帮助组织英语角的学生。只要你想锻炼口语，你总能在英语角找到Laihar的身影，因为不论晴天雨天，人数多或少，Laihar都在英语角等你，风雨无阻！

大爱延绵的传递者

外教 Laihar 做事默默无闻，勤勤恳恳。一身正气与爱心满满给我们留下了深刻的印象，也是我们学习的榜样。每年寒暑假放假一结束，她就会去福州福利院给那里的孩子送去自己掏钱买的生活用品。从书本到零食，多到数不过来。这对于我们来说，不仅仅只是为需要帮助的人伸出援手，更是明白了爱是一种传递。

鉴于 Laihar Wong 多年来对福建省女子高等教育事业所做的一切，福建省政府授予 Laihar Wong 外国人在我省工作的最高荣誉"友谊奖"，以表彰其在福建省经济建设和社会发展中做出的突出贡献。

第三章
1984年后的福建华南女子职业学院外教（续）

春色
任天涯
——福建华南女子
职业学院外教侧记
International Faculty with
Fujian Hua Nan Women's
College since 1908

456

第一节 道德教师
——记格雷戈里·盖尔切教授

2013年春季开学初，我第一次见到了格雷戈里·盖尔切教授，当时我正在应用英语专业办公室备课。一位戴着眼镜的高个子外国人走进了办公室，他身上斜挎着一个帆布包，是中国二十世纪七八十年代流行的那种军挎包款式。系副主任赖黎群和专业主任黄飞接待了他。黄飞把他介绍给我认识并让我介绍我教过的跨文化交际课程的情况，这学期将由盖尔切教授教这门课。第一次见面，盖尔切教授给我的印象是耐心，彬彬有礼且很合作。

接下来的几个月里，我对盖尔切教授有了更多的了解。他是美国人，1963年出生于土耳其。他的父亲被派遣到土耳其当空军医生。他是晨边大学（华南女院的姊妹院校之一）的历史学教授，热衷于社会活动。

盖尔切教授以访问教授的身份于2009年7月、2010年7月以及2013年春季先后访问了华南女院，他在华南女院教授英语和美国文化。在这三次访问中，他都带晨边大学的学生来华南女院交流学习。2009年7月，她的妻子由美子和女儿艾莉莎和他同行，母女俩在华南女院一起教授初级日语。他带来的三个学生乔丹·亚根、格雷·安德森、亚当·刚斯洛斯基则讲授公共演讲和美国文化课程，他的儿子亚历克斯·盖尔切从旁协助。在后来的两次访问中，和他同行的分别是学生德雷克·约翰逊（2010年）和托德·卡恩斯（2013年）。

盖尔切教授带来的学生可以通过完成去国外交流学习的任务获得相应的学分。例如，访问前，学生德雷克和托德首先要完成一份计划书，说明访问中国和华南女院的预期和想法，访问结束后他们要完成一份报告，评估他们自己在异国的文化体验。在华南女院期间，他们教学，同时协助几位中国教师教学。完成了这些任务，二者都获得了"五月课程"的学分。她的女儿艾莉莎针对中国当代女性做了研究，她用英文深度访谈了华南女院的6位学生，了解她们对当今中国女性地位变化的看法，并突出中国传统女性与学生自己希望成为的女性之比较。学生亚当则制作了一部关于华南女院的纪录片。该纪录片帮他成功考取了加州一个有名的研究生电影专业。学生格雷·安德森通过在华南女院教学完成了"五月课程"的学习。毕业后，他

盖尔切教授及其学生和华南女院教师（2010年）

在华南女院的经历和所学使他获得一份到海外教学的工作。学生乔丹在华南女院教学经历中受到启发，这促使他继续攻读研究生课程。

　　华南女院改变了晨边大学这些学生的生活。2016年接受采访时，盖尔切教授说："总而言之，我们希望来华南女院访问的学生能融入当地的文化，回去后撰写反思性文章。这些学生深受他们经历的影响，并有意识地利用访问华南女院的经历去发展日后的学习或职业生涯。他们都希望有朝一日还能重访华南女院"。

盖尔切教授和学生在玩传话游戏（2010年夏令营）

春色
任天涯
——福建华南女子
职业学院外教侧记
International Faculty with
Fujian Hua Nan Women's
College since 1908

458

　　盖尔切教授和他的家人以及他的学生的到来也给华南女院的师生带来新奇的体验。例如，2009年7月，盖尔切教授带了3名学生和他家人访问了华南女院，他们住在华南女院老校区，给华南女院学生上了一个月的课，课外请学生当导游带他们游览福州市区。他们给华南女院的学生讲授"公共演讲技能""美国文化概况""初级日语"等课程。下面摘录盖尔切教授在晨边大学校友杂志《晨边人》（2009年秋/冬季刊）上发表的一篇专题文章的部分内容和照片以飨读者。

盖尔切教授、学生德雷克和华南女院的学生（2010年夏令营）

　　第五天：

　　这也许是我所遇到的最有礼貌的学生。虽然这是上课的第二天，但她们的努力和能力给我留下了深刻的印象。我让学生以她们最为珍惜的东西为主题做一个象征性的演讲，即使大多数人是将演讲背下来的，但总体上学生的表现令人惊叹。虽然演讲中有些错误，有的学生也会紧张，但是她们的演讲使课堂有了良好的开端。

　　乔丹·亚根

　　亚当教女生玩扑克，而乔丹和格雷将他们负责的班级合并，教女生们玩美式足球（橄榄球）和Red Rover游戏。乔丹教授橄榄球的过程真是滑稽逗趣。他用一个篮球替代橄榄球来教学。悲催的是他不知道教英语为非母语的人玩橄榄球时，指令要非常简洁易懂！乔丹指定一名女生为中锋，并解释如何从两腿间发球，但他没提醒说中锋要等到四分卫提示后再发球。乔丹把球交给中锋，在他站回位置上还未及蹲下时，这名女生就从胯下将球扔出去了，正好打到乔丹身上。乔丹疼弯了腰，女生们则笑弯了腰。不过这算是打破了冷场。不久之后，就在乔丹示范如何传球时，被激动过头的四分卫给击中了脑袋。他那么卖力，真是不能说他什么了。

第九天：

在我的日语课堂上，这31名女生真是让我印象深刻。我上的是为期两周的高强度日语课，从周一至周五，早上8：30至11：30。教室在三楼，室内温度90～100华氏度，湿度达60%～95%，天花板上有几架风扇。早上8：20，当我进教室时，每个人基本已经坐好，许多人在学习。每天有两次10分钟的课间休息。当我说"好了，下课休息下吧"没有人站起来，她们还继续复习当天我所教授的内容。我也试着早一丁点放学，但无论如何，直到11：30才有人离开，她们只是不断地学习。课间时间，学生们会拿着记满问题的笔记本来问我。这使我想起我在日本的高中生活，但是我们当时的课时是50分钟，而不是180分钟。总之她们能够在那样又热又潮湿的天气里专心学习3个小时。如果相同的情况发生在美国又会怎样呢？

由美子·盖尔切2008

2010年7月，盖尔切教授带着他的学生德雷克·约翰逊访问华南女院。师生两人共同讲授"公共演讲技能"课程。德雷克尤其喜欢在福州购买衣服，他还学会打羽毛球，也和华南女院的学生和周边学校的学生一起打篮球。

晨边大学学生给华南女院学生上课
（2009年）

华南女院学生陪同晨边大学学生游览福州市区（2009年）

晨边大学学生乔丹·亚根和华南女院学生合影（2009年）

春色
任天涯
——福建华南女子
职业学院外教侧记
International Faculty with
Fujian Hua Nan Women's
College since 1908

460

2013年另一件令人愉悦的事是和盖尔切教授的学生托德·卡恩斯合作教学的经历。托德于当年5月份来到华南女院并在学校待1个月左右。在此期间，黄飞老师和我邀请他参与我们的教学。我们的中外教师合作教学模式是黄飞老师在2011年晨边大学的老师安德鲁·菲利普森博士和他的学生访问华南女院时开发的。托德与黄飞和我合作教授综合英语课程。我们从教学大纲和内容开始讨论，一起设计教学活动，一起选取教学方法。作为托德的导师，盖尔切教授也参加了我们的讨论会。但是大多数时候他只是听并启发托德产生自己的想法。最终我们决定托德负责教授"旅游"单元中不同国家的文化部分、部分阅读内容以及辅导学生的项目作业。令人高兴的是，托德制作了生动有趣的课件来吸引学生，并对基于项目的英语教学提供了很好的建议，尤其是他改进了评估学生项目作业的标准。有时托德还协助盖尔切教授教学。盖尔切教授在5月22日的日记中记下了一段课堂趣事："今天下午托德在英语听训与诵读课上协助我教学。有趣的是在第一节课学生得不断地提醒他我在班上定下的讲英语的规则：'慢慢地说，清晰地说，大声地说！'幸好，他很快掌握了窍门。"托德也从中学到了东西。2016年5月份他在写给盖尔切教授的一封邮件里谈论道："真有意思，我现在开始辅导学生进行软件开发，我想这是我在中国的经历带来的部分结果。"

和盖尔切教授合作真是令人愉快。当2013年春季学期结束时，他通过电子邮件送了我一份礼物——他教"跨文化交际"课程的教案和教学笔记，他希望这些材料对这门课程以后的发展有所帮助。从这份礼物里我发现盖尔切教授善于通过课堂上的问题讨论让学生真正地去思考课本上的内容，并将课堂所学应用于现实生活。有

晨边大学学生托德 Carnes 给华南女院学生上课（2013年）

些学生还保留着他改过的作业。此外，在期中对外教教学的评价问卷中，学生对他的教学和为人做出了积极的评价。学生们认为他耐心、认真、负责、幽默风趣、有风度、积极、细心、脾气好、帅。学生对他的教学更是赞赏有加：注重训练学生的发音，尽力帮助学生提高口语能力，授课内容丰富，注重师生互动。在接近期末的一堂课上，作为课堂的活动之一：模仿课文。在告别晚宴上作祝酒辞，学生发自肺腑地用祝酒辞表达了她们对老师的感激之情："同学们，今晚我们很高兴和格雷老师在一起。在过去的3个月里，他教我们英语。他是一位非常友善、耐心的老师。他总是准备了许多好玩的活动和有趣的故事。没有格雷老师的帮助，我们无法在小品比赛中获得二等奖。他就像一位父亲。没有格雷老师，我们无法享受到学习英语的乐趣。让我们敬格雷老师——干杯！"

盖尔切教授是一位真正的绅士，不仅外表长相绅士，行为举止更是透着绅士风度。他的一次小举动引起了我的注意。2013年的一天我在去校园专家楼的路上遇见了他。当我们经过路边一个垃圾桶时，他弯下腰捡起散落在垃圾桶外面的废纸丢进垃圾桶。这一切发生在瞬间，他的动作干净利落而且自然。虽然当时有学生从我们身边走过，但是没人注意到他的举动。几周后，当我在课堂上提及盖尔切教授的这个举动时，学生们并不惊讶，还告诉了我更多的信息。她们说她们经常看见教授在周末提个大大的塑料袋子在校园里、淑女湖旁捡垃圾。一位学生拍下了他捡垃圾的镜头并上传到微信群里，照片引起了热议并使学生深受教育。学生们开始称他为"道德教师"。

一位华南女院的学生在参加2013年12月份的省级英语演讲比赛中，以这位道德教师的事迹为例来支撑她演讲中表达的观点：孔子总是高度赞扬以真诚的道德情操为动机的道德行为。现场的外教评委对此印象深刻，并就这个例子提问以期引起观众对道德更深入的思考。后来，当我和学生们说我在写关于盖尔切教授的故事时，他们通过QQ给我发来许多关于教授的信息和照片，有的学生还保存着留有教授批语的作业。以下摘录部分学生发来的留言：

"每次上课他都会坐在门口等学生，然后和他们打招呼。"

"他上课挺好的，认真、严谨。但是他的考试超轻松。"

"每次上课都会给我们分组完成小组作业，然后提高我们的团队合作意识。"

"他平时还会去操场打篮球或羽毛球，参加各种像'3·7女生节''英语角'之类的活动。"

"他会和我们分享他们晨边大学的生活。"

春色
任天涯
——福建华南女子
职业学院外教侧记
International Faculty with
Fujian Hua Nan Women's
College since 1908

462

"他很爱护环境，不仅仅是口头上说说而已。经常看到他提个袋子在校园里、在淑女湖旁捡垃圾。"

"他很喜欢研究中国历史，特别喜欢解放军。"

"他喜欢喝中国龙井茶。"

"他喜欢拿着相机到处拍照，他自称是'照片控'。"

除三次的教学任务访问以外，盖尔切教授还对华南女院进行了两次非教学性质的访问：2008年5月随晨边大学的代表团来访，当时晨边大学赠送华南两棵"友谊树"；同年10月再次随晨边大学的代表团参加了华南女院的百年校庆，校庆期间两所大学还签订了校际交流协议。其中有一棵友谊树就种在华南女院新校区实训楼前面。友谊树茁壮成长，一如华南女院和晨边大学的友谊那样。

盖尔切教授对华南女院以及华南女院师生们有着特别的感念之情。他写道："华南女院就像我的第二个家，华南女院教职员工就像我的家人！外事处的老师们，吴瑗瑗和程铭茜，对外教们关怀备至，特别好！仅举一例：2013年春季，在华南女院期间，我年届五十。这是一个人生命中的重要里程碑，在美国我们通常会和家人及好友举行盛大的庆祝活动，但很显然，在中国的我远离家乡，无法那样做！然而，当外事处和教师们知道后，他们悄悄地为我安排了一场生日晚会，那个晚上，有美味的中国食物、温馨的陪伴，还有一个大蛋糕。因此，不仅没有伤心，这还成了我最难以忘怀的生日之一！一有机会，我就会和晨边的学生讲述华南女院的历史，分享华南女院的照片和故事。我期待着再次回到华南女院，见到我的朋友。"

种在华南女院新校区的友谊树（2016年）

第二节　普吉特海湾的十三朵金花

——记福建华南女子职业学院与美国普吉湾大学的友谊

2015年9月，国家主席习近平访美，这是习近平成为中国领导人以来对美国的首次国事访问，因此整个行程备受关注。其中一站就是拜访位于华盛顿州的塔科马。塔科马市是美国华盛顿州普吉特海湾南端的一个港口城市，位于西雅图和州府奥林匹亚之间。1994年，在时任福建省福州市市委书记习近平的推动下，塔科马与福州市成为姐妹城市。关于塔科马和福州建立友好关系还有这么一个小插曲：当年普吉湾大学的一位老师，前历史学教授苏珊娜开会走错房间，无意中听到塔科马市政官员正在讨论应该要和中国哪座城市建立友好关系，这位老师随口说了一句，如果是她的话，这个城市就一定是福州。没想到时隔不久，这位老师的无心之语竟成了事实。

福州市与塔科马市于1994年11月16日结成友好城市，两市结好以来主要在经济、教育、体育、研修生等领域开展多种形式的交流与合作。1996年和1997年两市间互派人员交流学习，也曾多次互派团组访问，就经贸投资、人才及文化交流等领域进行商谈。1998年塔科马市在福州举办《塔科马今昔》图片展，2000年塔科马市48人代表团来福州参加海交会暨国际龙舟邀请赛。2001年，福州市派友好代表团参加塔科马市举办的塔科马海事节及龙舟比赛。2006年，福州市文化代表团到塔科马市参加国际音乐节等交流活动。2011年，福州市援建的塔科马市中国协和园的"福州亭"还获得了美国国际友城联合会颁发的2011年艺术文化创新奖，"福州亭"三字由陈奋武先生题写。

在两个友好城市的互相交流蓬勃发展的同时，位于塔科马市的普吉湾大学和位于福州的华南女院也建立了交流合作关系，两所学校的结缘是在程氏家族（Trimble family）的大力推动下建立起来的。程氏家族四代人和福建有着深厚的百年情缘，程氏家族的第一代程吕底亚（Lydia Trimble）是华南女子文理学院的第一任外国人院长，家族的第三代程闽岱（Robert Trimble）更是出生在宁德古田，他的父亲在1927年回到美国后一直在普吉湾大学任校医。程闽岱也毕业于普吉湾大学，所以他对普吉湾大学有着深厚的感情，在这样的契机下，程氏家族积极推动了两所院校的

春色
任天涯
——福建华南女子
职业学院外教侧记
International Faculty with
Fujian Hua Nan Women's
College since 1908

464

程氏家族（Trimble Family）、华南女
院前任院长林本椿和普吉湾大学部分
教师在福州亭

塔科马市协和公园里的石雕描述
华人被赶走的景象

交流合作。普吉湾大学是一所私立的本科大学，注重培养学生的思考能力，鼓励学生自己讨论，用教育展现自我。而在1985年复办的福建华南女子职业学院是一所以培养高素质技能型人才为目标的三年制高职高专院校。由于两所学校的学制存在差异，两校间的交流合作要以哪种方式开始呢？华南女院有着很好的国际化背景，每年都有多名外籍教师来院任教，何不从选派外籍教师开始呢？

1996年11月福建华南女子职业学院正式与普吉湾大学签订英语教师专案协议计划书。按此协议计划，普吉湾大学定期选派一名女性毕业生至华南女院担任英语教师，每隔一年选派一名，工作任期为10个月（日后或许改为一年一任）。因两校校际关系的建立有其历史渊源，此协议计划不仅符合女子学院的教育方针，亦为普吉湾之中国研究课程的发展服务。普吉湾大学每次派任的英语教师均经过校方资格审查及严格选拔后产生，并得到华南女院认可。英语教师的教学工作及职务由华南女院分配决定，普吉湾大学负责教师往返美国与福州的旅程费用，并承担工作期间之健康保险。华南女院负责教师工作期间之吃住设施，提供洗衣服务及一般医疗需要，并协助办理教师入境与回国所需之文件及其他种种事宜。此协议一旦正式签订，将永久生效。若需终止或修改内容，必须获得两校有关单位主管双方同意后，才生效。

<u>普及湾华南英语教师专案</u>

中华人民共和国福建省福州市华南女子学院

与

美国华盛顿州塔可玛市私立普及湾大学

协议计划书

按此协议计划，普及湾大学定期选派一名女性毕业生至华南女子学院担任英语教师的职位。目前每隔一年选派一名，工作任期为十个月（日后或许改为一年一任）。普华两校校际关系的建立有其历史渊源；此一协议计划非但符合华南女子学院的教育方针，亦为普及湾大学之中国研究课程增拓发展。

1. 普及湾大学每次派任之英语教师均经过校方资格审查及严格选拔后产生，并将得到华南女子学院及有关政府单位之认可。

2. 英语教师之教学工作及职务由华南女子学院分配决定。

3. 普及湾大学将负责教师美国福州来回之旅程及费用并负担工作期间之健康保险。

4. 华南女子学院将负责安排教师工作期间之吃住设施，提供洗衣服务，一般医疗需要，并协助办理教师入境与回国所需之文件及其他种种。

5. 此协议计划一旦正式签订，将永久生效。若需终止或修改内容，必须获得两校有关单位主管双方同意后，才生效。

普及湾大学
校长

Susan R Piene

日期 16 October 1996

华南女子学院
副校长

陈钟英

日期 1996年11月5日

普及湾大学
教务长兼副校长

David B Potts

日期 16 October 1996

华南女子学院
副校长

陈琼林

日期 1996年11月5日

两校的协议计划书

　　普吉湾大学在选择合适的英语教师上是非常严格和谨慎的。由于华南女院是女校，所以普吉湾大学要求申请人必须是年轻女性毕业生，并且该名女性毕业生需要提供在普吉湾大学学习的成绩单和至少两封的教授推荐信。此外，个人的陈述也是必需的，在500～600字的陈述中，要说明申请人对华南女院教书岗位的兴趣，以及能胜任该教学岗位的能力。还要提及申请人的学术能力和个人准备，列举充分接触任何中国文化、语言、时事等的经历，尤其是要列出在普吉湾学习相关课程的证明。在申请人提交申请后由相关的委员会面试，最后选出合适的人选。此项遴选合适教师的工作在派遣老师的当年三月份左右结束，之后普吉湾大学的相关负责人和华南女院外事处的老师进行沟通和联络，做好派遣老师来华任教的相关签证事宜。

　　由于申请条件之一是要对中国感兴趣并且接触过跟中国相关的文化，因此所有

春色
任天涯
——福建华南女子
职业学院外教侧记
International Faculty with
Fujian Hua Nan Women's
College since 1908

466

派遣到华南女院的女毕业生们都曾经在学校上过不同程度的中国语言课程，并且她们中的大部分人都有在中国短期进修中文的经历。普吉湾大学选出当年符合条件的老师之后，还会安排老师在到达福州之前在北京参加TEFL培训。TEFL培训的英语全称是Teaching English as a Foreign Language，意为"作为外语的英语教学"，通常指在非英语国家教授非英语母语学生学习英语，目前国内的TEFL证书培训由中国国家外国专家局负责开展。TEFL或者TESOL证书是外国人到中国任教之前，若教学工作经验不满两年必须要提供的证书。不管网络还是实地授课，在全世界范围内要拿到TEFL证书不难。而普吉湾大学却愿意送学生千里迢迢来到北京接受培训，他们的重视程度可见一斑。在培训过程中，派遣来的老师们不仅可以了解即将面对的中国学生会是什么样，还会详细了解外国人如何在中国生活和工作，这对于远离家乡和亲朋好友的年轻人来说无疑起到了很大的帮助，使她们能尽快调整自己适应当地的工作、生活、饮食等各方面的问题。随着中国经济的迅猛发展，国门的打开吸引了越来越多的外国人来中国淘金。基于此，国家外专局对于外教的资历要求也水涨船高。除了要有TEFL证书之外，两年的相关教学经验也成了必要条件之一。普吉湾大学能很好地与华南女院进行沟通，及时调整申请条件，选择并派遣符合条件的申请人到福州。

两校签署协议之时，提出每隔两年选派一名年轻女教师，待他日时机成熟，或许改成一年一任。普吉湾大学派遣年轻女毕业生来华南女院任教，相关的费用由程氏家族专项奖学金全额支持，近些年来在程闽岱和他儿子程戈登（Gordon Trimble）的大力推动下，项目进行得比想象中顺畅得多。譬如，普吉湾大学会告知所有派遣来的学生，若是她们第二年还乐意继续留在华南女院任教，依然会得到程氏家族的全力支持。此外，程戈登不止一次跟普吉湾大学提过，若是有合适的人选，不需要每两年一人，一年一人，甚至一年两人也是没问题的！正是由于程氏家族的慷慨支持，自2010年起，普吉湾来华南女院任教的老师就再也没有中断过。

早些年，以志愿者身份来华南女院任教的外教偏多，因而从年龄上说都相对偏大。而普吉湾选送的都是刚刚毕业的女性，来华南女院当年都才二十二三岁左右。她们年轻漂亮，善良大方，受过良好教育，懂事礼貌。由于年纪相仿，总是很快和学生们打成一片，她们亮丽的身影构成了校园里一道独特风景。截至目前，普吉湾大学一共派遣了13名年轻女性教师到华南女院任教，让我们姑且把她们称作普吉特海湾的十三朵金花吧！

早在正式签署协议之前，普吉湾就派遣了第一名女教师，名字叫凯瑟琳·李·肖沃尔特（Catherine Lee Showalter），她的任期是从1994年8月到1995年8月。她长得挺高大的，经常俯下身子听学生说话，给刚接触外教的学生们很新奇的体验。一头卷卷的头发，很有热情但又略带一丝羞涩。学生们最初对于中美文化差异的认识始于这位给她们上英语读写课的朝气蓬勃的年轻老师。她印发《喜福会》的故事给学生读，之后让学生观看录像，通过阅读和观影，学生对于中美文化有了比较直观的了解。她还带领学生们阅读《罗宾汉》的故事，观看电影。课余她鼓励学生进行英文创意写作，主编了英文杂志*Sunshine Girl*，学生们对英语写作的兴趣就从那时候培养起来了。

　　在两校签署协议的当年，普吉湾送来了第二名教师珍妮弗·安·帕特森（Jennifer Ann Patterson），她的任期从1996年8月到1997年6月。1998年，梅根·莫利（Megan Morley）成为第一位在一年任期结束之后继续留任的老师，在2000年8月结束华南女院的两年教学之后，转至其他学院继续工作。接下来的两任老师分别是卡丽·安·理查森（Carrie Ann Richardson）和泰勒·艾丽森·布鲁诺（Tyler Alison Bruno），她们

程氏家族拜访华南女院，了解凯瑟琳在华南女院教书的情况

程闽岱和夫人与华南外事处徐道锋处长和负责校友
工作的刘贞琼老师亲切交谈

春色
任天涯
——福建华南女子
职业学院外教侧记
International Faculty with
Fujian Hua Nan Women's
College since 1908

468

的任期都只有一年。

2004年，第六任教师玛丽安·麦克劳德（Marian Mcleod）在华南女院任教满两年，紧接着2005年，普吉湾大学派来了丽莎·娄（Lisa Long）任教一年。从2005年到2006年间，是第一次也是到目前为止的唯一一次，有两名普吉湾老师同时在华南女院工作。在2004年到2006年间，华南年轻外教的人数非常多，除了玛丽安和丽莎之外，还有丽莎的姐姐麦洁高·娄（Mikiko Long）、建华基金会派来的香农（Shannon）、友好院校美国森坦纳瑞学院派来的杰西卡（Jessica）、两位年轻日本老师等，同龄人的相处，使得这些跨越重洋远离亲朋好友的年轻教师在心灵上多了一份慰藉。

丽莎·娄和部分外教在莆田湄洲湾

程氏家族三代人在华南女院前任副院长陈琼琳和前外事处处长
徐道锋陪同下和泰勒·布鲁诺参观华南女院在师大的旧校区

麦洁高、玛丽安和杰西卡参加
福建省政府组织的国庆招待会

　　下面这篇文章是第六任教师玛丽安写的，并刊登在普吉湾大学亚洲学习项目的
2005年春季新闻上：

　　当我寒假回到美国的时候，人们不停地问我中国怎么样。我明白大家都很好奇，
中国对于大多数美国人来说很陌生，但是印入我脑海的就是最简单的回答：中国
很好。

　　中国确实很好，尤其对于外国人来说那就更好了。在中国，我们外国人有当明
星的感觉。在福州，好多当地人都从来没见过外国人，所以在街上偶尔遇见外国人
对于他们来说简直是件大事，他们不停地瞪着我，低声叫我老外。虽然有时候我也
想尽力地融入，但这些已经成了我在这里生活的一部分；我的中国同事们，他们不
一样的面孔和眼睛，还有头发的颜色给我们打开了一扇扇的门。当我们在仓山的旧
街道上闲逛的时候，从院子里瞄进去，总有些正在扫地或是洗盘子的妇女把我们上
下打量，问我们是不是愿意进去参观。这里人们都很大方，这类小故事也常常发生，
这些使得我在中国的生活变得容易一些。

　　我和华南女院其他外教共同住在一栋楼里，所以这里就像一个小小的联合国，
或者说是个袖珍的美国。尤其是过感恩节和圣诞节的时候，我陶醉在熟悉的语言和
环境里，但对于这个小小联合国我又感到一些遗憾。我相信如果不是和一些说英文
的人待在一块儿的话，我的中文应该要好很多。因为楼里还住着两位日本老师，倒
是我的日语长进了不少。幸运的是，在福州出去逛逛是很容易的事，尤其是搭公交
车，只要一块钱，你就可以游遍整座城市。

　　在福州我过得很开心，我对道路也越来越熟悉，都可以给别人指路了，甚至还
会被本地人指错路。对于下个学期，我还是很期待开始我在华南女院的第二年工作，
希望到那时候我的回答不会再只是个简单的"中国很好"。

春色
任天涯
——福建华南女子
职业学院外教侧记
International Faculty with
Fujian Hua Nan Women's
College since 1908

470

　　丽莎·娄作为派到华南女院教书的第七任老师，和华南女院一直有着密切的联系，她于2008年、2011年先后两次带领普吉湾大学的学生来华南女院作短期访问。来华南女院教书是她人生中一次很适时的机会，在普吉湾大学念书的时候她就了解到学校有一个程氏家族资助来华南女院教书的机会，她希望自己在毕业时候可以申请这个项目。丽莎的专业是亚洲学习，在本科阶段曾专门学习过中文，在中国也学习过一段时间。但很遗憾的是，当她念完教育硕士的时候，申请普吉湾大学这个项目的时间不太合适，所以她决定独立申请。后来当丽莎发现可以独立申请的时候，她又鼓励也是大学刚毕业的姐姐跟她一起申请来华南女院教书。当时在华南女院教书的玛丽安也是丽莎的好朋友，当玛丽安告诉丽莎她决定第二年继续待在华南女院教书的时候，丽莎更高兴了，迫不及待地想立刻来到福州。对于丽莎来说，决定去华南女院任教，而不是去中国的其他学校教书的一个重要原因是在普吉湾念大学的时候，她多次获得程氏家族的奖学金。要做些什么才能回赠他们家族的慷慨呢？来华南女院教书应该是个很好的方式来表达丽莎对程氏家族的感激吧？

玛丽安和其他外教学习中国剪纸

丽莎正在学习中国剪纸

麦洁高是丽莎的姐姐，丽莎说服她一同和她来华南女院教书。姐妹俩从小就一起探险，有着许多共同的经历，她们俩能一起来中国教书看起来就非常合适。麦洁高是科罗拉多州立大学毕业的，一直对文化和语言很感兴趣。虽然她学习的是西班牙语，并且她的海外学习经历主要在中美洲，但她还是非常激动地决定跟丽莎一起来福州待上一年时间。

丽莎和姐姐麦洁高

麦洁高、玛丽安和日本老师Yoko

丽莎来到华南女院的时候，她刚刚拿到教育硕士，所以她觉得自己已经准备得很充分了，这大概是所有过分自信的老师都会有的想法。丽莎很快意识到不管接受过多少培训，受过多高的教育，只有通过教学实践才会真正知道如何教书。她的学生们都非常兴奋也非常愿意学习英文，但问题是大部分学生们都非常害羞。丽莎最大的挑战就是如何鼓励她们开口大声说话，她尝试着在上课内容里融入各种活动，比如学生感兴趣的话题，并且分享各自的经历。此外她在课堂上还努力培养学生分析和进行批判性思维的能力，虽然这和她上的英语听说课没有特别直接的联系，虽然这些加大了她的工作量，但她还是很愿意适时调整上课内容，使得学生对于人生能够思考得更深刻一些。

2006年普吉湾选送了第八名老师伊娃·谭（Eva Tam），并在2008年派来了兰·阮（Lan Nguyen），兰是一名美籍越南裔老师，同时也是华南女院在烟台山旧校区接待的最后一名普吉湾的老师。

玛乔丽·凯瑟琳·洛德威克（Marjorie Katherine Lodwick）是第十任教师，同时也是华南女院搬迁到大学城后接待的第一名普吉湾老师，大家都喜欢称她玛吉（Marjie）。玛吉是个充满活力的金发姑娘，勤劳踏实、肯干友善，几乎所有美好的

春色
任天涯
——福建华南女子
职业学院外教侧记
International Faculty with
Fujian Hua Nan Women's
College since 1908

472

伊娃（左一）和部分外教游玩
福州西湖公园

兰向普吉湾大学和华南女院院长做介绍

形容词用来形容她都不为过，所以她给大家的印象是不像一个真正的美国姑娘。玛吉的活力四射在课堂上得到了很好的体现，她上课充满了激情，因为担心学生听不懂就用手比画，还不小心用力过猛碰裂了墙壁。为了让学生们体验西方节日，在复活节来临之前她特意让远在美国的父母寄来颜料用于制作复活节彩蛋。等同学们画好彩蛋之后，玛吉把彩蛋藏在专家楼门口的草坪上让她们体验找蛋的乐趣。在华南女院教书期间，她还牵头成立了一个英语学习俱乐部，自愿在课余和周末时间，组织校内或是校外活动，帮助英语口语较弱的学生锻炼口语，同时坚持陪伴外教黄丽霞（Laihar Wong）组织每周五晚上的英语角活动。由于她开朗活泼的性格，很容易和其他中国同事打成一片。玛吉在大学修的是生物，所以对于自然界的动植物颇有心得。在和中国同事外出活动中，玛吉随便摘朵花，捉只昆虫，都能玩出乐趣来，给旅途增添了不少欢乐。玛吉顺理成章地继续留任一年，在2012年8月结束华南女院的教学任务之后，玛吉参加了和平护卫队。和平护卫队是一个由美国联邦政府管理的美国志愿者组织，组织使命包括三个目标：提供技术支持，帮助美国境外的人了解美国文化，帮助美国人了解其他国家的文化。一般来说，志愿者的工作大多跟社会和经济发展相关。和平护卫队的志愿者必须是美国公民，一般要具有大学本科学历。在接受几个月的培训之后，他们在美国境外需要至少服务两年。程戈登也参加过和平护卫队，他被派遣去了菲律宾，在那里遇上了他后来的太太程索妮娅（Sonia Trimble）。玛吉在华南女院的第二年就开始准备和平护卫队的申请工作，由于深深喜欢上了古老的东方文化，她希望去亚洲，不管哪个国家。虽然玛吉很愿意留在中国，但由于中国经济迅猛发展，在这方面并不需要美国的支援。后来玛吉被分派到了印度尼西亚，在东爪哇一个很偏远的村庄里，她依然在学校里教授英文。印尼的条件比中国艰苦太多，去最近的一个村庄都要翻山越岭，骑上个把小时的车。但玛吉乐观向上的生活态度，依然使得她苦中作乐。2015年7月，玛吉结束了3年在印尼的服务工作，准备返回美国，但她依然记挂着曾经生活过的福州和她认识的好朋友们。在回美国之前，她回到福州重游故地拜访老友，这让中国老师、学生还有她的朋友真是高兴坏了。她也非常激动地看到她教过的学生们成长起来，并实现了她们的梦想。在离开福州之后，玛吉坐高铁北上前往青岛，短暂停留后从青岛去美国的阿拉斯加。目前玛吉在距离华盛顿特区15英里的乞萨皮克和俄亥俄运河国家森林公园里工作，当公园讲解员，向游客们介绍公园的历史和自然风光。

玛吉和她的学生们

　　伊丽莎白·安·惠特克（Elizabeth Ann Whitaker）也是一位金发姑娘，高高的个子，笑容甚是可爱，性格有些腼腆，总是很虚心地向中国同事和其他外教请教，积极参与学生们的各种社团活动。协助外教黄丽霞组织的每周五晚的英语角活动，从始至终没有落下过。伊丽莎白来自俄勒冈，在普吉湾大学主修的是经济和中文。她对于中文的兴趣，源自高中时代参加的扶轮国际年轻人海外交流项目。伊丽莎白也跟她的上任玛吉一样继续留任一年，任教两年结束后，伊丽莎白回到美国继续工作。Liz之后的肯尼迪（Kennedy Holt）只任教一年，于2015年7月返回美国继续上研究生

春色
任天涯
——福建华南女子
职业学院外教侧记
International Faculty with
Fujian Hua Nan Women's
College since 1908

474

院。目前在我院任教的是第十三任老师，名叫奎西·利文斯顿（Quincy Livingston）。奎西在普吉湾大学主修中文，辅修生物。同样是位金发姑娘，她的祖父出生在福州，10岁才回到美国。奎西从小就被祖父家里各种中国艺术品和宝物深深吸引着。由于这段特殊的家族渊源，奎西产生了来福州教书的兴趣。奎西善解人意，适应能力强，她在福州感受教书带来的成就感的同时，也享受着福州这座平静安宁的城市中的平淡生活。

伊丽莎白·安·惠特克
在专家楼内

奎西在学院专家楼的圣诞晚会上

　　试想一个才20岁刚出头的女生，离开家人和祖国，跋山涉水来到完全陌生的一个环境里一待就是一年甚至是两年，需要对于东方文化有多少的热爱？需要有多少的勇气？需要有多少的自信心和责任心才可以使她在30位比自己小不了几岁的学生面前不胆怯地上课？所以我们非常理解为什么有些老师待完一年就迫不及待返回家人身边，我们也更加感激那些愿意留下来再待一年的老师们。学院对于普吉湾来的女生，上至领导，下到学生，总是给予更多的关心和照顾。学院领导看到普吉湾大学的老师去学生街上的大排档吃凉面，总会善意地提醒她们注意食物的卫生。系里的老师总会及时地跟普吉湾大学的老师沟通，带她们在校园内外走走，告诉她们将要面对的学生会是怎样的。其他有经验的外教也总是很热情地提供建议和经验，帮助年轻女生尽快地适应不同的文化差异。外事处的年轻老师和普吉湾大学的女生们年龄相仿，在上班时间之外经常和她们聊天或者出去散步，以减轻年轻女生的思乡之苦。学生们也总是很热情，邀请老师们到自己的家乡做客，逢年过节总是会带来家乡的特产跟老师一起分享。还有给外教做饭的阿姨，对于普吉湾大学的年轻女生们，总是照顾有加，总是细心留意女生们的口味。有的女老师喜欢吃茄子，阿姨就会在这个女老师来外教餐厅吃饭的时候多准备些红烧茄子。还有女老师因为怕骨头，连烤鸡腿也不肯吃的，阿姨总是会像慈母般地劝说女老师学着把骨头剔掉。为了让这些年轻女孩子能更快适应环境，外事处的老师特意把专家楼最好的房间之一留给普吉湾大学来的姑娘们。由于老师在离任前会留下一些教学资料或者其他的用品，所以每任新来的老师一进入房间，房间的布置、家具的摆放，总能让她们感受到来自同胞们的浓浓暖意。

普吉湾大学和华南女院的情缘由于程氏家族的大力推动，延续了近20年，这短短的20年承载了多少情深意切的中美友谊？在浩瀚的历史长河中写下了浓重的一笔。13朵金花，20年的中美友谊，虽然当初的老师和当初的学生已各奔天涯，但我们完全有理由相信当初的短暂师生缘分必定在她们各自的人生历程中留下深深的烙印。正如两校协议中的一句话：此协议一旦正式签订，将永久生效，普吉湾大学的年轻女教师和华南女院学生的情谊也必将一直延续下去！

普吉湾大学与华南女院的交流其实远远不仅限于派遣老师这一项，华南女院在2008年、2011年先后两次接待了普吉湾大学亚洲学习项目近30人的师生。亚洲学习项目的全称是The Pacific Rim/Asia Study-Travel Program，简称PRAST Program。每隔三年，普吉湾大学差不多就有30名学生有9个月完整的时间环游亚洲，进行学术和个人的研究探寻。他们要拜访8个亚洲国家，在这过程中，他们会体验到多国文化，面临文化、经济、政治、宗教和哲学等多领域的挑战。学生们在参加这项亚洲旅行学习项目之前，必须在学校里修完亚洲学习的相关课程。学生们在亚洲的那年，可以第一手接触到不同国家的文化，这些亚洲国家包括韩国、尼泊尔、越南、日本、印度、中国和其他由任课的教授所挑选的地点。学生们的中国一站，除会在北京、上海等大城市短暂停留之外，能让他们停留最长一站的，却不是那些大城市，而是福州。2008年11月感恩节前夕，二十几名学生千里迢迢从蒙古国赶到福州，和华南女院的师生共度感恩节。由于是第一次招待这么多的客人，外事处的老师和外教们非常重视，早早安排了住宿，细心到床品的布置和床垫的厚度都要符合美国人的需求。此外为了款待远道而来的贵宾，共同欢庆美国人最重要的节日之一——感恩节，在外教贝茨（Betts）的指导下，在客人来前一个月的时间里，烤火鸡要用的材料陆陆续续寄到了福州，大家着手烤起了火鸡。由于需要大概十几只的火鸡，当时麦德龙所有的火鸡都被华南女院买下来，这还不够，还得远赴厦门购回火鸡。外事处的烤箱不够用，食品营养专业借来的烤箱也派上了大用场。美国感恩节的食物除烤火

春色
任天涯
——福建华南女子
职业学院外教侧记
International Faculty with
Fujian Hua Nan Women's
College since 1908

476

鸡之外，南瓜派也是必不可少的，贝茨和外事处的老师特意去当时福州最好的五星级酒店香格里拉订了一些南瓜派。一切准备就绪，大家满心期待着这20多名年轻人的到来。2008年的感恩节，在华南女院旧校区的世静堂里，大家欢聚一堂，中外友人，你说我笑，心怀感激，共庆佳节。在饱餐了一顿正宗的感恩节大餐的同时，这些年轻的孩子们和大家开始分享了他们的感恩之情。有学生们说感谢一路上有这么多同学的互相照顾和帮忙；有人说感谢奥巴马当上了总统；有人说感谢普吉湾大学提供了这么好的一个旅行学习的机会；有人说感谢华南女院让他们有了回家的感觉；有人说感谢在异国他乡可以品尝到火鸡以及从来没有吃过的南瓜派，说完全场大笑。因为香格里拉做的南瓜派和美国传统的南瓜派完全是不一样的！

普吉湾学生在整个学习项目中，有几位老师带队。一位是项目负责人伊丽莎白·伯纳德（Elisabeth Benard）老师，还有一位随行校医，以及项目联络人、我们的老朋友丽莎，即上文提到的第七任普吉湾老师。他们前后在华南女院待了三周左右，不仅参观了福州当地的著名景点鼓山等，还请了林本椿教授、外教多琳·约翰斯顿（Doreen Johnston）作为嘉宾演讲，为他们介绍中国历史和文化。他们在福州期间需要完成一门课程的学习，为了上好这门课，华南女院给他们安排了专门的教室，授课老师是普吉湾大学派来的教授，同时也是当时亚洲项目的负责人田立凯（Karl Fields）博士，他所教授的课程主要跟亚洲政治相关。为了让学生能实地体验，在这次的福建之行中，普吉湾大学的学生参观了闽西古田会议遗址，古田会议是中国工农红军划时代的里程碑，田立凯教授的实地讲课给学生们上了生动的一课。学生们在参观古田会议遗址后，顺道去了永定土楼参观，中国古代精湛的建筑工艺给学生留下了深刻的印象，学生们纷纷竖起大拇指赞叹中国人建筑水平真棒！

担心这些年轻人在异国他乡人生地不熟，语言不通，华南女院特意从英语专业挑选了英语口语好的学生们，跟他们一对一结成对子。学生们带他们去学校餐厅吃饭，搜寻本地美食。花一元钱坐上福州的公交，走街串巷，融入当地生活。还有热情好客的华南女院学生把他们的搭档带回家做客，让这帮学生感受到中国人民的热情和好客。当年，普吉湾大学的校长雷诺·托马斯（Ronald Thomas）还特意从美国赶来见他的学生们。在2008年11月下旬到12月中旬之间，校园里，旧师大的学生街上，仓山老洋房建筑前，留下了许许多多年轻人的身影。

3年之后，也就是2011年，同样也是感恩节前夕，又一批普吉湾大学学生从越南千里迢迢来到福州。这一次，学生们特意选择在感恩节前两日到达，自己动手，准备一场丰盛的感恩节大餐。一些同学负责采购，一些同学做南瓜派，一些同学布

两校院长共庆姐妹校友谊

置餐厅，剩下的烤火鸡，或是做其他食物。感恩节前的那个夜晚，华南女院新校区的专家楼厨房里，彻夜灯火通明，学生们纷纷在制作的感恩卡上写下了感激的话语。这一次随访的依然是我们的老朋友，伊丽莎白·伯纳德教授和丽莎。此外，伊丽莎白·伯纳德教授的先生尼玛（Nima）也第一次来到了福州。这次福建之行，普吉湾大学的学生们要学习的课程是亚洲的宗教，教授的名字叫作黛博拉（Deborah），理学是她的研究领域之一。这一次他们去了武夷山，拜访理学大师朱熹生活过的五夫里。五夫里地处武夷山市东南部，朱熹曾在这里学习拜师长达40余年之久，也是朱子理学的形成地。学生们拜访朱子巷、紫阳楼，感受大师在那里生活的一点一滴。武夷山之行，部分学生还去看了印象大红袍，学生们评价说这是他们这辈子看过的最棒的演出！这次学生来访，华南女院依然为他们安排了一对一的对子，使得学生们能更好更快适应当地生活。华南女院的学生还特意为他们举行了联欢晚会，共庆中美友谊。在程氏家族的大力推动下，普吉湾大学和华南女院共同举办了东西方论坛，主题是"一个改变世界的词"。会上，中美学生互相交流探讨，体现了中美两国人民间的友好情谊。在福州行程结束之后，学生们前往香港，在香港他们会有短暂的假期，有的学生回到美国和家人小聚，有的学生待在香港，有的学生选择继续去亚洲国家如柬埔寨等探寻神秘的东方文化。临行前，学生们依依不舍，留恋福州人民的热情好客。普吉湾大学随行的老师告诉华南女院外事处的老师，一路下来，福州还有华南女院，是唯一一个让学生们感受到家的温暖的地方。非常可惜的是，由于项目课程设置的调整，普吉湾大学暂时取消了福建之行。但程氏家族依然在积极地协调和沟通，我们相信，或许在不久的将来，在条件许可的情况下，我们的校园里又会多些年轻的身影。

春色
任天涯
——福建华南女子
职业学院外教侧记
International Faculty with
Fujian Hua Nan Women's
College since 1908

478

　　不经意的一句话，福州和塔科马结成了友好城市；扯不断的情缘，程氏家族又将华南女院和普吉湾大学紧紧联系在了一起。我们在骄傲地看着华南女院学生拥有年轻外教的那份自豪感之外，也在深深感谢在背后为推动中美友谊努力过的人们，两所学校院长的相互理解、为推动派遣学生和亚洲学习项目沟通交流的两校老师的辛勤工作，当然，请大家别忘记了，从遥远太平洋过来，陪我们的学生度过求学生涯中难忘一刻的普吉特海湾的十三朵金花！

普吉湾大学的学生在武夷山下梅村

普吉湾大学的学生在武夷山
天游峰

两校学生联欢

普吉湾大学的学生游览三坊七巷

普吉湾大学的师生在厦门

第三节　玛丽安·戴维斯教授与她的"家政"情结

玛丽安·戴维斯教授，美国加州大学服装设计硕士，俄亥俄州立大学家政学博士，美国佛罗里达州立大学人类科学学院纺织品与消费者科学系教授，国际家政教育项目协调员。华南女院复办之初，戴维斯教授便来华开展调研，她对华南女院开设的食品营养、儿童教育、服装设计等家政学相关专业表现了极大的关注。自1987年起，她连续数年每年一次访问华南女院，为服装专业的学生开设学术讲座，为家政学研究开展问卷调查，查阅华南女院历史资料，访谈学院师生。1991年在美国《家政学期刊》发表了第一篇她对华南女院的研究论文：*Home Economics Heritage and Promise in China: A College Reborn*（《家政学在中国的传承与希望：一所学院的重生》）。她从家政学发展的视角出发，对华南女院的办学历史进行了深入了解，从早期华南女子文理学院办学者重视家政教育、引进美国家政教师设立家政学课程，并先后于1916年、1929年选送年轻教师到加拿大、美国攻读家政学硕士学位，到1932年正式成立家政专业，再到1951年全中国院校调整后家政学项目的取消，分析了家政学存在的现实意义及"美国式""贵族化"家政教育与新中国劳动人民需求的冲突，认为家政专业的取消是由于当时的中国政府对家政教育提升人民"生活福祉"基本功能的认识还不全面。家政学与每个人的生活息息相关，中国作为一个人口占世界五分之一的大国，其产生的影响是具有国际性的。

1985年，福建华南女子职业学院复办，在原华南女子文理学院家政专业的基础上，衍生出3个独立专业，即食品营养科学、儿童教育与咨询、服装设计工程专业。玛丽安·戴维斯教授来华南女院期间对这3个专业的招生、课程设置、教学方法、毕业生就业方向等方面展开了细致的调查。她首先认为这些专业的开设预示"家政学在中国复苏的希望"，但她又认为，家政教育在中国中断近35年，这些新生的专业普遍对家政学缺乏认同性，各自为政，专业知识多侧重于工商业时代的生产，以及在商业、经济领域的应用，远离了以人为中心的"家庭生活"。她一再强调，侧重人类生活品质提升的整合型的家政学科有其存在的必要。她向华南女院的领导们建议成立专门的家政学专业，得到了一致赞同。

玛丽安·戴维斯教授看到华南女院兼职的教师较多，认为作为全国第一个开设

春色
任天涯
——福建华南女子
职业学院外教侧记
International Faculty with
Fujian Hua Nan Women's
College since 1908

480

家政学项目的私立女子学院，最需要解决的是师资问题，她积极牵线华南女院和美国佛罗里达州立大学人类科学学院（前身为家政学院），1987年陪同余宝笙院长考察了佛罗里达州立大学。华南女院在玛丽安·戴维斯教授的帮助下，于1989年获准加入国际家政联盟，是全国第一所加入世界家政组织的中国院校，通过国际化的交流活动，华南女院的教师更好地了解了世界。

1990年华南女院与美国佛罗里达州立大学签订了首个合作备忘录，先期选派三名毕业留校的年轻助教和一名访问学者赴美国佛罗里达州立大学人类科学学院进修硕士学位和开展学术访问。

1995年9月，玛丽安·戴维斯再次来华南女院开展研究工作，并为我院师生作了3场关于服装设计的讲座。1996年7月，美国佛罗里达州立大学人类科学学院院长罗尔斯顿博士和玛丽安·戴维斯到我院访问。双方初步商定继续接收该院五位青年教师到该校学习，合作创办现代家政专业等事项。

华南女院先后共选派8位年轻助教赴美进修，分别获得食品营养、儿童教育、纺织与服装等专业的硕士学位。多位老师留学期间都选修了玛丽安·戴维斯教授开设的国际家政学课程，对她们各自专业领域与家政学的关系的认识有了很大的提升，为回国后的教学和科研奠定了基础。

两所院校合作期间，佛罗里达州立大学给予华南女院极大的援助。佛大人类科学学院先后捐赠华南女院各类专业书籍数百册。玛丽安·戴维斯教授还召集她们学院各系的教授成立了导师团队，为华南女院相关专业的建设和年轻师资的培养提供指导。作为服装纺织专业的教授，玛丽安·戴维斯还将她的学生制作的服装设计挂图及她自己制作的教具、幻灯片等捐赠给华南女院服装专业用于教学。华南女院留美助教及访问学者在美期间无论学习上还是生活上都得到戴维斯教授热情无私的帮助，她每年都向各基金会申请经费，使年轻老师有机会参加美国家政学会的学术活动。

经过10余年的努力，2002年华南女院终于被获准成立家政学专业。戴维斯教授获知此消息无比欣慰，在经历手术身体欠佳的状况下，仍积极帮助家政专业进行课程开发，通过各种渠道收集了大量的课程资料作为家政专业课程设置的参考，指导家政专业的教师将课程本土化，使其能符合中国的国情。她还拿出自己的经费，资助家政专业建设实验室。

玛丽安·戴维斯教授对家政学的执着感染了华南女院新老一代教育者，她为高等家政教育在中国的发展做出了突出的贡献。虽然家政教育在中国还处于起步阶段，但越来越多的学者已经加入了它的研究队伍，家政学的面纱在一层层揭开，它的魅力在逐渐展现，我们相信家政教育的前景是光明的。

第四节　芬兰黑美丽
——小记福建华南女子职业学院老朋友黑美丽

黑美丽其实并不"黑"，但却很"美丽"。"黑"来源于她的姓氏Köhler，意为手拿煤炭的人。"美丽"则源于她的名字 Elisabet的中文翻译伊丽莎白，而"美"源于中国女性名字的常见字。黑美丽，全名是Elisabet Rantschukoff，芬兰籍，1988年12月8日应联合国发展署的邀请，以志愿者身份来福建华南女子职业学院担任外籍教师，1989年学期结束后于6月7日回芬兰。1989年8月27日再次回到华南女院任教，1990年6月27日离开福州返回芬兰。当年黑美丽给学生们留下的印象是这样的：她喜欢各种各样的中国元素，尤其喜欢穿中国旗袍。黑美丽的学生回忆当年她们毕业前

1988年黑美丽参与世静楼和柯信谋夫人纪念楼的
破土动工仪式

黑美丽穿旗袍和其他外教一起表演

春色
任天涯
——福建华南女子
职业学院外教侧记
International Faculty with
Fujian Hua Nan Women's
College since 1908

482

夕准备拍集体照时，黑美丽故作神秘地提前跟学生们说到时要给她们一个惊喜。到照相那天，黑美丽以一身中国旗袍亮相，这让学生们眼前一亮，这身旗袍穿在年轻漂亮的外国女老师身上确实是一道曼妙的风景。黑美丽说她要把旗袍带回国珍藏纪念，直到多年之后黑美丽再次回到学校任教，华南女院的同事们还是能感受到她对旗袍的喜爱。凡是隆重正式的场合，必定以旗袍亮相。

黑美丽来华南女院教书前，在瑞典的移动设备通讯商爱立信公司工作了7年，主要负责培训咨询，同时负责公司的秘书培训项目。她觉得自己应该要做点别的事情，比如回到她的家乡芬兰。同时她一直对中国很感兴趣，总觉得自己将来会有一天探访这个东方古国，但暂时不知道该怎样实现这个梦想。黑美丽在1987年9月回到了芬兰，开始为芬兰的瑞典人民党工作。1988年夏天，芬兰当地最大的报纸刊登了一条来自联合国的广告，他们在寻找一位能来华南女院教授秘书实务课程的老师。命运就是如此神奇，黑美丽开始申请这个联合国发展署在中国的项目。当时联合国需要招聘两个岗位，一个在北京，一个在福州。那时候中国对外开放刚起步不久，需要针对准备进入合资企业尤其是鞋厂工作的人员进行培训。黑美丽经过了漫长而又烦琐的申请流程，包括书面申请、一整天的心理测试等。这一整套的申请都是通过芬兰外交部完成的，最后芬兰外交部推选她为这个项目的候选人。虽然黑美丽没有工商管理硕士学位，母语也不是英语，但是中国人选择了她！黑美丽是当时芬兰第一个也是唯一一个由联合国派到中国的志愿者，联合国发展署除了这个项目以外，

黑美丽和实用英语专业老师在班级

黑美丽和学生在课堂上开展活动

还在其他国家开展一些项目。黑美丽被选中之后，在芬兰外交部参加了两个星期的学习准备。1988年11月底，她被派去联合国在日内瓦的总部会见一些官员，探讨项目的具体问题，并且了解联合国发展署在中国的运作情况。1988年12月她来到北京，待了一周左右时间，之后来到华南女院教书。

20世纪90年代初，黑美丽来任教时候才30多岁，比起她的学生们其实年长不了多少。她总是跟学生"套近乎"，常常在午饭时间跑到食堂跟同学们一起吃饭，无形中学生的英语口语表达能力大大提高了，也同时跟她亲近了许多。虽然黑美丽的母语是瑞典语，但还是经常帮助学生练习英语口语。她常带着学生们去西湖公园溜达，或是去当时赫赫有名的东街口的上海西餐厅就餐，学生们也就趁此机会带本词典与她进行交流。黑美丽的专业背景是高级文秘，所以她来华南教书的主要课程是秘书实务。在20世纪90年代初，秘书实务对于中国学生们来说可是一门新课程，既要会外语，还要能操作办公自动化设备，在那个年代是要学会用打字机打字，此外还要掌握秘书工作的理论和技能。学生们在课堂上第一次接触到这么些理念和知识，感到特别新鲜，在后来的工作中，她们不止一次回忆起这门课程以及教授这门课程的老师。同时，黑美丽也为她的学生们感到自豪。她记忆最深刻的是当三年级学生参加毕业实习前，所有同学都已经靠自己努力找到了能提供一个月实习机会的单位。在学生毕业实习期间，她骑着自行车走遍了福州，去拜访她的每一个学生，并看看她们是否需要帮助。黑美丽受过专门的秘书实务训练，因此她对于学生们的行为时时提点，在课堂上让学生意识到什么是尊重。中国学生喜欢在课间趁老师不在场时偷看老师讲台上点名册的分数，有一次被她撞见了，大发雷霆之后她告诉学生们这是个人的隐私，应该学会尊重他人。同学们第一次被她的怒气吓坏了，但从此同学们多了一份"教养"。

在阔别中国这么多年的岁月里，黑美丽跟中国女性一样，工作、结婚、生子，虽然无数次想回到华南女院，但照顾家庭和工作的辛劳，使她实在无暇考虑其他。1996年开始，黑美丽换了工作，开始担任芬兰瑞典理工学院（2006年起改名为诺维尔大学）国际部主任。在此期间，她主要负责学院和欧亚学校间的联系。黑美丽想起是否可以利用她在福州的老朋友尝试建立一些合作关系的可能性，于是她联系了在福州的老朋友、福建省教育厅对外交流合作处的石茵，看看是否有这样的可能性。随后黑美丽在1997年拜访了华南女院，探讨中芬两校合作的可能性。在那之后，她先后共6次来到福州，每次来福州必定拜访华南女院。其中一次是2006年，她和芬兰学校的校长参加了福建师范大学的百年校庆。在2006年，诺维尔和华南女院签署了

春色
任天涯
——福建华南女子
职业学院外教侧记
International Faculty with
Fujian Hua Nan Women's
College since 1908

484

合作交流协议，但很遗憾的是并没
有进行学生和老师间的互换。但在
她的努力下，诺维尔大学和福建师
范大学、福州大学、福建中医学院
和福建医科大学也建立了友好合作
关系。黑美丽每次来福州，一定都
不会忘记拜访许道锋，还有一些她
的好朋友，比如石茵和陈纯甦，另
外还有一些她的学生们，后来这些
女生都成了她的好朋友。

黑美丽在福建省教育厅对外交流合作处石茵和
福建医科大学陈纯甦的陪同下拜访华南女院

以下是福建省教育厅对外交流合作处石茵老师对黑美丽的回忆：

本人与黑美丽女士结识于1989年夏天，当时省政府外事办组织在榕外籍教师赴
莆田参加第一届龙眼节活动，自那时起我们一直保持联系。1997—2005年，黑美丽
女士担任芬兰瑞典理工学院（现更名为"诺维尔大学"）国际部主任及信息部主任，
由黑美丽女士牵线联系，我省的福州大学、福建师范大学、福建医科大学、福建中
医学院及福建华南女子职业学院与芬兰瑞典理工学院、瑞典韦克舍大学（现更名为
"林耐奥斯大学"）建立交流合作关系。1998年5月，由时任省教育委员会副主任的陈
孔德先生率团赴芬兰、瑞典、丹麦，访问团成员有时任福建师范大学校长曾民勇先
生、时任福州大学党委副书记叶辉玲女士、时任福建医科大学校长陈丽英女士、时
任福建中医学院（现更名为"福建中医药大学"）院长杜建先生、时任福建中医药
大学国际交流处处长李灿东先生、时任福建省教育委员会外事处主任科员石茵女士。
代表团访问了芬兰瑞典理工学院、瑞典韦克舍大学、丹麦H:S护理学学校，双方就福
建省属大学与芬兰瑞典理工学院、瑞典韦克舍大学、丹麦H:S护理学校在教师交流、
学生交流等方面的合作交流进行了探讨。同年10月，芬兰瑞典理工学院由校长温格
伦先生率团访问了福建师范大学、福州大学、福建医科大学及福建中医学院，中芬
双方签订了合作协议。自1998年福建省教育代表团开启北欧先锋之旅以来，福建师
范大学、福州大学、福建医科大学、福建中医学院与芬兰瑞典理工学院、瑞典韦克
舍大学、丹麦H:S护理学校建立了校际交流关系，双方互派教师、学生的交流合作项
目进展顺利。

2005年、2006年黑美丽在阔别华南女院多年之后，利用机会故地重游，拜访老朋友。直到2013年，黑美丽给当时她的学生，华南女院前任院长张迅捷写信，表达了想回华南女院教书一个学期的愿望。由于黑美丽在芬兰工作非常忙碌，她对于来华南女院教书的想法整整酝酿并且准备了一年。黑美丽在芬兰的欧洲议会为尼尔斯·托瓦兹工作，尼尔斯·托瓦兹是一名活跃的共产主义者及电台记者，曾当选芬兰共产党中央委员会委员。托瓦兹家族属于在芬兰占6%的少数民族芬兰瑞典人。顺带提一下尼尔斯·托瓦兹有个比父亲名气还大的儿子林纳斯·本纳第克特·托瓦兹，他是全球最流行的电脑操作系统之一LINUX内核的发明者和该计划的合作者之一。

2014年8月27日黑美丽再次回到华南女院，回到了阔别将近20年的学校。这次重返校园，黑美丽打算教书一学期。由于她的工作背景和秘书实务有关系，所以外语外贸系把她安排在了应用英语专业。黑美丽很享受重回校园和学生一起相处的时光。此外，她也有更多的机会能和她之前的学生见面，老朋友聚会等等，不亦乐乎。黑美丽这么描述两次教学上的一些不同：1988年，学生用的是老式的英文打字机，办公文秘类的中英文书籍都没有。黑美丽必须自己准备所有的材料，把上课内容、练习和平时小测都打印出来，再誊印给学生们。那时候没有复印机、影碟机、电脑等。当她询问她所教的213名学生中有多少人去参观过办公室的时候，只有不到10人回答去过，而且有些人回答她们去过的可是邮局。那时候大部分学生都没有接触过外教，所以适应黑美丽还需要一段时间。对了，当时用的是黑板和粉笔。在五六月间，天气炎热而且潮湿，黑美丽在黑板上书写时候，感觉粉笔都要在指尖融化了。而到了2014年，教学条件得到了大大的改善。电脑和平板电脑广泛使用，课本也都

黑美丽重返华南女院拜访老朋友

黑美丽重返华南女院校园

春色
任天涯
——福建华南女子
职业学院外教侧记
International Faculty with
Fujian Hua Nan Women's
College since 1908

486

紧跟时代潮流，包含了上课内容、练习等。每个学生见到外国人和外教都习以为常，只不过有些学生还是挺害羞的。学生们对于小组任务和课堂介绍也更乐于接受。此外，教室都开始用白板了，这样上课容易了很多，除非不小心拿错了永久的记号笔。

但令大家当然包括她自己完全没有想到的意外发生了。2014年国庆放假期间，黑美丽感到身体不适，先是住进了省人民医院，后又改住到省立医院，外事处和英语专业的老师学生们轮流去医院照看她。她的挚友，在教育厅工作的石茵老师，还有福建医科大学的陈纯甦老师也几乎天天陪伴在她身旁，时任华南女院院长的张迅捷作为她的学生，也多次在医院陪伴她。但非常遗憾的是，黑美丽有哮喘病，这导致肺炎，她的家人、医生和老板都担心她不适应异国他乡的生活，加上她也不愿意麻烦中国朋友们，最终她不得已做了一个决定——离开中国。于是，黑美丽带着极大的遗憾于2014年10月27日再次离开了福州。这次离开后，等待下次的回来，又不知道要多少年了。

黑美丽在回国之后调养了一段时间，但还念念不忘她在华南女院生病期间帮助过她的同事们。2014年年底，她写信给华南女院，表示捐赠5000元人民币，自2015年起连续5年用来奖励一名优秀的应用英语专业老师。

2014年黑美丽参观烟台山校区的专家楼

2014年黑美丽在烟台山校区的世静堂门口

2014年黑美丽回到当年她住在专家楼的406房间

第五节　　心中有梦，缘定中国
——记玛莎·苏·托德

玛莎·苏·托德的中国缘

1988.8—1992.7　东南大学教学

1992.8—1995.6　福建华南女子职业学院教学　1994.9　获颁"福建省优秀外国
　　　　　　　　专家"奖

1995.8—1997.8　福建医科大学教学

1997.8—2000.7　闽江学院教学

2000.8—2001.6　福建华南女子职业学院教学

2004.6.13—7.2　福建华南女子职业学院访问

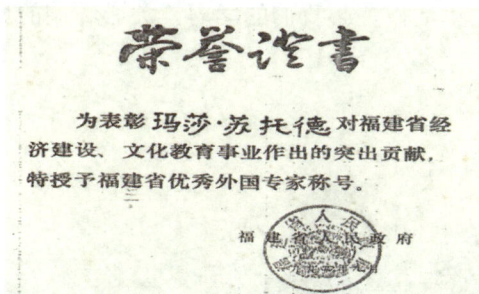

1994年9月获颁福建省优秀外国专家奖

玛莎·苏·托德

年少立志，梦牵中国

　　玛莎·苏·托德，生于1920年，是一个非常虔诚的基督徒。受教会影响，她在年少时就怀揣着到中国服务的梦想，年轻时候因为二战爆发未能实现。

　　命运安排她遇到了相敬如宾的人生伴侣，携手走过幸福的41年婚姻生活，成为一个儿子的母亲，一个孙子和一个孙女的祖母。丈夫离世后三周，苏的亲家母被诊断患上绝症，为了让儿媳从家务中解脱出来陪伴她的母亲走完人生的最后一段路，苏承担起照顾儿子及孙子、孙女生活起居的任务。14个月后，儿媳的母亲病逝，儿媳重新掌家，苏开始思考并寻找能让自己继续发挥作用的机会。彼时，苏一直藏在

春色
任天涯
——福建华南女子
职业学院外教侧记
International Faculty with
Fujian Hua Nan Women's
College since 1908

488

心里想要前往中国的梦想重新得到释放。苏从来都觉得来中国是她的宿命。她认为她前半生所做的很多事情都是在为前往中国做准备。亲家母的葬礼过后不久，苏得到消息，有机构组织志愿者去中国担任英语老师。苏没有犹豫，满怀激动、快乐和热情，当即提交申请，因各方面条件符合，她顺利通过审核。前往中国的梦想终于要实现。1988年8月，在亲人的送别下，68岁的苏登上了飞往中国的飞机。

梦想实现，结缘华南

爱德基金会成立于1985年4月，总部设于南京，旨在促进我国的教育、社会福利、医疗卫生、社区发展与环境保护、灾害管理等各项社会公益事业。基金会的成立对几乎同时初建的华南女院来说真是一大福音，诚如雪中送炭的天使。基金会每年无偿派来美籍英语老师支持华南女院的英语教学，少时一人，多时两人或三人。爱德基金会作为美国浸信会的对接机构，安排苏服务中国的第一站是在南京的东南大学。1993年，苏被派往福建，从此与华南女院结缘。

苏走进我的大学生活是在她来到中国的第6年。那一年她73岁高龄。虽然年过70，却不见一点老态。课堂上的她给我们留下的印象是充满激情的、温和随意的。课堂外她就像是我们的祖母，关心我们的生活，关心我们的学习，关心我们的烦恼。

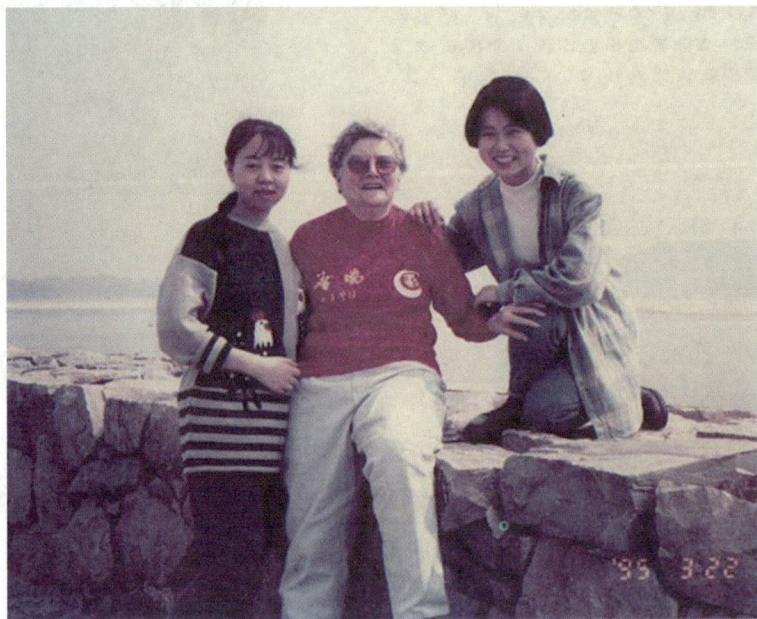

苏与学生们在一起

满满爱心，永生难忘

苏是一个充满爱心的老师。每逢学期第一节课，她总是按学号给每一个新学生拍一张近照，之后将洗出的照片贴在一本小册子里，边上记录着学生的姓名、学号和生日。

每逢学生生日，她一定会在课上带领全班同学唱起生日快乐歌，为寿星送上生日贺卡，表示祝福。每次探亲回来，苏一定会带回许多小礼物。学期初上课时她总是会给学生们分赠礼物。闲暇时，她时常自购食材带着学生们到外专楼厨房教她们制作美味的糕饼。她还常常分组带学生们去校外的麦当劳、肯德基或中餐馆，请学生们品尝美味的西式快餐或者中国菜。

"苏真心关爱着学生，很为学生着想。学生若因病或其他事情缺席，她一定会关心询问，甚至会让大家写信宽慰她们。当学生重新回到课堂，总能感受到苏热情的欢迎与温暖的问候。"（林丽华，1995）

聚会踏青（1995年）

特色教学，激发创造力

苏的课堂气氛轻松，上她的课鲜有沉闷的时候，她常适时带学生做做操，唱唱歌，玩玩小游戏。印象最深刻的是一次特色教学，在教室上课上到一半，苏竟带着全班同学离开教室，手上提着一台磁带录放机，按下录音键，大家一起走出校园，走下烟台山，经过解放桥头，沿着观海路、梅坞路，来到仓山电影院，穿过烟台山公园，回到学校，回到教室。大家坐下之后，苏开始播放录音，让学生们闭眼聆听

春色
任天涯
——福建华南女子
职业学院外教侧记
International Faculty with
Fujian Hua Nan Women's
College since 1908

490

苏与学生在教室里

各种录下来的声音，并回忆自己刚刚走过的路，之后要求大家用英文记录下听到的声音，想象的画面，描写出自己的体会与感受，写完之后与同学进行口头的分享和交流。与现实融合的教学，让我们感到既有趣，又有收获。

苏的自由谈话课组织形式灵活、十分贴近生活。为了给学生们创造良好的英语学习环境，让学生们在生活体验中对英语进行实践运用，她的课堂无处不在，有时在外专楼的厨房，有时在菜市场，有时在公园里，有时在录像室，有时在麦当劳，有时还在她的客厅。学生们常常在不知不觉中感知着、运用着英语。在她的推动影响下，说英语成为自然而然的事情。再害羞的同学经历过这一次又一次的现实场景训练之后，脱口而出流利的英语已然再也不是问题了。毫无疑问，苏对学生的英语语言训练是很成功的。

苏给学生们上英语写作课，她强调创造性写作。在课上，她给一个主题，然后

来自92C 班充满感恩之情的生日派对

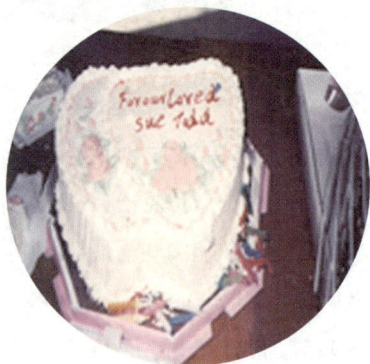

学生为苏准备的生日蛋糕

总是先启发学生，运用头脑风暴的方法广开言路，引导学生积极讨论，等大家的思路打开，讨论愈发热烈时，及时收住，要求学生各自静心整理思绪并开始写作。这样的方法，不但激发了学生思考、讨论的热情，也使学生们能够相互学习，互相促进。她在课上让我们写诗、写歌、写故事。我们的毕业任务则是写自传，对大多数学生来说，第一篇记录人生的英文自传就这样在苏的悉心指导下完成。她让学生对照美国的圣诞歌《圣诞十二天》，将其中的礼物替换成具有中国传统文化特色的名词，改写出中式的《圣诞十二天》。

写信是苏的另一个教学法宝。苏会找各种理由让学生写信。圣诞节，写给圣诞老人。开学时，写给学妹或学姐。新年到来，写给新年。她还发动她在美国的亲人和朋友与学生通信，在她的自传中展示的信件有写给她儿子的，写给她媳妇的，还有写给她孙儿的。

"在我们的国际商务英语课上，苏要求我们为不同的产品设计不同的包装或为未来的公司设计商标。她还要求我们为销售的产品设计广告、制作海报。之后在教室里开办海报展。从她的课上，我们不仅学到了很多，实践技能也得到了很大的提高。"（林丽华，1995）

苏认为想要学好英语，训练聆听带着不同地方口音的英语尤其重要。因此她总是尽可能多地给学生创造更多接触不同外国人锻炼听力与口语的机会。她常常邀请她的外教同事、她在福州认识的外国朋友、来探望她的各类亲友进入课堂，与学生们分享各种资讯。2001 年 5 月，苏的孙子和他的朋友来到福州探访时，苏就邀请他们来到课堂跟学生们说说美国年轻人的生活。

苏主持学生婚礼

春色
任天涯
——福建华南女子
职业学院外教侧记
International Faculty with
Fujian Hua Nan Women's
College since 1908

492

行善助人，播撒爱的种子

苏待人极其和善，把每一个人视同家人，只要有需要，她定尽力帮助。得到过她帮助的人真是数不胜数。在福州那些年，苏每年都去看望盲校的学生，并捐款4,500元为3个孩子缴纳一年的全额学费。她还定期带着礼物去探望学校附近的孤儿，给孩子们带去无限的快乐。为了帮人，苏几乎都要用光津贴，所以她常常需要动用以往的积蓄来贴补生活。常有毕业离校的学生邀请苏参加她们的婚礼，苏从未拒绝。不仅如此，她有时还应邀为学生主持西式婚礼。

学生离开苏的课堂之后仍然长期与她保持联系，成为永远的朋友。郑媚芳（May）就是一个最好的例子。她与苏一直保持密切的联系，甚至飞往美国去看望她。以下附郑媚芳文稿：

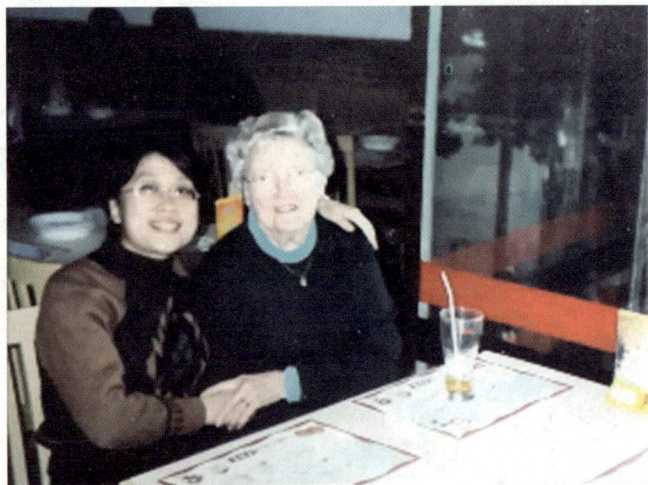

苏和郑媚芳共进午餐（1998年）

玛莎·苏·托德——不仅仅教会了我英语

玛莎·苏·托德——一个我永远也不会忘记的姓名。她是我在福建华南女子职业学院读书时三年级的老师。然而在我的心中，她早已不仅仅是老师了。毕业以后，我们一直保持联系至今。也就是说，我们已有20多年的友情了。

直到今天我还能常常记起她与众不同的授课方式。除正常的课堂教学之外，她会选择在公园、麦当劳（她买单）、外教厨房（厨艺课）等地方给我们授课。我总是觉得她的课非常有趣。她的音调和发音也很容易让我们接受，有助于我们掌握日常英语。记得有一次去她在教育学院的公寓时遇到了美国来的一位老师，她问我为

苏和郑媚芳，在苏美国北卡的家中

什么我的英语带着美国南部口音。苏替我回答了她："因为她的英语老师来自美国南部。"之后，苏告诉我她是多么为我自豪！

自从我们毕业，苏就被调到另外一个学校去了。虽然如此，我们还是每周见一次面。我们聊天，相互倾听。

她常来我家拜访并和我们一起共进午餐。她和我的家人关系很好。

她结束工作回国以后，曾经于2004年再次来到中国。那一次，她告诉我她老了，要我可能的话去美国看她。于是，我于2009年2月去美国探望了她。我们过得很开心。

我有一个女儿，她叫埃丝特（Esther）。苏以她祖母的名字为她命名。她告诉我，这个名字代表着闪烁的星星的意思。作为一个母亲，我总是疑惑该如何教好我的女儿。我和苏常常通过邮件探讨这个问题。苏给我提了一些建议。下面是她写给我的一封邮件：

亲爱的May，

帮助埃丝特的一个办法是按照你希望她如何表现的样子来表现自己。小孩子的不良行为都源于大人。你温和地和她讲话，她也会温和地和你讲话。我相信你已经这么做了。父母采用良好的行为举止处事，她也会学着她看到的大人的样子做的。

她的坏习惯可能受到托儿所里其他孩子不好的行为的影响。你们大人做好想让她学习的榜样，她就会养成良好的习惯了。

让她知道当你说"不"的时候就是代表绝对的不可以。小孩子总是要学会什么行为是可以接受的，什么行为是不可接受的。她们的年龄不足以让她们明白这些。因此大人必须要在生活中以家长认可的言行举止来行事从而教导孩子什么样的行为是对的。

春色
任天涯
——福建华南女子
职业学院外教侧记
International Faculty with
Fujian Hua Nan Women's
College since 1908

494

　　我知道你跟你妈妈一样爱着她，你们两个能够帮助她的。我觉得你一定会的。既要严格又要亲切。你能办到的。

　　希望这些建议能够帮到你。

　　爱你和你的家人

苏奶奶

　　上个月她刚度过她的95岁生日。我祝愿她长寿。目前正在安排旅程，准备再次探望她。

　　我只有一句话可以用来描述她，那就是：她不仅仅教会了我英语。

郑媚芳于福州

言传身教，激励众人

　　正如郑媚芳所言，苏不仅是一名耐心的英语教师，她更是一名引领人生方向的生命导师。就像她在邮件里教导家长该如何教好孩子一样，她在教会学生英语的同时，还用行动和言语时刻激励着学生积极、健康地学习、生活和工作。她说过的很多话，意味深长，至今影响着众人。

　　当学生遇到困难，想要放弃的时候，苏总是鼓励大家："任何事情只有不愿意，没有不可能。"很多学生在她的激励下，坚持到底并实现了梦想。

　　1994年苏因为在华南女院的工作表现突出，被评为"福建省优秀外籍专家"。苏低调，鲜见她提及此事。

　　苏说帮助别人，让别人快乐，自己也会很快乐。她不仅自己帮助别人，她还组织学生一起去帮助别人，让学生体验助人的快乐，比如她捐款给希望工程，比如她义务到附近小学教英语，比如她去探望孤儿等等。 当她看到学生们也开始自觉去助人的时候她总是特别特别开心和自豪。

　　郑先生，因为在公交上让座与苏相识，应邀到苏的课上分享纽约移民的奋斗经历与生活点滴。他的人生因为认识了苏和苏的一个优秀学生而变得不同。当年那个优秀的学生今天已经成为他三个小子的妈妈了。他说："苏让我觉得，或者说是学到了家庭的重要性，对社会的贡献，学习是为了更好地生活，等等，这些让我受益匪浅。我甚至也会学她在退休后去教书。"

　　"虽然一个人的年龄会老去，但内心却应该一直保持年轻。"当年75岁高龄的苏用她自己的行动告诉我们年龄不是停止奋斗，停止追求梦想的理由，任何时候都应

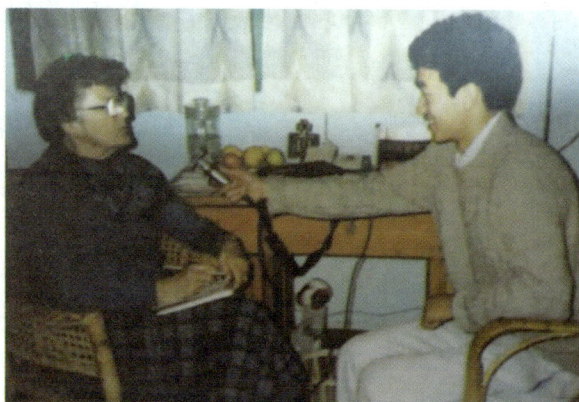

苏接受林海春采访

该保有一颗年轻的心，生命不止，奋斗不息，只有这样，生命的价值才能得到无限的延展。

苏曾经就话题"到了三十岁"接受记者林海春的采访，她的讲话引人深思：

"到了三十岁，大多数人都已经完成了学业，他们已准备开始工作，为自己设计了目标，一年年地追求那些目标并把目标同工作联系起来；

到了三十岁，大多数人已经从父母亲处独立出来，自己支持自己、开发自己，树立个人目标并努力完成；

到了三十岁，我相信大多数人开始认识到服务于某个团体或者国家的责任的重大；

2004年苏重返华南女院

春色
任天涯
——福建华南女子
职业学院外教侧记
International Faculty with
Fujian Hua Nan Women's
College since 1908

496

到了三十岁，很多人都有责任去照顾他们的父母亲，因为父母亲们已经年迈不能照料他们自己，所以在情感上、体力上，以及经济上要得到帮助；

到了三十岁，我相信很多人开始更多地思考她们未来的目标和需要，他们已经建立了自己的家庭，但不一定是每个人，她们同时开始考虑教育子女，制定一些计划为了孩子更好地成长。

我认为三十岁是人生中一个美好的里程碑，因为到这时已经完成了很多事情，你为了自己的目标抓紧了许多年。如果你不是二十九岁，也不能是三十一岁时，那么三十岁是最好的年龄！"

——摘自林海春《与话筒相伴》

在中国的大学服务于英语教学13年后，苏已年过80岁，上级机构不再允许她继续工作。 2001年6月，她不得不与她称作第二祖国的中国挥手说再见。2004年6月她想办法回到华南女院重温往日生活，享受了短短的两周与各方友人、学生重聚的快乐。那次以后，苏返回美国，与家人共享天伦之乐。

在这里引用苏2007年出版的自传《攀登长城，再老也不晚》中尾记里的一段话：

"我儿时要到中国服务的梦想终于成为完整的现实了。一个遗憾——没能再长些。我仍思念着自行车的铃声、街头的喧闹声、教堂里充满活力的歌声、学校课间吵闹的孩子们、轰鸣的公交在拥挤的街头躲避行人和骑行者的景象，以及一大早因佛教徒邻居离世而大声播放的悲凉的音乐声。想得最多的，还是好奇学生的到访……"

苏想要在中国待得再久一些，想为中国多做一些奉献。 她想念中国。

作为结尾，我愿与大家分享苏在课上强调过的一句话："一个女人的人生只有完成了结婚、生子、养育儿女的过程后才能算是完整的。"在我看来，苏的人生是完整的，但这并不仅仅是因为她结了婚，拥有很好的事业，拥有温暖的完美家庭，更重要的是她在68岁的时候，在她履行了她的家庭责任之后，她还能够设法追求并实现她的少年梦想。因此我想说的是，苏的人生不仅完整而且是精彩的、辉煌的。作为一个乐观的、积极的、友善的、善解人意的、谦虚的、具有坚强意志的女人，苏是所有女性的好榜样。玛莎·苏·托德，对她的故事发掘越多，我对她越发地崇拜。愿她在她的第一家乡美国安康祥和！

第六节　唯有爱，永不败
——忆念恩师丽莎

印象丽莎：桃李满天下，何用再种花

丽莎老师来自美国，在新西兰长大。她家有三姐妹，她是家中的老大。1994年9月至1995年6月，她担任福建华南女子职业学院实用英语专业94级A班的三门英语课程。94级A班共28人，如今，A班同学们回想起丽莎老师，大家都感慨万分。

在厦门太古机场工作的黄胜同学满怀激情地倾述了她对丽莎老师的思念之情：

2015年过去了，这一年比往年更加想念丽莎，因为2015年中国非常流行连衣裤，而我是在美丽的华南女院外教——丽莎身上与连衣裤第一次邂逅的，相信我的同学们也是如此不断地从连衣裤上看到丽莎的身影。

正如我所说的，丽莎是我到了华南女院后的第一位外教，所以她带给我的冲击力也是最大的。

她的年轻、她的金发碧眼是我第一眼的惊奇，我惊奇这样美丽年轻的妙龄女子竟愿意把她的青春岁月留在中国。但是接下来的日子里，我的惊奇还在继续，并且转变成敬佩：我见识了她的智慧、她的温柔……她从没有对我们大声斥责或是拍案而起，但她却是我这辈子见过最严厉的老师。她的课一开始，就开门见山地对我们明说，课堂上不允许见到中英文字典。如果她见到我们在课上使用字典，我们就会见到字典飞出窗外。于是，战战兢兢地，我在华南女院开始了我一生中最认真的学习生涯……也是我收获最多的学习生涯。

虽然丽莎只教了我们1年，但我们在华南女院的3年里，她一直关心我们，她的门总是对我们开放。及至如今，在时空的限制下我们不易相见，但我相信她仍是一如既往地关心着我们。丽莎一直是我们最美丽的老师、朋友、姐姐！

如今已是两个孩子妈的沈超尘同学是这样描述丽莎老师的：

丽莎·雷文希尔是我的第一位外籍教师，她给我留下了很深的印象。她非常优

春色
任天涯
——福建华南女子
职业学院外教侧记
International Faculty with
Fujian Hua Nan Women's
College since 1908

498

雅，金发碧眼，就像好莱坞电影里的一个角色。不像我见过的其他美国人，她完全是一位女士。你永远看不到她生气的样子或者大声狂笑的模样。她不仅教会我们知识，还非常关心学生。我记得有一次，我身体感到非常难受，无法集中精力学习。丽莎小心翼翼地问我，并给我建议。当时我真的很感激她。

她的课很有吸引力，尤其是自由谈话课。在课上，她教我们如何制作饼干并且一起分享。我们也做复活节彩蛋，并祝福我们的室友。在她的课上，带给我们很多的乐趣。这些美丽的记忆真的很值得我们去珍惜生活!

现担任福州创新英语培训学校校长及福州奥兰多贸易有限公司经理的程晓霞同学回忆道：

提起丽莎，我就会不由自主地想起美丽，敬业，专业，善解人意……

我把"美丽"放在第一位，那是因为她给我的第一印象就是如此。那是阳光明媚的一天，皮肤白皙的她穿着一袭蓝绿色的连衣裙，披着一头金黄色的头发，脚踩一双休闲的白色的平底单鞋，轻盈而优雅地走进教室。那双碧蓝色的眼睛被衬得更加清澈。她与中国老师是如此不同！我的全部感官立马都被她调动起来：竟然还有这么漂亮的"洋妞"教师！毋庸置疑，她的课我可是听得非常认真的。

丽莎人不仅长得好看，课程内容也精彩纷呈。上丽莎的课是一种独特的享受，伴随着她那清脆优美的美音，我们翱翔在英语的海洋中，领略着国外的风土人情。她时常鼓励我们"世上无难事，只怕有心人。只要你们努力学习，就一定能取得好成绩！"也时常警醒我们，不能放纵自己。在她的课上，我们不仅学到了英语的交流技能，还学会了许许多多基本的礼仪，如会面礼仪、用餐礼仪、交谈礼仪、商务礼仪等，她讲得形象生动，令我茅塞顿开。这些基本的常识让我受益匪浅，在日后的工作生活里能畅通无阻地与老外沟通。

在福州格致中学担任英语教师的王晓雁同学分享了她的感受：

丽莎·雷文希尔女士是我一生中的第一个外籍教师。在大学一年级的时候，她教我听力和口语，阅读和写作。她也是我人生中最重要的一个外国老师，她给我打开了一扇门，让我看到了一个全新的世界。在我看来，她是一个和蔼可亲、很负责任的老师，她的授课非常丰富和有趣。虽然我毕业了20多年，我仍然可以记得丽莎老师所教授的内容，仍然记得她带给我的快乐。那是一个非常美好的记忆。

在这里，我衷心地感谢丽莎·雷文希尔女士，就像我所敬重的导师、亲爱的姐姐一样，她一直在鼓励着我，引导着我。我将永远爱她，记住她。

远嫁美国的林娇同学细述道：

在所有的大学老师当中，丽莎绝对是我最喜欢的一位。此生所收到的祝福中，丽莎的祝福，一直是我生命中最有意义的祝福。对我来说，她是最有影响力的恩师。作为一位好老师，她不仅就就业业地准备最合适的教学方案，富有创意地传授专业知识，也激励着她的学生去思考更深层次的生活，并热忱地寻找真理。她用行动证明她所传授的知识是生命的真谛。在我的心里，她的引导让我大学毕业后不懈地寻求神圣和有目标的生活。我相信我能有今天，很大部分原因是受益于她的教导和指引。

总之，她指引我走向一个我前所未知的人生方向。因为她，我的心灵得到全新的改变。她本人可能从未想到她对教学的热爱和她的指导对我和其他同学产生的深远影响。每当我想起我最爱的英文歌《玫瑰花》，丽莎就浮现在我的脑海里。因为是她首次在大学时期介绍给我听的英文歌。她确确实实在我的心里是一朵最美丽的玫瑰花。

郑艳同学，曾供职于雀巢（中国）、厦门翔业集团（原航空港集团），近年来行走东南亚，致力于柬埔寨、中国台湾等自由行线路的跨国合作，道出了她压抑20多年的秘密：

我记得大学一年级那会儿，我贪玩，结果旷课，丽莎挺不高兴的。她主动找我谈话，很严肃，开始我很抗拒，渐渐地我听进去了。很奇怪，当时我很信赖她，我也把自己过去的经历和盘托出，她理解了，但最终还是给了我一顿批评，也给了我关于人生的建议。她说，人的性格是无法改变的，但是，我们可以改变处理事情的方法。当时的金玉良言我受用至今。

我还记得圣诞节的时候，我们在班级门上贴纵向的Merry Christmas，丽莎进来看半天不理解是什么意思，我才知道英文字母不能纵向写。

说真的，挺想念她的。有一次在曼谷机场看到一个特别像丽莎的人，差一点冲过去，仔细看看原来不是。

春色
任天涯
——福建华南女子
职业学院外教侧记
International Faculty with
Fujian Hua Nan Women's
College since 1908

500

时光荏苒，往事历历在目。如今已成就自己事业的纪玉美同学现任厦门蕴利进出口贸易有限公司销售经理，她将对丽莎的感恩之情娓娓道来：

丽莎·雷文希尔，我此生中碰到的第一个外籍教师，一个从遥远的大洋彼岸漂过来的美丽的年轻女子。她带着上帝的爱来到了我们的身边，不求报酬，不怕辛劳。

不知道我们是丽莎教过的第几届学生，但是，她是我这辈子一定不会忘记的老师之一。尽管离开学校已经快20年了，尽管这些年忙碌于恋爱结婚、生子创业，偶尔闲暇时光，回忆起三年在华南女院的日子，丽莎总是很轻易地走进我的脑海。她教我们听说和读写，每周要给我们上很多堂课，记忆中的她总是满面笑容，很多时候更像是我们的姐姐，而不是老师。

我是农村出来的，在去福州上学之前，平时都是满口的闽南语，普通话都讲不标准，我们中学学的英文基本就是"纸上谈兵"，从来没有真正开口说过一句，因此我的英文发音也非常不准确。记得很多次课堂上丽莎都是很耐心地纠正我的发音，一遍又一遍地在我面前读给我听，直到我念准确了她才微笑着走向下一位同学。正是在她的鼓励和影响之下，我才敢于开口说英语，并对它产生了浓厚的兴趣。毕业以后，我从事外贸工作，时常跟外国人交流。虽然，我知道自己的英语还是脱离不了闽南口音，但毕竟能靠着它找到一份非常不错的工作，并经过多年的努力经营，有了自己的事业，早早实现了所谓的财务自由。因此，我永远感激她。

一晃眼，离校庆时见到丽莎又过了8年多，但是，我知道她还在中国昆明执教，还在继续播种着爱心。每次想到，能有更多的中国学生享受到她的大爱，我就忍不住高兴。我常常认为丽莎简直就是在人间播种爱心的天使，她永远不吝啬付出她心中满满的大爱。她教给我们的东西，很多都是从书本上无法获得的知识。真的非常庆幸自己能遇到这样的外籍老师。

将近20年没有写过什么文章了，感谢能有这次机会让我说出对她的感想，无奈发现自己的文笔和措辞实在粗略，远远无法表达我心中真正的想法，只能借一句话来表达了："我感恩她一辈子！"

当时担任班级团支书的林影同学，眼前呈现出这样的一幅画面：

岁月，是一棵纵横交错的巨树。而生命，是其中飞进飞出的小鸟。又是一个普通的周六，照例去烟台山下的画室，接在那里学画的女儿。车子经过依然耸立在山头上的'华南女子学院'的校牌时，我总是不厌其烦地指给她看，然后喋喋不休地说起那些年的事。说得最多的还是她，我最亲爱的丽莎：第一次课堂提问，是考大家谁记住了她的全名，我抢答了，得到了她大大的赞扬。这是我在名气大、优生如云的中学里从未有过的体验，原来我也可以得到老师如此的肯定；第一次手工制作，是在自由谈话课，丽莎手把手地教我们做动物形状的小饼干，让我感受到原来语言学习并不是背单词记语法，它是世界上人与人沟通心灵的桥梁；第一次参加英语演讲比赛，她把我的稿子改了又改，还一直鼓励我，告诉我演讲是要用最真诚，最朴素自然的情感去表达，才能感染听众，而不需要浮夸的语气和表情；第一次在她温暖充满香气的房间里与她促膝谈心，她说不要把她当成老师，只当是好朋友（现在叫闺密吧），聊我爱慕已久的邻家大哥哥，这真的是第一次，这是包括父母姐妹都不知道的小秘密。然后她鼓励我要勇于追寻自己的梦想，哪怕结果不一定成功。我也终于明白，经历了高考失败陷入人生迷途的我真的打开了心扉，让她住进了我的心里。是她用爱照亮了我前行的路，坚定了我的步伐。我的女儿听我说这些就如同听故事，她挺好奇，会问丽莎漂亮吗。我说："那是当然，她是妈妈见过的这世上最美丽的女子。无论岁月如何变迁，她会一直住在妈妈的心里。"

亲爱的老师，我想骄傲地对您说："毕业以后，我从未忘记您对我的教诲，我很努力，我很好。遥祝您珍重珍重，天涯路远，后会有期……"

俄国教育家乌申斯基曾说："教师的人格对学生的影响是任何教科书，任何道德箴言，任何惩罚和奖励制度都不能代替的一种教育力量。"

不求回报，甘于奉献
走近丽莎：鹤发银丝映日月，丹心热血沃新花。

当时，杨方老师教授我们大学英语课，同时担任我们的班主任，1998年起至今一直在新加坡文中苑学校担任对外汉语教师。她是这样描述丽莎老师的：

我记得丽莎很文雅，口音清脆，她总是面带微笑，对学生解释说明时很耐心。

在外事处工作20多年的董秀萍与我们分享了她的回忆：

一说到丽莎，我们就会想到她非常优雅，教学非常认真，关心爱护学生，与学

春色
任天涯
——福建华南女子
职业学院外教侧记
International Faculty with
Fujian Hua Nan Women's
College since 1908

502

生关系非常融洽。决定来华南女院工作之前，她特意自费专程去台湾学了一年的汉语，就为了日后能够更好地了解学生，与学生进行沟通交流。

原在实用英语专业担任专业主任的何孝智老师高度评价了丽莎老师：

在我的印象中，丽莎的教学是非常有计划的。比如英语自由谈话课，她先从简单的内容着手，比如介绍家庭，介绍朋友，介绍老师等等，然后慢慢地变复杂一些。她是从简单到复杂这样的模式有计划地去安排教学内容的。

另外，她的教学是以学生为主体，采用合作式教学。一种是师生合作。虽然是以学生为主体，但是，老师起到很大的作用。另一种是生生合作，即学生与学生之间的合作。学生中间学习比较好的带一些学习基础比较薄弱的，用生生合作的方式互相带动。这个做得很好。特别是开始的时候，我觉得她用的那些方法非常好，这样很容易带动学生的积极性，避免她们害怕。

对于教学实践，丽莎都是着重于通过老师去调动学生的积极性。不是说你们调动积极性，你们自己讲，而是老师想尽办法去调动学生学习的积极性。这个很好，上课中一般都不会冷场，学生学得非常开心。有时，学生如果不会讲，丽莎就会有一个转弯的地方，这时，老师就起作用了。老师出来给学生扭转一下，安定一下学生害怕的情绪。与此同时，丽莎对学生的要求也很严格。她事先给学生布置讨论的话题，让学生去准备，查找一些资料，阅读一些书籍，要求学生自己要思考，自己做好话题准备，这样学生提前做好准备了，上课时就不会冷场。因此，她的课堂都是非常活跃的，给大家印象很深刻。此外，丽莎很会营造一种轻松愉快的课堂气氛，这样有利于学生克服紧张的心理。学生不会讲的时候，老师慢慢地插进去，好像很懂得学生要讲什么，接着她的话题讲，慢慢地引导学生去思考，由于丽莎耐心的引导，学生上课时都很开心，有说有笑。而且，丽莎上课都是用鼓励的语言，花样也很多。比如自由谈话课，丽莎会带学生到银行去，有时候一起到江心公园，坐在那儿谈，看到公园里有什么就谈论什么，非常自然。学生跟她一个学期，一年以后英语口语都变得很流利，经过三年这样的练习，毕业以后英语都是很流利很棒的。

与丽莎老师共事多年的外籍教师贝茨·里韦特博士（在华南女院服务近20年）回忆道：

　　1992年，我认识丽莎·雷文希尔，她和我一样，都是华南女院的外籍教师。那时共有14名外籍教师。我们完全是志愿来的，在华南女院连续服务了4年。我们不计报酬，自己支付所有的旅行费用。丽莎是个人缘很好的人。她为外籍教师筹办各种派对，如生日、圣诞节、情人节和复活节派对等。领导能力是她日常生活中很自然的一部分。她举止文雅，口齿清晰，脸上满是善良关怀的神情吸引了人们。

　　我不了解"教室里的丽莎"。然而，在当时，外籍教师备课、出考卷、给学生讲义都只能使用打字机打字。当时打字机只有两台，我们都得轮着用。教师图书馆的大部分材料是我们教学的素材。丽莎备课真是费尽心血。在过去，授课教材完全是由外籍教师来决定。对她而言，英语是第二语言。当时也没有任何人具体指导我们。我记得丽莎非常慷慨地与我们一起分享她的教案，以及来年教学所用的授课材料。1992年，华南女院只招收了约650名学生，所以都是小班上课。

　　也许通过联系学生，你会发现丽莎的教学方式：她是如何组织课堂，师生关系如何，她授课是否创新……你可以看看她的教学评价，她的个人档案，她的成绩册。最好的就是学生对她的评价了。我知道那是很久以前的事了，但我仍然和我的一些学生保持联系。她们分别毕业于1994年和1995年。我可以大胆地说，丽莎是一名优秀的老师……一名模范老师……在教室里，她为学生创造了一个积极的学习环境……她总是认真备课……她热衷教学。

　　我想起来了，我记得丽莎还和她的学生一起去购物，去公园放风筝，看龙舟……

良师益友，醇香馥郁

　　在大一与丽莎一起度过的那些日子，天天都是如沐春风，心花怒放，趣味盎然……除了上课时间，丽莎允许我们在课下任何时间都可以去找她，一起吃饭，一起游玩，一起分享……

　　活泼开朗的纪玉美同学晒出了她的画面：

　　丽莎偶尔也是个爱恶作剧的人，大一时候的愚人节，她和另外几位外籍老师突然光临我们宿舍，带来了很多很多的卫生纸，在每间宿舍挂得到处都是。那时候起我才知道，原来外国人可以在这一天'胡作非为'啊！她是一个完全能和学生玩在一起的大姐姐，我们宿舍全体人员周末去江心公园玩，邀请她和另外一个老师一起去，那次她和我们留下了很多珍贵的合影。还有全班同学去十八重溪、麦当劳……她都和我们在一起。如今这些照片都成了我珍贵的回忆。

春色
任天涯
——福建华南女子
职业学院外教侧记
International Faculty with
Fujian Hua Nan Women's
College since 1908

504

丽莎与学生在十八重溪游玩

丽莎与玛丽莎在江心公园

　　丽莎生日的时候，我们全班同学一起去台江麦当劳为她庆祝生日。

　　这就是我们敬爱的丽莎老师，她用人类最崇高的感情——爱，播种春天，播种理想，播种力量。用语言播种，用彩笔耕耘，用汗水浇灌，用心血滋润！

94级A班全体同学为丽莎庆祝生日

学生为丽莎庆祝生日

接下来就让我带着你们，一起走进丽莎老师的课堂，去欣赏一下丽莎老师那堂堂精彩、门门特色的课堂教学艺术与她的人格魅力吧！

著名的哲学家黑格尔曾经说过："教师是学生心中最美的偶像。"教师是学生心中景仰的道德标尺，学生都有"向师"的模仿心理。学高为师，身正为范。

灵魂教学，精益求精
深入丽莎：落红不是无情物，化作春泥更护花。

1994年9月，作为大一新生的我们，对华南女院的外籍教师满心欢喜。当时，丽莎老师是我们三门课程的任课老师："英语听力与口语""英语阅读与写作""英语自由谈话"。丽莎老师教授的每门课程都各有特色，让我们都非常喜欢上她的课。就让我们有代表地聊聊"英语阅读与写作"以及"英语自由谈话"课吧。

英语阅读与写作：把脉人生，扬帆起航

我印象中，当时的大学英语课上，中国老师的阅读教学模式通常为：教师介绍相关的文化背景→学生限时阅读后回答课后问题→教师的难点讲解；写作教学模式：写作要求的解释→写作技巧的介绍→学生写作→学生呈现作业→老师讲评。在丽莎老师的英语阅读与写作课上，她与传统的教学模式不同，她非常注重英语阅读与写作相互思维渗透的教学方法，她认为这种方法对学生英语应用能力的提高有很大的帮助，让学生不再为读不懂文章而担心，并提高了学生对英语阅读和英语写作的兴趣，培养了学生鉴赏英文文章与进行英语写作的能力。

在教授英语阅读中，丽莎老师用了灵活多样的教学方法。其中，她建议我们在阅读过程中应遵循几个原则：

（一）充分阅读

在阅读教学中，丽莎老师建议我们要进入到文章本身，沉浸在作者的语言中，体会文章本身的美感。

（二）阅读文章的内容而不是语言

老师说，在阅读中学习使用语言的方式是重要的，但是阅读的最终目的是为了掌握文章的意思和意义。如果阅读文章却没有掌握其中的意思，那么无论做了多少阅读都是无用的阅读。当时，丽莎老师鼓励我们要反复阅读以掌握文章的意义。

（三）猜测和预测

丽莎老师经常说，在阅读中，利用上下文来确定单词的意思是一个非常好的阅

春色
任天涯
——福建华南女子
职业学院外教侧记
International Faculty with
Fujian Hua Nan Women's
College since 1908

506

读策略，我们可以利用语感做出既符合语法又符合语意的正确猜测。

除了以上的建议，丽莎老师在选好文章给我们阅读的同时，她还寻找与任务相匹配的话题，提出各种问题让我们回答，这种富有想象力和挑战性的任务让我们倍感兴奋，当时，整个课堂都是一片热火朝天的沸腾景象。

丽莎老师教法不仅灵活，她还与时俱进，采用当时最新的适合学生程度的教学方法：流利领先教学法（fluency first approach）。丽莎老师运用的流利领先教学法注重读、写和说的流利性，把流利的阅读放在教学的第一位，在写和说的训练中，流利放在正确之前。

丽莎老师的阅读与写作课，充分体现了这一理念：

（一）选择适合高职学生层次和学生感兴趣的阅读材料

丽莎老师在语言输入上尽量以理想的语言输入为标准，首先是提高语言输入的趣味性，她选用了大量的经典小说和其他通俗读物作为学习材料，而不是选用以语言知识为主线的教科书。这些小说均为丽莎老师精心挑选的上乘之作，如《绿山墙的安妮》（*Anne of Green Gables*）、《死亡诗社》（*Dead Poets Society*）、《宾虚》（*Ben Hur*）、《回到未来》（*Back to the Future*）等。

（二）读写并进的作业模式

每天我们必须独立完成丽莎老师布置的阅读任务，然后自己进行口头和笔头练习；除了阅读任务之外，丽莎老师还要求我们完成相应的写作练习。一种是阅读摘要（Reading Log），即每天对老师布置的阅读部分，自己用两三句话概括出主要事件或情节。另一种是写"双栏日记"（Double-entry Journals），左栏是直接从阅读材料中摘抄自己认为有趣的、重要或感到疑惑的句子；右栏则对左栏的摘抄部分发表自己的看法和见解，通常包括以下四项内容：（1）自己的感受和想法；（2）将文中的事件和自己生活中事件联系起来；（3）对文中疑惑部分发表自己的看法；（4）对其中人物特征做出评价。当时作为学生的我，觉得丽莎老师这种阅读和写作并进的模式可以提高我们阅读的兴趣，激发我们勇于表达的信心，锻炼我们的写作表达能力。

（三）课堂形式多样

丽莎老师的课堂教学主要是以丰富的课堂活动来检查我们的阅读效果，围绕阅读的内容展开以听说能力为主的课堂活动。开展活动的主要形式有：（1）小组活动。分小组讨论阅读材料的重点、难点，同时训练我们的口语和听力。（2）双人角色对话。每两个同学选好两个文中的角色或话题，开展讨论。（3）速度测试（Speed Prediction）。把我们分成小组，老师针对阅读内容提问，同学以组为单位在阅读材料中寻找答案，然后派代表说明。在丽莎老师的课上，特别强调学生的参与，大部分课堂活动都是以学生为主角，如小组活动、个人陈述、小组讨论、角色扮演等活动都要求学生积极参与。丽莎老师在课堂的作用仅是引导。

（四）融入自由写作的教学活动形式

当时丽莎老师要求我们每周写两篇周记，将自己的思想感受自由表达出来，不需要太注意语言的形式，拼写错误、语法错误都允许存在。丽莎老师告诉我们，在写作过程中，要注重的是思想的流利表达，而不是语句的正确与否。我认为丽莎老师这种形式的训练对我们学生语言交流能力的培养，特别对写作能力的提高很有帮助。

（五）借助多媒体技术，使阅读和写作课程更加形象和立体化

当时，丽莎老师给我们播放了《绿山墙的安妮》《死亡诗社》《宾虚》等的录像带，借助多媒体的声音和视频，使文字形式的小说阅读更加形象、生动，帮助我们对文字的理解，从而提高我们的阅读速度和质量。

丽莎老师在处理我们的写作问题时，没有执着于我们在写作中的语法错误，没有一味地纠错，而是对我们所写的内容进行回应。在我们周记的最后，老师总是翔实地写上评语，与我们进行心与心的交流与沟通。我们在周记中，可以畅所欲言，老师总是和我们及时地沟通与交流。

接下来，让我们一起深入感受下丽莎老师所精选的小说中的两部代表佳作吧！

第一部：《绿山墙的安妮》（*Anne of Green Gables*）——健全人格

丽莎老师精选的《绿山墙的安妮》，由加拿大女作家露西·莫德·蒙格玛利所著，该书于1908年出版。故事发生在加拿大的安维利村里，在新斯科舍的孤儿院里，有一个叫作安妮·雪莉的小女孩，她出生不久，父母就相继离世，从此不得不寄人篱下，辗转在不同的家庭和孤儿院中，直到11岁时，她阴差阳错地被绿山墙农舍的马修和玛丽拉兄妹收养。卡斯波特兄妹本想领养一个男孩，以帮助马修干活，可因为经办人的失误，送来的却是小女孩安妮·雪莉。并且，这个小女孩还不是玛丽拉喜欢的类型。对新生活充满了渴望的安妮迅速爱上了绿山墙农舍和它周围的一切，但玛丽拉并不想收养安妮，这让安妮在短短的时间里从满怀欣喜沉入绝望的深渊。尽管如此，安妮并没有放弃对生活的信心，相反，安妮比普通人更快乐，她天真热情，有着各种奇妙的幻想。安妮拥有着天马行空的想象力，在她的世界里，溪水、玫瑰，甚至小树都是美丽的生命，她的影子和回声也是正在交流的知心朋友；安妮的想象力同时还充满了浪漫的色彩：在她的想象中，樱花是她的"白雪皇后"，苹果是她的

春色
任天涯
——福建华南女子
职业学院外教侧记
International Faculty with
Fujian Hua Nan Women's
College since 1908

508

"红衣姑娘",林荫道是"白色的欢乐之路","顽皮的小溪"在冰雪覆盖下欢笑,镜子中自己的倒影成了另外一个被魔法捆住的小姑娘山谷中传来的回声,在她听来却是一个叫维奥莱特——一个喜欢重复她说话的好朋友……多么丰富的想象力!多么天真可爱的孩子!

安妮不但爱幻想,而且乐观,积极向上。面对不幸的身世和遭遇,她没有丝毫抱怨,总是微笑以对。玛丽拉曾经问过安妮:"你的身世如此可怜,可你为什么还这么开心呢?"安妮严肃地回答:"生活就像一面镜子,只有你笑着对它,它才会笑着面对你,与其每天愁眉苦脸,还不如开开心心地过好每一天,这样我也可以让在天堂的父母安心。"

安妮的身上还有一种许多人都没有的品质——懂得感恩。为了报答玛丽拉与马修,她立下了远大的目标:考上女王学院并获得埃伯利顿奖学金。为此,她发奋学习,功夫不负有心人,安妮的愿望成真,成了玛丽拉与马修的骄傲。收养者马修受到刺激突然去世了,玛丽拉痛不欲生,从女王学校毕业的安妮为了照顾玛丽拉,不惜放弃了自己的梦想——读大学,留在了安维利教书,正如安妮所说:"我的未来就像一条笔直的道路,现在路上有了转弯,我相信那里一定有很好的风景。"

谈到上完丽莎老师《绿山墙的安妮》这部小说的阅读与写作课,94级A班的同学都各抒己见。陈宏,现担任香港罗氏建筑石材有限公司厦门代表处人事与财务主管,她回忆道:"在丽莎老师的阅读课上,我非常喜欢这部小说中的主人公安妮。安妮的故事告诉了我,我们现在还不曾有的东西,那就是,在任何时候都一如既往的优雅,一如既往的欢颜。"

郑艳同学说:"读了这本小说,让我的英文词汇与阅读质量有了很大的提高。特别是书中的安妮让我很感动。我切身体会到,我们要善待每一个人,这样别人也会善待你。"

"这部小说对我的震撼太大了。书中的主人公安妮跟我一样,没有漂亮的外表,有不服输的内心,蹦蹦跳跳像个男孩子。安妮在大家都不看好的成长背景中仍然笑脸面对,刚强努力,我也要加油,克服写作功底薄弱的困难,挑战英文写作难关。读了这本小说,我写英文读后感的时候,觉得下笔如有神,写得流畅欢快。"黄胜同学说,"安妮对知识和学习都有一股执着的劲头,那种积极向上、拼搏奋斗的精神令我感动,是我学习的楷模。"

《绿山墙的安妮》真的是一本感动上万个善良心灵的经典小说。安妮的坚强和勇气,安妮的善良和直率,安妮的乐观与执着,安妮的勤奋与努力,这一切的一切,都使得我们应该向安妮学习，学习安妮的执着，学习安妮的纯洁，学习安妮拥有一颗纯洁无瑕的心灵。感谢丽莎老师为我们精选了如此上乘的佳作，让我们在轻松愉快中完成了巨大的阅读量与写作任务。更可贵的是，丽莎老师带领我们身临其境地畅游在英文的海洋中，如海绵般不断地汲取营养精髓，让我们全身心受其精髓的滋润与浇灌，陶冶了情操，潜移默化地提升了我们的人格。

第二部：《死亡诗社》（*Dead Poets Society*）—— 指引人生

这是丽莎老师引入的第二部力作。看完录像带，读完剧本，我们的内心总有抑制不住的激动，我们的心灵深处在不断接受着这种撞击。我们从未遇见过像基廷（Keating）这样特别的老师。

影片中，威尔顿学院是一所传统的学校，培养了很多优秀的人才，他强调100年来始终坚持的四大信条：传统、荣誉、纪律和卓越。而新老师的到来使这一切有了改观，正是这位新老师为同学们带来了春风和细雨。约翰·基廷也是毕业于这所地狱学校威尔顿，但他没有传统的呆板与扼杀人性的作法，他喜爱诗歌，自称船长（captain），他打破传统教学方式，每一堂课都以幽默大胆的作风让学生对人生、对自己有了更深刻的理解。他鼓励学生独立思考，冲破牢笼的束缚。第一堂课，基廷让学生们来到教室的走廊里聆听前人的声音。他让大家撕掉那些刻板的理论教材，他带学生们来到户外感受什么是"一致"，他让每个人站在讲桌上用不同的角度去看事物。基廷老师很快走进了每一个学生的内心，他们喜欢这个不一样的老师。

重建死亡诗社（Dead Poets Society）毫无疑问是在基廷老师感染下的表现，这个不受学校欢迎的社团成了少年们的精神圣地，The Dead Poets was dedicated to "sucking the marrow out of life"。梭罗曾说死亡诗人致力于吸取生命的精华，这些诗歌、美丽、浪漫、爱情正是我们活着的意义。古诗人社的成员轮流朗诵，欢声歌唱，生命在这里得到了尽情绽放。

我步入丛林
因为我希望生活有意义
我希望活得深刻
汲取生命中的所有精华
把非生命的一切都击溃
以免当我生命终结时
却发现自己从未活过

春色
任天涯
——福建华南女子
职业学院外教侧记
International Faculty with
Fujian Hua Nan Women's
College since 1908

510

　　这首诗被写在尼尔朗诵的诗集的扉页上，一个人能在年轻时清楚地明白自己该干什么是多么大的快乐，在尼尔死后，基廷老师看见这首诗不禁潸然泪下。尼尔热爱演戏，他试图挣脱父亲的束缚，毅然参与演出，出色的演出并没有改变父亲的看法，父亲打算让尼尔退学入军校无疑是葬送了他的前程，直至死前，他仍呢喃道："我演得好，我演得真的很好。"尼尔死了，死在一个飞雪凄冷的夜晚。

　　我们本以为尼尔的死能改变些什么，但有些事情是无法改变的，威尔顿一如既往地恪守那四大信条，死亡诗社的一员卡梅隆出卖了大家，他们在校方和父母的施压下，将责任全部推给了基廷老师，基廷老师被辞退，死亡诗社被解散。在这最后的高潮，基廷老师来教室拿他的私人物品，校长诺论让他拿完东西后赶紧离开，就在基廷老师关门离去时，平时最胆小的托德站了起来，像老师教的那样，站在课桌上，含着泪大声呼喊："Oh, captain, my captain!"接着大家一个接一个地站起来，饱含深情地向这位伟大的船长表达敬意，基廷带着微笑欣慰地道声"谢谢"离开了。

　　片子至此结束，片尾的苏格兰风笛和鼓声，令人振奋，倘若没有最后学生们爬上课桌，这该是多么大的悲剧。这一站温暖了基廷，感动了大家，我们惊叹那些少年的勇气，基廷是胜利的，至少他们站起来了，这是多少积蓄的情绪的爆发，一种无畏的反抗精神。

　　在那个封闭的年代，在大多数人的眼里，基廷老师是一位十足的"另类"和叛逆者。但是，在他学生的心里，他却如春风细雨一般，给学生门打开了一扇窗，他为学生们带来不一样的生活体验，他用自己独特的教学方式让学生去感受文学的美。这样一位老师，他颠覆了传统教育理念，使学生摆脱了填鸭式教育的牢笼。在学生们惊异的目光中，他滔滔不绝地讲述该如何使生活变得有意义。

　　诚如片中的基廷老师，丽莎老师在实际的教学中也是一个导引青春航程的船长。她的授课方式有很多种，学生能够学到很多，不仅学到知识，也收获愉悦的感受。教师与学生的教与学的过程是一个交流的过程，把过程变得搞笑化，这会收获不一样的效果。丽莎老师注重我们的个性发展，不让陈旧的教学理论抹杀学生本有的天性。教育的目的是希望每一个渴求知识的人，都能够寻找到自身的价值，从而更精彩地活着，这正是丽莎老师所要倡导的教学理念。她在教学中践行着这一理念，用她的人格魅力感染着我们，不断地鼓励我们独立思考问题，用不同的角度去看事物，塑造培养我们的独立人格，教会我们如何选择自己的人生，教育引导我们对所做的每件事都必定经过思考，并且要敢于担负责任。

　　"一片树林里分出两条路/而我选择了人迹更少的一条/从此决定了我一生的道

路。"丽莎老师的教育宛若春风化雨，润物无声地留在我们每个同学的心里。

英语自由谈话：人文关怀，爱心浇灌

英语自由谈话课是我们华南女院的特色课程，当时我们班分成4组，每组7人，一组上课45分钟，课上我们学生当主角，充分自由地畅谈丽莎老师给定的任务话题。丽莎老师上"自谈课"，形式多样，独树一帜，精彩纷呈。她带我们去福州解放大桥对岸的台江麦当劳（1994年刚开业不久），边吃边聊，海阔天空；带我们去外国专家楼的厨房制作各种糕点。特别是自由谈话课上带我们一起玩 UNO 扑克牌，这对当时的我们而言实在是太新鲜，太新奇了。丽莎老师设定的玩牌规则，其中最基本的就是我们必须用英语交流，不许说中文。

丽莎老师告诉我们，UNO扑克是一种起源于欧洲，流行于全世界的年轻人最喜欢的普及型纸牌类游戏。在此游戏中考的是大家的集中和反应，还有相互间的思维较量。我们非常认真地倾听着丽莎老师耐心的说明。当时我们都很诧异，从丽莎口中冒出来的一长串的游戏规则，我们怎么就这么容易都听懂了呢？

如今回想起这些，黄胜同学说："UNO牌很好玩，我至今都一直在跟孩子们玩。玩UNO我可嘚瑟了，这是我唯一会玩的牌。'自谈课'上，玩UNO时我就慢慢放开了，不再拘谨，游戏紧张，情急之下就开口了。回想起来，这真是个很好的结合游戏的教学方法，解决了同学们不敢开口、不好意思开口的情形，在游戏中，大家慢慢地放开了，尽情地用英文表达。潜移默化中，口语表达能力自然得到了锻炼与提高，同时也提升了大家开口说英文的自信心。"

"丽莎老师给我们上的自由谈话课非常有趣，她鼓励我们要开口说英文，每次上课都有不同主题让我们自由发表观点。偶尔，我们碰到不会说的英文时就会偷偷

丽莎与学生共进午餐

春色
任天涯
——福建华南女子
职业学院外教侧记
International Faculty with
Fujian Hua Nan Women's
College since 1908

512

冒出中文来，她也从来不责备，总是微笑着提醒我们，并告诉我们英文要怎么表达。还记得复活节的自由谈话课，她煮了很多鸡蛋，让我们在鸡蛋上面自由涂鸦，完了大家拍照留念。每次看到这张照片，我总是觉得当时上的课就像昨天才刚发生的一样。"纪玉美同学回忆道。

郑艳同学说："我记得，有一次上'自谈课'，我肚子饿得咕噜咕噜叫，丽莎老师拿饼干给我吃。"

程晓霞同学谈到丽莎老师的自由谈话课时感触颇深：

"丽莎的自由谈话课是十分吸引我的：班上的同学分成几组，到外教楼的厨房里，一边做蛋糕、饼干之类诱人的美食，一边练习英语对话交流——这可是我以前从未接触过的。哈哈，那美味可口的饼干可是我的最爱！复活节我们就制作彩蛋，万圣节就有可爱的南瓜，万圣节有各种糖果……

可是，有一次自由谈话课，我被丽莎单独叫出门外，她一直泛着轻盈蓝光的眼睛在阳光下显得很深沉。她非常严肃地跟我说：'晓霞，你是学生会的干部，要知道你的一言一行都是别人的榜样，你觉得在自谈课上老用中文与同学交流合适吗？你这样做，别的同学也都跟着你讲中文，很不好的。'我顿时羞得面红耳赤，连连跟她说抱歉。丽莎那富有魅力的眼睛立即浮现出一丝欣慰的笑容。我非常感谢她给我留面子，没在同学面前批评我，此事给我印象之深刻，让我在以后从事教育工作中时刻提醒自己要顾及学生的自尊心和注意语气。"

正所谓"诚于中而形于外，慧于心而秀于言"，苏霍姆林斯基说过："学校里的学习，不是毫无热情地把知识从一个头脑里装进一个头脑里，而是师生间每时每刻都在进行的心灵接触。"在丽莎老师的自由谈话课上，不仅仅有我们师生间的知识信息的交流，更有彼此情感的交流。丽莎老师非常关爱我们。为了取得良好的教学效果，丽莎老师每一件事情都以爱学生为前提，一个鼓励的眼神与微笑、一次次与我们同学间坦诚的沟通交流都滋润我们的心灵，让我们感到温暖。我时刻感到在丽莎老师的课堂上，老师那亲切和蔼的笑容缩短了我们之间的距离，她那充沛的精力、饱满的情绪、昂扬的激情感染着我们，我们就在那和谐、温馨、亲和、快乐、放松、情感交融的氛围里以享受的心态愉悦地学习英语，游戏英语。

丽莎老师，您是大桥，为我们连接被割断的山峦，让我们走向收获的峰巅；您是青藤，坚韧而修长，指引我们采撷到崖顶的灵芝和人参。您真的是"不计辛勤一砚寒，桃熟流丹，李熟枝残，种花容易树人难。幽谷飞香不一般，诗满人间，画满人间，英才济济笑开颜"。

学院领导宴请丽莎

由左至右：黄胜，丽莎·雷文希尔，纪玉美

孔子曾经说过："与善人居，如入芝兰之室，久而不闻其香，即与之化矣。"

返校参加校庆

丽莎于2008年10月专程从美国回华南女院参加学院100周年校庆。

聆听恩师，教语菁华

对话丽莎：山重水复疑无路，柳暗花明又一村。

林校：您能否谈谈自己的教育背景和家人？

丽莎：我的父亲是英国人，母亲是美国人，我既懂得英式英语，也懂得美式英语，这是我的优势。在我的成长历程中，我们一家游历了不少地方，我也因此体验了许多不同的文化，并认识到英语真是一门国际语言。我在新西兰奥塔哥大学学习家庭科学，在美国得州女子大学修习职业家政学，并在以色列圣地大学获得了英语作为第二语言教学的资格证书。

林校：您从何处得知华南女院，来到这里无偿任教的原因是什么？

丽莎：我从某份专业科学杂志上了解到华南女院，并意识到我的教育背景很适合华南女院某些基于家政学的课程。既然我已经计划在未来前往中国任教，并有志于女性教育，这所大学似乎是一个显而易见的选择。对我来说，在新地方、新文化中获得的经验与知识，以及同中国人结交的机会比任何数额的金钱都更具价值。我相信我们都被赋予了令他人幸福的能力，因此我可以由衷地赞同华南女院的旧校训："受当施"。

林校：来华南女院执教前，我发现您曾去台湾学习汉语一年。您这么做的理念

春色
任天涯
——福建华南女子
职业学院外教侧记
International Faculty with
Fujian Hua Nan Women's
College since 1908

514

是什么？

丽莎：一位朋友建议为我在中国生活的目标找几块"垫脚石"，在台湾学习汉语一年就是垫脚石之一。我认为，学习汉语让我与一般语言学习者产生了更多共鸣，也让我对中国文化有了一些深刻了解。

林校：通过贝茨·里韦特博士，我才了解到，您在1992年至1996年间执教于华南女院时，实际上既是教师，也是课程规划师。您参与了教学内容选择、教学方法以及教材的选择、改编与评估。您开发了以学习者为中心的课程，这是您和学生们共同努力的成果，因为学生们积极参与了课程内容与教学方法的决策过程。这样的课程将包含几个要素，也就是规划（包括需求分析、目标设定、学生分组）、实施（包括内容选择与分级、教学方法和教材开发）和评估。您在1994年和1995年教授我们三门课程，即"英语阅读与写作""英语听力与口语""英语自由谈话"，您是如何处理这些要素的？能否和我们分享一些您的想法？

丽莎：我自1992年起在华南女院执教，在1994至1995年教授A班，我认为我已经相当确信自己了解一年级学生的平均英语水平，以及他们需要关注哪些方面来提高自己的英语。我的目标很简单，就是让学生相信他们能够学会英语，并带着这样的信心成长。为此，只要是我自己觉得有趣又确实想教的材料，我都会用（因为没有学生会认真听一个无趣的老师上一节无聊的课），希望学生们会觉得课程同样有趣，也希望我对英语语言的热情能够感染他们！

林校：教学方法包括学习活动和材料，通常在这方面，教师和学生之间的潜在冲突最大。在以学习者为中心的课程中，解决一切冲突是关键。近期的研究记录证实教师与学习者的预期存在普遍的不协调问题。因为，正如我们已经注意到的，相当一部分的学生倾向于对课程内容、学习活动、教学方法等抱有固定思维，而教师也似乎不得不继续面对一个抉择问题——要做出何种程度的妥协。但是，如果课程是要以学习者为中心，就应该征询和考虑学生的意愿，即使他们的意愿与教师的意愿有所冲突。您教我们的时候，是否遇到过和我们的某些冲突？如果曾有冲突，您是怎么解决的呢？

丽莎：我会很高兴地说："不，我与我的学生们在教学方法、活动或材料方面不曾发生任何冲突。"但这并不是说，我做的所有选择都是最好的，但我教授的学生都是（一年级）大学新生，他们就算对英语课程抱有固定想法或期望，也不会太多。我的优势是有幸成为他们的第一个外籍英语老师，因此我所做的一切看起来也就十分新奇且令人兴奋！

林校：众所周知，鉴于大多数学习环境存在局限性，要老师在课堂上将学生们所需的全部知识都传授给他们，是不可能的事情。因此必须尽可能有效地利用课堂的有限时间，教授学生们认为最迫切需要的语言知识，从而增加知识传授价值以及随之激发学习动力。以"英语阅读与写作"课为例，当课上发生这种情形时，您采取了什么措施来解决这个问题？

丽莎：这不是解决问题的事，而是关于优先传授基本知识，为学生打下一个良好的基础，以便二年级和三年级的其他英语教师能够在此基础上继续深入。为此，我十分注重学生们从阅读中获得乐趣，以及从阅读材料中寻找线索和主要观点的能力，即开头段落、标题、粗体字、斜体字和图表、图片和问题，以及新单词的语境。

林校：在教育界中，教师的 professeur（教授）身份遭到了某些质疑，认为他们可能是权利代理人，力求维护特权权利，教育学生们学会服从、听话。我们知道，互动中的权利行使与事务中的有所不同。在互动中，教师作为 professeur 占据优越的主导地位，这是社会赋予其的角色："我是你的老师。根据授予我的权限，我有权要求你做出一定的行为举止，不论你喜欢与否。而你根据你的角色，有必须服从的义务。"因此，互动中权利行使或多或少有些专制。但教师的 enseignant（教员）身份在事务中行使权利凭借的是自身获得的专家角色，其权利基于专业资格，其主导地位源于其执教能力，就指定目标而言即成功执行事务的能力。在这种情况下，不是对权力的主张，而是对知识的声明：不是"因为我告诉你要这么做，你就得这么做"，而是"我是老师，我知道什么对你而言是最好的"。因此，事务型权威行使或多或少具有一些权威性。同时，以学习者为中心的活动和课堂合作任务的增加并不意味着老师权威被削弱了。教师仍要设法获取所需的有利学习条件，还必须对进度进行监督和指导。在华南女院执教期间，您对教师与学习者的角色有何看法？

丽莎：教师在互动中和事务中扮演的权威角色，我都能理解。但我把教师更多地理解为学生的生活向导或导师。这对我来说并不难，因为那时我还是一位年轻的老师，因此仍在学习如何教学！不仅如此，我那时正在学习如何教授中国学生，这意味着我要了解他们的文化、背景和世界观。我要把自己放在一个谦虚的位置，而这与"老师总是知道什么是最好的"这一见解恰恰相反！

林校：我们知道，评估是在课程模式的最后组成部分，而评估是一个更加广泛的术语，牵扯到考查，但也包括其他程序。这些附加程序旨在帮助我们阐释和作用于我们的考查结果。从评估中得到的数据有助于我们决定某门课程是否需要进行某种方式的改进或修改，以便更加有效地实现目标。如果某些学生没能达到课程设置

春色
任天涯
——福建华南女子
职业学院外教侧记
International Faculty with
Fujian Hua Nan Women's
College since 1908

516

的目标，就必须确定导致这种结果的原因。我们还希望，作为课程的评估结果，能够想出一些弥补课程不足的可行措施。而且，评估不仅仅是获取信息的过程，这也是一个决策过程。在您曾经教授的课程中，您在这方面的实际做法是什么？

丽莎：除了小测验、大测验和考试成绩能为课程评估提供一些数据，我会与每位学生进行面谈或"聊天"，试图弄清他们为何没能达到所期望的目标——自信地进行英语听说读写。结果，作为一名老师，我需要做哪些努力来帮助该学生提高，这点通常是显而易见的，而某个学生遇到的困难往往表明了所有学生都在苦苦挣扎的问题。在这个时候，我可能会回顾某堂课，或以完全不同的方式重上某节课，再多多鼓励学生们！

林校：在"英语阅读与写作"课上，您选取了4部影片让我们观看，分别是《绿山墙的安妮》、《死亡诗社》、《回到未来》以及《宾虚》。在此期间，您还打印了所有原始资料作为我们的阅读任务，然后在课堂上进行热烈而深入的探讨。在那之后，我记得您还出了考卷，以便帮助我们更好地理解影片和小说。我想知道您挑选这4部影片的理由。您在挑选时抱着哪些确切的期望呢？

丽莎：这些电影的选择没有太多学术方面的考虑，因为在当时的中国无法提供很多电影方面的选择！（不同于现在，人们可在网上获取海量DVD和电影资源。）我只是单纯地喜欢这些电影，因为它们都以刻画人物为主，表达的主题很好，并且改编自不同题材的作品。我希望我的学生能从每部电影中学到点东西，给他们未来的人生带来积极影响。

林校：在您任教的课程中，我发现您实际上在不知不觉间将目标文化融入教学中。圣诞节，您告诉了我们西方人庆祝这个节日的原因以及圣诞老人姓甚名谁。您给每个人送了圣诞贺卡和圣诞礼物，我们共进圣诞晚餐，共唱圣诞颂歌。整个学年里，您把所有的西方节日都介绍给了我们，与我们一起过节，让我们也能够体验情人节、圣帕特里克节、复活节、愚人节、感恩节。不可否认的是，文化与语言密不可分。Kramsch（1996）强烈支持这一观点，他毫不含糊地表示："语言与文化从一开始就密不可分。"同样，Sapir（1970：207）说："语言无法独立于文化而存在，也就是说，语言源于社会继承的习俗和信仰之集合物，决定了我们生活的质感。"承载、阐释、记录无形文化的主要方式之一就是通过语言。有趣的是，在所有文化中，语言似乎是最具代表性的元素。

同理，文化是语言使用不可缺少的环境。首先，如果没有文化环境，外语教学将"十分枯燥"。对于学习外语的学生来说，如果他们对说该语言的人或国家一无所知，语言学习便显得毫无意义。因为文化是语言的组成部分之一，同样语言也是文化不可分割的一部分，要将文化从语言中分离出来几乎是不可能的。坦率地讲，一门外语的教学离不开对目标语文化的介绍。

其次，我们完全相信，文化构成了成功沟通的坚实基础。事实上，文化不仅规定了沟通的对象、内容以及进行方式，还有助于对话者进行信息编码，理解条件与情况，了解哪种信息可能或不能被发送，能否被人注意或者得到解读。简单地说，单靠语言学不足以让目标语言的学习者充分掌握该语言（Krasner，1999）。语言学习者需要注意某些问题，例如，如何以符合文化的方式称呼他人、表达感激之情、提出请求，在不同语境中同意或反对某人意见。他们应该知道，其母语社区中恰当的行为和语调模式，在目标语言言语社区的成员看来，可能会有不同的理解。因此，教师的责任就是帮助学生理解适应社会的沟通。在教学中，您圆满地完成了这项任务。您能否介绍您在这方面的理念，让大家都能听听您的心声？

丽莎：其实，我是有意识地将西方文化和国际文化的某些方面融入教学中，因为我希望我的学生能够去了解我，并理解从我的背景出发认为十分重要的故事、态度和信念。反过来，这也许能让他们从不同的角度更加清楚地看待自己的文化。

如前所述，语言和文化都是根深蒂固的，二者密不可分。因此，我要教给学生的不仅仅是英语单词、句子和短语。我必须教他们这些英语单词、句子和短语要怎么用，才能用得自然且符合文化背景。这不仅有助于他们在将来同我以及其他讲英语的人进行有效沟通，还会确保他们不会因不当的言行而使自己难堪——这对中国这样"顾全体面"的文化大国来说是个相当重要的问题。

最后，我希望学生们能够发现英语的乐趣，所以我通过介绍西方文化和国际文化的某些方面，让课堂充满乐趣、振奋人心。

林校：1992 年到 1996 年间，您在华南女院任教。当时的教学和生活条件实际上非常差。您对此有何感想，又是如何克服这些困难的呢？教学之外，您在业余时间还做些什么呢？

丽莎：我为能在中国生活而感到十分荣幸，而且华南女院外事办的工作人员是那么热情、善良、乐于助人，让我几乎感觉不到生活条件的艰苦。同样，我的生活十分充实，各种体验和众多友人让我根本不会去想自己缺少什么！偶尔也会碰到老鼠、食物中毒、停水的星期一、没有国际电话线的情况（那些日子里肯定没法上网），但这种"艰辛"却书写了一个个伟大的中国故事！

我们中的大多数人知道，贫穷与恶劣的生活条件并无多少关联。真正的贫穷源于

春色
任天涯
——福建华南女子
职业学院外教侧记
International Faculty with
Fujian Hua Nan Women's
College since 1908

518

缺乏对生活意义和目的的认识。在华南女院任教给我的生活赋予了许多目的和意义！

在业余时间，我结交中国朋友（他们中的大多数至今仍是我的朋友），探索福州城，到福建省其他有名的地方旅行，品尝各种当地美食，同其他外国教师进行交流，阅读书刊，做饭，摄影和绣十字绣。我还出演了三部中国影片！

林校：1996年起，您前往昆明执教，学生的年纪不同，英语水平各异。您能否分享一下您在那里的教学经历呢？

丽莎：我来到昆明是为了设立和经营一个全浸式英语学习营地，在这里所有活动的教学与引导都用英语进行。这是一个很好的机会，不仅为学生提供了一种全英语的语言环境，也让我学到了很多新的组织技能。我还在一家英语夜校工作了许多年，那里是专业人士下班后学习的地方。这份工作的内容包括帮助学生准备雅思考试。最近，我都在教授私人学生英语，他们中的大部分人已经在海外生活和工作。

林校：我想知道您选择在昆明执教20多年作为您职业生涯的延续，还有选择到中国而不是其他国家发展事业的原因。

丽莎：我不知道是我选择了在中国执教，还是这份工作选择了我，但我喜欢在中国生活。我来这儿不是为了发展自己的事业，而是为了创造美好生活——我相信后者更加重要。我的人生丰富多彩，因为我可以做我所爱，爱我所做！最后，我希望我以前的学生都能记住这一点：不论我们说着何种语言，没有爱，我们不过是在敲锣击钹罢了。唯有爱，永不败。

附录1：《死亡诗社》中沃尔特·惠特曼的诗《啊，船长，我的船长!》

啊，船长！我的船长！我们可怕的航程已经结束，
我们的船承受了每一次风浪，我们的奖赏已经得到，
港口近了，钟声响了，民众欢呼了，
在万众瞩目中，我们的航船庄重、威猛；
但是，啊心脏！心脏！心脏！
啊那些红色渗出、滴落，
我的船长躺在甲板上，
冰冷地倒下。

啊，船长！我的船长！站起来听那些钟声，

站起来，看那为你飘舞的旗帜、为你吹响的号角，

为你，鲜花和绸带结成花环——为你，岸上的人群集结，

人群为你欢呼，为你激动，他们热切的脸转向你；

在这里船长！亲爱的父亲！

这条胳膊枕在你的头下！

在甲板上就像是一场梦，

你已经冰冷地倒下。

我的船长没有回答，他的嘴唇苍白凝固，

我的父亲感觉不到我的胳膊，他的脉搏已然停顿，

这艘大船已安全地下锚，它的航程圆满完成，

从可怕的航程中胜利的航船实现了目标；

岸上人群欢呼，钟声响起，

但我低头悲伤，

走在我的船长躺着的甲板，

他已冰冷地倒下。

第七节　春风化雨，润物无声
——回忆佩罗特博士

有缘者，不以万里为远

1996年，佩罗特博士（Dr. Mary Carol Perrott）带着爱德基金会的使命，不远千里从美国来华南女院执教两年，从而拉开了与华南女院的20年情缘。

初识佩罗特博士

20世纪90年代初，对很多中国人而言，英语口语是英语学习中的一大弱项。我们有幸在华南女院学习英语，有很多的机会接触外教，克服哑巴英语并提高英语口语。记得第一学期接触外教时，上课前我们总会紧张地问自己："我们能行吗？"当

春色
任天涯
——福建华南女子
职业学院外教侧记
International Faculty with
Fujian Hua Nan Women's
College since 1908

520

听到佩罗特博士将执教我们，一方面我们很兴奋，就要见到美国外教，体验真正意义上的英语交流；另一方面，我们很紧张，担心沟通不来，特别是那些不是来自城市里的学生，她们发音不好是紧张因素之一，因为这些学生中学英语教学中极少用到英语口语，或很多英语老师本来英语就发音不准。

带着复杂的心情，我们期待着与佩罗特博士的见面。第一次的见面，记忆犹新。那天我们很早来到教室，没想到佩罗特博士更早。她，五十出头，中等个头，梨形身材，肤色白皙，留着一头利落的齐耳栗色短发，高鼻梁上架着一副黑色圆形眼镜，镜片背后是一双知性、亲切的大眼睛。她白里透红的脸上洋溢着笑容，唇红齿白，很像洋娃娃，一身的亲切感，顿时我们的紧张与担忧，随空而散。"大家好，我是佩罗特博士。呵，是否想到鹦鹉？对，联系它，就记住我了。"老师诙谐的开场白，一下子让大家放松下来，课堂气氛随之就轻松活跃起来。

大家争先恐后进行自我介绍，第一次体验了佩罗特博士轻松有趣的课。从此在佩罗特博士的鼓励下，我们忘记了胆怯，爱上了英语，爱上了佩罗特博士的课程，特别是英语的听与说。正是因为她，我们更好地开口说英语了；正是因为她，我们树立了自信；正是因为她，我们更加有动力学英语了；正是因为她，我们英语学习的目标更加明确，一步一个脚印，努力纠正个人的发音难点，练习英语的听与说。短短的第一学期，我们的听说能力有了较大的提高。

与佩罗特博士在一起的春夏秋冬

佩罗特博士以一首《小茶壶》在秋天开启我们的师生之旅。"我是一只小茶壶，又短又胖，这是我的手，这是我的嘴。"她教学独特，颇受学生欢迎。她一边唱，一边演示，她左手叉腰，右手做茶壶状。她的演示，幽默生动，很快活跃了课堂气氛。

福建的冬天，寒冷潮湿，有时候冷气直往骨头里钻。佩罗特博士的到来，总会将教室的寒意驱散。她告诉我们，在冬天里，戴一顶帽子，会阻止30%热量的散发。

"在专家楼上口语课时，她总将房间里的暖气开得很足，递给我们一杯热腾腾的可可，一口热可可喝下去，身子暖了，心更暖了。笑容可掬的佩罗特博士，充盈满屋的可可香，成为记忆深处最美的冬天画面。冬天佩罗特博士的口语课，成为女孩们最向往的一节课。"

对于许多女孩英语中轻辅音θ，浊辅音ð发不标准的情况，佩罗特博士想了一个巧妙的办法，她点燃了一段蜡烛，演示念一句特别设计的英语句子，轻辅音θ与浊辅音ð的单词前后相间。开始念句子时，她先把室内的灯关了，窗帘拉上，制造出一个黑夜的场景。然后她把烛台拖近，让嘴与烛焰成平行线，念到轻辅音 θ 时，烛焰随口中呼出的气息摇曳，而念到下一个浊辅音δ时，由于是喉咙的振动发音，烛焰便纹丝不动恢复如初。接下来，她便让同学们亲自实验，让大家掌握正确的发音方法。烛焰在黑暗中，有规律地忽暗忽明，年轻的女孩们借由这节游戏般有趣的发音课，永远记住并掌握了 θ 和δ的正确发音方式。

寒假一过，在万物复苏的春天，我们就以小草期待阳光的心情，盼望着上佩罗特博士的课。她临近教室门的像上课铃

佩罗特博士在专家楼的房间里

一样准点的熟悉的脚步声，总让我们的心雀跃。因为，在这第一课，她就要与我们分享她精彩的寒假生活，她的远游，她的收获。她很坦诚地与我们分享她的人生经历，她因爱嫁给了比她年长很多的丈夫，遗憾的是，不到五年，丈夫先她而去。她膝下无子女，但她并不孤独，她说她的外甥女和她的学生就是她的子女，她生活得那么充实，知识、爱与奉献让她的人生多彩多姿，她是那么独立与坚强。她告诉青春期的我们一定不要和已婚男人谈恋爱，她说那多半会是一个悲剧，一个未经世事的少女受骗是小菜一碟。

福州的夏季，炎热难熬，但跟她在一起的夏季，我们体验到更多的是夏季的清爽和丝丝凉意。她会在周末或期末时间，安排学生外出，自费带我们上麦当劳，体验西式的快餐文化，在实际的生活中使用口语。

美好的时光总是那么短暂，在知了的鸣叫声中，迎来了分别的夏季。在专家楼里，她为我们张罗了一个温馨的毕业告别会，临别时，她眼含热泪，张开双臂紧紧拥抱即将告别校园的我们，并告诉我们从今往后，我们就是一个成年人了，我们必须对自己的一言一行负责，要活出华南女儿的风采。

佩罗特博士的印象

佩罗特博士是我们喜欢的老师，她的课生动有趣，模式也很多样化。在她的课堂上经常充满笑声，她不计较我们的学习错误，宠着我们，激励着我们，我们的英

春色
任天涯
——福建华南女子
职业学院外教侧记
International Faculty with
Fujian Hua Nan Women's
College since 1908

522

佩罗特博士在福州解放大桥（桥的南面是华南女院）

语听说水平在愉悦的气氛中不知不觉提高了许多。

作为爱德基金会的援教老师，佩罗特博士有着常人没有的奉献精神，正是这种精神，支持并推动着她把教师工作做好。一路走来，她展现出来的是责任，是爱心，是无私，给华南女院带来的是福气。对基础薄弱的学生，佩罗特博士课外免费辅导，并且经常用自己的工资帮助生活困难的学生。同时注意收集材料，购买些学习资料，捐赠给班级。我们有幸成为她的学生，其他班级的学生都嫉妒我们能经常从她那边得到一些惊喜，包括教学中的小礼物及外出活动。感谢有她，我们克服了学习英语的恐惧；感谢有她，我们英语学习的路上充满欢乐；感谢有她，引导我们利用全英文的学习资料学习英语；感谢有她，我们不仅学会了相关英文知识，也学到了为人处世时积极向上的生活态度。

她是让我们感动的老师，她对学生一视同仁，公平对待她的学生。她不以貌取人，不偏袒好的学生，也不忽视弱势学生。（彭铿，她的学生）

她是一个很好的教育者。和蔼、大方、有思想、做事有条不紊，把生活安排得井井有条。（林娇，她的学生兼同事）

佩罗特博士是一位好老师，而且还是让我终生难忘的好老师。她独立、坚强、热爱生活、敬业、奉献的精神，时刻鼓舞我们，在人生的道路上勇敢前行。华南女院里许多优秀的中外教师，包括佩罗特博士，给我树立了闪光的精神典范，给我带来不同文化的精神养分，让我得以坚强地生长，成为一个自立、自强的现代职业女性。（卓小星，她的学生）

　　总之，她是个无私奉献的教师，用自己的行动，爱护华南女院学生，呵护学生的成长，支持华南女院的教育。她积极向上，尽管她早已经是心理学博士，仍不忘继续学习，努力学习选修她自己感兴趣的或其他实用的硕士学业。她自我教育的提升经历，让我们领悟了终身教育的概念。

润物无声

　　自从执教华南女院，佩罗特博士用自己的实际行动，默默地支持着华南女院的英语教育。

　　1. 通过午间播放原版英语电影，丰富教与学活动

　　作为爱德基金会派来的教师，佩罗特博士通过她的专业背景和实际行动帮助华南女院的很多学生。她是个有奉献精神的教师，她做了许多积极的事情，以提高华南英语教育的水平。在教学中，她首先引进英语电影来帮助提高学生的口语，加深她们对英美文化的理解，丰富学生的文化知识。当时原版的录像很贵，佩罗特博士都用自己的钱买，上完课后捐献给华南女院。"作为她的学生，我非常感激，她经常牺牲午间休息时间，来到语音室给我们播放原版英语电影。当时那种电影非常少，大家都很珍惜这样的机会。我记得我们总是尽快吃完午饭，然后冲向语音室，或实在来不及，就很快打个包，赶向语音室，等待午间电影的开始。"（林娇）

　　随着午间播放原版英语这份工作受到越来越多学生的青睐，包括外专业的学生也来观看。"从1998年留校后，我就加入午间播放电影的工作，加入那份受学生欢迎的工作。原版英语电影的播放，让许多华南女院学生受益匪浅。诚实地说，我的英语口语提高很多，就是因为佩罗特博士提供了这与众不同的原版英语电影。"（林娇）

　　2. 购买100多本英语字典给学生

　　在华南女院教学一年后，佩罗特博士意识到让学生拥有一本英英字典很重要，"经过精心规划，她有计划地安排自己的开支，用自己的钱从香港购买了100多本朗文英语字典给她的学生。这些字典的总费用在当时就超过1000美元"。（林娇）

　　3. 鼓励支持学生参加英语考证

　　在华南女院执教期间，佩罗特博士很关注学生的学习情况，经常鼓励大家从各方面提高英语水平。她的阅历丰富，见多识广，认为华南女院学生除要提升实用的英语听说能力、拥有良好的英语口语外，还要有相关的英语证书。为了让学生在未来就业的市场上更有竞争力，她又个人资助学生参加全国外语水平考试，并为学生取得的好成绩而自豪。

**春色
任天涯**
——福建华南女子
职业学院外教侧记
International Faculty with
Fujian Hua Nan Women's
College since 1908

524

师生情缘

佩罗特博士离开华南女院后，我们作为她的学生，以不同的方式，记着我们可爱可敬的老师。

多年来我一直在我的职业名片里写着Celina Zhuo，这个当年佩罗特博士给我取的名字，我以这种方式保持某种我与她之间的联系，感念佩罗特博士给我人生注入不一样的养分。（卓小星）

20世纪90年代，在相机不是很流行的时候，佩罗特博士用相机和华南女院的许多师生们合影留念，留下很多美好记忆。我们学生更多的是用传统的方法记着她的点点滴滴。她去日本后，我们主要通过华南女院固定联络点，与她信函联系。我们毕业后，她几次回福州，总会来看看在福州工作的学生，我们也乐意发起因她的到来而组织的班级聚会，聚会时她总会点些我们喜欢吃的菜；她随时关注我们的成长，总会给我们带来一些惊喜。

在国外留学期间，佩罗特老师的拜访是个大惊喜。佩罗特博士和她的丈夫新婚漂洋度假，联系看望她的学生并一起参观校园。那份惊喜与感动，难以用言语表达，感谢她对学生的体贴呵护。那个温馨体贴的拜访经历永远留在我记忆深处。（严涵）

每次见到她那可爱的脸，就拉近了我们年龄的差距；聆听她游览世界的故事，就让我们长了见识。与佩罗特博士联络越深，越能感知她对学生的付出与关爱，感知她身上传播的那份源自华南女院"受当施"的精神。

多年来，佩罗特博士的模样、谆谆教诲，犹在耳旁，从未远离。她独立坚强、热爱生活、无私奉献的精神，时刻鼓舞我们在人生的道路上勇敢前行。她把华南女院的精神，以润物细无声的方式，植入年轻的心灵，引领年轻的心走出迷惘，走向自尊、自爱、自立的现代女性的大美人生。

第八节　记Sandy

我不知道Sandy的中文名字叫什么，她大概也没有中文名字。她其实并没有教过我，我也从来没有听过她的课，说她是外教好像有点勉强。不过她是第一个来听我的课的老外，而且事先没有打招呼，搞了个突然袭击，让我十分意外。我们就是在那次课上认识的。转眼应该已经快20年了吧，当天的情形还历历在目。我们直到现在都还是朋友，我想这辈子也应该永远都是朋友了。遇到Sandy是我的幸运，因为不是每个外教都给我们留下美好的印象，更不是每个外教都会跟我们成为朋友的。出国以后，我自己成了外教，遇到了更多各式各样的学生，未必全都能跟他们成为朋友，自然也是一样的道理。

读硕士研究生的时候，导师要我去给自考班的学生上英美文学课，我很是紧张，一紧张就冒汗。那时候我的成绩虽然还可以，但基本上没有什么教学经验。英美文学是自考班最难的一门课，而且来听课的大概将近一百号人，老实说我第一次上课心里就直打鼓，下了课才发觉，自己的衬衫全都湿透了。不过一两堂课下来，我也没那么紧张了，一轮课讲下来，我心里就更有数了。我做事比较认真，接了课以后就没有过过周末，星期六、星期天都在备课、写讲稿。那时还没有互联网呢，我记得当时天天跑资料室和图书馆，查百科全书，或者其他各种能找到的资料。资料室的老师说，像你这样认真备课的，课一定上得不错。其实也许那时就是凭着一股热情和冲劲吧，要说上得多好倒也未必了。只是回头去看，现在我对那些作家作品的解读，也许会比当时更深刻一些，毕竟20年来摸爬滚打，世态炎凉，人情冷暖，也或多或少尝到了一些，对人生、对文学也有了新的理解。

那天晚上忘了是讲到哪一课了，我开始讲课的时候根本没有意识到教室里有什么不同，台下总是黑压压的一片，而且自考生上课总是很认真，从来没有人开小差或者开小会的。讲了一半我才发现，最后一排似乎坐了一个老外，也不知道是谁，心里很纳闷，但还是硬着头皮先把课讲完了。课间休息的时候我就走到她面前，小声地问她是哪位，怎么会来听课的。Sandy大概原来不希望被我发现，所以躲在最后一排，我们那时在外语系简易教室上课，最后一排离讲台总得有几十排座位吧，可她还是被我看到了。她笑容满面地告诉我，她是华南女院的老师，教学生写作的。

她班上的好几个学生都来选我的课，然后在作文里头写范老师如何如何，她就很感兴趣，想知道范老师究竟是何许人也，到底课上得怎么样，所以就跟着她学生Amy来听课。Amy也是华南女院的老师，正在进修本科。哦，原来是这样！我们简单聊了几句，我就接着回去把第二节课给上完了。一下课，同学很快都三三两两地离开了。我又走到最后一排她的面前，说："很高兴认识你，不然我们一起走吧？"Sandy说好，我们就跟Amy一起从简易教室慢慢走出来，一路闲聊，我一直把她们送到师大校门口才跟她们说再见。那时下了课就已经是八九点钟了吧，从简易教室到校门口的大道上，满是成荫的大树，晚风送来樟树、芒果、白玉兰和其他不知名的树的芬芳。离开福州多年后，回想起师大，记忆里挥之不去的还是那股淡淡的香气，而且好像只有在夜间才闻得到。

我已经忘记那天晚上都聊了什么，只记得过了几天就收到Sandy的信，很短，只是说感谢我让她听课，并邀请我去华南女院逛逛，还留了个电话号码给我。我们当时宿舍里是没有电话的，手机也不多见，一栋楼只在楼管员的房间里有一部电话，于是我立刻就去公话亭给她打了个电话，说很高兴收到她的信，一定会去拜访。老实说，我当时在师大已经待了五六年，华南女院在哪里都还不知道，正好借这个机会去了解一下。后来出了国，看到L. Ethel Wallace回忆华南女院的书 *Hwa Nan College: The Women's college of South China*，我才吃惊地发现，原来华南女院当年可是个响当当的大学！而翻到里面的插图，我就更惊讶了，我们再熟悉不过的师大校部大楼，原来全都是华南女院的！而且那些楼各有自己原来的名字，Cranston Hall（谷莲楼），Payne Hall（彭氏楼），Trimble Hall（程氏楼，又名立雪楼。这一楼两名含义却深，"Miss Lydia Trimble"是建校校长程吕底亚，"立雪"则显然来自"程门立雪"，用作大学建筑名称，再合适不过），都是以捐款人或者创建人命名的。师大还有一组风格特殊的建筑，就是现在的音乐系，原先则是陶淑女中的旧址，而陶淑女中也是教会建的学校。整个师大长安山，敢情都是这些教会学校奠定的基础。这些民国时期的建筑，比后来新建的楼群有独特风格得多，也美得多了。

华南女子文理学院，是美国基督教美以美女子布道会于1908年创办的，是民国时期全国13所基督教教会大学之一。如今的华南女院坐落在烟台山上，精巧的一个校园，说是"女院"倒也真是名副其实。当然，学生全都是女的，老师好像倒不一定了，但应该大部分都是女的。Sandy先带我逛了一圈校园，然后带我到教学楼顶楼去，我本来还以为她要带我去教室，上得楼来就明白了：眼前就是波浪起伏的闽江，蓝天上的白云缓缓飘过，船只在江面上往来穿梭，偶尔有几只飞鸟掠过，间或停在楼边的枝头乱啼。这一番壮阔的景象，跟刚才的小小校园，形成了极其鲜明的对比。我跟Sandy说："这里可比师大漂亮多了！"Sandy笑着说："对啊，所以要你来看看。"

我们从此就成了好朋友。人跟人之间其实是很奇妙的，那时我的英文也一般（当然现在也没有好到哪里去），Sandy则完全不懂中文，但我们就是聊得来。我们也没有特意要怎么样，只是互相觉得很亲切，所谓"白首如新，倾盖如故"，也许说的就是这个意思。Sandy知道我们从来都是"吃食堂"的，需要改善改善生活，所以她特意请我去华南女院的外国专家楼吃饭，而且是她亲自下厨。我还真是第一次尝西式烹调，对一切都很好奇，我已经忘记吃的是什么了，只记得她切菜的方式非常特别。我们切黄瓜是放在砧板上斜着削，她切黄瓜是把刀和黄瓜都握在手里用拇指推，切茄子也是一样（而且她用的是左手！）。我记得问她怎么不怕割到手，她说不会啊，从小习惯了。我认真观察了好一会儿，很想试试她的方法，但终究还是不敢。许多年后我在闵福德先生厨房里看他削土豆，也跟中国人习惯的方式不太一样，他还告诉我说以前英国人看厨师手艺好不好，其中之一就是看土豆削得好不好。虽然从文化差异的角度来说，这只是细枝末节，但也真是很有意思。

另一次Sandy请我去吃饭，不过是跟其他外教一起在她们专家楼的餐厅吃，是她们的厨师煮的菜，对我来说，是又多了一个跟外教聊天、了解她们的机会吧。师大当时外教少得可怜，我记得本科四年，就只上过两位外教的课，其中一位还显然是来中国混的。华南那些外教有来自美国的，有来自马来西亚的，还有新加坡、菲律宾的。她们虽然都很和善，但跟Sandy比起来，还是少了一点亲切，当然也许只是因为我跟她比较熟吧。

读研的时候我的扁桃体经常发炎，也不知道是太累还是怎么回事。有一次我又发烧躺在宿舍里，Amy突然提了满满一袋子东西进来，原来是Sandy让她送饭给我。Sandy特意做了土豆泥和果冻，说是这些咽喉痛也可以吃，虽然我实在没什么胃口，可还是把它们都吃完了。我只记得土豆泥放了黄油，很香，果冻则是浅红色的，不太甜，而且是冰镇过的，凉飕飕的。后来我出了国自己做土豆泥，也总喜欢放黄油，大概就是那次留下的印象。我不知道她对其他学生或同事是否也是这样，但对我来说，最真切的感受就是久违了的家的温暖，而这居然是从一位外教身上感受到的，所以更加难忘。

我硕士论文的主题是《红楼梦》和《汤姆琼斯》的比较，那时候对比较文学的理解还肤浅得很。我记得二年级定了题目以后就要去北京、上海查资料，其实也就是顺便去游学一番。我去了北京图书馆、北大图书馆、北师大图书馆，搜罗了一批

春色
任天涯
——福建华南女子
职业学院外教侧记
International Faculty with
Fujian Hua Nan Women's
College since 1908

528

资料回来，可还有些书根本没找到。Sandy知道了以后就自告奋勇地说她帮我找，我记得写了一个单子给她，她让她女儿在美国帮我找，没多久就都买到寄来了。我问Sandy要多少钱，她说这是送给我的，不要钱。我们当时都是穷学生，去北京查资料的时候住的地下室，或者借住北大或北师大同学的宿舍，怎么省钱怎么来。北图复印一页好像是两毛还是五毛，都觉得贵得不得了。收到这一包书我真是不知道怎么感谢Sandy才好。因为资料齐全，我几个月内就把论文写完了，按说三年级第二学期大概三四月份才交论文，我三年级第一学期末的十一月份就定稿了（其实那时早早写完论文还有一个目的，那就是准备专心考博）。最后定稿之前还是Amy帮忙打字输入（我那时候的论文都还是用纸笔写的，后来去了北京才开始用电脑），Sandy帮忙通读一遍，改正了不少错误。我在硕士论文致谢里特意提到了Sandy，没有她的鼎力相助，我的论文不可能完成得那么快。后来偶然有一次去Sandy的宿舍，她让我看她女儿写给她的Email，原来Sandy给她的单子上的书除了一本很贵她女儿没买，其他的都买了，不过她加了一句：Or if you like him that much, you can buy it for him. 那本很贵的书，就是后来闵先生大力推荐的余国藩（Anthony Yu）写的《重读石头记》（*Rereading the Stone*），怎么也得三四十美金吧（当时对我来说可是一笔巨款了，要知道我们每月生活费也就三四百元人民币，研究生的津贴每个月也就200多元）。钱多钱少倒不是重点，但可见Sandy对我喜欢的程度，以及她帮人帮到底的性格。

2000年，我硕士毕业那一年考上了北师大的委培博士。Sandy大概不明白委培是啥，但还是很为我高兴，不过同时她也告诉我说，因为要去加州照顾自己生病的弟弟，她要提前回国了。我一直以为她还会在福州待几年，所以当然很舍不得，但想想不久自己也要去北京读书，估计也很难再常见到她了。本来外教来华，就很少有一待好几年的。Sandy要回国之前，送了我一个小礼物，很简单的一个小摆设，她说是她朋友手工做的，上面是颗夜空中的星星，写着"Believe in yourself"。我到现在对自己还是很不自信，所以她这个礼物倒是送得很对。我从福州到北京读书，又从北京回到福州教书，再跨越大洋来到澳洲，这个小摆设一直放在我的书桌上，转眼15年了。

2001年还在北京读书时，我收到了一份特殊的圣诞礼物，夹在"For You, Son"的贺卡里面，贺卡上写着：Dear son Shengyu, Hope you have a Happy New Year and a wonderful Lunar New Year. Enclosed is a little something to help you celebrate. Love from Mum Sandy。她夹了一张二十美金的钞票！我还是第一次收到这样的礼物呢。我一直舍不得用掉。在北京读书的那几年，她每逢圣诞节必定给我寄贺卡。我记得偶尔也给她寄过福建茶叶什么的，那时她还在加州照顾她的弟弟，后来才搬回密苏里的家。我去了北京才开始用电脑，慢慢也开始用Email。不过Sandy写Email给我的时候不多，我倒是收到过好几封她的信。

2005年，我拿到哈佛霍顿图书馆的访学资助，去波士顿待了一个月，那时就很想去密苏里看看她。我给她打电话的时候，她知道我在哈佛非常高兴，忙说要替我找便宜机票，看什么时间我方便可以去看她。不过后来她建议我说因为只有一个月，还是好好在哈佛附近待着，密苏里来回至少要去掉一周。后来我听她的话，只去了纽瓦克，在Rutgers University的一位教授Barbara家住了两天，她带着我逛了一天纽约，其余时间都在哈佛附近待着。已经到了美国，却没能去看Sandy，想起来总觉得不免是个很大的遗憾。

Sandy送给我的那些卡片我都收在书架上，其中一张卡片上的一句话我觉得写得特别好，那就是："Your efforts will always reward you, maybe in unexpected ways."人生不可能老是一帆风顺，总有起起伏伏。遇到困难挫折，不妨把它看作暂时的风暴，总会过去。"不经历风雨，怎么见彩虹？"胸襟和眼光放得长远些，总是对的。Sandy好像是单亲妈妈，但我从来没有听她抱怨过谁。她为了照顾弟弟，中断在华南女院的教学生涯，为了照顾孙女让她搬来同住，而且从无怨言，这些都不是一般人能做到的。她豁达的心胸，温暖的笑容，从来都是令我一想起她来，就觉得很亲切。她过七十大寿的时候，我挑了一条澳洲产的羊毛围巾寄到美国给她。她特意打电话来道谢，说我选的大红颜色很适合她，各种衣服都可以搭配。听到她说喜欢我送的礼物，我自然也很高兴。

Sandy原来在密苏里州的Cassville有栋房子，她邀请我去了好几次，可我总也没能成行。就在我打算趁学术假去美国看她的时候，Sandy告诉我说，她把房子卖了，搬到Springfield的公寓里去住了。不能亲眼看到她在Cassville的房子，多多少少也是个遗憾。不过其实Sandy渐渐上了年纪，房子的琐碎事情总是很多，割草啊，修篱笆啊，剪树枝啊，要是想让花园好看点，得花不少时间和工夫呢，还是住公寓方便些。Sandy也计划来澳洲看我，但最后都没有成行。朋友总是聚少离多，何况我们相隔大洲大洋，就算最便捷的航班也要转个三五趟。我们虽然离得远，但还一直都保持着联系，偶尔打打电话，我还能听到她那熟悉的声音，也能想得见她那亲切的笑容。我跟Sandy福州一别至今就没有再见过，的确很是挂念。我衷心希望她健康长寿，也期盼我们再见的一天就在不远的将来。

2015年平安夜，堪培拉

春色
任天涯
——福建华南女子
职业学院外教侧记
International Faculty with
Fujian Hua Nan Women's
College since 1908

530

第九节　加州阳光
——小记福建华南女子职业学院的老朋友多迪

　　多迪（Dodie）全名是多琳·多萝西·约翰斯顿（Dorene Dorothy Johnston），但大家都喜欢叫她多迪。多迪来自阳光明媚的加州，而她开朗的性格，善解人意的笑容，总是给大家带来加州阳光的温暖。多迪常年在美国从事社会服务性工作，包括在特殊教育学校担任学校顾问、心理辅导师等。多迪于2000年第一次来华南女院教书，在接下来的十几年时间里，她先后于2002年、2003年、2004年、2005年、2008年、2011年共七次来华南教书，算得上是华南女院的老朋友了。大概在20世纪90年代，多迪在一本学校心理学家的专业杂志上读到一篇文章，这篇文章是华南女院的另外一位外教贝茨·里维特（Betts Rivet）写的，鼓励对中国有兴趣的学校心理学家来华南教书。多迪回信告诉贝茨她对这份工作有兴趣，但由于当时还未退休，希望将来有机会再去中国教书。几年之后，多迪和贝茨在澳大利亚举行的一场心理学专家的国际会议上相遇，贝茨继续鼓励她来华南女院。最终，在2000年，多迪做出了一个重要决定，那就是来华南女院任教。那年贝茨刚好有一个学期要待在美国，多迪非常担心她在华南女院教书会感到很孤单。但是当她在华南女院遇到了苏·托德（Sue Todd）和简·菲利普（Jeanne Phillips），还有桑德拉·卡勒斯（Sandra Cullers）、卡丽·理查森（Carrie Richardson），还有好多热情友好的中国老师，比如当时的外事处处长许道锋，英语专业教师林娇，多迪知道了她在华南女院根本不会感到孤独！

　　多迪来华南女院之前没有任何教书的经验，但每个人都那么友好地帮助她。第一年她所教授的学生们非常热情并充满激情，多迪很快就学会了在课堂上如何吸引学生们的注意力。但是她每个晚上都不得不花一些时间备课，因为多迪并没有经验也不自信，她总是需要比学生们先准备一步。多迪这么评价她2000级所教授的学生："她们实在是太可爱太天真无邪

多迪在学院欢迎外教晚宴上

了！我从来没有见过像她们一样的年轻人！她们对学习充满渴望，尊重老师。她们单纯又乐意参与，所以我们有很多机会练习英语口语，一起画复活节的彩蛋，在自由谈话课上畅所欲言。"

华南女院多年沉淀下来的国际文化也给外国友人们提供了一个"跋山涉水只为与一个知心朋友相见"的机会。多迪在华南女院教书的第一年遇到了简·菲利普，你会有这样的体会，当你遇到一个人，你有感觉就是她。从她说的话，从她的幽默感，你就知道你们一定会成为好朋友，简·菲利普之于多迪就是这样的一个人。从2000年多迪和她的初遇，到后来建立起了深厚的友情。两年之后，当简·菲利普由于身体的原因不能再回中国，多迪总是会去科罗拉多州看望她。多迪欣赏简·菲利普的智慧，在她脸上看到了坚强和对中国深深的眷恋。2013年当简·菲利普离开人世的时候，多迪也是第一个向华南女院老朋友传达噩耗的人。

2000年，多迪和简·菲利普在教学上决定做一些新的尝试，她们认为如果按照学生的英语水平来分班的话会是个好主意。在2000级英语专业新生里，她们给学生做了个简单的测试，根据她们的英文能力分成了一个重点班、一个弱班和两个普通班。多迪教最好的班级和一个普通班，简·菲利普教差班和另外一个普通班。她们忘了一个事实，所有的演讲比赛和其他各项竞赛都是以班级为单位，并不像在美国是以个人。在多迪的重点班学生赢得了所有的荣誉，因为她们又聪明又努力。多迪突然意识到她和简·菲利普的这个决定是如此糟糕，所有的获奖者都在一个班上，她们战胜了其他所有的班级。这并不应该是中国的方式，为此两位老太太感到非常尴尬和抱歉，以至于时隔多年，仍记忆犹新。

多迪和她的学生

春色
任天涯
——福建华南女子
职业学院外教侧记
International Faculty with
Fujian Hua Nan Women's
College since 1908

532

对于按程度分班教学而言，时任普通班级的班主任是这么说的：对于老师来说比较好管理和教学。分班有好处，教学上统一步伐的话进步更快。但对学生来说会产生心理压力、自卑等情绪，同时如果参加年段英语类比赛对弱班来说没有优势。虽然作为老师极力不挑明分班事实，学生还是很敏感。除非两个班由不同的老师教学，老师可以针对性选择教程，学生就不存在有被区别对待的疑心。分班的话，同班学生处于平均水平，学习上不会有先进弱后之分，也就和平共处了。但从另一方面讲，混班生、积极的学生可以带动弱后生，产生互补作用。据当时来自弱班的班主任的经验分享：从老师角度，给水平相当的学生上课，课堂备课授课安排组织会更顺手。从管理学生角度看，有很多不好的因素。当学生知道了自己被标记为差生后，很多学生就很自卑，班级整体情绪低，不愿意与其他班级接触。同时，因没有相关的计划按水平提升分班，有的学生直接就给自己标榜"我是差生"，对学生的整体心理发展并没有起到积极的作用。从学习方面考虑，她们的水平相当，合作学习工作是不错，但要找出特别好的引领帮助差的学生，这协调工作就难做。还好当时配的外教们都很用心，才抚平她们心中的那份不平衡，经过很长的时间才调整心态，进入学习轨道。也好在当时这批学生大部分都吃过苦，心理承受力也好些，勇于挑战，不自我放弃，配合老师，才慢慢提升学业。分班教学是一个孰是孰非的问题，不管对于老师还是学生来说，各有各的角度和看法，在2000级之后英语专业的学生再没有通过英语面试进行分班。我们暂且不论其优劣，但两位外教勇于尝试，对学生的良苦用心可见一斑。也难怪在多年之后她们还会记挂此事，并为此感到抱歉。

暂且抛开让这位老太太一直记挂的尴尬事，到底是什么样的动力让这位美国老太太一而再再而三返回中国到华南女院任教？在多迪年轻的岁月里，日子跟大多数中国女性一样过得紧张而忙碌，结婚，生子，离婚，回到校园拿到硕士学位，搬家，再婚，得到第一份工作在学校里当心理辅导师，积极投入到社区活动中，比如在社区里唱赞美诗，加入环保组织、文学组织、滑冰俱乐部等，再后来她成为一名白水漂流的导游和镶嵌玻璃的艺术家。在她身上可是把妇女解放体现得淋漓尽致！可是，当她的孩子渐渐长大，从校园毕业求得工作之后，她也由于年龄渐长不再适合当导游，自她从学校退休之后，对于拯救河流和保护当地环境的工作已经开始感到不耐烦了，生活开始变得平淡无味，她需要的是一些新挑战和新激情。

来中国对多迪是一个全新的挑战，教书更是一个全新的挑战，但幸而认识了一些给予她极大帮助的外教们，比如苏·托德，简·菲利普和贝茨。她深深喜欢学校的氛围，各个年龄层的人住在一座楼里。华南女院有如此大的魅力吸引着这么多人来

多迪参观永定土楼

多迪和美国普吉湾大学师生在古田

这里教书和访问。要是在美国就只能和同龄人、同样政治信仰的人在一起，而来到华南女院，生活实在有趣多了！

华南女院的老师实在是太友好了，非常细致耐心地照顾外教。她有无数多美好的回忆，比如和年轻老师外出活动一起参与项目。当时外事处的许道锋、董秀萍和姚亚美总是热心地帮助她，当然还有可爱的厨师准备可口的饭菜。就算时过境迁，新校区的环境已经完全不同了，但外事处的吴瑷瑷、程铭茜，还有新的厨师仍然把

多迪和其他外教在永泰游玩

春色
任天涯
——福建华南女子
职业学院外教侧记
International Faculty with
Fujian Hua Nan Women's
College since 1908

534

传统全部带到了新校区。你无法想象其他学校的外教是如何妒忌华南女院外教的福利待遇！

年复一年，岁月在改变，老太太也感到了自身的变化。当她成为更好的老师，对自己和对学生的要求也越来越严格。学生们开始变得复杂，开始关心化妆和穿衣打扮，开始变得像西方年轻人一样，埋头玩手机而不是专心上课。到了2008年，福州更像是美国一个大城镇，到处都是购物中心，旧校区已经被改造，华南女院也搬到了大学城。学校变大了，管理也更规范了，老师们也越来越忙，可以一起出去玩的时间也慢慢没有了。老太太在为学校发展感到由衷高兴的同时，也知道自己已经不适合继续待下去了！

多迪现在美国，退休后她写了一本关于中国的书。当多迪向他人介绍她的书时是这么描述的："我写的书叫作《中国是怎么样的》，这本书一部分是回忆录，一部分是小说，还有一部分是游记。当然也有非常生动的历史，因为我在有着百年历史的学校教书，这让我有10年左右的时间了解中国的崛起和富强，给我的创作提供了时间框架。这些故事从我的学生们到我的同事们，充满了幽默和深度。把他们全部融合到一块就是我冒险故事的生动体现，从教室到邻里，再到小村庄。读完这本书，你再也不会用旧眼光看中国了！"下面征得多迪的同意，摘录其在书结尾处的部分内容，以飨读者。

当一些中国老太太们从"文化大革命"的灰烬中让他们深爱的学校重生会发生什么事情？那些进入新华南女院念书的、乐观的年轻人是谁？那个没有任何英语教学背景的退休的心理学家，是如何度过了那10年，却仅仅只是发现，她自己才一直是学生的？

中国是怎么样的？用幽默、诚实和智慧来回答这些问题。部分回忆录，部分历史，部分插图，这本书让你知道一个你从未见过的中国。你会在老福州的街道上，快乐地享受生活；你还可以在市场上买到漂亮的瓷器。看着学生变成上班族，然后成为妻子和母亲。一个学校简短但生动的历史，也是中国共产党的胜利，中国的富裕和强大的历史。

中国是怎么样的？这本书描绘了两代女性不同的形象。当你读她们的故事，拜访她们生活的村庄，你甚至可以看到她们的未来。作为本书的作者，在2000年至2011年之间多次往返中国福州，观察她的学生文化和周边的变化。

第十节　高雅的郁金香
——记葛·凯伦博士

　　郁金香的花语是：高雅、博爱、聪颖、能干，用郁金香来形容葛·凯伦博士，应该是恰到好处。凯伦1938年5月出生于美国密歇根州，1959年于美国西密歇根大学获得学士学位，专业是英语与历史。本科毕业后，凯伦准备学以致用，开始在大学任教。由于对学术的兴趣不减，她一边工作一边继续深造，陆续获得了两个硕士学位，一个是1963年在密歇根州立大学获得的，专业是政治学；另一个是1970年在俄勒冈大学获得的，专业是亚洲研究。此时的凯伦虽然已经可以用学识渊博来形容，可是她对亚洲的研究还是意犹未尽，于是她继续攻读博士。功夫不负有心人，1980年凯伦获得美国俄勒冈大学历史学博士学位，她在读博士期间研究亚洲历史，尤其是现代中国历史，她的博士论文就是以中国二万五千里长征为研究对象的。看了凯伦的教育背景，你一定忍不住感到震撼吧。

　　来华之前，凯伦在美国南俄勒冈大学担任历史学教授，为人谦逊、和蔼。从1982年开始教授中国历史，一直教了近20年，从此与中国结下了不解之缘，称得上是一位中国通。在教学生涯中，她生动地向她的学生介绍文明古国之一的中国以及中国上下5000年的悠久历史，她还从历史的角度研究亚洲女性，多次以中国为主题举办讲座，搭建中西文化的桥梁，让美国人了解中国。此外，她多次在国际学术会议上提交论文，曾在马尼拉和新加坡的国际会议上提交了关于中国长征的论文，在曼谷的国际会议上提交了关于中国民间故事的论文，在香港的国际会议上提交了关于湄洲岛妇女生活的论文，还在莆田的国际会议上发表了关于妈祖（中国东南沿海的海神）的论文。这些都体现了葛·凯伦博士对中国历史，乃至对福建民俗的深入研究。如果说凯伦在读博士期间研究中国历史是在她的心中为日后来中国这片神秘的土地埋下了种子，那么教中国历史、举办讲座和提交论文就是这颗种子在渐渐生根发芽。

　　研究中国多年后，凯伦的"中国梦"终于在1979年9月实现了，当时中国刚刚改革开放，她得到一个机会来中国，在邮轮上给从大洋彼岸来的游客介绍中国历史和文化，邮轮沿途停靠上海、天津等港口。由于凯伦强大的知识储备，经过她生动

春色任天涯
——福建华南女子
职业学院外教侧记
International Faculty with
Fujian Hua Nan Women's
College since 1908

536

的讲解，旅客们对中国博大精深的文化和悠久的历史有了进一步的了解，给他们的旅途增添了不少乐趣。能让自己梦想成真并且学以致用，凯伦感到无比幸运。凯伦说，她热爱中国，现在依然如此。回想起当时对中国的印象，她觉得在那个年代中国人对外国人实在是太好奇了，有一次，凯伦在路边停下来换胶卷，一瞬间四周便围了几十个人，有的一直打量着她，有的向她提出各种问题。

凯伦摄于中国国家大剧院前

当时的上海还不是个现代化大都市，高楼大厦寥寥可数，一座十几层楼的酒店已经让人惊叹不已了。北京、上海这些大城市的交通可不像现在这么拥堵，街上车辆并不多，在大街上闲逛感到十分惬意。邮轮之行给凯伦留下了美好的回忆，三个月之后，凯伦怀着依依不舍的心情离开了中国，她有点伤感，因为不知道什么时候还能再来这个她喜爱的国家。

1987年1月，凯伦在俄勒冈州高等教育学习项目中兼任了俄勒冈大学与福建师范大学交换生项目的联络员，通过这个交流项目，福建的一些官员、学者可以到俄勒冈大学攻读硕士学位，而俄勒冈大学的在校生可以到福建师范大学学习汉语。凯伦作为俄勒冈大学的带队老师，随着学生一起来到中国。为了让学生们适应福州的生活，凯伦尽力地给他们提供帮助，在生活上无微不至地照顾他们，还与师大的老师一起带他们去厦门、泉州、武夷山等地方游玩。在担任联络员期间，凯伦结识了

凯伦和福建师范大学的老师
（右二为凯伦的翻译伙伴陈泽平）

凯伦被福建省人民政府授予福建
省第一届"友谊奖"

师大的老师，与他们建立了深厚的情谊。凯伦被中国朋友的热情好客深深打动了，所以第二年又申请当带队老师来中国。1988年，热心的凯伦为一位师大的老师写推荐信，帮助他出国深造，后来这位师大的老师获得了美国密歇根大学的博士学位。同一年，凯伦还帮助了另一位师大的老师到南俄勒冈大学教汉语。经过凯伦的努力，交流项目得以顺利进行。

20世纪90年代初期，通过凯伦大量的工作，南俄勒冈大学与福建师范大学启动了教工交流项目，两所院校各派12名教工到对方学校访学。为了促进福建与俄勒冈的教师交流项目顺利开展，凯伦积极地奔走于美国的俄勒冈州与中国的福建省之间，促进了两国之间的学术交流，无私地帮助了福建师范大学更多的老师到美国学习和深造。鉴于她为福建省的教育事业做出了重大的贡献，1999年9月29日，葛·凯伦博士被福建省人民政府授予"友谊奖"荣誉称号，值得一提的是，这是福建省的第一届友谊奖。

2000年，凯伦从美国南俄勒冈大学退休。退休后，她来到第二故乡——中国任教，她半年在福州教书，半年回美国。2001年至2003年，她在福建师范大学外国语学院担任访问教授，教外语专业研究生的英语写作课，2004年至2006年在福建师范大学协和学院教英语专业的口语课程。由于凯伦与华南女院的外教凯·格里姆斯是好朋友，在热心的凯的邀请下，凯伦经常到华南女院的外教餐厅与凯共进午餐。用餐时，凯伦结识了华南女院的其他外教和一些工作人员。2008年2月，在好朋友凯的引荐下，凯伦来到华南女院担任自由谈话课的授课老师。在教学中，凯伦秉持认真、严谨的态度，选取适合学生的话题进行讨论，努力创造轻松愉快的交谈氛围。她的自由谈话课不仅内容丰富，而且形式多样。有时她会用一些写着问题的卡片来提问学生；有时她会用扔球的形式来提问学生，接到球的学生要回答问题；有时她会把要学的词汇罗列在黑板上，让学生来造句；有时凯伦给出一个故事的开头，如"昨天，两个女生正在学生街走着……"，然后让学生发挥想象力接着往下编故事；天气晴朗的日子，她还会带学生去学校旁边的烟台山进行情景教学。2010年3月，在华南女院搬到大学城之后，凯伦再次来到华南女院，承担了两个班自由谈话课的教学任务。很多学生比较腼腆，因为怕说错而不敢开口，凯伦认为，要培养学生的自信心，就不要刻意去纠正她们的错误。

谈到对华南女院的感想，凯伦说，20年前，好友简·菲利浦告诉她，当时华南女院学生的英语水平非常棒，在福建省内是数一数二的，找工作都不用愁。可是多年后凯伦来这儿教书，发现有些学生在学业上不够努力，因此而感到有些失望。但

春色任天涯
——福建华南女子
职业学院外教侧记
International Faculty with
Fujian Hua Nan Women's
College since 1908

538

是凯伦还是觉得这儿的女孩子们都很贴心，都是好孩子。她十分敬佩华南女院的创办者，因为她们给女性提供了接受教育的平台。据她所知，在早期的华南女院，外教是没有工资的，他们身上都具有一种奉献精神。还有华南女院的"老太太"们，她们在华南女院也没有工资，却源源不断地付出了自己的时间和精力，因为她们相信华南女院。凯伦觉得大多数的华南女院教职员工都非常敬业。

凯伦不仅对中国文化很有研究，普通话也讲得很好，能够自如地与中国人沟通。凯伦是从1968年开始学习汉语的，当时她在俄勒冈大学读研究生。1970年她在台北参加了一个为期一年的汉语学习集训课程，当然在台湾学的是繁体字。后来，凯伦攻读博士学位的时候，由于她的博士论文是研究中国长征的，她翻阅了大量关于中国革命的历史资料，并且认识了中文的简体字，她的汉语阅读能力突飞猛进。在20世纪80年代，会说英语的中国人很少，交换生的带队老师，常常都是靠自己所学的汉语与中国人沟通，她的一口流利汉语就是在那个时候练出来的。

才华横溢的凯伦凭借着卓越的汉语表达能力以及对中国这片土地的了解，于1995年翻译了福建民间故事并将书名定为《想象妇女·福建民间故事》，该书在纽约Interlink出版社出版。后来，凯伦与师大中文系陈泽平教授合作又翻译了许多本书籍，例如，他们合作翻译中国作家残雪的书籍《天空里的蓝光》和《五香街》，分别在纽约New Direction出版社和耶鲁大学出版社出版。除了翻译书籍，凯伦和陈泽平教授还一起翻译了40多篇中国当代短篇小说，这些短篇故事多被美国文学期刊收录。由于凯伦精通汉语，2008年她应邀在福州大学陈小慰教授主编的《福建省情词汇表达速译手册》中任语言顾问和英文审稿工作，这本书后来成为英语专业学生的口译辅助教材。此外，凯伦曾担任过福建电视台的英文顾问。2014年，凯伦协助福建省外事办翻译了旅游资料。

作为教师，崇尚教育、热爱中国文化的葛·凯伦博士将这份热爱延续到了中国学生的身上，这些年来，许多中国学生得到了她的帮助。凯伦曾经推荐一位福建师大的学生到南俄勒冈大学留学，帮她解决住宿问题，还资助这位学生直到毕业。她与好友路易斯·罗默一起资助过一位中学生，后来该生考入福建卫生职业技术学院，凯伦又继续支付了三年的大专学费。充满爱心的凯伦听说有一个名叫"福建儿童"的组织专门帮助福建一些家庭贫困的孩子，她就联系了那个组织，并且慷慨相助。2006年起长达9年的时间里，凯伦一共资助了福建省福安市锦桌头小学的6名来自贫困家庭的小学生，直至他们小学毕业，有的升入中学后还继续得到凯伦的资助。其中的一位在凯伦的鼓励下考入华南女院，并且第一年的大学学费是凯伦资助的。当

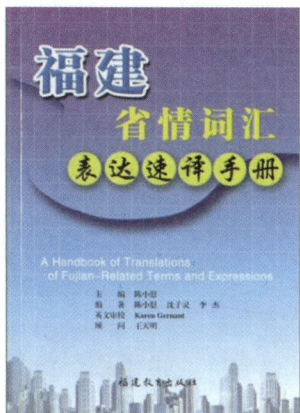

福建省情词汇表达速译手册

A Handbook of Translations of Fujian-Related Terms and Expressions

凯伦担任该书的语言顾问与英文审稿工作

时，凯伦去锦桌头看望孩子们，要先从福州坐火车到福安，然后还要坐一个半小时的汽车才能到达目的地，实在是非常辛苦，可是能给他人提供帮助，凯伦感到十分开心。来自美国的凯伦老师的爱心让这些锦桌头的孩子在学习的道路上增添了许多正能量，他们的家庭也少了些许负担。此外，胸怀博大的凯伦还为做心脏手术的孤儿捐款，为残疾儿童改善教室环境，为贫困儿童添置新衣。凯伦把她对中国这片土地的热爱化作一种关爱，她一直无私奉献，默默付出，不求回报。

热忱、真挚的凯伦人缘很好，有很多中国朋友，最近她还紧跟时代步伐开通了微信，与朋友们用微信交流呢。凯伦对中国的感情犹如涓涓细流，源远流长。她在这里安了家，在中国买了属于自己的房子，家里布置得很有中国味道。我在凯伦的家里和凯伦一边喝茶，一边聊天，甚感惬意，根本感觉不到中西方文化的碰撞，而是感觉到在和一位阅历丰富的朋友聊天。我们为身边有这样一位良师益友而感到无比幸运和自豪，凯伦的故事就像一本珍贵的书籍，耐人寻味。凯伦的好友路易斯评价凯伦是一个友好、有智慧、充满活力的人。的确，葛·凯伦博士就好比一朵绚丽高贵的郁金香，她的聪慧让她对中国有了丰富的了解，她的博爱使她帮助了许多人，她的芬芳洒满了八闽大地，她的才干让她促进了福建教育事业的发展。

凯伦和她资助的学生（左二）

葛·凯伦与本文作者摄于阳光新村（凯伦在中国的家）

春色
任天涯
——福建华南女子
职业学院外教侧记
International Faculty with
Fujian Hua Nan Women's
College since 1908

540

第十一节 一生的坚守：做个有用的人
——记路易斯·罗默博士

初识路易斯·罗默博士

2006年暑期，外事办向我负责的专业推荐了一位美国外籍教师，给了我一份长达8页的简历，他就是路易斯·罗默：在美国高校从教35年，教授，应用科学（电子工程）博士，工程师，雷达和通信专家，科研论文、著书、专利总计多达近100项。如此博学、专业的专家会乐意来我们华南女院这样的"小庙"吗？我带着疑问再次和外事办确认，得到的答案是肯定的。我随即通过电子邮件与路易斯·罗默博士取得联系，希望他能在新学期教授学生《英语毕业论文写作》课程，他欣然答应，并告诉我他8月24日下午到达福州，并不顾时差反应，要求26日下午约见，交流新学期课程的相关事宜。

我如期赴约，在外事办专家楼的会客室第一次见到了这位心目中的资深教授，一眼看去活脱脱就是一个圣诞老人，身材高大魁梧，胡子花白，和蔼可亲，虽已年届古稀之年，但仍然精神矍铄，思维极其敏捷，走起路来健步如飞。

路易斯·罗默博士出生在美国一个军人家庭，父亲是一名军官。童年是在巴拿马运河区和马里兰州度过的，二战时他父亲在菲律宾，他则生活在加利福尼亚州。后来，他迁往特拉华州上大学，就读于特拉华大学的物理专业。获得物理理科学士后，在美国海军服兵役三年。退役后，又回到特拉华大学攻读电子工程硕士和博士。毕业后，在俄亥俄州阿克伦大学任教21年，1989年被路易斯安那理工大学聘为电子工程系主任。其间他还在美国国家航空航天局（NASA）和美国工程教育协会（ASEE）兼职，从事雷达和通讯研究，他说这些经历使他获得了更多的实践经验。

2003年路易斯从路易斯安那理工大学退休后，一心想着要继续让自己成为有用的人！他便申请参加美国护卫队工作（US Peace Corps，美国联邦政府管理的志愿者组织），但在等待审批的过程中，一位中国朋友安排他前往青岛科技大学任教。一年后，他回到了美国，但仍惦记着自己要成为有用的人，便想再回中国帮助那些需要他帮助的人。正在寻找合适的单位时，他意外接到了当时在华南女院任教的美国老师贝茨·里韦特博士（Dr. Betts Rivet）的电话，问他是否乐意到华南女院任教，他欣然答应。这一答应，便使他与福州结下了不解之缘，一待便是10年，他在这里不仅收获了浓浓的友情，而且实现了他成为有用之人的梦想，不断地发挥自己的余热。

路易斯的筑梦之旅

"英语毕业论文写作"是路易斯到华南女院教授的第一门课，他负责商务英语专业2004级两个班、80个学生的教学工作，指导和批改任务艰巨。由于远道而来，初来乍到，各种的不适应，而且9月的福州恰逢"秋老虎"，酷热难当，对于怕热的他，是严峻的考验，每次一进教室便是大

路易斯·罗默博士

汗淋漓。教室设备又非常简陋，讲台只有一台风扇，但他心疼学生，于是把风扇朝向了学生，结果他没能顶住，中暑发烧病倒，辗转多家医院病情一直反反复复，但他没落下一次课，仍然坚持走进课堂。这门课从指导学生选题、拟提纲、写开题报告、正文语言组织、论文格式规范，他都一一手把手指导，逐字逐句批改，课后还约见每位同学，而且每周固定给我一封电子邮件，反馈学生学习的情况。

有一次，外事办同事看他在电脑边一边修改学生论文，一边摇头，表情甚是失望。原来，有同学的论文经他查重，被发现有抄袭行为，他无奈地说："我要向主任反映了！"他很快找到我，交给了我一个光盘和一本厚厚的笔记本。光盘是标准规范的论文样文以及引言规范书写的指导。笔记本的封面赫然用大写字母写着"建议的商务论文题目（供下届参考），2007年4月4日，署名：路易斯·罗默"。翻开笔记本是他为了最大化避免学生抄袭，一笔一画拟写了20个与福州本地实际相结合的调查论文题目，并附调查研究的思路，结尾用语重心长的寄语，希望学生能严谨治学，诚实做人，为自己和母校赢得良好声誉！

面对大专学生的实际英语水平和论文撰写功底，要上好这门课确实不易，但是路易斯做到了。除了承担这门课，他还主动请缨帮忙毕业论文的安排工作，如《毕业论文答辩工作指南》的撰写，全过程组织学生答辩。

春色
任天涯
——福建华南女子
职业学院外教侧记
International Faculty with
Fujian Hua Nan Women's
College since 1908

542

乐善好施，大爱无疆

"与人分享，力所能及地帮助别人，总是一件很快乐的事。"路易斯常常这么说，也一直是这么做的。

据原华南女院外事办的一位老师回忆，路易斯刚刚应聘来华南女院教书的那个暑假，他在西安交大教法律的女儿因为要回国，把所有家用电器和行李都寄到华南女院给他。他到任后发现华南女院提供了所有的生活用品，就把他女儿给他的电器都悉数送给临时工了。有同事建议他留些电器放在自己的房间里，方便时还可以用用。他却回答说，餐厅里有公用的电器了，还是把东西留给更需要的人。

至今路易斯在外事办的老邻居仍清楚地记得她女儿懂事后的第一个圣诞节是怎么过的。当时女儿问她为什么专家楼到处挂着圣诞袜，她妈妈，也就是路易斯的邻居就告诉她，只要她好好表现，圣诞前夕圣诞老人会往她的袜子里放礼物。原本以为只是随便一说，没想到圣诞节那天，小女孩一大早就起床去翻挂在铁门上的袜子。那时她妈妈又紧张又担心，因为自己什么都没放进去，担心这样会让孩子伤心失望。结果小女孩惊喜地掏出了好多礼物，有玩具、水果、巧克力。本以为事情到此就告一个段落了，但是小女孩坚持认为自己是个好孩子，圣诞老人应该每天都来看她。所以她每天都表现得很好，主动问好，自己能做的事情都自己做。路易斯一直扮演着圣诞老人的角色，他在中国的每一天对这个小女孩来说都是圣诞节。因为挂在铁门上的那只袜子里永远装满礼物。如今这位小女孩已长大，成了他的忘年交。这位老邻居感叹道："做一次两次好事不难，可一辈子做好事真不容易！"路易斯正是这样拥有一颗善良的心，他愿意尽自己所能去帮助身边的每一个人，哪怕是一个小孩。

路易斯老邻居的侄女为了得到更好的教育，随她到福州一起生活。然而，有次老邻居家里遭窃，家里给侄女准备的学费也被偷了。路易斯和他的好朋友得知后，一起把邻居侄女的学费全都垫上，而且从初一开始一直资助她到中专毕业。期间老邻居多次婉言谢绝，但他总是淡淡地说，他只是做了自己能做的小事而已。如今，这位邻居的侄女已经成为一名医务工作者，路易斯也成了她心目中常常惦记的爷爷，时常去看望他。

路易斯到福州后认识的挚友葛·凯伦，他们有共同的爱好、相同的价值观，都热爱中国，喜欢阅读、听音乐、看戏，一起参观展览、旅游、烹饪，兴趣广泛。说起路易斯，葛·凯伦对他总是赞不绝口，说他心地善良、对人体贴、善待他人且聪明睿智。最让她感动的是，路易斯曾经为了帮助一个盲人同学功课而自学盲文。一般而言不管什么年龄的外国人学习中文都是令人有点望而却步的事情，但是令她和其他人感到惊讶的是，路易斯能在这个年龄，把中文学到游刃有余，并记了很多汉字；更令她佩服的是，他很有孩子缘，这是美国老年人中少见的，孩子们很顺从他。她很喜欢看着他和孩子们——如他的孙子们和学生们交流，孩子们是那么敬重他。

与生同乐，永葆童心

2010 年因华南女院迁到大学城新校区，交通不便，路易斯便辞去了该校专任教学工作，但心中想成为有用之人的梦想依然如初。他主动承担起每个周末在华南女院旧址外籍专家楼义务帮助华南女院员工孩子学习英语的任务，分文不取，直到 2013 年该旧址转让。华南女院应用英语专业一位老师深有感触地说："路易斯是一个很有绅士风度的外教，永远不跟别人争名夺利，永远是谦谦君子。印象最深刻的是他对孩子的那份耐心，他对着一群年龄和兴趣相差悬殊的孩子，采用生动的绘本、丰富的肢体语言和有趣的游戏让学生开心学习英语。他那圣诞老爷爷一般慈祥的笑容，让孩子们觉得特别亲切，孩子们都亲切地叫他 'Grandpa'，因为这位可爱的 '圣诞老爷爷'，英语学习在孩子眼里变得有趣起来。我对他充满敬意，感受到他对于中国孩子们深深的爱。"

2011 年初，我接到外事办一位老师热情洋溢的电话，问我家小孩子是否需要外教辅导英语，并说路易斯很乐意帮助有需要的孩子学英语，我当即表示愿意，并给他发了一封邮件，同时推荐了华南女院几个同事的同龄孩子一起参加他的英语学习班。他欣然同意，并希望此举作为一份礼物无偿地送给孩子们，理由很简单，他说他在中国收获了很多人的帮助，希望自己有机会回馈，举手之劳而已。不曾想，他的这一举手之劳一直坚持至今，每周六风雨无阻地陪伴在这群孩子的身边，循序渐进地引导孩子们掌握英语知识点、拓展阅读；带孩子们做游戏、表演剧本、逛超市、参观创意园；边学习制作西点，边学习英语，其乐融融。他说引导孩子做中学能让孩子真正体会到学习的快乐。为了使孩子拓宽阅读面，激发孩子的兴趣和达到教育孩子的目的，他不辞辛苦，亲自编写英文故事，一个个孩子也成了故事中的主人公，活灵活现于每个充满友爱的、温情的、对中国传统文化满怀敬畏之心的故事中。如今他创作的 80 多个故事已被编辑、印刷成两本精美故事集（第三本即将与读者见面），并赠给华南女院的学生、初中生和亲朋好友，为的是让更多的孩子受益于这些故事。

"5 年前，从一位好友那儿得知有一位美国朋友愿意在周末义务为孩子们上英语口语课。于是带着些许好奇心与孩子加入这个特殊的班级，结识了这位特殊的老师，

春色
任天涯
——福建华南女子
职业学院外教侧记
International Faculty with
Fujian Hua Nan Women's
College since 1908

544

来自大洋彼岸的老者——路易斯·罗默。5年多来，无论刮风下雨，这位身材魁梧、精神矍铄的老者总是如约而至，与孩子们共度周末时光。他不仅教孩子们英语单词与表达，还教孩子们如何染布；闲暇之余他带孩子们到他的住所亲自动手做西点，到麦德龙超市比对商品价格与重量，指导孩子们如何合理购物、经济持家……在他的课堂上，孩子们学到了中国课堂学不到的知识。几年来，他成了孩子们周末的期盼。虽然我不信基督教，不是基督徒，但请允许我说：'感谢上帝！给我们送来一位如此慈祥、乐善好施的异国友人！'他给予我们和孩子们的关爱和帮助，时时萦绕在我们周围，成为我们生活中的一抹亮丽的色彩，激励我们如他一般热情、友爱地对待身边的每一个人。他的大爱精神，无关宗教，无关国籍，直指人的本心。请允许我在此代表这个班级所有孩子和家长向路易斯说：'遇上你真好！'"一位孩子的妈妈动情地如此说道。

孩子们课后都亲切地叫他路易斯爷爷，每逢节日都会给他送上最真挚的祝福和谢意。看到孩子们渐渐长大，他很是欣慰，常说："这些孩子很棒！英语水平远远超过美国同龄孩子！"

由于他年事已高，我们不希望他过于劳累，但他总说："我已经老了，但还对孩子们有用，我很开心！和他们一起成长，我感觉自己还不老！"为了成为一个有用的人，他依然乐此不疲。

行走福州，其乐无穷

有人说："爱上一座城，是因为城中住着某位喜欢的人。"而路易斯说："我每年都要回到福州，是因为城中有我喜欢的一切！"他喜欢福州的生机勃勃，深深爱上这座欣欣向荣的城市。他说他最爱每日坚持行走于福州城的大街小巷，去感受福州深厚的文化底蕴，去见证福州的变化，去珍惜福州的温情和友谊。

坐落小区两边的剧院，是他常去的地方，听戏、看演出，成了他了解福州传统文化的窗口；在学生街的早市，他乐于穿梭于熙熙攘攘的人群中，挑选新鲜的蔬菜和水果；沿着学生街往里走，是他常常要介绍朋友认识的文化创意园，院子里的一砖一瓦，每个创意工作室，他可以娓娓道来；他爱走街串巷，沿路他总喜欢经停一些老工厂，和工人们聊聊天；有时从闽江公园步行至花海公园，一路风景宜人，公园里，孩子与父母和祖父母间的那份天伦之乐会让他感动不已。行走时，他说偶尔还可以踱步到远离城市喧嚣的寺庙，享受一份宁静，品尝一份美味素食，而行走于泥泞老路上，他沉醉于人们如何习惯于新的马路和建筑。

　　看到福州城日新月异的变化，他和城中人一样激动，并用手中的相机记录了城市每个角落的点滴故事，当看到路边需要帮助的人，还可以及时搭把手，这一切都是他爱上行走福州的理由。

　　为什么已入耄耋之年了，路易斯还千里迢迢在中国寻梦、追梦？他如是说："人生就是一场旅行，做有用的人是人人之所需。我将之比作种树。'前人种树，后人乘凉。'当我们长大时，必须要为后人种树。希望世界也会因我们的努力付出而变得更加美丽。我们无法左右别人的生活，但我们可以为他们开启一扇门，通往更美好的路，帮助他们实现目标。我视之为责任，但更多的是一种乐趣。常言道：'教育是使火焰燃烧，而不是灌输。'如果一个人想学习，我们就要帮助他。如果一个人没有丝毫学习动力，我们能做的也就是祝福他的人生。久而久之，人们就从生活中吸取教训。"

第四章

福建华南女子职业学院的外教文化内核

春色
任天涯
——福建华南女子
职业学院外教侧记
International Faculty with
Fujian Hua Nan Women's
College since 1908

548

第一节　福建华南女子职业学院的外教政策

1984年10月，福建华南女子职业学院复校，这是旅居海内外的老华南女院校友以华南女子文理学院暨附中校友会的名义，在余宝笙博士的带领下努力的结果。学院奉行国际化道路，自建校以来，学院除得到省和市政府、爱德基金会，以及香港董事会的帮助外，还得到了国际友好组织，如亚洲高等教育基督教联合董事会（以下简称亚联董）和美国联合卫理公会全球事工属下的妇女部的长期支持。自1985年起，在亚联董和爱德基金会的大力帮助下，学院引进美国、英国、澳大利亚等国的外籍教师80多人近200人次。

为了进一步了解华南女院复办之初的外教政策与外教管理，我们采访了陈钟英理事长、林本椿顾问、原外事处许道锋处长、原应用英语专业主任何孝智老师，以及原教务处处长马秀发老师。

华南女院自复校之初就非常看重外籍教师的引进。一方面，是出于对老华南女院办学过程中外籍教师所扮演的不可或缺角色的充分认识，另一方面，是以余宝笙博士为代表的老华南女院校友对外教特色这一传统的继承与推崇。在采访中，陈钟英理事长回忆："余院长很看重外教工作。余院长把她的办公室设在外专楼（外籍教师居住的独栋建筑），每当余院长给我们开完会后，她就会端着一杯茶继续到外专楼与外籍教师交流，因此外籍教师有什么反馈或者建议，余院长即刻就会知道。"深受余院长的影响，陈钟英理事长担任华南女院院长期间也十分重视外教建设。

陈钟英理事长

采访中许道锋老师说道："外教是老华南的特色，也是保证教学活动正常进行与教学质量稳固的重要条件，尤其是英语专业。"因此，华南女院复办初期，余宝笙院长以及陈钟英教授等老一辈华南女院校友就通过各种方式联系外教来到华南女院任教。在初期阶段，亚联董给予华南女院很大的帮助，亚联董选派了多位外教前来华南女院任教。其中有一部分是复办前就来过华南女院教学的外教，一部分是亚联董以及这些外教们介绍来的。这些外教为复办后的华南女院的发展注入了巨大的力量。

林本椿教授担任华南女院院长期间，延续了余宝笙博士与陈钟英理事长重视外教的传统。一方面，他加强与亚联董的沟通，请亚联董帮助派遣优秀的外教来华南女院任教，丰富华南女院的外教资源，使学生受益；另一方面，林本椿顾问通过邮件与老华南第一任校长程吕底亚后代程戈登联络，诚挚邀请他来华南女院看看。程戈登与其父程闽岱先生所在的程氏家族与华南女院有着百年情缘。在林本椿教授联系程戈登之前，程戈登和父亲程闽岱先生就曾多次回到中国寻根。当时担任美国夏威夷州参议员的程戈登恰逢立法会休会时间，因此他快乐地答应了邀约，与妻子索妮娅踏着祖辈的足迹来到华南女院任教。同时，在担任夏威夷州参议员期间，戈登积极推动华南女院与福州的姐妹城市华盛顿州塔克马市的普吉湾大学进行合作。自1994年起，程戈登担任主席的程氏基金会，每两年资助一名普吉湾大学的毕业生到华南女院任教，选派25名学生赴华南女院进行学术和文化交流。

外教对华南女院来说是一笔珍贵的财富。学院不仅在思想上重视引进外教，在外教的教学管理与生活服务方面也尽量做到细致与周到，力图为外教提供一个舒适的教学环境。林本椿教授担任华南女院院长期间，外教的管理主要由外事处负责，当时的负责人是许道锋老师。

林本椿顾问、前院长

春色
任天涯
——福建华南女子
职业学院外教侧记
International Faculty with
Fujian Hua Nan Women's
College since 1908

550

据担任应用英语专业主任多年的何孝智老师回忆，每一位外教都会认真编写教学大纲、教案和教学总结等，并且经常在他们的教案当中有很多创新的地方。何孝智老师会搜集外教的教学资料，专门存放起来，供其他中国老师学习、交流和讨论，以提升她们的教学能力。许道锋老师积极推动外教组织英语角、英语演讲比赛、英语话剧比赛等英语第二课堂活动，让外教融入学生的学习与生活。

生活方面，外教集中居住在外国专家楼，起居在一起，像一个大家庭一样。由专职的阿姨为外教提供营养均衡丰富的饮食，如果外教愿意，也可以选择到外教专用的厨房自己做饭菜。外事处还有专门的洗衣房。这样的传统源自老华南女院时期，即便是抗战时期校区转移到南平，也没有丢失这个传统。如果外教生病了，外事处老师会亲自去医院照顾，关心问候。外事处还会与外教私下交流，根据每位老师的兴趣爱好做出行程表，在节假日带他们到福州或省内其他地方游玩，鼓山、鼓岭、西湖、厦门，这些地方外教们都走过。因此外事处的老师们与外教私交都很不错。

许道锋老师担任外事处处长期间，每学期都会组织外事处和英语专业所有的老师们为外教开欢迎会，表示对外教到来的热烈欢迎；每次有外教要离开华南女院，她便会组织欢送会，真诚欢送即将离开华南女院的外教。欢送会上，她虚心听取外教的反馈，了解外事处将来如何能更好地为外教服务，并用有说服力的话语，真诚地表达希望外教尽快再次回来任教的愿望。总而言之，不管是教学方面还是生活方面，只要外教提出要求，许道锋老师都会尽力去满足他们的需要。她说："管理外教，关心外教，服务外教，这些是我的职责与乐趣。"

因为学院对于外教不论在教学需求还是生活需求方面都给予最大限度的满足，以及外事处老师们对外教的了解、懂得和尊重，华南女院复办以来，众多外教在华南女院有了家的归属感。他们在自己的岗位上默默坚守，无私奉献。他们对学生因材施教，不仅培养学生的综合素质，而且教学生为人处世。他们与中国老师结下了深厚的情谊，并将这份情谊延续至今。外教凯·格里姆斯博士不时从国外给道锋老师寄来益智杂志，如数独或填字游戏杂志，并且估摸着道锋老师快要填完一本的时候就寄来另外一本，她希望通过杂志上的游戏让道锋老师的生活充实而快乐。这也从侧面说明了许道锋老师在外教工作上的出色表现。2003年国家外国专家局授予许道锋老师"全国聘请外国文教专家工作先进个人"荣誉。

有了丰富的外籍教师资源、华南女院校友会，以及社会各界的支持，秉承着"受当施"的精神，复办后的华南女院培养了一批批的优秀女大学生。不论是教学水平还是毕业生能力都得到了社会的广泛认可，社会对于华南女院的关注也越来越多。1990年9月27日，时任福州市市委书记的习近平率领福州市各部门领导一行8人亲临华南女院视察。当时，习书记满脸笑容地对我院院长余宝笙博士说："感谢华南女院为福州市培养这么多人才，我们将一如既往地支持华南女院办学，

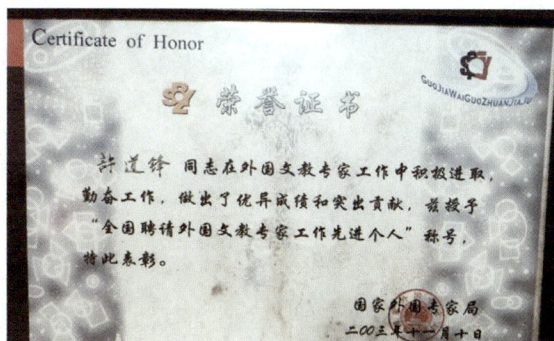

国家外国专家局授予许道锋老师的证书

希望你们总结社会力量办学的经验，有什么困难可以书面寄给我。我当召集有关人员一起解决。"1992年国家教育部开展民办教育会议，我院被邀请参加，余院长在会上做了题为《解放思想 大胆探索 华南女子学院闯出一条民间办学之路》的发言，提出外教的重要性。

1995年4月，时任福州市委书记的习近平在我院庆祝校庆10周年前几个月，曾为华南题词："巾帼不逊须眉，华南女杰辈出。"

华南女院的影响力，不仅仅是女校特色，更在于综合实力，其中外教的影响至深且巨。以下是获中国政府以及福建省政府奖的华南外教：

序号	奖项	专家姓名	性别	国籍	获奖年份
1	国家友谊奖	贝茨·里韦特	女	美国	2006
2	福建省友谊奖	贝兹·里韦特	女	美国	2001
3	福建省友谊奖	简·菲利浦	女	美国	2003
4	福建省友谊奖	凯·格里姆斯	女	美国	2005
5	福建省友谊奖	程戈登	男	美国	2010
6	福建省友谊奖	黄丽霞	女	澳大利亚	2015
7	外国专家奖	朱迪丝·威廉逊	女	美国	1992
8	外国专家奖	玛莎·苏托德	女	美国	1994
9	福建省"荣誉公民"	贝茨·里韦特	女	美国	2010

春色
任天涯
——福建华南女子
职业学院外教侧记
International Faculty with
Fujian Hua Nan Women's
College since 1908

552

第二节　师者仁心，教无定法
——福建华南女子职业学院外教教学思想探微

华南女院外教上课总是富有活力，深深吸引着华南女院学子。华南女院毕业生对母校怀有深厚的感情，与外教共度的时光是她们美好的回忆。出于对华南女院外教教学方式的好奇，我针对部分外教进行了邮件采访，询问他们以下问题。

一、你的总体教学理念是什么？

Ms. Elisabeth Kohler提出了四个A：

Attendance（出勤）＝从不缺勤

Activity（活动）＝尽可能活跃，因为这是学习的唯一途径

Appreciation（欣赏）＝光学习是不够的，欣赏不但要求洞见，也需要心灵去体会

Awareness（意识）＝获得的知识必须付诸实践，并分享给他人

Dr. Louis Roemer 给出了一个路线图：

1. 弄清学生需要什么；

2. 确定课堂任务的可用资源；

3. 准备教学材料；

4. 判断学生是否听明白；

5. 返回第一步。

Lai Har Wong：

我的教学理念是传授有用的知识给学生，以身作则，引导学生向上，从而为社会做出贡献。

Senator Gordon Trimble：

我从来没有考虑过教学理念这个问题。我的"教学"生涯始于我十二三岁的时候，当时同学们常常请我解释老师的话。我一直这样帮助他人学习。我不是从自己的角度出发去解释问题，而是让学生解释他们的理解，直到他们能够自如地用自己的语言解释。我觉得我不能算是老师，因为所有的工作都是由学习者本人完成的。我觉得自己更像一个拉拉队长或教练。孩子们之所以来找我，也许是因为我上课不记笔

记，自己开口之前会专注地看着他们，认真倾听。他们认为这是聪明人的特点。我觉得没有必要向他们解释，我的做法其实与智力没有什么关系。我相信任何追求进步的人都是值得重视的。他们有自己的思想和感情，当他们意识到自己作为一个人而受到尊重的时候，会更快地成长。

Dr. Betts Rivét:

作为一名教师，需要具备一些重要的个人素质，我的教学理念就蕴含其中。

对每一个学生表现出真诚的兴趣。比如关心学生的学业进步，主动去了解他们，愿意在他们需要帮助时伸出援手。

从不批评学生。相反，去发现他们值得赞美的地方。

让课堂充满正能量。换句话说，不要只是坐着教书，要走动，接近学生，并且每天都带着微笑走进教室，快乐地和学生打招呼。

让课堂既充满乐趣，又富有挑战。用各种创新的方式，让学生去开动脑筋，不要让课堂流于无聊。

严格而公平。

通过实地考察（我曾带学生参观博物馆和五星级酒店）、游戏、比赛以及一些别出心裁的方式激发学生兴趣。

鼓励学生。让每个班级都感觉自己是特别的。

如果不能拥有积极的心态，对每一个学生都怀有真诚的关爱，并认真准备每一堂课，以上这些就都无从谈起了。

Ms. Dodie Johnston:

我认为学生信任老师、敢于尝试的时候，能够取得最佳的学习效果。师生关系融洽时，双方就能放松、自由地交流。当时我负责口语课教学，但我也教导学生相信自己，开拓思维，从而有益于自身和社会发展。

让每一堂课的内容对学生有意义，并寻求个性化的教学材料，这一点非常重要。当孩子们对所学的内容真正感兴趣的时候，学习效果是最好的。用个人亲身经历的故事、不具威胁性的比赛、正面的反馈来激发学生的兴趣，不是一件容易的事。我所教的内容是由课程所决定的，但我可以选择教学的方法。在我的课堂上，我尽量做到以学生为中心。

二语学习者要取得进步，必须操练语言基础知识，学习新词汇和语法，还要参与课堂活动，将所学知识应用于实践。我经常组织讨论、辩论和演讲，尽量每日都为班上的每一个学生创造表现的机会。

春色
任天涯
——福建华南女子
职业学院外教侧记
International Faculty with
Fujian Hua Nan Women's
College since 1908

554

每个学生的能力起点、家庭背景、所受教育都各不相同。教授新材料的时候，我尽量考虑到这些因素，确保学生参与课堂活动时，不会为自己的表现而自惭形秽。我经常进行小测，考核学生的学习情况，让学生可以针对自己的缺漏进行强化。我告诉她们，小测的目的是为了评估教学效果，从而了解哪些学生需要额外帮助。

Dr. Karen Germant:

我曾在美国南俄勒冈大学教授历史，我认为学生积极参与到学习过程中，能更好地记住课程内容。因此，我逐渐形成了这样的教学方式：课前布置大量阅读材料，然后利用课堂时间进行集中讨论。我的学生必须为此做好充足的准备，因为他们在讨论中的参与度会计入课堂成绩当中。我不举行正式考试，相反，我提供两到三个问题，让学生就其中的一个问题写一篇文章。通常来说，我的问题会要求他们就历史的某一方面选择立场，他们选择哪个立场不重要，重要的是他们如何支持所选的立场，即他们是如何利用证据的。

这类教学方法或理念并不适用于语言类课程，因为老师教授的是技巧而不是内容。但尽管如此，学生在学习语言的时候参与到课堂中来也是至关重要的（在英语口语和自由会话课上可能尤为重要）。我在华南女院，以及早前在协和学院教授口语类课程时，要求每一位学生都参与到每一堂课当中。我明白有些学生生性腼腆（我小时候也是这样），因此我努力去营造一个相互促进、相互鼓励的环境。我告诉学生不要互相批评嘲笑，我也一般不会在课堂上批评或纠正学生的错误。我告诉他们认真倾听也是谈话的一部分，我决不允许有人在别人发言的时候窃窃私语。（有时候为了检查他们是否认真倾听，我会询问他们刚才别人说了什么。）我在自由会话课堂上的目标就是让学生能放松自在地用英语交流。交流并不意味着要说得很完美。如果我能听懂学生说的话，那就够了。要是有学生想让我纠正他们的错误我会照做。虽然语音练习有些枯燥，但是学生觉得有必要在自由会话课上进行语音训练。我的每一堂课都先进行语音训练，这时我会纠正他们的错误，或让他们互相纠正。一般来说，我每节课会专门就一个句型进行语音训练，这样可以向他们灌输正确的语法而无需对他们进行刻意的纠正。

在华南女院和协和学院任教时，我努力使课堂幽默有趣。如果学生能在他们的谈话内容中发现幽默并且开怀大笑，他们就会放松下来，也就更愿意学习了。看到学生笑起来，我就会感觉到他们正在学习，因为在我看来，如果一个人可以用另一种语言玩文字游戏、玩幽默，那这就是进步。

课堂上我自己尽量少开口，这样学生就能利用课堂时间多开口。有时候为了确保学生有更多的时间发言，我会把他们分成几个小组。

我不仅仅把自己当作一位老师，可能更重要的是看作一名啦啦队队长。我认为提升他们的信心是我的责任，所以我尽量给予他们积极的反馈。我每堂课结束时都会总结学生在课堂上的精彩表现以及他们获得的巨大进步（虽然有时这不是真的），除非我忘了。我能看出来这会使他们感到愉悦。（然而我不确定这样是否会激励他们进步。）

外教们对第一个问题的回答可以总结为以下四点：（1）教学的基础在于态度，真正的教学之道需要专注与热忱。（2）教学的关键在于学生参与，没有参与就没有学习。（3）为了激发学生参与学习过程，必须通过有趣的活动给课堂注入活力。（4）老师必须真诚地为学生提供学业及精神上的支持，使学生能够长期保持良好的学习状态。我建议中国的英语教师，不要把课堂变成要学生一较高下的竞争场所。从长远来看，教师帮助学生树立信心，也许比教授知识或训练技能更重要。

二、怎样让课堂生动有趣？

Elisabeth Kohler:

充分备课，设计好"讲什么"以及"如何讲"：我会仔细思考要教授的话题，以及关于此话题最适宜的教学方法。我认为理想的课程应包括以下部分：

1. 教师介绍本堂课的主要任务。

2. 把单词、习语和概念从头到尾地过一遍，确保每个人都理解。

3. 学生的意见得以倾听，问题得以解答。

4. 分小组或大组讨论。

5. 口头或笔头的个人练习或小组练习。

6. 小组内的演讲或是全班性的演讲。

7. 教师和其他同学对演讲进行评价（语音、声音、肢体语言以及逻辑顺序）。小组和大组活动我都很重视，但是个人思考的时间也是必要的。思考能帮助学生理解并充分领会话题。

Louis Roemer:

我会寻找我认为有趣的材料，这些材料必须是学生力所能及的，有能力理解的。确定学生的兴趣所在不是件容易的事。

Lai Har Wong:

以下是我的一些做法：

春色
任天涯
——福建华南女子
职业学院外教侧记
International Faculty with
Fujian Hua Nan Women's
College since 1908

556

1. 教授新内容时要与学生已学过的内容联系；

2. 选择与学生生活相关的、有趣并引人深思的话题；

3. 避免单调乏味、难以驾驭的话题；

4. 在教学过程中增添点趣味——解释单词、佐以例证、讲述故事和学生开玩笑；

5. 尽量让学生参与到教学中来，避免教师一言堂；

6. 始终满腔热情、准备充分。

Gordon Trimble:

学习是一个艰难的过程。我会努力去确定学生的兴趣所在，但我更关注学习的过程。老实说，是学生使得课堂变得有趣，奠定了课堂的基调和标准。学生的注意力可能只能保持7分钟。有时候她们需要站起来伸个懒腰，使头脑清醒过来，把氧气输送给大脑。在课堂上她们要阅读，要写作，要发言，哪一件都并非易事，但是当她们看到自己正在进步，就会愿意再付出一点努力。我会花时间去解释，为什么明白这一点或是能够做到这一点，能使她们成为一个更幸福、更成功的人。我尽量把学习和大学毕业后的生活联系起来。每一节课的开展似乎都不是事先确定的，而是随着学生的影响而随时变化，这时学生似乎会投入到学习当中。学生多练习写作，就会越写越好；多开口说话，沟通技巧就会日渐成熟。我们教师并不是可供复制的模型。课堂上需要有一定程度的随机性和令人兴奋的东西。这一点需要教师要形成自己的风格才能做到。

Betts Rivét:

在每次一个半小时的课堂时间里，我会开展好几个不同的活动。我教授读写课和听说课，通常都是进行小组活动（四人为一组），而我在教室里四处走动，聆听学生的交谈，给她们提供帮助或建议，或向他们提问。我利用图片来激发写作灵感、刺激学生交谈，有时甚至给她们开头第一句，让她们接着往下编。每次上课，我会先在黑板上写一个很有哲理的句子（比如：人生短暂，勿留遗憾），询问她们对这个句子的理解。这件事情每周都做，慢慢地，师生互动越来越好。我还得到学校许可带我的学生去校外参观学习（由我支付车费），参观博物馆、五星级酒店，学生由此学到很多，之后她们写下参观感想，并与其他同学分享。另一个活动是两人一组，发给她们各人一张图片，她们手中的图片大体相似但有诸多不同的细节，她们需要互相提问，找出8到10处不同来。另一个我所记得的活动是根据当天的主题或是阅读材料讲述个人的故事或是生活经历。这可以让学生认识到她们所学的内容是与自己的生活切实相关的。

有些时候学生仅仅需要做一些演讲，或是词汇小测，或是根据我给她们的图片写一则故事。我从美国带来许多阅读材料，阅读课上我的学生阅读故事，然后写一则简短的概述（他们必须学会写概述），给出她们的看法。不管我安排什么课堂活动，都不会让学生有半刻空闲。如果我在课堂最后还有5分钟的时间，我会利用黑板或者白板做一个叫"吊死鬼"的猜字游戏……每个学生给出一个字母，直到有人猜出这个单词为止。

无论学生的水平如何，我都尽量公平对待每一个人。我让每个人都有机会进步，哪怕这需要我进行一对一的指导。我想让她们成为最好的自己。我告诉她们："我不允许你们失败。"有些学生不知道她们的"最好"可以到什么程度，我会证明给这些需要关注的学生看。我已经记不清有多少次我的努力得到了丰厚的回报。

Dodie Johnston:

英语口语课的理念就是让学生们多开口，所以在我的课堂上，词汇和语法的教学围绕符合这些年轻女性背景和兴趣的话题展开，从我们所熟知的事物开始，例如我们的家庭、家乡以及食物偏好等，然后逐渐拓展话题的广度，使英语口语基础的学习变得生动有趣。

每天早晨都安排一个学生向全班同学介绍一句习语或动词词组。我们进行传统的轮唱，也唱披头士的歌；我带来建筑图纸，让她们设计理想中的房子，然后向大家讲解她们的设计；我们向彼此描述完美的假期；我让她们向我介绍中国的民间故事；我们分组讨论课上提出的问题。

她们用各种各样的形容词来给我讲的故事编造结局。她们设计了新颖的产品和服务，并试图销售给班上的同学。我把《中国日报》带到班上，让每一个人都挑选一则她们感兴趣的报道，在全班同学面前总结报道的内容，并思考其中的含意。我带来《国家地理》杂志，让同学们选择一个感兴趣的国家，然后说服其他同学到这个地方去旅行。每个小组的成员都会轮流担任协调员和发言人，协调员负责确保组内每个人都有发言的机会，而发言人代表本组向全班报告讨论结果。

我从不坐着上课。介绍新材料的时候我通常站在黑板前，但我更多的还是在过道上走来走去，带着问题和建议穿梭于各小组之间。这样能使班级保持活力，让每个人都能参与进来，开口说英语。

Karen Germant:

我尽量使用不同的方法，有些方法在上述的第一个问题里提到了。

春色
任天涯
——福建华南女子
职业学院外教侧记
International Faculty with
Fujian Hua Nan Women's
College since 1908

558

外教们对第二个问题的回答可以概括为两点：一是多样化。如果教师没有与生俱来的幽默感，怎么才能把课上得生动有趣、引人入胜呢？训练有素的教师知道，课堂的多样化是一把金钥匙。也就是说，通过设计多样化的课堂活动，提供多样化的教学材料，使得学习成为一个有趣的、能激发学习动力的、丰富多彩的体验。二是个人化。在外语教学中，教材中往往是别人的故事，有时学生很难有认同感。然而，个人化的教学是强化学习动力的有效手段。个人化意味着让语言学习的内容对学习者个人富有意义。如果课堂教学的内容与学生本人的经历、感情、价值观、观点相结合，学生参加课堂活动时就会更加投入，也更有兴趣去学习目标语言。

三、在中国任教期间，你们如何解决文化差异呢？

Elisabeth Kohler:

我尽量用宽容、好奇的态度对待其他文化的思维方式、行为方式和表达方式，对文化差异保持高度的敏感。我接受过肢体语言的训练，可以轻易看懂非言语表达方式，虽然有时听不懂别人说的汉语。如果有什么疑问，最好的做法就是询问："亲爱的，我觉得你好像很困惑/生气/开心/难过。是这样的吗？"如果你没有正确领会那个人的心情，你最好通过询问弄清楚，这样才能在和谐的氛围中继续交流。

每一种文化都有它特有的面部表情和肢体动作，你只需要去学习就好。这是与不同文化背景的人打交道的乐趣所在！

如果你非常好奇，渴望去了解别人的思维方式，那么，与人相处就会变得更容易。

同样你需要尊重他人和他们的文化。不要趾高气扬，认为只有自己的文化才是唯一正确的。每种文化都各有优缺点，人无完人。

Louis Roemer:

我尽量让材料贴近学生的兴趣，在她们的理解能力之内。如果文化差异妨碍了理解，我会解释问题出现的原因。

Lai Har Wong:

当我遇到文化差异的时候，首先，我会判断什么是正确的，什么是错误的。如果其他国家的文化没有影响我的信仰或良知的话，我会去尊重、理解并支持这个国家的文化。但有些事情是错误的，由于我的个性和所受的教育，我很难像大多数中国人一样容忍这种事情并保持沉默，这时我会直言不讳。

Gordon Trimble:

上课的第一天我想要我的学生明白两件事情。第一，生活是艰难的。第二，他们需要将压力变成成功的动力。在接下来的四个半月里，我担任导演，而他们要把自己当成初涉影坛的演员，扮演许多不同的角色。"走出你的舒适区，尝试新事物，看看什么最适合崭新的自己。到学期末，你将有能力调整自己的行为，你将更能适应真实的自己。"我和我的学生性别不同，年龄也相差好几代。我不会戴上文化的有色眼镜来看待我的学生。我在乎的是她们能够成长，无论她们选择在什么样的文化背景下工作生活，都能有所成就。多样性是好事。我看见你的时候，会注意到你有两只眼睛，一个鼻子，每只手都有四个指头和一个拇指。我想你至少和我一样优秀，我会努力，以免你觉得我不如你。我用眼睛观察四周，从而避免撞到东西；我用大脑发挥想象。我把每个人都当成单独的个体，我想要了解他们的所思所想。这个过程比简单武断地给人贴上文化标签要缓慢得多。所以我们来到中国，向我们的学生学习，和她们分享我们的经历。她们可以自主选择了解对她们有用的东西，忽略其他的部分。我们并没有兴趣去改变中国。我们只是去寻找一个平台，利用这个平台建立连接，构建桥梁，使得我们能够更好地相互了解和沟通。

Betts Rivét:

45年前我与伙伴创立国际学校心理协会。每年夏天我们都在不同的国家举行会议，迄今为止我去过48个国家了。说实话，不管在哪个国家我都不会觉得不自在。在中国也是如此。我很快就能适应不同的文化。"适应"就是关键所在。我没觉得自己需要解决什么文化差异。我只是去适应我所在的地方。我曾在说西班牙语的波多黎各生活了14年。我驾驶自己的飞机载着内外科医生和牙医到墨西哥的一个小村庄提供医疗服务。我甚至学会了在中国讨价还价。要适应在异乡生活，还有一个关键词，那就是"学习"，学习并融入他们的生活方式。正如古话所说"入乡随俗"，这很容易！

Dodie Johnston:

我并不觉得文化差异能算得上需要我们去解决的问题，事实上，它只是需要在大环境下去考虑和了解的社会习惯。刚开始，中国人不经意间的一些行为会让我感到惊讶，甚至震惊：在公共场合清嗓子、随地吐痰；在等候服务或入场的时候推推搡搡；在作业和考试中作弊；在别人出现状况或发生争执的时候发笑。但当我开始了解每一个人，和他们成为朋友之后，我才明白他们都是善良、有礼貌、友好的人，那些都是从艰苦时期遗留下来的传统行为方式。几个世纪以来，生活对普通的中国老百姓来说很是艰难，有些在我看来粗鲁莽撞的行为，曾经也是生活所迫。

例如，外国人经常需要依靠中国朋友或同事来"干预"（比如在议价的时候），

春色
任天涯
——福建华南女子
职业学院外教侧记
International Faculty with
Fujian Hua Nan Women's
College since 1908

560

因为我们不够强硬。每当我看到父母让患了唐氏综合症的孩子在火车站乞讨的时候，或是店主将商业垃圾清扫到大街上的时候，或不断在课堂上强调不要作弊的时候，我都大为不快。但我对那些情况又了解多少呢？是什么导致了这些行为呢？

我回到中国的次数越多，就越希望自己对中国能够有个开放性的判断，并且接受这个事实：当我在这个国家的时候，我必须接受他们处理事情的方式并尽量去理解背后的原因，而不是觉得烦躁或是愤怒。我相信在美国的中国人也是这样去适应美国的生活方式的。

Karen Germant：

我尽量从学生的角度去理解他们。但有时候，我觉得有必要挑战一下她们认为可以接受的一些观念。我在师大教研究生写作的时候发现了大量的剽窃现象。我记得，我把他们的作业都评为了不及格，并告诉他们如果剽窃的话，就可能要挂科。我向他们解释道，如果他们身处西方的话，甚至会因为剽窃而被开除。我不确定他们是否相信我所说的话，有些人仍然在剽窃，但我觉得我需要把这些都说出来。

在华南女院，有一个文化差异与系院（或是学校本身？）的规定有关。如果学生考试不及格，老师必须让这个学生继续考试，直到通过为止。我相信在华南女院教书的大多数外教（或是全部）都把这看成是对老师的惩罚。关键是，我们大都不想如此宠溺学生。所以如果学生本该挂科的，我们就给他最低的及格分（60分）。

另一个文化差异是"关系"。有些学生不在乎他们是否学到了什么，因为他们有"关系"，无论他们在华南女院成绩如何，都会找到工作。对此我们也无能为力。

当学生明显没花时间和精力学习的时候，我会很失望气馁。她们往往会欣然承认。"你的时间都用来做什么了？"我问。"听音乐、购物、睡觉、上网、玩游戏。"如此等等。我告诉她们，在美国，学生对每一个小时的课堂时间一般要花费两个小时的课后时间来配合学习，她们都不相信。（当然，中国学生的上课时间会比美国的学生多好几个小时。）当学生告诉我她们上课的时间有多少之后，我对她们微乎其微的课外学习也没那么失望了。或者说，至少我更能理解她们了。

20多年前我应要求为福建省的职业学校编写一本英语教材，教材中有好几课涉及文化差异。当时国际交流无论深度还是广度都不及如今，人们对文化差异还不是很熟悉。在针对教材召开的研讨会上，有人对我提出质疑，因为我在教材中提出我们应该去适应西方文化，当时有些人认为这是缺乏文化自信的表现。20多年过去了，情况发生了巨大的变化。文化差异已经成为英语教学中必不可少的部分。一方面中国人努力通过本地化的方式去更好地接受西方的产品或服务，西方人也一样通过本地化让他们的产品或服务更容易为中国人接受。比如诺基亚的网站，针对不同文化，网站风格也不同。面向欧洲国家的网站，背景是蓝色的；而面向中国的网站，背景是红色的。东西双方正本着互惠互利、互相理解的原则，积极地看待文化差异。无论好坏，事物都有其存在的理由。这就是相互理解的基础。

相对于其他行业，大学中文化差异造成的问题不是那么突出，在华南女院尤其如此，因为外教们对学生宽容大度，充满爱心、同理心。本书撰写即将结束之际，部分作者谈到他们对华南女院外教的感情，他们对外教的爱、尊敬和感激，这些都是超越文化差异的。

第三节　福建华南女子职业学院与亚洲基督教高等教育联合董事会

1949年前，基督徒传教士在中国建立13所基督教教会大学：燕京大学、齐鲁大学、东吴大学、圣约翰大学、之江大学、华西协和大学、华中大学、金陵大学、福建协和大学、华南女子文理学院、金陵女子文理学院、沪江大学、岭南大学。教会大学数量不多，起点很高，水平接近了同时代欧美一般大学的程度，在中国教育近代化过程中起着示范和导向作用。华南女子大学由美以美会（1939年以后称卫理公会）于1908年创办（时称华英女子学堂，1916年改称华南女子大学），简称华南女大，民国元年（1912）由美国基督教女布道会出资奠基兴建，位于仓山区上三路8号，现为福建师范大学仓山校区校部。民国十七年（1928）向中华民国教育部登记，因不满足普通大学至少三个学院的要求，改称华南女子文理学院，简称华南女院。1951年与福建协和大学合并为福州大学，1953年改称福建师范学院，1972年改称福建师范大学。1984年由华南女子文理学院暨附中校友会复办成立民办福建华南女子学院，位于福州仓山乐群路6号。

亚洲基督教高等教育联合董事会简称亚联董，英文为United Board for Christian Higher Education in Asia（UBCHEA），总部设在美国纽约，是非营利性的非政府组织（NGO）。它最早成立于1922年，中国的三所基督教大学在美国纽约成立了一个联合办公室，后来逐渐发展成为中国基督教大学联合董事会，在北美为中国13所基

**春色
任天涯**
——福建华南女子
职业学院外教侧记
International Faculty with
Fujian Hua Nan Women's
College since 1908

562

督教大学联合募集办学经费，制定高等教育整体发展规划与政策。中国基督教大学联合董事会的工作赢得了中国政府的认同，合作开展了不少基督教高等教育项目。此外，中国基督教大学联合董事会还吸引了很多美国高等院校参与与中国基督教大学的合作及相关援助，对加快中国高等教育现代化进程、提高中国高等教育国际化程度和推进中西文化交流产生了一定的积极影响。1951年中国基督教大学联合董事会与中国的联系中断了，它转而向中国大陆以外的亚洲其他国家和地区的高等教育提供支持，名称也变更为亚洲基督教高等教育联合董事会，直至今日它已经与亚洲14个国家和地区的80多所高校形成了合作关系。

Ethel Wallace撰写的《华南学院》（*Hwa Nan College*）一书这样描述亚联董对华南女子文理学院的支持：日本侵华战争结束后，亚联董的现场代表（field representative of UB）Dr. William P. Penn、亚联董秘书（secretary of UB）Dr. Robert J. McMullen于1946年春天和夏天分别访问了华南女院。1947年，亚联董华南分委会（the Hwa Nan Committee of the UB）拨付5万美金用于重修被烧毁的彭氏楼（Payne Hall）。同年，华南女子文理学院通过亚联董获得了理科实验室所需的仪器设备。总之，抗日战争结束后，亚联董为华南女院恢复在福州办学提供了重要的支持。

1980年亚联董应邀恢复了在中国的工作，中国项目仍占亚联董工作最大的比重，获得亚联董最多的项目资金支持，是亚联董拥有最多合作院校的国家。1984年，华南女院复办后开始与亚联董再续前缘，翻开了双方合作的新篇章。30年来，亚联董不离不弃，始终陪伴，默默注视，积极支持，对华南女院的建设和发展做出了突出的贡献。亚联董与华南女院紧密合作，不是亲人胜似亲人缘起于三点：一是时间的契合。亚联董1980年应邀恢复在中国的工作，而华南女院是在1984年复办。二是身份的吻合。华南女院是13所教会大学中唯一复办的独立的民办学院，是中国改革开放的产物，是充满生机活力的新鲜事物，华南女院独立的、民办的身份与当年的华南女子文理学院是吻合的，因此迅速得到了亚联董的认同，获得了亚联董特别的关注。三是目标的一致。亚联董恢复中国业务后的重点放在师资培养方面，与复办后华南女院迫切的需求高度契合。由华南女子文理学院暨附中校友会老校友们复办的华南女院由于当时中国的人才分配政策，正苦于如何吸引青年教师加入。唯一的出路在于吸引一批优秀华南女院毕业生留校，继续深造，经过长期的培养和学历提升的过程，达到在高校担任教师的资格。以余宝笙院长为首的老校友们殚精竭虑，积极为年轻人寻求深造的途径，为华南女院培养新鲜血液和事业接班人。而学历的提升在当时中国高等教育环境下，在国内是没有门路的。寻求亚联董的资金支持，选送优秀教师出国留学深造，用最短的时间达成学历迅速提升的目的，这既是老华南女院培养接班人的传统，在当时也是一条非常明智的道路选择，得到了亚联董积极的响应。

复办30年来，华南女院与亚联董往来频繁，亚联董主席和副主席都曾到访过学院，亚联董中国项目负责人定期来院访问。访问期间，他们通过与学院领导的会面，与青年教师的座谈，与学生的交流来关心学院的发展，了解学院的需求。学院领导也访问过亚联董在纽约的总部和在香港的办公室，利用参加亚联董组织的国际会议间隙与亚联董官员会谈。值得一提的是，2002年11月14日至15日，美国亚洲基督教高等教育联合董事会主席Dr. Light率领董事成员8人来院调研考察，学院安排年轻的院长助理徐欧介绍新旧华南女院的概况，院长助理王凌做关于华南女院与中国高等教育以及中国妇女教育的报告，此次到访给亚联董全体董事留下了深刻的印象，中国项目负责人Anne Ofstedal在随后的感谢信中表示董事们在访问后召开的董事会上对华南女院的发展赞不绝口，对华南女院培养青年教师的工作给予了高度的肯定。

学院与亚联董往来情况一览表

1986	亚联董主席 Dr. Lauby 来院访问并给学生讲座，林本椿老师陪同翻译。
1987.1.21-1.30	学院作为中国唯一代表应邀参加了在泰国清迈帕亚大学（Paya University）召开的亚洲妇女高等教育研讨会，大会由美国亚洲基督教高等教育联合董事会主持。
1993.4.7	美国亚洲基督教高等教育联合董事会中国委员会主席、美国威尔斯利女子学院 Roger Johnom 约翰逊教授到我院，与我院商讨拟选派准备攻读硕士研究生学位的本科毕业生到我院进行教学实习等有关事宜。
1993.5.18	美国亚洲基督教高等教育联合董事会主席文德惠先生访问我院，他到医院看望了余宝笙院长，与学院领导小组成员、外事处、实用英语专业负责人等座谈关于支持学院青年助教赴美留学以及选派外籍教师到该院任教等事宜。
1994.5.7	美国亚洲基督教高等教育联合董事会中国项目联络员安妮·奥夫斯特达尔（Anne Ofstedal）访问我院。
1995.1.19	南京大学 United Board 师资培训班教授 Kate Parry 向我院英语专业助教们介绍她在美国和中国的教学经验，并就助教们提出的"怎么上好听说课、读写课"等问题作了指导。
1995.2.12	我院陈琼琳副院长应邀前往美国佛罗里达州立大学作为期半年的访问学者。

春色
任天涯
——福建华南女子
职业学院外教侧记
International Faculty with
Fujian Hua Nan Women's
College since 1908

564

1995.7.20	美国亚洲基督教高等教育联合董事会主席 Dr.David Viednetr 文德惠和南京爱德基金会教育组丁言仁教授一同到学院考察，商谈资助学院发展的项目。
1997.9	美国亚洲基督教高等教育联合董事会通过南京爱德基金会专项资助我院 1997 学年清寒助学金 U.S$5000（折合人民币 4 万元），共资助了 101 名学生。
1999.7.24-7.26	United Board 中国项目负责人 Ms.Anne Ofstedal 来我院访问。
2001.3.21-3.22	美国亚洲基督教高等教育联合董事会亚洲项目负责人 Anne Ofstedal 来我院调研。
2002.3.8	美国亚联董副主席 Dr.Rita Pullium 由该会中国项目官员 Anne Ofstedal 陪同来我院访问。
2002.11.14-11.15	美国亚洲基督教高等教育联合董事会（简称 U.B.）亚洲主席 Dr.Light 率领董事成员 8 人来院调研考察。
2003.5	学院院长助理王凌访问亚联董 UB 总部。
2005.3.20-4.3	学院陈钟英理事长、林本椿院长、王炜书记、外事处许道锋主任，以及副院长王凌一行 5 人应学院香港董事会邀请赴港参加 2005 年董事大会期间拜访亚联董香港办公室。
2005.9.24-9.29	由美国亚洲基督教高等教育联合董事会赞助，学院主办的"以创造写作与文学在英语教学中的应用"为主题的第三届国际学术会议及 TESL（Teaching English as A Second Language）研讨班在福建省福州市召开。
2006.3.8-3.10	美国亚洲基督教高等教育联合董事会中国项目负责人 Birgit Linder 博士来学院访问。
2006.8.17	美国驻广州总领事馆经济政治部副领事高大年先生受美国 ASHA 基金会的委托来学院考察。
2006.9.22	美国驻广州领事馆总领事金瑞柏、政治经济领事、新闻文化领事，在省外办人员的陪同下对我院进行访问。
2008.10	亚联董 AvronBoretz 和 Birgit 来院参加百年校庆。
2009.1	亚联董 Jonathan 拜访华南女院讨论 ASHA 项目。
2010.2.1	亚联董（United Board）主席 Patricia Stranahan 和亚联董捐赠管理负责人 Jonathan Wolff 到访我院。
2011.6.12-7.16	我院青年教师吴瑷瑷赴港参加由美国亚联董（United Board）资助的亚洲文化和神学的高级研讨班（IASACT）。

2012.3.11-3.13	亚联董主席 Dr. Nancy Chapman 和副主席 Ricky Cheng 到访我院。Ricky Cheng 以"大学筹募的概念、原则、策略和方法"为题，与院领导、中层干部及发展办、校友办等部门的老师进行了面对面的交流和分享。
2012.11.1-11.2	学院图书馆接受美国开发计划总署官员对 ASHA 项目建设的验收和审查，该项目建设成果获得资助方官员的认可。
2012.8.19	亚联董中国项目负责人熊舟女士到访我院，张迅捷院长、徐欧副院长、理事会秘书长王凌、图书馆长郑惠玲、外事处副处长吴瑗瑗参加了座谈。
2014.8	亚联董亚洲项目联络人 Vivica 拜访我院，主要探讨 faculty program 的内容。
2015.8	亚联董亚洲项目负责人 Cynthia 拜访我院，主要探讨 UB 项目。

亚联董对华南女院青年教师的培养投注了很多心力，不遗余力地支持华南女院培养自己年轻的教师队伍，复办至今已为华南女院培养了院领导、中层管理干部、专业带头人和骨干教师队伍。亚联董不仅出资培养青年教师，还一直关注着她们的成长，关心她们在学院的工作状况，直至华南女院能够依靠自己培养的中青年骨干教师队伍独立生存发展，于是有了华南女院师资队伍的不断壮大，有了华南女院的新老交替，有了华南女院的新局面。亚联董对华南女院师资建设的资金支持主要通过项目资金的形式，华南女院每年定期向亚联董申请项目，每年定期向亚联董汇报学院的发展、亚联董项目的执行情况和资金的使用情况。华南女院较好的项目执行能力及与亚联董频繁有效的沟通，获得了亚联董的赏识和信任。学院每年申请的项目基本都能够得到亚联董的支持。项目主要集中在国内外师资培训和干部管理能力的培训上。初期，国外进修项目集中在教师赴美国佛罗里达州立大学提升学历学位，在国内每年派3～4名青年助教到高等院校进修学习。后期，国外培训渐渐转移到亚洲地区亚联董联系的泰国和菲律宾的相关院校。再后来由于亚联董的教师培训项目开始逐渐关注欠发达的中西部地区的高校，华南女院留校的青年教师也分批次完成了学历学位的提升，华南女院向亚联董申请的项目转向社区服务、教师科研，以及领导人培养等方面。学院先后派遣两任院长和两位副院长参加亚联董UB Fellow项目，他们赴美国和亚洲高校分别进行一个学期的访问学习，期间还参与了亚联董安排的为期一周的学习总结交流会，管理水平和治校能力得到了提升。

在亚联董对华南女院青年教师培养工作中不得不提的一个人是Anne Ofstedal女

**春色
任天涯**
——福建华南女子
职业学院外教侧记
International Faculty with
Fujian Hua Nan Women's
College since 1908

566

士。Anne Ofstedal女士长期在亚联董担任中国项目负责人。在任期间对亚联董支持华南女院青年教师进修工作起到了重要的作用，她为人低调，柔软坚定，总是能够想到学院的需要并及时伸出援手，给予学院坚定的、持久的和适合的支持。下表为亚联董资助学院教师出国学习情况一览表。

福建华南女子职业学院教师出国（境）进修学习情况一览表

专业	序号	姓名	进修项目	进修院校	专业	进修年限	学习起止日期
应用英语	1	李小武	攻读学士学位	美国弗吉尼亚州林曲堡大学	工商管理	1年	1989.8-1991.5
	2	张　华	攻读硕士	美国佛罗里达州立大学	多语言多文化教育	2年	1991.8-1993.12
	3	林　寒	攻读硕士	美国佛罗里达州立大学	儿童发展	2年	1992.8-1994.12
	4	王　凌	攻读硕士	美国佛罗里达州立大学	图书情报学	2年	1995.9-1997.12
	5	董秀萍	攻读硕士	美国佛罗里达州立大学	多语言多文化教育	2年	2002.1-2003.12
	6	黄　飞	攻读硕士	泰国易三仓大学	英语语言教学	2年	2003.9-2005.1
	7	赵　卉	攻读硕士	日本广岛女学院大学	英语语言文学	2年	2002.4-2004.4
	8	严　涵	攻读硕士	泰国易三仓大学	英语语言教学	2年	2004.9-2007.1
	9	潘　樱	攻读硕士	泰国易三仓大学	工商管理	2年	2006.12-2008.12
服装鞋帽	10	徐　欧	攻读硕士	美国佛罗里达州立大学	服装商品学	2年	1999.9-2001.12
	11	周　玲	攻读硕士	日本广岛女学院大学	衣生活	2年	2004.4-2006.3
	12	余荣敏	攻读硕士	美国佛罗里达州立大学	服装设计	2年	1998.11-2000.11

春色
任天涯
——福建华南女子
职业学院外教侧记
International Faculty with
Fujian Hua Nan Women's
College since 1908

568

序号	专业	姓名	进修项目	进修院校	专业	进修年限	学习起止日期
13	商务英语	林丽华	攻读硕士	泰国易三仓大学	英语语言教学	2年	2003.9-2005.1
14		林校	攻读硕士	泰国易三仓大学	英语语言教学	2年	2004.9-2007.1
15		朱卿	攻读硕士	菲律宾雅典耀大学	英语语言与文学教学	2年	2006.6-2008.8
16		杨淑琴	攻读硕士	菲律宾德拉刹利大学	教育管理	3年	2006.9-2008.10
17	国际贸易	林晓鸿	攻读硕士	美国世纪大学	工商管理	2年	2004.9-2006.9
			学术交流会	美国纽约	妇女高等教育研讨会		2008.5
18	涉外旅游	陈薇薇	攻读硕士	泰国易三仓大学	旅游管理	2年	2006.12-2008.12
19	食品营养	张迅捷	攻读硕士	美国佛罗里达州立大学	营养食品与运动科学	2年	1993.12-1995.12
20		苏萌娜	攻读硕士	美国佛罗里达州立大学	食品与营养	2年	2000.8-2002.12
21	学前教育	蔡巧英	攻读硕士	美国佛罗里达州立大学	儿童发展	2年	1995-1997
22		任建红	攻读硕士	美国佛罗里达州立大学	家庭和儿童科学	2年	2004.6-2006.8
23	学前教育	任建红	访问学者	香港浸会大学		半年	1999.9-2000.5
24	学院领导	王凌	访问学者	美国 Randolph-Racon college	"领导人培训"项目	1学期	2003.2-2003.5
			访问学者	韩国梨花女子大学	"领导人培训"项目	1学期	2004.4-2004.6

序号	专业	姓名	进修项目	进修院校	专业	进修年限	学习起止日期
25	商务英语	林校	学术交流会	泰国曼谷	第25届TESOL国际会议		2005.1.20-1.22
			学术交流会	菲律宾马尼拉	高等教育亚洲妇女领导艺术国际研讨会		2007.12.3-12.8
26		钟福连	学术交流会	菲律宾马尼拉	女性教育与性别平等		2008.5.12-5.26
27		杨文燕	进修	菲律宾马尼拉大学	英语语言		2007.9-2007.11
28	服装鞋帽系	余荣敏	学术交流会	菲律宾Sain Scholastica College	性别平等教育		2006.6-2006.11
			学术交流会	瑞士卢塞恩	国际家政联盟（IFHE）第21届国际年会暨国际家政联盟成立100周年大会		2008.7.26-7.30
29	食品营养	苏萌娜	访问学者	菲律宾马尼拉玛利诺女子学院	"领导人培训"项目	1学期	2007.1-2007.5
30	基础部	姚光平	学术交流会	菲律宾马尼拉	女性教育与性别平等		2008.5.12-5.26
			访问学者	台湾辅仁大学	"领导人培训"项目	1学期	2009
				香港岭南大学	"领导人培训"项目	1学期	2010
31	学院领导	张迅捷		香港	UB的AULP亚洲高校领导论坛		2009.2.6-2.11
				印尼	领导人论坛		2010.7.26-8.1
			学术交流会	香港	UB的AULP亚洲高校领导论坛		2011.1.24-1.28
				香港	UB的AULP亚洲高校领导论坛		2012.2.2-2.6
32	学院领导	徐欧	访问学者	美国Faiefield大学	"领导人培训"项目	1学期	2014.9-2015.1
			访问学者	韩国首尔女子大学	"领导人培训"项目	1学期	2016.3-2016.6

570

春色
任天涯
——福建华南女子
职业学院外教侧记
International Faculty with
Fujian Hua Nan Women's
College since 1908

亚联董资助项目一览表（1997-2017）

	国外师资培训	员工福利	国内师资培训	科研、教研、出版	奖学金	干部培训	图书馆自动化	聘请客座教授	UB fellow	会议	合计
1997-1998	26,000	19,590		2,000	5,000						52,590
1998-1999	34,000	21,000	10,000	5,000							70,000
1999-2000		15,000	6,000	3,670							24,670
2001-2002	42,217		4,813			6,600	7,118	8,700	15,000		84,448
2002-2003	82,950		5,788			6,270					95,008
2003-2004	33,762		15,000	8,487				1,100	13,500		71,849
2004-2005	10,070		8,000								18,070
2005-2006	31,300									18,000	49,300
2006-2007			13,750					6,000	12,500		32,250
2007-2008	29,457.14		5,438						12,600		47,495.14
2008-2009	2,300		7,114						12,700		22,114
2010-2011				1,100							1,100
2012-2013				3,000							3,000
2014-2015									15,000		15,000
2015-2016				5,000					15,000		20,000
2016-2017				26,400							26,400

注：未完全统计　633,294.14

2007年，出于对学院的高度信任，亚联董提议并支持学院在首山旧校区承办学院复办以来唯一的一次国际会议，此次会议在学院对外交流和学术交流史中具有里程碑的意义。2007年12月17日、18日两天，由亚联董主办、学院承办、福建师范大学社会历史学院和云南大学社会工作研究中心协办的"亚洲妇女与社会工作"国际研讨会在华南女院举行。学院院长林本椿教授和美国亚洲基督教高等教育联合董事会中国项目负责人Linder博士分别在开幕式上致欢迎词。云南大学社会工作研究中心向荣主任应邀在开幕式上做主题发言，介绍中国女性主义社会工作教育的实践研究。研讨会期间，来自9个国家和地区的近30名从事社会工作教育的专家学者就社会工作教育理论和实践的研究专题展开交流，此次研讨会还研究制定了"亚洲妇女与社会工作"的课程大纲，建立起在社会工作教育研究和学生服务学习方面的合作和交流。此次国际研讨会促进了学院在妇女社会工作领域与国内外学者的联系和交流，帮助学院将妇女社会工作教育的内容融入课程体系。

亚联董对学院的另一个重要贡献是其在学院图书馆的建设中所起到的关键性的作用。早在2000—2002年，亚联董就曾拨付7118美元用于图书馆自动化项目的建设，图书馆因此购置了几台电脑，购买了ILLAS软件，开始建立机读图书数据库，实现了借、阅、访的自动化。2007年、2008年，亚联董和学院共同向美国国际开发署申报ASHA项目——图书馆网络化学习项目。ASHA（American School and Hospital Abroad）即美国海外学校和医院项目，是属于美国国际开发署（USAID, United States Agency for International Development）的一个项目，主要为美国的海外院校和医院等机构的发展提供资助。该项目每年申请一次，必须由一家美国本土机构和一个海外机构一起申请完成。2008年ASHA项目申请成功，学院获得了美国国际开发署40万美元的资金援助。2009—2012年，图书馆分两阶段完成了项目建设任务。2009年9月至2011年6月，完成图书馆服务台、门禁系统、服务器、存储设备、书架、阅览桌椅、自助打印复印扫描系统和设备、电子阅览室设备和管理软件、防病毒软件、电子图书、VOD点播系统和资源等设备和软件的采购、安装。2011年10月至2012年6月，完成远程访问管理系统、三人钢排椅、空调、图书监测仪、图书、安防监控系统的采购安装。截至2012年10月底，所采购的ASHA项目的设备、软件、图书全部投入使用，这使全院师生受益。该项目成果通过了ASHA的审核验收。

亚洲基督教教育联合董事会的作为感动着华南女院人，派往国外学习的华南女院人心怀感恩，心系学院，绝大部分都如期回到华南女院，坚守在各自的岗位，成为学院的中坚。谨此代表许多曾获得过亚联董帮助的华南女院人感谢亚洲基督教高

**春色
任天涯**
——福建华南女子
职业学院外教侧记
International Faculty with
Fujian Hua Nan Women's
College since 1908

572

等教育联合董事会长期以来对福建华南女子职业学院无私的帮助和支持，对学院青年教师的大力培养。近年学院新区建设暂告一段落，财务压力有所缓解，自2014年开始，学院决定每年定期向亚联董捐赠一小笔资金表达对亚联董的感谢，更重要的是传递学院在不断发展壮大的时候能够饮水思源，能够传承校训"受当施"的精神，其精髓在于无私，在于奉献，在于不求回报。

附录 福建华南女子职业学院外教名单

Appendix Album of International Faculty with Fujian Hwa Nan Women's College

	姓名 / Name & 在华南女院任教时间 / Teaching periods at Hwa Nan		姓名 / Name & 在华南女院任教时间 / Teaching periods at Hwa Nan		姓名 / Name & 在华南女院任教时间 / Teaching periods at Hwa Nan
1.	哈拿·普拉斯格 Hana Prashker 1985.8—1986.7	2.	阿曼达·爱基 Amanda Agee 1985.9—1986.7	3.	玛利·巴克利 Mary Buckley 1985.9—1987.7
4.	刘永和 Liu Yung Huo 1987.9—1988.7; 1989.11—1990.4; 1993.1—1993.5	5.	雪伦·米勒 Sharan Miller 1986.9—1987.7	6.	杰拉尔丁·谢尔顿 Geraldine Sheltor 1986.9—1987.7
7.	詹姆斯·柯比 James Kirby 1987.1—1987.9	8.	莱斯丽·希尔 Leslie Hill 1986.11—1987.7	9.	伊内兹·弗莱明顿 Inez Flemington 1986.9—1987.7

春色
任天涯
——福建华南女子
职业学院外教侧记
International Faculty with
Fujian Hua Nan Women's
College since 1908

574

10.		11.		12.
	玛德琳·丹尼斯 Madeline Dennis 1987.7—1989.6		拉里·摩根 Larry Morgan 1987.7—1989.6	南希·摩根 Nancy Morgan 1987.7—1989.6
13.		14.		15.
	贝思·马丁利 Beth Mattingly 1987.8—1988.7		菲尔·拉尔斯 Phil Ralles 1987.4—1989.6	克里斯坦·奥莉豪斯（柯素汀） Christine Olinghouse 1987.4—1989.6
16.	 奥加·韦贝 Olga Webb 1988.9—1989.7	17.	 简·菲利浦 Jeanne Phillips 1987.8—1988.2； 1989.9—1990.7； 1992.9—1993.8； 1997.10—1997.12； 1998.9—1999.2； 1999.8—2000.9； 2001.8—2002.1； 2002.10-2003.2	18. 洛尔丝·科尔（高如玉） Lois Cole 1987.9—1989.7

19. 萨拉·考夫曼 Sarah Kauffman 1987.9—1989.7	20. 玛丽·阿利 Mary Alley 1988.9—1989.2	21. 刘焕新 David Low 1988.9—1989.7
22. 帕特里夏·麦吉乐 Patricia McGill 1988.9—1989.7	23. 克里斯丁·格兰柏利 Krystin Granberg 1988.9— 1991.8	24. 伊丽莎白·科勒（黑美丽） Elisabet Kohler 1988.12—1989.7； 1989.7—1990.6； 2014.9—2014.10
25. 多萝西·麦克迈克尔 Dorothy McMichael 1989.2—1989.7	26. 朱迪丝·威廉逊 Judith Williamson 1989.9—1992.7	27. 安德鲁·威廉逊 Andrew Williamson 1989.9—1992.7
28. 玛丽·洛格斯登 Mary Logston 1989.9—1991.8； 1992.8—1994.2	29. 阿莱西娅·托马斯 Alethea Thomas 1989.9—1992.1	30. 朱尼弗·雷古德 Judnifer Reyngoud 1990.12—1991.1

春色
任天涯
——福建华南女子
职业学院外教侧记
International Faculty with
Fujian Hua Nan Women's
College since 1908

576

31. 罗沙·西特勒 Rosa Sitcher 1991.2—1991.5； 1992.2—1992.6	32. 安吉拉·威廉斯 Angela Williams 1991.7—1994.6	33. 玛亚塔·蓬基宁 Marjatte Punkkinen 1991.9—1995.6
34. 塞亚·皮耶蒂宁 Seija Pietinen 1991.9—1992.1	35. 玛丽安·戴维斯 Marian Davis 1988.5/1989. 5/1990.5/1992.5/1995.9	36. 玛莎·苏·托德 Martha Sue Todd 1988.8—1995.6； 2000.8—2001.6
37. 丽莎·雷文希尔 Lisa Ravenhill 1992.8—1996.8	38. 黄丽霞 Lai Har Wong 1993.8—1997.8； 1998.8—2000.8； 2002.8—2003.8； 2007.2—2010.2； 2010.9—至今	39. 梅利莎·阿博特 Melissa Abott 1994.8—1995.8

40. 米歇尔·朗 Michelle Long 1993.2.9—1996.8	41. 卡伦·约翰斯顿 Karen Johnston 1994.7—1995.8	42. 凯瑟琳·肖沃尔特 Catherine Showalter 1994.8—1995.8
43. 贝茨·里韦特 Marion Betts Rivét 1992.8—1993.7； 1995.2—1996.8； 1997.8—2000.8； 2001.2—2003.9； 2004.8—2009.10； 2010.2—2011.6	44. 宫城裕子 Yu Ko (Miyagi) 1995.4—1997.2	45. 玛丽·格温德琳 Mary Gwendoline 1995.8—1996.8
46. 米茨·哈里斯 Mitzi Harris 1994.7—1997.8	47. 迈拉·曾（曾王荷道） Myra Chang 1992.9—1993.7	48. 夏洛特·科布 Charlotte Cobb 1995.8—1996.8
49. 杰恩·李（李子仁） Jain Lee 不详	50. 玛莎·M·托德 Martha M. Todd 1987.10— 1989.9	51. 邓迪·麦克罗利 Dendy McLeroy 1992.2—1992.7

春色
任天涯
——福建华南女子
职业学院外教侧记
International Faculty with
Fujian Hua Nan Women's
College since 1908

578

52. 坎迪·卡恩 Candi Cann 1992.9—1993.7	**53.** 托马斯·詹金 Thomas Jenkins 1993.2—1993.7	**54.** 苏珊·麦卡锡 Susan McCarthy 1993.7— 1994.8
55. 柏特里夏·乔治 Patricia George 1993.7—1994.8; 1996.9—1997.8; 2011.3—2011.5	**56.** 鲁斯·科尔文 Ruth Colvin 1994.3—1994.6	**57.** 罗伯特·科尔文 Robert Colvin 1994.3—1994.6
58. 夏洛特·科布 Charlotte Cobb 1995.8—1996.8	**59.** 德鲁·汉普希尔 Drew Hampshire 1994.10—1995.1; 1995.10—1996.10	**60.** 琳达·罗 Linda Low 1996.2—1996.7
61. 珍妮弗·帕特森 Jennifer Patterson 1996.8—1997.6	**62.** 玛丽·帕骆德 Mary Perrott 1996.8—1998.7 1998.3—1998.6	**63.** 威廉明娜·波特 Wilhelmine Porter 1997.2—1997.6; 1998.3—1998.6

64. 卡伦·林赛 Karen Lindsay 1997.8—1998.2； 2002.8—2004.8	65. 艾琳·萨默维 Eileen Summerville 1997.8—1998.6	66. 高文·阿秀德 Gavin Archard 1997.8—1998.5； 2002.6—2003.7；
67. 萨拉·巴克利 Sarah Buckley 1997.12—1998.5	68. 梅甘·莫利 Megan Morley 1998.8—2000.8	69. 凯·格里姆斯 Kay Grimmesey 1998.9— 2000.8； 2001.8—2002.8； 2003.8—2007.2； 2007.9—2008.2； 2008.9—2009.2； 2009.9—2010.2； 2010.9—2011.1
70. 桑德拉·卡勒斯 Sandra Cullers 1998.9—2001.8	71. 米克拉·罗德里格斯 Mirzah Rodriguez 1998.9—2000.8	72. 杰拉尔·斯廷森 Gerald Stinson 1998.9—1999.8

580

春色
任天涯
——福建华南女子
职业学院外教侧记
International Faculty with
Fujian Hua Nan Women's
College since 1908

73.

乔·斯廷森
Jo Stinson
1998.9—1999.8

74.

海伦·凯博
Helen Cable
1999.2—2000.2；
2005.9—2006.2

75.

玛丽·梅尔罗斯
Marie Melrose
1999.2—1999.7

76.

萨拉·莫里森
Sarah Morrison
1999.2—1999.7

77.

格伦·鲁克丝
Glenna Roukes
1999.9—2000.8；
2004.2—2005.8

78.

李温迪（李文）
Wendy Lee
1999.8—2000.8

79.

希瑟·斯特鲁姆
Heather Strum
1999.8—2000.8

80.

南茜·怀特
Nancy Wight
2000.2—2001.1

81.

卡丽·理查森
Carrie Richardson
2000.8—2001.8

82. 多琳·约翰斯顿 Dorene Johnston 2000.8—2001.8; 2002.8—2003.8; 2004.8—2005.8; 2011.9—2012.1; 2016.11—2017.1	83. 拉塔沙谢里·格洛弗 Latosha Glover 2000.8—2001.8	84. 珍妮·法勒 Jeanne Farrer 2000.9—2001.8
85. 珍奈尔·林赛 Jenelle Lindsay 2001.2—2001.6	86. 寒竹真美 Mami Kantake 2001.2—2001.3; 2001.4—2002.8	87. 池田莫里子 Mariko Ikeda 2001.4—2003.2
88. 德里克·培顿 Derek Patton 2001.8—2002.8	89. 伊娃·盖尔贝 Eva Gereb 2001.8—2002.8	90. 沃尔特·韦斯特 Walter West 2002.3—2006.2
91. 梅本佳子 Yoshiko Umemoto 2002.8—2004.8	92. 吉永理华（吴鲁华） Rika Yoshinaka 2002.9—2008.7	93. 伊丽莎白·斯图尔特 Elizabeth Stewart 2002.8— 2003.8

春色
任天涯
——福建华南女子
职业学院外教侧记
International Faculty with
Fujian Hua Nan Women's
College since 1908

582

94. 泰勒·布鲁诺 Tyler Bruno 2002.8—2003.8	95. 贝弗莉·肖尔茨 Beverly Scholz 2002.8—2003.8	96. 沈茂杨 Maw-Yang Shen(Judy) 2002.8—2003.8
97. 康赛普西翁·马丁内斯 Concepcion Martinez 2001.2—2001.6	98. 诺尔玛·克洛普 Norma Korpopp 2002.8—2003.8	99. 吴森 Idongesit Isong 2002.9—2004.8
100. 弗蕾达·肖尔茨 Fraeda Scholz 2002.10—2003.8	101. 玛丽莎·汤普森 Marissa Thompson 2003.2—2003.8	102. 香农·瑞思 Shannon Rise 2003.2—2004.8; 2005.4—2006.8
103. 艾伦·蒲伯 Alan Pope 2003.2—2004.2	104. 松本真智子 Machiko Matsumoto 2003.2—2004.2	105. 韦尔纳·柯林斯 Werner Collins(Larry) 2003.9—2004.8

106. 樋田明子 Toyoda Akiko 2003.9—2004.8	107. 丁潔玲 Kit Ling Ting 2003.9—2004.8	108. 欧普鲁瓦 Opaluwa Nwaife 2003.12—2004.8
109. 伊桑·克莱恩 Ethan Crane 2004.2—2005.2	110. 沈蕾 Shen Lei 2003.12—2006.12	111. 何永欣 Hor SZ Yoong Hin 2004.9—2005.8
112. 平泽叶子 Yoko Hirazawa 2004.9—2005.8	113. 莱纳·帕尔默 Laynah Palmer 2004.9—2005.2	114. 玛丽安·麦克劳德 Marian McLeod 2004.9— 2006.8
115. 池卫明 Weiming Chi 2005.2—2005.8	116. 吴蓁华 Kathryn Baker 2005.2—2005.8	117. 彼得·姆博亚 Peter Mboya 2005.9—2006.7

春色
任天涯
——福建华南女子
职业学院外教侧记
International Faculty with
Fujian Hua Nan Women's
College since 1908

584

118.	程戈登 Gordon Trimble 2005.9—2006.2； 2007.9—2008.1； 2009.9—2010.12； 2011.9—2011.12； 2012.9—2013.1； 2013.9—2013.12； 2014.9—2014.12； 2015.9—至今	119.	程索妮娅（家属） Sonia Trimble (dependent)	120.	杰西卡·詹森 Jessica Jansyn 2005.9—2006.8
121.	伯纳黛特 Bernadette Nuque(Bern) 2005.9—2007.2	122.	对尾幸华 Sachika Tsushio 2005.9—2007.2	123.	正月萌子 Moyoko Masatsuki 2005.9—2007.2
124.	麦洁高·朗 Mikiko Long 2005.9—2006.8	125.	丽萨·朗 Lisa Long 2005.9—2006.8	126.	玛丽亚·吉娜·门索托 Maria Gina Monsanto 2006.9—2010.6； 2014.3—至今

127. 史蒂文·沃菲尔德 Steven Warfield 2006.9—2007.2	128. 鲁兹·加尔维斯 Luz Galvez 2006.9—2010.6	129. 路易斯·罗默 Louis Roemer 2006.8—2008.7； 2009.3—2009.7； 2010.3—2010.7
130. 伊娃·谭 Eva Tam 2006.7—2007.8	131. 古斯塔夫·弗兰克 Gustav Franck 2006.9—2007.7	132. 梅丽莎·格洛弗 Melissa Glover 2007.2—2007.6
133. 斯坦尼斯劳斯·库萨克 Stanislaus Cusack 2007.2—2008.2； 2008.9—2009.2	134. 丽贝卡·曾斯克 Rebecca Zensky 2007.9—2008.2	135. 马修·兰伯特 Mattew lambert 2007.9— 2008.8
136. 妮可·兰伯特 Nicole Lanbert 2007.9—2008.8	137. 宝拉·曼利 Paula Manley 2005.10—2006.2	138. 斯蒂芬妮·基莉 Stephanie Kearley 2008.9—2009.7

春色
任天涯
——福建华南女子
职业学院外教侧记
International Faculty with
Fujian Hua Nan Women's
College since 1908

586

139. 安东尼·路易斯 Antony Louis 2005.9—2006.7	140. 彼得·马修斯 Peter Mathews 2008.9—2008.12	141. 兰·阮 Lan Nguyen 2008.9—2009.7
142. 比约恩·维斯 Bjorn Weis 2008.9—2010.9	143. 琳恩·西蒙森 Lene Simonsen 2008.9—2010.9	144. 特丽萨·略伦特 Treresa Llorente 2008.7—2010.2
145. 陈宝凤 Elisa Tan 2008.9—2010.7； 2011.2—2011.6； 2012.2—2012.6； 2013.2—2014.1； 2014.9—2015.1； 2015.9—至今	146. 杰伊·科德尔 Jay Coder 2009.2—2010.7	147. 邓肯·弗朗斯 Duncan France 2009.9—2010.1
148. 特雷莎·泰勒 Theresa Taylor(Teri) 2009.9—2010.1	149. 凯伦·杰南特 Karen Gernant 2006.2—2006.6； 2010.2—2010.8	150. 罗伯特·弗瑞尔 Robert Frail 2010.3—2010.7

151.	帕特丽夏·莫尔 Patricia Moore 2010.3—2010.7	152.	玛乔丽·洛德威克 Marjorie Lodwick (Marjie) 2010.9—2012.7	153.	伊丽莎白·帕萨 Elizabeth Passas(Kitty) 2010.10—2010.11
154.	拉里·雷克 Larry Lake 2011.2—2011.6； 2012.9—2012.12； 2013.9—2013.12； 2014.9—2015.4	155.	威利·霍尔本 Willi Holbron 2011.2—2012.1； 2012.9—2013.6； 2014.9—2015.1； 2015.9—至今	156.	格雷戈里·盖尔切 Gregory Guelcher(Greg) 2013.2—2013.7
157.	凯瑟琳·康 Catherine Connor 2011.5—2011.6	158.	卡罗尔·尼米克 Carol Nimick 2011.9—2012.1	159.	艾米丽·布罗克尔曼 Emily Brockelman 2011.9—2012.11
160.	马里亚诺·普拉多 Mariano Martin Prado 2011.9—2013.6	161.	约翰·卡特 John Carter 2012.9—2013.1	162.	伊丽莎白·惠特克 Elizabeth Whitaker (Liz) 2012.9—2014.6

春色
任天涯
——福建华南女子
职业学院外教侧记
International Faculty with
Fujian Hua Nan Women's
College since 1908

588

163.	金伯利·伯德 Kimberly Byrd(Kim) 2012.9—2013.6	164.	拉腊·泰勒 Lara Taylor 2013.9—2014.6	165.	马克·泰勒 Marc Taylor 2013.9—2014.6
166	唐纳德·班尼特 Donald Bennett(Don) 2013.9—2016.6	167.	丹尼斯·比尔 Dennis Beal 2014.3—2015.1	168.	肯尼迪·霍尔特（何佳蒂） Kennedy Holt 2014.9—2015.6
169.	罗伯特·迪克 Robert Dick(Bob) 2015.3—2016.1	170.	奎西·利文斯顿 Quincy Livingston 2015.9—2016.6	171.	埃米·博德纳（柏艾敏） Amy Bodner 2016.9 至今
172.	琳达·莫尔 Linda Moore 2016.9-2016.12				

参考文献

References

1. Campbell, Barbara E. To Educate Is to Teach to Live [M]. A publication of the Women's Division General Board of Global Ministries. The United Methodist Church, 2005.

2. Davis, Mary Virginia. Hwa Nan Women's College: Heirs of a Great Faith [D]. A senior thesis submitted to the East Asian Studies Department of Princeton University in partial fulfillment of the requirements for the degree of Bachelor of Arts, 1991.

3. Wallace, L. Ethel. Hwa Nan College [M]. New York: United Board for Christian Colleges in China, 1956.

4. Wallace, L. Ethel. Hwa Nan College [M]. Zhu, Feng and Aiju Wang translated. Zhuhai: Zhuhai Press, 2005.

5. Xie, Bizhen. Hwa Nan Women's College: A Century of Progress (1908-2008) [M]. Fuzhou: Fujian Education Press, 2008.

6. Zhou, Yifang. Hwa Nan Women's College and Fujian Modern Society [D]. MA dissertation submitted to Fujian Normal University, 2006.

7. Genesee, Fred. Some Holes in Whole Language [J]. TESOL，1994（4）：6，7.

8. Goodman，K. I didn't Found Whole Language [J].The Reading Teacher，1992（46）：3.

9. Kramsch, C. Cultural Components of Language Teaching [Z/OL]. www. Spz.tu-darmstadt.com, 1996.

10. Kraner, C. Language and Culture [M]. Oxford: Oxford University Press, 1999.

11. Krashen, S. We Acquire Vocabulary and Spelling by Reading：Additional Evidence for the Input Hypothesis [J]. Modern Language Journal，1989（73）：440-464.

12. Rigg, Pat. Whole Language in TESOL [J].TESOL Quarterly，1991，（25）：3.

13. Sapir, E. Language. An Introduction to the Study of Speech [M]. London: Rupert Hart-Davis, 1970.Tomlinson.

14.B. and Masuhara, H. Developing Cultural Awareness: Integrating Culture into a Language Course [J]. Modern English Teacher. 2004, 13（1）. Oxford: Oxford University Press, 2004.

春色
任天涯
——福建华南女子
职业学院外教侧记
International Faculty with
Fujian Hua Nan Women's
College since 1908

590

后 记

Postscript

本书为集体创作的结晶。具体分工如下：

岳峰设计、审阅全书，直接编写第四章第二节、第一章第三节等内容。

吴瑗瑗编写并翻译第三章第二节"普吉特海湾的十三朵金花"、第三章第四节"芬兰黑美丽"、第三章第九节"加州阳光"以及中英文附录。

赖黎群编写并翻译第二章第五节"印象程氏家族"。

黄飞翻译第三章第三节"玛丽安·戴维斯教授与她的'家政'情结"，编写并翻译第二章第四节"空谷幽兰"，翻译第二章第四节最后一小节，修改并翻译第三章第一节"道德教师"。

余俊英翻译序言、第一章第一节"华南女子文理学院（1908—1951）与外教"与第四章第二节"师者仁心，教无定法"。

叶林编写并翻译第二章第三节"生如夏花之璀璨"、第三章第十节"高雅的郁金香"。

林校编写并翻译第三章第六节"唯有爱，永不败"，翻译第四章第三节"福建华南女子职业学院与亚洲基督教高等教育联合董事会"。

乐荣妹编写并翻译第一章第二节"春风化雨总关情"、第三章第一节"道德教师"。

程铭茜编写并翻译第二章第二节"加州玫瑰"。

林娇（Amy Lin West）翻译第三章第八节"记 Sandy"。

林晓鸿编写并翻译第三章第五节"心中有梦，缘定中国"。

林丽华编写并翻译第三章第十一节"一生的坚守：做个有用的人"。

潘樱翻译第二章第一节"因为爱中国，她来了"，合译第二章第六节"丽霞老师的理想与行动"。

严涵、卓小星合编第三章第七节"春风化雨，润物无声"，严涵翻译此文。

汴梁编写第一章第一节"华南女子文理学院（1908—1951）与外教"。

王凌编写第四章第三节"福建华南女子职业学院与亚洲基督教高等教育联合董事会"。

范圣宇编写第三章第八节"记 Sandy"。

董秀苹编写第二章第一节"因为爱中国，她来了"。

陈晴编写第二章第六节"丽霞老师的理想与行动"，并翻译其中一部分。

韩艳艳编写第四章第一节"福建华南女子职业学院的外教政策"。

余荣敏编写第三章第三节"玛丽安·戴维斯教授与她的'家政'情结"。

张琳编写第二章第四节"空谷幽兰"最后一小节。